SAP R/3
Certification
Exam Guide

SAP R/3
Certification
Exam Guide

Stewart Miller

McGraw-Hill
New York   San Francisco   Washington, D.C.
Auckland   Bogotá   Caracas   Lisbon   London
Madrid   Mexico City   Milan   Montreal   New Delhi
San Juan   Singapore   Sydney   Tokyo   Toronto

Library of Congress Cataloging-in-Publication Data

Miller, Stewart S.
    SAP R/3 certification exam guide / Stewart S. Miller.
        p.   cm.
    Includes index.
    ISBN 0-07-134161-7
    1. SAP R/3.   2. Business—Computer programs.   3. Client/server
computing.   I. Title.
HG5548.4.R2M55   1999
650'.0285'53769—dc21   98-39249
                                                                            CIP

McGraw-Hill

A Division of The McGraw-Hill Companies

The views expressed in this book are solely those of the author, and do not represent the
views of any other party or parties.

1 2 3 4 5 6 7 8 9 0   DOC/DOC   9 0 4 3 2 1 0 9

P/N 134162-5
PART OF ISBN 0-07-134161-7

The sponsoring editor for this book was Simon Yates and the production supervisor was
Clare Stanley. It was set in Sabon by Patricia Wallenburg.

Printed and bound by R. R. Donnelley & Sons Company.

McGraw-Hill books are available at special quantity discounts to use as premiums and sales
promotions, or for use in corporate training programs. For more information, please write
to the Director of Special Sales, McGraw-Hill, 11 West 19th Street, New York, NY 10011.
Or contact your local bookstore.

"SAP" is a registered trademark of SAP Aktiengesellschaft, Systems, Applications and Products in Data Processing, Neurottstrasse 16, 69190 Walldorf, Germany. The publisher grate-
fully acknowledges SAP's kind permission to use its trademark in this publication. SAP AG
is not the publisher of this book and is not responsible for it under any aspect of press law.

Portions of this text are copyright SAP AG.

 This book is printed on recycled, acid-free paper containing
a minimum of 50% recycled, de-inked fiber.

This book is dedicated to:

All the members of my family whom I love most dearly.

Contents

Preface

It is my experience that knowledge is power, and power is best expressed in thorough preparation. In writing this book I wanted to provide you with the most knowledge you can have about both SAP as an organization, and their partner academy as the means of transferring knowledge.

SAP is an excellent organization with a very good product. However, becoming certified is often a challenge that can prove very difficult. Finding the basic information you need to get to the right department can often be difficult. This text will give you clear information regarding whom you can contact to register and take the exam.

Knowing contact information and background is only the beginning. There are MANY certification options you could choose. You may wish to take several courses and then become certified, or you may choose to go directly to the exam and obtain your certification as soon as possible.

Many people know they WANT to become certified, but they are not certain which course best suits their needs. This book will explain all of the courses that the SAP Partner Academy offers and explain what certification and courses are most appropriate for your needs. In this way, you have a guide that can point you in the right direction. The last thing you want to do is pass a certification cost at considerable expense of time and money only to find you are not certified in the track that you need most!

Finally, this book will provide you with the knowledge that is MOST IMPORTANT. Once you have decided which course to take and where you are going to take it, this book will provide you with both questions and answers to all of the primary tracks and course information that you will encounter.

Carefully read and KNOW all of the questions, answers, and tips presented in this book. This book provides you with the edge you need to pass over the competition and obtain your certification. This book was carefully prepared to provide you with the information that you need to meet your objectives. It will help you determine your best course of action and give you a competitive edge to deal with R/3 effectively and satisfy your certification requirements efficiently.

I lecture, consult, write, and speak about all Enterprise Resource Planning issues. As a well-known "efficiency expert" I encourage you to contact me should you require my services to assist your organization or gain a competitive edge in today's aggressive industry.

I can be reached at:

Telephone# 1-800-IT-MAVEN

or by e-mail at: Miller@ITMaven.com

Sincerely,

Stewart S. Miller

President/*CEO*

Executive Information Services

Introduction

The *SAP R/3 Certification Exam Guide* gives you the chance to become familiar with not only the requirements, but to know exactly what each certification course within the SAP Partner Academy involves. This book covers areas including Accounting and Controlling, Human Resources, Materials Management, Production, Production Scheduling, Sales Order Processing, Application Development, and ABAP/4 Development Workbench.

In the exams that you will be expected to take in these courses, you can expect multiple-choice examinations that last approximately three hours. These tests sometimes allow you to refer to R/3 online documentation. Each question can contain three to five choices as the answer. You will find that there is more than one answer that will appear to be correct.

The way this book is set up is to test you on specific concepts. I don't necessarily believe in showing you a multiple-choice question that gives you answers that are very close to one another. I feel that approach during the learning process is confusing and an ineffective way of teaching.

My job is to present you with concepts that ask you the question in plain, simple English. Then you can refer to the answer section of each chapter and look at the correct answer. If you look at multiple-choice questions, you do NOT want to look at two choices and not be able to tell the difference between them.

I am teaching you the way I prefer to learn. As a student, I always excelled when a book laid out the information in a clear format. My goal is that when you take the test, you can look at the multiple-choice question and the correct answer will pop out at you.

When you actually take the exam, note that each track often relies on technical knowledge, but in addition common-sense answers will often help you decide on a correct answer as opposed to an incorrect one.

The examination for becoming an R/3 consultant for the Accounting and Controlling area gives you the chance to demonstrate your knowledge of this area of R/3 as well as your ability to apply this knowledge within an example project environment.

You can expect a typical exam to consist of about 80 multiple-choice questions with the following format:

1. General Questions
2. Master Data
3. General Ledger
4. Accounts Receivable
5. Accounts Payable

6. Fixed Assets
7. Cost Element Accounting
8. Cost Center Accounting
9. Internet Orders
10. Profitability Analysis
11. Integration

The Human Resources course track often gives you tests that also have about 80 multiple-choice questions. The format for this test has the following specific subject areas:

1. General Questions
2. Basic HR Principles
3. Master Data
4. Time Recording
5. Recruitment
6. Gross Payroll
7. Organizational Management
8. Personnel Development
9. Training and Events Management
10. Reporting

The Materials Management course track teaches you the basic knowledge you need about the R/3 system and tests you in that knowledge in the area of Materials Management. You must be able to apply this knowledge to customer projects. Each exam is composed of about 80 multiple-choice questions in the following areas:

1. General Questions
2. Master Data
3. Material Planning and Forecasting
4. Purchasing
5. Inventory Management
6. Invoice Verification
7. Valuation and Account Determination

The Production Planning course track exams also contain about 80 multiple-choice questions from the following areas:

1. General Questions
2. Material Master
3. PP Master Data
4. Sales and Operations Planning
5. Demand Management and MRP

6. Production Orders
7. Capacity Planning
8. Product Costing
9. Repetitive Manufacturing
10. Logistics Information System
11. Integration

As a consultant in sales order processing you will have to pass a test similar in format to the ones above. This test is also about 80 multiple-choice questions from the following areas:

1. General Questions
2. Organizational Structures
3. Master Data in Sales and Distribution Processing
4. Sales
5. Pricing
6. Shipping
7. Billing
8. Credit Management
9. Sales Information System
10. Integration

This book is designed to present each course track in a clear and detailed way. I have created this text specifically to help you identify what course certification you need and then give you an edge in preparing you for the course itself.

These certification courses cost an average of $12,000. When you decide to spend this much money on a course that will no doubt change your future, you can rest in the knowledge that this book will help you plan your career efficiently and effectively.

I wish you good luck in your pursuit of a career in SAP. I advocate SAP and believe your future in relation to this company will be a bright one!

Stewart Miller
President/CEO
Executive Information Services

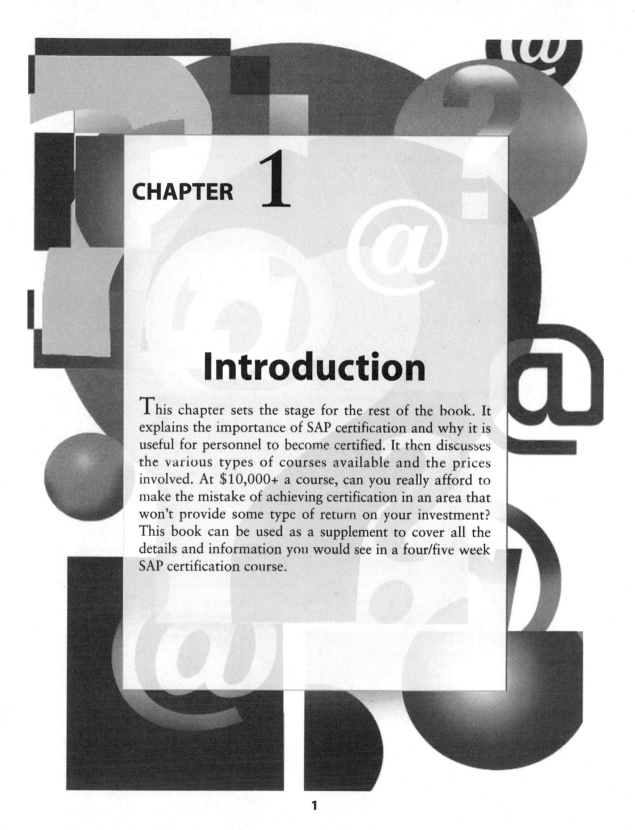

CHAPTER 1

Introduction

This chapter sets the stage for the rest of the book. It explains the importance of SAP certification and why it is useful for personnel to become certified. It then discusses the various types of courses available and the prices involved. At $10,000+ a course, can you really afford to make the mistake of achieving certification in an area that won't provide some type of return on your investment? This book can be used as a supplement to cover all the details and information you would see in a four/five week SAP certification course.

SAP Partner Academy

The SAP Partner Academy is composed of an international institute of higher education in SAP applications. It is unique in offering the most comprehensive training academy in the business software industry. This resource is open to all SAP partners; it is an accessible entity providing a direct pathway to getting the most out of your SAP R/3 investment.

The SAP Partner Academy is important because it allows people to gain the necessary expertise and knowledge needed to receive an important level of certification from SAP. This certification gives people the ability to consult on many different facets of SAP R/3 and various aspects of its implementation. This chapter will briefly review the types of courses the Partner Academy offers, and delve into specifics that make it possible to determine which course track is right for you and your company. We also look into specific course titles and important price points, to allow you to see some of the major certification courses offered.

SAP's Training Activities

SAP's consultant training activities focus on the SAP Partner Academy, which offers its services at various SAP locations around the world.

The courses offered are specifically geared to the requirements of R/3 consultants who must be highly knowledgeable in order to help customers get the most out of R/3 applications. At the SAP Partner Academy, students learn about individual applications, implementation, customizing and customer services.

There are Partner Academy locations around the world to make certain to offer a consistent level of quality for global SAP support. Each Academy location provides the same core curriculum of high-level training courses that is supplemented and expanded by courses individualized to specific local needs and business practices.

The result is an exceptional resource base of expertise in all parts of the world: professionals who are fully knowledgeable, up to date, and trained to help customers get the most from SAP integrated software solutions.

Certification Benefits

SAP consultants all have the same goal when jointly implementing R/3 with SAP: to enhance productivity, profitability, and leadership in their market segment.

Certified SAP R/3 consultants have passed a test to "certify" that they possess the R/3 product know-how required to successfully implement R/3 for customers. Certified SAP R/3 consultants are integrated in a closely coupled information network with SAP that provides quality and up-to-date knowledge to benefit customers.

Personal experience that certified SAP R/3 consultants gain is complemented by access to information and experience accumulated by other SAP consultants, such as contact with developers at SAP. A certified SAP R/3 consultant can help customers efficiently and quickly derive full benefits from their R/3 installation.

Creating Experts in SAP Software

The SAP Partner Academy is open to all SAP partners and independent consultants who are on the "waiting list" and has two primary responsibilities:

1. It must train consultants in the features, functions, and most efficient use of SAP products in order to satisfy customers' business goals
2. It must provide continuing education and advanced training for experienced consultants

SAP Partner Academy has locations worldwide. The Academy makes certain to offer consistent quality of SAP support on a global basis. Each Academy location provides core training curriculum coursework that is supplemented and enhanced by courses individualized to specific local requirements and business processes.

All of these factors combine to produce a comprehensive resource that offers expertise across the globe. This results in SAP's ability to offer a substantial resource base of expertise offering knowledgeable, up-to-date, and trained professionals who can help customers achieve the greatest benefit from their SAP integrated software solutions.

Partner Academy

The Partner Academy is well known for its standards and its comprehensive instruction in SAP Certification. The SAP Partner Academy is one of a kind. It was the first entity to offer an international partner academy in the industry. Worldwide locations offer intensive programs. Each of these programs provides detailed coursework in both SAP products and applications.

The Partner Academy has a strong level of training, offering certifying consultant expertise in SAP systems and best-business practices.

The SAP Partner Academy provides a diverse range of detailed training programs in all of the most current SAP products and business applications. These applications are the cornerstone of what is taught in the instruction centers. The Academy concentrates on a core curriculum that deals with product training courses; these courses are significantly expanded by more advanced technical material on specialized subject matters.

In the core curriculum, five primary application and instructional tracks are provided for new consultants. Each of these tracks focuses on a specific functional area tailored to specific interests and business practices. This information can be used to supplement current duties or offer a company a high level of expertise in a given track. These primary functional areas include:

1. FI (Financials)
2. CO (Controlling)
3. PP (Production Planning)
4. MM (Materials Management)
5. SD (Sales/Distribution)
6. HR (Human Resources)

Each of these process-specific tracks involves four to five intense weeks of instruction in SAP capabilities and applications. Each class starts with a comprehensive overview of the R/3 system concepts. Once the concepts are reviewed, the course then concentrates on how components can effectively be integrated. The classes then cover the current best-business practices and the best methods for implementing these practices with SAP in a real-world environment. The knowledge the students gain can be used to determine exact detail on configuring SAP systems so they can perform specific functions.

Common Course Offerings

The programs include certification in new product releases and special courses that deal with technological advancements that can enhance business process productivity.

The most common course offerings include the following:

- SAP Business Workflow products
- Application Link Enabling (ALE)—Partner or R/3
- SAP R/3 Business Engineering Workbench (BEW)
- Internet capabilities—Partner or R/3

Successful completion of your Partner Academy training means something substantial has been achieved. Consultants who embark on this route must complete a detailed instructional series and must demonstrate mastery of the subject by passing SAP certification exams.

These standardized examinations deal with specific products and business processes. Achievement of expertise leads to focus on attaining an effective implementation within specific functional areas. The tests are often administered with Academy courses. However, any consultant who has enough SAP expertise can immediately take the exams to acquire certification.

Location and Enrollment

Enrollment in a course is contingent upon simultaneous receipt of the completed enrollment form and payment in full. Submission of the enrollment form and funds is not a guarantee of course admission. Due to the high volume of initial registrations, SAP is not able to confirm enrollment within two business days.

SAP notifies applicants of enrollment status by fax or e-mail as soon as enrollment has been processed. To request an enrollment form, e-mail the request to **academyinfo@sapacademy.com**.

Those unable to attend a course for which they have enrolled should advise SAP as soon as possible. Cancellations received within 14 business days of the class start date are subject to a 50% cancellation fee. No cancellations are accepted after 8:00 a.m., five business days before the course start date. After this cancellation deadline, a refund of course fees is not possible.

All the necessary information on SAP's curriculum content, course offerings, dates, locations, and hotel accommodations can be found in the following resources:

- ✎ SAP Training Catalog. SAP training can be reached by calling 1-800-USA-1SAP.
- ✎ SAP Online Service System (OSS) for customers and businesses
- ✎ Internet: **http://www.sap.com/**
- ✎ SAP Education and Training Central—Registrants can call: 1-888-777-1SAP or 1-800-872-1727

Those interested in more information should get in contact with:

SAP Partner Academy for SAP Consultants
Telephone (800) 790-7750
(612) 376-7750
Fax: (612) 376-7755
e-mail: academyinfo@sapacademy.com

SAP R/3 project team training ties together new instructional approaches and a well-integrated multimedia experience. The courses deliver a high level of quality and help provide superior job performance quickly and cost-effectively.

SAP's methodology can emulate realistic implementation of project team activities. Real-world business models are used to promote a quick grasp of R/3 by adhering to business process flows and test cases.

A knowledgeable instructor is available to help the skills transfer process. Students share this person's R/3 expertise and build their own in a real-world environment. This book will facilitate understanding of the intricacies of R/3 use of learned information.

The SAP R/3 All-in-One Certification Exam Guide is meant to help students prepare for the certification process. The goal is to know and truly understand the material, pass the certification exams, and to be able to proceed with normal business process activities.

SAP Partner Academy Class Schedules

The SAP Partner Academy classes are held outside Boston, in Waltham, MA, and are filled on a first-come, first-served basis.

Primary certification courses are held in Waltham within the U.S. Partner Academy courses in various subject areas are held at several locations around the country at various SAP satellite training sites.

It is important to note that submission of the enrollment form and funds does not guarantee course admission.

Partner Academy classes are not available to customers of SAP America. These courses have been so crowded because of initial registrations that SAP is not able to confirm enrollment within two business days. Notification of enrollment status is by fax or email as soon as an enrollment has been processed.

Request a current enrollment form for the most current classes by sending an e-mail request to **academyinfo@sapacademy.com**. If it is impossible to attend a course you have enrolled in, it is very important to inform the Partner Academy immediately.

Experienced Consultant Workshops

The Partner Academy provides workshops specifically addressed to students who need information from experienced consultants, in a forum that allows sharing their experience.

Sessions are taught by consultants who have personal experience of the subjects under discussion. They use state-of-the-art media to focus on significant issues. There are extensive discussions and it is easy to benefit from colleagues and peer experiences.

SAP created these workshops as a forum for building on and intensifying existing experience. Participants should be SAP consultants who have at least one year of experience and a sound technical knowledge of the system including basics of the applications.

Continued Training

There is a guarantee of long-term qualification. Continual further training makes a crucial contribution to keeping this support at a high level of quality on a long-term basis. The SAP Partner Academy also offers further training. In that way, certified consultants can continually update their product- and consultancy-related knowledge through integration with SAP's information network and systematically promoted events.

Alliance Management

Alliance Management conducts programs specifically to address partner companies, encouraging them actively to provide further training to their R/3 consultants.

Course Pricing

US SAP Partner Academy Course Schedule:

- ABAP/4—$8,000.00
- Unix/Oracle (Introductory Basis Classes TCC)—$12,500.00
- Unix/Oracle (Advanced Basis Classes TCC)—$7,500.00
- CIM—$4,000.00
- FI-CO—$10,000.00
- HR—$12,000.00 (sponsored by employer) to $14,000.00 (individuals)
- MM—$10,000.00
- PM—$8,000.00
- PP—$10,000.00
- SD—$10,000.00
- Full Track and ABAP/4—$200.00
- TCC (BASIS)—$300.00

Classroom Capacity

Classroom capacity for many SAP courses has increased to accommodate the growing interest in becoming certified. In order to meet students' needs, in 1998 SAP supplemented current training centers with extra classrooms. Overall capacity has increased in the Atlanta, Dallas, Cleveland, and Chicago area locations. New training locations have been developed in Detroit and San Diego.

SAP Canada has added several courses in all their training centers at the request of Canadian customers.

Training Preparation

Training is synonymous with success. Return on investment is increased through R/3 training.

Complementary software education is available (at an additional cost) that supports R/3 throughout specific industry-solution workshops. In addition, SAP offers CSP, The Complementary Software Partner program, which supports SAP's goal of actively promoting a comprehensive solution for specific industries. This program is widely accepted by customers, and continues to prove an effective means of training. To support this important aspect of business, SAP has an extensive course offering for CSP training.

R/3 Training

SAP's R/3 Training uses advanced learning techniques that allow students to learn how to gain knowledge via the most modern techniques in adult education.

Many students find that training is more palatable with goal-based learning achieved through objectives and associated methods. Different learning styles—video, audio, business models, demonstrations, process flows, documentation, and exercises—are used.

Instructors also encourage exploration of the business models by offering expert feedback throughout the course.

Self evaluation is a helpful tool that allows mastery of the material at hand. Consistency is an important factor throughout the courses. All project team members are trained with the same materials throughout the entire enterprise project around the world.

The objective of this type of learning is to learn much more quickly, to retain knowledge better, and more effectively apply your R/3 coursework to real-life core business processes. Continuing Professional Education (CPE) credits for SAP courses are available.

Results

After completing SAP certification courses, students can significantly increase the return on their information investment. SAP R/3 Training integrates courseware, business models, online help and documentation.

This type of information infrastructure supports the learning process and on-the-job performance. It makes it possible to answer important questions about mission-critical R/3 tasks, including:

- What does that mean?
- What does the flow look like?
- How does it work in practice?

This level of support is offered through a variety of tools and media that is tightly integrated into the R/3 course material. The experienced professional instructors are intimately familiar with R/3 operations and can impart knowledge of how to take advantage of R/3's rich functionality in specific areas of interest to individual students.

Training Course Levels

SAP R/3 training incorporates three distinct levels of courses. The curriculum was created in a hierarchy that allows students to delve into specific detail levels that match their individual criteria. This type of course modularization allows students to reduce the total amount of project training time because they can choose to take only those courses that satisfy their individual needs.

The separate levels of training courses include:

1. **Awareness**—Introductory courses offer an overview of features and functionality of:
   — R/3
   — Services
   — Support
   — Implementation framework
   — SAP-specific terminology

2. **Readiness**—Core Business Process courses provide the skills needed to be ready to apply SAP R/3 to any company's individual business processes.
3. **Proficiency**—Advanced courses foster the ability to gain expertise specific to supporting the students' individual requirements.

SAP offers more than 100 advanced courses each year. Students can always remain competitive by using the power of SAP R/3 education.

Each of the levels of R/3 Project Team Training discussed gives students the ability to move from overviews to processes to advanced subject matter.

Business Application and Technology Expertise

The objective of the Academy is to create extensive knowledge of and expertise in business applications and technology.

The Academy finishes its courses with a one-week case study where a cross-functional team of students creates a company from the ground up within a simulated environment. Technical training offered is one of the most crucial elements in making sure that systems get up and running. This level of instruction also makes certain that a system goes through both customization and testing.

Customization is represented in the following courses: Technical Consultant Training, ABAP/4 Development Workbench, and Advanced Studies.

Advanced training programs are provided to update the knowledge of experienced SAP consultants with respect to new developments. These programs are designed to enhance skills and give new perspectives on SAP implementation. This information can be used for effective handling of new situations that might arise and could possible cause loss in productivity.

R/3 Customer Needs

Many people install SAP R/3 Release 4.0 for their first implementation of the R/3 product. Several new courses cater to new Release 4.0 customers. SAP Education's objective is to offer an original and detailed array of training products and services that will permit quick and efficient implementation of SAP R/3 as a viable business solution in your organization.

SAP Education is an important part of TeamSAP. The team acts to reinforce a total commitment to ensuring complete success with an R/3 business solution. The SAP education product and services were created based on individual requirements in combination with SAP's dedication efforts to meeting customers' needs.

On-Site Training

SAP continues to enhance its onsite training so that customers can use the training delivery option. Customer experience demonstrates that onsite training offers savings in both cost and time while adding focus and pliancy for project team training. In addition, portable classroom equipment has been significantly enhanced to meet training needs so that SAP can offer the most flexible possible level of training.

Business Process Models

The R/3 curriculum is arranged around key business processes that cross various application modules. This can best be illustrated by customer order management training doing tasks that include:

- Sales
- Shipping
- Delivery
- Accounts Receivable.

Project team methodology allows students to start using important success factors that deal with the implementation of a complete business solution.

Business process model courses offer a tightly integrated cross-application instruction set for R/3. An interdisciplinary method allow students to satisfy real-life enterprise requirements. Exercises get students integrally involved and provide the ability to follow business process flows as well as to execute R/3 transactions.

Business models allow students to explain their organizations' business requirements. Project team members can create a comfortable level in combination with the expertise they need to begin their R/3 implementations effectively and quickly.

SAP Standard Training

In R/3 Release 3.0, SAP offers an R/3 training program, redesigned to go with Releases 3.0 and 3.1 of the R/3 system. The training package is primarily for customers and partners. Benefits can accrue from key R/3 business processes the product knowledge required to identify and use the best R/3 implementation options for any company.

Level 1 courses offer an overview of the R/3 environment. They are by design compact, so they can offer an initial understanding of R/3 applications, R/3 basic technology, integration concepts, and SAP Internet solutions. They do not cover the breadth of functions in specific applications but focus on mission-critical business processes as well as the interaction with other modules. The course were created for company managers, project managers, and project teams.

Level 2 courses discuss fundamental business processes that can be modeled through the R/3 system. These courses act as an introduction to specific areas that may include procurement and production planning.

Level 2 courses do not use the entire range of functions for specific applications, but do focus on key business processes and the interaction with other modules. They were designed for members of project teams and company managers to set an in-depth look at R/3 business processes and functions.

Level 3 courses concentrate on offering detailed information regarding individual application areas. Their goal is to focus on R/3 customizing and function descriptions. They often build on information dealt with in associated level 2 courses, and are tailored to meet the requirements of project teams.

Curriculum Design

The improved curriculum design offers three important categories:

Delta Training Courses

Those wishing to upgrade from R/3 Release.3.x to R/3 Release 4.0, can obtain significant benefits from attending SAP's training courses and reading this book. Release 4.0 is covered in Chapter 17.

Management Courses

These are attended by people who have not yet attended any other SAP course and are not a prerequisite for attending any other courses. They provide attendees with a compact and fast introduction for the key processes in R/3 and are individualized to the requirements of project managers and decision-makers who require a firm knowledge of R/3 quickly.

Industry-specific Training Courses

These illustrate the growing trend at SAP toward providing tailor-made industry solutions. In each industry sector, SAP offers a planned curriculum or workshops that concentrate on expert knowledge about that sector.

Training for R/3 Application Consultants

The basic training program for R/3 application consultants is created specifically for consultants who need a solid foundation for important business-related issues but do not have previous experience of working with the R/3 System or comparable software.

Courses are supplemented with extensive practical exercises based on case studies. The final element of the basic training is an integration workshop that occurs over several days. In it consultants from various different business areas jointly execute a given implementation.

The core training courses are usually held between 9 a.m. and 5 p.m. each day, permitting further study and additional exercises later in the day. There are also frequent extra sessions scheduled in the evenings.

Courses that result in certification as an SAP consultant are also held by large consulting partners with their own training facilities. These partners have absorbed SAP's R/3 consultant training program for their own staff.

Testing and certification can be supervised and monitored by SAP.

PAAC10 Financial and Controlling

The goal of the Financial and Controlling course is to provide a solid foundation for SAP functions. It gives an introduction to SAP implementation tools as well as a detailed study of functions in the Financial Accounting (FI) module, including Asset Management (AM), Overhead Management (CO) and Cash Management (TR-CM).

The module know-how acquired can be used to establish an integrated model company based on predefined business processes. There is work on SAP implementation projects under expert guidance and supervision. Requirements are sound business know-how in financials and controlling and basic knowledge of graphical user interfaces (GUIs) including Microsoft Windows.

This course provides an overview of the SAP implementation tools Procedure Model and Implementation Guide Business Navigator. It investigates SAP master data, SAP architecture, the Financial Accounting (FI) module, G/L accounting, accounts payable accounting, accounts receivable accounting, the asset management module, the controlling (CO) module, overhead management configuration, and organization.

FI/CO—Financial and Controlling Track

The objective of the FI/CO track is to provide an entry-level overview of the Financial Accounting, Controlling, and Special Purpose Ledger modules. The case study enhances the exposure to integration with the functionality of SM, MM and PP. This includes re-engineering a company using SAP software. Students who successfully complete the examination at the end of this course are awarded SAP Certification in FI/CO.

FI/CO Prerequisites

The FI/CO prerequisites include:

- Solid business background in accounting
- Solid business background in finance and control
- Basic knowledge of a graphical user interface (GUI) such as a foundation in the Microsoft Windows environment

Course Contents

- Familiarization and system navigation
- New position of IMG
- Customizing customer-specific IMG projects
- Integration of the navigator into configuration
- Financial accounting
- General ledger
- Accounts receivable
- Accounts payable
- Controlling
- Cost centers
- Internal orders
- Profitability analysis
- Special purpose ledger
- Report Painter

Financial/Management Accounting and Reporting Process

Financial/Management Accounting and Reporting means the planning and recording processes, and monitoring business events through both report and analysis. The R/3 application module that supports this process, Financial Accounting (FI), includes:

- General Ledger
- Accounts Receivable
- Accounts Payable
- Fixed Assets
- Consolidation
- Special Ledger
- Treasury

Financial/Management Accounting and Reporting Process deals with planning, recording, and business event monitoring. The primary functions of this process include general ledger accounting and legal/management reporting.

PALO10 Materials Management

The goal of the materials management course is to provide SAP functions. There is an introduction to SAP implementation tools and an in-depth study of functions in the Materials Management (MM) module.

Module know-how acquired is used to set up an integrated model company based on predefined business processes. There is comprehensive preparation for the R/3 Application Consultant test for materials management and work on SAP implementation projects under expert guidance and supervision.

This course requires a good foundation in business know-how in materials management and basic knowledge of graphical user interfaces (GUIs) such as Microsoft Windows.

The business processes in Materials Management provides an overview of SAP implementation tools, including the following elements:

- Implementation guide business navigator
- SAP master data overview of SAP architecture
- Materials Management (MM) module
- Consumption-based planning
- Procurement
- Inventory management
- Physical inventory invoice
- Verification
- Material valuation configuration
- Organization integration workshop
- Setting up a model company

✎ Mapping and presentation of business processes
✎ Review and certification check.

Materials Management (MM)

The materials management track uses a combination of lecture and hands-on training to provide an overview of the capabilities and integration in SAP R/3 of the functional areas of materials management. The course also gives an overview of the integration of these functions with the areas of FI/CO, SD, PP, and re-engineering a company using SAP software. Students who successfully complete the exam at the end of this course earn SAP Certification in MM.

MM Prerequisites

MM prerequisites include:

✎ Solid business background in materials management
✎ Basic knowledge of a graphical user interface (GUI) such as the Microsoft Windows environment

Manufacturing Planning and Execution Process

Manufacturing Planning and Execution specifies the process of recognized demand, achieving requirements, planning for material procurement or production, and determining the capacity to meet demand.

Application modules that support demand include the following:

✎ Materials Management (MM)
✎ Financial Accounting (FI)
✎ Sales and Distribution (SD)
✎ Production Planning (PP)
✎ Controlling (CO)
✎ Human Resources (HR)

The manufacturing planning and execution process deals with the demand forecast activity, close-loop planning phase, and the control of production activities via inventory valuation, order settlement, and product costing.

Primary functions of these business processes include:

✎ Master Production Scheduling (MPS)
✎ Materials Requirements Planning (MRP)

- ✎ Planned order processing
- ✎ Production order
- ✎ Goods issue
- ✎ Production order receipt

Contents

- ✎ Materials management
- ✎ Inventory management
- ✎ Vendor evaluation
- ✎ Invoice verification
- ✎ Material requirements planning
- ✎ Batch management

PALO20 Production Planning

The goal of the production planning course is to provide an overview of SAP functions and give a foundation for SAP implementation tools in the Production Planning (PP) module. Module know-how is used to set up an integrated model company based on predefined business processes.

There is comprehensive preparation for the R/3 Application Consultant certification test for Production Planning and the chance to work on SAP implementation projects under expert guidance and supervision.

The requirements for this course are: solid business knowledge in the production planning area and basic knowledge of graphical user interfaces (GUIs) such as Microsoft Windows.

Course contents include understanding of business processes in Production Planning and discussion of the SAP implementation tools Procedure Model and Implementation Guide Business Navigator.

There is an overview of SAP master data:

- ✎ SAP architecture Production Planning module (PP)
- ✎ Discrete manufacturing basic data, including production planning and requirements planning
- ✎ Production order processing
- ✎ Capacity planning
- ✎ Product costing
- ✎ Repetitive manufacturing
- ✎ Logistics information system
- ✎ Configuration and organization integration workshop
- ✎ Setting up a model company

✎ Mapping and presentation of business processes
✎ Review
✎ Certification check.

Production Planning (PP)

The production planning track uses a combination of lectures and hands-on training to provide an overview of the capabilities and integration within SAP R/3 of the functional areas of production planning.

The course also presents an overview of the integration of these functions in the areas of FI/CO, SD and MM, as well as reengineering a company using SAP software. Students who successfully complete the examination at the end of the course earn SAP certification in PP.

PP Prerequisites

✎ Solid business background in production planning
✎ Basic knowledge of a graphical user interface (GUI) such as the Microsoft Windows environment

Procurement Process

Procurement indicates the requisitioning process, vendor sourcing, purchasing, receiving, and paying for materials and services used in a company. R/3 application modules that support this process include:

✎ Materials Management (MM)
✎ Financial Accounting (FI)
✎ Production Planning (PP)
✎ Controlling (CO)
✎ Plant Maintenance (PM)

Contents

✎ Menu navigation
✎ Materials master
✎ Vendor master
✎ Positioning of production planning
✎ Bill of Material
✎ Single BOM
✎ Multiple BOMs
✎ Variant BOM

- Group BOM
- All plant allocations
- Reporting
- Work centers
- Allocation cost centers
- HR assignment
- Formulas Scheduling Capacity
  - long-term capacity
  - finite planning
  - individual capacity
- Routings
- Normal parallel & alternate phantom processing
- Multi-level planning
- Work centers
- Trigger points
- Mass function scheduling and material master update
- Planning
- Forecasting
- Sales and operational planning
- Long Range
- MRP
- Demand management
- Production planning
- MPS
- Materials requirements planning
- Production orders
- Capacity planning

PALO30: Sales and Distribution

The goal of the sales and distribution is to provide a solid foundation in SAP functions, SAP implementation tools and a comprehensive study of functions in the Sales and Distribution (SD) module.

It explores the module know-how necessary to establish an integrated model company based on predefined business processes and the requirements for the R/3 Application Consultant certification test for Sales and Distribution. Work on SAP implementation projects is guided by experts.

Requirements for this course include: sound business know-how in sales and distribution and basic knowledge of graphical user interfaces (GUIs) such as Microsoft Windows.

The content of the course includes:

- Knowledge of business processes in Sales and Distribution
- Knowledge of SAP implementation tools
- Procedure Model and Implementation Guide
- Business Navigator
- Knowledge of SAP master data
- Knowledge of SAP architecture Sales and Distribution (SD) module
- Sales Partner concept
- Pricing
- Conditions
- Shipping
- Billing
- Sales information system
- Integration workshop in setting up a model company
- Mapping and presentation of business processes
- Review
- Certification test.

Sales and Distribution (SD)

The Sales and Distribution track's purpose is achieved through a combination of hands-on system exercises and case-study situations where participants learn the functionality of the SAP R/3, the sales and distribution module and key points of integration with other SAP Modules (FI/CO, MM and PP). The case study furthers the exposure to integration with the other tracks' functionality and includes re-engineering a company using SAP software. Participants who successfully complete the examination at the end of this course earn SAP Certification in SD.

SD Prerequisites

SD Prerequisites include:

- Solid business background in sales and distribution
- Basic knowledge of a graphical user interface (GUI) such as the Microsoft Windows environment

Contents

- General system navigation
- Introduction to the R/3 Business Navigator

- Corporate structure definition
- Pre-sales activities and support
- Sales order processing
- Pricing techniques
- Shipping
- Billing system configuration
- Integration with financial accounting, materials management and production planning
- Technical Consultant Certification program.

Human Resources (HR)

The HR Partner Academy has been designed to offer basic requirements for a consultant to advise, configure, and implement the SAP HR module.

This five-week course is based on a company model. Each student creates a division within the company and assigns his own corporate, personnel, and organization structures for this company.

At the completion of this course the company should be fully implemented. This requires a team effort to successfully complete the company as portrayed. Utilizing the company model gives the student a hands-on approach to learning the SAP HR configuration/implementation.

HR Prerequisites

The HR prerequisites include:

- Technical background (strongly recommended)
- Solid business background in human resources administration
- Basic knowledge of a graphical user interface (GUI) such as the Microsoft Windows environment

Course Contents

- Full HR system demonstration
- System familiarity and navigation
- Overview and configuration of:
  - corporate structure
  - personnel structure
  - payroll subunits
  - time management
  - organizational structure
  - applicant administration

- Qualifications and career and succession planning
- Cost planning
- Workforce planning/shift planning
- Organization management
- Seminar and convention management
- Security
- HR reporting
- Gross payroll configuration
- Payroll interface
- Authorization and system controls
- Time evaluation

PABC40: Application Development in the ABAP/4 Development Workbench

The ABAP/4 Development Workbench course lasts 4 weeks and its objective is to assist ABAP/4 beginners and application consultants who have appropriate IT know-how, and need to acquire certification as R/3 consultants for the ABAP/4 Development Workbench. Experienced R/3 ABAP/4 Development Workbench consultants can take the certification test without attending the course.

Students learn about the ABAP/4 programming language as well as the ABAP/4 Development Workbench tools necessary to create their own business applications and to enhance the standard SAP software to meet specific customer requirements.

This course deals with the benefits of the client/server architecture for: programming, performance issues, procedures, and special features of development projects.

The content for this course is presented using documented and process-oriented training examples taken from practical project contexts. Course examples are structured and documented so that students can refer to them on the R/3 demo systems at their own companies.

Course requirements include:

- Solid foundation in IT
- Knowledge of operating systems
- Experience in another programming language
- Basic knowledge of graphical user interface (GUIs) such as Microsoft Windows.

The contents of the course includes:

- ✎ Basic technology overview
- ✎ Architecture of client/server organizational units
- ✎ Application hierarchy of navigation SSCR (SAP Software Change Registration)
- ✎ ABAP/4 Development Workbench data modeler
- ✎ ABAP/4 dictionary
- ✎ ABAP/4 language
- ✎ ABAP/4 editor
- ✎ Screen painter
- ✎ Menu painter debugging
- ✎ Runtime analysis of ABAP/4 Workbench programs
- ✎ Organizer Programs in background processing in ABAP/4
- ✎ Repository info system
- ✎ CATT (Computer Aided Test Tool)
- ✎ Authorization concept in data transfer
- ✎ Data interfaces
- ✎ Batch input processing
- ✎ RFC interface Asynchronous
- ✎ RFC sequential buffered data transfer
- ✎ Local files desktop integration
- ✎ OLE additional analyses
- ✎ Interactive reporting
- ✎ ABAP/4 query function enhancements
- ✎ Improvements to standard software through customer exits
- ✎ Inhouse developments
- ✎ Basics of online programming
- ✎ Update concept
- ✎ Lock concept.

ABAP/4—(aka PABC 40)

This track uses a combination of lecture and intensive hands-on training to offer an introduction to SAP's R/3 development environment, emphasizing the ABAP/4 programming language. Students who successfully complete the examination at the end of this course are awarded SAP Certification in ABAP/4.

ABAP/4 Prerequisites

The prerequisites involve a minimum of two years of recent (within 5 years) professional business programming experience using structured programming languages and techniques. Experience with common business programming constructs and algorithms such as looping structures, conditional tests, and other common programming conventions is required.

It is important to have knowledge of basic data modeling and system architecture as well as basic knowledge of graphical user interface (GUI) in the contents of the Microsoft Windows environment.

Course Contents

- SAP Development Workbench
- ABAP/4 Editor
- ABAP/4 Debugger
- Screen Painter
- Menu Painter
- R/3 Repository and Information System
- Data Dictionary and Information System
- Workbench Organizer
- Data types
- Control statements
- Program modularization
- Windows techniques
- Logical database processing
- Interactive reporting
- Background Processing
- File handling
- Batch input (batch data communication)
- Call transaction
- On-line programming
- Data validation
- Database table updates
- Transaction maintenance
- Overview of the R/3 System Architectural and Information Systems

R/3 Application Consultant Certification

When consultants have sufficient SAP experience or have completed the training program, they can take an examination for certification as an R/3 System consultant. The standardized examinations deal with specific product releases, business processes, and effective implementation in specific functional areas and are often given in combination with Academy courses. However, any consultant with sufficient SAP experience can take the examination to obtain certification.

Technical Consultants—Initial Training

The SAP Partner Academy provides a special training program to prepare candidates for certification as SAP R/3 Technical Consultants. Expert competence level training courses are held in a block. Block training participants need to have a solid foundation in the operating system and database concerned.

Technical Consultant Certification

Students can acquire certification as SAP R/3 Technical Consultants for the basic module in R/3 Release 3.x. This certification deals with a specific R/3 release as well as the combination of operating system and database tested.

There are no specific eligibility requirements for certification. Certification candidates must have knowledge that can be obtained in corresponding courses in the SAP training program, and preparatory courses provided by SAP's partners for the operating system and database. Partner certificates are not necessary for admission to the certification test.

PABC10 Technical Consultant Training for UNIX/ORACLE

This course lasts 4 weeks and is meant for consultants who are knowledgeable system administrators and database administrators. Its objective is to acquire comprehensive expert-level training in R/3 System management. It prepares participants for the SAP R/3 Certified Technical Consultant test.

Course requirements include knowledge of: UNIX, ORACLE database, and TCP/IP network administration.

This course offers knowledge regarding R/3:

- Basic technology
- Implementation planning
- System management
- Advanced R/3 system management
- Technical core competence

✎   Workbench organizer and transport system
✎   System upgrades
✎   Going live
✎   Installation
✎   Workload analysis
✎   Database administration/ORACLE.

The first three weeks of the course covers topics that do not depend on databases. Database-related topics are covered in the fourth week of the courses.

The training course does not involve the installation of an actual system. In order to derive the greatest benefit from the course, students must perform additional study and exercises beyond the normal 9–5 contact hours.

When taking this course, students should bring a laptop with CD drive for additional study.

On the last day of the course, students will need to take the SAP R/3 Certified Technical Consultant test, but the test fee is included in the course fee.

PABC90 R/3 Installation under Windows NT

The main audience for the Windows NT installation course is consultants responsible for installing R/3. This usually involves system administrators. The goal of this course is to provide an overview of R/3 installation in combination with a comprehensive discussion of critical implementation themes.

PABC91 Installation Course for R/3 under UNIX

The installation course under UNIX lasts 2 days. Students who take this course are usually Basis consultants. The goal of the course is to offer an overview of the technical process of installing an R/3 system.

Course prerequisites include:

✎   Knowledge and experience with the UNIX operating system
✎   Knowledge and experience with database administration
✎   Knowledge of R/3 Technical Core Competence (BC31x).

This course covers issues pertaining to installation and hardware planning, with demonstration of:

✎   R/3 System installation

✎ Language transports
✎ Desktop integration
✎ Setting up a remote connection to SAP
✎ Setting up additional R/3 systems.

Technical Training

The TCC program consists of tracks that are operating system- and database-specific. For a specific operating system and database, the TCC program consists of two tracks (introductory and advanced):

1. The introductory track uses a combination of lectures and intensive hands-on training to offer the fundamentals of the R/3 basis system and all R/3-specific aspects of planning and implementing an R/3 systems environment center from a consultant's perspective.
2. The advanced TCC track uses a combination of lecture and intensive hands-on training to offer details of the expert knowledge required by a consultant to analyze, fine tune, and support a R/3 installation as it goes live.

Participants who successfully complete the certification examination acquire SAP certification in TCC. SAP recommends that a participant complete the introductory track and spend between three and six months utilizing and reinforcing the skills learned on an actual R/3 project before trying to complete the advanced track. It is necessary to register to take the TCC exam in addition to any TCC tracks. The TCC exam is not the concluding event of a TCC track.

TCC Prerequisites

TCC prerequisites include:

✎ Solid technical knowledge/experience using the appropriate operating system
✎ Solid technical knowledge/experience using the appropriate data base
✎ Solid technical knowledge/experience using a graphical user interface (GUI) such as the Microsoft Windows environment

Contents

✎ UX/OR
✎ INTRO (UNIX/Oracle Introduction) consists of:
  – SAP50

- BC040
- BC360
- PABC91
- BC325 NT/OR
- INTRO (NT/Oracle Introduction) consists of:
  - SAP50
  - BC040
  - BC310
  - PABC90
  - BC325 NT/SQL
- INTRO (NT/SQL Introduction) consists of:
  - SAP50
  - BC040
  - BC314
  - PABC90
  - BC325
- ADVANCED (UNIX/Oracle Advanced and NT/Oracle Advanced) consists of:
  - BC505
  - BC305
  - BC340
  - BC315

Resources and Service

IDES: International Demonstration and Education System

One of the most important aspects in an R/3 project is the creation of the necessary R/3 knowledge in a company. In order to make certain that learning does not end with the training courses but is intensified, SAP has created the International Demonstration and Education System (IDES), which offers a comprehensive R/3 system that functions with the data of a multinational model company. It allows R/3 users to learn quickly with all functions provided in the R/3 system.

Besides the business process model both current and future technological advances are incorporated in the IDES system. It is possible to prototype Internet/intranet-to-R/3 business scenarios using the prepared examples delivered with the IDES system. IDES is currently available at no charge for customers and partners with an existing R/3 installation.

The international nature of the group of companies in IDES and its range of products allow this system to reflect real-life situations and assure a high degree of integration of all business processes.

IDES models very specific business situations. You can use the Unlimited Information due to the fact that there is no sensitive corporate information to be protected including the current liquidity or sales plans. This allows you to remain free to move around the IDES corporation as needed. Should you wish to look behind the Profit Center Accounting scenes or locate a decision model for a simplified production procedure (i.e. KANBAN[1]) you can because there is no limit to the information available in the IDES system.

You can also produce high-quality prototyping without prior preparation. Your complete organizational structure and master data have been established to assure that the general business context is always at the fore-front of activities. This allows prototyping function to satisfy specific elements of the current structure and individual requirements of an organization without having to neglect integration.

It is also possible to incorporate management in all the design decisions so that the most suitable business solution can be arrived at rapidly. An R/3 consultant or project manager gains a high level of responsibility necessary to perform required tasks and a foundation on which to base decisions. As part of the R/3 system, IDES depicts an integrated model company.

The international specifications are a motivating force and offer a range of products managed within the system so that information needed to make decisions is readily available.

SAP Training

The whole R/3 training program is full of exercises and examples adapted to IDES, so that it is possible to use training materials, course exercises, and the extensive system details.

Release upgrades are accessible at any given time. As the time between releases decreases because of technical advances, the most current information must be available as quickly as possible. IDES represents the most current version of the R/3 System and provides direct access to the new functionality, making it possible to carry out system upgrades without problems.

---

[1] Kanban is a Japanese management methodology that was created in the 1980's in an effort to reduce costs in the manufacturing industry. Kanban is designed to reduce costs by producing an output that is equal to the current levels of demand within your industry sector. As a result, your need to keep excess goods in a warehouse and investment costs are both reduced.

Information Databases and Your Return

SAP customers and partners have continued to demonstrate an ability to achieve superior results with the licensing of SAP courses in combination with associated technology via the Information Database. The Information Database is used for project team training as well as for a foundation for end-user training. This latter use is an important aspect in training many of SAP's customers. Education, support staff, and the Education Account Manager Program have expanded to support this area.

SAP and CBT: A Mutually Beneficial Relationship

SAP and CBT Systems joined forces to develop high-quality, interactive computer-based training (CBT) on SAP R/3 for end-users, power-users, business professionals, and all management levels. This training is complementary to SAP's courses, but is not intended to replace SAP classes.

CBT tools can be an important supplement to an effective training session before the class actually begins. CBT and this text will provide a good foundation for building the information base needed to thrive in an R/3 environment.

These course supplements expedite the learning process and increase understanding of the differences in what is offered between SAP R/3 Release 3.0 and Release 4.0. These options allow students to make important distinctions in the way they learn so they can better control the learning process.

Using the Internet

Like many other organizations, SAP has embraced the Internet. Customers often use the online Education Catalog through the Internet on both the SAP America and Canada Training Home Pages. The catalog is frequently accessed by customers and partners. This medium allows customers to instantly see exactly what courses are being offered through:

- Direct navigation of HTML encoded Web pages
- Adobe Portable Document Format files that are:
  — Viewed directly through the Web browser
  — Downloaded at leisure to be viewed offline

The Internet has developed into the most effective medium for distributing information of practically any type. The direct-access course catalog is updated on the SAP World Wide Web site every week to include new and additional course information. Go to the Web page at **http://www.sap.com/usa** and follow the training link.

Online Help

Online help can assist in navigation through business processes. It was created especially for IDES. To those familiar only with working in a new application area, the detailed documentation on processes helps in moving efficiently through the process flows. All the application and department-specific restrictions can be avoided.

Detailed descriptions of the process flows can be accessed and quit at will. At any point users can move to background information that has business data and important examples that have been both tried and tested.

R/3 software is based on client/server architecture. R/3 is designed as an open system that can be used on operating systems from a variety of vendors. Along with the software, SAP provides a complete spectrum of services, professional consulting in organizational and technical issues ranging from project planning to system implementation, qualified staff training, and 24-hour hotline support. SAP's quality management process for software development meets international ISO 9001 standards.

Customer Satisfaction

One of the driving factors behind SAP's high status in the industry is customer satisfaction. The Award of Excellence is a primary indicator of how SAP expertise is certified within its consultant base. The Partner Academy exemplifies this driving force and represents the SAP Award of Excellence, originally created to recognize partner organizations that achieve the highest possible levels of customer satisfaction. This award is given every year to SAP partner firms who have achieved top scores in independent worldwide surveys of customer satisfaction.

The award represents the highest possible achievement by the organization and/or the SAP consultant.

This level of certification verifies comprehensive and current SAP expertise. It represents a significant benchmark of consultant expertise and the dedication consultants possess to provide the highest-quality support. Customers always realize that working with a certified consultant provides substantial benefits that represent the cornerstone of success. Success is then translated into maximizing business performance and profitability with SAP.

Worldwide SAP Support

SAP support quality translates into the best possible level of support around the world. This support allows customers to increase their business performance and profitability. The support process begins with the best software solutions and grows to offer complete support via an international network of SAP partners and consultants.

This comprehensive group of certified professionals works toward a common goal: achieving business objectives. SAP is dedicated to success through an effective educational infrastructure with the SAP Partner Academy.

The Partner Academy's first priority is to offer consultants the highest level of SAP knowledge and applications expertise. The result is a high level of skilled global support and consistency.

In classrooms around the world, consultants receive intensive training in the most current SAP systems, tools, and implementation techniques. Quality training significantly benefits all SAP customers by improving implementation effectiveness and business performance.

Summary

This chapter has covered all of the preliminary information leading to your certification classes, including the basic structure of SAP's certification courses and to prepare for the subject matter or appropriate course track.

Chapter 2 provides more information on SAP Partner Academy and resources for the professional consultant.

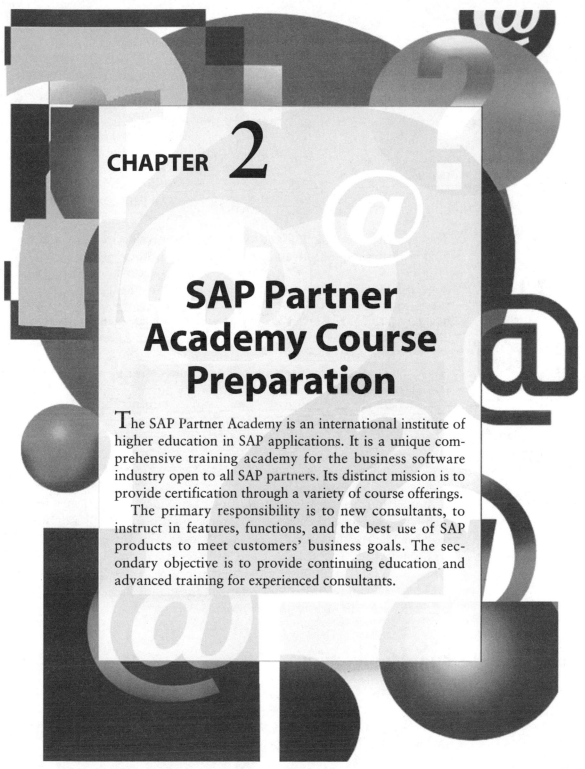

CHAPTER 2

SAP Partner Academy Course Preparation

The SAP Partner Academy is an international institute of higher education in SAP applications. It is a unique comprehensive training academy for the business software industry open to all SAP partners. Its distinct mission is to provide certification through a variety of course offerings.

The primary responsibility is to new consultants, to instruct in features, functions, and the best use of SAP products to meet customers' business goals. The secondary objective is to provide continuing education and advanced training for experienced consultants.

Common Questions About Courses

What is involved in successful completion of Academy training?

Successful completion of Academy training is a significant achievement. Consultants must finish a rigorous, comprehensive course of instruction and demonstrate mastery of subject matter by passing SAP's certification exams.

What do the standardized exams cover?

The standardized examinations cover specific product releases and business processes and effective implementation in those areas.

When are the tests usually given?

The tests are usually given in concert with Academy courses, though any consultant who has sufficient SAP experience can take these exams to obtain certification.

SAP has consistently introduced automated testing tools and other methods in an effort to increase the efficiency of the certification process.

Training Centers

SAP classroom training facilities offer extensive access to education in several locations. In the United States, SAP has facilities in Philadelphia, Boston, Parsippany, Atlanta, Houston, Dallas, Chicago, Detroit, Minneapolis, Cleveland, St. Louis, Los Angeles, and San Francisco. Overseas, SAP has facilities in Canada (Toronto, Ottawa, Vancouver, Calgary, Montreal) and Latin America (Mexico City, Argentina, Brazil, Venezuela, and Columbia). If a company has global training requirements, SAP-AG schedules the same curriculum offerings throughout the world. SAP also offers on-site training.

Education Account Management

As customers work together with SAP to create their SAP R/3 implementation strategy, one vital focus is the training plan for the project team. Currently, a member of the SAP consulting organization works with customers to develop their training plans.

The Education Account Manager Program offers an additional resource to assist the consulting organization and customer in planning education for customers with 30 or more in their project implementation team.

The education professional will work with the SAP and customer project team members to make certain the customer optimizes the return on investment in SAP Education's array of services and delivery options. The customer gets the best people, training, time, and place at the SAP Education Center or on-site.

Consulting Partners

Consulting Partners are business and technology consulting firms who offer assistance in all phases of an R/3 implementation project: Going live, training, and education.

They have proven expertise in using the best practices for effective business process reengineering and work closely with clients in redefining roles and systems to optimize performance with SAP software. Several partners maintain SAP solution centers for specific industries and business needs.

Helping Customers Through SAP Support

Enhancing the quality of SAP support globally assists customers by increasing business performance and profitability. This level of support involves world-class software solutions, and extends to complete support through a global network of SAP partners and consultants. This extensive pool of certified professionals is dedicated to achieving customers' business goals.

SAP is dedicated to assuring success through the strong educational infrastructure provided by the SAP Partner Academy, whose primary mission is to provide consultants with the highest degree of SAP knowledge and applications expertise.

The result is an unequalled measure of skilled support and consistency worldwide. Consultants receive intensive training in the latest SAP systems, tools, and implementation techniques, quality training which benefits every SAP customer by increasing implementation effectiveness and business performance.

SAP People

SAP consulting partners are sub-divided into three categories based on business scope:

1. **Global Consulting Partners**—These are the largest and most experienced consulting partner firms with multinational and multi-industry SAP support capabilities.

   Partners include:
   - Andersen Consulting
   - CAP GEMINI Coopers & Lybrand
   - CSC
   - Digital
   - Deloitte & Touche
   - EDS
   - Ernst & Young
   - Hewlett-Packard
   - IBM
   - KPMG
   - ORIGIN
   - PLAUT
   - Price Waterhouse
   - SNI

2. **National Consulting Partners**—These are large firms with resources and capabilities to offer SAP support services in one particular country.

3. **Implementation Partners**—These firms offer more localized or specialized SAP support in one region of a country or in a specific industry.

Hardware Partners

Hardware partners are leading hardware vendors who offer the computing hardware required for a customer's system requirements. When a company works closely with both SAP and its customers, hardware partners constantly develop and optimize products to meet the real-world requirements of operating business applications with SAP software.

Hardware partners have created dedicated organizations to offer comprehensive SAP support dealing with product selection, system setup, installation, and continuous performance tuning, as well as other needs.

Every hardware partner maintains one or more competence centers to be certain of the correct sizing of customer computer systems and full compatibility with SAP software.

SAP hardware partners include:

- Amdahl
- Bull
- Compaq
- Data General

- Dell
- Digital
- Fujitsu
- Hewlett-Packard
- Hitachi
- IBM
- Intergraph
- NCR
- NEC
- Sequent
- Siemens Nixdorf
- Sun
- Tandem
- Unisys

SAP Expertise Award of Excellence

Certifying through SAP Expertise Award of Excellence illustrates the high level of customer satisfaction which is the motivating force behind SAP. This award was established to recognize partner organizations that achieve the highest levels of customer satisfaction. It is given annually to SAP partner firms who earn outstanding scores in independent surveys of customer satisfaction conducted around the world.

The award is a significant achievement for companies and their consultants that proves a high level of recognition of top SAP support. This release-based certification verifies comprehensive, up-to-date SAP knowledge and is an important benchmark of consultant expertise. It also demonstrates dedication to providing the highest degree of quality support.

Customers have found that working with a certified consultant delivers substantial benefits integral to success in maximizing business performance and profitability with SAP.

New Content Approach

In combination with a new instructional approach, there is a new content approach which concentrates on a business process perspective of the SAP R/3 system. It also highlights the integration of the software's components. This methodology provides participants with the core knowledge they need to implement and use the SAP R/3 system and its tools.

Global Partnerships

SAP supplements its own capabilities and resources by creating an international network of strategic alliances with highly reputable companies in the information technology industry. These alliances draw on the strengths of all concerned. They offer additional capabilities for further development and use of the R/3 system and permit extension of the range of customer support for implementation and use of SAP's applications.

Partner Awards

SAP has set up specific programs to recognize partner organizations that achieve the highest levels of customer satisfaction. The partner award is given annually to SAP partner firms who earn outstanding scores in independent surveys of customer satisfaction conducted around the world. The awards mean companies and their consultants have achieved a high level of recognition. The release-based certification verifies comprehensive, current SAP knowledge. It is an important benchmark of consultant expertise and it demonstrates a company's dedication to offering the highest degree of quality support.

Customers have found that working with certified consultants provides substantial benefits. Such interaction is a key element of success in maximizing business performance and profitability with SAP.

Consultants

Knowhow Transfer

"Knowhow transfer" is the term used by SAP for promoting the creation of successful alliances, which depend on systematic transfer of information, experience, and knowhow. The SAP Partner Academy uses internationally standardized teaching methods to transfer this know how.

Advanced Teaching Methods and Multimedia

R/3 self-study units are used. Course participants have online access to current information related to products and applications, and can also take advantage of system resources to conduct supplementary independent studies.

The first training block usually lasts five weeks. Students learn about application functionality in a practical, hands-on manner. They work with business processes, illustrated by a model company called IDES (International Demo and Education System).

Case studies allow students to test what they have learned. The first training sequence finishes with a one-week integration workshop at which consultants from various fields jointly conduct a practice implementation.

SAP Consultant Certification

Proven R/3 competence happens after completing training. Students take a test to qualify as "certified SAP R/3 consultants." This certificate is written proof that a participant has completed the course and mastered its subject matter.

Customers know that certified consultants have direct access to SAP's information network; they can therefore benefit from the practical experience accumulated by SAP's consultants.

Certificates can be earned in the following areas:

- Accounting and controlling
- Handling of customer orders
- Materials management
- Production and production planning
- Human resources
- Development of applications with ABAP/4
- R/3 system support

In order to gain certification, a test lasting several hours must be passed. Attendance at the Partner Academy is not required and experienced R/3 consultants may take tests to document knowledge acquired elsewhere.

Complementary Software Certification

Interoperability is the seamless integration of applications and components from different vendors. Customers need interoperability when they choose add-on products, but there is often no guarantee that this important requirement will be fulfilled.

SAP has implemented a process for certifying add-on components for its own application interfaces. This involves a detailed technical evaluation of the connection between the third-party complementary product and the SAP software, but does not examine the actual application functionality of the product itself.

Third-Party Complementary Product Certification Program

SAP has created a special certification program for third-party complementary products allowing software to benefit from short implementation cycles for ready-to-use solutions.

Regardless of where certification is obtained, it is valid worldwide. SAP certification labs have been set up in the USA, Germany and Japan.

SAP is dedicated to enhancing its open nature for its customers to guarantee seamless integration of third-party products with the SAP applications that run core business.

Customers who choose from the list of certified products know they can achieve specific benefits, including:

✎ Reduced implementation times by buying a ready-to-use solution
✎ Reduced costs by installing a product with an interface that works with the dedicated R/3 application
✎ Good investment in a complementary product with a stable interface to SAP's enterprise software.

Third-Party Benefits

Third-party benefits accrue beyond what is gained from SAP's certification process. When interfaces are tested, software partners know that their add-on solutions will work with the tested interface at all customer sites. Partners also receive marketing support and increased visibility through association with SAP.

NOTE

See Chapters 15 and 16 for more information on complementary software certification.

Summary

SAP intends to provide further interfaces for certification. Interfaces to system management tools will become part of the certification process as will database backup tools. SAP is also interested in providing standardization of interfaces between applications, and is actively involved in the Open Applications Group (OAG). After the successful integration of Object Linking and Embedding (OLE), SAP continues to pursue its policy of incorporating widely accepted standards in the R/3 system.

These first two chapters have discussed the variety of tracks that define the SAP Partner Academy and provided a better understanding of the specific types of certification SAP offers. Use this information to refine your own certification objectives and find the most helpful course(s) to suit your own career goals.

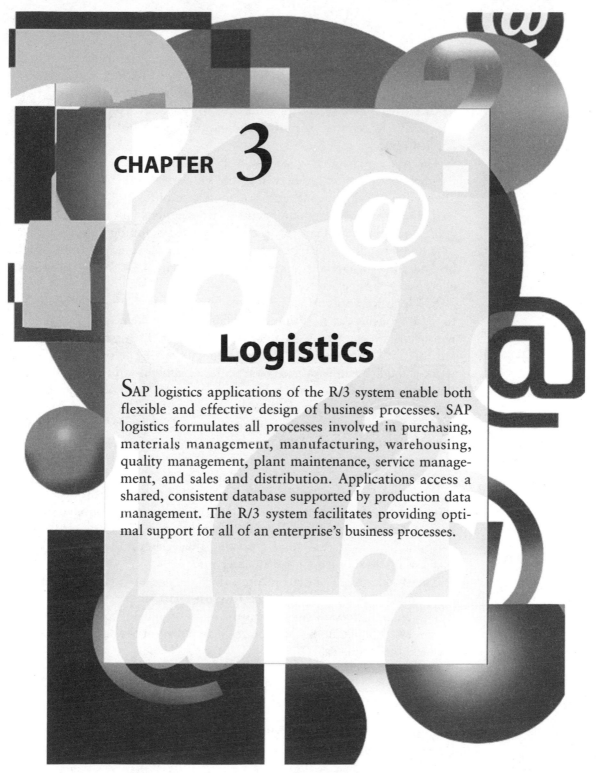

CHAPTER 3

Logistics

SAP logistics applications of the R/3 system enable both flexible and effective design of business processes. SAP logistics formulates all processes involved in purchasing, materials management, manufacturing, warehousing, quality management, plant maintenance, service management, and sales and distribution. Applications access a shared, consistent database supported by production data management. The R/3 system facilitates providing optimal support for all of an enterprise's business processes.

A company must adjust effectively to changing customer needs in order to remain competitive. Logistics applications of SAP's R/3 system provide all sizes of organizations with optimized processes and simple workflows for improving quality and productivity to reduce costs and time-to-market. SAP's R/3 system supports the supply chain with fully integrated applications.

The process chains of each application ease the processes and accelerate the flow of information within the enterprise. When these processes are used across applications, the true potential of the R/3 software is realized. Thus managers can consistently base decisions on information gathered from planning material requirements, developing sales forecasts, scheduling production capacities, or gaining production costs on a single, body of up-to-date information. SAP provides essential integrated client/server business software.

R/3 logistics applications work to help improve the supply chain. All functions of these applications are planned, controlled, and coordinated within the system across all organizational units. Because the R/3 system automatically links all the elements that logically belong together, no work is duplicated. Data need to be entered only once. In the R/3 system, the processes involved in logistics, financials, and human resources all synchronize, creating an efficient business model. The primary areas of sales and distribution, materials management, and production compose the foundation for this integrated system.

It is possible to enhance this functionality by constantly expanding the system with respect to an organization's particular requirements. The flexibility of R/3 applications makes it possible to modify the R/3 system to changes in the market, when needed. In addition to complete integration of R/3 applications, SAP business workflow offers a powerful, application-independent tool for supporting the design and optimization of business processes throughout an enterprise.

The standard R/3 system incorporates a range of executable example workflows that can be customized to satisfy particular requirements. SAP business workflow allows definition of company-specific workflow processes. Organizational boundaries may not be at the same point where business processes cease.

Logistics Information

Logistics tasks are useful for all sections of an enterprise. R/3 logistics applications offer solutions for thousands of organizations in more than 50 countries around the world to integrate logistics, financials, human resources, SAP business workflow, and links to the Internet. More than 800 business processes are part of this comprehensive software system. It is possible to use a single R/3 component or a combination of components and subcomponents to satisfy requirements.

SAP and the Internet

SAP offers at least 30 complete Internet applications that will make it possible to place a product catalog from R/3 directly on the Internet, or create sales orders from customers using the Internet.

Services

R/3 users benefit from an extensive range of services, both consulting and supplementary, provided by individual product providers who work in close cooperation with SAP. SAP service partners ensure that consulting and system requirements are met. There are an increasing number of business activities that involve crossing national borders.

Logistics Tasks

Logistics tasks are pertinent to all sections of an enterprise. In order to support the complex ways where these interact, it is important to have comprehensive integrated software applications. R/3 logistics applications yield solutions for thousands of organizations in more than fifty countries around the world. The R/3 System incorporates Logistics, Financials, Human Resources, SAP Business Workflow, as well as links to the Internet.

There are more than 800 business processes that are part of this comprehensive software system. You can employ one single R/3 component or a combination of components and sub-components to best satisfy your requirements.

NOTE

Although computing tasks are executed locally, components and subcomponents remain integrated with the rest of the system. R/3 functions have access to shared central data, effectively eliminating data redundancy and ensuring data integrity.

Functional Integration

The integration of all functions provides a high-level of performance features for SAP software. In the R/3 System, data is instantly relayed to where it is needed. Automatic linking between components accelerates and eases business procedures.

Production Planning and control data can flow directly into Time Management. Results from Payroll Accounting can be passed on to Financial or Cost Accounting. Financial controlling and analysis capabilities provide reliable help in making decisions, permitting you to introduce any necessary changes in your business immediately.

An increasing number of business activities involve crossing national borders. The R/3 System supports international requirements of your organization with country-specific versions that take account of different languages and currencies, and creating provisions for pertinent legal requirements.

Year 2000 Compliance

SAP makes certain they have year 2000 compliant software by developing its R/3 System with a four-digit year code from the start.

R/3 Logistics

The R/3 logistics components provide a high-level of performance in several areas and permit easy access to complete and current data. The R/3 logistics applications allow creation of individualized decentralized solutions using an enterprise-wide information system that allows easy integration of additional functions.

Product Data Management

Another important R/3 component involves the Product Data Management (PDM) system or a single-source PDM solution offered within the R/3 system. PDM functions work in combination with other R/3 application components to provide a single-source integrated solution.

The R/3 PDM solution reflects knowledge gained through the implementation of business processes for entire organizations. This action benefits from the interdependencies between engineering and production.

Logistics Component

The logistics component includes a complete suite of customer service functions such as call management, warranty management, and service and maintenance contract processing. On-time delivery should be the standard. Shipping management provides easy-to-use functions for managing picking, packing, and loading tasks, and monitoring delivery deadlines. The system offers a list of all sales orders due for delivery and offers the choice of delivering the order completely or partially, individually or collectively.

Bill of Material

PDM provides product structure information instantly. Bill of Material (BOM) management makes the distinction between engineering BOMs and production BOMs in a company. By maintaining the distinction between the different uses of a BOM it is possible to create entirely separate BOMs or to define different views on the same BOM.

The product structure browser allows easy movement between objects in the product structure. All data pertinent to the product, including data from areas outside the actual design environment, can be accessed. Relationships among all the objects in the product structure are viewed in graphical form. PDM functions are supported for large product development projects in the R/3 Project System.

Bill of Material Management solves the problem of making the distinction between engineering BOMs and production BOMs in your company. It is possible to maintain the distinction between the different uses of a BOM. You must create either an entirely separate BOM or define different views on the same BOM. There is a definite trend toward products with a large number of variants. Product configurations must be completely integrated in the logistics process chain of your company. When you configure a product, you can inspect it to determine whether the configuration is complete and consistent. This inspection allows you to avoid impossible combinations.

Document Management System

The Document Management system provides the ability to manage a variety of technical, commercial, and administrative documents consistently.

Original documents can be linked to all types of objects in the R/3 system: material master records, BOMs, or change master records.

Classification System

The Classification System is a system-wide function that permits you to classify all types of object in the R/3 System. It is possible to classify and structure data on materials, operations, production resources/tools, documents, inspection characteristics, customers, and vendors according to criteria you designate.

Designers use the classification system to find similar parts, thus reducing duplication on parts in the company.

R/3 supports a standardized dialog interface. It is an important module for integrating engineering and design processes in the logistics process chain of a company. This interface is both used for integrating CAD systems, and connecting all kinds of engineering applications to your R/3 System.

Engineering Change Management

Engineering Change Management ensures that planned changes to master data are automatically available in the productive functions of Sales and Distribution, Demand Management, MRP, Production Control, Product Costing, Quality Management, and Materials Management at a specified time.

Product Structure Browser

The product structure browser allows you to move easily between objects in the product structure. You can access all data that is pertinent to the product such as data from areas outside the actual design environment. You can view relationships between all the objects in the product structure in graphical form.

PDM functions are supported for large product development projects in the R/3 Project System. R/3 Logistics Applications enhance your customer service with a reliable, fully integrated sales system.

Sales Support Component

The Sales Support component gives you tools to manage information on sales leads, sales calls, inquiries, quotations, marketing campaigns, competitors, and their products. Sales and marketing personnel can access this data constantly to perform sales activities or produce direct mailings. You can use Sales Support not only to make your sales process more efficient, but to also increase service to existing customers.

Identifying Business Sources

You can identify new sources of business, save time, and reduce errors with user-friendly order entry. Order entry in the R/3 System is mostly automatic. You can reference information that you wish to input in the simple user interface. The system assembles information, including the terms of payment and delivering plant. It then proposes this information in the sales order.

Customer Sales and Distribution

Sales and Distribution

R/3 system's sales and distribution applications offer access to real-time, online information from sales support to the billing process. They have all the functions and information needed for easy automation of sales tasks, to allow a company to focus on expanding its business. The sales support component makes it possible to manage information on sales leads, sales calls, inquiries, quotations, marketing campaigns, competitors, and their products. Sales and marketing personnel can access this data constantly to perform sales activities or produce direct mailings. Sales support makes the sales process more efficient and customers benefit from increased service.

Sales and distribution offers a detailed level of support for foreign trade processing that provides an automated export control to determine whether it is possible to export specific products to a specific country or customer at a given time. The system handles all the necessary customs forms automatically.

The R/3 system gathers all the data required for the declarations and creates the proper forms for declaration of shipments of goods to government authorities.

Preference agreement processing assists in managing the shipment of products eligible for customs tariff preferences, tracking the origin of component parts, and designating a tariff classification for materials.

Customer Information

Customer information is displayed according to your preference. This information can be from a customer, material, region, or any other means. You can receive the information in an easy-to interpret list or informative graphic. You can use the Sales Information System to put you in a strategic position to address market trends and changes.

Customer Billing

Automatic customer billing is possible for your orders and deliveries. The system automatically executes billing for all due items. The system then creates an invoice, debit memo, or credit memo for each item or collectively for several transactions. You may then send a billing document directly to the customer either by mail, fax, or EDI.

Revenues and receivables are immediately visible in the Financial Accounting (FI) and Controlling (CO) components. In addition, you can also process rebates based on a customer's purchase volume. All of this information works towards recognizing market trends so that SAP can give you the best possible level of support, so that you can make decisions for your Sales Information System. When you input a Sales and Distribution document into the system, the relevant information is updated in the Sales Information System. This makes certain that the information you access is always up to date.

Availability

You can review availability in multiple locations. When dealing with customers requiring specific quantities of a product, you can use the make-to-order production features in Sales and Distribution. This indicates that your organization can make sales order decisions with current information, helping you complete business processes quickly and efficiently. Offer your customer the best possible service Sales and Distribution supports a wide range of contracts, from general contracts to more specific rental contracts. With them, you can specify delivery quantities, delivery dates, and prices. Scheduling agreements and more complex requirements such as just-in-time delivery schedules are also supported. Or you can follow up on your products with the Service Management

It can be used in all sectors of industry and provides a whole palette of production methods ranging from make-to-order production/variant processing to repetitive manufacturing or mass production. Similarly to R/3 Logistics applications, PP is fully integrated in the complete R/3 system.

It doesn't matter whether you have a standalone system or a worldwide network of distributed R/3 systems, linked by ALE. Your data is available within seconds within the Production Planning and Control, Financial Accounting, in Sales & Distribution, and in Human Resource Management modules.

Availability Check

The availability check can work in combination with the Materials Management (MM) and Production Planning (PP) applications. It verifies that you have enough quantities on the requested delivery date to satisfy a sales order. If you are not able to satisfy the requested delivery date, the system immediately determines when the desired quantity will become available.

Many organizations work with conflicting goals that involve products or services which must be provided or received from colleagues, associates, or clients. However, customers expect delivery times and product life cycles to be shorter now than they ever were before.

Pricing

Pricing starts automatically in the sales order. It is possible to determine pertinent predefined prices, surcharges, and discounts. A system works from price lists and customer agreements, or can determine an amount according to the product, product group, or product cost.

The pricing functions are flexible and can manage even the most complex price structures, making it possible to maintain pricing information with data from sales deals and promotions. A system can also execute a dynamic credit limit check, checking against credit, financial, SD (sales and distribution), and sales data to verify the customer's credit limit.

Transportation

The transportation module provides functions for transportation planning, processing, monitoring, and controlling. It does not matter where products are sent, the transportation chain can represent the R/3 system for individual shipments or stop-off shipments involving several deliveries and several destinations. It is also possible to select forwarding agents and track shipments.

Transportation Activities

Transportation activities are made easy through functions such as shipping point determination and route determination. Foreign trade processing is made possible by quickly preparing the necessary data for customs declarations, for export, or for import activities.

NOTE

SAP has Application Link Enabling (ALE); this makes it possible to execute business processes throughout multiple systems. SAP makes available distribution scenarios gained from the actual requirements of a large number of customers. ALE facilitates the integration of individual applications operating on different systems. The integrated turnkey system ensures the consistency of all functions.

Production and Manufacturing

Production Planning and Control

The R/3 system's Production Planning (PP) and Control application enables achieving the greatest potential when planning, executing, and controlling production. Several market pressures, including high-level globalization, influence organization to move away from traditional processes and toward customer orientation and flexible production methods. PP satisfies the business requirements of manufacturers whose processes are continually changing and developing.

This component offers solutions for three areas: production planning, production execution, and production control.

The integrated solution for all industry sectors, PP deals with the production process, creation of master data, production planning, MRP, and capacity planning, and with production control and costing.

Production planning modules employ Sales & Operations Planning (SOP) to provide the ability to create consistent planning figures and dates with respect to expected sales or other key figures of choice.

Repetitive Manufacturing

Repetitive manufacturing is created specifically for manufacturers of products that are typically produced repetitively on a given production line over a longer period. R/3's repetitive manufacturing module offers a tool based on production rates and lines to cover the requirements of this type of production.

Production Control

Production can be controlled using KANBAN techniques. KANBAN is a production order primarily used as a tool for discrete, job-shop production that provides many status management functions. Replenishment or the production of a material is not triggered until a higher production level actually requires the material. In R/3's KANBAN module, various replenishment methods are available for in-house production, external procurement, and stock transfer.

Project Systems

Project Quality Management

Quality management, interfaces to PDC systems, distributed control systems, laboratory information systems, and extensive data analysis functions in the Open Information Warehouse are all also integrated in R/3's Production Control.

Successful project management is synonymous with planning, carrying out, and monitoring important undertakings economically and with your objective always in mind. Increased performance of your organizational tools and technical systems means more successful your project management will be.

Extensive functionality and integrated project processing are the indicators of a high-performance project management system. Project planning and control become an integral part of your business organization and management regimes. The functions available in the R/3 System guarantee reliable support during all phases of an undertaking and meet the requirements typical of projects of all types.

Project System

The project system's graphical interface can be used to create structures quickly. Cost and schedule planning become more refined as the project becomes more detailed and easier to view. The project system can be integrated with other modules in the R/3 system to permit planning of resources in cooperation with purchasing, inventory management, and material requirements planning. Human resources can be designated by individual employee or by group.

The project system checks and monitors availability of funds, capacities, and materials to ensure that there is enough of each for the project to be executed. It is possible to restrict and control project expenditure using the tools for approving and releasing project budgets.

Workflow

WBS Project System

The central structures in the Project System are work breakdown structures (WBS) and networks with its activities. You can also use these structures in combination with sales orders for sales and distribution, with BOMs for production and procurement, and to model complex projects in the system.

SAP Business Workflow for Projects

SAP Business Workflow is available for you to improve communications within large projects. It allows you to use workflow to make certain that the purchasing department is immediately notified of any changes in schedule or quantity requirements.

Throughout project processing, the system offers a flexible information system that allows you to tailor the layout and degree of detail of reports to suit your own requirements.

Listings and Graphical Analyses

Listings and graphical analyses provide all of the information you need on the budget, planned and actual costs, revenues, commitments, payments received and made, schedules, and resources.

Standard Interfaces

Standard interfaces offer a two-way communications base required for further planning and calculations in additional systems and at a local level.

Production Planning

Production Planning Application Tools

PP application tools ensure a high performance level for the planning and control of the complete material flow in production processes. It offers several easy-to-use information systems that can be adjusted to suit specific requirements. Planners, work schedulers, and production schedulers are relieved of routine tasks and therefore have more time to concentrate on more business-critical activities.

Materials Management

Materials management can help improve the procurement process and the logistics pipeline within an organization. The R/3 system's materials management application contains all the functions required to simplify business processes in terms of requirements planning, purchasing, inventory management, warehouse management, and invoice verification, and also offers a high degree of automation of standard procedures.

MM application components allow optimization of material procurement processes, offering powerful cost-effective purchasing tools, timely acceptance, and billing of services.

R/3 functions are tightly coupled with each other and with other functions in R/3. This indicates that the most up-to-date information is always available to users within Materials Management and to other users in Logistics and Financials. The system does all the routine tasks for you, resulting in giving you time for more important activities.

Material Master Record

A central theme throughout any R/3 application involves the material master record, a data object that allows recording of general data which are valid throughout the company and defined within the design or standards department, including the material number, descriptions in multiple languages, weight, basic material, and classification data. It is also possible to maintain data relevant to specific functions, such as sales and distribution, Material Requirements Planning (MRP), and work scheduling. The different perspectives on a material master record allow maintenance of separate data for different departments.

Dealing with Materials

R/3 can work easily with materials. You can enter materials manually, choose from customer-based product proposals, or work with variant configurations to configure a product to meet customer requirements.

Material Requirements Planning

In Material Requirements Planning (MRP), the system computes the quantities and procurement dates for the necessary raw materials. Capacities can be planned at this phase and bottlenecks can be recognized. Capacity planning is integrated with production order processing in combination with repetitive manufacturing. Various dispatching strategies and a flexible graphic-planning table support planning of resources.

Production order processing, repetitive manufacturing, or KANBAN production control can make a production order primarily a tool for discrete, job-shop production that offers a number of status management functions, controlling per order, and various operation-related functions.

Vendor Evaluation Application

You can compare prices during the procurement process or automate the vendor selection or order creation processes. The Vendor Evaluation application enables you to determine the best vendors using criteria of your choice. You also have the option of requiring purchasing documents to be part of a release and approval procedure before they can be further processed.

Evaluated Receipt Settlement

The Evaluated Receipt Settlement (ERS) function permits elimination of vendor invoices. It automatically and periodically creates invoices based on the goods receipts posted in the system for purchase orders.

Invoice verification provides a special method of entering vendor invoices that is much faster than standard procedures. It is possible to integrate further processes in materials management. The MM application comprises several additional functions to assist the shaping of a materials management system as efficiently as possible.

Purchasing Information Systems

A purchasing information system provides the power to negotiate with vendors. It allows choice of which data to integrate in reports and how to present the information. Inventory controlling can be used to determine stock values and inventory turnover rates, and to execute analyses. The information systems help identify trends and developments, the foundation for making decisions.

Purchase Activities and Order History

Purchasing activities are approved by authorized members of staff via electronic signature. You can transmit purchase orders or forecast delivery schedules to the vendors either on paper or electronically. The purchase order history allows you to monitor the status of your order and track deliveries or invoices already received.

Product Quality and the Purchasing Department

Your purchasing department receives the latest quality scores for vendors as well as quality data for requests for quotations and purchase orders. Since product quality is crucial, the quality function can release a vendor for delivery. The control data you predefine in QM determines which materials will be inspected and posted to inspection stock to undergo a goods receipt inspection, production inspection, or source inspection. This action makes certain that only products conforming with the predefined quality requirements will be released for further processing.

You can reduce your administrative tasks through company-wide quality planning. If you organize your quality planning activities centrally, you can make sure that the quality requirements for quality characteristics, inspection methods, and specifications will be documented and up to date.

Integrated Use of Master Data

The integrated use of master data ensures that your inspection planning activities will be consistent and efficient. The R/3 System has inspections that are documented by an inspection lot as well as the corresponding inspection results. When you record inspection results, you can record the results directly in the R/3 System, create a quality notification on the Internet to allow your customers to interact directly with the problem management process, and you can document your product quality using quality certificates.

Besides shipping documents that accompany the delivery of goods to the customer, you can incorporate a quality certificate to verify the product quality. In addition to printing a quality certificate, you can also transmit a certificate by fax or your customer can retrieve the certificate via the Internet.

Goods Movements

Goods movements postings automatically result in an update of values in Financial Accounting, Asset Accounting, and Controlling. Whether you execute physical inventories periodically or continuously, use total stock, or use sampling or cycle counting methods; the system supports you with several convenient aids for entering data and with a variety of automatic evaluations. You can several inventory valuation methods, such as LIFO or FIFO, for balance sheet valuation.

Inventory Management

Inventory management gives companies the ability to keep stock of materials and to manage on both value and quantity bases. The application component supports all the most common types of receipts, issues, and stock transfers, and permits management of special stocks (such as batches, consignment stocks, project stock, returnable transport packaging, or components stocked at a subcontractor's facilities).

Warehouse Management

Costs can be reduced with efficient warehouse management. The Warehouse Management (WM) module provides an automated means of support that allows processing of goods movements and maintenance of a current record of all materials stored in highly complex warehousing structures. WM is integrated with and linked directly to other SAP applications, including Inventory Management (IM), Sales and Distribution (SD), Production Planning (PP), and Quality Management (QM). It is possible to use advanced put-away and picking techniques, so that WM optimizes material flow and capacity in the warehouse, storing goods in the most favorable locations.

WM can be interfaced to hand-held terminals, bar-code scanners, and automated warehousing systems, so that the many automatic processes available in the WM component are easily accessible.

Quality Management

Quality Management (QM) complies with both R/3 logistics applications and quality management standards. QM is an important factor in producing high-quality products that foster long-lasting customer/vendor relationships, reduce expenses, and improve competitiveness.

QM makes it possible to achieve a high degree of quality for all processes in the logistics chain. QM is closely integrated with the other R/3 system modules. Implementing it in a logistics system offers several advantages over the use of isolated systems.

Whenever product quality is crucial, the quality function can release a vendor for delivery. The control data predefined in QM determine the specific materials to be inspected and posted to inspection stock to undergo a goods receipt inspection, production inspection, or source inspection. This action ensures that only products conforming with the predefined quality requirements will be released for further processing.

The QM component functions in the R/3 system to create a computer-integrated quality management system (CIQ) and offer a foundation for total quality management. Materials can be maintained in batches on the basis of quality characteristics. The batch characteristics defined in QM can be used as a method of searching for batches in a delivery.

The QM information system can be used at different management levels to plan, monitor, evaluate, and control quality. Quality notifications offer a flexible means of solving quality-related problems of products or services. Quality notifications in the R/3 system can be used to process complaints against vendors, internal problem reports, or complaints filed by customers.

QM Information System

As part of the central Logistics Information System (LIS), you can use the QM Information System at different management levels to plan, monitor, evaluate, and control quality.

Furthermore, you can manage problems efficiently by using quality notifications. Quality notifications provide a flexible and efficient means of solving quality-related problems for products or services. You can use the quality notifications in the R/3 System to process complaints against vendors, internal problem reports, or complaints filed by customers.

You can define corrective actions (tasks), assign tasks to persons responsible, and link the processing activities to the SAP Business Workflow to help you solve a problem quickly. Through the integration of the R/3 System's Controlling (CO) application, you can easily identify all costs incurred while processing a quality notification.

SPC Functions

The functions for Statistical Process Control (SPC) offer a means of monitoring, controlling, and improving the processes. R/3 also supports the use of quality control charts.

Plant Maintenance

Plant maintenance, production planning, and the project system need materials or services to be procured externally. Individual departments can enter purchase requisitions manually. The system passes these purchase requisitions directly to purchasing, where they are converted into purchase orders.

The PM application is a software solution that covers every maintenance task in a company. PM supports the planning and execution of all maintenance activities with regard to system availability, costs, material, and personnel deployment. Plant Maintenance (PM) supports different options for structuring technical systems with its object-, type-, and function-related views, and eases navigation. Data on the planning, processing, and history of maintenance tasks are documented in the system to comply with business verification requirements.

PM provides technical and business reports and various presentation options, according to the criteria used. These criteria include organizational units, locations, execution periods for tasks, or system manufacturers. This information helps reduce the duration and costs of plant downtimes as a result of damage, and makes it possible to recognize weak points within a technical system. As a result, optimum maintenance is achieved through what is called "risk optimized maintenance," also commonly referred to as Total Productive Maintenance, or "TPM." The interface-free integration of plant maintenance in the R/3 system forms the basis for fast and efficient communication and cooperation among the different enterprise areas.

PM provides a complete, industry-wide management system that makes maintenance an integral component of enterprise resource planning. The PM component fulfills the requirements of technical and commercial enterprise areas in its role as a complete plant information system. The standard user interface and the careful implementation ensure reduced implementation times.

The integrated service management system is essential. Because of globalization of markets, worldwide competition between companies has grown. As a result of changing company objectives, the demands of customer service have increased the importance of how everything in your organization is regarded.

Service Management

R/3 Service Management Module

The R/3 System's Service Management module provides highly integrated functionality and is suitable for all types of industry. Long-term service agreements and/or warranty conditions are checked when a call is logged. Services described in these documents can be freely configured with characteristics such as service window, response time, and service area. Pricing is determined with respect to options that you select.

Call Management Process

Throughout the call management process, logged customer calls are automatically checked against service contract commitments and warranty conditions. You can use an extensive catalog system as well as free format data to record and codify activities, type of damage, cause of damage, etc. All service activities are stored in a comprehensive history database. A powerful information system is also available in SM that you can adjust to suit your own particular needs.

Service Billing

Billing can be performed for service contracts on a periodic basis, and also for service orders, based on time and material consumption.

Summary

In this chapter, we covered significant concepts that help plan SAP courses appropriately. These ideas teach global functionality with SAP logistics tasks. R/3 logistics applications provide a background on the integrated functions of data networks, and lead to the types of logistics services that SAP offers.

NOTE

The continuous evolution of SAP will ensure technological superiority. In addition, there will be access to a business model that incorporates the newest advances and developments.

In Chapter 2 we saw how the SAP Partner Academy, which facilitates logistics planning and makes it possible to schedule core curriculum studies efficiently and effectively to suit individual needs.

This chapter helps participants achieve the best and most successful SAP career paths and quickly excel through certification testing. The questions pertaining to logistics that follow will aid in preparation for the logistics portions of the SAP certification exam.

In the following chapters we will explore the specific SAP certification tracks in more detail. As technology changes and SAP develops, these tracks are expected to change.

3-1   Briefly state what SAP offers as far as Internet applications are concerned.

3-2   Explain what type of global functionality is present within logistics tasks.

3-3   What do R/3 logistics applications provide?

3-4   What is the scope of the R/3 application?

3-5   Explain how data networks have integrated functionality.

3-6   What does automatic linking between components do?

3-7   Explain how R/3 supports international requirements.

3-8   Is SAP Year 2000-Compliant?

3-9   Explain how tasks relate to integrated data administration.

3-10 What do the R/3 logistics applications allow users to create?

3-11 What is PDM?

3-12 What does the R/3 PDM solution do?

3-13 How important is the installed base management?

3-14 What does the document management system do?

3-15 What is a material master record?

3-16 Define the "classification system."

3-17 Describe product life cycles.

3-18 Does the R/3 system support a standardized dialog interface?

3-19 What does Engineering Change Management do?

3-20 What type of information does PDM provide very quickly?

3-21 How do users maintain the distinction between different BOM usages?

3-22 What does the product structure browser allow users to do?

3-23 How is PDM used for development projects?

3-24 How can R/3 logistics applications improve customer service?

3-25 What does the R/3 system's sales and distribution application provide?

3-26 What types of tools are found in the sales and support component?

3-27 What are the benefits to order entry?

3-28 How is pricing executed in a sales order?

3-29 Explain the "pricing function."

3-30 What is an availability check?

3-31 What kind of customer service functions are found in the logistics component?

3-32 What specific functions does shipping management provide?

3-33 What does the transportation module do?

3-34 Does sales and distribution provide support?

3-35 How are shipments of goods declared to the government?

3-36 How is automatic billing of customers done?

3-37 Explain how customer billing information is displayed.

3-38 Describe the benefits of Production Planning and Control.

3-39 What three primary areas allow PP requirements to be satisfied?

3-40 In what industry sectors can PP be used?

3-41 Under what conditions can data be available, how fast are data available, and under what modules are they found?

3-42 What is it possible to do with production planning modules using SOP?

3-43 What happens with MRP?

3-44 Explain the significance of production control modules.

3-45 What is repetitive manufacturing and how is it designed for product manufacturers?

3-46 Explain what R/3's repetitive manufacturing module provides?

3-47 What is the role of capacity planning?

3-48 What happens in R/3's KANBAN modules?

3-49 Name some of the entities integrated into R/3's Production Control.

3-50 What types of tools does the PPP application provide?

3-51 What is PS: Project System?

3-52 What signifies high performance project management?

3-53 What can the project system be used for?

3-54 Define WBS.

3-55   Explain how to use the project system's graphical interface.

3-56   What are the benefits of integration with other modules?

3-57   Explain the project system checks and monitors.

3-58   What does SAP Business Workflow do?

3-59   During what phase is it possible to tailor the layout and degree of detail of reports for particular needs?

3-60   What do listings and graphical analyses provide?

3-61   What do standard interfaces provide?

3-62   How can materials management help improve the procurement process in any company?

3-63   What does R/3's material management application contain?

3-64   Explain the level of functional integration present in R/3.

3-65   Name three items that require either material or services to be produced externally.

3-66   What does the Vendor Evaluation Application allow users to do?

3-67   Who approved purchasing activities?

3-68   What does the purchase order history allow users to do?

3-69   What are the benefits to proper inventory management?

3-70   What results from goods movements postings?

3-71   What can the Warehouse Management module do?

3-72   Explain the capabilities of warehouse management.

3-73   How can the efficiency of invoice verification be improved?

3-74   Explain ERS Functionality.

3-75   What is invoice verification?

3-76   Explain what composes the MM application.

3-77   What are some of the functions that make transportation activities easier?

3-78   What other functions do MM application components provide?

3-79   What does the purchasing information system do?

3-80   Explain how quality management fits in with logistics applications.

3-81   Explain Quality Management in a logistics environment.

3-82   How can the quality of your procured goods be verified?

3-83   In what way can administrative tasks be reduced?

3-84   What will the integration of a master date make sure of?

3-85   Explain how an inspection is documented in the R/3 system.

3-86   Describe what composes "CIQ?".

3-87   Describe how materials can be maintained.

3-88   What is SPC, and what kind of functionality does it provide?

3-89   Does R/3 use quality control charts?

3-90   Can the QM Information System be used at various management levels?

3-91   What do quality notifications do?

3-92   What does Plant Maintenance do, and what kind of options does it offer?

3-93   Explain what Total Productive Maintenance is.

3-94   Explain how PM provides and that integral to any ERP implementation.

3-95   Explain what R/3's application tasks covers for a company.

3-96   Explain the open aspects of your R/3 system.

3-97   Explain Integrated Service Management.

3-98   What does R/3's Service Management module do?

3-99   Explain service agreements.

3-100   What happens during call management?

3-101   When can billing be performed?

3-1 SAP currently offers nearly 30 complete Internet applications. These applications allow placement of a product catalog from R/3 directly on the Internet creation of sales orders from customers using the Internet. The result is that a company and its products are present anywhere worldwide all the time. SAP will continue to implement new industry-specific processes.

3-2 Logistics tasks are pertinent to all sections of an enterprise. In order to support the complex ways in which these interact, there must be comprehensive, integrated software applications.

3-3 R/3 logistics applications provide solutions for thousands of organizations in more than 50 countries around the world.

3-4 The R/3 System incorporates logistics, financials, human resources, SAP business workflow, and links to the Internet. More than 800 business processes are part of this comprehensive software system. It is possible to use one single R/3 component or a combination of components and subcomponents to best satisfy a company's requirements.

3-5 The integration of all functions offers a high level of performance features for SAP software. In the R/3 System, data is instantly relayed where it is needed.

3-6 Automatic linking between components greatly speeds up and eases business procedures. Production planning and control data can flow directly into Time Management. In the same way, results from Payroll Accounting can be passed on to Financial or Cost Accounting. Financial controlling and analysis capabilities offer reliable help in making decisions, permitting immediate introduction of any necessary changes into a business.

3-7 A growing number of business activities involve crossing national borders. The R/3 System supports international requirements of organizations with country-specific versions that take account of different languages and currencies and create provisions for pertinent legal requirements.

3-8 Yes. SAP makes certain there is Year 2000-compliant software by developing its R/3 system with a four-digit year code from the start.

3-9 Even though tasks are executed locally, components and subcomponents remain integrated with the rest of the system because all R/3 functions have access to shared central data eliminating data redundancy and making certain data integrity is maintained.

3-10 R/3 logistics applications permit creation of a decentralized solution based on an efficient, enterprise-wide information system where additional functions can easily be integrated as necessary.

SOLUTIONS

3-11 The Product Data Management (PDM) System is a single-source PDM solution offered within the R/3 system. SAP continues to work closely with its partners to enhance functionality of the interface and implement support for other PDM systems. SAP provides its own PDM functions in combination with other R/3 application components to offer a single-source integrated solution.

3-12 The R/3 PDM solution illustrates the expertise gained from the implementation of business processes for entire organizations, especially in the interdependencies between engineering and production. PDM records all master data.

3-13 Managing the configuration and history of the customer-installed base, regardless of whether it is a proprietary or a competitor's product, is one of the core activities in the system.

3-14 The Document Management System makes it possible to manage a wide range of technical, commercial, and administrative documents consistently. Original documents can be linked to all types of objects in the R/3 system: material master records, BOMs, or changed master records. External optical archiving systems can also be accessed.

3-15 The material master record is a data object that is the cornerstone of the R/3 system. In a material master record, general data valid throughout the company and defined within the design or standards department (i.e. material number, descriptions in multiple languages, weight, basic material, and classification data) can be recorded. Data relevant to specific functions, such as Sales and Distribution, Material Requirements Planning (MRP), and Work Scheduling can be maintained. The different perspectives on a material master record permit separation of data for different departments.

3-16 The classification system is a system-wide function that permits classification of all types of objects in the R/3 system. In fact, data on materials, operations, production resources/tools, documents, inspection characteristics, customers, and vendors can be classified and structured according to personalized criteria. Designers use the classification system to find similar parts, and thereby reduce duplication of parts inventory.

3-17 Most organizations must deal with conflicting goals because of the complexity of products, as the range of product variants is constantly increased. However, customers expect delivery times and product life cycles to be shorter than ever. A company needs a competitive edge in the long term, and must therefore meet these challenges on a daily basis. Those working with these issues face, the same types of questions.

SOLUTIONS

3-18 Yes, the R/3 system supports a standardized dialog interface. It is an important module for integrating engineering and design processes in the logistics process chain of a company. This interface is used not only for integrating CAD systems, but for connecting all kinds of engineering applications to an R/3 system.

3-19 Engineering change management makes certain that planned changes to master data are automatically available in the productive functions of sales and distribution, demand management, MRP, production control, product costing, quality management, and materials management at a specified time.

3-20 PDM provides product structure information instantly. Bill of Material (BOM) management solves the problem of making the distinction between engineering BOMs and production BOMs in a company.

3-21 In order to maintain the distinction between the different uses of a BOM, either entirely separate BOMs must be created or different views of the same BOM must be defined. There is a definite trend toward products with a large number of variants. Product configurations must be completely integrated in the logistics process chain of a company. Configuring a product, should entail inspection to determine whether the configuration is complete and consistent. This inspection allows avoidance of impossible combinations.

3-22 The product structure browser permits easy movement between objects in the product structure. All data pertinent to the product, such as data from areas outside the actual design environment, can be accessed. Relationships between all the objects in the product structure can be viewed in graphical form.

3-23 PDM functions are supported for large product development projects in the R/3 project system.

3-24 R/3 logistics applications enhance customer service with a reliable, fully-integrated sales system.

3-25 The R/3 system's sales and distribution application offers access to real-time, online information from sales support to the billing process. It has all the functions and information required for easy automation of sales tasks so that a company can focus on expanding its business.

3-26 The sales support component provides you with simple tools to manage information on sales leads, sales calls, inquiries, quotations, marketing campaigns, competitors, and their products. Sales and marketing personnel can access this data constantly to perform sales activities or produce

SOLUTIONS

direct mailings. Sales support can be used not only to make sales process more efficient but to increase service to existing customers.

3-27 New sources of business can be identified, time saved, and errors reduced with user-friendly order entry. Order entry in the R/3 system is nearly automatic. Information that must be input in the simple user interface can be referred to and the system assembles information including the terms of payment and delivering plant. It then arranges this information in sales order.

3-28 Pricing is executed automatically in the sales order. In order to determine pertinent predefined prices, surcharges, and discounts, the system works from price lists and customer agreements, or it determines an amount according to the product, product group, or product cost.

3-29 The pricing function is flexible and can manage even the most complex price structures. Pricing information is maintained with data from sales deals and promotions as well. The system also executes a dynamic credit limit check, checking against credit, financial, SD (Sales and Distribution), and sales data to verify the customer's credit limit. It is possible to set the system to automatically alert credit or sales personnel when a sales order fails the check.

3-30 The availability check can work in combination with the Materials Management (MM) and Production Planning (PP) applications. It verifies that sufficient quantities exist on the requested delivery date. If the requested delivery date cannot be satisfied, the system immediately determines when the desired quantity will become available so that a new date can instantly be quoted.

3-31 The logistics component includes a complete suite of customer service functions such as call management, warranty management, and service and maintenance contract processing.

3-32 On-time delivery should be the standard. Shipping management provides easy-to-use functions for managing picking, packing, and loading tasks, and monitoring delivery deadlines. The system offers a list of all sales orders due for delivery and gives the choice of delivering the order completely or partially, individually or collectively. It is also possible to start picking for the available quantities with full integration to the warehouse management system.

3-33 The transportation module offers functions for transportation planning, processing, monitoring, and controlling functions. Regardless of where the products are sent, your transportation chain can be represented in the R/3 system for individual shipments or stop-off shipments involving several deliveries and several destinations. It is also possible to select forwarding agents and track shipments.

SOLUTIONS

3-34 Yes, sales and distribution also provides a detailed level of support for foreign trade processing that provides an automated export control to determine whether it is possible to export specific products to a particular country, to a particular customer, and at a given time. The system handles all the necessary customs forms automatically.

3-35 In order to declare shipments of goods to government authorities, the R/3 system collects all the data required for the declarations and creates the proper forms. Preference agreement processing is another feature that aids in managing the shipment of products eligible for customs tariff preferences, tracks the origin of component parts, and assigns a tariff classification to materials.

3-36 Automatic billing of customers with respect to orders and deliveries is possible. The system automatically executes billing for all due items. It then creates an invoice, debit memo, or credit memo for each item or collectively for several transactions. A billing document may be sent directly to the customer by mail, fax, or EDI. Simultaneously, revenues and receivables are immediately visible in the Financial Accounting (FI) and Controlling (CO) components. In addition, rebates can be processed based on a customer's purchase volume. All of this information works toward recognizing market trends so that SAP can provide the best possible level of support for making decisions for a Sales Information System. When a sales and distribution document is put into the system, the relevant information is updated in the Sales Information System. This makes certain that the information accessed is always up to date.

3-37 Customer information is displayed according to preference by customer, material, region or any other means. The information comes in an easy-to-interpret list or informative graphic. The Sales Information System can create a strategic position to address market trends and changes. Availability in multiple locations can be reviewed. If customers require specific quantities of a product, the make-to-order production features in Sales and Distribution can be used. All of this means an organization can make sales order decisions with current information and complete business processes quickly and efficiently. Offer customers the best possible service, since Sales and Distribution supports a wide range of contracts, from general contracts to more specific rental contracts. With these, it is possible to specify delivery quantities, delivery dates, and prices. Scheduling agreements and more complex requirements such as just-in-time delivery schedules are also supported. Follow-up on products can be done with the Service Management.

3-38 The R/3 system's Production Planning and Control application, can help achieve the fullest potential when planning, executing, and controlling production. Since there are increasing market pressures, high-level globalization, and increasing customization, companies today are moving away from traditional processes and toward a customer orientation and flexible production methods. PP satisfies the business requirements of manufacturers whose processes are continually changing and developing.

3-39   It offers ideal solutions for the three areas, including production planning, production execution, and production control. The integrated solution for all industry sectors, PP covers the complete production process, dealing with the creation of master data, production planning, MRP, and capacity planning, as well as production control and costing.

3-40   It can be used in all sectors of industry and provides a palette of production methods ranging from make-to-order production/variant processing to repetitive manufacturing or mass production. As with R/3 logistics applications, PP is fully integrated in the complete R/3 system.

3-41   Regardless of whether there is a standalone system or a worldwide network of distributed R/3 systems, linked by ALE, data are available within seconds within production planning and control, financial accounting, sales and distribution, and human resource management modules.

3-42   Production planning modules using Sales and Operations Planning (SOP) allows the creation of realistic and consistent planning figures and dates on the basis of expected sales or key figures of choice.

3-43   In material requirements planning (MRP) the system computes the quantities and procurement dates for the necessary materials, as well as the raw materials. Capacities can be planned at this planning phase so that possible capacity bottlenecks can be identified with plenty of time to take the necessary preventive measures.

3-44   Depending on methods of production, it is possible to use Production Order Processing, Repetitive Manufacturing, or KANBAN Production Control—a production order is primarily a tool for discrete, job-shop production that offers many status management functions, controlling per order, and various operation-related functions.

3-45   Repetitive manufacturing is created especially for manufacturers of products typically produced repetitively on a particular production line over a longer period. Production planning and control are usually carried out based on periods and quantities.

3-46   R/3's repetitive manufacturing module provides a tool based on production rates and lines to cover the requirements of this type of production.

SOLUTIONS

3-47 Capacity planning is integrated with production order processing as well as with repetitive manufacturing. Various dispatching strategies and a flexible graphic planning table support planning of resources. If production is controlled using KANBAN techniques, replenishment or the production of a material is not triggered until a higher production level actually requires the material.

3-48 In R/3's KANBAN module, various replenishment methods are available for in-house production, external procurement, and stock transfer. The signal for replenishing a material can be triggered by bar code or by using a graphic KANBAN board.

3-49 Quality management, interfaces to PDC systems, distributed control systems, laboratory information systems as well as extensive data analysis functions in the Open Information Warehouse are all also integrated in R/3's Production Control.

3-50 The PP application provides tools that guarantee a high-performance level of planning and control of the complete material flow in the production processes. It also provides easy-to-use information systems that can be adjusted to suit particular needs. The result is that planners, work schedulers, and production schedulers are relieved of routine tasks and therefore have more time to concentrate on more business-critical activities.

3-51 Successful project management is synonymous with planning, carrying out, and monitoring important undertakings economically, with the objective always in mind. Better performance of organizational tools and technical systems leads to more successful project management.

3-52 Wide-ranging functionality and integrated project processing are the hallmarks of a high-performance project management system. Project planning and control become an integral part of business organization and management regimes. The functions available in the R/3 system guarantee reliable support during all phases of an undertaking and meet the requirements typical of projects of all types.

3-53 The central structures in the project system are WBS and networks with their activities. These structures can also be used in combination with sales orders for sales and distribution, with BOMs for production and procurement, and to model complex projects in the system.

3-54 WBS stands for work breakdown structures.

3-55 The Project System's graphical interface can be used to create structures quickly. Cost and schedule planning become more refined as the project becomes more detailed and easier to view.

3-56   Integration with other modules in the R/3 system makes it possible to plan resources in cooperation with purchasing, inventory management, and material requirements planning. Human resources can be assigned by individual employee or by group.

3-57   The Project System checks and monitors availability of funds, capacities, and materials, making certain that there is enough of each for the project to be executed. Project expenditure can be controlled using the tools for approving and releasing project budgets.

3-58   SAP Business Workflow is available to improve communications within large projects. It permits use of workflow to make certain that a purchasing department is immediately notified of any changes in schedule or quantity requirements.

3-59   Through project processing, the system offers a flexible information system that allows tailoring of the layout and degree of detail of reports to suit individual requirements.

3-60   Listings and graphical analyses provide the information required on budget, planned and actual costs, revenues, commitments, payments received and made, schedules, and resources.

3-61   Standard interfaces provide the two-way communications base required for further planning and calculations in additional systems and at the local level.

3-62   Materials Management can help improve the procurement process and the logistics pipeline within a company. The efficiency of business processes for procuring raw materials and the effectiveness of the logistics pipeline through which materials flow are factors that are essential to corporate success.

3-63   The R/3 system's materials management application not only contains all the functions required to simplify business processes in terms of requirements planning, purchasing, inventory management, warehouse management, and invoice verification, but it also offers a high degree of automation in standard procedures.

3-64   All functions are closely integrated with each other and with other functions in R/3. This means that the most up-to-date information is always available to users within Materials Management and to other users in Logistics and Financials. The system does all the routine tasks, thereby providing time for more important activities.

3-65   Plant maintenance, production planning, or the project system can also require materials or services to be procured externally. Individual departments can enter purchase requisitions manually. The system passes these

SOLUTIONS

purchase requisitions directly to Purchasing, where they are converted into purchase orders. It is at this point that buyers have a plethora of sophisticated tools, from special purchasing master data and requests for quotations, to quotations and outline agreements.

3-66 It is possible to compare prices during the procurement process or automate the vendor selection or order creation processes. The vendor evaluation application makes it possible to determine the best vendors using individualized criteria. There is the option of requiring purchasing documents to be part of a release-and-approval procedure before they can be further processed.

3-67 Purchasing activities are approved by authorized members of staff by electronic signature. Transmission of purchase orders or forecast delivery schedules to vendors can be on paper or electronically.

3-68 The purchase order history makes it possible to monitor the status of an order and track deliveries or invoices already received.

3-69 Inventory management facilitates keeping a stock of materials. Effective management can be done in terms of both value and quantity. The application component supports all the most common types of receipts, issues, and stock transfers and allows management of special stocks (such as batches, consignment stocks, project stock, returnable transport packaging, or components at a subcontractor).

3-70 Goods movement postings automatically result in an update of values in financial accounting, asset accounting, and controlling. Whether physical inventories are done periodically or continuously, or total stock, sampling or cycle counting methods are used, the system offers support with several convenient aids for entering data and with a variety of automatic evaluations. Several inventory valuation methods, such as LIFO or FIFO are available, for balance sheet valuation.

3-71 Reduced costs can be achieved with efficient warehouse management. The Warehouse Management (WM) module provides flexible, automated support that permits processing of goods movements and maintaining a current record of all materials stored in highly complex warehousing structures. WM is integrated with and linked directly to other SAP applications, including Inventory Management (IM), Sales and Distribution (SD), Production Planning (PP), and Quality Management (QM). Advanced putaway and picking techniques are available, so that WM optimizes material flow and capacity in the warehouse, storing goods in the most favorable locations.

3-72   The capabilities of WM to be interfaced to hand-held terminals, bar-code scanners, and automated warehousing systems complements the automatic processes already available in the WM component.

3-73   Invoices received on paper or by EDI are inspected automatically in the system. If an invoice referencing a purchase order is input, the system can automatically produce the invoice it expects to receive. An invoice is automatically blocked for payment if impermissible variances in delivery date, quantity delivered, or agreed price occur.

3-74   The Evaluated Receipt Settlement (ERS) function permits elimination of vendor invoices. The system automatically and periodically creates invoices based on the goods receipts posted in the system for purchase orders.

3-75   Invoice verification offers a special method of entering vendor invoices which is much faster than standard procedures.

3-76   Additional processes can be integrated into MM. The MM application comprises several functions that can assist in shaping a materials management system as efficiently as possible.

3-77   Transportation activities are simplified through several functions that include shipping-point and route determination. Smooth and efficient foreign trade processing can be assured by quick preparation of the necessary data for customs declarations, export, or import activities.

3-78   The MM application components make it possible to optimize material procurement processes, provide powerful cost-effective purchasing tools, timely acceptance, and billing of services performed.

3-79   The Purchasing Information System presents all the facts and figures required for negotiating with vendors. Select which data to integrate in reports and how to present the information. Inventory Controlling can help determine stock values, find out inventory turnover rates, and carry out analyses. The information systems enable identification of trends and developments, creating a sound basis for decision-making.

3-80   Quality Management is integrated with R/3 Logistics Applications Compliance. This is an important factor in producing high-quality products that foster long-lasting customer/vendor relationships, reduce expenses, and improve competitiveness.

3-81   QM facilitates achieving a high level of quality for all processes in the logistics chain. QM is closely integrated with the other R/3 System modules. Implementing it in a logistics system offers several advantages over isolated CAQ systems.

SOLUTIONS

3-82   The purchasing department receives the latest quality scores for vendors as well as quality data for requests for quotations and purchase orders. Whenever product quality is crucial, the quality function can release a vendor for delivery. The control data predefined in QM determine which materials will be inspected and posted to inspection stock to undergo a goods receipt inspection, production inspection, or source inspection. This makes certain that only products complying with the predefined quality requirements will be released for further processing.

3-83   It is possible to reduce administrative tasks through company-wide quality planning. If quality planning activities are centrally organized, requirements for quality characteristics, inspection methods, and specifications will be documented and up to date.

3-84   The integrated use of master data ensures that inspection planning activities will be consistent and efficient.

3-85   In the R/3 system, an inspection is documented by an inspection lot as well as the corresponding inspection results. Inspection results can be recorded directly in the R/3 system, quality notification can be created on the Internet to allow customers to interact directly with the problem management process, and your product quality can be documented using quality certificates. The shipping documents that accompany the delivery of goods to the customer, and certificate to verify the product quality can be created. A quality certificate can be printed, faxed or posted for customer retrieval via the Internet.

3-86   The functions of the QM component in the R/3 system compose a computer-integrated quality management system (CIQ) and offer a foundation for "Total Quality Management."

3-87   Materials can be maintained in batches on the basis of certain quality characteristics. The batch characteristics defined in QM can be used as a way to search for batches in a delivery.

3-88   The functions for Statistical Process Control (SPC) offer a means of monitoring, controlling, and improving the processes.

3-89   Yes, the R/3 system supports the use of quality control charts.

3-90   Yes, as part of the central Logistics Information System (LIS), the QM Information System can be used at different management levels to plan, monitor, evaluate, and control quality.

3-91   Problems can be managed efficiently by using quality notifications, a flexible and efficient means of solving quality-related problems in products or services. The quality notifications in the R/3 system can be used to process complaints against vendors, internal problem reports, or complaints filed by customers. It is possible to define corrective actions (tasks), assign tasks to those responsible, and link the processing activities to the SAP business workflow to help solve a problem quickly. Through the integration of the R/3 system's Controlling (CO) application, all costs incurred while processing a quality notification can easily be identified.

3-92 Plant Maintenance (PM) supports various options for structuring technical systems with its object, type, and function- related views, and enables flexible navigation. Data concerning the planning, processing, and history of maintenance tasks are documented in the system to comply with business verification requirements.

3-93 PM provides technical and business reports and various presentation options, with respect to the criteria used. These criteria can include organizational units, locations, execution periods for the tasks, or system manufacturers. This information helps reduce the duration and costs of plant downtimes as a result of damage, and makes it possible to recognize possible weak points within a technical system in a timely fashion. The information forms the basis for defining an optimum maintenance strategy in the sense of "Total Productive Maintenance" (TPM) or risk-optimized maintenance. The interface-free integration of PM in the R/3 system forms the basis for fast and efficient communication and cooperation among the different enterprise areas.

3-94 PM provides a complete, industry-wide maintenance management system that considers maintenance an integral component of enterprise resource planning. Whenever the PM component is well established, it has fulfilled the requirements of technical and commercial enterprise areas in its role as a complete plant information system. The standard user interface and the careful implementation both ensure reduced implementation times.

3-95 The R/3 system's PM application is a software solution that covers all maintenance tasks for a company. PM supports the planning and execution of these activities with regard to system availability, costs, material, and personnel deployment.

3-96 The open aspects of the R/3 system provide many options for integrating PM and external systems, which may include geographical information systems, CAD systems, plant data collection systems, systems for entering measurement, and/or counter readings 4SCADA). This allows creation of an information base that takes business, technical, and process-related criteria into consideration. It is then possible to achieve optimized maintenance objectives.

SOLUTIONS

3-97   The integrated service management system is essential because of globalization of markets; worldwide competition among companies has grown. As a result of changing company objectives, customer service has increased the importance of how everything in an organization is regarded. The system infrastructure is often characterized by a lack of integration between business systems such as service contract management and invoicing, and more technical systems such as installed base management and call management. It is difficult to make quick decisions based on service contract obligations and resource availability.

3-98   The R/3 system's service management module offers highly integrated functionality and is suitable for all types of industries.

3-99   Long-term service agreements and/or warranty conditions are checked when a call is logged. Services described in these documents can be freely configured with characteristics such as service window, response time, and service area. Pricing is determined with respect to options selected.

3-100 During the call management process, logged customer calls are automatically checked against service contract commitments and warranty conditions. An extensive catalog system and free-format data can be used to record and codify activities, types of damage, causes of damage, etc. All service activities are stored in a comprehensive history database. A powerful information system is also available in SM and can be adjusted to suit individual needs.

3-101 Billing can be performed for service contracts on a periodic basis, and for service orders, on a time and material consumption basis.

CHAPTER 4

Production Planning (PP)

Production planning is important for performing various order confirmations, observing the results of entering partial quantity confirmations, and entering confirmations with time but no quantities.

This chapter lays the groundwork for handling the PP course track: it covers knowing methods for correct entry of the proper confirmation so that it is possible to determine the cost and capacity impact it may have on a production order. This information will facilitate confident preparation for the the certification course and the exam.

Introduction

The Production Planning (PP) course track provides you with a detailed overview of SAP functionality with respect to their implementation tools and methodology. This chapter will help you become familiar with the specific details of the PP module. The text in this section will give you the chance to use the module specifics you learn here so that you know how to set up an integrated business model that includes specifics business processes.

After reviewing this chapter you will be more prepared to take the R/3 Application Consultant Certification test. You will be one step closer to working on SAP implementation projects because you will have gained a solid foundation in using the SAP Procedural model, implementation guide, production order processing, capacity planning, product costing, repetitive manufacturing, and presentation of business processes.

Material Master

This section explains how to create and maintain material master records. We start by examining the specific users of the material master and providing an overview of this course track.

In an overview of the SAP process consider elements including basic data, sales and distribution (SD), production planning (PP), sales planning, project system, quality management (QM), materials management (MM), and plant maintenance (PM). Within these categories note the connection between processes within the SAP R/3 environment.

Material and Industry Sector

In this sector it is possible to organize materials in different ways depending on industry sector or material type.

The material type designates which specific departments can maintain a material master record. It can also be used to define whether quantities and value are updated in inventory management and how numbers are assigned. Permitted procurement types can be determined as can the method by which fields are displayed while maintaining material master records. G/L accounts determined through automatic means can be defined.

It is important to note that the industry sector is in control of field selection and screen sequence when maintaining material master records.

Each user department has its own view on a material master record. In each material type, designate what views are possible and what views each user may maintain or display on each material master record. The user can define what views to maintain or display and what views are normally provided when maintaining material master records. In addition, the data in some of these views require designation of specific organizational units for which the data maintained.

In material master maintenance, a standard sequence is defined for each data screen at the main working level. In addition, this standard sequence can be interrupted by changing screens at the main working level through the Goto menu. It is also possible to gain access to these screens at the extras data level through the Extras menu.

Material Type

Material types are important in the PP course because they permit definition of a type for each material that is included in the general data on the material. User departments are defined for a material type to designate what views can be maintained for a material of a specific type. In each material type, it is possible to define whether internal or external procurement is permitted. This can be achieved with a warning message to inform the user exactly what is proceeding at each stage.

The specific type of inventory management can be defined in terms of quantity and value for each material type with respect to a given plant. Specific price controls can be set and designated as default values or mandatory standard values. Assigning stock accounts and consumption accounts through the valuation class is clearer in the unit called "Valuation."

Material Master Record

In any given material master record the general data are valid for the entire client or whole group. Descriptions can be entered in as many languages as required. Entering sales data about a sales organization and distribution channel is also possible. In a warehouse management system, data an be entered for each warehouse number as well as for each storage type of a specific warehouse number.

Units of Measurement

Specific dimensions can be used for easier execution of conversions that occur between different units of measurement. Remember that for each dimension there is a specific and unique SI unit.

```
SI unit = International Unit System
```

Calculations must be done through a system of internationally standardized units. There are seven base (metric) units, but the remaining units are derived units including the square meter and kilogram per cubic meter.

Besides the internal key for a unit of measurement, there are two language-specific external keys. An internal key for the units of measurement standard on an SAP R/3 system cannot be changed. If during the certification process it appears that the internal key has been altered, there is something obviously wrong.

TIP

When taking the test keep an eye out for errors that are simple to catch, but can cause a wrong answer to be derived. In calculations, many items can go wrong and it can take too much time to go through each process. Therefore, look for something elementary to do a quick check of figures including watching the units of measurement on the internal key as described above.

When dealing with the units of measurement for the same dimension, conversion factors for the SI unit of the dimension must be maintained so that all conversions between these measurement units can be executed. When dealing with dimensionless units of measurement, remember the entry "AAAADL," because this is defined in the dimension field in the standard SAP R/3 system. Use this unit of measurement in purchasing operations, but make certain that it is marked as a commercial unit.

Measurement Units Defined

It is extremely important to ensure familiarity with units of measure to derive precise calculations. A simple error can cost points, so memorize the following definitions:

1. **Base Unit of Measure**—This is the unit reserved for managing stocks. Each quantity manages in other units of measure is converted to the base unit of measure. If it is necessary to work with measurement units that cannot be converted into a standard format, then designate a conversion factor in the material master maintenance.

2. **Order Unit**—This is a unit of measure used to order a material in purchasing calculations.
3. **Sales Unit**—This is the unit under which material is sold. It is used in an order where it can be changed to meet conditions.
4. **Issue Unit**—This is the unit under which the material is issued from the warehouse. The physical goods issues and inventory options can be entered.

Material Data in Accounting

It is possible to designate material to a group of G/L accounts. One of the aspects that determines G/L accounts costs in the valuation class. These account costs are posted when a transaction pertinent to a valuation is executed. The material type defines which valuation classes are permitted. It is then possible to display all of the possible entries for a given material type. A material type may permit more than one valuation class. In addition, a valuation class is permissible for more than one material type.

Changing or Extending a Master Material Record

Each department within an organization can have its own view for each material master record. Note that the specific material type designates which material master record views are permitted. It is then possible to designate which views each user is permitted to maintain or display and to define specific views on a material master record to see what is normally shown in maintenance functions when logging on with a user. It is important to note that some views require entry of specific organizational aspects.

PP Basic Data

What Is a BOM?

A Bill of Materials Management (BOM) is defined as a completely formal structured list for an object that lists all of the necessary parts given the name, reference number, quantity, and unit. BOMs are useful for materials management and production control. BOMs and routings are composed of significant master data. A given department within an organization can produce a design for a new product that can function correctly and also be manufactured. The product phase is the result of multiple drawings as well as a list of all of the parts and materials needed to construct it.

The required bills of material are located where finished products or partly manufactured materials are constructed of several elementary parts and materials called the *recipe* or *ingredient list*.

Any data saved within a BOM creates a large foundation for various areas within production planning. Material requirements planning explodes BOM to determine the correct order quantities for a specific time to produce the most cost-effective plans possible.

BOMs function well for work scheduling because they form the foundation for planning of operations and production control. In addition, production order administration utilizes BOMs to plan for part preparation.

BOMs are employed in sales orders to assist in entering data, in reservation and goods issues to assist in data entry, and in product costing to determine the material usage costs associated with the completed product.

It is important to note that BOM can be used data in several organizational areas. This represents a significant advantage that integrated modules have: they can be linked to promote the flow of data between different work areas. This permits all users to access current values at any given time.

Classification

There is a classification system whose purpose is to locate appropriate objects, locate similar objects, and ascertain that no appropriate object exits. In the absence of a logical arrangement, it is exceedingly difficult to achieve objectives within this classification system. The SAP classification system is a mechanism that extends beyond numerical objectives to create a correct ordering system.

The main aspects of the classification system are arranged in four key areas:

- Characteristic Maintenance
- Class Maintenance
- Classification
- Object Search.

Bill of Materials Management

BOM categories include the material master record, equipment master record, and document information records. Object references are created through BOM categories, while material BOMs usually depict the structure of the completed product produced within an organization. Equipment BOMs are employed to depict the structure of a given piece of equipment in addition to allocating spare parts to some equipment for plant maintenance.

Documents can be composed of several documents including:

- Programs
- Technical Drawings
- Writing
- Photographs.

BOMs can be combined to create a document information record (document BOMs).

BOM Terms Defined

A number of terms used when dealing with BOMs must become familiar during study for certification.

Assembly indicates a group of components for a product which are all linked together for manufacturing purposes. Assembly can be use as a component in another assembly project as well.

Simple-level BOMs indicate the quantity of all components that can be used to depict one or more assemblies. Single-level BOMs and assemblies have only one level.

BOMs are composed of data directly responsible for production. The plant is the workplace where all essential preparation for work is completed. This work includes planning material requirements as well as creating routings.

To create a material BOM, there must be a valid material master in the same plant. Several checks must be made before creating any given item. If material components are created, then plan data needs to exist for all plant materials.

Validity

The validity time period is the time in which the BOM is valid. This time period is linked through entries in the BOM headers and in the BOM item that include:

- **Valid-from date**—When establishing a BOM, this date determines the exact point in time for which the BOM is utilized. If a BOM is created or altered by entering a change number, then the system will use the valid-from date from the change master record.

✎ **Valid-to date**—This date signifies the end of the temporal validity for the BOM. The system determines this date dynamically with a default value of 12/31/9999. The valid-to date can only be modified by using the change number established through Engineering Change management. This component is valid only until midnight on the valid-to date.

A single BOM "_" doesn't have variants or alternative. A variant BOM of type "V" is a combination of several BOMs that provides a combined description of at least one object that has a large proportion of common identical parts. A multiple BOM of type "M" is a combination of several BOMs that provides a combined description of several alternative material combinations for one and the same product.

BOM data are arranged in an organized structure. It is possible to maintain the data for the whole BOM in a header or to maintain data that only pertain to a specific section of the given BOM item. In addition, BOM items can be further segmented into subitems whenever partial quantities for a BOM items are represented by the place where they are integrated.

BOM validity areas are designated by the plant. Validity areas can be enhanced by allocating the same BOM to an object in another plant. However, if only one BOM exists, then changes will take effect within all plants. The BOM material must be allocated to another plant, so it should have a valid material master in the new plant. In addition, all of the material items within the BOM must also have material masters in the plant as well.

BOM Usage

Usage can allow establishment of to separate BOMs for various areas within an organization. The design BOM ties together all components for the product from the design perspective and holds all of the technical data. A manufacturing BOM is established from the manufacturing perspective.

It is possible to work with just one BOM for all areas. However, if a BOM has several uses for one material, then the system can save the BOM for each use under its own internal number. The authorization concept of BOM maintenance takes the use into account as well.

Items

Whenever a new BOM item is created, every item must be allocated to an *item category*. Each item category designates the functions of a BOM item. This signifies that special item information is processed and controls future system activities.

Make certain to know if a material must be entered, on an item involved where there is quantity management; determine if the quantity indicator is permitted, see what subitems are used for, and see what screen selections or screen layouts of item detail appear to be.

TIP

It is not possible to alter an item category once the item has been created. The entry for the item category can be corrected by deleting the items or creating another one.

A subitem depicts various integration points for partial quantities of a given item. Each subitem can also maintain a short text adjacent to the subitem quantity. Subitems have no operative meaning within the BOM, indicating that operation assignment is only at the item level while scrap calculation is only at the item level.

BOM explosion indicates the composition of a product. This is important in various situations, including the requirements calculation executed for a product. It also indicates the overall structure of a product (a consideration in the engineering departments of most organizations). It provides an overview of all pertinent parts and materials that will be created as well as the costs, or effects of cost changes, that need to be calculated.

The application is composed of specific search procedure elements that involve the sequence for the BOM usage, the priority of a given alternative for a specific multiple BOM, production versions from the material master, and the inspection of specific status indicators. In the user master, it is possible to enter a default value for the application field that has a value designated through the SET/GET parameters.

Routing Management

Routing indicates material-specific production. Reference operation sets are not established for a given material, but can be used to duplicate and reference routings. It is possible to create reference operation sets that have internal or external number assignments.

Rate routings depict material-specific production that takes place within a production line, while a reference rate routing can assist in creating rate routings.

Task lists are an important concept. They exist inside a group used to produce similar materials. Task lists that have analogous manufacturing procedures within a group can also be linked. There are alternative sequences that allow choosing alternatives to a sequence of operations.

This can result when various work procedures are used for different lot sizes or when working under restricted capacity.

It is also possible to employ a *parallel sequence*. This sequence will permit processing of operations in parallel with other operations. Parallel sequences are useful in depicting the special operations can be overlapped. They are used in mechanical engineering for assemblies that have production of individual components. In the chemical industry they are used for detailed analytical processes that function in parallel with the production process.

Routing Management Terms Defined

The terms for Production Resources/Tools (PRT) that can be assigned to each production are defined by a material master or a *PRT master*. This leads into routing sequences that are best depicted through alternative sequences tied to the standard sequence. The start operation number for the alternative sequence cannot be less than that for a standard sequence. The number of the last operation of the alternative sequence should also not be more than the number of the link operation that exists within the main sequence.

Scheduling

Scheduling is a very important aspect of production planning. There are two methods of scheduling used in production planning. Production orders are scheduled by executing lead time scheduling on operations. Lead time scheduling permits compulation of capacity requirements for planned order within the materials requirement.

NOTE

Production order always employs both basic and target pairs of dates, where target dates are the date most pertinent to production.

In-house and ordered time elements are also extremely important in scheduling. In-house production time can be maintained within the material master. Basic dates can be computed within requirements planning, but remember that in-house production time within the material master complies with the results achieved from the lead time scheduling used in routing.

Operations last for a given amount of time that consists of no more than five time elements:

1. Queue time
2. Setup time
3. Processing time

4. Teardown time

5. Process-related wait time.

Time elements are important for specific events. Material requirements are scheduled to take place at the earliest possible start date, but this can be customized to meet specific needs. It is important to maintain time elements for lead time scheduling in various places with the PP applications. Make certain to employ the correct settings and use the system correctly in order for the scheduling effort to be achieved successfully.

Standard values are designated for the routing, and formulas originally defined in the work center are employed in lead-time scheduling to compute the execution time for individual segments including: setup, processing, and teardown.

There is a connection between formula and standard values. It is possible to designate formula definitions for computing both execution time and capacity requirements within a work center.

Reduction

Reduction measures are one final aspect that must also be considered. A system can execute reduction tasks in lead time scheduling for orders. It is then possible to set the time elements that can be reduced in addition to the reduction strategy for customizing each order category. Reduction can then be designated for the floats both before and after production to proceed in the order or in the customizing for each type or group.

Allocating Materials

At any point when the material component overview is displayed, it is possible to allocate and display material components for individual operations. A material component list can be sorted or filtered by different criteria. The lists also have functions for reallocation and deletion of material allocations, moving between operations if several were chosen.

Materials can be allocated to several routings, in a plant to several routings, or a route can be designated to several materials.

Work Centers

Work centers have several functions that determine the place where a given operation is to be executed. They contain default values that are duplicated or referenced within operations when you routings lists are created. They also hold the data important for costing operations. In addition, they contain the scheduling and capacity data necessary for lead-time scheduling and capacity planning.

Work centers can be used for popular work center categories. Each work center category is defined by the work center category field. Work center categories have specific uses including routing or networking. Work center data are important at each work center, which contains several groups of data which can be entered on various screens.

Standard text for operations permits duplication of or reference to standard texts. It is used for frequently repeated descriptions of a specific cycle.

Each work center has a specific capacity. It is possible to sustain the available capacity for users. The validity of a given capacity can even be interrupted by an interval of given capacity with a limited validity period. This permits maintenance of intervals of available capacity using shift sequences. Available capacity is useful with shift sequences because the work start, finish, and break periods can be defined for all work centers within a shift definition. Furthermore, shift sequences permit maintenance of the sequence of individual shift definitions for all shift sequences.

Work centers are designated to a cost center and each cost center can be composed of several work centers. Input activity types pertinent to costing at a work center in the cost centers.

The work centers at a plant can be formulated as work center hierarchies that have as many levels as required. These hierarchies are used as repositories for available capacities and their requirements in capacity planning. Work centers may also be designated to several hierarchies.

Variant and Multiple BOMs

Sometimes numerous products are made with parts that only differ in very minor ways. Different products can be illustrated through a variant BOM. However, only a basic material BOM can be extended to a variant BOM; a multiple BOM may not be converted to a variant BOM.

It is not possible to create a variant for an existing BOM without using a material that does not already have a BOM. Furthermore, the BOM for the material whose variant must be created cannot be a multiple BOM. Base units of measure for all variant materials must be all the same because the base unit of measure for the BOM needs to match the base unit of measure within the material master.

The field for the BOM group can also be employed as a mnemonic external BOM number because whenever several products are created as variants of a variant BOM, they are saved under an internal BOM number. All of the variants of one variant BOM can be named through the BOM group or header.

Products can be manufactured in different versions with respect to the quantity that needs to be made. These products are depicted numerous times through alternative BOMs that only differ from each other with respect to terms of the component quality.

The field BOM group can be employed as a mnemonic external BOM number because all of the terms for a multiple BOM are saved under an internal BOM number. Just remember that the plant and usage are elements of the complete designation of the BOM.

More Functionality

Reference operation sets are an important aspect of routing. However, they do not permit parallel and alternative sequences. It is possible to allocate a material to a reference operation set. The copy from function can be used to duplicate a reference operation set from a routing or reference operation set, but it is not possible to copy from a routing that has a reference to a reference operation set.

Suboperations are hierarchically arranged under the operation, and employed to execute a more comprehensive costing and capacity planning.

NOTE

The control key has an important function. But scheduling occurs at the operation level and standard values of suboperations can accumulate to the appropriate operation with respect to the dimension and unit of measure.

Suboperation dates are designated by the reference to the beginning or completion of an operation just by inputting an offset. Pertinent reference dates for a given suboperation can occur either before or after the operation segments undergo setup, processing, teardown, or wait.

Recursiveness is used to describe a BOM when a product has an element with the same object number. It often deals with entry fields on purpose. Should a system identify recursiveness online, there is a message that the "BOM is recursive." There are some events where recursiveness is only identified by the update program. In addition, the individual who creates the recursive BOM also receives a message. If a recursive BOM is invented, it is important to set the indicator "Recursiveness Permitted" in the proper area.

When dealing with each BOM, it is possible to input a distribution function for each item in a BOM. When a distribution function is input for a given component, numerous planned orders are established with respect to the distribution function. Planned orders often deal with partial quantities of whole dependent requirements for different dates for the planned or production order. Therefore, materials planning can execute a daily provision of partial quantities and then send them over the order duration period.

The lead time offset field allows planning of the individual component in greater detail. When the lead time offset has a positive value then the component is not needed immediately. It will be available for a given number of days subsequent to production. Should the lead time offset have a negative value, then the component must available for a given number of days prior to the start of production.

There is a "where-used list" that includes work centers, PRTs, reference operation sets, materials, and documents. This list tells where a material is used and how much is used. This is important to know if there are are many parts and materials used. This information is necessary to compute requirements for a given model, choose products affected by changed to individual parts, determine the assemblies produced late, and compute the cost effects on a product should the costs of materials change.

In addition, there is a method of replacing as well as deleting components when dealing with mass replacement in BOMs. It is also possible to mass replace routing data so that the replace function is used to execute mass changes to work centers, PRTs, and reference operation sets.

Managing Change

Engineering change management involves many tasks that revolve around the change in the master record. The structure of the change master record involves:

- ✎ **Changing the master header**—Dealing with a reason for change and its validity
- ✎ **Object type**—Material, BOMs, routings, and documents
- ✎ **Object management**—Working with material BOMs, equipment task lists, and routings.

Change can be documented but is only effective when precisely defined. The changes object is saved twice: in the state before and after the change.

The state before the change concludes with the valid-to date, while the state after the change begins with the valid-from date. All of these changes are ultimately recorded in the "change master record."

Planning

Executing a production order begins with MRP and leads to purchase requisition and production order. Planned order can translate into a production order or a purchase requisition. In order to complete a purchase order, release the order, issue materials to the production order, execute the completion of confirmation, receive the finished product, and sell the order. The MRP planning level produces a planned order or internal request, the production activity control will add order-specific data, dates, and quantities to current information.

Production order is used both to control and to monitor production in an organization and as the controlling mechanism for cost accounting. Production orders determine what is to be produced, the production dates, where the capacity load is dispatched, and finally the actual and planned production expenses.

Sales and operations planning (SOP) is a generic planning and forecasting tool which has main SOP steps that include creating a sales and production plan, dispersing planning values, and transferring planning values to demand management. SOP permits users to accumulate data from various internal and external sources for the purpose of setting obtainable operational objectives. They can plan more effectively. In addition, SOP tasks are executed through a planning table similar to a spreadsheet. This table allows users to record previous planning data, forecast market demand, run analyses, and execute hypothetical simulations.

Differentiating MPS and MRP

Almost any material can be designated as an MPS material. Usually any item that has a direct relationship with mission-critical resources is part of MPS. Any frequent changes in a completed product can cause the complete planning run to become unstable. In order to alleviate this instability, MRP controllers that do not use MPS usually plan high safety stock levels and floats to make certain material is available.

Planning master schedule items before executing a material requirements planning operation helps increase planning stability while reducing storage levels and storage costs. The result is that the planner has the opportunity to plan master schedule items more often without a system performance degradation.

MPS created planned order for top-level items to meet independent requirements from SOP. The master production scheduling (MPS) and material requirements planning (MRP) guarantee material availability. They are used to achieve or produce required quantities for internal use as well as sales and distribution. Independent requirements from SOP catalyze the master scheduling process. MPS run results are a planned order for the master schedule item. They rely on requirements for the level just below the MPS item. There are no planned orders created for component material during an MPS run.

In an MRP run, MRP creates dependent requirements and planned orders for remaining material inside a BOM structure. For all components of a BOM during a multi-level MRP run, dependent requirements and associated planned order are produced. Material requirements are observed for sales orders, planned independent requirements, material reservations, and dependent requirements received from BOM explosions.

The system compares warehouse stock or scheduled receipts from purchasing and production with net requirements in MRP. When dealing with material shortage, a system can create an order proposal. Order proposals are also scheduled that involve determining the delivery and release dates for materials gained externally and computing production dates for materials procured in-house. When exact required quantities are needed for MRP, work with especially low safety stocks.

Finally, let us consider the production planning environment and all associated planning levels. Note how controlling and profit planning proceed into capacity planning and production.

Sales and Operations Planning (SOP)

SOP helps establish a product group hierarchy, execute planning tasks with standard SOP, and transfer values to demand management. There are various levels within SOP that allow refining of organizational operations with various levels of planning and feedback.

The first step is to establish a planning hierarchy and select a planning method to implement in a standard SOP. This can be accomplished by establishing a product group and following a level-by-level planning method.

A sales plan can be taken from a sales information system, profitability analysis, or material forecast, or can be duplicated from another plan. A production plan is created at the product group level with respect to various planning strategies.

Planning types can be created using a table painter and planning screen. Planning types permit users to establish different views on an information structure to assist the input of planned data.

BACKGROUND

A macro is useful when a mathematical operation composed of a sequence of instructions is carried out. Macros take existing fields, execute mathematical equations, and produce a new calculation of field values.

It is important to be able to forecast how any event can have an impact on promotions, sales deals, and competitor sales activities. Cumulative events can be designated by whole positive or negative numbers, while proportional numbers are determined as percentages. Events can be assigned to information structures and can be time-dependent or relate to specific characteristics or key figures.

Determining Objectives

Planning objectives is an important part of any process (particularly certification). Independent requirements can be created in demand management and the functions of planning strategies and their resultant demand management impact can be explained. This also makes it possible to determine the availability of checking options during sales order entry.

In setting goals, a sensible logistics chain must be developed. A demand program is constructed the way independent requirements are used to start a planning run, so that it is possible to tell when material shortage happens. Such a shortage is usually indicative of available stock being less than a requirements quantity.

In-house production refers to planned orders created first and then converted into production orders. External procurement refers to purchase requisitions or scheduling agreements that are created. When materials are produced in-house, dependent requirements are created for material components by the BOM explosion.

The strategy is depicted by the proper procedure for planning a material and is defined by a requirements type from independent requirements management or from sales order management. A combination of both may be the correct answer, and designating different planning strategies to the material in the material master record through an MRP group is possible. This information can be used by the system to locate the correct requirements type when maintaining planned independent requirements and customer requirements. Should the MRP group be maintained in the material master record, then the system can automatically find the correct requirements type within the demand management.

Production Levels

The different levels of production include make-to-stock production and production by lots. In make-to-stock there is a reduction from the demand program to MRP to warehouse stock finished product, and finally to sales orders from the warehouse. In production by lots, the requirements are sent to the materials planning sin sales order processing. In fact, warehouse requirements can also be planned in demand management. They are groups with respect to lot sizing procedures. Sales order are also covered by warehouse stock. The availability check with respect to ATP logic can be executed in SD.

Planning with final assembly is important because planned independent requirements are entered at the finished product level. This effectively spurs production and procurement in the product structure. Note that customer requirements consume planned independent requirement quantities. Planning quantities that are not consumed end up increasing warehouse stock. Should the actual customer requirement quantity be greater than the planned quantity, then the system automatically adjusts the master plan to deal with these extra requirements. It is then possible to choose to check availability in sales order processing with respect to ATP logic or by employing the check when designating independent requirements.

Make-to-order production also follows a logical arrangement, in that a reduction process occurs from sales order, to MRP, to customer stock finished product, to delivery. Note that in make-to-order production, individual sales orders are planned separately and maintained in an individual segment of the MRP list. The lot-for-lot order quantity is used regardless of entry in the material master record. In addition, all production costs are recorded individually for a sales order.

It is possible to plan without final assembly. Here the independent requirements are planned at the finished product level. Dependent requirements are passed on to the lower-level assemblies. Production and procurement are initiated at the assembly and component level. Sales order triggers make-to-order production level, while final assembly is started on receipt of sales order and planned independent requirements are consumed.

A planning model is a good strategy when specific assemblies are employed in several finished products. Planning materials defined are composed of common assemblies and associated elements. Planned independent requirements are established for planning material and initiate production and procurement. The sales order for a completed product references the planning material and reduces the planned independent requirements of planning material while initiating final assembly.

It is also possible to plan at the assembly level because during the planning strategy, independent requirements for an assembly are planned individually. They are established at the assembly level and initiate the production of assembly. Dependent requirements are established for the assembly of a product once the sales order has been received.

Production Scheduling

When considering production scheduling; remember the specific advantages of MPS as well as the purpose of planning time fence in R/3. These objectives can be achieved by considering the execution of the executive planning run. The master schedule items are planned in an individual planning run, while master items incorporate finished products or assemblies.

Planning the time fence is an important aspect of this section. Note that the MRP controller can employ a planning time fence to designate a period so that the system is not permitted to execute automatic changes to the master plan.

Firming a planned order involves the planned order, planning run, and conversion. If a planned order is manually changed, then the system automatically establishes the firmed indicator for the planning order indicating that the header data of the planned order is not altered in the next planning run. When a component is manually changed, the system sets the firmed indicator for the components so that the planned order will not be changed in the next planning run. The firming indicators for the planned order or its component cannot themselves be changed. By resetting the conversion indicator in the planned order it is possible to stop the planned order from being converted into a production order or purchase requisition.

Material Requirements

In considering a plan for material requirements, look into the exact steps for the planning run and examine the different lost sizing procedures involved. Let us examine these objectives in the MRP procedures where all existing requirements and receipts with quantities are considered. The foundation of the planning run involves sales orders, planned independent requirements, material reservations, and dependent requirements.

TIP

Improving the performance of a planning run makes it possible to limit the planning horizon so that the system will only create receipt elements for the requirements that lie in the planning horizon itself.

The planning run can be executed even for single items. Any single item multilevel planning involves planning for a BOM structure and/or manually changing the master plan for each material in the bill of material. However, single-item single-level planning involves altering the master plan manually through the create, delete, change, and reschedule commands. In a single-item multilevel planning run, the materials planned through MRP methods are planned with respect to the structure of the bill of materials. In fact, the MRP controller can view the planning results of the assemblies or components during the multilevel planning run and execute manual changes prior to the system's continuing the planning run.

Scrap Terms Defined

When dealing with any scrap operation it is important to know the following terms:

- ✎ **Component Scrap**—This scrap pertains to the individual component in an assembly group. When a BOM explosion occurs, the system increases the component quantity by the computed scrap quantity.
- ✎ **Assembly Scrap**—This scrap is maintained in the master of the MRP screen. In the MRP, the system increases the material requirements for all of the components within the assembly group by the scrap quantity computed for the components.
- ✎ **Scrap Operation**—This scrap is a precursor of the scrap-adjusted quantity in the next operation and pertains to scheduling and costing.
- ✎ **Operation Scrap BOM**—This scrap pertains to the quantity of a component that an operation processes. This entry replaces the blanket assembly scrap for high-value materials and affords a more precise materials planning.

Calculating Lot Size

Lot-size calculations require quantities in the individual order proposals. In order to achieve optimum lot-sizing procedures, numerous net requirements should be grouped together. In addition, the lot size may be restricted by specifying that the system should round the lot size with regard to a present rounding value.

There are six lot-sizing procedures:

1. **Static lot sizing**—Future material shortages are not considered, so when a material shortage happens the system creates an order proposal for the amount designated in a static lot size without any checks.
2. **Lot-for-lot order quantity**—The system establishes an order proposal for the amount designated for the material shortage.
3. **Fixed order quantity**—The system establishes an order proposal for the quantity designated as a fixed lot size.
4. **Replenishment up to stock level**—The system creates an order proposal for the quantity needed to make stock level rise as much as possible.
5. **Period lot sizing**—All requirements within a predefined period are grouped together into one lot.
6. **Dynamic lot sizing**—Procedures optimize the total costs that result from adding order and storage costs.

Procurement

Procurement types designate whether a material is produced in-house or outside. If the procurement type permits both in-house and external procurement, then the system will employ in-house production.

Procurement often relies on the ability to determine order dates for in-house production. Goods receipt processing time determines the number of workdays necessary for the purchasing department. In-house production time is computed by adding the lead time and the floats before and after the production. An opening period represents the processing time needed by the MRP controller for converting the planned orders. Both order start date and completion dates for a planned order are computed during scheduling, where the order start date is the soonest and the order finish date is the latest used for production. When dealing with materials using MRP or any prediction planning, order dates are computed by backward scheduling.

Phantom Assemblies

Phantom assemblies often depict an assembly established during the production process. It is not placed in stock, but used instantly. The phantom assembly can also depict a logical grouping. An assembly may be indicated as a phantom just by entering a special procurement type in the material master record. During a planning run, the dependent requirements of a higher-level assembly are directly passed on to the components of a phantom assembly. In some situations, phantom assemblies are placed in stock where they can be removed.

Scheduling Agreements

There are two planning time fences within a scheduling agreement. Once a schedule line exists within a planning time fence it is not altered in the planning run. Should additional requirements emerge, the system will create another schedule line.

When a requirement is displaced external to the planning time fence, then the associated schedule line is deleted in the planning run. It is often not possible to tell the vendor in a sufficient amount of time about the schedule line fixes. The only answer is to use both planning time fences. The planning time fence for the planning run can be used as the period used for fixed schedule lines.

Planning

Various planning elements include gross requirements planning, net requirements planning, storage location MRP that involves locations planned both separately and excluded from the planning run, individual customer segment, individual project segment, direct production, and planning without final assembly.

During a planning run the system compares exception messages in the new MRP list with the exception messages in the old list. When one exception message is listed, it is called an old exception message. Under the collective list display, there is the option of choosing a new exception message. In the individual display of the MRP list, it is possible to search for new or old exception messages.

Under a collection conversion, an MRP controller can choose the planned orders for the materials for which it is responsible and then convert them collectively into production orders, process orders, or purchase requisitions.

An *opening period* is the time period between the opening date and the start date in the planned order. This period represents the processing time needed by the MRP controller to convert the planned orders. When dealing with collective conversion, the system chooses the planned order through the opening date, making it possible to choose planned orders with opening dates that occurred in the past.

Material Discontinuation

An overview of a business background indicates that its objective is to have no wasted warehouse stock. This means that a new material is only planned when the stock of the old material has been exhausted. The discontinuation of dependent materials involves parallel discontinuation, definition of the main part for discontinuation, and dependent components that are discontinued along with the main part.

When maintaining data, note that simple or parallel discontinuation involves material that is to be discontinued as well as main material in the group of materials that are to be discontinued.

Shop Floor Control (SFC)

We start by examining the data in PP. First, the master data involve the factory calendar, material master, work centers, BOMs, routings, PRTs, and CAPP formulas. The transaction data deal with production orders, confirmations, CO-object or cost collection, and material movements.

Any long-term data are referred to as PP master data. Transaction data are composed of documents that only exist for a limited period of time. Documents used for confirmation, costs (CO objects), and material movements are designated for production orders.

Production order management is a component used in a complex functional procedure that begins with independent requirements and extends to dealing with finished products. In an SAP system, production order management controls the overall procedure for in-house production. Production order management employs system components such as word processing, factory calendar, classification, communication, customization, and graphics.

Procurement types are defined through the use of material types. Material types permit both in-house production and external procurement and define procurement types using material master maintenance, quotation, and per-procurement transactions. In addition, production orders support in-house production of finished products, assembly groups, and individual parts and other services as well.

When dealing with a production order, it is important to consider several aspects. Items that are produced include finished products and services. The time frame in which these items are produced involves planned order dates, basic dates, calculated dates, reported dates, release, start, and finish dates. The quantities produced involve planned order quantities, production order quantities, and reported quantities. The quantities are produced for materials, cost centers, orders, and plants. The people for whom these items are produced are often referred to as cost carriers. The items used to manufacture these products include material implementation, PRTs, and checks. The costs involved with production often include planned and actual costs.

It is important to note that specific elements can be added to the order structure displayed. It is also possible to allocate material components as well as PRTs to the operations as required. Several alternative or parallel operation sequences may then be created. Costs are computed at the operation level, but only processed at the order header level.

Sub-operations are arranged hierarchically within operations so as to facilitate more detailed costing and capacity planning. Control keys are very important in this regard. Since scheduling always occurs at the operation level, standard values can collect on the operation they are property of with respect to both dimension and unit. In addition, no material components or PRTs can be allocated under these circumstances.

Item categories are designated in customizing. They have the responsibility of controlling data and processing material components such as stock items, non-stock items, variable size-items, and text items. The indicator called lot independent or fixed lot controls required quantities. There must be a bulk indicator to define a material component as an overhead material. Components that have an item category of non-stock item automatically establish a purchase requisition that can be displayed using a further item screen.

Creating Orders

Production orders can be created manually or converted directly from a planned order. There can be at least one operation, but the system can create more if needed. The lead time scheduling is executed automatically; it computes the start and finish dates in the order as well as the detailed dates in the operation itself.

There are several options for the creation process. In the material reference there is the choice of the manual route, with planned order, with/without routing, with/without BOM, with sales order, or with an assembly order. If an option has no material reference, the manual route can be selected.

Material reservations are created for all material components for a type of stock material. Reservations are considered when designating MRP requirements. Goods movements for components within the production order are established with a reference to the reservation. An order determines the requirements for every item, while an indicator controls whether goods movements are permitted for reservation items. Reservations are assigned for material components in the production order. Lists of reservations for material or account assignments can then be produced.

The issue of routing comes into play because routings contain order-independent data that can be employed for repeated manufacture of products. Routing data can be duplicated and put into the production order. When routing is later changed, orders that currently exist will not be affected. The routings within a routing group can be used to manufacture similar materials. In addition, routings with similar manufacturing procedures can be combined in a routing group.

Alternatively, a sequence can be used that provides the chance to choose alternative operations in a given sequence. In fact, this may pertain to production runs with different lot sizes as much as it applies to capacity bottlenecks.

When using customization, define possibilities for routing selections, but remember that all the criteria are always checked. It is possible to designate whether a routing is necessary, but if the indicator selection of alternatives in the material master does not call for the selection by production version, then the specifications that involve the production version in the material master must have priority over the others.

It is possible to employ the function "new routing" to alter the routing that was originally copied for an alternative routing. This change can also be made until the routing has been released for production. Note that the allocation of BOMs and PRTs is the same as long as there is the same operation.

BOM selection is important because BOMs contain material structure and order independent input quantities of individual components for a product. BOM data are duplicated to the production order, while future changes to the BOM have no effect on existing orders. With order creation that deals with pertinent selection criteria, they are used for accurate choice of one BOM.

Remember than creation of production orders from planned orders is the most important type of application in PP. When dealing with the data flow in order creation, the production order is automatically created from the master data copy operation. Furthermore, nearly all of the data in a production order can be changed on creation. In addition, data are created when the order is created.

Converting planned order to production orders involves several steps. Planned order possess a basic start date (BS), a basic finish date (BF), and a creation date (CD). During the creation date, a planned order needs to be converted to a production order or a purchase requisition. Planned orders can be converted online in the form of either individual or collection conversion. When a planned order is converted into a production order, the planned order and its associated material components, along with any capacity that exists, are deleted. Conversion also occurs when the creation of a production material reservation record occurs for the material components and capacity requirements.

During the entire product structure, only planned orders are provided for conversion dealing with the planned creation dates that exist within the creation horizon to be specified. The size of the creation horizon in customization must be determined with respect to the current date. Furthermore, the MRP controller also converts the planned orders for a product structure step by step on the time axis.

Order Changes and Releases

An order release is the foundation for a follow-up process for the production order. This involves the printing of documents and material withdrawal. Production orders are managed using the status, while an order release has an appropriate status set. Availability checks can be executed automatically, and individual operations, an entire order, or several orders can be released simultaneously.

Status management involves four steps: the application, status type, system status, and user status. In the application phase the sequence of business transactions for a production order can be controlled, and it is possible to work with the order, operation, material component, and PRT. In the status types phase there is the system and user status. The system status phase deals with the system internal status, items the user cannot change, fixed quantities of predefined status, and fixed sequences for status assignment. In the final user status phase there are freely definable terms, items set by the user, and links through the status profile.

Material availability checks are controlled through multiple part inspection requirements. Checking requirements involve several elements. Checking groups involve the designation of the material master or MRP 2 screen. The checking rule involves the designation of order types. The scope-of-check concerns the specifications of checking details for each checking rule and group.

The scope-of-check deals with limiting the time period of the availability check and designates the elements to be incorporated into the check. The checking group deals with the assignment of a checking requirement to a material. The checking rule deals with the assignment of a checking requirement to an application. The checking control for production orders deals with defining checking rules for a specific order, specifying controlled-by operations that are created or released, activation or deactivation of the availability check, and the control-of-order release option with missing parts.

Dealing with production resources and tool availability checks involves the checking control for production orders. It is possible to see that the orders deal with defining the checking rule for specific orders, specify controlled-by operations that are created or released, activate or deactivate availability check, or the control-of-order release option for missing PRTs. The checking rule is the second component that checks for material stock or material status, document status, and PRT status.

Printing Documents

Production order documents may be printed online, in the background, or during a status update. Printing can be accessed directly as a collective print, from production order processing, or for each job.

Print control involves print modes that permit printing the original, reprinting, or a partial print. It offers a selection of plant, MRP controller, order type, material, dates, order status, or production schedulers. Finally, there are control tables involving lists, transactions, forms, reports, document types, print flow, output device, and table accesses.

The last ingredient is spool maintenance that supports printing of production orders on any printer. The SP01 is used for daily administrative business by all users, while SPAD deals with the actual administration, printer setup, and setup modification.

Goods

Any issues dealing with goods can be either planned or unplanned. The data input relies on the specific types of goods issues involved. In a goods movement, a material document as well as one or more accounting documents are created. A material document defines goods movements from one warehouse perspective. An accounting document defines the goods movement from the perspective of the accounting department. It is possible to branch from the material document display to the accounting document display and designate individual goods movement types whether or not a material document can be printed. Or it is possible to specify whether or not printing is allowed, so that a material document can be printed directly when inputting a goods movements, or later using a specific function.

Movement types are central to defining material movements. They control both the creation and update of a material movement. Individual items in a material document can be created with different movement types, and you can also control the reference to a production order on material withdrawal can be controlled through a specially created movement type.

References to a reservation define whether a material withdrawal for a production order will be planned or unplanned. Planned material withdrawals are only executed for components kept in stock. Creating goods movements without references involves a single record entry and a collective entry. Creating goods movements with a reference is for an order or reservation. The effect of a goods movement involves the reservation, G/L accounts, stock quantity consumption statistics, and the point of consumption (cost center or order).

Backflushing or material withdrawal is the opposite of components kept in stock. Backflushing is employed if physical staging of materials from the warehouse needs to be avoided. Materials are staged at the work center and the areas of application have continuous flow and assembly lines as well as less value-intensive materials. It is essential to rework successful backflushes to achieve success with zero stock totaling.

Order Confirmation

Order confirmation helps keep a record of internal activities that have been achieved for an order. The order confirmation can be used to monitor the work progress in the production order.

It is possible to control the confirmation using parameters which can be defined or fixed in customizing and then altered during confirmation. Order confirmations involve confirmation at the order header level. Confirmation can be executed through the control key with automatic goods input. The backflushed components can be corrected within a material overview or as many unplanned material movements as required can be created. A confirmation for an order can only be executed when no confirmation is created for an operation.

Confirmation of date involves specific selection options that include order overview, operation sequence, confirmation number, and sub-operations. It then involves the confirmation of data that include quantity of work, forecast, dates, personnel, and descriptions.

Receipt of Goods

Goods receipts automatically follow when the last operation in confirmed. Before this can happen an indicator must be chosen in the control key for this operation. Goods receipts from production for a pertinent warehouse occur in the same way as to normal goods receipts for a purchase order.

It is possible to designate specific conditions during the goods receipt from a production order that include items of plant, storage location, batch, stock type, and final delivery.

The final delivery indicator tells whether an order will count as a completed entity from the perspective of a goods receipt. Therefore, no additional goods receipt will be expected for an order so that the open quantity is zero. Goods receipt postings of leftover quantities are possible, but do not change the open order quantity. When a return delivery occurs for an item that has a final delivery indicator and a further delivery is expected, then transverse the final delivery indicator.

When dealing with a goods receipt that references a production order, the system introduces an open order quantity for the goods receipt. It is possible to alter this quantity if the delivered quantity is different. When a goods receipt is created, the goods receipt quantity is compared to the open order quantity. This allows the system to make certain there is no over- or underdelivery.

Underdelivery is allowed in the standard system. An underdelivery tolerance can be input in the order indicated in percentage terms. A goods receipt quantity less than the order quantity less the underdelivery tolerance is interpreted and accepted as what is called a partial delivery. The system indicates that the underdelivery to the user occurs when it takes the underdelivery tolerance into account for the online message.

No overdeliveries are allowed within a standard system. When overdeliveries are allowed, then an overdelivery tolerance can be input in percentage terms within the order. The overdelivery tolerance within an order can be overridden but no unlimited overdelivery is permitted.

Order Settlement

Controlling order settlement is achieved through a settlement profile. It is possible to credit an order through each cost element. Employing a settlement structure is necessary to designate cost elements between debit cost element/production order and the credit cost element/cost receiver. Each conclusion is achieved through the differences that produce postings to price difference accounts for revenue or expense or the correction of the allocation price.

Settlement profiles for production orders are designated by specific order type, while permissible settlement receivers exist in the settlement profile. Cost assignments within an order occur through the settlement profile for specific settlement rules.

It is important to note that the act of archiving or deletion occurs in stages. The actual physical deletion or archiving of a given order occurs after various conditions have been checked. In addition, individual or mass deletion can also occur.

Application Difficulties

Producing a material in a different plant is controlled through a special procurement key. Special procurement keys can be designated in the material master or in quota arrangement, or production values can be changed manually within a planned order. Remember that planned order variables can be controlled by procurement.

Production orders are specific to a given plant, but individual operations cannot be completed at another plant. Plant specifications can only be altered on the operation detail screen of General View.

External processing of a given operation is effected by an operation control key or external processing indicator. When an order is created, a purchase requisition or BANF is automatically created. A requisition type is just a standard purchase order (NB) and cannot be altered. Purchase orders can be created for a requisition when an order has been created, but the requisition and its purchase order are allocated to the production order. The two types of external processing data needed for order operation are:

- Purchasing group and planned delivery time needed for requisition
- Material class and short term information necessary for information record retrieval.

Note specific time elements and how they originated. Maintain time elements for lead time scheduling in various areas within a PP application. Use appropriate settings correctly to achieve successful scheduling.

Reduction measures are extremely important. The system can execute reduction measures for orders that have lead time scheduling. Reducible time elements and reduction strategy can be designated in customizing per-order type and planner group. In addition, floats may be reduced both prior and subsequent to production in order to designate reduction in customizing for each plant, order type, and planner group.

Scheduling sub-operations is also critical because sub-operation dates are designated by using references for the start and finish of a given operation with an offset specification. Specific reference dates for a sub-operation can occur before or after element setup, process, teardown, and wait.

Logistics Information System (LIS)

There can be automatic updating of the logistics data base from logistics applications, and accumulation of data from external systems. It is also possible to establish statistical data in a given information system. When an LIS information structure is analyzed, a flexible analysis offers the option of adding a mixture of more data from the SAP R/3 system.

This introduces the concept of information structures that form the foundation for all of the logistics information systems. These include tables of statistics where data are from the operative applications that are constantly updated and aggregated.

Information structure is composed of three primary elements of information:

1. Characteristics that involve common business criteria with no time reference usable for aggregation
2. Unit of periodicity that is designated to an information structure. This deals the period unit and how frequently data is collected and compressed as part of the updating process.

Standard R/3 systems support several information structures for each application. They permit analysis of events with respect to operative applications from various angles. The tools within the statistics database permit designation of personalized information structures composed of characteristics and key figures (values that offer information of specific business relevance). All of these combine to form the foundation for creating individual update and analysis programs.

Whenever data are recorded within an application, the system will try to determine whether they have been defined to be used within a LIS. These data are then reduced and sent to the LS interface as a communication structure. Physical updates of LIS tables often occur asynchronously. Asynchronous updating of LIS is a prelude to an individual Logical Unit of Work (LUW) that makes certain that periodic posting turns on the operational systems are not at risk when problems develop during a statistics update.

Application Link Enabling

Application Link Enabling (ALE) is integrated with the LIS. ALE is the foundation upon which data can be exchanged between a central application and distributed applications operating on various logical systems.

ALE permits recording of consolidated statistics during events where different business areas are processed on different R/3 systems. The update of distinct statistics can be unique in the central system and in the local systems to satisfy individual information needs.

When ALE is implemented in LS statistical data are transferred on two different levels. The first is composed of all data needed for updating any information structure. The second is composed of data that have been aggregated and created as part of updating in the local system. The benefits are that in level 1, ALE makes certain that all data that relate to updating are transferable so that an individual update occurs in the central system. In the second level, a smaller amount of data than from level 1 is transferred. There is also a way that ALE is filtered to permit restricting the amount of data transferred with respect to individual needs.

Summary

In this chapter we explored the background of the production planning environment provided by R/3. The productivity and efficiency of an organization are vital. This chapter has discussed planning, inventory, and maintaining material master records to ensure the best possible solution for any company. The menu paths described in this chapter, have opened the way to a better understanding of R/3.

4-1 What is a standard material master menu path?

4-2 What is the base unit of measure?

4-3 What alternative unit of measures exist?

TIP

Remember always to press the units-of-measure button. To display any classification information, choose the class type or material class.

4-4 What is the MM/PP status field used for?

4-5 What lot size rule is being used for planning?

4-6 How is inventory being valued in a general ledger?

4-7 Name two material master views that are not plant-specific?

4-8 Create a menu path for material master creation.

TIP

When creating a finished product, select all views available for the material type and enter additional fields where required. Then record the screen on which each piece of information is entered.

Always make certain to select the Enter icon as each view is displayed to indicate acceptance of the data displayed. Always remember to save the material master file record by selecting the Save icon. Then create the next material master file assembly.

4-9 Create the following material master records by using the copy command (see Figure 4.1) define a menu path leading to the step where copy can be entered from data (Figure 4.2).

If there is a bill of material display, with the following menu path: Logistics to Production to Master Data to Bills of Material to Bills of material to Material BOM to Display.

4-10 What is the definition of BOM usage 1?

4-11 What is the BOM status?

4-12 In a typical bill of material creation, define a logical menu path that leads from Logistics to Create.

4-13 Define a menu path for routing creation.

FIGURE 4.1
Master Record

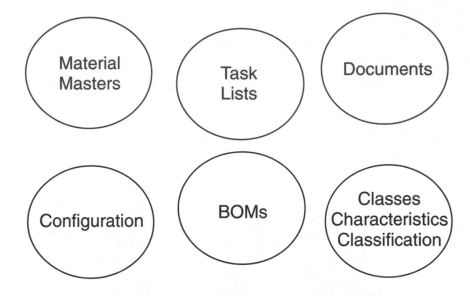

FIGURE 4.2
Structural Change of
Master Records

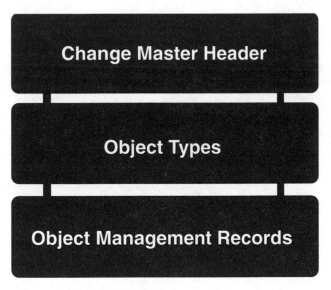

TIP

Select the Header icon or use the menu path that leads from Details to Header to enter your routing header information. The menu path leading from Details to Operation may be required to input the standard values for each operation. Use the Arrow icons to move forward and backward between individual operations.

4-14 Determine the base quantity and operation in order to define how these relate to standard values.

4-15 Define a menu path for routing display.

4-16 Define a menu path for routing maintenance.

4-17 After a component is allocated to an operation, what additional parameters can be defined?

Work Center Maintenance

4-18 Define a menu path for work center creation.

Always select the Enter key or click on the Basic Data button to access the Basic Data view.

TIP

4-19 Define the impact the labor efficiency rate has on the labor time entered for operations using this work center.

4-20 Can operations using the work center be defined without entering a setup time?

4-21 Can the work center be used to define routing operations based on the data entered to this point?

4-22 Can capacity, scheduling, and costing activities be executed for operations using the work center?

4-23 Define a menu path for work center maintenance.

Select the Capacities button or use the menu path Goto to Capacity to Overview to enter capacity data. Once the formulas are entered, press the Enter key. Remember to clear any errors before proceeding, then choose the Capacity header button, or use the menu path Goto to Capacity to Header to enter the header data.

TIP

4-24 Is it possible to define a labor capacity for a work center?

Select the back icon from the header screen, position the cursor on the formula and select the Formula button, or use the menu path Extras to Formulas to Display.

TIP

4-25   What is the value of the capacity processing formula selected?

TIP   Select the Scheduling button or use the menu path Goto to Scheduling to access the scheduling data.

4-26   Determine the value of a processing formula.

4-27   Determine why the definition of a capacity category on the Scheduling view is important.

4-28   What time parameter default is defined by Location Group?

4-29   Why is the activity type so important?

4-30   Specify three views for which formulas can be entered.

4-31   Is it necessary to have more than one formula for the same work center?

4-32   How could any additional views of the work center be defined?

Routing Maintenance

4-33   Define a menu path for routing maintenance.

4-34   Explain why the activity type for the machine standard value should be maintained.

TIP   When looking up the work center (Figure 4.3), clear the work center category field and enter *insp* in the description field. This will ensure all inspection work centers are displayed.

4-35   Explain why it is not possible to make an entry for the control key in certain operations.

4-36   Define an alternative sequence creation menu path.

TIP   Always select the Sequence Overview button or use the menu path Goto to Sequence Overview. Choose the New Entries push-button and choose Alternative sequence in the pop-up window.

FIGURE 4.3
Work Center

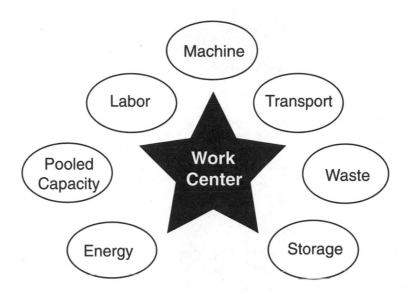

4-37   Define a menu path for parallel sequence creation.

4-38   In addition to alternative and parallel sequences, what other schedule reduction methods can be used reduce operation lead-times?

4-39   Explain where reduction values are defined.

TIP

Select the Header icon or use the menu path Details to Header to access the routing status. Change the status to Released (General).

KEY CONCEPT

In order to illustrate the integration of the applications in the SAP R/3 system this section examines the entire planning process, (Figure 4.4) which starts with the creation of independent requirements. A sales order is then created to determine if and how the independent requirements are consumed. MRP is executed to compute lower level requirements. The planner, must review the results and take all necessary actions such as converting planned orders to production orders or purchase requisitions, converting requisitions to purchase orders, and checking the accuracy of the data in the BOMs, routings, and the material master.

4-40   Create a planned independent requirements menu path.

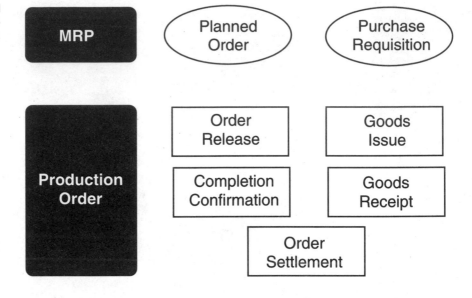

FIGURE 4.4
Production Orders

KEY CONCEPT

To illustrate the integration of the applications in the SAP R/3 system, this section allows review of the use of SOP in planning. The functionality of product group planning is used and the information is disaggregated down to its members. Ultimately these plans to are transferred demand management. The process starts with the creation of production master data.

4-41   Create a production plan that illustrates the menu path for a given product group.

KEY CONCEPT

In order to illustrate the integration of the applications in the SAP R/3 system, it is important to demonstrate how the Make-To-Stock Planning strategy functions.

In the manufacturing stage, imagine that the company has decided to keep production levels constant for the year in order to balance the work force and fully utilize the current equipment capacity. Before starting to forecast the material, set-up the master data:
1. Create the material master
2. Cycle count the material in the plant.

4-42   Define a menu path that allows creation of a new part by copying a part number from one plant to another?

KEY CONCEPT

In order to illustrate the integration of an applications in the SAP R/3 system, it is to demonstrate how the Make-To-Order Planning strategy operates. The next group of questions helps provide you the opportunity to determine the impact of Make-To-Order sales orders on inventory and planning.

Imagine that in the company there are several items manufactured specifically for individual customer orders. It is not necessary to forecast these items as demand is never constant and the BOM structures are subject to change. It will be necessary to create a make-to-order item (Figure 4.5).

FIGURE 4.5
Product
Manufacturing

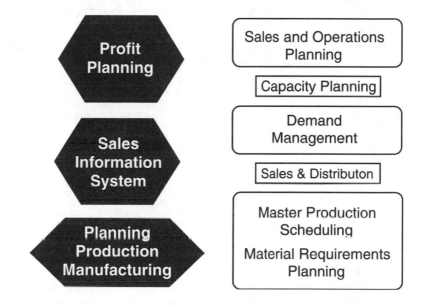

The purpose of the following questions is to create a production order using various methods. How to create an order without a routing, create a production order with a routing, and create a production order using a planned order are covered.

KEY CONCEPT

On the path to certification, it will be necessary to release an operation on the order and then release the entire order created, as well as to verify that the configuration is set up correctly for this order in respect to availability checking.

The purpose of the next question is to execute a goods receipt transaction for the production order. When tackling this kind of question, check whether the system expects a goods receipt for the order and then note the underdelivery and overdelivery tolerance.

4-43 Define a menu path for the for stock overview dealing with a given material.

4-44   Define a menu path for a goods receipt that deals with a partial quantity for a given order.

4-45   Define a menu path for a good receipt that has a final quantity of 25.

4-46   Define a menu path that deals with the review of material and accounting documents of the posted goods receipts.

KEY CONCEPT

The purpose of this next set of questions is to settle the production order. The goal here is familiarity with the various steps performed to settle a production order.

The purpose of this section is to illustrate how to set up the function of trigger points for reporting rework operations. Familiarity with creating a rework operation to be inserted is the basis for, change the routing to indicate where the rework operation should be automatically inserted. Check configuration, and then set up a new order. In the report of actual completion, invoke the trigger point by defining a reason code.

It also necessary to be familiar with the standard analysis function in the Shop Floor Information System.

4-47   Define a menu path to display the material master data for any given material.

KEY CONCEPT

It is important to become familiar with the basics of the Early Warning System. An exception EX-SCRAP-XX for scrap deviation for the information structure (production orders) will be created. Select (or be given) a period of time to analyze. Then display these lines in red if the exception occurs in the standard analysis, for periodic analysis send mail to yourself.

4-48   Define a menu path that illustrates a a periodic analysis, by creating an area to analyze and a variant.

KEY CONCEPT

Achieve familiarity with the techniques of creating flexible analyses. To create a flexible analysis to select data for checking the cost variances of the evaluation structure, the characteristics are plant, material number and order. Key figures are the planned value and the actual value. The variance (planned value–actual value) must also be displayed (insert formula).

4-49   Create a menu path that illustrates flexible analysis.

4-1 Menu path: Logistics to Production to Master Data to Material Master to Material-to-Display to Display, Current.

4-2 EA (Each)

4-3 PAL (Pallet)

4-4 To exclude materials from certain business activities.

4-5 EX (Lot for lot-order quantity)

4-6 The Price Control is S (Standard Cost)

4-7 Basic data and Classification

4-8 Menu path: Logistics to Production to Master Data to Material Master to Material to Create (general).

4-9 Menu Path: Logistics to Production to Master Data to Material Master to Material-to-Create (general) to Immediately 4Enter Copy From Data.

4-10 Production

4-11 1 (Active)

4-12 Menu path: Logistics to Production to Master Data to Bills of Material to Bills of material to Material BOM to Create.

4-13 Menu path: Logistics to Production to Master Data to Routings to Routings to Routing to Create.

4-14 1 Each: The standard values entered are the setup, machine, and labor time required to manufacture one pump.

4-15 Menu path: Logistics to Production to Master Data to Routings to Routings to Routing-to-Display

4-16 Menu path: Logistics to Production to Master Data to Routings to Routings to Routing to Change.

4-17 The Backfush Indicator can be set to identify if the component will be backfushed at the operation.

4-18 Menu path: Logistics to Production to Master Data to Work Centers to Work center to Create.

4-19 The labor standard time entered will be divided in half because the real operation time is less than that entered.

4-20 Yes, but a warning message will appear prompting for entry of a setup time.

4-21 Yes.

4-22 No, because these views and their individual calculation formulas have not yet been defined.

4-23 Menu path: Logistics to Production to Master data to Work Centers to Work Center to Change.

4-24 Yes; each work center can have multiple capacity views so that it is possible to look at the operational load for multiple resources consumed at a work center.

4-25 The value displayed is formula-specific. The value is: machine standard value from the routing operation X operation quantity divided by base quantity.

4-26 The value displayed is formula-specific. The value for SAPOO2: is Machine standard value from the routing operation X operation quantity ÷ base quantity ÷ operation splits.

4-27 Definition of a capacity category is important because it determines which capacity category is to be used in the calculation of schedule dates of production at the work center. This would typically be the critical capacity resource for the work center.

4-28 Move Time; This value is defined in a matrix indicating the default move time between one location group and other location groups.

4-29 The activity type contains the cost center's cost rate for the activity that will be performed.

4-30 Three views for entering formulas are capacity, scheduling, and cost center assignment.

4-31 Multiple formulas must be designated because the formula used for costing might not be appropriate for the calculation of capacity load or operation schedule times and dates.

4-32 Additional work center views are:

   1. Technical Data
   2. Hierarchy Detail
   3. Assignment of a Person
   4. Qualification Assignment
   5. Position Assignment.

4-33 Menu path: Logistics to Production to Master Data to Routings to Routings to Routing to Change.

4-34   When the cost center assignment was performed for the work center, this activity was defined as not maintainable.

4-35   When the work center defaults for MONT-xx were defined the control key was designated not maintainable.

4-36   Menu path: Logistics to Production to Master Data to Routings to Routings to Routing to Change.

4-37   Menu path: Logistics to Production to Master Data to Routings to Routings to Routing to Change.

4-38   Other schedule reductions are Overlapping operations or operation splitting.

4-39   Overlap between operations and operation splitting are defined on the Operations Detail view of the operation.

4-40   Menu path: Logistics to Production to Master Planning to Demand Management I–Planned Independent Requirements to Create.

4-41   Menu path: Logistics to Production to SOP to Planning to For Product Group to Change.

4-42   Menu path: Logistics to Production to Master Data to Material Master to Material to Create (General) to Immediately.

4-43   Menu path: Logistics to Materials Management to Inventory Management to Environment to Stock to Stock Overview.

4-44   Menu path: Logistics to Production to Production Control to Environment to Goods Movement to Goods Receipt.

4-45   Menu path: Logistics to Materials Management to Inventory Management to Goods Movement to Goods Receipt for Order.

4-46   Menu path: Logistics to Materials Management to Inventory Management to Material Document to Display.

4-47   Menu path: Extras to Master Data to Material.

4-48   Menu path: Logistics to Logistics Controlling to SFIS to Early Warning System to Periodic Analysis to Area to Analyze to Create.

4-49   Menu path: Logistics to Logistics Controlling to Flexible Analysis to Evaluation to Definition to Create.

SOLUTIONS

CHAPTER 5

Supply-Chain Management

Mission-critical information gives a distinct competitive advantage today. Competition is marked by increased demand, decreased customer loyalty, shorter product life-cycles, and mass product customization. Businesses must effectively gather vital information and quickly act on it. Companies must recognize that tight interaction and coordination among the members of the supply chain will be key ingredients in their continued success.

The objective of the supply chain is to support the flow of goods and materials from the original supplier through multiple production and logistics operations to the ultimate consumer.

Supply-chain management is the planning and control of this flow to speed time-to-market, reduce inventory levels, lower overall costs, and, ultimately, enhance customer service and satisfaction. The time has come when companies can no longer afford to look at their operations in a vacuum. What they now need is the ability to collect comprehensive, accurate, and timely information over the entire supply chain.

Study of this information will help prepare for answering questions on the certification exam, questions about how changing conditions affect businesses. It will be possible to make informed business decisions and help the organization accomplish business goals while at the same time helping it use information for competitive advantage.

Supply Chain Management Course Information

Achieving successful supply chain management involves the integration of information as the first step: analysis of information to determine which actions to take within the context of automated business processes. The most effective goals are achieved by automatically triggering a corresponding product transition. The tight coupling of execution and decisionmaking is an essential ingredient in effective supply chain management.

Information technologies reduce communication barriers to enable an improved flow of information among all members of the supply chain. The way to start is to develop a step-by-step approach to chart the course of a business toward high-performance supply chain management; steps include:

1. Achieving execution excellence by fully automating and optimizing business practices
2. Extending the enterprise to accept all members of the supply chain
3. Integrating business systems with those of customers, suppliers, and partners to create a common information foundation
4. Deploying real-time decision support to increase responsiveness
5. Investing in re-educating and reorienting employees, vendors, and other members of the supply chain on the practices needed to optimize business processes
6. Making a company-wide commitment to creating and managing a more complex organization capable of tackling global business issues.

TIP

The topics in supply-chain management courses include:

- Introduction to supply-chain concepts
- Evolution of MRP/ERP supply-chain model
- Cross-industry best practices
- Contemporary demand management best practices
- Collaborative/concurrent product development
- Automated replenishment
- Advanced planning systems
- Introduction to optimization
- Theory of constraints
- Process flow theory
- JIT, KANBAN, and other best practices
- Electronic commerce
- The supply chain and the Internet
- Introduction to APO server
- Implementing APO within SAP's business framework
- Integrating APO with third-party systems
- Supply chain cockpit
- Graphical supply-chain modeling and monitoring
- Configurable user interface forecasting and demand planning
- Core set of forecasting
- Demand planning functionality ATP
- Simulate and load orders
- Aggregated ATP check
- Allocations
- Rule-based ATP advance planning and scheduling
- Detailed finite scheduling
- High-performance master planning and material planning
- Internet-enabled forecasting and demand planning
- Additional statistical forecast methods of advance planning and scheduling
- Distribution and deployment planning
- Synchronized material and capacity planning algorithms and heuristics
- Optimization techniques.

In SAP's Business Framework in Enterprise Execution Excellence, an organization must be capable of implementing and executing its business processes to maximize business benefits. Business applications must be able to process high volumes of information. They must be open, robust, highly flexible, and easily configured and managed, and they must ensure a high level of data integrity throughout the organization. R/3 offers business functions such as sales and materials planning, production planning, warehouse management, financial accounting, and personnel management to form an integrated workflow of business events.

SAP offers solutions that automate crucial supply chain processes in ways that improve performance and provide a competitive edge. SAP's solutions deliver robust functionality, a high degree of configurability, and real-time data integration to provide benefits from information that gives a company a distinct advantage.

Business Framework

Business Framework allows a company to reduce deployment time, institute continuous business improvement, and dynamically reconfigure R/3 without disrupting the business. The component and messaging-based architecture makes it possible to deploy new R/3 functionality incrementally.

R/3 interfaces are standards-based and provide benefits from the full interoperability between SAP and third-party components. Business Framework makes systems simpler to maintain; different components can be upgraded on different release cycles. The highest levels of execution excellence and a new level of flexibility and agility are possible. The open interfaces foster the integration of a company's business systems with those of partners and suppliers.

Messaging techniques support businesses in the same way that enterprise does and adopt the methodologies of high-performance supply chain management.

Business Information Warehouse also employs highly tuned data structures to add a new level of supply chain-oriented decisionmaking capabilities to Business Framework. Business Framework works in combination with Business Information Warehouse to offer organizations the tools to achieve execution excellence in today's competitive environment.

To participate in a high-performance supply chain, a company must be taken forward and extended beyond the bounds of the traditional enterprise. The enterprise extends beyond formal boundaries to meet business challenges and consider factors that affect decision making.

Business Component Access

SAP provides extensive access to R/3's independent business components through BAPIs that conform to accepted, open object standards published by CORBA and DCOM.

SAP offers Internet-enabled R/3 that added several Internet Application Components to the standard Business Framework. These improvements have enabled features such as remote order entry over the Internet in R/3's Sales and Distribution component.

SAP's goal is to further integrate business processes across the supply chain. The result is that SAP delivers a very high level of data integration available in supply chain software allows for integrated decision-making.

Extended Enterprise

The extended enterprise incorporates all of the members of a company's supply chain: the different legal units within the company, suppliers and their vendors, customers and their customers, and external service providers. The introduction of low-cost communications media such as the Internet facilitates integration across the extended enterprise and allows any enterprise to compete regardless of size.

The extended enterprise is much like the typical direct-order computer manufacturer. Consumers access the company's Web site, where they can browse through available options and configure a machine to their exact specifications and budget. Customers receive an immediate price quote and, once an order is placed, a firm delivery date and a confirmation number to track the order. They can shop without pressure, customize the purchase, know exactly when it will be delivered, and receive a price break that reflects the manufacturer's lower cost of doing business.

Orders are collected directly from the customer and the company can use valuable point-of-sale (POS) data to distribute real-time feedback to various points within its business processes. Manufacturing knows precisely what to build, procurement knows what to order, and marketing can immediately determine the success of a given program. The extended enterprise helps feed material requirements and fulfillment data directly to the systems of suppliers of parts and distributors of finished goods.

Business information systems must satisfy several fundamental criteria to allow a company to extend the enterprise and participate in a high-performance supply chain.

A system must be highly flexible, in order for users to individualize it to their exact business requirements and adapt it to meet changes in processes. A system must be powerful enough to integrate the vast flow of information among all members of the extended enterprise. It must also be open, so all participants can benefit from the power of shared information in ways that meet productivity, customer service, and other key strategic objectives. The system should also be dynamic and highly automated, to react effectively to changing variables and ensure that changing business conditions trigger appropriate, coordinated responses across the chain.

SAP's Business Framework satisfies all the extended enterprise conditions and provides several other important benefits as well. Enterprise open connectivity provides greater compatibility between multiple instances of R/3 and between third-party systems to facilitate higher levels of intraenterprise and interenterprise communication.

Internet Applications

R/3 has several Internet application components for consumer-to-business, business-to-business, and intranet applications. Employees can use a standard Web browser anywhere in the world to access authorized portions of a corporation's R/3 system to gain information and transact real-time business securely.

R/3 permits integrated business systems to cooperate across the Internet through open BAPI standards for business transactions. This level of open connectivity allows business components to interact with multiple business systems in fully electronic supply chain management.

Messaging Techniques

Messaging techniques support businesses as well as extending your enterprise and adopt the methodologies of high-performance supply chain management. It gives you the chance to get your company ready for future initiatives.

Information Integration

Integrating information is the cornerstone of many corporate efforts for improving business processes. ERP systems are designed to accomplish this task and to provide organizations with a system for planning, controlling, and monitoring business processes.

ERP systems acquire high levels of integration by using a standard mechanism for communications. This creates a common understanding of what shared data represent and establishes a set of rules for accessing data. Like ERP solutions, supply chain solutions must integrate information consistently. They differ from ERP systems because supply chain systems must deal with the complexity of integrating information from disparate information systems anywhere in the supply chain.

An ERP system uses different methods to integrate operations. A database is the basis of communications within the organization, while individual applications access data through a variety of standard networking protocols. Different members of a supply chain can use any number of different database architectures, but, companies will likely not influence every member of the supply chain to agree on one standard database architecture.

Businesses must also agree on what shared data represent as well as on rules governing access, including authorization procedures. Agreement is facilitated through the adoption of a common set of standards, which for SAP users is uniform throughout the organization.

ERP systems integrate data within the organization, and supply chain solutions must integrate decisions within the extended enterprise. Real-time decision support is crucial, though it cannot be applied to just one or a few links in the supply chain. High-performance supply chain solutions must monitor all the elements of the chain, execute critical decisions, and continuously effect process change.

Flexible supply chain solutions can work with market changes by acting quickly on changing conditions. Real-time data on materials availability, transportation, labor, and other factors can be used to facilitate change across the product cycle as conditions mandate. On the demand side, predictions based on up-to-the-minute data from point-of-sale and marketing help set safe inventory levels based on realistic projections, not historical data.

Should production fall behind schedule due to labor shortages or machinery downtime, supply planners, customer service representatives, and logistics planners can execute changes both upstream and downstream. Companies that acquire execution excellence as a result of their R/3 implementations can realize the potential of a vast store of business information.

R/3 Benefits

R/3 benefits from the optimized business data in the business information warehouse and messaging capabilities which offer the real-time decision support required to perform effective supply chain management. Third-party programs using memory-resident analytical engines have benefited from R/3's messaging and extended its capabilities to include supply chain functions.

Tools range from supply planning, plant scheduling, and demand planning to logistics. These communicate directly with R/3 to help with timely decisions to optimize supply chain performance.

SAP's Business Framework provides the solid foundation needed to build a robust supply chain solution. There should be additional functions to complete this solution. Because no single vendor can address all aspects of the supply chain, customers may find they need to work with more than one supply chain component vendor.

Third-party solutions are largely decisionmaking only and lack the ability to effect change in an automated fashion. This critical detail of execution is resolved by the integration process.

Open Interfaces

SAP's Business Framework helps you achieve the highest levels of execution excellence as it provides you with a new level of flexibility and agility. Its open interfaces permit for the integration of a company's business systems with those of partners and suppliers.

Supply Chain Optimization

Supply chain optimization is a complex task that involves the integration of additional supply chain components into current business processes, intensifying the complexity. SAP enhances the extensibility of R/3 and assists in implementation of supply chain solutions.

Seamless integration provides benefits for all supply chain activities, involving the interface between the decision support for planning and optimization as well as the execution of business processes. These processes are crucial for achieving the highest level of performance in supply chain solutions.

R/3 benefits include:

✎ Availability of information required to make informed business decisions
✎ The underlying architecture required for automatic execution of the appropriate changes in business processes.

Advanced planning and optimization extend into areas beyond available solutions, including architecture. SAP's planning and optimization capabilities are integrated in memory-resident computing technologies capable of processing huge volumes of information and making decisions in near real time.

Supply Chain Differences

NOTE

Different members of a supply chain can use any number of different database architectures. However, companies won't usually influence every member of its supply chain to agree on any given single, standard database architecture.

Businesses must agree on what shared data represents as well as rules governing its access. This includes authorization procedures. This type of agreement is facilitated through the adoption of a common set of standards. SAP users benefit from their supply chain standards uniform throughout the organization.

Implementation Levels

SAP's implementation achieves a high level of decision and data integration by maintaining real-time synchronization of information between execution and decisionmaking. Higher levels of integration provide a higher degree of functionality.

In contrast to other third-party solutions, SAP offers tighter control over execution and decisionmaking and advanced tools for global visualization of the entire supply chain. These tools enable supply chain decision makers to view an industry-specific graphical representation of flow, constraints, and other factors within the supply chain.

SAP has created implementation solutions based on open standards for messaging and data sharing. These include the publishing of additional BAPIs along with powerful new business data objects that will synchronize data and decisions among all participants in the supply chain.

Supply chain functions are built into R/3, to eliminate concerns with integrating supply chain functions into existing business processes and help companies focus on areas of the business that improve competitiveness.

SAP has simplified implementation of the supply chain solution by producing improvements to the configuration tool, R/3 Business Engineer.

The long-term cost of SAP ownership is less than that of multivendor solutions. Advanced supply chain planning functions come through the implementation of SAP's Business Framework and third-party add-on supply chain solutions.

APO

Advanced Planner and Optimizer (APO) builds on SAP's Business Framework to improve information flow and incorporate real-time collaborative decision support, advanced planning, and optimization into R/3.

APO is composed of a memory-resident analytical engine and specialized data objects that will be configured to offer four areas of function:

1. Supply Chain Cockpit and Forecasting
2. Advanced Planning
3. Scheduling
4. Available-to-Promise decision support.

Supply chain solution is required to inform decisionmakers of exception conditions as they occur and empower them to make the appropriate changes in business plans.

APO Forecasting is a performance tool to help partners throughout the supply chain create powerful collaborative forecasts that integrate individual vendor forecasts and real-time data including point-of-sale information. This tool allows marketing departments to plan promotions based on up-to-the-minute market data.

APO's Advanced Planning and Scheduling (APS) methods incorporate tools to handle distribution, deployment and transportation, production planning, and shop floor scheduling. The primary objective of APS is to synchronize the supply plan with actual demand captured by forecasting. It achieves this by combining various algorithms such as linear programming, heuristics, classical material and capacity planning with real-time decision support and response capabilities as well as multiplant sourcing logic to provide complete supply chain synchronization.

Supply Chain Engineer

Supply Chain Cockpit is composed of Supply Chain Engineer and Supply Chain Controller to provide decisionmakers the insight and control for effective management of the supply chain.

Supply Chain Engineer enables planners and decision makers to perform graphical maintenance of extended supply chain models including plants, distribution centers, and constraints, as well as factory layouts with associated machinery, storage locations, and constraints.

Supply Chain Controller allows users to review forecasts, plans, and schedules based on the actual status of a system, performance figures or any exceptions or problems that exist.

Supply Chain Cockpit minimizes the complexity of conditions that exist within the entire supply chain, providing decision makers with greater control over their business processes and permitting them to respond more quickly and with more accuracy.

Cockpit is highly configurable to conditions within several industries and business configurations. It incorporates an Internet-enabled user interface to provide remote viewing and control over the entire supply chain.

Forecasting

Forecasting can also be used to enact Vendor Managed Inventory (VMI), shifting the responsibility for replenishment to suppliers. It combines advanced statistical forecasting methods with real-time data from a variety of sources, and provides tight integration with SAP's Business Information Warehouse.

When Forecasting is used in combination with Cockpit, it allows businesses to capture changes in demand signals and patterns as early as possible so that the supply side of the business can respond quickly and appropriately.

Advanced Planning and Scheduling methods are closely integrated with Supply Chain Cockpit to offer planners and schedulers highly graphical representations for the control and accuracy required to optimize business processes.

ATP Server

SAP acquires Available-to-Promise decision support through a high-performance global ATP Server. The server uses a rules-based strategy to acquire results that incorporate factors including customer/plant preferences and approved product substitutions. The server also executes multi-level component and capacity ATP checks in real-time and simulation modes. It can execute these ATP checks against aggregated, memory-resident data for even better performance. The ATP server maintains simultaneous, immediate access to product availability across the supply chain and allows companies to have the highest degree of confidence in the precision of delivery commitments.

Supply Chain Planning

In conjunction with APO, SAP provides Supply Chain Planning Interface (SCPI), a high-fidelity interface that offers access to all R/3 3.1 and 4.0

supply chain components needed by SAP third-party supply chain partners. SCPI+ provides open access to memory-resident APO data for third-
party planning and optimization tools. It allows APO to accept refined
forecasts and schedules from third-party supply chain systems. Integrating
supply chain decision support into Business Framework allows SAP to
assure the highest performance solutions on the market.

Benefits from real-time integration include automatic notification of
incremental changes, exception handling, ATP integration, and backward
communication of plans and schedules.

Supply chain decision support systems require various memory-resident
data models capable of handling large amounts of complex data in real
time. SAP's supply chain solution employs technology that provides the
capabilities required for optimizing supply chain management. Accessibility to APO's primary functions is acquired through the SCPI+ interface, a
collection of high-fidelity BAPIs.

APO's high-performance processing capability is liveCache, which uses
advanced computing technologies that take advantage of multiprocessor
configurations and will support multi-gigabyte memory layouts. live-
Cache enables the APO server to perform supply chain calculations and
other complex tasks, such as semantic synchronization, in real time.

APO's data objects are similar to SAP business objects: a grouping of
complex planning and optimization data and the procedures to manipulate the data. These objects represent SAP's expertise in business processes
and the techniques and methodologies required to perform supply chain
planning and optimization. APO data objects are directly accessible by
R/3 and by third-party systems through the SCPI+ interface.

Data objects are optimized representations of complex supply chain properties, and systems are able to calculate complex properties such as total
material requirements with simple method calls to the APO data objects.

Data within the APO servers are intelligent representations of the same
data objects that exist within the R/3 transaction system as well as those
contained within individual forecasts. Since these objects are more comprehensive than simple business data objects, they cannot simply share the
accompanying business systems' database. The APO server must filter
business data in order to build the APO data objects.

R/3 must maintain two different representations of the same information. In order to achieve this goal, the APO server is equipped with algorithms that perform real-time synchronization of various instances of data
across the supply chain.

The APO server integrates with R/3's Business Information Warehouse
to provide unprecedented access to vital business decision data. The APO

server contains a library of advanced optimization algorithms that can be used to develop forecasts and optimized plans and schedules. It also can generate real-time notification to the underlying business framework and third-party systems.

It is also possible to use event notification to indicate incremental changes in stock, demand, and other factors, and handle exceptions like material shortages, transportation problems, or production problems. Event notification also helps propagate and synchronize plans and schedules throughout the supply chain. Since the APO server is easily configured, it supports several applications within the supply chain across a wide range of industry environments.

It is possible to perform Forecasting, APO, ATP, and supply chain Cockpit functions in a variety of operational, tactical, and strategic ways. When an organization implements supply chain solutions, it must initiate and adopt new business practices and personnel must be trained. Those who are skilled in piloting the real-time information the new systems will produce can integrate it with current knowledge bases to optimize supply chain decision making.

Supply Chain Solutions

There is increased demand for high-performance supply chain solutions to manage and integrate data from different systems. These solutions also must tie together powerful decision-making capabilities with the ability to perform change within an organization's business processes.

Much like ERP systems that integrate data within the organization, supply chain solutions must integrate decisions within the extended enterprise. While there is a definite need for real-time decision support, this need is complicated by the fact that this support cannot be applied to just one or a few links in the supply chain.

NOTE

High-performance supply chain solutions must monitor all the elements of the chain, execute critical decisions, and continuously affecting process change.

BACKGROUND

Organizations have used powerful computers to analyze business process data and provide decision support. This analysis occurs on an "as-needed" basis and changes are frequently executed with little understanding of the effect on other functional areas of the business.

Because there isn't any single vendor can address all aspects of the supply chain, customers may find they need to work with more than one supply chain component vendor. Customers will also find that third-party solutions are largely decision making only and just lack the ability to affect change in an automated fashion. This critical detail of execution is left to the integration process for resolution.

Advanced Planning and Scheduling Methods

APO's Advanced Planning and Scheduling methods includes several tools to handle Distribution, Deployment and Transportation, Production Planning, and Shop Floor Scheduling. The primary objective of APS is to synchronize the supply plan with actual demand that has been captured by Forecasting. It accomplishes this by combining various algorithms such as linear programming, heuristics, classical material and capacity planning with real-time decision support and response capabilities as well as multi-plant sourcing logic to provide complete supply chain synchronization.

Similar to forecasting, Advanced Planning and Scheduling methods are tightly integrated with Supply Chain Cockpit to provide planners and schedulers with rich graphical representations for the control and accuracy required to optimize business processes.

Production Planning Results

Production Planning can generate production plans that incorporate constraints such as supply levels, labor availability and maintenance schedules. Production Planning can operate on single or multiple plants, juggling production loads between facilities with similar production capabilities.

Shop Floor Scheduling

Shop Floor Scheduling to produce optimized schedules that are tightly integrated with the production plan. These methods use a variety of industry and task-specific algorithms and heuristics to produce desired results.

Summary

In this chapter we have seen how supply chain management plays a crucial role in improving communication flow and achieving the best approach to supply chain management, and how it is possible to extend an enterprise with Business Framework.

The most important goal of doing business in the future is making sure that R/3 financials are there assure that a business is run cost-effectively. Chapter 6 discusses R/3 financials in detail.

5-1 What is the first step to achieving success in supply-chain management?

5-2 How can the information in supply-chain management be more effective?

5-3 What does information technology do to improve the flow of communication?

5-4 What has been a primary factor for companies expecting to realize a successful supply-chain management approach?

5-5 Describe in detail the approach needed to obtain success in a supply chain management approach.

5-6 What benefits can be expected when SAP's business framework execution strategy is used? What does this involve in the way of business processes?

5-7 What is the driving force behind business applications? What capability must they have to realize this potential?

5-8 What primary business functions does R/3 offer to assist supply chain management strategy?

5-9 What solutions does SAP offer and how do they relate specifically do critical supply chain processes? How do they relate to performance?

5-10 What specifically do the SAP business framework and business information warehouse enable?

5-11 Explain what specific layer is placed over R/3's business components.

5-12 What does the business framework provide in terms of benefits?

5-13 What does the component and messaging-based architecture allow to be deployed?

5-14 How does the business framework benefit a company with respect to upgrades?

5-15 Explain how the business framework helps a company acquire the highest levels of execution in providing a certain kind of interface. Define these interfaces and explain what they actions enable.

5-16 What do messaging techniques support?

5-17 What does the business information warehouse do for your supply-chain decisionmaking capabilities?

5-18 What does the combination of SAP's business framework with the business information warehouse provide?

QUESTIONS

5-19   What does the "extended enterprise" consist of?

5-20   State specifics about the extended enterprise and what kinds of capabilities it may have.

5-21   What other benefits can result from an extended enterprise with respect to material requirements?

5-22   What is involved in creating the extended enterprise with the business framework?

5-23   Why must the system be highly flexible? What kinds of benefits does this allow users to do?

5-24   Why must the system be robust, and how does this involve the flow of information?

5-25   Why must the system be open?

5-26   What benefit is there to the system's being dynamic and highly automated?

5-27   What SAP solution is highly flexible, robust, open, dynamic, and automated?

5-28   Explain what enterprise open connectivity offers.

5-29   What do R/3 Internet application components provide?

5-30   What can users do with a standard Web browser?

5-31   Specifically what does R/3 allow integrate business systems to do?

5-32   What is involved in integrating supply chain information?

5-33   How do ERP systems achieve a high level of integration? What mechanism do they use to do this?

5-34   How are ERP solutions the same as supply chain solutions when it comes to integrating information? How these solutions differ?

5-35   Explain how the methods used in an ERP system are also applicable to supply chains. How are they not applicable?

5-36   Can different members of a supply chain use different database architectures?

5-37   How specifically must businesses agree with respect to shared data and rules that govern data access?

5-38   What facilitates the agreements between businesses?

5-39   Give an example that illustrates SAP's desire to have a uniform set of supply-chain standards.

5-40   What is the primary benefit to working toward a uniform set of open standards and how does this relate to business processes across the entire supply chain?

5-41   Explain how to optimize real-time data for effective decision support.

5-42   What must supply-chain solutions integrate and how is this similar to the action of ERP systems?

5-43   What factor complicates the need for real-time decision support?

5-44   What must high-performance supply-chain solutions monitor?

5-45   Describe the analysis that a company usually performs to analyze business process data and provide decision support.

5-46   What problems can result from a company's trying to launch a marketing campaign for a new product?

5-47   What do agile supply-chain solutions deal with?

5-48   What happens if production falls behind schedule?

5-49   How can a company convert business data into business intelligence?

5-50   How does R/3 fit in the modern supply chain?

5-51   Describe the tools that extend R/3's capabilities.

5-52   Explain how the activities in an isolated organization differ from the operations of new virtual organizations.

5-53   What must an organization do if it is looking for immediate, high-performance supply-chain solutions?

5-54   Why would it be necessary to work with more than one supply-chain component vendor?

5-55   How is supply-chain optimization made more complex by the integration of supply-chain components?

5-56   Explain the benefits of seamless integration of all supply-chain activities.

5-57   Explain SAP's goal of advanced intelligence.

5-58   What are the benefits of advanced intelligence?

5-59 How does the method of advanced planning and optimization go beyond other solutions? Explain what key areas are involved in SAP's planning and optimization capabilities.

5-60 How is the method of advanced planning and optimization unlike architecture that synchronously exchanges information with underlying business processes?

5-61 What do higher levels of integration provide in terms of functions?

5-62 What do advanced tools for global visualization of the entire supply chain enable?

5-63 Describe the open nature of SAP R/3.

5-64 Explain the ease of implementation within R/3.

5-65 How has SAP worked to ease implementation efforts for company supply—chain solutions?

5-66 Explain the benefits of R/3's more diverse modularity.

5-67 How does the fact that SAP uses object-oriented techniques help deploy supply chain solutions?

5-68 Explain what is involved in the expense of implementation.

5-69 How does the long-term cost of ownership differ from multi-vendor solutions?

5-70 What is SAP's APO? Explain in detail.

5-71 What does APO consist of and what four functional areas does it offer?

5-72 What is the supply chain cockpit?

5-73 Explain the action of the SAP integration of a GUI in the supply chain.

5-74 What does the supply chain engineer allow planners and decision-makers to do?

5-75 What does the supply chain controller allow users to do?

5-76 How does the supply chain cockpit minimize the complexity of supply-chain conditions?

5-77 How is the supply chain cockpit highly configurable?

5-78 Explain APO forecasting.

5-79 Explain in detail how forecasting can be used to enact VMI.

5-80   What does forecasting combine?

5-81   What happens when forecasting is used in combination with the supply chain cockpit?

5-82   What does the advanced planning scheduling method include?

5-83   What do distribution, deployment and transportation incorporate, and what do they offer?

5-84   What can production planning generate?

5-85   How can shop floor scheduling be used?

5-86   Explain how advanced planning and scheduling is like forecasting.

5-87   How does SAP achieve available-to-promise decision support?

5-88   What does the ATP server provide for companies?

5-89   What is the SCPI?

5-90   What is SCPI+?

5-91   What is the result of integrating supply-chain decision support into the business framework?

5-92   What benefit accrues from real-time integration?

5-93   Is it possible to model extended supply chains that incorporate existing R/3 business models?

NOTE

SAP knows that supply-chain practices are a dramatic departure from the standard business practices employed by organizations. It responds to the need for education on the practices and techniques associated with supply-chain management and optimization.

5-94   What is the Supply Chain Institute?

5-95   How does SAP help enable optimized supply-chain management?

5-96   What kind of technology exists in SAP's supply-chain solution.

5-97   What does the Advanced Planner and Optimizer server consist of?

5-98   How is accessibility gained with API's primary functionality?

5-99   What is APO core processing? Define how liveCache relates.

5-100   What are APO's data objects?

5-101   How are APO data objects accessible by R/3 and third-party systems?

5-102   Why are systems able to calculate complex properties ?

5-103   What is semantic synchronization?

5-104   Why must the APO server filter business data?

5-105   With what does the APO server integrate and what kind of access does it provide?

5-106   What can the server be configured to provide?

5-107   What can the APO server generate?

5-108   What can event notification be used for?

5-109   What benefit is there in the APO server's being easily configurable?

5-110   What can the common techniques provided with APO enable?

5-111   What must an organization do to implement a supply-chain solution?

5-1 Identifying courses to help achieve successful supply-chain management involved the integration of information as the first step in supply-chain management. It is important to have the ability to analyze information to determine which actions to take within the context of automated business processes.

5-2 In order to be most effective this information should automatically trigger a corresponding product transition. The tight coupling of execution and decision making is an essential ingredient of effective supply-chain management.

5-3 Information technologies remove communication barriers and enable an improved flow of information among all members of the supply chain.

5-4 The most successful companies realize they need a step-by-step approach to chart a business's course toward high-performance supply-chain management.

5-5 Those steps include:

1. Achieving execution excellence by fully automating and optimizing business practices
2. Extending the enterprise to accept all members of the supply chain
3. Integrating business systems with those of customers, suppliers, and partners to create a common information foundation
4. Deploying real-time decision support to increase responsiveness
5. Investing in re-educating and reorienting employees, vendors, and other members of the supply chain on the practices needed to optimize business processes
6. Making a company-wide commitment to creating and managing a more complex organization capable of tackling global business issues.

5-6 When a company deals with execution in SAP's business framework in enterprise execution excellence it must possess the capability of organizing to implement and execute its business processes to maximize business benefits.

5-7 The business applications driving this effort must be capable of processing extremely high volumes of information. They must be open, robust, highly flexible, easily configured and managed, and they must ensure a high level of data integrity throughout the organization.

5-8 R/3 provides business functions such as sales and materials planning, production planning, warehouse management, financial accounting, and personnel management for an integrated workflow of business events.

SOLUTIONS

5-9   SAP provides solutions that automate critical supply-chain processes in ways that improve performance and provide a competitive edge. SAP's solutions deliver robust functionality, a high degree of configurability, and real-time data integration so a company can benefit from information that gives a distinct advantage.

5-10 The SAP business framework and business information warehouse enable a flexible infrastructure to respond quickly to new business demands through an open business framework and a strategic architecture for R/3.

5-11 As part of SAP's development effort, there is an objects-based communications layer over R/3's business components (Figure 5.1).

FIGURE 5.1
Business Component

Customer Prospect Managment

Pricing and Configuration

Opportunity Management

Workbench

Sales Analysis and Workflow

Quotations and Orders

5-12 The business framework permits reduction of deployment time, instituting of continuous business improvement, and dynamic reconfiguration of R/3 without disrupting a business.

5-13 The component and messaging-based architecture allow deployment of new R/3 functions incrementally. R/3 interfaces are standards-based and make it possible for a company to benefit from full interoperability between SAP and third-party components.

SOLUTIONS

5-14 Business framework makes systems simpler to maintain because different components can be upgraded on different release cycles.

5-15 Business framework helps a company achieve the highest levels of execution excellence while delivering a new level of flexibility and agility. Its open interfaces enable the integration of a company's business systems with those of partners and suppliers.

5-16 Messaging techniques also support businesses as they extend their enterprise and adopt the methodologies of high-performance supply-chain management. The techniques facilitate immediate participate or readies companies for future initiatives.

5-17 The business information warehouse uses highly tuned data structures to add a new level of supply chain-oriented decisionmaking capabilities to the business framework.

5-18 SAP's business framework and the business information warehouse provide organizations with the competitive tools to achieve execution excellence in today's competitive environment. In order for a company to be able to participate in a high-performance supply chain, this combination must extend beyond the bounds of the traditional enterprise.

5-19 The extended enterprise goes beyond formal boundaries when looking for the answers to business challenges and the factors that affect decision-making. Many of these answers exist in the virtual or extended enterprise. The extended enterprise includes all of the members of a company's supply chain: the different legal units within the company, suppliers and their vendors, customers and their customers, and external service providers. Low-cost communications media such as the Internet facilitate integration across the extended enterprise and allow any enterprise to compete, regardless of its size.

5-20 The extended enterprise is similar to a typical direct-order computer manufacturer. Consumers access the company's Web site, where they can browse in available options and configure a machine to their exact specifications and budget. Customers receive an immediate price quote and, once an order is placed, a firm delivery date and a confirmation number to track the order. Customers can shop without pressure, customize the purchase, know exactly when it will be delivered, and receive a price break that reflects the manufacturer's lower cost of doing business. The company reaps benefits from this type of situation too. Because orders are collected directly from the customer, the company can use valuable point-of-sale (POS) data to gather real-time feedback to various points within its business processes. Manufacturing knows precisely what to build, procurement knows what to order, and marketing can immediately determine the success of a given program.

5-21   A company can benefit from the extended enterprise to feed material requirements and fulfillment data directly to systems of parts suppliers and distributors of finished goods. If a company automates its own business processes and integrates them with the automated processes of its supply chain partners, then in combination they can develop a mechanism for dealing with the volatility and variability of the market.

5-22   Business information systems must satisfy several fundamental criteria to permit a company to extend the enterprise and participate in a high-performance supply chain.

5-23   The system must be highly flexible; this allows users to individualize it to their exact business requirements and adapt it to meet changes in processes.

5-24   The system must be robust to integrate the vast flow of information among all members of the extended enterprise.

5-25   The system must be open so all participants can benefit from the power of shared information in ways that meet productivity and customer service, as well as other key strategic objectives.

5-26   A system must be dynamic and highly automated to react effectively to changing variables and ensure that changing business conditions trigger appropriate, coordinated responses across the chain.

5-27   SAP's business framework satisfies all of these conditions and offers several other important benefits in dealing with a supply-chain management plan.

5-28   Enterprise open connectivity offers greater compatibility between multiple instances of R/3 and between third-party systems. This facilitates higher levels of intra-enterprise and inter-enterprise communication.

5-29   R/3 has several internet application components to provide consumer-to-business, business-to-business, and intranet applications.

5-30   A standard Web browser can be used anywhere in the world to access authorized portions of a corporation's R/3 system to gain information and transact real-time business securely.

5-31   R/3 allows integrated business systems to cooperate across the Internet through open BAPI standards for business transactions. This open connectivity allows business components to interact with multiple business systems, enabling fully electronic supply-chain management.

5-32 The concept of integrating information is the cornerstone of many corporate efforts for improving business processes. ERP systems are designed to accomplish this task and to provide organizations with a system for planning, controlling, and monitoring an organization's business processes.

5-33 ERP systems achieve high levels of integration by using a standard mechanism for communications. This effectively creates a common understanding of what the shared data represent. It also establishes a set of rules for accessing data.

5-34 As with ERP solutions, supply-chain solutions also must integrate information consistently. They differ from ERP systems in that supply-chain systems must deal with the complexity of integrating information from several disparate information systems anywhere along the supply chain.

5-35 Among the methods an ERP system uses to integrate operations are some that are applicable to supply chains and others that are not. ERP systems inside a single company use a database as the basis of communications within the organization, while individual applications access data through a variety of standard networking protocols.

5-36 Yes, different members of a supply chain can use any number of different database architectures. However, companies will not likely influence every member of its supply chain to agree on a single, standard database architecture.

5-37 Businesses must also agree on what shared data represent as well as rules governing its access, including authorization procedures.

5-38 Agreement is facilitated through the adoption of a common set of standards. SAP users benefit from supply-chain standards that are uniform throughout the organization.

5-39 SAP provides extensive access to R/3's independent business components through BAPIs that conform to accepted, open object standards published by CORBA and DCOM. SAP also offers Internet-enabled R/3 that has added several Internet application components to the standard business framework. These improvements have enabled features such as remote order entry over the Internet in R/3's sales and distribution component.

5-40 SAP continues to work toward open standards in an effort to integrate business processes across the supply chain. The result is that SAP delivers a very high level of data integration in supply-chain software to promote integrated decision-making.

5-41 The demand is great for high-performance supply-chain solutions to manage and integrate data from different systems. These solutions must also

SOLUTIONS

associate powerful decisionmaking capabilities with the ability to perform change within an organization's business processes.

5-42   As in ERP systems' integrating data within the organization, supply-chain solutions must integrate decisions within the extended enterprise.

5-43   There is a definite need for real-time decision support. This need is complicated by the fact that the support cannot be applied to just one or a few links in the supply chain.

5-44   High-performance supply-chain solutions must monitor all the elements of the chain, execute critical decisions, and continuously effect process change.

5-45   Organizations have used powerful computers to analyze business process data and provide decision support. This analysis has occurred on an "as-needed" basis and changes have frequently been executed with little understanding of their effect on other functional areas of the business.

5-46   The decision for a company to launch a marketing campaign can produce several orders for a product and a series of problems across the entire product supply chain. These problems start with procurement's inability to secure parts and end with customer dissatisfaction with delivery.

5-47   Agile supply-chain solutions can deal with market volatility by acting very quickly on changing conditions. As far as the supply side is concerned, real-time data on materials availability, transportation, labor, and other factors can be used to foster change across the product cycle as conditions mandate. On the demand side, predictions that are based on up-to-the-minute data from point of sale and marketing help set safe inventory levels based on realistic projections, not historical data.

5-48   If production falls behind schedule due to labor shortages or machinery downtime, supply planners, customer service representatives, and logistics planners can execute changes both upstream and downstream.

5-49   Companies that achieve execution excellence as a result of their R/3 implementations can realize the potential of a vast store of business information. SAP has taken this byproduct of R/3, filtered it, and converted it into valuable business intelligence in the business information warehouse. The result is that SAP provides customers with an effective supply-chain solution. Companies can combine the core transaction system with all of its business intelligence and real-time information handling and decision-making. These added functions helps combine business data with information from the extended enterprise to illustrate the entire supply chain.

A company can then make informed decisions that will cut the time-to-market, reduce inventory, lower costs, and improve customer satisfaction.

5-50   R/3 benefits from the optimized business data in the business information warehouse and the resulting messaging capabilities to offer the real-time decision support required for effective supply-chain management. Third-party programs using memory-resident analytical engines have benefited from R/3's messaging and extended their capabilities to include supply-chain functions.

5-51   The tools range from supply planning, plant scheduling, and demand planning to logistics. They communicate directly with R/3 and facilitate timely decisions to optimize supply-chain performance.

5-52   As opposed to the sequential activities of an isolated organization, the operations of these new virtual organizations require redesign and support supply-chain activities as collaborative, synchronized processes that respond rapidly to changing business conditions.

5-53   Organizations searching for an immediate, high-performance supply-chain solution must look beyond their traditional ERP vendors for a total solution. SAP's business framework provides the solid foundation required to build a robust supply-chain solution. It is important that companies add additional functionality to complete the supply chain solution.

5-54   Since no single vendor can address all aspects of the supply chain, customers may find they need to work with more than one supply-chain component vendor. Customers will also find that third-party solutions are largely decisionmaking and cannot effect change in an automated fashion. This critical detail of execution is left to the integration process to resolve.

5-55   Supply-chain optimization is a complex task in itself, and integrating additional supply-chain components into current business processes only intensifies the complexity. SAP tries to enforce the extensibility of R/3 and assist in implementation of supply-chain solutions.

5-56   The benefits of seamless integration of all supply-chain activities involve the interface between the decision support for planning, and optimization and execution of business processes. These processes are crucial to achieving the highest level of performance in supply-chain solutions.

5-57   SAP's product involves the combination of advanced intelligence resulting from the R/3 business processes with intelligence collected from the extended enterprise to build a memory-resident model of the supply chain. This model is used as the basis for the advanced decision support that is necessary for effective supply chain management.

SOLUTIONS

5-58 The resulting benefits include the availability of information required to make informed business decisions, and acquiring the underlying architecture required for automatic execution of the appropriate changes in business processes.

5-59 The method of advanced planning and optimization reaches beyond all other available solutions in several areas including architecture. SAP's planning and optimization capabilities are integrated on memory-resident computing technologies capable of processing huge volumes of information and making decisions in near real time.

5-60 In contrast to other competing architectures that asynchronously exchange information with underlying business processes, SAP's implementation achieves a higher level of decision and data integration by maintaining real-time synchronization of information between execution and decisionmaking.

5-61 Higher levels of integration provide a higher degree of function. SAP provides precise control over execution along with decisionmaking, as well as advanced tools for global visualization of the entire supply chain.

5-62 These tools will enable supply chain decisionmakers to view an industry-specific graphical representation of flow, constraints, and other factors within the supply chain.

5-63 SAP continues to create solutions based on open standards for messaging and data sharing. These plans include the publishing of additional BAPIs as well as powerful new business data objects to synchronize data and decisions among all participants in the supply chain.

5-64 Because supply-chain functions are inherent in R/3, integrating supply-chain functions into existing business processes need not be a concern. It is therefore possible to concentrate on areas of business that improve competitiveness.

5-65 SAP has eased efforts to implement a supply-chain solution by producing improvements to the configuration tool R/3 Business Engineer.

5-66 Most R/3 users are accustomed to deploying components of their business systems incrementally. SAP uses an architecture that makes it possible to deploy solutions analogously.

5-67 SAP uses object-oriented techniques; supply-chain solutions can be deployed as components and in stages.

5-68 Organizations that have recently implemented third-party planning products as well as those currently evaluating their options realize the expense of implementing such solutions. With planning and execution integrated in R/3, the cost of integrating multiple vendors' products is nearly eliminated, as are concerns about version compatibility.

5-69 The long-term cost of SAP ownership is much less than that of multi-vendor solutions. Advanced supply chain planning functions accrue through the implementation of SAP's business framework and third-party add-on supply-chain solutions. Functions within R/3 essentially provide the supply-chain solutions required.

5-70 SAP's Advanced Planner and Optimizer (APO) builds on the business framework to improve information flow and incorporate into R/3 real-time collaborative decision support, advanced planning, and optimization.

5-71 APO consists of a memory-resident analytical engine and specialized data objects that will be configured to offer four areas of functioning:

1. Supply chain cockpit and forecasting
2. Advanced planning
3. Scheduling
4. Available-to-promise decision support.

5-72 A supply-chain solution must primarily inform decisionmakers of exception conditions that occur and empower them to make the appropriate changes in business plans.

5-73 SAP produces a graphical interface to the supply chain that synthesizes large amounts of collaborative business and decision data into important information requiring action. The supply chain cockpit consists of the supply chain engineer and the supply chain controller to provide decisionmakers with the insight and control for effective management of the supply chain.

5-74 Supply Chain Engineer enables planners and decision makers to perform graphical maintenance of extended supply-chain models including plants, distribution centers, and constraints, as well as factory layouts with their associated machinery, storage locations, and constraints.

5-75 Supply Chain Controller allows users to review forecasts, plans, and schedules based on the actual status of a system, performance figures or any exceptions or problems that exist.

5-76 Supply Chain Cockpit minimizes the complexity of conditions that exist within the entire supply chain, providing decisionmakers with greater control over their business processes and permitting them to respond more quickly and with greater accuracy.

SOLUTIONS

5-77 The cockpit is configurable to conditions within several industries and business setups. It includes an Internet-enabled user interface to provide remote viewing and control over the entire supply chain.

5-78 APO Forecasting is a performance tool to help partners throughout the supply chain create powerful collaborative forecasts that integrate individual vendor forecasts and real-time data including point of sale. This tool allows marketing departments to plan promotions based on up-to-the-minute market data.

5-79 Forecasting can also be used to enact Vendor Managed Inventory (VMI), shifting the responsibility for replenishment to suppliers.

5-80 Forecasting combines several advanced statistical forecasting methods with real-time data from a variety of sources, and tightly integrated with SAP's business information warehouse.

5-81 When forecasting is used in combination with Supply Chain Cockpit, it allows businesses to capture changes in demand signals and patterns as early as possible so that the supply side of the business can respond quickly and accordingly.

5-82 APO's advanced planning and scheduling (APS) methods include several tools to handle distribution, deployment and transportation, production planning, and shop-floor scheduling. The primary objective of APS is to synchronize the supply plan with actual demand that has been captured by forecasting. This syncronicity is achieved by combining various algorithms such as linear programming, heuristics, and classic material and capacity planning with real-time decision support and response capabilities as well as multiplant sourcing logic.

5-83 Distribution, deployment and transportation incorporate warehouse and transportation constraints to offer decisionmakers the business intelligence needed to make informed decisions on issues including inventory allocation and alternative transportation routes and methods.

5-84 Production planning can incorporate constraints such as supply levels, labor availability and maintenance schedules. It can operate at single or multiple plants, juggling production loads between facilities with similar production capabilities.

5-85 Shop Floor Scheduling is used to generate optimized schedules that are tightly integrated with the production plan. A variety of industry and task-specific algorithms and heuristics are used to produce desired results.

5-86 As in forecasting, advanced planning and scheduling methods are tightly integrated with Supply Chain Cockpit to provide planners and schedulers with rich graphical representations for the control and accuracy required to optimize business processes.

5-87   SAP achieves available-to-promise decision support using a high-performance, global ATP server. The server uses a rules-based strategy to acquire already determined results that incorporate various factors, including customer/plant preferences and approved product substitutions. The server also performs multilevel component and capacity ATP checks in real-time and simulation modes. It can also perform these ATP checks against aggregated, memory-resident data for even better performance. The ATP server maintains simultaneous, immediate access to product availability across the supply chain.

5-88   The ATP server gives companies the highest degree of confidence in the precision of delivery commitments.

5-89   In combination with APO, SAP offers Supply Chain Planning Interface (SCPI), a high-fidelity interface that provides access to all R/3 3.1 and 4.0 supply-chain components needed by SAP third-party supply-chain partners.

5-90   SCPI+ offers open access to memory-resident APO data for third-party planning and optimization tools. It allows APO to accept refined forecasts and schedules from third-party supply chain systems.

5-91   By integrating supply-chain decision support into Business Framework, SAP assures the highest performance solutions on the market.

5-92   Benefits from real-time integration include automatic notification of incremental changes, exception handling, ATP integration, and backward communication of plans and schedules.

5-93   Yes, it is possible to model extended supply chains that incorporate existing R/3 business models.

5-94   The Supply Chain Institute is a global forum to educate clients and assist in the development of the skills required for supply-chain optimization planning and execution.

5-95   Existing ERP systems use data models different from those of supply-chain decision support systems, which require memory-resident data models capable of handling vast amounts of complex data in real time.

5-96   SAP's supply-chain solution employs powerful technology that provides the capabilities required for optimizing supply chain management.

5-97   The advanced planner and optimizer server consists of a collection of complex data objects specifically designed for planning, optimization, and real-time event notification. It offers enhanced graphical capabilities, a library of advanced optimization algorithms, and a high-performance, memory-resident data processor.

5-98   Access to APO's primary functions is provided through the SCPI+ interface, a collection of high-fidelity BAPIs.

5-99   At the center of APO's high-performance processing capabilities is live-Cache, it employs advanced computing technologies that benefit from multiprocessor configurations and will support multigigabyte memory layouts. liveCache enables the APO server to perform supply chain calculations and other complex tasks, such as semantic synchronization, in real time.

5-100 APO's data objects are similar to SAP business objects. They are a collection of complex planning and optimization data and the procedures to manipulate the data. These objects represent SAP's expertise in business processes and the techniques and methodologies required to perform supply-chain planning and optimization.

5-101 APO data objects are directly accessible by R/3 and by third-party systems through the SCPI+ interface.

5-102 Because the data objects are optimized representations of complex supply-chain properties, systems will be able to calculate complex properties, such as total material requirements, with simple method calls to the APO data objects.

5-103 Data within the APO servers are intelligent representations of the same data objects that exist within the R/3 transaction system, as well as those contained within individual forecasts. Since these objects are more comprehensive than simple business data objects, they cannot simply share the accompanying business systems' databases.

5-104 The APO server must filter business data in order to build the APO data objects. The system must maintain two different representations of the same information. In order to achieve this goal, the APO server is equipped with algorithms that perform real-time synchronization of various instances of data across the supply chain.

5-105 The APO server also integrates with R/3's business information warehouse in order to provide customers with unprecedented access to vital business decision data. The APO server contains a library of advanced optimization algorithms that can be used to develop forecasts and optimized plans and schedules.

5-106 The server can be configured to provide task-specific, industry-specific, and company specific optimization and automated decisionmaking.

SOLUTIONS

5-107 The APO server can also generate real-time notification to the underlying business framework and third-party systems.

5-108 Event notification can be used to indicate incremental changes in stock, demand, and other factors, and to handle exceptions like material shortages, transportation problems, or production problems. Event notification also helps propagate and synchronize plans and schedules throughout the supply chain.

5-109 Since the APO server is easily configurable, it supports several applications within the supply chain across a wide range of industry environments.

5-110 Common techniques provided with APO can be used to perform forecasting, APO, ATP, and Supply Chain Cockpit functions in a variety of operational, tactical, and strategic roles.

5-111 When an organization implements supply-chain solutions, it must initiate and adopt new business practices, employees must be trained and strategies developed. Those who are skilled in piloting the real-time information the new systems will produce can integrate it with current knowledge bases to optimize supply-chain decisionmaking.

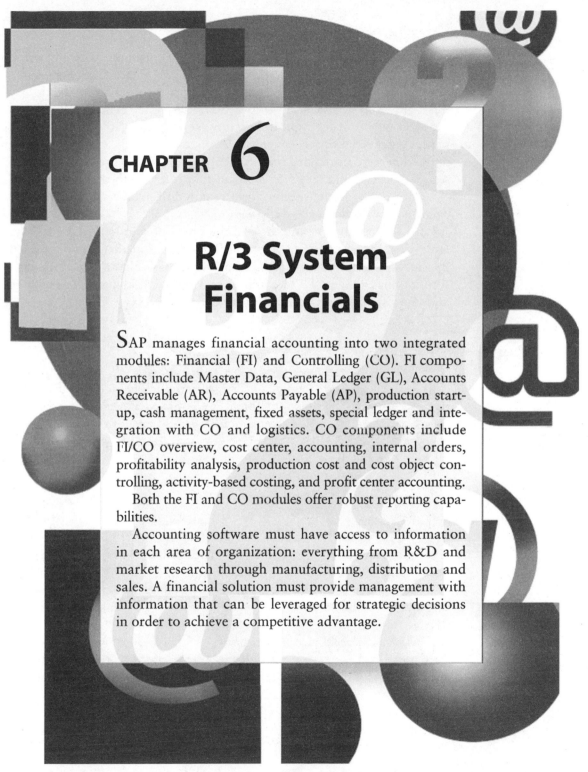

CHAPTER 6

R/3 System Financials

SAP manages financial accounting into two integrated modules: Financial (FI) and Controlling (CO). FI components include Master Data, General Ledger (GL), Accounts Receivable (AR), Accounts Payable (AP), production start-up, cash management, fixed assets, special ledger and integration with CO and logistics. CO components include FI/CO overview, cost center, accounting, internal orders, profitability analysis, production cost and cost object controlling, activity-based costing, and profit center accounting.

Both the FI and CO modules offer robust reporting capabilities.

Accounting software must have access to information in each area of organization: everything from R&D and market research through manufacturing, distribution and sales. A financial solution must provide management with information that can be leveraged for strategic decisions in order to achieve a competitive advantage.

Strategic Solutions for Managing Your Accounting is an important objective discussed in this chapter. Processes and Improving Competitiveness is the foundation for the entire concept of information technology; this philosophy is based on the idea that offering the right information to the right people at the right time can make a crucial difference to a company. A great deal of this key information is often in the form of financial data. However, just having financial data is not sufficient; there must be a set of processes and views of the data that offer up-to-the-minute financial information in the specific form required to make that critical difference and help with crucial decisions.

This chapter gives an overview of the financial solutions in the R/3 system, depicting a portion of the total R/3 solution available. This suite of application components produces a world-class client/server financial solution that allows SAP to continue to work with its partners to extend and improve the R/3 System to satisfy client's needs.

FI/CO Course Information

This chapter discusses the FI/CO certification track in an effort to provide details leading to the functions found in the financial accounting, controlling, and special-purpose ledger modules. It also examines how this track is connected with SM, MM and PP functionality and how a company can be re-engineered using SAP R/3.

Financial and Controlling Tracks

The purpose of the financial and controlling tracks is to provide an entry-level overview of the functionals of the following modules: financial accounting, controlling, and special-purpose ledger.

These courses were designed to demonstrate the integration of the FI/CO track with the functions of other tracks, including SM, MM, and PP.

This includes reengineering corporation with SAP software. Those who participate and correctly finish all the examinations at the conclusion of the course are awarded SAP certification in FI/CO.

NOTE

Recently SAP divided the FI/CO certification into separate tracks.

Course Prerequisites:

- Solid business background in accounting
- Solid business background in finance and control
- Basic knowledge of a graphical user interface (GUI), such as that of Microsoft.

The windows environment contents include:

- Familiarization and system navigation
- New position of IMG
- Customizing customer specific IMG projects
- Integration of the navigator into configuration
- Financial accounting (FI)
- General ledger (GL)
- Accounts receivable (AR)
- Accounts payable (AP)
- Controlling (CO)
- Cost centers
- Internal orders
- Profitability analysis
- Special purpose ledger
- Report painter.

Financial Information

R/3 financials offer integrated functionality to an organization. It is important to know that financial decisions are based on current data as opposed to numbers from outdated records. The current data must illustrate every segment of a company's activities, no matter how large or small the enterprise.

R/3 financial application components function in cooperation to improve a business. The internal quality of the components and the financial functions of R/3 produce a tight level of integration throughout all business and geographic areas. This tight integration includes the R/3 components that deal with everything from financials to human resources to logistics.

The R/3 system automatically links related areas and reduces the need to repeat procedures. In the R/3 system, all areas function together in order to develop a new level of efficiency in handling financial data.

Financial Functions

R/3's financials components provide financial functions as well as analysis support for thousands of businesses.

Installation

R/3 can be installed on a large number of hardware platforms using the most advanced operating systems. The open R/3 system environment provides the flexibility to choose the computing platforms and systems that best satisfy particular needs. SAP R/3 is designed for open client/server environments so it can include a simple graphical user interface as well as menu-driven functions that are the same across all R/3 components.

R/3 also offers a three-tiered client/server structure that provides several choices of hardware systems to use. It also allows users to add to the R/3 system without multiplying costs. R/3 financials components provide a high level of performance in several areas and provide easy access to more complete and current data.

When tasks are executed locally, components and subcomponents remain integrated with the rest of the system since all R/3 functions have access to shared central data. This effectively eliminates data redundancy and ensures data integrity.

R/3 financial components can help establish local and enterprise-wide solutions. In addition, tight integration of non-SAP products with components in the R/3 system is possible as is maintaining integrated central financial records within highly decentralized organizations.

Financial Accounting

R/3 financial accounting permits central tracking of financial accounting data within an international framework of multiple companies, languages, currencies, and charts of accounts.

At any point where raw materials move from inventory into manufacturing, the system reduces the quantity values in inventory while at the same time subtracting from the balance sheet dollar values for inventory accounts.

The financial accounting component complies with international accounting standards including GAAP and IAS. R/3 financial accounting transactions are processed individually and integrated with all other relevant financial areas.

General Ledger (GL)

The R/3 GL is essential for a financial accounting system and strategic decisionmaking. It is used with active integration in business processes, R/3 logistics, and accounting subledgers. R/3 GL serves as a central pool of financial data for reporting and other accounting areas. The origin of centrally stored data can be traced at any time by researching data from a given transaction.

The general ledger supports all the functions needed in a financial accounting system. These functions involve flexible structuring of the chart of accounts at group and company level, distributed application scenarios using Application Link Enabling (ALE), real-time simultaneous update of subledgers and the general ledger, elimination of time-consuming reconciliation, and parallel views of data in both the general ledger and managerial accounting applications.

R/3 GL offers document parking, posting, reporting, an integrated financial calendar for automating periodic activities, and the option of displaying documents and reading them into the system memory.

The Special Purpose Ledger

The special purpose ledger system is an enhancement to the general ledger. It provides summary information from other components at a user-defined level of detail. Creation of combinations of entered data, produces data summaries that can be used in planning, allocation, distribution, and reporting. It also facilitates taking advantage of more functions in general ledger and in cost-center accounting.

The special purpose ledger includes parallel charts of account and currencies, planning and allocation tools, direct data entry in special purpose ledgers (i.e. for adjustment postings), and user-defined reporting.

R/3 provides a financial overview of global business partner relationships in the accounts receivable and payable subledger functions. These subledgers are integrated with the general ledger as well as with areas in R/3 SD and MM, where financial data originate.

Asset Accounting

R/3 asset accounting manages a company's fixed assets. From inside the financial accounting system, FI-AA acts as a subledger to the general ledger and offers detailed information on asset-related transactions. Significant features include country-specific charts of depreciation that comply with local legal requirements, full support throughout the asset life cycle (from acquisition to retirement), depreciation simulation, interest calculation, integration with project management, and order accounting for management of capital assets. Asset accounting offers integration with plant maintenance for management of machinery and equipment, management of leased assets and assets under construction, mass processing with workflow integration, and interactive reporting.

Legal Consolidation

R/3 Legal Consolidation (FI-LC) is tightly coupled to the financial accounting system to permit direct data transfer from individual statements into the consolidated report. This simplifies the workload of staff and reduces data-entry errors.

In addition to the consolidated statements required by law, legal consolidation allows development of multiple views of consolidation data. These views permit creation of reports about legal entities or segments of a business. User-defined fields provide further details.

Controlling Component (CO)

The controlling component in the R/3 system gathers the functions required for effective internal cost accounting and offers a flexible information system with standard reports and analysis paths for the most common questions.

Overhead Cost Controlling (CO-OM)

When dealing with overhead cost controlling, there is a sizable increase in the percentage of indirect costs which cannot be directly assigned to the products manufactured or services rendered.

Both cost monitoring and optimization are advanced in production areas, but transparency is usually absent in overhead cost areas. CO-OM focuses on monitoring and allocation of overhead.

Cost Components

Cost Center Accounting (CO-OM-CCA) analyzes the point at which overhead occurs within the organization. Costs are assigned to the subareas of the organization where they started. The R/3 system provides several methods for allocating posted amounts and quantities. Activity accounting allows for the allocation of many costs to products based on cost sources. This permits hitherto impossible assignments.

Overhead Orders (CO-OM-OPA) collect and analyze costs based on individual internal criteria. The R/3 system can monitor and automatically check budgets assigned to each measure. Product Cost Controlling (CO-PC) determines the costs that occur when manufacturing a product or providing a service.

The Activity-Based Costing (CO-OM-ABC) module is a response to the need for monitoring and control of cross-departmental business processes in addition to functions and products. Organizational transparency in overhead areas is greatly improved by observing costs from a different perspective.

Cost Object Controlling (CO-PC-OBJ) helps with monitoring manufacturing orders. Integration with the R/3 logistics components results in a logistical quantity flow that offers instant information on actual cost.

Profitability Analysis (CO-PA) inspects the sources of returns and is the last step in cost-based settlement. It is here that revenues are designated to costs with respect to market segment. It is possible to define any market segment and distinguish among products, customers, orders, sales organizations, distribution channels, and business areas. The market segment can then be evaluated it with respect to contribution and revenue margins.

Investment Programs

Investment Management (IM) provides extensive support for investment processes that involve everything from planning through settlement. Corporation-wide budgeting is important in R/3.

Investment planning and budgeting can be controlled at a level higher than specific orders or projects. It is possible to define an investment program hierarchy by using any criteria. When specific investment measures, such as internal orders or projects, are designated for positions in the hierarchy, there is always current information on available funds, planned costs, and actual costs already incurred from internal and external activities.

The investment program provides the opportunity to distribute budgets used during the capital spending process. The system assists in monitoring and avoiding budget overruns.

Appropriation Requests

Appropriation requests provide tools to help plan and manage capital spending projects from their earliest stages. The capital spending process begins with entry of the application for the spending project as an appropriation request. The evaluation and approval process is then defined. When the system has a detailed history of the status of the appropriation request, the data can be transferred from the appropriation request to the investment measure after the request is approved for implementation.

Detailed plan values can be input for the appropriation request as can variants to be used in the preinvestment analysis. Investment measures to be monitored individually can be represented as internal orders or projects.

Financial Investment Management (IM)

The financials IM system automatically separates costs requiring capitalization from costs that are not capitalized. It debits the correct costs to the asset under construction. When dealing with different accounting needs, the system can employ different capitalization rules for making this split. The investment measure can then be settled to various receivers by line item.

Asset accounting offers precise proof of origin for all transactions dealing with acquisition and production costs. IM budgeted balance sheets and cost planning are based on current values. Planned depreciation values for investment measures and appropriation requests can be transferred directly to continuous overhead cost planning. The system recalculates expected depreciation amounts whenever planning data are updated.

Treasury Cash Management

The R/3 treasury component offers a basis for effective liquidity, portfolio, and risk management. The cash management component affords the opportunity to analyze financial transactions for a given period. Cash management also identifies and records future developments for the purposes of budgeting.

With R/3 treasury cash management, a company's payment transactions are segmented into cash holdings, cash inflows, and cash outflows. Cash management provides information on the sources and uses of funds to secure liquidity to satisfy payment obligations when they become due.

Cash management monitors and controls incoming and outgoing payment flow. Treasury mines the data required for managing short-term money market investments and borrowing. The cash management component makes certain that all information relevant to liquidity is available for analysis purposes, creating a basis for the necessary cash management decisions.

The treasury management component provides functions for managing financial deals and positions, from trading through to transferring data to financial accounting. It also supports flexible reporting and evaluation structures for analyzing financial deals, positions, and portfolios.

Market Risk Management

Market risk management is important within treasury because it makes certain that a company stays competitive. This process involves a complex feedback loop that deals with data collection, risk measurement, analysis, simulation, and active planning of financial instruments. It parallels other treasury and corporate functions. The complexity of this management process and its interaction require a powerful tool set. Market risk management acts as an integrated, central risk-control station with monitoring and management functions.

Cash management pools all cash flows from business sectors that include sales, distribution, or purchasing. As a result, all cash flow from the company's operating business can be accessed for the purpose of risk management.

All financial transactions are managed in treasury management. They can be evaluated together with the cash flows produced from different operating divisions. This component offers several measurements for analyzing and assessing interest rate and currency risks.

Funds Management

R/3 Funds Management (TR-FM) handles the funds-management process in terms of budgeting and payments. It incorporates monitoring expenditures, activities, resources, and revenues. Budgeting in TR-FM offers functions ranging from original budget through approval and release, budget supplements, returns, and transfers. There is also support for all stages of the budgeting process. Budgets are input for areas of responsibility that deal with as many management levels as necessary.

Funds Management Components

EC (Enterprise Controlling) optimizes shareholder value as it satisfies internal objectives for both growth and investment. R/3 EC integrates the executive information system, business planning and budgeting, consolidation, and profit center accounting.

Executive Information System (EC-EIS) offers an overview of the information critical to managing an organization. This component integrates data from other EC components as well as from R/3 components and non-SAP data sources both inside and outside an enterprise.

Business Planning and Budgeting (EC-BP) deals with the management teams of business units and groups in the computation of business targets, including ROI. It supports central investment planning, budget release, and consolidation.

Legal Consolidation (FI-LC) is a user-friendly entity that provides excellent reporting tools.

Profit Center Accounting (EC-PCA) analyzes the profitability of internal responsibility centers. The organizational structure is depicted as a profit center hierarchy with the profit center as the smallest unit of responsibility. This module automatically transfers data about investment requirements from transaction applications, and offers extensive analysis functions for budget monitoring.

Consolidation (EC-CS) demonstrates the next generation of consolidation in the R/3 system. It provides consolidated reports for both legal and management requirements. The result is increased flexibility in creating corporate structures for consolidated processing. These user-defined structures illustrate the legal, and business segment views, or a view specific to a company's own internal reporting structure.

Note that all business transactions in Financial Accounting, MM, Asset Management, and SD affect profits and are automatically reflected in Profit Center Accounting.

Profit Center Planning

Profit center planning is a component of total corporate planning. Profit centers stress the integration aspect of corporate planning that permit plans from other application areas to be combined, extended, and altered in EC-PCA. Profit center-related postings are also analyzed through the EC-PCA information system, to facilitate running standard reports and creating custom reports for special analyses. EC-PCA offers profitability information to appropriate management and controlling departments. Since data transfer from other R/3 components is automatic, this component automatically executes internal billings and elimination between profit centers.

Obtaining Data

R/3 EC automatically receives the information it needs from such other elements of the R/3 system as logistics, human resources, or other financial components. When detail is required, it can be found in those components.

In addition, EC can be used even if an organization is decentralized and uses a distributed computing system. EC is useful for decentralized accounting and reporting in local business units, while leveraging its controlling functions in the central office. EC's standard data structures can act as multiple purposes in different parts of an organization. End users can even pull their data down to a PC and develop further analyses. Regardless of whether an enterprise is centralized or decentralized, R/3 EC offers timely availability of business control information, for business units and for top management.

Summary

This chapter provides a sound foundation in R/3 financials, critical to a company's financial well-being. The chapter covered specifics of how R/3 is integrated throughout each business area in a given organization and how financial functions provide with a useful open environment in daily activities such as financial accounting, data administration, and working with activities-based costing.

6-1 What do R/3 financials provide?

6-2 Explain how R/3 functionality is integrated throughout different business areas.

6-3 What is the result when R/3 automatically links to related areas?

6-4 What kind of global functionality is seen within R/3 components?

6-5 Is it possible to combine components to satisfy requirements?

6-6 Describe functional integration.

6-7 What does automatic linking between components do?

6-8 What do financial controlling and analysis capabilities offer?

6-9 What kind of services are available for R/3?

6-10 Explain the scope of international versions.

6-11 Give an example of R/3's open environment.

6-12 What does a three-tiered client/server structure provide?

6-13 What is the EMU?

6-14 What kind of performance level can be expected in R/3 financials components?

6-15 Explain integrated data administration.

6-16 What is involved in financial accounting?

6-17 What type of control and integration is essential to decision making?

6-18 What does R/3 financial accounting make possible?

6-19 Give an example of what R/3 financial accounting can do.

6-20 What standards does the financial accounting component comply with?

6-21 What financial areas is the R/3 financial accounting transactions integrated with?

6-22 What is the general ledger?

6-23 What types of functions does the general ledger support?

6-24 Specify what does R/3 GL provide?

6-25 What does the special-purpose ledger system provide?

6-26 Give an example of what the special-purpose ledger can provide.

6-27 Name other important features in the special-purpose ledger.

6-28 When are financial accounting payable transactions performed?

6-29 What do accounts receivable and payable functions include?

6-30 Explain how R/3 fits in with global business partner relationships?

6-31 What is included with accounts receivable and support for EDI processing?

6-32 What other functions are found in the financial accounting module?

6-33 What does R/3 asset accounting manage?

6-34 Describe the elements of financials legal consolidation.

6-35 What takes place with the link between R/3 legal consolidation and the financial accounting system?

6-36 Besides consolidated statements, what does legal consolidation permit?

6-37 What does the controlling component in the R/3 system do?

6-38 What is involved with overhead cost controlling?

6-39 What does cost-center account do?

6-40 What are overhead orders?

6-41 What happens in activity-based costing?

6-42 Explain product cost controlling.

6-43 Explain the significance of plan and standard values?

6-44 What does the activity-based costing module do?

6-45 Explain how R/3 determines the utilization of business processes.

6-46 Define cost object controlling, and explain what integration with R/3 logistics components results in.

6-47 What do follow-up calculations determine?

6-48 Explain what the profitability analysis does.

6-49 What can be done with the information from profitability analysis?

6-50 Describe investment management.

6-51 What can corporation-wide budgeting facilitate?

6-52 What benefits does an investment program provide?

6-53   What do appropriation requests offer?

6-54   What do internal orders or projects provide the means for?

6-55   Define settlement.

6-56   What does automatic settlement to fixed assets recognize?

6-57   What does the financials IM do?

6-58   What can the system do for different accounting needs?

6-59   What is the purpose of asset accounting?

6-60   Explain depreciation forecasts.

6-61   What does the R/3 treasury component offer?

6-62   What does the cash management component do?

6-63   What does R/3 treasury cash management do?

6-64   What does the cash management component ensure?

6-65   What does the liquidity forecast function do?

6-66   What do the cash position and liquidity forecast components cover?

6-67   What is involved in treasury management?

6-68   What exactly does the treasury management component offer?

6-69   What can be done for short-term liquidity and risk management?

6-70   When do securities and loans come in?

6-71   What happens during active management of interest rate and currency?

6-72   What happens during back-office processing?

6-73   What specific elements can be used to represent organizational structures in a system?

6-74   What is market risk management?

6-75   How important is gaining access to information on current and future cash flows?

6-76   Explain the evaluation process of financial transactions managed in treasury management.

6-77   What can be determined by simulating market data?

6-78   Explain R/3 funds management.

6-79 What areas have budget responsibility?

6-80 What do funds centers and their hierarchical structure provide?

6-81 What can the information system supply?

6-82 How does enterprise controlling optimize shareholder value?

6-83 What does the executive information system provide?

6-84 What tools are needed to evaluate and present data?

6-85 What types of users can benefit from the report portfolio?

6-86 What do business planning and budgeting support?

6-87 Describe legal consolidation.

6-88 What does profit-center accounting do?

6-89 Explain consolidation and how it is related to reporting.

6-90 How does financial accounting reflect business transactions?

6-91 How is profit-center planning part of the total corporate planning effort?

6-92 How does component integration play an important role?

6-93 Explain how R/3 enterprise controlling receives the information it needs.

6-94 Is it possible to benefit from EC if an organization is decentralized?

6-95 What purposes can EC's uniform data structures be used for?

6-1 Financials from general ledger and funds management to activity-based costing and profitability analysis are covered. R/3 financials offer integrated functionality for an organization, though it must be emphasized that financial decisions are based on current data instead of numbers from out-of-date records. There current data must represent every segment of a company's activities, regardless of the size of the enterprise.

6-2 R/3 financial application components work together to improve the bottom line because of the internal quality of the components themselves and because the financial functionality of R/3 is tightly integrated throughout all business and geographic areas. This tight integration (Figure 6.1) includes the R/3 components that deal with everything from financials to human resources to logistics.

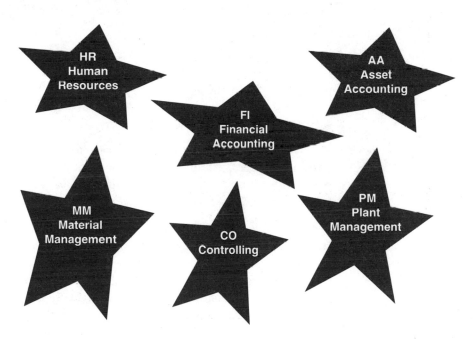

FIGURE 6.1
Integration

6-3 Because the R/3 system automatically links related areas, it eliminates the need to repeat procedures. Data are input only once. In the R/3 system, all areas work together, creating a new level of efficiency in handling financial data.

6-4 R/3's financials components offer financial functionality and analysis support to thousands of businesses in more than 80 countries. The R/3 system includes financial application components, human resources (HR), logistics, business workflow, ALE, and links to the Internet. More than 800 business processes are part of this comprehensive software system.

6-5   It is possible to use one individual R/3 component or a combination of components and subcomponents to best meet requirements.

6-6   The integration of all functions offers many performance features within SAP software. In R/3, data are immediately relayed where needed.

6-7   Automatic linking between components greatly speeds up and simplifies business procedures. Production planning and control data can flow directly into time management. In the same manner, results from payroll accounting can be passed on to the financial or cost accounting components.

6-8   Financial controlling and analysis capabilities offer reliable help in executing decisions, so the necessary changes can immediately be introduced into a business.

6-9   R/3 users can benefit from an extensive range of services: consulting services and supplementary services provided by individual product providers who work in close cooperation with SAP. SAP service partners make certain that a company's consulting and system requirements are satisfied.

6-10   International versions offer business activities that involve crossing national borders. The R/3 system supports the international requirements of a corporation with country-specific versions that work with different languages and currencies. It also makes provisions for relevant legal requirements.

6-11   It is possible to install R/3 solutions on a large number of hardware platforms using the most advanced operating systems. The open R/3 system environment provides freedom to select the computing platforms and systems that best satisfies individual needs. SAP R/3 is designed for open client/server environments and therefore includes an easy-to-use graphical user interface as well as menu-driven functions that are the same across all R/3 components.

6-12   A three-tiered client/server structure gives provides many choices when choosing hardware systems. It also allows additions to the R/3 system without multiplying costs.

6-13   The European Monetary Union (EMU) presents a technical and organizational challenge that affects nearly all areas of business including accounting, human resources management, and logistics. However, changes and adjustments may seriously affect on an entire data processing system. SAP makes the transition to the new currency as smooth as possible and also provides relevant conversion tools, through an extensive range of services.

6-14 The R/3 financials components have a high level of performance in several areas and provide easy access to complete and current data.

6-15 Even when tasks are executed locally, components and subcomponents stay integrated with the rest of the system, because all R/3 functions have access to shared central data. This effectively eliminates data redundancy and ensures data integrity.

6-16 It is possible to use the R/3 financial components to create local and enterprise-wide solutions and also tightly to integrate non-SAP products with components in the R/3 system. Integrated central financial records can be maintained with R/3 financials, even in highly decentralized organizations.

6-17 Company-wide control and integration of financial information is essential to strategic decision making.

6-18 R/3 financial accounting provides the ability for central tracking of financial accounting data within an international framework of multiple companies, languages, currencies, and charts of accounts.

6-19 When raw materials move from inventory into manufacturing, the system lowers the quantity values in inventory while at the same time subtracting dollar values for inventory accounts in the balance sheet.

6-20 The financial accounting component complies with international accounting standards such as GAAP and IAS. It also satisfies the local legal requirements of many countries and fully reflects the legal and accounting changes resulting from European market and currency unification.

6-21 R/3 financial accounting transactions are processed individually and integrated with all other relevant financial areas.

6-22 R/3 General Ledger (GL) is essential both to the financial accounting system and to strategic decision making. It is used with active integration in business processes, R/3 logistics, and accounting subledgers. R/3 GL serves as a central pool of financial data for financial reporting and other accounting areas. The origin of centrally stored data can still be traced at any time by researching data from a given transaction (see Figure 6.2).

6-23 The general ledger supports all the functions needed in a financial accounting system, including flexible structuring of the chart of accounts at group and company level, distributed application scenarios using Application Link Enabling (ALE), real-time simultaneous update of sub-

SOLUTIONS

ledgers and the general ledger, elimination of time-consuming reconciliation, and parallel views of data in both the general ledger and managerial
accounting applications.

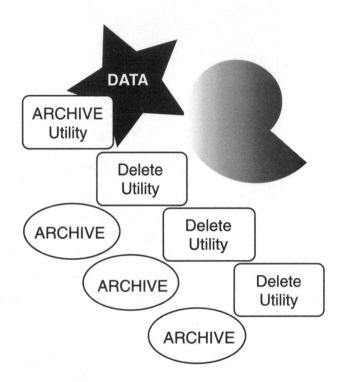

6-24 R/3 GL provides document parking, posting, reporting, an integrated
financial calendar for automating periodic activities, and the option of
displaying documents (see Figure 6.3) and reading them into the system
memory.

6-25 The special purpose ledger system is an enhancement to the general
ledger. It provides summary information from other components at a
user-defined level of detail. Combinations of entered data, produce data
summaries that can be used in planning, allocation, distribution, and
reporting. It is also possible to take advantage of more functions in general ledger and in cost-center accounting (see Figure 6.4).

6-26 This tool makes possible the creation of individualized database tables
and define non-standard fields to satisfy specialized accounting or reporting requirements. The special purpose ledger allows selective grouping
and updating of data in ledgers individually defined (see Figure 6.5).

FIGURE 6.3
Document Types

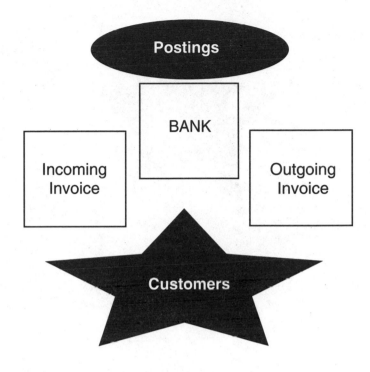

FIGURE 6.4
Cost Centers

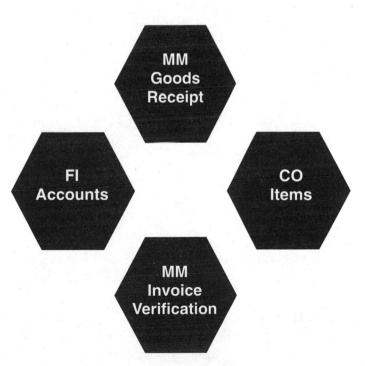

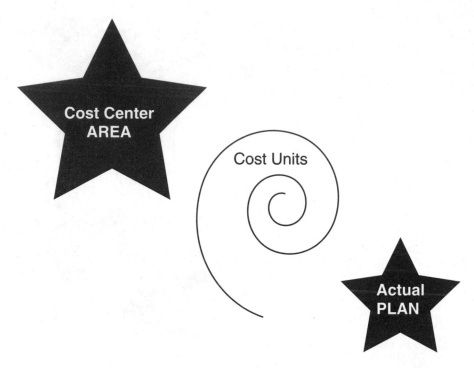

FIGURE 6.5
Reporting

Cost Center
AREA

Cost Units

Actual
PLAN

6-27 The special-purpose ledger includes parallel charts of account and currencies, planning and allocation tools, direct data entry in special-purpose ledgers (i.e. for adjustment postings), and user-defined reporting.

6-28 Financial accounting payable transactions are performed automatically when associated processes occur in other R/3 components. The financial-accounting module uses standard business rules for procedures dealing with data entry, reporting, processing payments, and bank transactions (see Figure 6.6).

6-29 Accounts receivable and payable functions include: Internet integration; document management and full accounts receivable and payable.

6-30 R/3 offers a financial overview of global business partner relationships in the accounts receivable and payable subledger functions. These subledgers are integrated with the general ledger and with areas in R/3 Sales and Distribution (SD) and Materials Management (MM), where financial data originate.

6-31 Processes included are automatic clearing by lockbox processing, integration with cash management, and flexible reporting using customer and vendor information systems.

SOLUTIONS

FIGURE 6.6
Payment Advices

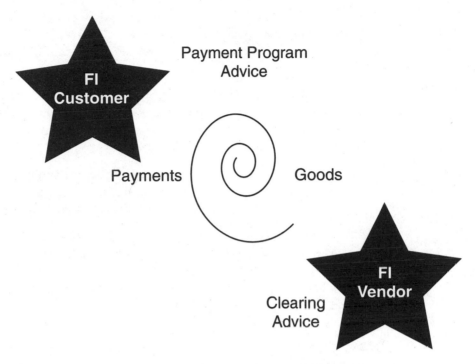

FIGURE 6.6
Payment Advices

6-32 The module also offers flexible dunning, enterprise-wide credit management with workflow integration, payment automation with EFT and check processing, as well as document parking with different approval procedures.

6-33 R/3 asset accounting manages a company's fixed assets. From inside the financial accounting system, FI-AA acts as a subledger to the general ledger that offers detailed information on asset-related transactions. Significant features include country-specific charts of depreciation that comply with local legal requirements, full support throughout the asset life cycle (from acquisition to retirement), depreciation simulation, interest calculation, integration with project management, and order accounting for management of capital assets. Asset accounting offers integration with plant maintenance for management of machinery and equipment, management of leased assets and assets under construction, mass processing with workflow integration, and interactive reporting.

6-34 Consolidated financial statements must be integrated effectively with operational data at the individual company level. Different valuation methods, facilitate planning balance sheet strategies to satisfy individual requirements.

SOLUTIONS

6-35   The R/3 legal Consolidation (FI-LC) is closely linked to the financial accounting system, allowing direct data transfer from individual statements into the consolidated report. This simplifies staff workload and reduces data-entry errors.

6-36   Legal consolidation helps create the consolidated statements required by law, permits multiple views of consolidation data. These views facilitate generating reports about legal entities or segments of a business. User-defined fields provide further details.

6-37   The Controlling (CO) component in the R/3 system collects the functions necessary for effective internal cost accounting, providing a flexible information system with standard reports and analysis paths.

6-38   Overhead cost controlling (CO-OM) emphasizes, significant increases in the percentage of indirect costs which cannot be assigned to products manufactured or services rendered. Although cost monitoring and optimization are advanced in production areas, transparency is usually absent in overhead cost areas. CO-OM concentrates on monitoring and allocation of overhead.

6-39   Cost Center Accounting (CO-OM-CCA) analyzes where overhead occurs within the organization. Costs are assigned to the subareas of the organization where they started. The R/3 system provides several methods for allocating posted amounts and quantities. Specifically, activity accounting allows for the allocation of many costs to products based on cost sources. This allows hither to impossible assignments.

6-40   Overhead Orders (CO-OM-OPA) gather and analyze costs based on individual internal criteria. The R/3 system can monitor and automatically check budgets assigned to each measure.

6-41   Overall corporate goals come before the goals of individual departments when business-process reengineering is concerned.

6-42   Product Cost Controlling (CO-PC) determines the costs that occur in manufacturing a product or providing a service.

6-43   Plan and standard values are concerned with valuing warehouse stock and in contrasting revenues received with costs. The specific values in CO-PC are critical for finding the lowest price limit that makes a product is profitable. The effects of changes in production methods on the cost of goods manufactured can be noted.

6-44   The Activity-Based Costing (CO-OM-ABC) module is a response to the need for monitoring and control of cross-departmental business processes,

SOLUTIONS

as well as functions and products. Organizational transparency in overhead areas is greatly improved by observing costs from a different perspective.

6-45 The R/3 system automatically determines the use of business processes by products, customers, and other cost objects based on the cost drivers taken from the integrated accounting environment. This greatly decreases the effort involved in maintaining a business-process model in a separate system.

6-46 Cost Object Controlling (CO-PC-OBJ) assists in monitoring manufacturing orders. Integration with the R/3 logistics components results in a logistical quantity flow that offers instant information on actual cost.

6-47 Follow-up calculations determine and analyze the variances between actual manufacturing costs and the plan costs resulting from product cost planning. R/3 can valuate work in process and post the results to financial accounting.

6-48 Profitability Analysis (CO-PA) inspects the sources of returns. As an element of sales controlling, CO-PA is the last step in cost-based settlement. This is where revenues are designated to costs with respect to market segment. It is possible to define any market segment and make a distinction among products, customers, orders, sales organizations, distribution channels, and business areas. Individual areas can then be evaluated with respect to contribution and revenue margins.

6-49 Information from profitability analysis facilitates important decisions in areas that include determining prices, selecting customers, developing conditions, and selecting distribution channels.

6-50 Investment Management (IM) offers major support for investment processes dealing with everything from planning through settlement.

6-51 Corporation-wide budgeting is useful in R/3 IM for better control of investment planning and budgeting at a level higher than specific orders or projects. It is possible to designate an investment program hierarchy by using any criteria. Once the specific investment measures (i.e. internal orders or projects are designated to positions in the hierarchy, then information on available funds, planned costs, and actual costs already incurred from internal and external activities remains current.

6-52 An investment program facilitates distribution of budgets used during the capital spending process. The system assists you in monitoring and avoiding budget overruns.

6-53 Appropriation requests offer tools for planning and managing capital spending projects at their earliest stages. In the initial stage of the capital

SOLUTIONS

spending process, the application for the spending project is entered as an appropriation request. At that point an individualized evaluation and approval process can be defined. The system keeps a detailed history of the status of the appropriation request. Data from the appropriation request can be transferred to the investment measure when the request is approved for implementation. Detailed plan values are input in the appropriation request, as are variants to be used in the preinvestment analysis. Investment measures that need to be monitored individually can be represented as either internal orders or projects.

6-54 These internal orders or projects provide the means for executing capital investment. They act as the objects for gathering primary and secondary costs, calculating overhead and interest, managing down payments and commitments, and handling other related tasks.

6-55 Settlement is flexible and almost fully automatic. This type of settlement assures complete integration with business planning and control and offers consistently current values.

6-56 Automatic settlement to fixed assets recognizes the importance of the asset-accounting aspects of investment measures.

6-57 The Financials IM: Investment Management system automatically separates costs requiring capitalization from costs that are not capitalized. It debits the correct costs to the asset under construction.

6-58 For different accounting needs, the system can use different capitalization rules. Once completed, the investment measure can be settled to various receivers by line item.

6-59 Asset accounting provides precise proof of origin for all transactions dealing with acquisition and production costs.

6-60 IM budgeted balance sheets and cost planning are always based on current values. Planned depreciation values for investment measures and appropriation requests can be transferred directly to continuous overhead cost planning. The system recalculates expected depreciation amounts whenever planning data are updated.

6-61 The R/3 treasury component provides a basis for effective liquidity, portfolio, and risk management.

6-62 The cash management component permits analysis of financial transactions for a given period. Cash management also identifies and records future developments for the purposes of financial budgeting.

6-63 In R/3 treasury cash management, a company's payment transactions are grouped into cash holdings, cash inflows, and cash outflows. Cash management offers information on the sources and uses of funds to secure liquidity to satisfy payment obligations when they become due. Cash management monitors and controls incoming and outgoing payment flows. Treasury mines the data required for managing short-term money market investments and borrowing. Depending on the time element, a distinction can be made between cash position, short-term cash management and medium- and long-term financial budgeting.

6-64 SAP's R/3 cash management component ensures that all information relevant to liquidity is available for analysis purposes, creating a basis for the necessary cash management decisions. Bank account management, electronic banking, and control functions provide support for managing and monitoring your bank accounts.

6-65 The liquidity forecast function integrates anticipated payment flows from financial accounting, purchasing, and sales to create a liquidity outlook for the medium to long term.

6-66 The cash position and liquidity forecast components generally cover both foreign currency holdings and expected foreign currency items.

6-67 A treasurer must take the results of current liquidity, currency, and risk positions and consider the conditions prevailing on the money and capital markets before implementing concrete decisions in the form of financial instruments in treasury management.

6-68 The treasury management component offers functions for managing financial deals and positions, from trading through to transferring data to financial accounting. Treasury management also supports flexible reporting and evaluation structures for analyzing financial deals, positions, and portfolios.

6-69 During short-term liquidity and risk management, money market or foreign exchange transactions can be used to refine liquidity or eliminate currency risks.

6-70 Securities and loans come in during the medium and long term.

6-71 Financial risks are eased by derivative financial instruments. The trading area contain functions for recording financial deals, exercising rights, performing evaluations, and computing prices.

6-72 In back-office processing, additional data required for processing deals include account assignment and payment details. Automatic confirmations are then generated. Position management functions (i.e. securities account transfers or corporate actions relating to securities) are also supported in the back-office area. The general ledger is updated in the accounting area, which also offers flexible payment processing functions, valuation, and accrual/deferral methods.

6-73 When common organizational elements are used, various organizational structures can be represented in the system, including a central enterprise-wide treasury department or in-house banks. This also assures full integration of treasury into other SAP R/3 components.

6-74 Market risk management plays a key role within treasury in making certain that a company remains competitive. The process involves a complex feedback loop encompassing data collection, risk measurement, analysis, simulation, and active planning of financial instruments. This process parallels other treasury and corporate functions. The complexity of this management process and its interaction demand a powerful toolset. Market risk management serves as an integrated, central risk-control station with monitoring and management functions.

6-75 Access to information on current and future cash flows and on financial deals already processed is exceedingly important. Cash management pools all cash flows from business sectors (i.e sales and distribution or purchasing), and consequently, all cash flows from the company's operating business that can be accessed for the purpose of risk management.

6-76 All financial transactions managed in treasury management can be evaluated together with the cash flows produced by the various operating divisions. The component provides various measurements for analyzing and assessing interest rate and currency risks. Market-to-market, effective rate and effective yield calculations are based on current market data, uploaded through data feed, and financial transactions/positions.

6-77 When market data are simulated, it is possible to determine the risk structure of "what-if" analyses including crash scenarios or worst-case scenarios as well as to measure and compare the impact of alternative hedging strategies by using simulated transactions.

6-78 R/3 Funds Management (TR-FM) supports the funds management process with from budgeting to payments. It includes monitoring expenditures, activities, resources, and revenues. Budgeting in TR-FM provides functions ranging from original budget through approval and release, budget supplements, returns, and transfers. There is also support for all stages of the budgeting process.

6-79 Budgets are entered for areas of responsibility that deal with as many management levels as required.

6-80 Funds centers and their hierarchical structure offer a base for top-down budgeting and represent responsibility areas within budget control. The commitment management system allows control of various funds commitments and determines how much of a budget has already been used, through availability checking.

6-81 The system can supply information at any time, with respect to the particulars of funds commitments. Analyses by responsibility area and commitment items permit identification of budget bottlenecks.

6-82 Enterprise controlling optimizes shareholder value while meeting internal objectives for both growth and investment. R/3 enterprise controlling integrates the Executive Information System (EC-EIS), business planning and budgeting, consolidation, and profit center accounting.

6-83 EC-EIS provides an overview of the critical information needed to manage an organization. This component integrates data from other EC components, other R/3 components, and non-SAP data sources both inside and outside the enterprise.

6-84 Drill-down reporting and the report portfolio are available to evaluate and present the data. In drill-down reporting, data are analyzed interactively. Exceptions are defined to highlight areas of concern. The drill-down reports can also be made available in the graphical report portfolio for less-experienced users.

6-85 The report portfolio is meant for users with basic knowledge of the system who want to access information put together for their specific needs.

6-86 Business Planning and Budgeting (EC-BP) supports the management teams of business units and groups in the computation of business targets including the return on investment. EC-BP supports central investment planning, budget release, and consolidation.

6-87 Legal Consolidation (FI-LC) is user-friendly, flexible, and offers excellent reporting tools. EC-CS coexisted with FI-LC in 1997, and in 1998 FI-LC will migrate to EC-CS. Tools to assist existing FI-LC customers in the migration process to EC-CS will be provided.

6-88 Profit Center Accounting (EC-PCA) analyzes the profitability of internal responsibility centers. The organizational structure is represented in the form of a profit center hierarchy with the profit center as the smallest unit of responsibility. This module automatically transfers data about invest-

SOLUTIONS

ment requirements from transaction applications, and offers extensive analysis functions for budget monitoring.

6-89 Consolidation (EC-CS) illustrates the next generation of consolidation in the R/3 System. EC-CS offers consolidated reports for both legal and management reporting. The user will have a greater amount of flexibility in creating the corporate structures for consolidated processing. These user-defined structures can represent the company's legal view, business-segment view, or a view specific to the company's own internal reporting structure.

6-90 All business transactions in financial accounting, materials management, asset management, and sales and distribution that affect profits are automatically reflected in profit center accounting. Selected balance sheet items can be analyzed by profit center and used for calculation of ratios (such as ROI).

6-91 Profit center planning is part of total corporate planning. Profit centers stress the integration aspect of corporate planning to allow plans from other application areas to be combined, extended, and altered in EC-PCA. Profit center related postings can be analyzed via the EC-PCA information system, which makes it possible to run standard reports and create custom reports for special analyses. EC-PCA provides profitability information to appropriate management and controlling departments. Since data transfer from other R/3 components is automatic, this component automatically executes internal billings and eliminated duplication between profit centers.

6-92 Full integration with other systems is important because R/3 enterprise controlling is most powerful when it is fully integrated with other R/3 application components.

6-93 R/3 EC automatically receives the information it needs from the rest of the R/3 system from logistics, human resources, or other financial components. When detail is required, it is possible to drill down to data that reside in those components.

6-94 It is possible to take advantage of enterprise controlling even if an organization is decentralized and uses a distributed computing system. EC can be used for decentralized accounting and reporting in local business units, while its controlling functionality is leveraged in the central office.

6-95 EC's uniform data structures can serve multiple purposes in different parts of an organization. End-users can even pull their data down to a PC and develop further analyses. Regardless of your enterprise is centralized or decentralized, R/3 EC offers timely availability of business-control information, for business units and for top management.

SOLUTIONS

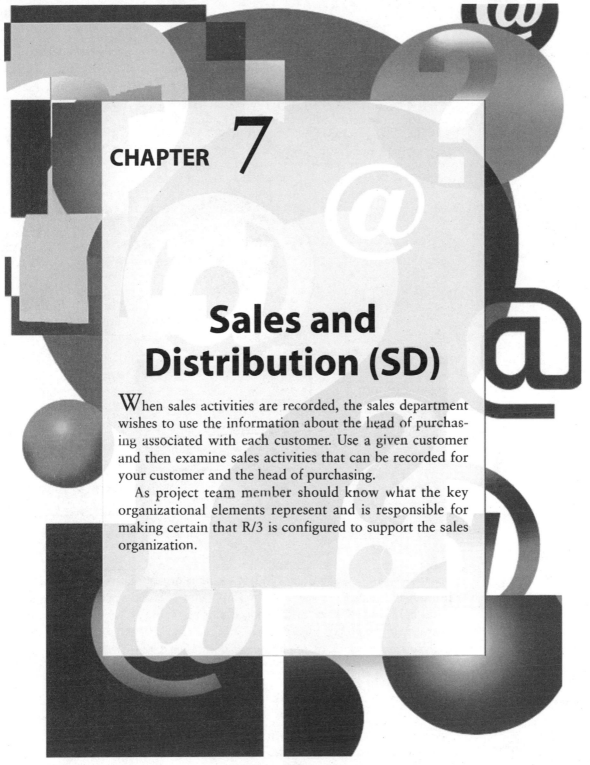

Sales and Distribution (SD)

When sales activities are recorded, the sales department wishes to use the information about the head of purchasing associated with each customer. Use a given customer and then examine sales activities that can be recorded for your customer and the head of purchasing.

As project team member should know what the key organizational elements represent and is responsible for making certain that R/3 is configured to support the sales organization.

This chapter you covers several key aspects of the Sales and Distribution (SD) program that must be known to achieve SAP certification in this primary course track. Review of this information you will have a better command of the type of material the SD track offers and of how to prepare for successful completion of the course.

Sales support includes (Figure 7.1) reporting requirements and key interfaces to Finance and Materials Management.

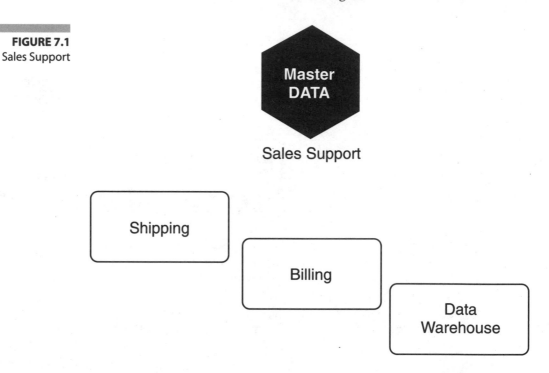

FIGURE 7.1
Sales Support

Sales Support

Shipping

Billing

Data Warehouse

TIP

Use the Implementation Guide (IMG) to examine organizational elements and their relationships. Organizational data are found in financial accounting, logistics general, and sales and distribution. Before doing the IMG exercises, answer the following questions regarding organizational structures. The questions refer to the group presentation regarding organizational data.

Sales and Distribution Information

Sales and Distribution (SD) information is an important factor in R/3. The features it affords include:

- Delivery scheduling
- Transfer of requirements
- Pricing
- Availability check
- Text processing
- Update of the sales information system
- Printing of documents (output)
- Credit limit checking.

The flow of documents in the sales, delivery and billing cycle could include:

- Inquiry
- Quotation
- Sales order
- Delivery
- Invoice.

Sales documents are composed of the document header and any number of items. The items can be subdivided into schedule lines. Discounts are calculated as a percentage of an item's value and the discount scale entries are based on the value of the order item, instead of on its weight, volume, or other factors.

Pricing procedures offer a determination that uses the sales area (sales organization, distribution channel, division), the document pricing procedure from the document type, and the customer pricing procedure from the customer master record.

SAP R/3 offers new standards that allow for a more effective level of integration between business administration and data processing. R/3 system components are depicted by a detailed business functionality that offers a higher level of integration between applications. This makes certain that all of the functions that this product offers within the sales and distribution modules are directly available within the system and your organization.

Condition Technique

The SAP Conditioning Technique allows the user to define and create only the rules that he needs. This reduced database access that is not necessary and accelerates response time. In addition, it prevents any code changes from occurring that are difficult to maintain. When dealing with some legacy systems you will note that either the pricing or procedure method was very difficult to hard code into a a given program. Although, prices could be established for individual materials, the method that would allow you to determine the net prices was often handled by the program itself. In order to deal with exceptions, sub-routine calls were create so that you could be able to process unusual conditions.

SAP R/3 allows you to define and create rules that you need for pricing, discounting, and surcharges. The conditioning technique reduces database access that is not needed due to the fact that the pricing procedure possesses only the conditions that are necessary. You will also find your response time is much better when you use the conditioning technique as compared to the hard coded programs that require you to sort through several exception call routines. Due to the fact that the user both defines and creates the needed requirements within your software, there is a no need for program code changes.

The conditioning technique is just a series of tables that are set up by the user. They are used to define a pricing procedure that acts very similarly to a program. An application then causes the system to search the Implementation Guide (IMG) for the pricing procedure table. At that point, the pricing procedure table requires the sales organization, distribution channel, division, and document pricing procedure from the document type, and the customer pricing procedure from the customer master record itself.

IMG Pricing Procedure

The IMG Pricing Procedure Table is based on the sales organization, distribution channel, division, document pricing procedure, and customer pricing procedure that has the proper pricing procedure assigned to it.

The Pricing Procedure contains all of the condition types that include prices, discounts, surcharges, rebates, and costs in the order or use for the purpose of determining the sales pricing and discounts for a given item. In addition, each condition type can define the data requirements for the condition records on the application level. The condition type also designation if it is a price or discounts depending on what quantity is needed.

Access Sequence

You must also note that an access sequence is designated to a condition type. An access is a search strategy that tells the system which table to locate the condition record value for the condition type. A search strategy is developed to start looking for the value that has the most specific condition until the last item in the search becomes the most general condition.

Specialized Business Transactions

R/3 comes standard and pre-configured with various kinds of sales transactions that include supporting rush orders, cash sales, and deliveries at no cost. When rush orders are saved, a delivery is automatically created for the warehouse.

When doing cash sales you believe you are receiving cash right away for the goods of services such that the invoice receipt is printed automatically. When delivery is created automatically, billing needs to be operated without the generation of an invoice.

Whenever you provide deliveries at no cost, you can freely distribute product samples to your customers or give away products to satisfy customers with complaints.

CPG

When working with the consumer packaged goods (CPG) industry, you will find that products are often sold in different forms with respect to varying design or packaging. Even though the product itself is always the same, each variation has article number due to the fact that the packaging is different depending on when the products is sold and for what promotion.

Whenever you determine specific materials in a sales order, your system automatically substitutes a given article number with others so that you have the same information as defined in your master record. In addition, you can also configure your system to automatically replace articles in an order with respect to your own material availability.

When you create an order, you can display a dialog box that has all of the different alternative products for your own material. You may then only determine materials within a sales document that has been set with the function within customizing. In addition, you may also determine each sales type indicating you should check material listings or exclusions. You also be able to determine that material listings and exclusion are based on the condition technique.

Pricing Configuration

Condition tables are composed of fields in the sales and distribution documents and forms the primary element for condition records. It is possible to create more condition tables when customizing.

Access sequences are able to designate the sequence where the system can access the condition tables. At least one condition table is designate to an access sequence. They can define an access sequence to a given condition type. Each condition type must be recorded in to the pricing procedure when you wish that it be considered during pricing configurations.

Billing Process

When dealing with the billing process, it is highly important to remember that you can control the flow of data by using different programs, billing document types, and exercising copying control.

Additionally, you can designate copying control for both the header and items. This allows you to determine that at billing, pricing is determined again based on the pricing type field in the copy control at item category level.

NOTE

A billing plan is a schedule that has billing data for a specific sales document item. Each billing process that is used will find that your system will automatically suggest one or two billing plan types namely:

1. Periodic Billing
2. Partial Billing

When working with an installment plan, you can either print an invoice listing payment and its amounts or use another customer posting line that is established in accounting for each individual installment time frame.

Definitions

- ✎ **Condition Table**—The key of the condition record.
- ✎ **Access Sequence**—A search strategy to locate the proper condition record.
- ✎ **Condition Types**—A calculation or formula used for a component of pricing.
- ✎ **Pricing Procedure**—A sequential list of condition types and subtotals.
- ✎ **Condition Records**—The data used by condition types to calculate pricing.

Showing Value

Accessing the "detail screen" in R/3 for a specific condition type from the item pricing screen shows a value in the Inactive field, indicating that the condition is not active because of condition exclusion.

A comparison of condition types is defined in exclusion groups assigned to the pricing procedure. An exclusion group selects the largest single discount and deactivates the others in the group.

Should an item net value be determined as less than the minimum price, the system computes the condition value of minimum price (PMIN) as the difference between the minimum price and the gross amount less any discount amount. The item net value per each will then correspond to the minimum price per each.

Schedule line categories use specified movement types to determine which stock values and stock accounts are updated during a goods movement. Movement types will reduce the available stock in the issuing plant and update consignment stock at the customer end. Other movement types reduce the available stock at the customer site.

Third-Party Processing

When dealing with third-party processing, a company does not deliver the items requested by the customer, but passes the order to a third-party vendor who ships the goods instantaneously to the customer and then bills you.

A sales order is often composed partly or entirely of third-party items. At some point, a vendor might deliver items you normally delivered by the company. Saving a sales order composed of one or more third-party items automatically creates a purchase requisition in purchasing. Should a sales order item have more than one schedule line, the system creates a purchase requisition item for each schedule line.

SD Distribution Channels

It is possible for you to use various distribution channels in sales and distribution so you can obtain the market with the best possible service. You will find sample distribution channels such as wholesale trade, sales to industrial customers or direct sales from a plant.

Distribution channels are established with respect to the market strategy or for some reasons of an internal organization. In a given sales organization you can give a customer his supply through several different distribution channels. You can also vary the material master data that is pertinent for sales, prices, minimum order quantity/delivery quality for each sales organization and distribution channel.

You can define a division-specific sales organization as well as product groups and divisions for several different projects. It is possible to make customer-specific agreements for each division such as deliveries, pricing, and terms of payments. In a division you can execute statistical analysis or create your own specific marketing methods.

NOTE

Whenever you designate organizational structures try to keep them as simple as you possibly can.

Sales

A sales office is often seen as a subsidiary where the geographical elements of an organizational structure within business development and sales that are defined through using sales offices. Sales offices are designated to sales areas such that if you enter a sales order for a sales office in a given sales area where the sales office can be assigned to a given sales area.

In a sales group, data on the employees of a sales office is stored in sales groups such that a sales group can be defined for each given division.

A sales group is composed of a specific number of salespersons. Each salesperson is designated to a sales group in a user master record. The data for each salesperson is managed under a personnel master record within a personnel number. You may also execute sales analyses on different internal organizational levels as well.

Creating a Sales Order

Whenever you create a sales order, the R/3 system injects most of the data from master records. This is why SAP asks that you record as much data as possible within these records. As a result, this will save you much time and effort whenever you enter data.

Customer data is recorded in customer masters, while vendor data is managed in vendor masters. However, employee data in you own organization is stored in the human resources master so that you can assign employees a personnel number that can be used in all business transactions where they are involved. In addition, this employee data at a partner company can be stored in files on contact persons.

Sales Area

A sales area is a combination of sales organizations, distribution channels, and divisions. You can use a sales area so that you can determine what materials within a division can be sold though a distribution channel. Furthermore, you can execute analyses in a given sales area such as an analysis of sales within a sales area. For example, you can define a customer-specific price agreement for any given sales area.

Sales and Distribution Documents

By simply using the menu path for Sales and Distribution to Sales. To Sales Documents, it is possible for you to control sales documents as well as develop new sales document types.

The specific sales and distribution document categories include:

- **Sales Document Types:** inquiries, quotations, and standard orders
- **Delivery Types:** deliveries and return deliveries
- **Billing Types:** invoices, credit memos, and debit memos

NOTE

A sales document can possess any amount of items. Knowing this, you can create several subdivisions as needed for each item with regards to both date and quantity.

There are several documents available in both sales and distribution processing. This allows you to illustrate various types of business transactions in sales. You can then add to the documents available in the R/3 system.

You can take pricing and availability functions and execute them within sales documents. You can turn these functions on and off as needed within different document types. You can then determine which functions you need to activate in the document types during each project phase.

Sales documents can be composed of a header, items, and schedule lines. You can then take header data and make it valid for all items when data on a given item level does not deviate from data you would find on the header level. Finally, you can input data in the header, items, and schedule lines in several screens within the sales document.

Processing Sales Orders

In its most basic form you can create an order on "one" interview screen. You can create orders and use customer-specific material numbers as well. An order entry screen is very useful for this situation.

In Customizing mode, you can execute specific settings such that you can require your R/3 system to send a message for all existing quotations or contracts for a customer.

It is also possible for you to block orders for shipping or billing temporarily such as when a returned product that must first be authorized. You can also establish an in-kind or free rebate on a order simply by linking the item to a higher-item level item.

Controlling Sales Documents

When you define a sales document type, you must maintain a series of control data. However, some settings for the number range in internal assignment and must be designated prior to assigning specific document types.

You are able to create your own sales document types to meet the specific needs of your own organization. The simplest way to create a new type is by duplications and then modifying existing document types.

You can execute specific settings for general sales and distribution or pricing functions before assigning document types. You can also manage status in sales documents so that you can deal with permitting future transactions. Furthermore, you can also restrict sales documents from being processed for specific sales areas by connecting them to the permitted sales areas in customizing.

Inquiries and Quotations

The order process starts with an inquiry or quotation. In this situation all information is sustained in this period and is employed as a reference for future orders. At that point, you can restrict the validity periods for inquiries and quotations.

It is possible for you to break off a transaction prematurely when the ordering group rejects an inquiry or quotation.

NOTE

The documents are not immediately deleted because it may have information that can be employed in future analyses.

You can provide an inquiry or quotations without reference to a material. You can also provider alternative materials for a n item. You can also alter inquiries and quotations using a work list. Hie structure of this list can also be modified within through customization.

Items and Schedule Lines

You can set item category functions through several customizing control settings. At that point you can determine if an item is acceptable for delivery or billing.

A delivery relevance indicator is good only for items that do not have schedule lines that are to be copied to the delivery of text items. Usually schedule items are in an order to be items in the that delivery. You can also establish you own items and schedule line categories to satisfy your organizations specific needs.

You can finally assign item categories to sales document types when you establish an order. Once the order is established, the R/3 system automatically suggests an item category so that the use can overwrite the suggestions with other item categories that are valid for the pertinent document type.

Whenever you make assignments you must remember that the item category group in the material master must also be considered such that the item is used and applies to the item category of the high-level item.

Control parameters are use for several schedule line categories and established in customizing. You may also designate line categories to item categories. Whenever you establish an order, the R/3 system automatically suggests a schedule line category. These suggestions can be overwritten with other schedule line categories that are valid for the pertinent line category.

Contracts

Contracts and scheduling agreements are actually outline agreements that are pertinent for a specific time interval. Scheduling agreements often have many schedule lines for each item. They get selected from the delivery process at the time where each schedule line is due.

Date determination rules are created especially when functioning with contracts that can be established in customizing and designated to each contract type. You can employ each one when you establish a contract to automatically define the beginning and end dates within a contract.

You find it useful to know that you can use cancellation rules so that you can check if each customer maintains contract conditions when that person tries to cancel it. In addition, contracts can also be used to determine special pricing agreements that can be used at any time when a order is created with respect to pertinent contracts.

Purchase Orders

Purchase orders are created from purchase requisitions through normal methods. During purchase order processing the system automatically duplicates the delivery address of a customer from the associated sales order. In the sales order it is possible to create purchase order text for each third-party item; the system will automatically copy the text into the purchase order. The purchase order number appears in the document flow information of the sales order. All changes made in the purchase order are automatically made in the sales order.

During the automatic delivery scheduling of third-party items, the system considers lead times specified by the purchasing department. Third-party orders appear in the billing due list depending on what has been set in the item category.

Order-related Billing

An item category must be set to a value suitable for order-related billing on the basis of the order quantity. The third-party order is completely billed only at the point at which the invoiced quantity is equal to the order quantity of the sales order item.

It is also possible to opt for order-related billing on the basis of invoice quantity. The indicator can be set so that the system will not include the order in the billing due list until an invoice from the vendor is received and processed by the purchasing department.

Ingredients of A BOM

The BOM is composed of selection criteria for each component. These selection criteria are set values in the BOM for batch. The system only looks for a search methodology when no characteristic values are recorded in the BOM. The search criteria is then used from the classification record analogous to the sales area.

Summary

In this chapter we covered the sales and distribution track. The information in this chapter is vital to adequate preparation for the certification course. We discussed sales document structure, partner functions, and specific circumstances that must be dealt with when creating an order. We also covered billing documents, sales organization specifics, and delivery and goods issues.

7-1 What does a company code represent in SAP?

7-2 Define the term "business area." How can it be used?

7-3 Which three organizational elements make up a Sales Area? Briefly explain their function.

7-4 Define two internal organizational elements within a sales organization and briefly explain their function.

7-5 Explain sales organizations and company codes.

7-6 Describe how sales organization and the distribution channel can be linked to plants?

7-7 How are divisions assigned to sales organizations?

NOTE

The Customer Group field can be defined by using the help function within R/3: position the cursor on name. The customer group is used to identify a particular group of customers for pricing or statistics purposes.

7-8 When accessing the sales data fields for the sales view, what steps are involved to make a customer group a required entry?

7-9 Go to the sales data fields and access the fields for the billing view. How can terms of payment be made a required entry?

BACKGROUND

It is necessary to select the following views:

- Basic data
- Sales: sales organization data
- Sales: general/plant data
- Purchasing
- MRP1
- MRP2
- Storage
- Accounting.

KEY CONCEPT

When altering the customer master record of a given customer to add a contact person as the head of purchasing, check to see if the new contact person and accompanying data can be viewed from the Customer Master.

Check the customer at the Partner Function window to see which partners are proposed for this customer master record. It is important to know how to add a partner function and to know if R/3 is using the partner determination procedure.

QUESTIONS

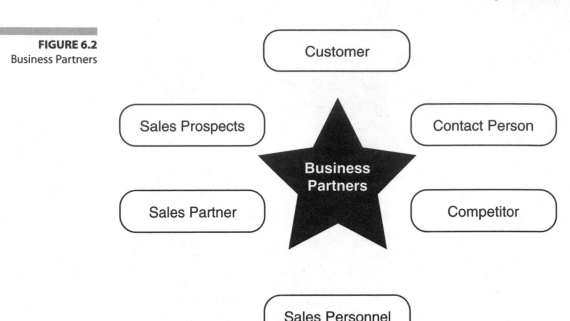

FIGURE 6.2
Business Partners

7-10   Define a menu path that may illustrate how logistics can lead to a central change.

7-11   Define what functions can be performed during order entry.

7-12   Define a possible document flow in sales and distribution.

7-13   Describe the basic structure of all sales documents.

7-14   Display the schedule line for a given order and define a path for the data contained in a schedule line?

7-15   Once data are entered, a partner pop-up screen appears, prompting choice of a ship-to party. Explain why this happens.

7-16   Examine the requested delivery date, the default data entry format, the item numbering, and the partners on this order. Can the Head of Purchasing be added as a partner function on the Partners window? If not, explain why.

TIP

The partner procedure created and used in the Partner Determination chapter is affiliated with the creation of customer master records, but not with the creation of sales orders.

7-17 How can this order be saved and the number recorded?

7-18 Choose the Partner Object Sales Document header and click the Partner Procedures icon. Enter the description and save this entry, then choose the procedure and click the Procedure Details icon. The procedure is composed of five partner functions:

1. Sold-to-party
2. Ship-to party
3. Bill-to party
4. Payer
5. Purchasing.

Produce a sales order using the sales document type. Check whether the head of purchasing is a partner in the sales order header by using the following menu path: Header to Partner.

TIP

All five partner functions are mandatory, and the Sold-to party cannot be changed.

OBJECTIVE

Add the five partner functions to the procedure, then use the check boxes to mark these selections prior to hitting the Enter key. Then save the entry.

Then go back to Maintain and proceed to the Partner Procedures Sales Document Header window and choose the Procedure Assignment icon. Locate the sales document type. Designate the newly created procedure to the sales document type. Save this entry and exit this table.

7-19 The customer receives a quotation and rejects the first item because it is too expensive. Use the change function, input the appropriate reason for rejection for the first item in the quotation, then save the quotation. Enter a menu path to reflect these actions.

7-20 At the Change Quotation: Overview window, use the following menu path then explain the procedure that would permit expanding on the reason for rejection: Overview to Reason For Rejection.

7-21 Create a quotation (QT) with reference to a given inquiry. At the Create with Reference pop-up window, input the inquiry number and click the Copy icon. Input a given numeric identifier in the Material field so that it fulfills the customer's specifications. The quotation should be valid until the end of next month. Then look at the order probability for the item, and finally save the quotation.

Define a menu path that leads from logistics to an inquiry.

NOTE

Imagine responding to an inquiry by creating a quotation (QT) with reference to the inquiry. The warehouse says that only X pieces can be offered for the first item.

7-22 Copy both items into the quotation. Modify the quantity of the first item in the overview screen. Check the validity dates. If there are none, make the quotation valid from today to the end of next month, then save the quotation.

7-23 Display the document flow of the quotation. Examine the reference status of the inquiry, then develop a menu path that illustrates the process.

NOTE

Fully referenced/completed refers to all quantities of this item on the quotation have been copied into the sales order.

7-24 Attempt to produce a standard order (OR) for the quotation and explain why this can or cannot be done.

7-25 Define a menu path that leads from logistics to a quotation.

7-26 Determine if it is or is not possible to create an order with an order type from a quotation.

7-27 Where is the copying from quotation to order controlled? Explain the process in detail.

7-28 Define a menu path that focuses on sales and distribution.

7-29 When are the entries in the document flow control for an order type created?

7-30 Which item numbers are created by R/3 if an order with order type is created from a quotation? What field controls this?

7-31 When dealing with the sales document type, explain the procedure to follow that would allow testing of configuration changes.

7-32 Exhibit the list of open quotations for a given customer, then select quotations valid for the next few months. If there are any open quotations for this customer, create a single standard sales order (OR) with reference to these quotations. Copy ALL remaining items and quantities into the sales order, then save. Define a menu path, then explain the solution.

KEY CONCEPT

When an order is created, a dialog box with a list of ship-to parties appears. Select the customer as the ship-to party, then choose the second item and then create a viable menu path to change the ship-to party to another customer.

When a sales order is created, the order header suggests the payment terms of the first item. The payment terms of the second item are different from those of the order header. The payment terms for the new item are gained from the order header. Orders that have different terms of payment at the item level result in separate invoices for the each payment term.

7-33 Inspect a plant that has defaulted from the customer-material information record and decide how R/3 has determined the plant for the other items. What areas could be checked to find a solution?

7-34 Produce a sales order for the customer using a given order type. Include two items with the second being a Rebate in Kind. Make certain to enter the Material number in the Material field, not in the Batch field.

7-35 Check the pricing at the header and item levels. Follow the path from Logistics to Sales/Distribution to Sales to Order to Create, then input the first item and then select Overview to double-line the entry.

TIP

The shipping point is in the business data of the first order item.

7-36 Create a delivery for this order. At the Create Delivery window, designate the shipping point. In the Selection Date field, input the end of next month. Determine the order number that has just been changed. Reduce the quantity of the first item by half on the delivery, then save the delivery.

7-37 Define a menu path to use for an order delivery.

7-38 Create and save another delivery for the order and review the order status again.

NOTE

Reviewing the status of the items, will show that only specific items have a rejected status. Although the text item does not generate a schedule line, the flag "Item Relevant for Delivery" is turned on. This happens when a text or value item is passed on to delivery processing only for informational purposes.

7-39 Check to see which item categories R/3 found for the main item and individual components. How is the material priced, at the main item or at the component level?

KEY CONCEPT

Display Scope of Check involves the following:

✎ Purchase orders
✎ Reservations
✎ Sales requirements
✎ Delivery requirements.

Planned orders are included. Purchase requisitions are not included. Replenishment lead time is considered because the indicator saying "no check" is not selected.

7-40 Explain how replenishment lead times affect the delivery date.

7-41 Define a menu path that illustrates substitution reasons.

7-42 Explain how R/3 reacts.

KEY CONCEPT

If the customer is interested in ordering other things as well, delete the excluded item to continue to enter items.

It is important to make certain that order entry operators have access to important information about customers when creating sales orders. Record this important information in the customer master record. Test R/3 so that it has the ability to meet this business requirement.

Create the text type in Customizing, specifically in Sales and Distribution, basic functions.

Observe the following menu path from the SAP Enterprise IMG: Sales and Distribution to Basic Functions to Text Determination to Define Text Types.

The definition procedure is linked with customer master records, specifically Sales and Distribution. The work is with the Text Object Customer who is specifically SD.

OBJECTIVE

Create an order with Customer Y.

The text input in the customer master record for Customer Y looks like a pop-up note here. No additional data entry is required. Exit without saving the order.

Observe the following menu path: from the SAP Reference IMG: Sales and Distribution to Sales to Incompleteness of Sales Documents to Define Incompletion Procedures.

1. Select Group 1 Sales-Header and then click the Procedures icon.
2. To assure Change mode, use the menu path: Table View to Display to Change.
3. Select the Sales Order procedure.
4. Click the "Copy as" icon.

TIP

A dialog box appears that states, "Specify target entries"; remember to click the OK icon.

When copying the existing procedure, choose the Copy All icon at the pop-up window, "Specify object to be copied".

Remember to save the new procedure.

KEY CONCEPT

In addition to the fields copied, must be added a field for the ordering party to the new procedure. Choose the new procedure and select the Fields icon. Click the New Entries icon to add fields to the procedure. These fields appear in the order screen as Header-Purchase order data.

7-43 Define a procedure for the sales document type, indicate all possible steps to take and what fields to use.

7-44 Input all data and press Enter. What does R/3 do?

7-45 Review the incompletion log and observe the following menu path: Edit to Incompletion log.
Determine what data is missing.

7-46 Explain why this causes an error message.

7-47 Explain what effects these settings have.

7-48 What elements are used for pricing procedure determination.

7-49 Check the results of pricing by viewing the pricing analysis for the order item. What is different about this order's pricing?

KEY CONCEPT

For copying: Customer to Customer, click the Execute button. Choose the resulting line and click the Continue button.

An individualized "Group Pricing Report" may be created. It should list condition records that contain the fields Customer, Material, or Sales Organization. Position the fields and select formatting options as desired.

Observe the following menu path: Tools to Business Engineering to Customizing to Implement.

Projects to SAP Enterprise IMG to Sales and Distribution to Basic Functions to Pricing to Define Screen Layout For Pricing Reports to Pricing Report to Create.

KEY CONCEPT

Input the name of the pricing report and click on the Enter button. Select the fields Customer, Material and Sales Organization. Click on the Select tables button.

The option to select only tables where all selected fields appear together will be presented. Remember to answer no. From the displayed list of tables, click on the Position Fields button.

Use the Position column to place each field in the Page header, Group header or Item level of the report. Use the Sort field to sequence each group of fields as required. Use the Text field to choose when the description of the item should be shown beside the key.

Click on the Format button to display either the validity period or the scales assigned to the condition records.

Define Terms

Describe and give an example of the following terms:

7-50 Condition Table

7-51 Condition Types

7-52 Pricing Procedure

7-53 Condition Records

7-54 In the Design phase. a pricing strategy will be built from the ground up. Management has asked to institute a new percentage discount based on the sales organization, distribution channel, ship-to party and material. This discount will only be used on a special-order type.

Create and save a new condition table called Test1. This table should reflect the discount criteria of sales organization, distribution channel, customer and material. These fields must be selected in the sequence they should appear on when creating a condition record. Incorporate the group number in the description.

Explain why both are active?

TIP

Instead of Ship-to Party, choose the Customer field for the condition table. It will be changed to reference the ship-to party in the next exercise.

7-55 Explain what happens during pricing for the item.

7-56 Define a billing document menu path.

7-57 Define a sales organization menu path.

7-58 Explain what is involved in changing the sequence for a given delivery that needs to be moved.

7-59 Explain specifically what must be done first to post goods issue for this delivery.

7-60 Describe exactly what effect posting goods issue has on making changes to the delivery.

7-61 Describe other factors involved with a given delivery before it can be billed.

KEY CONCEPT

The billing type is displayed on the detail screen, and can also be found in the title bar of the overview screen in the billing document.

To create a reference to an order, press the Ref to Order button. In addition, observe the following menu path: Sales Document to Create with Reference to Order.

It is also possible to use the selection list when Creating with Reference and select only the material and the quantity being credited.

7-62 Once the billing department is ready to issue credit, a credit memo must be created for the Released Credit Memo request. How is this done?

7-63 Define a menu path to illustrate issuing a credit memo request.

7-64 Create a menu path that permits checking the document flow for the accounting documents.

7-65 Define a menu path for a return with reference to an order.

7-66 Explain how to display the accounting documents for both orders.

7-67 Explain the specific factors used to determine the general ledger accounts. Observe the following menu path: Logistics to Sales/Distribution to Billing to Billing Document to Display.

7-68 Detail all the factors a standard system may use to determine which accounts should be posted.

7-69 Where in the configuration should the account determination procedure to be used be defined? Explain and detail the menu path.

7-70 Compare the configuration of the two schedule line categories by using the following menu path from the SAP Enterprise IMG: Sales and Distribution to Sales to Sales Documents to Schedule Lines to Define Schedule Line Categories.

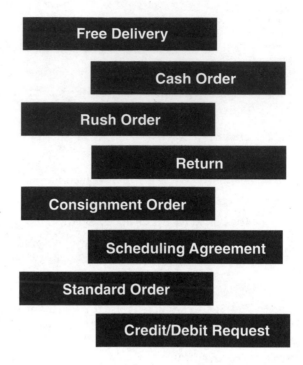

FIGURE 7.3
Sales Documents
Copyright by SAP AG

7-71 Define which processes would have to occur in the system for the third-party transaction to be complete all the way through to billing.

7-72 Specify which controls have to be set in the system for a third-party transaction to appear automatically in the billing-due list.

7-73 Inspect the material document. How are the accounting documents viewed?

7-74 Determine the impact of the transfer on the receiving plant.

7-75 Define a menu path that leads to entering a given material and quantity.

7-76 Explain how to view documents by following a menu path that starts with choosing the material document.

7-77 Determine the impact of the transfer on a receiving plant.

7-78 Make certain that there is enough stock on hand at the supplying plant. Define a path leading to stock overview.

7-79 Enter material number, but do not set the plant number to display stock for all plants for the material; then select Execute Green Check Mark.

Create the delivery and hit the Additional Screen button to key in only the material in question. Now define a menu path that illustrates the delivery process.

7-80 Explain the process that makes it possible to record the delivery number.

7-81 Describe inter-company sales processing.

7-82 Produce the billing document to send to Receiving Plant. Define a menu path that illustrates this process.

7-83 Explain what is involved in creating the inter-company invoice.

7-1 A company code is an independent legal accounting unit for which balance sheets and profit and loss statements are created.

7-2 A business area is an optional internal financial accounting organizational unit. Business areas are used to create internal profit and loss statements and balance sheets for one or more companies. As an example, business areas could be used to represent the different product lines that an organization manufactures and sells. They are used for flexible reporting across company codes.

7-3 The three elements of a sales area are:

1. **Sales Organization**—a legal selling unit responsible for product liability and claims. This can be a geographic area or industry sector e.g., industrial chemicals or Western Canada and is responsible for negotiating sales.
2. **Distribution Channel**—The means though which sales materials reach the customer. This can be a basis for terms of sale, e.g., retail, wholesale, direct sale.
3. **Division**—A grouping of products or services, e.g., solvents. This can represent a product line.

7-4 Two internal organizational elements are:

1. **Sales Office**—Geographical aspects of the organizational structure in business development and sales are defined using sales offices. A sales office can be viewed as a subsidiary. Sales offices are assigned to sales areas such as Toronto, Ottawa, or Boston.
2. **Sales group**—A group of people within one sales office which is responsible for the sale of certain products and services or a market segment, e.g. wholesale cleaning products. One or more sales groups are assigned to one sales office.

It is not. If a company is set up for business area balance sheets, it can post to any business area defined for that client.

7-5 Many sales organizations can be assigned to one company code; however a sales organization cannot be assigned to more than one company code.

7-6 Many sales organizations and distribution channels (together) can be linked to many plants—as long as they are within the same company code.

7-7 Many divisions can be assigned to many sales organizations.

7-8   In the Field status section of the window, double-click on Sales Data. In the Select Group section of the window, double-click on Sales. Make Customer Group a required entry and save this entry.

7-9   In the Field Status section of the window, double-click on Sales data. In the Select Group section of the window, double-click on Billing. Make Terms of Payment a required entry and save this entry.

7-10   Menu path: Logistics to Sales/Distribution to Master Data to Business Partners to Sold-to Party to Change to Change Centrally

7-11   Functions performed during order entry include:

- Delivery Scheduling
- Transfer of Requirements
- Pricing
- Availability check
- Text processing
- Update of Sales Information System
- Printing of Documents (output)
- Credit Limit Checking.

7-12   A possible flow of documents in the sales, delivery and billing cycle could include:

- Inquiry
- Quotation
- Sales Order
- Delivery
- Invoice.

7-13   All sales documents are made up of the document header and any number of items. The items can be subdivided into schedule lines. See Figure 7.4.

7-14   Menu path: Logistics to Sales/Distribution to Sales to Order to Display.
    Within the overview screen select an item using the check box and hit the Schedule Line button. The schedule lines contain the requested quantity and date and the confirmed quantity and date.

7-15   Two ship-to parties appear, since a second potential ship-to party was added to the customer master record for a customer in the Partner-Determination chapter. Choose either party.

7-16   The default data entry format is double-line entry that shows both plant and net price. The requested delivery date defaults as defined.

The partner does not appear in the sales order, nor can it be added. The partner procedure assigned to the new order type does not contain this partner.

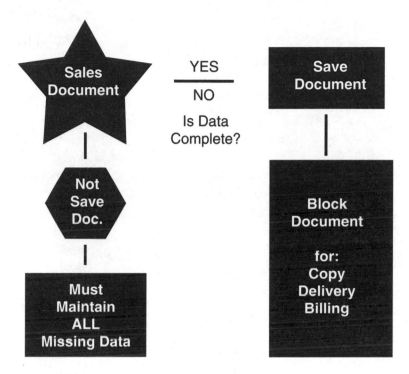

7-17 To save this order and record the number: from the SAP Enterprise IMG: Sales and Distribution to Basic Junctions to Partner Determination to Define; then assign partner determination procedures.

7-18 At the Header Partner window, verify that the head of purchasing has been copied into the order, then save the sales order. Save this entry and exit this table.

Go back to the Maintain: Partner Procedures Sales document header window and select the procedure. Click the Procedure Details icon. Locate the Purchasing Partner Function and delete the line. Save this entry and exit this table.

Use quotation type QT. Click the Ref to Inquiry icon. At the Create with Reference pop-up window, input the number of the inquiry then click the Copy icon.

7-19 Menu path: Logistics to Sales/distribution to Sales to Quotation to Change.

7-20   To proceed, choose the first line item and input the appropriate reason for rejection of this line item, then save this change.

7-21   Menu Path: Logistics to Sales/Distribution to Sales to Quotation to Create to Sales Document to Create with Reference to Inquiry.

7-22   Use quotation type QT. Click the Ref. to Inquiry icon. At the Create with Reference pop-up window, input the number of the inquiry and click the Copy icon. Input a valid-from and valid-to date. Then, alter the item quantity of the first material, and save this quotation.

7-23   See Figure 7.5. Reference status of inquiry: From the Document Flow window, choose the inquiry and click the Status overview icon. Position the cursor on the quotation and click the Status Overview icon.

   Menu path: Logistics to Sales/Distribution to Sales to Quotation to Display to Environment to Document Flow.

FIGURE 7.5
Document Flow

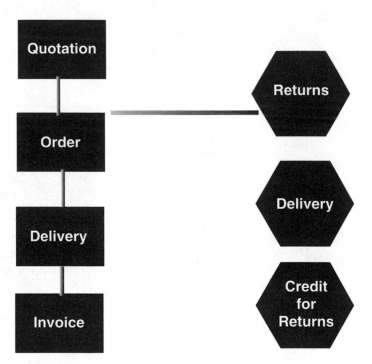

7-24   Use order type OR. Click the Ref. to Quotat. icon and enter the number of the quotation, then click the Copy icon. R/3 issues an error message indicating that the reference has already been completely copied or rejected.

7-25   Menu Path: Logistics to Sales/Distribution to Sales to Order to Create to Sales Document to Create Reference to Quotation.

7-26   Yes, it is possible to create an order with an order type from a quotation.

7-27   The control is in the copy control for sales document. Choose: Copying control: Sales Document by Sales Document. Use the Position icon to find ZGG as the target and QT as the source.

7-28   Menu path: From the SAP Reference IMG: Sales and Distribution to Sales to Maintain Copy Control for Sales Documents.

7-29   An order type is created by copying the standard order type (OR). When copying an order type, the copy control is also maintained for the new order type.

7-30   "Copy item number " field in copy control at header level. Controls the creation of item numbers. Copy control indicates if R/3 is copying the item counter from the source document to the target document or if R/3 is looking to the target document to specify the item counter.

7-31   In the copy control, choose the Target Document type and Source Document type QT, then go to the Detail window. If Copy Item Number is selected, R/3 uses the item number of the source document. If Copy item number is not selected, R/3 uses the numbering specified in the target document.

7-32   Menu path: Logistics to Sales and Distribution to Sales to Quotation to List. Two solutions exist:

1. Note the quotation numbers, exit this work list, create a single standard sales order (OR) and call in each of the quotations listed here by using the Create with Reference function.
2. Access each quotation from this list in Change mode and use the Subsequent Functions feature to convert the quotation to a standard sales order (OR). Once that sales order is saved, R/3 will return to this work list where the next quotation can be selected for conversion to a sales order. Repeat the steps listed above until all quotations appearing on the work list have been converted into standard sales orders.

7-33   The plant is visible from the double-line overview, which is then copied from the master data. The customer-material info record has the highest priority and will override a plant specified on the customer which in turn will have priority over the plant specified in the material master (see Figure 7.6).

7-34   Display the overall, delivery, and rejection status of the order with the purchase order number.

SOLUTIONS

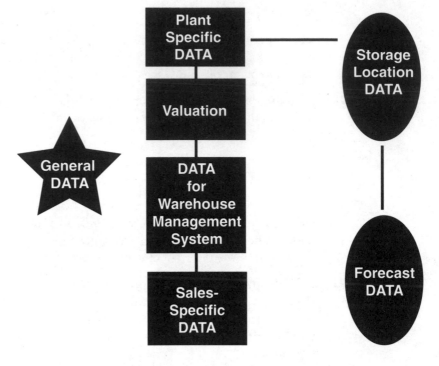

FIGURE 7.6
Material Master
Record

7-35 Using the change mode, reject the third item using any rejection code. Check the shipping point determined for each order item. Save the order.

7-36 Use the following steps:

1. At the Create Delivery window, specify the shipping point, end of next month, and sales order number. Press Enter.
2. Change the quantity of the first item and save the delivery.
3. Review again the overall, delivery, and rejection status of the order.

From the Change Standard Order: Overview window, use the menu path in solution 37 to look at the overall, delivery, and rejection status of the order.

7-37 Menu path: Logistics to Sales/Distribution to Shipping to Delivery to Create.

7-38 At the Create Delivery window, specify the shipping point, end of next month, and sales order number. Press Enter. Save the delivery.

7-39 Item categories for higher-level items and item categories for the sub-items have been entered for sales document type ZGG and item category group.

7-40 Replenishment lead times may be used to promise availability if sufficient stock is not available. For example, if there is a replenishment lead time of four days, the system confirms delivery of that ordered material four days from the order date regardless of stock availability at order time.

7-41   Menu path: From the SAP Enterprise IMG: Sales and Distribution to Basic Functions to Material Determination to Define Substitution reasons.

7-42   R/3 displays a dialogue box with a warning message indicating that a given item will be replaced due to material determination. If presented with a pop-up window, click the Green Check Mark icon to acknowledge the message. When Enter is pressed, the given material will replace an original item on this sales order.

7-43   At the Select Transaction pop-up window, select Error Procedures of the Sales Document header and click the Choose icon. Use the Position icon to find the sales document type ZGG. In the InP field for the sales document type, enter GG + 60 (the newly created procedure) by typing over the existing procedure. Save the entry.

7-44   R/3 issues the warning: Please Enter Name. Press Enter at the Warning pop-up window.

7-45   At the Configuration: Change List Sales Orders window, use the menu path: Environment to Generate.

This produces all the display variants created by the class during this exercise. This is the last step when creating display variants at a site.

7-46   It causes an error message because a mandatory pricing condition record for the material is missing.

7-47   The discount is calculated as a percentage of the item's value and the discount scale entries are based on the value of the order item, instead of its weight, volume, and other factors.

7-48   Pricing procedure determination uses the sales area (sales organization, distribution channel, division), the document pricing procedure from the document type, and the customer pricing procedure from the customer master record.

7-49   Select the line item and then use the following menu path: Item to Pricing to Edit to Analysis. None of the conditions has assigned requirements in the pricing procedure that are taken into account during pricing. This method can be used when discounts and surcharges are not intended to affect the net price.

Choose Copying Control: Delivery Slip to Billing Document. Select the line for Source and click on the Item button in the Navigation section. Choose the intended item category and click on the Details button.

Choose Maintain Pricing Procedure, then select the pricing procedure required and click on the Control button. In customizing, when defining the pricing procedure, it is possible to designate a condition type as manual only (Man.). So that the condition is not automatically designated during pricing but can only be entered manually.

Choose Maintain Access Sequences, and then click on the Accesses button.

7-50 Condition Table is the definition of the key of the condition record. Access Sequence is a search strategy to locate the proper condition record.

7-51 Condition Types are a calculation or formula used for a component of pricing.

7-52 Pricing Procedure is a sequential list of condition types and subtotals.

7-53 Condition Records are data used by condition types to calculate pricing.

7-54 Accessing the detail screen for a given condition type from the item pricing screen shows a value in the Inactive field. This indicates that the condition is not active due to a condition exclusion.

Comparison of different condition types is defined in exclusion groups assigned to the pricing procedure. The exclusion group selects the largest single discount and deactivates the others in the group.

Observe the following menu path: Tools to Business Engineering to Customizing to Implement. Projects to SAP Reference IMG to Sales and Distribution to Basic Functions to Pricing to Pricing Control to Condition Exclusion to Condition Exclusion For Groups Of Conditions.

Choose Maintain Condition Exclusion for Pricing Procedures. Double-click on the pricing procedure.

7-55 If the item net value determined is less than the minimum price, the system calculates the condition value of minimum price (PMIN) as the difference between the minimum price and the gross amount less any discount amount. The item net value for each will then correspond to the minimum price for each.

7-56 Menu path: Tools to Business Engineering to Customizing to Implement. Projects to SAP Reference IMG to Sales and Distribution to Billing to Billing Documents to Define Billing Types.

7-57 Menu path: Tools to Business Engineering to Customizing to Implement. Projects to SAP Reference IMG to Enterprise Structure to Definition to Sales and Distribution to Maintain Sales Organization.

7-58 To change the sequence, double-click on the delivery required to move and position the cursor on the line preceding where that for the delivery (the system inserts the delivery after the line selected).

7-59 The delivery must first be fully picked (and, if required, confirmed).

7-60 The delivery can no longer be changed in any way, especially with regard to quantity. The system should propose the delivery note as output to be issued in the delivery document.

7-61 If the delivery has not been "goods issued", then this must be done before continuing.

7-62 Enter the number of the credit memo request from above. Press the Execute button. Save the Credit Memo.

7-63 Menu path: Logistics to Sales and Distribution to Billing to Billing Document to Create.

7-64 Menu path: Logistics to Sales and Distribution to Billing to Billing Document 4Display to Environment to Document Flow.

7-65 Menu path: Logistics to Sales/Distribution to Sales to Order to Create.

7-66 While in document flow for the order click on the Accounting Document number then select the Display Document button to view the accounting document.

Alternatively use the menu path: Logistics to Sales/Distribution to Billing to Billing Document to Change Select Overview to Accounting and then double-click on the Accounting Document number to view the accounting document.

7-67 Double click on Individual Condition Types to view the factors for account determination.

7-68 Factors used to determine account posting include: chart of accounts, sales organization, distribution channel, division, customer account group, material account group, and account key.

7-69 Menu path: From the SAP Enterprise IMG: Sales and Distribution to Basic Functions to Account Assignment4 Revenue Account Determination to Define and Assign Account Determination Procedures to Billing: Document Types–Account Determination.

The account determination procedure is assigned to the billing document type.

Go to Item and then to Business Details in the sales order through either Change or Display mode.

7-70 Schedule line categories use specified movement types to determine which stock values and stock accounts are updated during a goods movement. Movement types will reduce the available stock in the issuing plant and update consignment stock at the customer. Other movement types will reduce the available stock at the customer site.

7-71 In third-party processing, the company does not deliver the items requested by the customer. Instead, the order is passed to a third-party vendor who then ships the goods instantaneously to the customer and bills the company. A sales order is usually composed partly or entirely of third-party items. Occasionally, it may be necessary to let a vendor deliver items normally delivered by the company.

When the sales order that contains one or more third-party items is saved, the system automatically creates a purchase requisition in Purchasing. If a sales order item has more than one schedule line, the system creates a purchase requisition item for each schedule line.

Purchase orders are created from purchase requisitions through standard methods. During purchase order processing the system automatically duplicates the delivery address of the customer from the corresponding sales order. In the sales order, purchase order text can be created for each third-party item and the system will automatically copy the text into the purchase order. The number of the purchase order appears in the document flow information of the sales order. All changes made in the purchase order are automatically made in the sales order.

During the automatic delivery scheduling of third-party items, the system takes into account lead times specified by the purchasing department. Third-party order will appear in the billing-due list depending on what has been set in the item category.

7-72 The item category has to be set to something pertinent for order-related billing on the basis of the order quantity. The third-party order is completely billed only when the invoiced quantity equals the order quantity of the sales order item.

It is also possible to choose to implement conditions relevant for order-related billing on the basis of the invoice quantity. The indicator can be set so that the system will not include the order in the billing-due list until an invoice from the vendor is received and processed by the purchasing department.

7-73 In order to view the documents, select Material Document, select Display and press Enter. When the document is displayed, select the Follow on Documents icon to view the related accounting document.

7-74 To view the impact on stock return to the material document initially screen select Environment to Stock Overview and enter the material number and the receiving plant; then press the Execute button. Double click on the plant to view stock type and stock screen. The transferred material quantity is in the Transfer (plant   bucket.

7-75 Logistics to Materials management to Inventory Management. Choose the Transfer Posting icon. Choose from the menu path: Movement Type to Transfer Posting to Plant to plant to PLin.stor.in.plant. This effectively sets the movement type so that the plant and storage can be entered before inputting the material and quantity.

TIP

Always remember to save the document.

7-76 To view the documents, choose the menu path Material Document to Display and press Enter. When the document is displayed, choose the Follow on Documents icon to view the related accounting document.

WARNING

A warning message appears to indicate that no accounting document has been created.

7-77 To view the impact on stock return to the material document initially screen select the menu path that leads from Environment to Stock Overview and then input the material number as well as the receiving plant.

At that point, press the Execute button. Double click on the plant to view stock type and stock screen. Note that the transferred material quantity in the Transfer (plant) bucket has been removed.

7-78 Menu path: Logistics to Materials Management to Inventory Management to Environment to Stock to Stock Overview.

7-79 Menu path: Logistics to Sales/Distribution to Shipping to Delivery to Delivery Due List.

7-80 Enter the shipping point and change the selection date to find the stock transfer order. Make sure that the document to be selected is stock transfer. Save the delivery then follow the menu path: Goto to Log to Deliveries; record the delivery number.

Enter the delivery document and then choose the Picking button for Replenishment. Inspect the screen to verify the data and enter the picked quantity and post goods issue.

SOLUTIONS

7-81 Enter the shipping point and change the selection date to find the stock transfer order. Make sure that the document to be selected is stock transfer. Save the delivery then follow the menu path: Goto to Log to Deliveries. Then record your delivery number.

Enter the delivery document and then choose the Picking button for Replenishment. Inspect the screen to verify the data and enter the picked quantity and post goods issue.

Enter the movement type, purchase order number, and storage location. Choose the applicable line item and press the Copy + Details button. Finally, press the Copy button again and save.

7-82 Menu path: Logistics to Sales/Distribution to Billing to Billing Document to Billing Due List.

7-83 Enter the billing date, select inter-company items and enter the sold-to party. Press execute and the system will create the inter-company invoice.

CHAPTER 8

SAP R/3 Human Resources Management

SAP R/3 Human Resources (HR) components offer detailed, process-driven solutions that deal with an organization's human resources global requirements. This global approach covers both country and local requirements, combining all the key functions required by HR departments to provide powerful human resources solutions.

Human resources management is an essential factor of any successful business. Many factors affect an HR department, therefore HR managers must constantly review and optimize their business processes.

SAP R/3 HR components are easily integrated with all R/3 business components and work to improve productivity. They offer company-wide solutions for HR departments and permit other departments to access specific employee data. A human resource management system has to be adaptable to company-specific requirements, as well as to constantly increasing HR requirements.

HR functions work exceedingly well within integrated standard application systems as they deal with all the functions required in business practices. They offer a great deal of flexibility in R/3 system components and make it possible to optimize business processes by adjusting the R/3 solution to meet the organization's needs.

Human Resources Course Information

HR functions work well within integrated standard application systems as they deal with all the functions required in business practices. They offer a great deal of flexibility in R/3 system components and allow optimization of business processes by adjusting the R/3 solution to an organization's needs.

In this section we examine functional HR and the specifics about the SAP HR Partner Academy, the basic requirements involved in being a consultant in this area. The result will be expertise in how to advise, configure, and implement the SAP HR module. This chapter gives real examples to help create a division in a company and assign corporate, personnel, and organizational structures for that company. There are lessons in fully implementing the company and creating a team effort to achieve the goal of a solid company model that will give afford a hands-on feel for SAP HR configuration and implementation.

International Versions

International Versions deal with business activities regarding situation involving the crossing of national borders. R/3 supports international requirements with country-specific versions that benefit from different languages and currencies. It also makes provisions for pertinent legal requirements.

European Monetary Union

EMU is the European Monetary Union has a technical and organizational challenge that deal with practically all areas of business including accounting, Human Resources management, and logistics. There is a need for changes and adjustments. If these modifications are not implemented, they could have a devastating effect on your entire data processing system. SAP makes it possible for you to make an easy transition to the new currency.

Country Specific Versions

SAP provides you with country-specific versions of R/3 Payroll Accounting where you can fulfill language, currency, and regulatory requirements. SAP offers solutions for over twenty countries such as Austria, Belgium, France, Germany, Great Britain, Japan, the Netherlands, Switzerland, and the USA. However, SAP is constantly adding new country-specific solutions.

SAP offers standardized communication channels in Time Management. It is used for connecting to external time recording systems. An additional communication channel for plant data collection (PDC) indicates that data relevant to HR can be transferred automatically to Time Management.

Basic Functional HR

The HR Partner Academy was created to offer the basic requirements for a consultant to have the power to do the following actions for a SAP HR module: advise, configure, and implement.

All students create their own divisions within their organizations. Then they designate their own corporate, personnel, and corporate structures for their company. When the course is completed the company should be fully implemented. This requires a team effort. The corporate model provides a hands-on workshop methodology to learn the SAP HR configuration and implementation.

Prerequisites

The prerequisites include:

- Technical background (strongly recommended)
- Solid business background in human resources administration
- Basic knowledge of a graphical user interface (GUI) such as the Microsoft Windows environment

The course covers:

- Complete HR system demonstration
- System familiarity and navigation

✎ Overview and configuration of:
  – corporate structure
  – personnel structure
  – payroll subunits
  – time
✎ Management
✎ Organizational structure
✎ Applicant administration
✎ Qualifications
✎ Career
✎ Succession planning
✎ Cost planning
✎ Workforce planning
✎ Shift planning
✎ Organization management
✎ Seminars
✎ Convention management
✎ Security
✎ HR reporting
✎ Gross payroll configuration
✎ Payroll interface
✎ Authorization
✎ System controls
✎ Time evaluation.

Human Resource Components

Human resource components provide a flexible structure for quickly and easily customizing a system to meet specific needs. Logging on in a specific language, causes screens, messages, and documents to appear in the language determined and provides access to all the system's functions.

Components can be used individually or in combination with other components. When they are entered, data are maintained centrally and are available to all other applications that provide immediate access to any data required.

Human resources components, in particular, administer to millions of employees around the world, providing support to more than a thousand businesses in over 50 countries in executing a multitude of HR tasks. R/3 offers integration of all functions as performance features of SAP software. Automatic linking between components greatly speeds up and simplifies business procedures. Production planning and control data can have a direct impact on time management.

HR Components

HR components have a high level of performance and provide easy access to data in a complete and up-to-date fashion. The R/3 system can be customized to suit the specific requirements of an organization.

Employee Master Data is where SAP R/3 Human Resources has a centralized database with integration to multiple components that deal with processing employee information. SAP provides tools to save you time and help you tailor the system to fit your needs.

R/3 has predefined sequences of information screens for various personnel events. This can be depicted through a sequence of screens necessary for processing a new hire or a promotion. These sequences can be tailored to conform to specific business practices.

Master Data

SAP R/3 HR contains information types for storing any desired information about your employees. You can add your own information types. R/3 Human Resources allow you to enter data through the time saving fast entry feature, processing data in two modes:

1. Online
2. Background

Personnel

Personnel management inside SAP R/3 HR integrates numerous software components that permit dealing with human resources tasks more quickly, not only as part of a company-wide R/3 solution, but also as a stand-alone solution.

Personnel administration facilitates creating a global, fully integrated HR data structure. Information is no longer owned by specific departments, but is instead shared by multiple entities across an organization. This eliminates duplicate entries, reduces the chance for error, and improves data accuracy.

Employee master data is SAP R/3's human resources centralized database with integration to multiple components for processing employee information. SAP offers tools to save time and help tailor the system to fit specific needs.

Personnel Cost Planning

Personnel cost planning offers the benefits of a systematic and forward-looking planning tool that considers the final effects of all personnel events. A company is better of organized when it can accurately forecast personnel costs, so that the management team has a more complete cost picture to assist them in making informed decisions.

Personnel cost planning permits cost comparisons between target and actual personnel costs. Cost previews can be created and wages, salaries, and other cost elements can be predicted for open and filled positions, based on simulated, planned, or actual payroll figures. Results can be displayed through the R/3 business graphics feature. The standard link to Microsoft Excel helps to provide results in a spreadsheet format and these results are transferred to SAP R/3 cost accounting as needed.

HRIS

The Human Resources Information System (HRIS) and Executive Information System (EIS) display graphical information such as organization charts or employee data through the HRIS. HRIS incorporates both standard and customer-defined reports. SAP has condensed vast amounts of HR information into smaller, more meaningful units of data in the EIS. EIS key figures offer an organization information in a quantified and summarized format.

Information Screens

R/3 has predefined sequences of information screens for different personnel events. This specific sequence of screens can be tailored to conform to your specific business practices.

It doesn't matter whether your business operates solely in one country or has expanded to international locations, SAP helps you with your payroll requirements.

HR Travel Management

HR travel management facilitates processing of a business trip from start to finish, from the initial travel request to posting in financial accounting and controlling. It incorporates any subsequent corrections and all retroactive accounting requirements. Integration with several R/3 components and subcomponents makes certain the correct posting, taxation, and payment of trip costs.

Travel data can be entered by the person traveling, by a secretary, or by the relevant department. This can take place either before or after the trip. The entry of a travel request automatically generates a workflow that makes the administrator's work much simpler. Business, employee, and country-specific trip provisions can be implemented through system settings.

Travel management automatically calculates tax and processes credit card transactions for a specific trip. The receipts can be entered in any currency and include supplementary receipt information. There is an optical archive available for long-term archiving of travel receipts. Travel costs can be divided into different levels: employee, trip destination, and receipt. Expenses can be posted to several account assignment objects such as cost center, order, project, or cost object.

Travel management provides multiple report formats. Receipts can be input in any currency and reports in the native currency. Travel expense accounting provides with self-explanatory forms, statements, and an electronic approval process to improve communications and reduce unnecessary calls to the HR department.

KEY CONCEPT

The integrated functionality of room reservations planning assists in choosing a room with respect to capacity, room design, and available facilities. When a training course is completed, appraisal forms can be automatically issued.

Appraisals can be executed for instructors, attendees, business events, and training courses. Criteria can be defined for every appraisal type.

Price determination, invoice training, and event management automatically determine a price per attendee with respect to required resources. Attendee charges can be calculated internally through SAP R/3 cost accounting and invoiced externally through SAP R/3 sales and distribution.

SAP R/3 Component Integration

SAP R/3 components integrate with e-mail, kiosk, and IVR technologies. These capabilities afford managers and employees access to benefits information from any location, at any time.

KEY CONCEPT

Internal and external communication can be increased. Both the global Internet and company intranet indicate easy data access and exchange. The common graphic web browsers, open standards, and protocols (i.e. TCP/IP) provide the latest information. The R/3 system is the first business application software that provides special Internet functionality for a large number of business processes, including personnel marketing.

The Internet provides the opportunity to advertise vacancies in a company to a large number of potential applicants all over the world. Applicants are then able to execute a general inquiry or be more selective by designating a preferred geographical region.

The application may be executed online by referencing an application form, completing it, and returning it as an e-mail. The application can then be processed automatically in R/3 HR. When applicants are sent their own ID or password via e-mail, they have the option of monitoring the progress of their application. When working on company-internal level, R/3 HR also makes searching for the right contact person simpler, especially in larger organizations.

Benefits Administration Reporting

This component tracks employee changes and investment histories. SAP R/3 HR Benefits Administration offers a variety of standard reports meant for savings plan administration.

HR Organizational Management helps maintain an accurate portrayal of the organization's structure, working with a graphical environment to make it easier to review moves, additions, or changes in employee positions.

HR Payroll Accounting

HR Payroll Accounting Processing makes it possible to keep careful control over payroll requirements and maintain sufficient flexibility to respond to future needs. R/3 HR payroll accounting deals with payroll functions from a global perspective. It is possible to centralize payroll processing or decentralize the data based on country or legal entities. HR Payroll Accounting has options for creating business rules without modifying the existing payroll.

The R/3 payroll accounting date reminder feature provides an online tickler system to notify about transactions due for processing. When the process is completed, an integrated audit trail date stamps the record for future reference. The system automatically produces a history record for every payroll transaction.

Payroll accounting makes it possible to individualize the system to an organization's requirements. When policy or legislative changes happen, the system can be adapted. Payroll accounting offers several standard reports as well as the ability to create reports to meet particular requirements.

HR Payroll Accounting maintains information on employees in a master file shared with all other human resources components. The R/3 system writes payroll data to controlling, financial accounting, and logistics.

HR Time Management

HR Time Management helps simplify administration and evaluation of time data. It assists in administering and evaluating data related to the time employees spend working. This component can assist whether an organization uses centralized or decentralized data to resolve employee working hours.

HR Time Management manages work schedules efficiently and effectively by automating schedule generation and permitting flexible definition of time models and schedules with respect to location and organization level. Time management facilities setting flexible working hours and processes. The time evaluation component stores an organization's business rules and automatically validates hours worked and wage types. Time evaluation results are illustrated on a time sheet that offers a detailed overview of daily balances and time wage types.

Time management review in R/3 HR Time Management offers special transaction abilities created to support time clerks in their daily tasks. It offers both information and tools to review and maintain employee time data. If input data is not correct, an error-handling feature makes the corrections.

Time Management Component

Reports and Analyses in SAP R/3's Time Management component give you several standard reports that assist you in tracking and analyzing employee time with both completeness and accuracy.

Reporting and Analysis features provide the training coordinator with reports on event data ranging from catering requirements to registrant qualifications for each business event. The Reporting feature offers measurements of education and training performance.

Time Evaluation

The time evaluation component allows for daily processing of employee time data. This tool supports complicated evaluation rules to satisfy regulatory requirements and determine overtime and other time-related data.

HR Salary and Benefits Administration

SAP R/3 HR salary administration helps in the salary review process by considering standard salary changes within the company in addition to individual compensation exceptions.

The R/3 HR benefits administration component offers capabilities and flexibility to manage benefits programs effectively for diverse employee populations. Benefits Administration uses a hierarchical structure for the ability and flexibility to add new programs at any time.

The Benefits Administration can maintain an unlimited number of benefits types and individual plans that are offered to employees. It permits establishing benefits groups based on specific employee demographics. The benefits administration component permits definition of eligibility groups and rules based on several factors, as well as the specific variables, rules, and cost formulas for each benefits plan.

Benefits enrollment is used when a company needs options for enrolling employees in benefits programs. Benefits Administration provides real-time processing and the ability to prepare employee specific enrollment forms using any and all employee data.

HR's Benefits Administration, permits an unlimited number of savings plans for employees to consider and allows users to maintain both deferred and non-deferred options in addition to employer-matched and unmatched contributions. This component tracks employee changes and investment histories.

HR Benefits Administration provides you several reports designed for savings plan administration as well as standard reports to assist in administering programs. The component's reporting capabilities make it possible to respond to requests quickly, accurately, and confidently. Benefits Administration allows employees to have direct access to their individual benefits information, so that personnel staff have to deal with fewer time-consuming questions on a daily basis.

Shift Planning

Shift planning facilitates efficient planning of workforce requirements by providing the option of arranging a target plan that can be drafted for any given period. Shifts can be planned with respect to requirements, considering factors including absences because of leave, sickness, and time off.

Shift planning makes it possible to stay informed at all times of staff excess or deficit. It offers a convenient planning board to guide entering and copying of shifts for any designated time period. The plans can be checked at any time against rules dealing with employee working time to detect non-compliance with relevant legislation.

All time data relating to employees is centrally administered by R/3 HR Time Management. As a result, planned working time and short-term changes to the shift plan due to sickness or overtime are relayed directly to the time management component.

Shift planning is beneficial because it facilitates temporarily assigning an employee or employees to another organizational unit, as they are needed. This allows for a temporary change of cost center. Shift planning also permits viewing and printing of plans in Microsoft Excel.

HR Recruitment Component

HR recruitment interfaces with Microsoft Word for Windows to produce standard applicant letters. SAP's office communication facilitates linking to send e-mail messages to internal applicants. SAP offers tools to analyze costs incurred during advertising and interviewing for each open position. The HR recruitment component manages job openings, applications and applicant data, costs, and hiring process.

The recruitment component includes processes for managing open positions/requisitions, applicant screening, selection and hiring, correspondence, reporting, and cost analysis. The component gives direct access to data stored in other components of HR such as personnel administration, payroll, and personnel planning. These links eliminate duplication of data entry and increase productivity.

HR Qualifications

The HR qualifications and requirements/career and succession planning components provide advanced tools to automate the labor-intensive process of matching internal job requirements to qualified candidates.

HR qualifications helps profile predefined tasks and prerequisites of each position in an organization. Qualifications of employees and external candidates under consideration for each position can be profiled. Comparison of qualifications and profiles, helps when selecting individuals for future consideration.

HR Career and Succession Planning

Planning benefits provide improvements in employee performance, employee potential, staff quality, working climate, and employee spirit. HR Career and Succession Planning provides an organization with a method of modeling appropriate career opportunities for employees within the company.

KEY CONCEPT

The education and training programs of R/3 Human Resources make it possible to determine the specific areas where employees need further training. Individual plans can then be drawn up for further education. Detailed information for each of the events is maintained to ease production of event catalogs and schedules.

Training programs and business events are essential components that include tools to maintain information on the internal or external organizers of each event, as well as prerequisites, objectives, content, time schedule, prices, capacity, locations, attendee billing information, and budgets.

Resources such as instructors, rooms, equipment, and course materials can be automatically suggested to save data-entry time.

With the assistance of fast data entry, it is possible to book, rebook, and cancel attendees at very short notice, as well as, check course prerequisites and confirm the availability of attendees.

HR Employee Self-Service

SAP's customary authorization and data security measures also apply to employee self-service components. Employees can access only their own data and require a user ID specified by the system and a personal password. It is possible to specify whether employees can modify their personnel data or be authorized only to view their own data. Changed data can be sent to the human resources department for checking and confirmation.

HR employee self-service components are simple Intranet scenarios that permit employees to display and even update their own personnel data. This means that the HR department no longer has to execute such time-consuming and costly activities as issuing information and maintaining data.

HR staff can now focus efforts on corporate areas of greater strategic value. Employee self-service components also enhance the quality of information at an organization. Employees can check, supplement, and even change their address and dependents data. Employees can check their current leave entitlement and submit leave requests. Using SAP R/3 Business Workflow, these requests can be forwarded directly to the person responsible for authorizing leave.

Employee Self-Service Transactions

Employee self service is a collection of self-service applications to provide access to your HR records using the Internet. Applications available include personal information, time entry, purchase requisition, employee directory, benefits, travel expenses, electronic paystubs, employment/salary verification, and the ability to change a password.

Data Security Measures

SAP's customary authorization and data security measures also apply to Employee Self-Service components. Your employees can only access their own data and require a user ID specified by the system and a personal password.

You can delegate each of your employees to modify their personal data or become authorized to view only their own data. Changed data can be sent to the human resources department for checking and confirmation.

Summary

This chapter provides a solid background in the R/3 human resources management component. The chapter covered HR component performance issues, personnel management and administration, HR benefits administration, and how the HR recruitment interface component functions.

8-1 What is SAP's upgrade policy about?

8-2 Describe the human resource components.

8-3 Explain SAP R/3's modular structure.

8-4 Explain how components can be used.

8-5 Describe SAP R/3's global functionality.

8-6 Describe functionality integration with data networks.

8-7 What does automatic linking do?

8-8 What do financial controlling and analysis capabilities offer?

8-9 What kind of services can R/3 users take advantage of?

8-10 What do service partners do?

8-11 What do international versions involve?

8-12 Can R/3 take advantage of open systems?

8-13 What is the EMU?

8-14 What has SAP done about Year 2000 compliance?

8-15 What kind of performance can be expected for SAP R/3 HR?

8-16 Can R/3 be individualized for an organization? If so, how?

8-17 Explain integrated data administration.

8-18 Explain personnel management.

8-19 Explain personnel administration.

8-20 Explain employee master data.

8-21 What are information types?

8-22 Explain ArchiveLink and what it has to do with optical storage.

8-23 How do personnel and dynamic events play into information screens?

8-24 What do HIS and EIS mean and how do they relate to the HRIS?

8-25 What is involved for personnel management recruitment, management selection, and hiring?

8-26 Can HR Recruitment interface directly with other programs? If so, which program (s)? Give an example.

8-27   Why use automation for the recruitment process?

8-28   What does the recruitment component do?

8-29   Give examples of shared data.

8-30   What can shared data information be used for?

8-31   How can HR travel management be dealt with?

8-32   Describe integration of several R/3 components and subcomponents.

8-33   Who can enter travel data?

8-34   What countries are considered standard for trip provisions?

8-35   What does travel management do?

8-36   Describe the different levels into which travel costs can be divided.

8-37   How are costs reimbursed?

8-38   Does travel management provide multiple report formats? If so, why?

8-39   What exactly does HR travel management make possible?

8-40   Why is integration with several R/3 components and sub-components important?

8-41   In what currency form can receipts be entered?

8-42   How can salary administration be dealt with effectively?

8-43   What exactly does HR salary administration do for you?

8-44   Who is involved in personnel management benefits?

8-45   What does the HR benefits administration component offer?

8-46   How many benefits types and individual plans can be offered to employees with HR's Benefits Administration?

8-47   What does benefits enrollment provide for a company?

8-48   What does plan management do?

8-49   How are the costs associated with each benefits plan option calculated?

8-50   Explain how savings plans relate to HR's benefits administration?

8-51   What does the benefits administration component do?

8-52   Specify the advantages of HR benefits administration.

8-53   What kind of information access capabilities can be expected from HR benefits administration?

8-54   Explain what SAP R/3 components can integrate with.

8-55   Explain the process of salary administration.

8-56   Describe "plan management".

8-57   Explain how savings plans can be implemented for employees with HR's benefits administration.

8-58   Explain "direct access" and how it relates to your employees.

8-59   What is involved in maintaining an accurate portrayal of organizational structure?

8-60   Describe planning features and how they can assist you.

8-61   What can R/3 business workflow do for you?

8-62   Explain how personnel cost planning can be a strategic success factor.

8-63   What can performing cost planning make possible?

8-64   Explain the HR payroll accounting process.

8-65   What does the R/3 payroll accounting date reminder feature do?

8-66   What does payroll account do?

8-67   Explain how integration plays an important role with HR payroll accounting.

8-68   What are the effects of operating in a global environment? What do country-specific versions of R/3 offer?

8-69   Explain the concept of time management.

8-70   How does HR time management deal with work schedules?

8-71   What does the time evaluation component do?

8-72   Explain "time management review".

8-73   What does the time evaluation component do?

8-74   What is the standardized communication channel? How does it relate to time management?

8-75   How does time management relate to reports and analyses?

8-76   What does the shift planning component do?

8-77 Explain the personnel development process.

8-78 What do HR qualifications do?

8-79 How can career and succession planning be effectively executed?

8-80 What are the benefits of career and succession planning?

8-81 What do the reporting analysis features offer?

8-82 Explain SAP's customary authorization and data security methods.

8-83 Explain HR employee self-service components.

8-1 SAP's upgrade policy ensures that a company is technically up-to-date and has constant access to a state-of-the-art business model. Today, many businesses cross boundaries. The R/3 system supports an organization's international needs with country-specific versions of the HR strategic solutions from recruitment to career planning.

8-2 Human resource components offer a flexible structure that allow quick and easy customization of a system to suit individual requirements. When a user logs on in a particular language, screens, messages, and documents appear in the language selected, providing acccss to the system's complete functionality.

8-3 SAP R/3 has set the standard for integrated client/server application software and has a distinct advantage in its modular structure, since is composed of a system which provides the basic elements needed to control and coordinate business application programs.

8-4 Components can be used on their own or in combination with other components. When they are entered, data are maintained centrally and available to all other applications that provide immediate access to any data required.

8-5 R/3's human resources components cover millions of employces around the world, providing support to more than a thousand businesses in over 50 countries in executing a multitude of HR tasks.

8-6 R/3 offers integration of all functions as performance features of SAP software. In the R/3 system, data are immediately relayed where needed.

8-7 Automatic linking between components greatly speeds up and simplifies business procedures. Production planning and control data can flow directly into time management. In addition, results from payroll accounting can be passed on to financial or cost accounting.

8-8 Financial controlling and analysis capabilities provide reliable help in making decisions, allowing immediate introduction of any necessary changes into a business.

8-9 SAP R/3 users can take advantage of consulting and supplementary services offered by individual product providers who work in close cooperation with SAP.

8-10 SAP service partners make certain that consulting and system requirements are met.

8-11 International versions involve business activities that deal with crossing national borders. The R/3 system supports international requirements

SOLUTIONS

with country-specific versions that benefit from different languages and currencies. It also makes provisions for pertinent legal requirements.

8-12   It is possible to install R/3 solutions on a wide variety of hardware platforms using the most advanced operating systems. The open R/3 System environment provides the flexibility to choose the computing platforms and systems that meet individual needs. SAP R/3 was created for open client/server environments, and therefore includes a simple graphical user interface, as well as menu-driven functions that are uniform across all R/3 applications. A three-tiered client/ server structure affords the ability to determine which hardware systems are needed, and to add to the R/3 system without multiplying costs.

8-13   EMU is the European Monetary Union, presenting a technical and organizational challenge that affects nearly all areas of business including accounting, human resources management, and logistics. It requires changes and adjustments. If these modifications are not implemented, they could have a potentially serious effect on the entire data processing system. SAP makes possible an easy transition to the new currency.

8-14   SAP's client/server applications are year-2000 compliant. SAP has made certain to develop its R/3 System with a four-digit year code from the very beginning.

8-15   The R/3 HR components have a high level of performance in several areas, offering easy access to data in a complete and up-to-date fashion.

8-16   The R/3 system can be tailored to suit the specific requirements of an organization. It is possible to add non-SAP functions, develop individualized solutions using R/3 components, or use one of several industry-specific components that supplement R/3 functions.

8-17   Integrated data administration is useful even when tasks are executed locally. Components and subcomponents remain integrated with the rest of the system because all R/3 functions have access to shared central data, eliminating data redundancy and ensuring data integrity.

8-18   Personnel management within SAP R/3 HR incorporates several software components that make it possible to deal with human resources tasks more quickly, accurately, and efficiently. These components can be used not only as part of a company-wide R/3 solution, but as a standalone solution. Non-SAP features can be seamlessly integrated within the R/3 system.

8-19   In personnel administration a global, fully integrated HR data structure can be created. Information is no longer owned by specific departments, but is shared by multiple entities across the organization. This eliminates duplicate entries, reduces the chance for error, and improves data accuracy.

8-20 Employee master data is on SAP R/3 Human Resources centralized database with integration to multiple components for processing employee information. SAP offers tools to save time and help tailor the system to fit individual needs.

8-21 SAP R/3 HR contains information types for storing any desired information about your employees. It is possible to add personalized information types. R/3 HR permits entry of data through the time-saving fast-entry feature, processing data in two modes; online and background.

8-22 Original documents can be scanned into HR for optical storage with SAP's ArchiveLink.

8-23 R/3 has predefined sequences of information screens for various personnel events. This concept can be illustrated with the sequence of screens necessary for processing a new hire or a promotion. The sequences can be tailored to conform to specific business practices.

8-24 Human Resource Information System (HRIS) and Executive Information System (EIS) display graphical information such as organization charts or employee data using the HRIS. HRIS incorporates both standard and customer-defined reports. SAP has condensed vast amounts of HR information into smaller, more meaningful units of data in the EIS. EIS key figures offer an organization information in a quantified and summarized format.

8-25 In personnel management and recruitment management selection and hiring, employee and applicant qualifications are matched with the requirements of the job to select candidates.

8-26 HR recruitment interfaces directly with Microsoft Word for Windows to produce standard applicant letters. SAP's Office Communication link can be used to send e-mail messages to internal applicants. SAP provides tools to analyze costs incurred during advertising and interviewing for each open position. The HR recruitment component permits efficient and effective management of job openings, applications and applicant data, costs, and the hiring process.

8-27 Use automation to hire the right people with the right skills. Reducing the cost of recruiting and hiring new employees is a challenge for the HR professional responsible for placing people in the right job, at the right time, and with the right skills and education. These requirements are fulfilled only through effective automation of the entire recruitment process.

SOLUTIONS

8-28   The recruitment component includes processes for managing open positions/requisitions, applicant screening, selection and hiring, correspondence, reporting, and cost analysis. Open positions effective management of an organization's job openings helps HR recruiters, managers, and interested candidates. The R/3 HR recruitment component allows direct access to data stored in other components of HR such as personnel administration, payroll, and personnel planning. These links eliminate duplication of data entry and increase productivity.

8-29   Shared data related to job openings include: position open date, location and reporting specifics, job descriptions, and skills and education requirements.

8-30   This information can be used for both internal job postings and external advertisements with newspapers, magazines, colleges, or recruitment firms. When a selection has been made and an applicant has been hired, the data gathered during the recruitment process turn into new-hire information, effectively eliminating duplicate data entry and the possible introduction of errors caused by re-entering the data.

8-31   Travel expenses can be easily processed in several currencies and formats. HR travel management permits processing a business trip from start to finish, from dealing with the initial travel request to posting in financial accounting and controlling. This incorporates any subsequent corrections and all retroactive accounting requirements.

8-32   Integration with several R/3 components and subcomponents assures correct posting, taxation, and payment of trip costs.

8-33   Travel data can be entered by the person traveling, by a secretary, or by the relevant department. This can take place either before or after the trip. The entry of a travel request automatically generates a workflow that makes the administrator's work much simpler. Business, employee, and country-specific trip provisions can be implemented via system settings.

8-34   Trip provisions for the following countries are included as standard: Austria, Belgium, Germany, Japan, Netherlands, Switzerland, and USA.

8-35   Travel management automatically calculates the tax. It also automatically processes credit card transactions for a specific trip. The receipts can be entered in any currency and include supplementary receipt information. There is an optical archive available for long-term archiving of travel receipts.

8-36   Travel costs can be divided into different levels: employee, trip destination, and receipt. Expenses can be posted to several account assignment objects such as cost center, order, project, or cost object.

SOLUTIONS

8-37   Costs incurred during a trip are reimbursed through payroll accounting, accounts payable accounting, or by data medium exchange.

8-38   Travel management provides multiple report formats. Receipts can be entered in any currency, with reports printed in native currency. Travel expense accounting provides self-explanatory forms, statements, and an electronic approval process to improve communications and reduce unnecessary calls to the HR department.

8-39   HR travel management permits processing of a business trip from start to finish. It deals with the initial travel request as well as posting in financial accounting and controlling. This incorporates any succeeding corrections as well as all retroactive accounting requirements.

8-40   Integration with several R/3 components and subcomponents assures correct posting, taxation, and payment of trip costs.

8-41   Management provides multiple report formats. Receipts can be entered in any currency and reports printed in the native currency. Travel expense accounting provides self-explanatory forms, statements, and an electronic approval process to increase communications and decrease unnecessary calls to the HR department.

8-42   The process of rewarding employees can be greatly simplified. Administration of salaries is continuous process within the human resources department. It is especially important during the review process when the goal is to justly rewarding good performance.

8-43   SAP R/3 HR Salary Administration assists in the salary review process by considering standard salary changes within the company as well as individual compensation exceptions.

8-44   Personnel management benefits administration provides both flexibility and power for a benefits program.

8-45   As organizations grow, laws change, and employee requirements expand, it is important to have a flexible system to satisfy requirements. The R/3 HR benefits administration component offers capabilities and flexibility to manage benefits programs effectively for diverse employee populations. Benefits administration uses a hierarchical structure that affords the ability and flexibility of adding new programs at any time.

8-46   R/3 HR's benefits administration can maintain an unlimited number of benefits types and individual plans that are offered to employees. Benefits administration allows the establishment benefits groups based on specific employee demographics.

SOLUTIONS

8-47   Benefits enrollment is important when the company needs options for enrolling employees in benefits programs. Benefits administration provides real-time processing that gives the chance to prepare employee-specific enrollment forms using any and all employee data.

8-48   With the benefits administration component, eligibility groups and rules based on several factors can be defined. The specific variables, rules, and cost formulas for each benefits plan can be determined. The types of benefits plans that most closely parallel employee demographics can be designed. SAP provides the tools to maintain plans. Each company must determine the options offered to employees. The benefits administration component provides the framework to administer these options efficiently.

8-49   The costs associated with each benefits plan option are automatically calculated to ensure consistent and accurate reports.

8-50   With HR's benefits administration, it is possible to sustain an unlimited number of savings plans for employees to consider.

8-51   The benefits administration component makes it possible to maintain both deferred and non-deferred options in addition to employer-matched and unmatched contributions. This component tracks employee changes and investment histories.

8-52   SAP R/3 HR benefits administration provides several standard reports designed for savings plan administration.

8-53   R/3 HR benefits administration provides standard reports to assist in administering programs. The component's reporting capabilities assist in responding to requests quickly, accurately, and confidently. Benefits administration allows employees to have direct access to their individual benefits information, obviating the need for time-consuming questions your staff must deal with every day.

8-54   SAP R/3 components integrate with e-mail, kiosk, and IVR technologies. These capabilities provide managers and employees access to benefits information from any location, at any time.

8-55   Administration of salaries is a continuous process within the human resources department. It is especially important throughout the review process when the goal is sufficient reward of good performance. SAP R/3 HR salary administration assists in the salary review process by considering standard salary changes within the organization as well as individual compensation exceptions.

8-56   Plan management utilizes the benefits administration component, permitting definition of eligibility groups and rules based on a wide range of factors. It is possible to determine the variables, rules, and cost formulas for each benefits plan, as well as to design the types of benefits plans that best fit employee demographics.

8-57   HR's benefits administration, makes it possible to maintain an unlimited number of savings plans for employees to consider. The benefits administration component provides the ability to have both deferred and non-deferred options, as well as employer-matched and unmatched contributions. This component also tracks employee changes and investment histories. SAP R/3 HR benefits administration offers a variety of standard reports meant for savings plan administration.

8-58   HR benefits administration offers standard reports to assist in administering programs. The component's reporting capabilities assist in responding to requests quickly, accurately, and confidently. Benefits administration allows employees to have direct access to their individual benefits information, eliminating the need for time-consuming questions that staff must deal with on a daily basis.

8-59   An HR organizational management can assist in maintaining an accurate portrayal of an organization's structure. A graphical environment makes it easier to review moves, additions, or changes in employee positions. It is also possible to create multiple simulations for an organization as ways to execute adjustments in personnel are explored.

8-60   Planning features designed to assist include graphical organization charts, staffing schedules by headcount, percentage, and working hours, job and work center descriptions, and job tasks and descriptions.

8-61   R/3 business workflow offers built-in integration and automatically updates routing paths and other data in workflow as soon as a change in organizational management is executed.

8-62   Personnel cost planning is a strategic success factor for every company. A systematic and forward-looking planning tool considers the final effects of all personnel events. A company will be in a better state of organization, with the ability accurately to forecast personnel costs. These costs provide the management team with a more complete cost picture to assist in making informed decisions.

8-63   R/3 personnel cost planning makes it possible to perform cost comparisons between target and actual personnel costs as well as to create cost previews. Wages, salaries, and other cost elements can be predicted for open and filled positions, based on simulated, planned, or actual payroll figures. In addition, results can be displayed through the R/3 business graphics feature. Another benefit is the standard link to Microsoft Excel, and results can be viewed in a spreadsheet format before they are transferred to SAP R/3 cost accounting as needed.

8-64 Payroll can be processed with SAP R/3 HR payroll accounting. Maintain a careful control over payroll requirements and sufficient flexibility to respond to your future needs. R/3 HR payroll accounting addresses payroll functions from a global perspective. Payroll processing can be centralized, or decentralize, as country or legal entities require. HR payroll accounting affords options to create business rules without modifying the existing payroll.

8-65 The R/3 payroll accounting date reminder feature provides an online tickler system that indicates when transactions are due for processing. When the process is completed, an integrated audit trail date stamps the record for future reference. The system automatically produces a history record for every payroll transaction.

8-66 Payroll accounting provides the ability to individualize the system to the organization's requirements. When policy or legislative changes happen, the system can be adapted. Payroll accounting offers several standard reports as well as the ability to create reports that meet the organization's needs.

8-67 HR payroll accounting maintains information on employees in a master file shared with all other human resources components. The R/3 system writes payroll data to controlling, financial accounting, and logistics.

8-68 Regardless of whether the business operates solely in one country or has expanded to international locations, SAP helps with payroll requirements by offering country-specific versions of R/3 payroll accounting to fulfill language, currency, and regulatory requirements. SAP currently offers solutions for over 20 countries, including Austria, Belgium, France, Germany, Great Britain, Japan, the Netherlands, Switzerland, and the USA and is constantly adding new country-specific solutions.

8-69 Time management helps ease administration and evaluation of time data. HR time management helps administer and evaluate data related to the time employees spend working. This component can be useful whether an organization uses centralized or decentralized data to resolve employee working hours.

8-70 HR time management manages work schedules efficiently and effectively by automating schedule generation and permitting flexible definition of time

SOLUTIONS

models and schedules with respect to location and organization level. Time management makes it possible to set flexible working hours and processes.

8-71 The time evaluation component stores a company's business rules and automatically validates hours worked and wage types. The results of time evaluation can be depicted on a time sheet that offers a detailed overview of daily balances and time wage types.

8-72 Time management review in R/3 HR time management provides special transaction abilities created to support time clerks in their daily tasks. It offers all necessary information and tools to review and maintain employee time data. If incorrect data are input, an error-handling feature makes the corrections.

8-73 The time evaluation component permits daily processing of employee time data. It is a flexible tool designed to support complicated evaluation rules to satisfy regulatory requirements and determine overtime and other time-related data.

8-74 SAP offers a standardized communication channel in time management that is used for connecting to external time-recording systems. An additional communication channel for Plant Data Collection (PDC) indicates that data relevant to HR can be transferred automatically to time management.

8-75 Reports and analyses in SAP R/3's time management component provide several standard reports that assist in tracking and analyzing employee time with both completeness and accuracy.

8-76 Shift planning makes it possible to plan workforce requirements quickly by affording the ability to arrange a target plan that can be drafted for any given period. In addition, shifts can be planned with respect to particular requirements, considering all criteria such as absences because of leave, sickness, and time off. Shift planning makes it possible to stay informed at all times of any staff excess or deficit. It offers a convenient planning board for guidance in entering and copying shifts for any designated period of time. The plans can be checked at any time against rules dealing with employee working time to detect non-compliance with relevant legislation. All time data relating to employees is centrally administered by R/3 HR time management. Therefore, planned working time and short-term changes to the shift plan due to sickness or overtime are relayed directly to the time management component. Shift planning is also advantageous because it enables planners temporarily to assign an employee or employees to another organizational unit where they are needed, with a temporary change of cost center. Shift planning also permits viewing and printing out of plans in Microsoft Excel.

8-77   Personnel development allows choosing the best people and effective fostering of careers. HR qualifications and requirements/career and succession planning components offer advanced tools to automate the labor-intensive process of matching internal job requirements to qualified candidates.

8-78   HR qualifications allow profiling of predefined tasks and the prerequisites of each position in an organization. The qualifications of employees and external candidates under consideration for each position can be profiled. When qualifications and profiles are compared, there is assistance in choosing individuals for further consideration.

8-79   Effective personnel development planning makes it possible to assure that organizational objectives and employee goals are in synch.

8-80   The benefits of planning include improvements in employee performance, employee potential, staff quality, working climate, and employee spirit. HR career and succession planning offers a company a method of modeling appropriate career opportunities for employees within the company.

8-81   Reporting and analysis features offer the training coordinator reports on event data ranging from catering requirements to registrant qualifications for each business event. The reporting feature offers measurements of education and training performance.

8-82   SAP's customary authorization and data security measures also apply to employee self-service components. Employees can only access their own data and require a user ID specified by the system and a personal password. It is possible to designate whether employees can modify their personnel data or are authorized only to view their own data. Changed data can be sent to the human resources department for checking and confirmation.

8-83   HR employee self-service components are simple intranet scenarios that permit employees to display and even update their own personnel data. This means that the HR department no longer has to execute such time-consuming and costly activities as issuing information and maintaining data. HR staff can now focus on their efforts on corporate areas of greater strategic value. Employee self-service components also enhance the quality of information at an organization. Employees can check, supplement, and even change address data, entering data on new family members, or changing existing information on other family members. They can check current leave entitlement and submit leave requests. Using SAP R/3 business workflow, the latter can be forwarded directly to the person responsible for authorizing leave.

CHAPTER 9

ABAP Workbench: Client/Server Application Development

This course is designed for ABAP/4 beginners and application consultants with appropriate IT know-how, who wish to obtain certification as R/3 consultants for the ABAP/4 Development Workbench. Experienced R/3 ABAP/4 Development Workbench consultants can take the certification test without attending the course.

Participants will learn about the ABAP/4 programming language, how to use the ABAP/4 Development Workbench tools to develop their own business applications and to enhance the standard SAP software to meet specific customer requirements.

This course also covers the advantages of the client/server architecture for programming; performance issues; procedures; and special features of development projects.

The course content is presented using documented and process-oriented training examples taken from practical project contexts.

All the examples are structured and documented in such a way that participants can refer to them on the R/3 demo systems at their own companies.

Requirements

- ✎ Sound IT know-how, preferably operating system know-how
- ✎ Experience in another programming language
- ✎ Basic knowledge of graphic user interface (GUI), such as Microsoft Windows

Contents

- ✎ Basic technology overview
  - Architecture
  - Client/server
  - Organizational units
  - Application hierarchy
  - Navigation
  - SSCR (SAP Software Change Registration)
- ✎ ABAP/4 Development Workbench
  - Data Modeler
  - ABAP/4 Dictionary
  - ABAP/4 Language
  - ABAP/4 Editor
  - Screen Painter
  - Menu Painter
  - Debugging and runtime analysis of ABAP/4 programs
  - Workbench Organizer
  - Programs in background processing
  - ABAP/4 Repository Info System
  - CATT (Computer Aided Test Tool)
  - Authorization concept
- ✎ Data transfer, data interfaces
  - Batch input processing
  - RFC interface
  - Asynchronous RFC

- – Buffered data transfer
- – Sequential local files
- – Desktop integration
- – OLE
- ✎ Additional analyses
  - – Reporting
  - – Interactive reporting
  - – ABAP/4 Query
- ✎ Function enhancements
  - – Enhancements to standard software via customer exits
- ✎ Inhouse developments
  - – Basic of online programming
  - – Update concept
  - – Lock concept

Since more and more organizations use client/server technology, the demand for application development tools is rapidly growing. Most IS departments report that the application backlog for corporations is as long as 36 months. This backlog is poison for corporations looking to maintain a competitive business advantage. Investments must offer faster and more productive development.

Companies have three options to address this problem:

1. Purchase packaged software applications
2. Modify packaged applications to meet specific company requirements
3. Use powerful client/server application development tools to develop their own business solutions

However, the majority of IS professionals feel there are few development tools available that meet their needs for power, openness, and flexibility.

SAP offers the ABAP Workbench, a powerful, integrated set of fourth-generation (4GL) client/server development tools (see Figure 9.1). Consisting of the same tools used to develop SAP's R/3 system, the ABAP Workbench allows developers to quickly and easily customize and extend existing SAP applications. This makes it possible to create unique new applications to meet their needs.

ABAP Workbench Information

ABAP stands for Advanced Business Application Programming. It yields increased productivity, makes applications available faster, and reduces both costs and labor. The ABAP workbench is used to develop diverse client/server applications and is a repository-driven development platform designed for client/server applications.

FIGURE 9.1
4GL

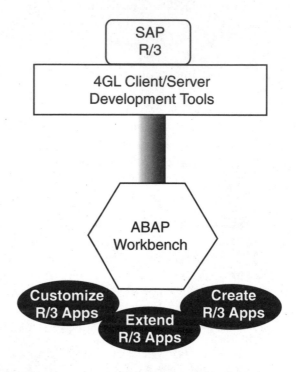

NOTE

 It is important to achieve increased productivity to make your applications operate more quickly, while reducing both costs and labor.

TIP

The application development process is supported by team management and promotion facilities that are needed for complicated client/server development projects.

Applications created with the ABAP workbench can be used with a variety of database systems, networks, operating systems, hardware platforms, and graphical user interfaces.

Integration into client/server architectures is where the ABAP workbench consistently supports distribution of computing power and resources on various levels. Instead of being tied to a single host computer, all developed applications can be distributed to run on multiple applications servers.

The ABAP workbench has the following characteristics:

✎ Flexibility to distribute applications among various servers, resulting in optimization of hardware utilization
✎ Hardware scalability
✎ Portability of applications across different platforms and operating systems
✎ Support for all popular graphical user interfaces
✎ Integration of desktop applications using open RFCs
✎ OLE (Object Linking and Embedding)

The ABAP dictionary makes certain that critical information about development objects is always available. Extensive prototyping capabilities help assure that the finished product is the right product.

The ABAP workbench organizer supports the project's systematic procedure. ABAP developers need not be familiar with the details of a specific technological environment to write applications. ABAP is keyword-oriented, making it easy to read through and understand program code. ABAP also supports prototyping-based program development.

One of most significant advantages of the ABAP workbench is that it permits standardized access to different database systems. Programs can be developed and maintained independently of the underlying relational database.

Database Operations

It is possible to transfer data records between application programs; the database is coordinated by the database interface on the basis of definitions stored in the ABAP dictionary. Database access operations are based on SQL.

Libraries of reusable program and business function modules help you speed and streamline the developer work. Both modules and programming assist you in managing and documenting modules that are in the library that are easy to identify and incorporate into other programming projects. These modules can be used in homogeneous SAP environments. Otherwise, they can be called by external applications.

Remote Function Calls (RFCs) allow ABAP function modules to be accessed from applications such as Microsoft Excel and Access, or Lotus 1-2-3. Therefore, data can be taken from the R/3 System and integrated into a spreadsheet to permit PC application users to benefit from R/3 functions without straying from their PC interface.

Developers can use their own modules and store them in the library for future use. Teamwork Application development is carefully coordinated and documented to make certain you have a successful collaborative effort. Developers can also create their own modules and store them in the library for future use.

The Workbench Organizer supports the project's systematic procedure. The version manager administers all development objects, as well as all associated corrections and changes. All versions can be reactivated at any time. The promotion system handles moving development objects and applications into test or productive operation.

Using ABAP, developers do not need to be familiar with the details of a specific technological environment to write applications. ABAP is keyword-oriented, so it is easy to read through and understand program code. In addition, ABAP supports prototyping-based program development.

The ABAP Workbench is advantageous because it gives you standardized access to different database systems. As a result, programs can be developed and maintained independently from the underlying relational database. Transfer of data records between application programs and the database is coordinated by the database interface on the basis of definitions stored in the ABAP Dictionary.

Database access operations are based on SQL. Fourth Generation Language ABAP is a high-level 4GL, meaning it works well for developing business applications.

ABAP Workbench

ABAP supports structured programming, and the syntax of the language enables programmers to deal with mission-critical client/server application needs. The ABAP workbench is used by experienced professionals who are concerned with issues such as tool integration and ergonomics.

ABAP Workbench facilitates programming by providing useful navigation and organization tools and standardizing access to all development objects and tools. Methods and utilities for accessing data, programming communications, and implementing GUIs and an extensive library of reusable ABAP modules are all contained in the ABAP workbench.

A program editor is integrated into the environment of the ABAP workbench. This editor permits text operations (i.e., syntax check with automatic correction facility). The structured outline view of the editor makes it possible to collapse or expand syntactical blocks. The user gains a good overview of the overall application structure.

The ABAP workbench is essentially a collection of sophisticated development tools. The browser tool lists all development objects with respect to a relaxed project management model, while the navigator launches any development object and activates the associated tool.

The R/3 Repository is a central storage facility for all development objects such as the ABAP modules, screens, ABAP Dictionary objects, data models, and authorizations.

The R/3 Repository Information System is used to evaluate this data, and determine where it is used. Developer teams working on objects can use the R/3 Repository simultaneously. An open repository interface guarantees that even with non-SAP tools, users can process all repository objects.

The ABAP Dictionary

The ABAP dictionary is an integrated component of the ABAP workbench. It has a central reference point for developers and manages all application-related meta-data including table definitions, internal structures, foreign key relationships views, conversion rules, and online help information. In addition, the integration of the ABAP dictionary with other development tools ensures that all tools can access common meta-data and retain global consistency. Any changes made in the ABAP dictionary are effective within all applications concerned. Enhancements to the ABAP dictionary enable users to attach fields to tables and structures in the customer system without changing the original.

The Report Builder is composed of a powerful interactive list processing and reporting tool, as well as a graphical query product. The list processing facility makes reporting simple. Reports can be stored hierarchically, in a tree structure.

The ABAP Query is a graphical tool that allows users to execute quick and simple database calculations. The result is that it allows you to focus on other tasks, including very complex data queries.

Other Workbench Features

The ABAP Workbench can be used to create applications and user interfaces in a number of different languages. It has the ability to work with international capabilities that permit multi-byte code pages (such as Kanji and Mandarin) to be supported.

In addition to OLE (Object Linking and Embedding), open Remote Function Calls (RFCs) are used to control function module calling and programs across system boundaries that communicate with external systems. RFCs can be used to establish asynchronous communication links. Furthermore, it is possible to operate user dialogs within modules called by an RFC. Integrated correction and transfer systems as well as version managers help you meet the needs of both centralized and distributed development.

Because of automatic version management, all changes and newly developed objects are coordinated so that they can be accessed at any given time. Complete information can be called up about all corrections and transfers made. Furthermore, all versions and releases are administered so that developed applications can be easily revised.

A Debugger helps locate and correct errors in application logic or data handling. It also offers you insights into the application runtime patterns and performance of individual modules, and helps keep track of the use of program parts, variables, and type conversions.

CATT (Computer Aided Test Tool) is an integrated facility of the ABAP Workbench that allows you to comprehensively test software quality. It creates and automates business processes in test procedures that you can repeat as often as you like. Each test procedure generates a detailed log.

The ABAP workbench possesses a library of reusable program modules. Business function modules and programming aids are managed and documented in the library. They are easy to identify and integrate into new development projects. Developers can create and store their own modules for future use. There is also an interactive test tool used for checking the functions and runtime requirements of modules. This can save years of programming time.

There are monitoring tools in the ABAP workbench that create precise resource and performance data. Applications are optimized from extensive runtime analyses and evaluations. Utilities like SQL Trace and ABAP Trace assist in performance optimization.

Trace

The SQL trace facility produces performance statistics for the Processing of SQL statements. In fact, you can enable and disable the SQL trace facility for all sessions through the initialization parameter called SQL_TRACE.

Whenever you start a session, you can either enable or disable the SQL trace facility with respect to this parameter's value. It is also possible for you to enable or disable the SQL trace facility for your session with the SQL_TRACE option of the ALTER SESSION command.

The ABAP workbench can be used for modifying or individually enhancing standard R/3 applications. It can also develop individual solutions separate from SAP standard software with an integrated, professional toolkit.

ABAP offers a structured training plan in combination with a detailed online help function that makes it simpler to work productively. There are specific advantages to using its user-friendly tools, intuitive GUI, and extensive navigation capability.

It is important to note that ABAP is completely platform-independent. It supports all high-end operating systems, databases, and front ends. This assures that investments are protected. Applications created on one platform run on others. This means that if a company wishes to, it can change its hardware.

Object-Oriented Programming

SAP uses object technology from a business perspective when creating enterprise business systems. The main focus is on the design and implementation of business processes based on business objects. SAP offers a comprehensive business-driven approach with the business framework. After developing object-oriented solutions for modeling, interfacing, and workflow in earlier R/3 releases, SAP has enhanced to ABAP in Release 4.0 to permit object-oriented programming.

Reusability of program components is supported by business-oriented modeling tools. The incorporation of object-oriented concepts into ABAP is advantageous because each object has its own well-defined interface. The internal structure is hidden and modifications can be made without affecting other program components.

SAP's object strategy is based on Business Objects and deals with modeling, programming, interfacing, and workflow. SAP uses principles such as encapsulation, inheritance, and polymorphism.

The object-oriented extensions of ABAP support real object-oriented development. Therefore, you see improvements in the areas of reusability, maintenance, and quality of code.

SAP's object approach has advantages from their customers' investments in existing business processes, functionality, and data. SAP uses object technology when creating enterprise business systems. The main focus is on the design and implementation of business processes based on business objects.

SAP supports object strategy and provides a comprehensive business-driven approach with the Business Framework. After developing object-oriented solutions for modeling, interfacing, and workflow in earlier R/3 releases, SAP's enhancements to ABAP in Release 4.0 makes object-oriented programming easier. Programmers benefit from the enhancements made to ABAP through increased productivity with both high quality and easier code maintenance.

Application developers are most productive when they are able to focus their efforts on solving the application problem itself as opposed to other aspects of program development. The incorporation of object-oriented concepts into ABAP moves the language a step closer to this goal.

NOTE

Each object has a well-defined interface that can only be accessed through this interface. This hides the internal structure and permits modifications to be made without affecting other program components.

Object Attributes

Reusing both designs and program components becomes simpler when object-oriented enhancements to ABAP permit the development of object-oriented frameworks. An object component is designated as public, protected, or private. Objects have attributes. These describe the current state of the object.

Object Interaction

Object Behavior

Object behavior is determined from it's individual operations. A *method* allows for you to implement an operation for a given object.

NOTE

Various objects may have different methods for the same operation.

When either a request or message is sent to an object, that object sends both a specific method and message to another object. Messages are used for object interaction, whereas methods are executed as a reaction to a message. Methods are usually the only interface through which you can communicate with an object.

The attributes of an object can be directly manipulated. However, this manipulation relies on the type of encapsulation a system offers. In some systems, methods must be offered to either get or set attribute values.

ABAP Objects

ABAP objects are an object-oriented extension of SAP's ABAP/4 language and run-time engine. It provides a new extended virtual machine (VM) capable of running both new applications implemented by ABAP objects as well as all existing ABAP/4 applications.

RFCs

Remote function calls (RFCs) provide an alternative way to access R/3 business logic on a more in-depth level. Developers usually use RFCs whenever BAPIs are not available. The problem with RFCs, however, is that unlike BAPIs future releases of R/3 may not support all current RFCs.

Objects interact with each other in three very specific ways:

1. **Direct data access**—An object has direct read and write access to the visible attributes of other objects.
2. **Calling a method directly**—When a method is called directly, a unique object (the server or supplier) is called and this object is known to the calling object (the client).
3. **The publish-subscribe mechanism**—If an event is raised while a method is being executed, all objects currently registered as interested in this event (the subscribers) will be informed of it.

Subclasses and Superclasses

The objects that are the property of a class are also defined as instances of the class. A new class is defined as a specialization of an existing class. A more specialized class is defined as a *subclass*, while a more generalized class is called a *superclass*. Furthermore, any statements that are true for the outward behavior of the superclass are also true for the subclass.

All of the public attributes and methods of the superclass will also be found in the subclass. In addition, there will be the same semantics valid in both subclass and superclass. Subclasses achieve implementations of all the superclass methods, though these methods may be overridden within the subclass.

The definition of a class holds the specifications of the interfaces and the structure of the objects in that class. Two objects that have the same interface may be treated identically by clients even though each may have been implemented differently.

ABAP offers the "interface construct" for this purpose. The use of this construct means that two objects may offer a common interface even though they do not have a common superclass. A client can treat two objects that have the same interface similarly without forcing both objects to be instances of the same superclass. The definition of a class can determine if the class implements one or more interfaces.

A method body is essentially the implementation of a method. It must be specified for each method contained in the interface whenever a class is implemented. Classes that implement a composite interface must provide implementations for each interface it contains.

ABAP provides an interface so that two objects may offer a common interface even though they do not have a common superclass. A client can treat two objects that have the same interface the same way, without forcing both objects be instances of the same superclass.

Attributes can have one of the data types available in the existing ABAP language as well as a new object or interface reference type. Attributes are variables that are local to the object and are therefore not normally visible from the outside.

Attributes can be made visible so that they can be used from the outside as variables. The components of an object that are only visible within a class definition are designated as private.

Virtual Attributes

Components of objects visible in the definitions of the direct and indirect subclasses are designated as protected, while all other components are public. Virtual attributes, however, can be accessed analogously to normal attributes, though the implementing class can use an access method instead of making a direct attribute access.

When virtual attributes are used, it is possible to defer the decision on whether attribute accesses should be replaced by access routines until later. Furthermore, changes need not be made to all the program components that access the attributes concerned.

Virtual attributes in ABAP make it possible to determine at runtime whether the current value of an attribute is valid. If the value is valid, it can be accessed directly. If it is not, it must be recalculated by a method call.

Class Attributes

Class attributes can be specified as public, protected or private, READ-ONLY, and/or virtual analogously to instance attributes. A method permits operations to be performed on a particular instance of a class. It can read and change the state including all attributes such as public, protected, private, and READ-ONLY attributes.

NOTE

Class methods are methods that can only access class attributes.

Methods do not access the instance-specific attributes, however they can be used even when no instance of this class has been created yet or if no instance is known. Analogous to instance-specific methods, class methods can be declared as public, protected, or private.

When an event is raised, other actions can occur as a consequence of the event. A consequence of an event may include a given process that is started or when other events are raised. Examples of events include: changes in the state of an object (i.e. "posting cancelled") or the creation of a new object such as "new account created" that are known to all other interested objects.

Attributes defined for a class are those that are common to all the instances of both the class and all its subclasses.

ABAP allows constants to be designated as common to all the instances of a class. Methods, much like function modules, have parameters so that they can pass back a return value. Methods are also used to determine how objects handle events.

Events in Detail Events are characterized as occurring at a specific time. When an event is raised, other things can occur as a consequence.

Objects in ABAP can raise events. Other objects can react to these events in an appropriate way. An object that raises an event does not guess about the number of objects that will handle the event, when they will do so or how. The raising object does not know which objects will handle the event. This means that the event concept of ABAP must be distinguished from a callback concept where exactly one object is expected to react in a specific way. Before an object is in a position to react to the events raised by another object, at least one of its methods needs to be registered as an event-handling method for that object.

The Callback Concept

The callback concept is used to attach application-specific functions to a given product. Whenever a product is activated by the user, a callback function that has been registered by the application is executed. The callback function can be used to influence the user interface or to execute application tasks.

Callbacks are composed of two phases. The first is called the callee (the application) registers a callback function to the caller. During this phase, the callee is in control of program execution. The registration function terminates and execution of the callee program continues. The second phase consists of an execution control that has been passed to the caller, the callee's function is activated by an object that belongs to the caller.

The benefits of this feature of the callback concept includes the proper data and control separation of both the caller and callee. All information that needs to be passed within the callee from callback registration to callback execution (the client_data) is shielded from the caller's point of view.

The callback concept is similar to the Action routines. This concept is not confined to the user interface. It can be generalized and applied wherever an event-driven interface between software modules is needed.

Event-Handling Methods

The user can act on a component just by choosing it or pressing the Return key to create an Event object. The event-handling system passes the Event up the Component hierarchy and allows each component the opportunity to react to the event before platform-dependent code can implement or process it completely.

Each Component's event handler can react to an event by ignoring the event and allowing it to be passed up the Component hierarchy such as default component implementation. Whenever an event is intercepted, it is possible to stop it from being processed further. Should an invalid character be entered in a text field, an event handler may stop the Event from propagating upward. Furthermore, the platform-dependent implementation of the text field would never see the event.

From the component's perspective, the event-handling system is similar to an event-filtering system. Platform-dependent code produces an event, however components have the opportunity to modify, react to, or intercept the event before the platform-dependent code completely processes the event.

An Event Object includes the type of the event (i.e. key press or mouse click). The object (event objective) has a timestamp indicating when the event occurred, the location where the event occurred, the key that was pressed, an arbitrary argument, and the state of modifier keys.

You can implement an Event Handler just by realizing that the Component class defines many event-handling methods and you can override any of them. With the exception of the all-purpose method (handleEvent()), each event-handling method can be used for only one particular type of event.

However, instead of using the all-purpose method, you can use the override event-handling method that's specific to the type of event you need to handle. This method tends to have less unintended side effects.

When this type of an event occurs, the event-handling method that matches the event type is called. Specifically, the Event is first passed to the handleEvent() method that calls the appropriate method for the event type. All the event-handling methods have at least one argument (the Event) and return a boolean value.

An event-handling method may be registered for the events of a single object, multiple individual objects, all instances of a class, or all instances that implement a certain interface. This method may be registered for the events of a single object, multiple individual objects, all instances of a class, or all instances that implement a certain interface.

Should an object wish at any time to stop handling the events raised by another object, it can cancel the registrations of its methods. If the object raises an event, each event-handling method that registered for this kind of event is informed. Should there be several handling methods registered for the event, the order in which they are processed is determined by the system.

Event-handling methods can also be called directly to inform a non-registered object that an event has been raised so that the object can handle the event as if it had received the event directly, and to allow the raising of events to be reproduced. Events can have parameters as methods do.

Event-handling methods can determine the object that raised the event. Classes in a system will often require several objects that possess the same attributes and methods and can raise the same events. Class descriptions contain the declarations of both the public and the private components of the objects and specify their implementation.

Class definitions possess specifications of the attributes and methods of the individual instances and also of the class attributes and class methods. They describe events that can be raised by instances of the class and the interfaces that can be used to provide access to the instances. They also specify events that can be handled by instances of the class.

Classes can be declared as subclasses of other classes. Even though it is possible to define class attributes and class methods, classes are not designated as objects with an existence of their own nor can they be referenced as objects. Classes are therefore not instances of meta-classes.

A class can implement at least one interface. All objects that implement the same interfaces can be treated identically by clients, regardless of the class to which they belong; a client can access all these different classes by the same type of interface reference.

A class can also be declared as a subclass of another class. Although it is possible to define class attributes and class methods, classes cannot be seen as objects. Therefore, classes are not instances of meta-classes. The methods of a subclass do not have access to the private methods and attributes that are defined in a superclass—unless the superclass specifically permits this form of access. The superclasses of a class includes both the direct superclass as well as all the indirect superclasses.

The subclasses of a class includes all the direct subclasses and all of their subclasses. All the pertinent properties including the meaning and types of the attributes, parameters, and events are defined by the superclass. Subclasses are also able to define additional attributes, methods, and events as well as support additional interfaces. The components of subclasses live in the same name space as the components of their superclasses. This means that once a name has been used for a public (or protected) component in a superclass, it cannot be used again in a subclass.

The smallest unit of encapsulation is the class, but not the object. This means that all methods defined in a class can use the private attributes and methods of all the instances of the class, but not just those of the current instance.

Generalization and Specialization ABAP allows classes to be declared as direct subclasses of a class that are already defined such as their direct superclass.

Subclasses can syntactically be used like any of their superclasses. The implementation of the subclass must guarantee that the subclass also functions like a special case of the superclass (semantic specialization).

Naming conflicts can not occur between identically named attributes and methods in different interfaces even if a class implements several of these interfaces. As a result, each class can support any number of interfaces at any time, without changing the clients of this class to resolve name conflicts.

Sometimes two classes need to cooperate so closely, that it is convenient to allow one class to access another class's private components. This special relationship is designated as the friend concept, which must be agreed upon by both classes.

Friendship relationships are directed relationship. This means that if class A gives friendship to class B, so that B gains access to it's private components, it doesn't follow that class B has to offer friendship to class A.

Interfaces

An interface reference only illustrates the components defined directly in that interface. Implementing an interface involves defining a method body for each method contained in the interface. If a class implements composite interfaces then it must implement the interfaces contained in the composite interfaces. The attributes defined in the interface are automatically added to the instances of the class that implements these interfaces.

Each interface and class definition has a separate name space for components (attribute, method and event definitions). If classes implement interfaces, the name spaces of the implemented interfaces are not incorporated in the name space of the class, so that the components of the implemented interfaces do not automatically appear at the top level as components of the class.

An interface permits objects to be used independently of their implementation. Common aspects of the interfaces of two objects can be expressed even when objects do not have a common superclass. As opposed to class definitions, interface definitions do not contain an implementation section. An interface definition only describes the interaction possible with an object of any class that supports the interface.

Only public components of objects can be specified in interface definitions: public attributes, public methods, and the events that the object can raise.

Interfaces are usually created in a bottom-up fashion by using existing protocols and standardizing similar interfaces. A development always starts with small interfaces, so that there will be a frequent need to define new higher interfaces that integrate existing interfaces.

ABAP provides a method of defining hierarchy and abstraction in interfaces. An interface can contain other interfaces and also add to them by defining its own attributes, methods, and events. The attributes, methods and events specific to this interface form a separate interface that supplements the contained interfaces.

An interface contains other interfaces as components (i.e. is a composite interface). This allows arbitrary interface hierarchies to be defined.

Composite Interfaces

A class that implements a composite interface also has to implement all the interfaces this composite interface contains. Each interface has a separate name space for its components. If interfaces contain other interfaces, the name spaces of the contained interfaces are not part of the name space of the composite interface.

Note that in ABAP, the extension of interfaces is achieved by making the extending interface contain the original interface and map all its components under the same name in its own name space using aliases. A class implementing a new interface must implement the bodies for the new methods.

Clients can use the old and new components uniformly through the one new interface. This permits a gradual migration of clients and implementers of interfaces.

Interface References

At any point where an interface reference variable is defined, an interface name must be specified. All objects that can be referenced by these variables must have implemented this kind of interface. ABAP allows the creation of reference variables that can reference arbitrary objects. The contents of any other reference variable can be assigned to them.

Objects are always created both explicitly and dynamically. The class of the object has to be specified either explicitly or implicitly. A reference is returned to the creator, and this can then be used to access the newly created object. An object with an encapsulated internal state can guarantee its own consistency and must be true from the moment it is created.

ABAP offers a "constructor method" for every class. This method is automatically designated by the system when the object is being created; it has the task of initializing the object. There is only one constructor for each class, a special method whose parameters can be set. Any mandatory parameters must be supplied when an object is being created.

The Runtime System

There entity called the runtime system makes certain that no object is deleted if there is still a valid reference to the object anywhere in the program. When there are no more references to the object, then the system can delete the object. This procedure assures that invalid references do not happen. The system, by itself, is responsible for deciding when an object should be deleted.

At any point at which an interface is defined, the common client-visible aspects of two objects can be expressed, even though the objects do not have a common superclass. A class definition can determine the class implements of one or more interfaces.

Finally, the class itself must designate a method body for each of the interfaces' methods. Interfaces can contain other interfaces. Classes that implement a composite interface must also implement all contained interfaces.

ABAP allows interfaces to be extended and thus further developed by adding more attributes, methods and events. This means that existing program components need not be modified unnecessarily. Objects do not have to be deleted explicitly. Instead, the runtime system offers a garbage collection mechanism.

Summary

In Chapter 6 we discussed several important issues in the ABAP work-bench—from the 4GL programming language to the R/3 repository. We explored crucial components and architectural advantages that will appear on the SAP certification exam.

We learned how mission-critical applications can run cross-platform. This chapter stressed SAP's object strategy. Use of object technology will be prevalent in R/3 release 4.0, and will play an important role in the way business is conducted in the future.

The knowledge gained from sales and distribution can be applied to Chapter 10, dealing with the business framework, the enterprise and specific details on employees, client information, and Internet strategies.

9-1   What does the acronym ABAP stand for?

9-2   How can a good development environment pay off in several ways? Name them.

9-3   ABAP Workbench is a software tool that permits the power, versatility and flexibility necessary to create what?

9-4   Define ABAP Workbench.

9-5   Explain what SAP delivers.

9-6   Describe specifically where front-end applications can communicate and exchange data with ABAP programs.

9-7   Describe the components of ABAP Workbench.

9-8   Explain the advantages of this architecture are.

9-9   In detail, explain how ABAP Workbench's tools support the whole development cycle to produce a more effective use of development talent.

9-10   Describe how reusable program and business function models assist in speeding and refining a developer's work.

9-11   How do Remote Function Calls (RFCs) assist the developer's work?

9-12   Explain teamwork application development.

9-13   How can Workbench Organizer support a project?

9-14   What does a version manager administer?

9-15   Do ABAP developers need to be familiar with the details of a specific technological environment in order to write applications?

9-16   Does ABAP Workbench offer standardized access to different database systems? If so, how?

9-17   Are the unique features of the database system the main concern of the developer?

9-18   How is the transfer of data records between applications programmers and the database coordinated?

9-19   On what protocol are database access operations based?

9-20   What type of programming does ABAP support?

9-21   Who uses the ABAP workbench?

9-22   What does the user interface builder screen painter do?

QUESTIONS

9-23 How does ABAP Workbench speed programming?

9-24 Explain what the screen painter does.

9-25 Explain what the program editor does.

9-26 Explain the browser tool and what it does.

9-27 Explain what the navigator does.

9-28 What benefits does the combination of the browser and navigator tools offer?

9-29 Explain in detail the ABAP R/3 repository.

9-30 What can developers use the R/3 repository information system for?

9-31 What does an open repository interface guarantee?

9-32 Describe what the ABAP dictionary is.

9-33 What benefits are there to integrating the ABAP dictionary with other development tools?

9-34 How quickly do changes in the ABAP dictionary become effective in all concerned applications?

9-35 Explain what the report builder does.

9-36 What is the ABAP query tool?

9-37 Can ABAP Workbench work in other languages? If so, explain.

9-38 Name two mechanisms that use interprogram communications.

9-39 Describe a method used for calling function modules and programs across system boundaries and to communicate with external systems.

9-40 What does the repository infosystem show?

9-41 What systems are essential to help meet the requirements of centralized distributed development?

9-42 Explain why a debugger is useful.

9-43 What is a function library?

9-44 What does a performance monitor do?

9-45 Define CATT and explain in detail what it does.

9-46 Explain what ABAP Workbench is designed for.

KEY CONCEPT

The ABAP Workbench enhances productivity and the economic viability of development work. Professional Fourth-Generation Language, SAP's development, is based on the business-oriented language, ABAP. The strengths of this fourth-generation language are derived from its high performance and flexibility. Its prototyping functionality offers maximum programming support. The ABAP Workbench contains a multitude of powerful, integrated development tools that provide support throughout the development process.

The ABAP Workbench makes certain that all the development work is carried out properly, easily, and error-free. Changes to objects are precisely documented and registered. Version management also makes it possible to track and compare changes, and reactivate previous versions.

9-47 How does SAP support open communication?

9-48 What are some factors that make ABAP easy to use?

9-49 What does the ABAP Workbench support?

9-50 Can applications run cross-platform?

9-51 What is SAP's Object Strategy?

9-52 Explain SAP's Object Strategy.

9-53 Describe SAP's approach towards objects.

9-54 Explain how business objects reflect SAP Business Goals.

9-55 Describe how SAP uses object technology.

9-56 Explain SAP's approach to Business Framework.

9-57 Explain how the reusability of program components can improve both quality and productivity.

9-58 How does the incorporation of object-oriented concepts into ABAP help application developers?

9-59 Can any object be accessed by different interfaces?

9-60 Can an implementation be facilitated through reuse?

KEY CONCEPT

Interfaces to standards such as OLE/DCOM and CORBA become easier to use and to develop. It is now very simple to develop SAP Business Objects and support SAP Business Workflow for future GUI developments. Object-oriented enhancements help ABAP contribute to the SAP's object strategy. The next section illustrates the programming model of ABAP with objects, without referring to the syntax. It offers the basic information necessary for developing object-oriented applications with ABAP.

In order more fully to explain object-oriented concepts, we deal with an object as central to object-oriented development. The concept of objects is such that the entities involved in a problem should be represented as far as possible one-to-one by objects in a given solution. An object is a self-contained entity having a state, a behavior, and an identity. Because objects are self-contained entities, many of their aspects are not visible from the outside. This is why we must distinguish between the outer view and the inner view of an object.

9-61   What factor determines whether an object component is designated public, protected, or private?

9-62   What describes the behavior of an object?

9-63   Explain how ABAP objects can raise and handle events.

9-64   Explain, in detail, how objects can interact with each other.

9-65   Define "Class."

9-66   Define the objects that are property of a class.

9-67   Define a "New Class."

9-68   How is a more specialized class defined?

9-69   How is a more generalized class defined?

9-70   What factors are prevalent in terms of the behavior of the answers from the previous two questions?

9-71   What happens if two objects have the same interface?

9-72   What has to be specified for each method contained in an interface during the implementation of a class?

9-73   What must classes that implement a composite interface provide for all contained interfaces?

9-74   Explain how objects can possess attributes that contain information about their internal state?

9-75   Is it ever appropriate to make certain attributes visible?

9-76   Define protected and public components.

9-77   Explain where protected and public components are visible.

9-78   How can public attribute be flagged?

9-79   How can virtual attributed be accessed?

9-80   Using the response to the previous question, determine if virtual attributes can be references with field symbols or passed as reference parameters to a routine.

9-81   What special abilities do virtual attributes provide in ABAP?

9-82   Describe "lazy evaluation."

9-83   Can class attributes be defined for a class?

9-84   Describe how class attributes can be specified.

9-85   Does ABAP allow constants to be defined for all instances of a class?

9-86   Does a method operate on any given instance of a class?

9-87   How are methods similar to function modules?

9-88   How is a method in a class uniquely identified?

9-89   What are class methods?

9-90   Can these methods be used if no instance of a class has been created?

9-91   How are class methods defined?

9-92   Can class methods raise events?

9-93   What identifying factor is representative of events?

9-94   Give an example that describes what can happen as the direct result of a given event.

9-95   What is the connection between objects in ABAP and events?

9-96   Explain what an event-handling method can be registered for.

9-97   What happens if an object wants to stop handling the events raised by another object?

9-98   What happens if an object wants to raise an event?

9-99   Explain how to determine the order in which several handling events are handled by your system.

9-100   Can event-handling methods be called directly? If so explain how this is accomplished.

9-101   Explain why objects are defined in classes instead of by any other means.

9-102   What does a class description contain?

9-103   Explain the specification that a class contains.

9-104   Can a class be declared as a subclass of another?

9-105   What is the smallest unit of encapsulation?

9-106   The methods of a subclass do not have access to _____ and _____ unless _____ specifically permits this form of access.

KEY CONCEPT

This concept gives the options of informing more than one event-handling method that an event has been raised and allows events be processed asynchronously. These parameter restrictions may be eased in the future for events for which there is always just one event-handling method, or when synchronous handling is desired.

This method is different from that of Smalltalk 80, where a method has access to the private attributes of the current server only and to the public attributes of all other objects.

9-107   Explain what two items permit ABAP classes to be declared as direct subclasses of a class that has already been defined.

9-108   What does a superclass of a class include besides the direct superclass?

9-109   Explain the connection between superclass supported interfaces and subclass supported interfaces.

9-110   What can be overridden in subclasses?

9-111   What makes certain that access is possible to methods that have been redefined?

9-112   Describe what subclasses are able to define in order to support additional interfaces.

9-113   Explain how classes can implement interfaces.

9-114   What can language guarantee?

9-115   How can naming conflicts and aliasing be avoided?

9-116   Give an example of how to avoid a naming conflict.

9-117   What is the "friend concept?"

9-118   Explain the friendship relationship.

9-119   Define an interface.

9-120 How can interfaces be combined?

9-121 What is a composite interface?

9-122 Must each component have a separate name space?

9-123 Explain what it means to have extended interfaces.

9-124 How does ABAP accomplish the extension of interfaces?

9-125 Describe how references relate to objects and interfaces.

9-126 Explain what is involved in copying reference variables.

9-127 Describe specific types of reference variables.

9-128 Must an interface name be specified when defining an interface reference variable?

9-129 Can arbitrary objects be referenced?

9-130 Explain the object life-cycle.

9-131 What is the "constructor method"?

9-132 Can a subclass override the constructor that it inherits?

9-133 Explain object storage management.

9-134 What does the runtime system do?

9-135 Is there currently a way to use language for special methods executed before an object is deleted?

9-136 How can local and global classes and interfaces be defined?

9-137 How can local classes be defined?

9-138 What happens when you define an interface?

9-139 What must the class itself define?

9-1 ABAP stands for Advanced Business Application Programming.

9-2 A good development environment pays off by:

- Yielding increased productivity
- Making applications available faster
- Reducing costs and labor.

9-3 It is used to develop diverse client/server applications.

9-4 It is a repository-driven development platform designed for client/server applications.

9-5 SAP provides a completely open development environment. Regardless of what systems are used for the actual programming work, applications constructed with the ABAP Workbench can be used with a broad range of database systems, networks, operating systems, hardware platforms, and graphical user interfaces.

9-6 The entire development process is supported by team management and promotion facilities necessary for complicated client/server development projects.

9-7 Integration into client/server architectures is where the ABAP Workbench consistently supports distribution of computing power and resources on various levels. Instead of being tied to a single host computer, all developed applications can be distributed to run on multiple applications servers.

9-8 The advantages of ABAP Workbench are:

- Flexibility to distribute applications among various servers resulting in optimization of hardware utilization
- Hardware scalability
- Portability of applications across different platforms and operating systems
- Support for all popular graphical user interfaces
- Integration of desktop applications using Open RFCs (Remote Function Calls, see Figure 9.2)
- OLE (Object Linking and Embedding).

9-9 The ABAP Dictionary ensures that critical information about development objects is always available. Extensive prototyping capabilities help make certain that the finished product is the right product.

9-10 A library of reusable program and business function modules helps speed and streamline the work of developers. The modules and programming aids managed and documented in the library are easy to identify and incorpo-

SOLUTIONS

rate into other programming projects. They can be used in homogeneous SAP environments, or they can be called up by external applications.

9-11   The assistance of Remote Function Call (RFC) allows ABAP function modules to be accessed from applications such as MS-Excel, MS-Access, or LOTUS 1-2-3. In this way, data can be taken from the R/3 System and integrated, for example, into a spreadsheet, enabling PC application users to take advantage of R/3 functions without ever having to venture outside of the familiar PC interface.

9-12   Developers can create their own modules and store them in the library for future use. Teamwork application development is carefully coordinated and documented to make certain of a successful collaborative development effort.

FIGURE 9.2
Remote Function Calls

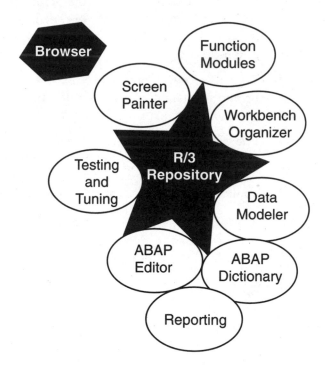

9-13   The workbench organizer supports the project's systematic procedure.

9-14   A version manager administers all development objects and associated corrections and changes. All versions can be reactivated at any time. The promotion system takes care of moving development objects and applications into test or productive operation.

9-15   No! With ABAP, developers do not need to be familiar with the details of a specific technological environment, to write applications. (See Figure

9.3.) ABAP is keyword-oriented, making it easy to read through and understand program code. Most important, ABAP supports prototyping-based program development.

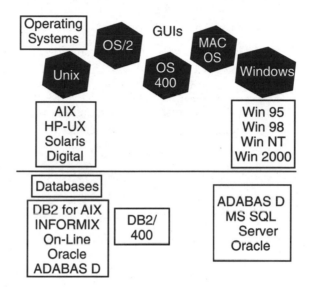

FIGURE 9.3
ABAP Technological Environment

9-16   One of most significant advantages of the ABAP Workbench is that it allows standardized access to different database systems. Programs can be developed and maintained independently of the underlying relational database. See Figure 9.4.

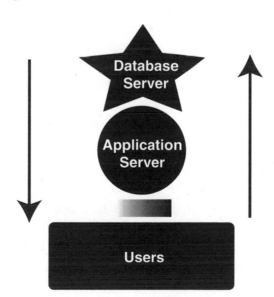

FIGURE 9.4
Representation of SAP Database/Application Server

SOLUTIONS

9-17   No, the unique features and attributes of the database system are not as much the main developer concern.

9-18   Transfer of data records between application programs and the database is coordinated by the database interface on the basis of definitions stored in the ABAP Dictionary.

9-19   Database access operations are based on SQL. Fourth-Generation Language ABAP is a high-level 4GL that works well for developing business applications.

9-20   ABAP supports structured programming, and the syntax of the language enables programmers quickly and easily to address mission-critical client/server application needs.

9-21   ABAP Workbench is used daily by experienced professionals concerned with issues such as tool integration and ergonomics.

9-22   User Interface Builder Screen Painter creates graphical user interfaces by supporting a broad range of graphical user interface controls.

9-23   ABAP Workbench facilitates programming by offering useful navigation and organization tools and standardizing access to all development objects and tools. Methods and utilities for accessing data, programming communications, and implementing GUIs as well as an extensive library of reusable ABAP modules are contained in the ABAP Workbench.

9-24   The screen painter creates a graphical interface by allowing the user to make menus and function key assignments for applications.

9-25   The program editor is integrated into the overall environment of the ABAP Workbench. It permits text operations (i.e. syntax check with automatic correction facility). The structured outline view of the editor makes it possible to collapse or expand syntactical blocks. The user gains a good overview of the overall application structure.

9-26   ABAP Workbench is a collection of sophisticated development tools. The browser tool lists all development objects with respect to a relaxed project management model.

9-27   The navigator launches any development object and activates the associated tool.

9-28   Both of these tools facilitate the development process so that the programmer can comfortably organize his work.

9-29   The R/3 repository is a central storage facility for all development objects including the ABAP modules, screens, ABAP dictionary objects, data models, and authorizations.

9-30 Developers can use the R/3 repository information system to evaluate and determine where data are used. Teams of developers working on development objects can use the R/3 repository simultaneously.

9-31 An open repository interface guarantees that even with non-SAP tools, users can process all repository objects.

9-32 The ABAP dictionary is an integrated component of ABAP Workbench. It is a central reference point for developers and manages all application-related metadata such as table definitions, internal structures, foreign key relationships, views, conversion rules, and online help information.

9-33 The integration of the ABAP dictionary with other development tools ensures that all tools can access common metadata and retain global consistency.

9-34 Any changes made in the ABAP dictionary are immediately effective in all applications concerned. Enhancements to the ABAP dictionary enable users to attach fields to tables and structures in the customer system without changing the original.

9-35 The report builder is composed of a powerful interactive list processing and reporting tool as well as a graphical query product. The list-processing facility makes reporting simple. Reports can be stored hierarchically in a tree structure.

9-36 ABAP Query is a graphical tool that allows users to execute quick and simple database calculations. Development staff can then focus on other tasks. Even the most complex data query can be handled by this full-featured tool.

9-37 ABAP Workbench can be used to devise applications and user interfaces in a number of different languages. Its ability to work with international capabilities allows support for multi-byte code pages such as Kanji and Mandarin.

9-38 Communications using RFC and OLE (Object Linking and Embedding) SAP make use of two mechanisms for interprogram communications.

9-39 OLE, the standard for desktop integration and open RFCs are used to control calling of function modules and programs across system boundaries as well as for communicating with external systems. RFCs can be used to establish asynchronous communication links. It is possible to operate user dialogs within modules called by RFC.

9-40 The repository infosystem shows the system-wide use of all development objects.

9-41 An integrated correction and transfer system and the version manager help meet the requirements of both centralized and distributed development. Due to automatic version management, all changes and newly developed objects are coordinated and can be accessed at any time. Complete information can be called up about all corrections and transfers made. All versions and releases are administered so that developed applications can be easily revised.

9-42   The debugger helps locate and correct errors in application logic or data handling. It also provides insights into the application runtime patterns and performance of individual modules and helps keep track of the use of program parts, variables, and type conversions.

9-43   ABAP Workbench contains a library of reusable program modules. Business function modules and programming aids, managed and documented in the library, are easy to identify and integrate into new development projects. Developers can create and store their own modules for future use. There is also an interactive test tool included for checking the functions and runtime requirements of modules. This can save years of programming time.

9-44   The monitoring tools in ABAP Workbench generate precise resource and performance data. Applications are optimized as a result of extensive runtime analyses and evaluations. Utilities like SQL Trace and ABAP Trace assist in performance optimization.

9-45   CATT (Computer Aided Test Tool) is an integrated facility of ABAP Workbench that allows comprehensive testing of software quality. (See Figure 9.5.) It creates and automates business processors in test procedures that can be repeated as often as required. Each test procedure generates a detailed log.

9-46   ABAP Workbench can be used for modifying or individually improving standard R/3 applications. It is also of interest to organizations wishing to develop individual solutions separate from SAP standard software with an integrated, professional toolkit.

9-47   The SAP technology infrastructure permits easy communication with other systems. It concentrates on RFC and OLE to make certain there is smooth program-to-program communication.

9-48   ABAP has structured training plans as well as a detailed online help function that makes it easier to work productively. Benefit can be derived from all the advantages offered by the user-friendly tools, intuitive GUI, and extensive navigation capability.

9-49   ABAP is entirely platform-independent. It supports all high-end operating systems, databases, and front ends to make certain that investments are protected.

SOLUTIONS

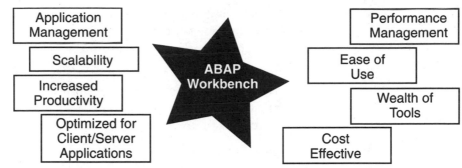

FIGURE 9.5
Illustration of Quality

9-50 Applications created on one platform run on others. If a company wants to change its hardware, it can do so.

9-51 Object-As part of SAP's commitment to object technology, Release 4.0 of R/3 will contain object-oriented enhancements to the ABAP programming language.

9-52 SAP's object strategy is based on SAP business objects and deals with modeling, programming, interfacing, and workflow. SAP employs principles such as encapsulation, inheritance, and polymorphism, the object-oriented extensions of ABAP that support real object-oriented development, so that it is possible to see improvements in the areas of reusability, maintenance, and quality of code.

9-53 SAP's approach toward objects benefits from customers' investments in existing business processes, functionality, and data.

9-54 Implementation of software systems that satisfy rapidly evolving business requirements is abated by business objects that reflect real business entities and are simultaneously represented by true software objects.

9-55 As opposed to using a stolid technical view, SAP uses object technology from a business point of view in developing enterprise business systems. The main focus is on the design and implementation of business processes based on business objects.

9-56 In order to support this strategy, SAP provides a comprehensive business-driven approach with the Business Framework. After developing object-oriented solutions for modeling, interfacing, and workflow in earlier R/3 releases, SAP's enhancements to ABAP in Release 4.0 pave the way for object-oriented programming. Programmers benefit from the enhancements made to ABAP through increased productivity with both high quality and easier code maintenance.

9-57   The increased reusability of program components supported by business-oriented modeling tools indicates that R/3 is able to make the quality and productivity of application development even better.

9-58   Applications developers are most productive when able to concentrate their efforts on solving the application problem itself as opposed to other aspects of program development. The incorporation of object-oriented concepts into ABAP moves the language a step closer to this goal.

9-59   Each object has a well-defined interface, and can only be accessed through this interface. This hides the internal structure and permits modifications to be made without affecting other program components.

9-60   Faster and more standardized implementation can occur through reuse. The reuse of designs and program components becomes simpler, while object-oriented enhancements to ABAP permit the development of object-oriented frameworks.

9-61   Depending on its visibility, an object component is designated as public, protected or private. Objects have attributes that describe the current state of the object.

9-62   The behavior of an object is described by its methods. Each object has a unique identity that never changes and allows it to be distinguished from other objects that have the same set of attributes and the same attribute values.

9-63   When one object raises an event, one or more other objects can be informed that this event has occurred, and can then react as public, protected, and private components.

9-64   There are three different ways in which objects can interact with each other:

1.   **Direct data access**—An object has direct read and write access to the visible attributes of other objects

2.   **Calling a method directly**—When a method is called directly, a unique object (the server or supplier) is called and this object is known to the calling object (the client).

3.   **The publish-subscribe mechanism**—If an event is raised while a method is being executed, all objects currently registered as being interested in this event (the subscribers) will be informed of it.

It is therefore possible for an event to occur and for no object to handle it, only because no object has subscribed to the event. The object that raised the event does not know which objects have subscribed to this event.

9-65   A class holds the specifications of the interfaces and the structure of the objects in that class.

9-66 The objects that are property of a class are also defined as instances of the class.

9-67 A new class is a specialization of an existing class.

9-68 The more specialized class is a subclass.

9-69 The more generalized class is a superclass.

9-70 Any statements that are true for the outward behavior of the superclass are also true for the subclass. Specifically, all of the public attributes and methods of the superclass will also be found in the subclass and will have the valid same semantics as those in the superclass. Subclasses also get the implementations of all the superclass methods, but these methods may be overridden within the subclass.

9-71 Two objects that have the same interface may be treated identically by clients even though each may have been implemented differently. ABAP offers the interface construct for this purpose. The use of this construct means that two objects may offer a common interface even though they do not have a common superclass. A client can treat two objects that have the same interface in the same way, without forcing both objects be instances of the same superclass. The definition of a class can determine if the class implements one or more interfaces. Each instance of this class then has all the attributes of these interfaces, can be called using the associated methods, and can raise the events defined in the interfaces.

9-72 A method body is essentially the implementation of the method. It must be specified for each method contained in the interface in the implementation of the class.

9-73 Interfaces can contain other interfaces. Classes that implement a composite interface have to provide implementations for all the contained interfaces.

9-74 Objects can possess attributes that contain information about their internal state. Attributes can have one of the data types available in the existing ABAP language (i.e., integer, character field, structure or internal table), and also the new object or interface reference type. Attributes are variables that are local to the object and are therefore not normally visible from the outside.

9-75 It can be appropriate to make certain attributes visible so that they can also be used from the outside as variables. The components of an object that are only visible within a class definition are called private.

SOLUTIONS

9-76 Components of objects that are only visible in the definitions of the direct and indirect subclasses are called protected. All other components are public.

9-77 These are visible to all clients of the object such as other program components and other class definitions.

9-78 Public attributes can be flagged as not-modifiable or read-only from outside the object. Attributes can also be flagged as virtual.

9-79 Virtual attributes can be accessed in the same way as normal attributes, but the implementing class then has the freedom to use an access method instead of making a direct attribute access.

9-80 Virtual attributes cannot be referenced with field symbols or passed as reference parameters to a routine (method, function or form). When virtual attributes are used, it is possible to postpone the decision to replace attribute accesses by access routines, without the need to make changes to all the program components that access the attributes concerned.

9-81 Virtual attributes in ABAP make it possible to determine at runtime whether the current value of an attribute is valid. If the value is valid, it can be accessed directly; if not, it must be recalculated by a method call.

9-82 In a lazy evaluation, a class can defer recalculation of a value until it is really needed, using virtual attributes.

9-83 Class attributes are common to all the instances of both the class and all its subclasses.

9-84 Class attributes can be specified as public, protected or private, read-only and/or virtual, just as for the instance attributes.

9-85 ABAP allows constants to be defined that are common to all the instances of a class (i.e. variable class attributes). These can be thought of as class constants. Methods in detail objects are able to execute operations. The methods of an object are the means for accomplishing the task.

9-86 A method always operates on a particular instance of a class. It can read and change the state, such as all attributes including public, protected attributes (which store the object state), and private read-only attributes.

9-87 Methods, like function modules, can have parameters so that they can pass back a return value. Methods are also used to determine the way objects handle events.

9-88 Each method in a class must be uniquely identifiable using its name. Method names may not be "overloaded".

9-89 Class methods can access class attributes only.

9-90 Since these methods do not access the instance-specific attributes, they can be used even if no instance of this class has been created or if no instance is known.

9-91 Like instance-specific methods, class methods can be declared as either public, protected, or private.

9-92 Class methods cannot raise events.

9-93 Events in Detail Events are represented by the fact that they occur at a particular point in time. When an event is raised, other things can occur as a consequence of the event.

9-94 A consequence of an event could be that a process X is started or that other events are raised. Examples of events include changes in the state of an object such as "posting canceled" or the creation of a new object such as "new account created", that have to be made known to all other interested objects.

9-95 Objects in ABAP can raise events. Other objects can react to these events in an appropriate way. An object that raises an event makes no assumptions about the number of objects that will handle the event, when or how they will do so. The raising object therefore does not generally know which objects will handle the event. This means that the event concept of ABAP must be distinguished from a callback concept where exactly one object is expected to react in a specific way. Before an object is in a position to react to the events raised by another object, at least one of its methods needs to be registered as an event-handling method for that object.

9-96 An event-handling method may be registered for the events of a single object, multiple individual objects, all instances of a class, or all instances that implement a certain interface.

9-97 If an object wishes to stop handling the events raised by another object at any time, it can cancel the registration of its methods.

9-98 If an object raises an event, every event-handling method currently registered for this kind of event is informed. The object that raised the one process can be characterized as existing over a particular period of time.

9-99 If there are several handling methods registered for the event, the order in which they are processed will be determined by the system.

9-100 Yes, the event-handling methods can also be called directly. The two reasons for doing this are:

SOLUTIONS

   1. To inform a non-registered object that an event has been raised so that the object can handle the event just as if it had received the event directly

   2. To allow the raising of events to be reproduced. Events can have parameters just as methods do.

From the point of view of the event-handling method, all event parameters are input parameters. No provision is made either for reference parameters or for a return value.

9-101 The event-handling method can find out the object that raised the event. Classes in a system will often require several objects that possess the same attributes and methods and can raise the same events. These objects will often differ only in their current state. For this reason objects are defined in classes rather than in a one-off fashion.

9-102 The description of a class contains the declarations of both the public and the private components of the objects and specifies their implementation.

9-103 The definition of a class contains specifications of the attributes and methods of the individual instances and also of the class attributes and class methods. It describes the events that can be raised by instances of the class and the interfaces that can be used to provide access to the instances. It also specifies the events that can be handled by instances of the class.

9-104 A class can also be declared as a subclass of another class. Even though it is possible to define class attributes and class methods, classes cannot be seen as objects with an existence of their own, nor can they be referenced as objects. Therefore, classes are not instances of meta-classes.

9-105 The smallest unit of encapsulation is the class, not the object. This means that all methods defined in a class can use the private attributes and methods of all the instances of the class, not just those of the current instance.

9-106 The methods of a subclass do not have access to the private methods and attributes that are defined in a superclass, unless the superclass specifically permits this form of access.

9-107 Generalization and specialization permit ABAP classes to be declared as direct subclasses of a class already defined—their direct superclass (simple inheritance).

9-108 The superclasses of a class include not only the direct superclass but also all the indirect superclasses, in other words, the superclasses of the direct superclass. In the same way, the subclasses of a class include all the direct subclasses and all of their subclasses.

9-109 The attributes, methods, events and supported interfaces of superclasses are also implicit attributes, methods, events and supported interfaces of each of their subclasses. All the pertinent properties including the meaning and types of the attributes and the meaning and parameters of methods and events are defined by the superclass.

9-110 Only the implementation of methods can be overridden in subclasses.

9-111 A scope resolution operator ensures access even to methods that have been redefined.

9-112 Subclasses are also able to define additional attributes, methods and events and to support additional interfaces. The components of subclasses live in the same name space as the components of their superclasses. This means that once a name has been used for a public (or protected compo-nent in a superclass, it cannot be used again in a subclass.

9-113 Classes can implement one or more interfaces. All objects that imple-ment the same interfaces can be treated identically by clients, regard-less of the class to which they belong. A client can access all these dif-ferent classes by the same type of interface reference. An interface reference only exposes the components defined directly in that inter-face. Implementing an interface involves defining a method body for each method contained in the interface. If a class implements compos ite interfaces, then it must also implement the interfaces contained in the composite interfaces. The attributes defined in the interface are automatically added to the instances of the class that implements these interfaces.

9-114 The language guarantees that subclasses can be used syntactically like any of their superclasses. The implementation of the subclass must guarantee that the subclass also functions like a special case of the superclass (semantic specialization).

9-115 Each interface and each class definition has a separate name space for its components (attribute, method and event definitions). If classes implement interfaces, the name spaces of the implemented interfaces are not incorpo-rated in the name space of the class, such that the components of the implemented interfaces do not automatically appear on the top level as components of the class. In addition, this rule applies when interfaces con-tain other interfaces as well. This eliminates naming conflicts that could occur when classes implement interfaces, and with composite interfaces.

9-116 No naming conflict can occur between identically named attributes and methods in different interfaces—even if a class implements several of these interfaces. As a result, each class can support any number of interfaces at any time, without the need ever to change the clients of this class to resolve name conflicts.

9-117   At certain times two classes need to cooperate so closely that it is convenient to allow one class to access another class private components. This special relationship is designated as the "friend concept" and it has to be agreed upon by both classes.

9-118   The friendship relationship is a directed relationship. Even though class 1 gives friendship to class 2, so that 2 gains access to its private components, it does not follow that class 2 has to offer friendship to class 1.

9-119   An interface allows objects to be used independently of their implementation. Common aspects of the interfaces of two objects can be expressed even when objects do not have a common superclass. Unlike class definitions, interface definitions do not contain an implementation section. An interface definition only describes the interaction possible with an object of any class that supports the interface. In interface definitions only public components of objects can be specified: public attributes, public methods, and the events the object can raise.

9-120   Interfaces are often created in a bottom-up fashion by drawing from existing protocols and standardizing similar interfaces. A development always starts with small interfaces, so that there will be a frequent need to define new higher interfaces that integrate existing interfaces. ABAP offers a means for defining hierarchy and abstraction in interfaces. An interface can contain other interfaces and also add to these by defining its own attributes, methods, and events. The attributes, methods and events specific to this interface form a separate interface that supplements the contained interfaces.

9-121   An interface that contains other interfaces as components is also called a composite interface. This allows arbitrary interface hierarchies to be defined. Classes that implement a composite interface also have to implement all the interfaces that this composite interface contains. If a class implements several different interfaces that contain an other interface, then this other interface and its affiliated attributes exist just once for each instance of the class.

9-122   Each interface must have separate name space for its components. If interfaces contain other interfaces, the name spaces of the contained interfaces are not part of the name space of the composite interface.

9-123   The first version of an interface is often not complete; it should therefore be possible to define new interfaces as extensions to existing interfaces.

The extended interface integrates the original interface and contains all components defined by that original interface.

9-124 In ABAP, the extension of interfaces is accomplished by making the extending interface contain the original interface and map all its components under the same name in its own name space using aliases. A class implementing the new interface must implement the bodies for the new methods. Clients can utilize the old and new components uniformly through the one new interface. This permits a gradual migration of clients and implementers of interfaces.

9-125 Whenever an object is created, a reference to the new object is returned to the creator and can be used for subsequent access to the object. The reference is recorded in a reference variable. Before the first assignment of a reference to a reference variable, the reference variable contains a null reference "Initial".

9-126 If the contents of one reference variable are copied into another reference variable, the referenced object itself is not duplicated. The result is that the two reference variables now reference the same object.

9-127 References to objects are introduced as new primitive data types in ABAP where reference variables are typed. When an object reference variable is defined, a class name has to be specified. All objects that can be referenced by these variables are property either of this class or of one of its subclasses.

9-128 Whenever an interface reference variable is defined an interface name must be specified. All objects that can be referenced by these variables must have implemented this kind of interface.

9-129 ABAP permits creation of reference variables that can reference arbitrary objects. The contents of any other reference variable can be assigned to them. There is a predefined class called "object" for these universal reference variables. The object class can be thought of as an implicit superclass of all other classes.

9-130 Objects are always created both explicitly and dynamically. The class of the object has to be specified either explicitly or implicitly. A reference is returned to the creator, and this can then be used to access the newly created object.

9-131 If an object with an encapsulated internal state can guarantee its own consistency, then it must be true from the moment when it is created. ABAP provides the "constructor method" for every class. This method is automatically called by the system when the object is being created and has the task of initializing the object. This method is called the constructor. There is one constructor for each class. This special method may be given parameters. Any mandatory parameters have to be supplied when an object is being created.

9-132 A subclass cannot override the constructor it inherits. Instead, the constructor of the subclass must explicitly call the constructor of its direct superclass and supply the required parameters. The number and the types of the parameters of the subclass constructor may vary from those of the superclass.

9-133 With storage management for objects objects are created explicitly, but cannot be deleted explicitly. If a program component no longer needs an object, it can designate a "null" reference to the appropriate reference variable. This indicates that the object is no longer referenced by this variable.

9-134 The runtime system makes certain that no object is deleted if there is still a valid reference to the object anywhere in the program. Only when there are no more references to the object is the system free to delete the object in the future. This procedure makes certain that invalid references do not happen. The system, by itself, is responsible for deciding when an object should be deleted.

9-135 There is no provision at this time in the language for special methods executed immediately before an object is deleted. There is provision, however, automatically to release external resources when an object "dies" or the whole program terminates.

9-136 Classes and interfaces can be defined either globally or locally. Global classes and interfaces are stored in the class library, known as the object repository.

9-137 Local classes can be defined as ordinary types on the top level of programs, reports, module pools, and function groups.

9-138 In defining an interface, the common client-visible aspects of two objects can be expressed, even though the objects do not have a common superclass. A class definition can determine whether the class implements one or more interfaces.

9-139 The class itself must define a method body for each interface method. Interfaces can contain other interfaces. Classes that implement a composite interface must also implement all contained interfaces. ABAP also enables interfaces to be extended, and thus further developed, by adding more attributes, methods and events. This means that existing program components need not be modified unnecessarily. Objects need not be deleted explicitly. Instead, the runtime system provides a garbage collection mechanism.

Business Framework

Business Framework is a combination of SAP and non-SAP products that produces an open, integrated, component-based enterprise business application solution for companies, regardless of size, in any industry.

There are several primary factors that control the design of enterprise business IT systems. This is best seen through the differences in the products of the automotive and aeronautics industries. The products can be assembled from different prefabricated components, each of which can also be integrated in different technical solutions.

Business Framework allows global enterprises to create their own information systems quickly with respect to individual components. The greatest benefit of this type of distributed network solution is that it can be constantly maintained even when the release or technical implementation for an individual component changes. Business Framework provides a strategic architecture for the R/3 system, permitting quick and flexible establishment of enterprise-critical distributed IT systems using independent components.

Business Framework Benefits

The business framework is a combination of SAP and non-SAP products that provides an open, integrated, component-based enterprise business application solution for companies, regardless of size, in any industry.

Issues that shape the design of enterprise business IT systems are illustrated through the differences in the products of both the automotive and aeronautics industries. These products can be assembled from various prefabricated components, each of which can also be integrated into different technical solutions. This method permits production cycles to be greatly shortened so that new high-quality products can be placed on the market quickly at reduced cost.

The business framework permits global enterprises to develop their own information systems quickly with regard to individual components. The best advantage of this type of distributed network solution is that it can be constantly maintained at a point where the release or technical implementation for an individual component changes.

Business Framework provides a critical architecture for the R/3 system and makes it easy to establish enterprise-critical distributed IT systems through independent components.

R/3 Component Family

R/3 is constantly evolving into a family of components that can be linked into integrated and continuously maintainable network solutions regardless of the release of the components. The result is an open Business Framework so that components from other vendors can also be integrated into network solutions.

When dealing with Business Framework, the R/3 system also evolves into a family of autonomous components that can be combined into integrated network solutions that illustrates the needs of individual users.

R/3 Component Strategy

Whenever different components are integrated, company-specific process and organization structures can produce results quickly with a great deal of flexibility. This powerful functionality resolves the conflict between purchasing packaged software or developing custom business applications. Components can be added to both industry solutions and customer-specific software to core R/3 system modules including areas such as Human Resources, Logistics, Financial Accounting or R/3 Internet application components.

Maintenance (as opposed to development) is critical whenever components are integrated in network solutions. The open nature of Business Framework can handle different upgrade strategies. The component network always stays functional.

R/3's component strategy designates how an enterprise can enhance its business processes into the Internet. Within Business Framework a company's IT systems can be coupled with those of customers and vendors. This creates new markets and allows individual business processes to be supported more quickly and cost effectively.

Internet orders can be transferred to the order management system where they are automatically executed to all the proper processing steps to delivery. Vendors have access to specific parts of their customers' warehouse management system that allow them independently to schedule their just-in-time deliveries. A local Java client can be used to execute defined personnel tasks that are automatically processed in the Human Resources system. This can greatly assist in alleviating demands on the HR department for personnel planning.

R/3 Internet applications can be beneficial because of a close interaction between the software components of different manufacturers and the extension of business processes beyond system and enterprise boundaries. The R/3 system can also support a powerful platform for mission-critical high-load operation. Tasks can be quickly executed inside Business Framework with assistance from multi-tier R/3 network architecture as well as implementation of object-oriented technologies in the R/3 system.

R/3 Repository

An R/3 system with its integrated repository allows for centralized management and control. It makes it possible to maintain a consistent application environment. The R/3 repository is the foundation for all other tools.

The R/3 repository is the central place that holds all of the production system's information such as technical and business objects. This stops the storage of redundant information, and permits software to be reused through centralized management and documentation of these reusable repository objects.

The repository consists of the technical objects that possess dictionary information such as data and table definitions, screens, ABAP programs, and reusable function modules important for application development.

The repository contains the business objects for the R/3 reference model. This model maps all functions, business objects, processes, information flows, technical features of system organization, the organizational structure, and distribution of applications.

The global R/3 reference model is an important part of the R/3 repository. When changes are executed in one area of the R/3 system, they are automatically executed in all other affected areas.

There are more than 1,000 business processes describing the R/3 system functions contained in the reference model. The model offers more than 100 basic business situations seen as value chains.

The R/3 Repository stores the attributes for each function in a process model. It allows users to navigate directly from the Process Model to an operating R/3 System. These options are supported by a comprehensive repository meta-model.

Multi-Tier Network Architecture

Multi-tier network architecture is at the core of the R/3 system. The multi-tier R/3 architecture offers high-performance middleware. There is a break between presentation, application, database, and Internet-enabling layers. The multi-tier R/3 network architecture provides a flexible platform for distributed IT scenarios. The presentation layer of the R/3 system (with its SAPGUI) provides a front-end technology that permits users to experience the full potential of the R/3 system.

In addition, the popular Windows/MAC GUIs for Internet browsers can act as user interfaces. Browsers have the distinct advantage of doing away with the need for additional administration within the enterprise.

An Internet-enabling layer was added to the three-tier client/server architecture of the R/3 system for the purpose of assisting users in the creation of business potentials for the Internet market. This layer is the link between Web browsers and R/3 applications that operate on the application layer. Application servers possess the complete business process logic of R/3 applications. These applications can function on Windows NT systems, major UNIX operating systems, and AS/400 systems.

The component strategy defines how an enterprise can extend its business processes beyond its own limitations into the virtual marketplace of the global business village.

R/3 Distributed Layers

The database layer manages the R/3 application programs as well as the enterprise's working data. Tasks are executed through relational database management systems that meet strict R/3 system requirements for enterprise-critical processing during high-load operation. Platforms currently supported include IBM's DB2, Informix' Online, Microsoft's SQL Server, and Oracle.

R/3 can be distributed among layers where each layer has its own unique defined tasks. In each of these layers, the ABAP VM (Virtual Machine) supports business application logic of the R/3 system separate from the technical points of the networks, operating systems, databases and front ends.

NOTE

The messaging infrastructure employs TCP/IP as the network protocol. This offers transparency against COM/DCOM, CORBA or RMI (Remote Method Invocation) for defining communications mechanisms between distributed components.

R/3 provides an extremely cost-effective solution and gives comprehensive investment protection. A system can be ported to all platforms that comply with open systems computing standards. R/3 is highly scalable, allowing accurate computation of the cost/benefit advantages of required hardware and software resources at each of these levels.

R/3 offers a high-performance messaging infrastructure that controls the integration of additional application components through uniquely defined messages. This makes it possible to implement nearly any distribution situation.

BAPIs

BAPIs act like interfaces for controlled method calls between SAP business objects and objects of external providers. SAP business objects are closely linked to the development of the R/3 infrastructure as the successive implementation of object-oriented technology is the key to enhancement of the R/3 system.

R/3 systems have more than 200 different SAP business objects each of which has encapsulated data structures and methods. These objects make business objects that incorporate customer, material, order, quotation, and request for quotation.

Object technology offers several distinct advantages that permit modeling and structure of business application systems on a high semantic level. Individual objects interact through specifically defined interfaces. BAPIs are implemented as methods of SAP business objects that play a central role.

BAPIs are open interfaces ensuring that two application systems communicate with each other. Business-related information such as order, customer, or part number, all uses the same semantics. This allows the exchange of transactions directly across enterprise boundaries.

BAPIs also comply with Microsoft's COM/DCOM specifications as well as related CORBA specifications, and can be used in a Java environment as of R/3 Release 4.0.

Business Framework is refined through numerous high-performance tools supplied with the R/3 system. These tools permit making several company-specific adjustments quickly so that the R/3 system can be extended to respond to new market challenges.

Business Engineer

The R/3 Business Engineer is the cornerstone of the AcceleratedSAP Program (ASAP). It permits quick implementation of the R/3 system. The R/3 repository guarantees the consistency of metadata in an environment that comprises both customer-specific developments and standard components.

The business object repository is the object-oriented extension of the R/3 repository and contains about 200 SAP business objects.

Standard business objects include: customers, vendors, articles, and materials lists.

Business objects must possess encapsulated data and functions. Communication between these objects happens through clearly defined method calls. The business object repository illustrates SAP's object-oriented technologies for modeling, workflow, interfacing, and programming. R/3 users can communicate with their more technically-oriented colleagues using a common language.

R/3 Business Engineer is founded on the "configure-to-order" concept that provides the framework for choosing and configuring the R/3 applications necessary in different companies. Its objective is fast and customer-specific implementation for integrated process chains together with a view to continuous optimization of the value chain. This approach applies both to initial installation of the R/3 system and to the optimization of processes during continuous operation.

Business Engineer is based completely on the R/3 reference model. There are more than 1,000 R/3 business processes within the reference model that have been combined into 100 business situations. Enterprises can create their organizational plans and configure systems with regard to their individual needs quickly and efficiently via Business Engineer, which offers a knowledge-based configuration that can easily guide users through the initial implementation phase. It also contains an interactive question-and-answer procedure that handles continuous change of the business situation and system improvements.

Business Engineer provides for integrated checks for consistency, context and cross references to ensure that configuration decisions conform to the relevant business rules and are supported by the R/3 functions. This applies to the entire configuration process that starts with the business plan and goes through the organizational units and all associated distribution models (i.e. the process and function level).

Business Engineer allows customers to develop most of their required changes during normal operation. Its knowledge-based configuration connects enterprise modeling with the live R/3 system. This effectively connects application design and implementation.

ABAP Workbench

ABAP Workbench supports the entire development cycle of enterprise-wide client/server solutions. It is based on the principles of rapid prototyping. The GUIs and easy operation with object-oriented navigation make it simple to use the tools. The ABAP programming language has evolved to integrate object-oriented elements.

ABAP objects (a new generation of the ABAP virtual machine) permit component integration using ActiveX or JavaBeans. They also permit additional forms of structuring to be introduced within the R/3 application components. ABAP objects contain mechanisms for defining both local and global categories.

Open repository development objects including ABAP modules, screens, data models, and HTML templates are recorded in the R/3 repository. This permits fast and easy access to all objects and guarantees a transparent view of the data structures.

The development of the R/3 repository as an open repository permits users to store the objects they have developed in specially assigned name ranges and to mix these with SAP business objects.

ABAP Workbench provides a set of carefully matched professional tools that can be used to enhance R/3 applications for individual needs and to add enhancements. These tools can be used independently of SAP software to create individualized applications.

R/3 application enhancements that have been programmed by users can be managed individually and can be maintained compatible with current releases.

When an R/3 software upgrade is performed, custom extensions can be transported to the new release where they continue to work as they did before. SAP does not provide any defined user exits, so developers can program enhancements to the standard system through the Modification Assistant. An integrated Workbench Organizer registers and documents all activities performed. It also ensures that program changes are executed in a coordinated way.

ABAP Workbench functionality is completed with tools for quality assurance and performance optimization. These tools can perform targeted analyses of either individual programs or a complete system. They can also create detailed statistics of resource consumption and performance.

Applications created with ABAP Workbench can be ported to various platforms, operating systems, databases, and graphical user interfaces. Communication with other systems is executed reliably through the R/3 technology infrastructure.

SAP Business Workflow permits enterprises to obtain a high level of flexibility when designing and automating business processes. This works to accelerate the processes beyond their own boundaries.

SAP Business Workflow

SAP Business Workflow provides an easy working environment that satisfies the specific needs of both regular and occasional users. It is also possible to illustrate business processes that can be actively controlled using SAP Business Workflow through the complete processing of a customer order from its receipt through delivery of the goods and issuing the invoice.

A workflow can be triggered in SAP Business Workflow through different front ends or applications. During the workflow, users can continue to use the environment familiar to them. They can process the individual work items in a working environment they know, request information on the current status of specific workflows at any time, and trace the history of the work process. All these functions can also be accessed through the Internet.

SAP Business Workflow is not possible without the open nature of the business framework. This also deals with linking of customer and vendor systems that may be non-R/3 applications. Staff do not have to use different systems to process workflows. SAP's consistent use of open interfaces and industry standards helps because SAP is a member of the Workflow Management Coalition (WfMC). SAP has already supplied the first published workflow standard for workflow client applications. Business Workflow functions can be accessed from all MAPI (Messaging Application Programming Interface) compatible clients. Users can continue using their familiar mail front ends.

SAP Business Workflow also provides form integration that makes it possible to use Visual Basic, Outlook, or JetForm forms when automating business processes. These can be used to start workflows, both offline and online, and to accelerate form-based tasks within a business process.

Semantic Synchronization

Semantic synchronization is the situation where something can be implemented with the R/3 System resulting from the development in the areas of interface and integration technology. These developments are based on open systems computing standards. The mechanism is the semantic synchronization of the business data exchanged between various components.

Integration Technologies

The R/3 System provides special integration technologies to achieve semantic synchronization such as: Application Link Enabling (ALE). ALE allows the exchange of business messages between autonomous applications. You will also find that it provides SAP Business Workflow that empowers the design and automation of business processes throughout enterprise boundaries.

The Interfaces provided involve the Object-oriented Business Application Programming Interfaces (BAPIs). These are compatible with Microsoft's COM/DCOM specifications (i.e. Distributed Component Object Model) and the Object Management Group's CORBA specifications (Common Object Request Broker Architecture). Due to the fact that BAPIs are Java-enabled, they also allow communication between components in a Java environment.

By integrating different components, company-specific process and organization structures can be produced quickly with a great deal of flexibility. This powerful functionality resolves the conflict between purchasing packaged software or developing custom business applications. You can simply add a couple additional components to both industry solutions and customer-specific software to core R/3 System modules such as Human Resources, Logistics, or Financial Accounting.

Maintenance is more important than development when components are integrated in network solutions. The open nature of the Business Framework supports different upgrade strategies. The component network always remains a functioning entity.

Application Link Enabling

ALE allows loose coupling of different components. These components can be installed with respect to a decentralized plan and can be technically independent of each other. They do not all have to be at the same release level.

A standard distribution situation can be the centralized management of purchasing agreements for decentralized procurement applications, or the coupling of centralized financial systems that have decentralized logistics applications.

ALE is based on an exchange of messages controlled by business processes. Applications are integrated using asynchronous communications mechanisms under time control. ALE permits business processes from different systems (each with their own database) to be integrated.

ALE is not based on the concept of distributed databases because this generally requires a great deal of management effort at the same release levels on all network nodes. This is in contradistinction to the concept of autonomy in economically independent units, and cannot always be realized because of time and cost.

ALE in the R/3 system provides another important integration technology within the business framework next to SAP Business Workflow. An array of prefabricated distribution scenarios is supplied together with ALE.

Workflow designs can be greatly simplified and accelerated by the use of the Workflow Wizards that are integrated in SAP Business Workflow. Workflow Wizards, are assistants found in many PC applications and guide the designer in a controlled dialog based on carefully prepared questions and decision options, producing an executable workflow definition.

Synchronizing business processes of the communicating systems is a crucial task for ALE. ALE uses standardized intermediate documents

(IDocs) to exchange messages containing application data. These documents are similar to those used by the R/3 functions that support electronic data interchange (EDI).

IDocs have a neutral data structure and can be used by non-SAP components as a standard interface for data transfer. R/3 release 4.0 IDocs can be called via BAPIs.

In the SAP business framework, ALE ensures that process integration between components ALE and BAPIs is achieved. Object-oriented development of R/3 interface technology and a uniform business framework, lead to combining ALE with the BAPIs. Existing ALE distribution situations are equipped with BAPIs at each step and new situations are implemented using BAPIs.

Internet Applications

Users can use the Internet to shop using a Web browser. Their Internet orders are transferred to the order management system where they are automatically executed to all the proper processing steps to delivery. Vendors have access to specific parts of their customers' warehouse management system, allowing them to independently schedule their deliveries just in time.

Employees can use a local Java client to perform specifically defined personnel tasks that are automatically processed in the Human Resources system. This assists in alleviating HR department capacities for the task of personnel planning.

R/3 Internet applications productively by using a close interaction between the software components of different manufacturers and the extension of business processes beyond system and enterprise boundaries. The R/3 System is even better able to offer a powerful platform for mission-critical high-load operation. You can execute tasks quickly and efficiently within the Business Framework with the help of multi-tier R/3 network architecture and the implementation of object-oriented technologies in the R/3 System. Chapter 14 gives more information about the Internet.

Summary

In this chapter we have discussed the open nature of the business framework and how it can play a critical role in an enterprise information system. The business framework allows an R/3 system to grow into a powerful network enterprise solution. We covered semantic synchronization, component integration, Internet strategies, and what the business engineer offers its users.

Just as the business framework can help an enterprise more effectively integrate R/3, Windows NT and UNIX integration across each desktop in a computing environment are essential to success throughout the client/server environment.

10-1 What exactly is SAP's Business Framework?

10-2 What factors govern design of enterprise business IT systems?

10-3 Define some practical uses for Business Framework.

10-4 What kind of benefits can be expected from the open nature of Business Framework?

10-5 Explain how Business Framework allows the R/3 system to grow into a more powerful network solution.

10-6 Explain semantic synchronization.

10-7 What kinds of integration technologies does the R/3 system provide?

10-8 Name the interfaces and integration technology interfaces that R/3 offers.

10-9 What can a company achieve by integrating different components?

10-10 Which is more important: development or maintenance, and why?

10-11 Clearly state Internet strategies that define how it is possible to work with extended business processes.

10-12 Can a company's IT systems be coupled with those of its customers and vendors?

10-13 What type of client can employees use to execute personnel tasks?

10-14 Describe a means by which SAP customers can use R/3 Internet applications productively.

10-15 Exactly what do object-oriented methods permit?

10-16 Describe exactly what the multi-tier network architecture is and what it does.

10-17 What is the Internet-enabling layer and how does it relate to the three-tier client/server architecture of the R/3 system?

10-18 What do the application servers contain?

10-19 What does the database layer manage?

10-20 Describe how the R/3 system can be distributed among three distinct layers.

10-21 In what way can the R/3 system act as investment protection?

10-22 What does the messaging infrastructure use?

10-23 What is the most common language in the business environment?

10-24   What special entity do BAPIs act like?

10-25   Approximately how many different SAP business objects are there in an R/3 system?

10-26   What is the advantage of object technology?

10-27   What primary function do BAPIs have?

10-28   What are some tools that allow for quick R/3 implementation?

10-29   What does R/3's integrated repository do?

10-30   Where is all of the production system's information kept?

10-31   Explain the connection between the R/3 repository and technical objects.

10-32   Explain the connection between the R/3 repository and business objects.

10-33   Explain standard order processing. Is it a process model?

10-34   How can a user's needs be met through faster implementation?

10-35   What is the R/3 business engineer?

10-36   Explain the business object repository.

10-37   What does the configure-to-order concept involve?

10-38   What is the business engineer?

10-39   What does the business engineer offer?

10-40   What does the business engineer allow customers to do?

10-41   What is a customer cross-section?

10-42   Explain the significance of ABAP objects.

10-43   What are open repository development objects and where are they stored?

10-44   What does the ABAP class library provide?

10-45   What allows you to develop customized applications? Explain in detail.

10-46   Explain the active ABAP dictionary.

10-47   Describe how R/3 application enhancements can be managed.

10-48   Explain the integrated Workbench Organizer.

10-49   What does Web reporting allow?

10-50   How does quality assurance play an important role?

10-51 What can be accomplished with applications developed with the ABAP Workbench?

10-52 How does SAP Business Workflow integrate all of the business processes?

10-53 What kind of working environment can be expected from SAP Business Workflow?

10-54 Explain what work items are.

10-55 How is a workflow triggered?

10-56 Explain the workflow process.

10-57 Explain the open nature and workflow standards of SAP Business Workflow.

10-58 Explain MAPI support and forms integration.

10-59 Describe asynchronous communications.

10-60 Explain what ALE (Application Link Enabling) is based on.

10-61 How is cooperative processing between components achieved?

10-62 What are workflow wizards?

10-63 What is semantic synchronization?

10-64 What does ALE do in Business Framework?

10-1 Business Framework (Figure 10.1) is a conglomerate of SAP and non-SAP products that produces an open, integrated, component-based enterprise business application solution for companies, regardless of size, in any industry.

10-2 The factors that control the design of enterprise business IT systems are best seen through the differences in the products of the automotive and aeronautics industries. The products can be assembled from different pre-fabricated components, each of which can also be integrated in different technical solutions. This method allows production cycles to be significantly shortened; new high-quality products can be put on the market quickly and at minimum cost.

FIGURE 10.1
R/3 Components

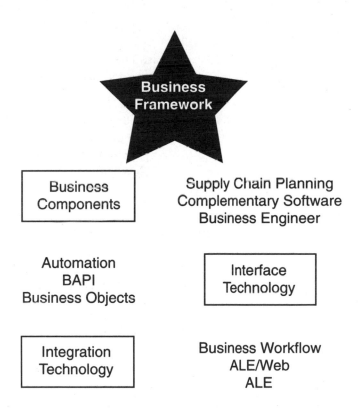

10-3 Business Framework allows global enterprises to create their own information systems quickly with respect to individual components. The advantage of this type of distributed network solution is that it can be constantly maintained even when the release or technical implementation for an individual component changes. Business Framework provides a strategic architecture for the R/3 system, while permitting quick and flexi-

SOLUTIONS

ble establishment of enterprise-critical distributed IT systems using independent components.

10-4 The R/3 system is growing into a family of components which can be combined into integrated and continuously maintainable network solutions regardless of the release of the components. The benefit of the open Business Framework is that components from other vendors can also be integrated into these network solutions.

10-5 In Business Framework, the R/3 system is growing into a family of autonomous components which can be combined into integrated network solutions that reflect the needs of individual users.

10-6 Semantic synchronization occurs when something can be implemented with the R/3 system because of development in the areas of interface and integration technology. These developments are based on open systems computing standards. The mechanism is the semantic synchronization of the business data exchanged between various components.

10-7 The R/3 system provides special integration technologies to achieve semantic synchronization including Application Link Enabling (ALE). ALE allows the exchange of business messages between autonomous applications. It also provides SAP Business Workflow that empowers the design and automation of business processes throughout enterprise boundaries.

10-8 Interfaces provided involve the Object-Oriented Business Application Programming Interfaces (BAPIs). (See Figure 10.2). These are compatible with Microsoft's COM/DCOM (Distributed Component Object Model) specifications and the Object Management Group's CORBA (Common Object Request Broker Architecture). Because BAPIs are Java-enabled, they also allow communication between components in a Java environment.

10-9 When different components are integrated, company-specific process and organization structures can be produced quickly with much flexibility. This powerful functionality resolves the conflict between purchasing packaged software and developing custom business applications. A few components can be added to both industry solutions and customer-specific software to achieve core R/3 system modules such as human resources, logistics, or Financial Accounting (i.e. R/3 Internet application components).

10-10 Maintenance, not development, is the crucial aspect, especially when components are integrated in network solutions. (See Figure 10.3) The open nature of Business Framework supports different upgrade strategies. The component network always remains a functioning entity.

SOLUTIONS

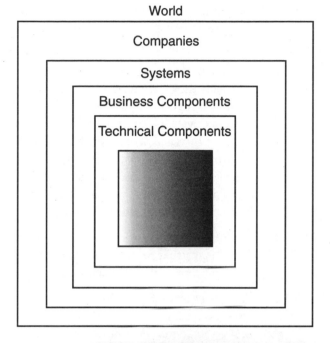

—Upgrade All

—Upgrade Several Small Components

—Upgrade Several Large Components

SOLUTIONS

10-11   The component strategy defines how an enterprise can extend its business processes beyond its own limitations into the virtual marketplace of the global business village.

10-12   Yes, inside Business Framework a company's own IT systems can be coupled with those of customers and vendors. This creates new markets and permits individual business processes to be handled more quickly and cost-effectively. Users can employ the Internet to shop using a Web browser. Their Internet orders are transferred to the order management system and automatically executed through all the proper processing steps to delivery. Vendors have access to specific parts of their customers' warehouse management systems, allowing them independently to schedule their deliveries just-in-time.

10-13   Employees can use a local Java client to perform specifically defined personnel tasks that are automatically processed in the human resources system. This assists the HR department in personnel planning.

10-14   SAP customers employ R/3 Internet applications productively by using a close interaction between the software components of different manufacturers and the extension of business processes beyond system and enterprise boundaries. The R/3 system is even better able to offer a powerful platform for mission-critical high-load operation. Tasks can be executed quickly and efficiently within Business Framework with the help of the multi-tier R/3 network architecture (See Figure 10.4) and the implementation of object-oriented technologies in the R/3 system.

FIGURE 10.4
Multi-Tier R/3
Network Architecture

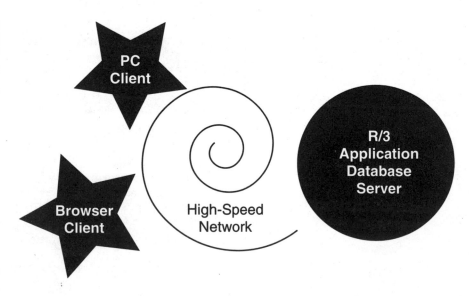

10-15 Object-oriented methods permit mapping of real-life situations to satisfy the IT environment required by the enterprise.

10-16 The multi-tier R/3 network architecture provides high-performance middleware. There is a definite break between presentation, application, database, and Internet enabling layers. The architecture offers a flexible platform for distributed IT scenarios. The presentation layer of the R/3 system (with its SAPGUI) offers a front-end technology that allows users to benefit from the full potential of the R/3 system. MS-Windows GUIs or popular Internet browsers can act as user interfaces. Browsers have the distinct advantage of doing away with the need for additional administration within the enterprise.

10-17 The Internet-enabling layer was added to the three-tier client/server architecture of the R/3 system in order to assist users in creating business potentials for the virtual Internet market. This layer is the link between Web browsers and R/3 applications that operate on the application layer.

10-18 Application servers contain the complete business process logic of R/3 applications. These applications can operate on Windows NT systems, major UNIX operating systems, and AS/400 systems.

10-19 The database layer manages both the R/3 application programs and the enterprise's working data. This task is executed using relational database management systems that satisfy strict R/3 system requirements for enterprise-critical processing during high-load operation. Some of the platforms currently supported include IBM's DB2, Informix' Online, Microsoft's SQL Server, and Oracle.

10-20 The R/3 system can be distributed among these layers where each layer has its own specifically defined tasks. In each of these layers, the ABAP VM (Virtual Machine) maintains the business-application logic of the R/3 system separately from the technical points of the networks, operating systems, databases and frontends.

10-21 The R/3 system is extremely cost-effective and offers comprehensive investment protection. The system can be ported to all platforms that comply with open systems computing standards. In addition, it is highly scalable to permit accurate computing of the cost/benefit advantages of required hardware and software resources at each of these levels. The R/3 system also provides a high-performance messaging infrastructure that controls the integration of additional application components through uniquely defined messages. This permits implementation of almost any distribution situation.

SOLUTIONS

10-22   The messaging infrastructure uses TCP/IP as the network protocol and provides transparency against COM/DCOM, CORBA or RMI (Remote Method Invocation) for designating communications mechanisms between distributed components.

10-23   The most common language in the global business industry is object-oriented.

10-24   The BAPIs act like interfaces for controlled method calls between SAP business objects and objects of external providers. SAP business objects (see Figure 10.5) are tightly coupled to the development of the R/3 infrastructure. The successive implementation of object-oriented technology is the key to enhancement of the R/3 System.

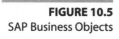
FIGURE 10.5
SAP Business Objects

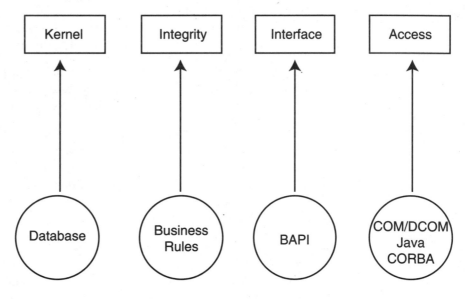

10-25   R/3 systems contain more than 200 different SAP business objects, each with encapsulated data structures and methods to create business objects that include customer, material, order, quotation, and request for quotation.

10-26   The advantage of object technology is that it allows modeling and structure of business application systems on a high semantic level. The individual objects interact through clearly defined interfaces. BAPIs are implemented as methods of SAP business objects and play a central role.

10-27 BAPIs are open interfaces to make certain that when two application systems communicate with each other, the business-related information such as order, customer, or part number, all uses the same semantics. This allows the exchange of transactions directly across enterprise boundaries. BAPIs comply with Microsoft's COM/DCOM specifications and related CORBA specifications, and can also be used in a Java environment as of R/3 Release 4.0.

10-28 Tools that allow fast R/3 implementation while satisfying individual needs focus on the speed with which R/3 infrastructure offers Business Framework. Business Framework is enhanced through several high-performance tools supplied with the R/3 system. These make it possible to perform several company-specific adjustments quickly, so that the R/3 system is constantly extended in response to new market challenges.

10-29 The R/3 system with its integrated repository permits centralized management and control. It makes it possible to maintain a consistent application environment. The R/3 repository is the foundation for all other tools. There are no redundancies or reusable software.

10-30 The R/3 repository is the central container that holds all of the production system's information, such as technical and business objects. This method prevents the storage of redundant information, and allows software to be reused through centralized management and documentation of these reusable repository objects.

10-31 The R/3 repository (see Figure 10.6) makes up the technical objects that contain dictionary information including the data and table definitions, screens, ABAP programs, and reusable function modules important for application development.

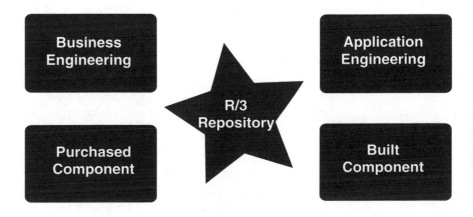

FIGURE 10.6
R/3 Repository

Business Engineering

Application Engineering

R/3 Repository

Purchased Component

Built Component

SOLUTIONS

10-32   The R/3 repository also contains the business objects for the R/3 reference model. The reference model maps all functions, business objects, processes, information flows, technical features of system organization, the organizational structure, and distribution of applications. The global R/3 reference model is an integral part of the R/3 repository. When changes are made in one area of the R/3 system, they are automatically made in all other affected areas. There are over 1,000 business processes describing the R/3 system functionality that are contained in the reference model. The model provides more than 100 basic business situations that are interpreted as value chains.

10-33   Standard order processing is described as a process model. The R/3 repository stores the attributes for each function in a process model. This allows users to navigate directly from the process model to an operating R/3 system. These options are supported by a comprehensive repository meta-model.

10-34   Fast implementation tailored to users' specific needs is a crucial factor in maintaining a competitive edge that involves timely implementation of business application software. The point is to achieve a smooth implementation of the software to new organizational structures without disruption of normal operation.

10-35   The R/3 business engineer is the central tool of the AcceleratedSAP Program (ASAP). It allows for quick implementation of the R/3 system. The R/3 repository guarantees the consistency of meta-data even in an environment that comprises both customer-specific developments and standard components.

10-36   The Business object repository (Figure 10.7) is the object-oriented extension of the R/3 repository and stores approximately 200 SAP business objects. Typical objects include customers, vendors, articles, and materials lists. Business objects must contain encapsulated data and functions. Communication between these objects occurs through clearly defined method calls. The business object repository illustrates SAP's object-oriented technologies for modeling, workflow, interfacing, and programming. R/3 users are thus able to communicate with their more technically-oriented colleagues using a common language.

10-37   The business engineer is based on the "configure-to-order" concept that offers the framework for selecting and configuring the R/3 applications required in different companies. The goal is fast and customer-specific implementation of integrated process chains with a view to continuous optimization of the value chain. This approach applies not only to initial installation of the R/3 System but also to the optimization of processes during continuous operation.

FIGURE 10.7
Business Object
Repository

10-38 The business engineer is based entirely on the R/3 reference model. There are over 1,000 R/3 business processes contained in the reference model that have been combined into 100 business situations. Enterprises can develop their organizational plans and configure systems with respect to their individual needs quickly and efficiently using the business engineer. The business engineer is the central tool in the ASAP Program for quickly customized implementations of the R/3 system enterprise modeling.

10-39 The business engineer offers a knowledge-based configuration for quick guidance through the initial implementation phase. In addition, it also contains an interactive question-and-answer procedure that supports continuous change of the business situation and system improvements. It offers integrated checks for consistency, context and cross-references to make certain that configuration decisions conform to the relevant business rules and that they are supported by the R/3 functions. This applies to the entire configuration process, from the business plan through the organizational units as well as the associated distribution models and the process and function level.

10-40 The business engineer enables customers to create the majority of their required changes during normal operation. The knowledge-based configuration connects enterprise modeling with the live R/3 system. This effectively links application design and implementation.

10-41 The customer cross-section is the result of an enterprise model documented in the R/3 repository of the R/3 reference model. The additional open R/3 repository API conforms to COM/DOCM model specifications that allow other modeling tool suppliers to use the R/3 reference model and develop their own industry-specific models.

10-42 ABAP Workbench supports the complete development cycle of enterprise-wide client/server solutions, and is based on the principles of rapid prototyping. The graphical interfaces and simple operation with object-oriented navigation make it easy to use the tools. The ABAP programming language has also been evolved to include object-oriented elements. ABAP objects (a new generation of the ABAP virtual machine) allow component integration using ActiveX or JavaBeans as well as the introduction of additional forms of structuring within the R/3 application components themselves. ABAP objects contain mechanisms for defining both local and global categories.

10-43 Open repository development objects, including ABAP modules, screens, data models, and HTML templates, are stored in the R/3 repository. This allows fast and easy access to all objects and guarantees a transparent view of the data structures. The development of the R/3 repository into an open repository allows users to store the objects they have developed in specially assigned name ranges and to mix these with SAP business objects.

10-44 The ABAP class library provides a view of R/3 system categories as well as their subordinate relationships.

10-45 ABAP Workbench offers a set of carefully matched professional tools that can be used to extend R/3 applications for individual needs and to add enhancements. These tools can also be used independently of SAP software to create individualized applications.

10-46 The active ABAP dictionary is the central information base for developers. This is where all application-specific data are managed and made available in a uniform method to the integrated development tools. This library with reusable program modules promotes a rational approach to software development both within the R/3 system environment and for customers' own developments.

10-47 Enhancements to R/3 applications programmed by customers can be managed individually and kept compatible with current releases. When an R/3 software upgrade is performed, these custom extensions can be transported to the new release, where they continue to work as they did before. This is true in cases where SAP does not offer any defined user exits; developers can program enhancements to the standard system using the modification assistant. Since SAP and customer development objects are clearly separated, these controlled customer enhancements may also be reused almost automatically following a release upgrade.

10-48   The integrated Workbench Organizer registers and documents all activities that are performed, and makes certain that program changes are executed in a coordinated way.

10-49   Web reporting allows reports and report hierarchies to be output as HTML documents using a browser.

10-50   The large number of features offered by the ABAP Workbench is completed by tools for quality assurance and performance optimization. These tools can execute targeted analyses of either individual programs or a complete system. At that point, they can create detailed statistics on resource consumption and performance.

10-51   Applications developed with ABAP Workbench can simply be ported to various platforms, operating systems, databases, and graphical user interfaces. Communication with other systems is executed reliably through the R/3 technology infrastructure.

10-52   SAP Business Workflow allows enterprises to achieve a great deal of flexibility when designing and automating business processes. This works to accelerate the processes beyond their own boundaries.

10-53   SAP Business Workflow offers an easy working environment that meets the specific needs of both regular and occasional users. The result is that employees are immediately and actively integrated in the enhanced value chains.

10-54   With work items it is possible to illustrate business processes that can be actively controlled using SAP business workflow through the complete processing of a customer order from its receipt through delivery of the goods and issuing the invoice. All steps within this business process can be automated in chronological order, while the roles of the affected employees are defined. Check a customer's credit line and creditworthiness, query the stock on hand, and automatically place an order.

10-55   A workflow can be triggered in SAP Business Workflow through different front ends or applications.

10-56   During the workflow, users can continue to use the environment familiar to them. They can process the individual work items in a working envi-

SOLUTIONS

ronment they know, request information on the current status of specific workflows at any time, and trace the history of the work process. All these functions can also be accessed through the Internet.

10-57   SAP Business Workflow would not be possible without the open nature of Business Framework. This also deals with linking of customer and vendor systems which may be non-R/3 applications. Consider also the fact that staff do not have to use different systems to process workflows. SAP's consistent use of open interfaces and industry standards is useful because SAP is a member of the Workflow Management Coalition (WfMC). SAP has already supplied the first published workflow standard for workflow client applications.

10-58   The functions of SAP Business Workflow can be accessed from all MAPI-compatible clients. Users can continue using their familiar mail front-ends. SAP Business Workflow also offers form integration which permits use of Visual Basic, Outlook, or JetForm forms when automating business processes. The forms can be used to start workflows, both offline and online, and to accelerate form-based tasks within a business process.

10-59   ALE allows loose coupling of different components. These components can be installed with respect to a decentralized plan and be technically independent of each other. They do not all have to be at the same release level. A typical distribution situation could be the centralized management of purchasing agreements for decentralized procurement applications, or the coupling of centralized financial systems that have decentralized logistics applications. The R/3 reference model within the R/3 repository forms the foundation for these situations.

10-60   ALE is based on an exchange of messages controlled by business processes. Applications are integrated using asynchronous communications mechanisms under time control. ALE allows business processes from different systems (each with its own database) to be integrated. ALE is intentionally not based on the concept of distributed databases as this generally requires a great deal of management effort at the same release levels on all network nodes. This is in opposition to the concept of autonomy in economically independent units, and cannot always be realized because of time and cost.

10-61   ALE in the R/3 system offers another important integration technology within Business Framework besides SAP Business Workflow. An array of prefabricated distribution scenarios is supplied with ALE.

10-62   Workflow designs can be simplified and accelerated by the use of Workflow Wizards integrated into SAP Business Workflow. These Workflow

Wizards, or assistants, resemble those found in many PC applications. They guide the designer in a controlled dialog based on carefully prepared questions and decision options, and produce an executable workflow definition quickly and reliably.

10-63 Synchronizing the business processes of the communicating systems is one of ALE's most important tasks. ALE employs standardized intermediate documents (IDocs) to exchange messages containing application data. These documents are analogous to those used by the R/3 functions that support electronic data interchange (EDI). IDocs have a neutral data structure and can also be used by non-SAP components as a standard interface for data transfer. R/3 release 4.0 IDocs can be called via BAPIs.

10-64 In Business Framework, ALE assures achieving process integration between components of ALE and BAPIs. In dealing with object-oriented development of R/3 interface technology and staying within a uniform business framework, the next logical step is to combine ALE with the BAPIs. Existing ALE distribution situations are equipped with BAPIs at each step and new situations are implemented using BAPIs.

SOLUTIONS

CHAPTER 11

Windows NT and UNIX Integration

This chapter discusses three critical areas most organizations need to address for successful integration of Windows NT into UNIX environments: NFS, X terminal emulation, and X access to Windows applications. There are many third-party options in all three areas, as well as other, more specialized aspects of NT/UNIX integration.

The rapid growth of NT/UNIX integration solutions demonstrates the industry's interest in moving Windows NT systems into UNIX environments. It also shows how fortunate Microsoft is to have such a wide array of third-party companies addressing NT/UNIX integration issues. The result is a favorable situation for users, third-party software developers, and especially Microsoft.

All this information can be useful with R/3 applications. Knowing how SAP R/3 functions is not enough. Knowledge of how its client platforms such as UNIX and Windows NT co-exist makes is easier to handle client side issues when running R/3.

BACKGROUND

In many respects, Windows NT is ideally suited to succeed where UNIX has previously been dominant. Windows NT offers powerful workstation and server features that rival of UNIX. On the other hand, Windows NT is rarely in a position to replace existing UNIX systems entirely because it is not binary-compatible with any UNIX version, and many UNIX-based applications have not been moved over to the Windows NT environment.

As a result, Windows NT must be able to coexist and interoperate with UNIX systems in the same network. IT professionals contemplating deploying Windows NT in a UNIX environment face special issues that need to be addressed in the planning stage.

UNIX and NT interoperation can provide the best of both operating system worlds. If some clients still run UNIX, or an element to the Web server that better in that environment, then use the power of the Windows NT platform to manage those capabilities.

NT/UNIX Integration Information

Windows NT is readily moving into UNIX environments. It provides a powerful workstation and server features that rival even the most powerful UNIX workstations and servers. However, it is rarely in a position to replace current UNIX systems entirely because it is not binary-compatible with any UNIX version, and many UNIX-based applications have not been moved over to the Windows NT environment.

Windows NT must be able to coexist with UNIX systems in the same network. An IT professional contemplating deploying Windows NT in a UNIX environment, faces special issues that need to be addressed, in the planning stage.

Integration Tools

A high level of integration between Windows NT and UNIX is possible regardless of the fact that integration services come from Microsoft. The majority of these products and services come from third-party companies that are well known in both UNIX and Windows NT markets. Third-party companies provide essential Windows NT and UNIX integration.

It is imperative to evaluate options for integrating UNIX and Windows NT, explore key third-party products that help with SAP integration, and apply the most straightforward interoperability solutions to common NT configurations. First examine the UNIX integration services that come with Windows NT.

Once Windows 2000 is installed, there are a handful of relatively lackluster tools with which to handle UNIX coexistence and interoperability issues. Microsoft offers a TCP/IP stack, but only provides a weak implementation of Telnet and ftp to go with the TCP/IP stack.

Although Microsoft's Telnet and ftp can be used to access applications and share data on UNIX systems, neither of these tools is as powerful or flexible as any of the commercial versions of Telnet or ftp available from third-party companies.

Telnet implementation only supports basic VT52 and VT100 emulation and the ftp utility is a command-line, character mode program. The least expensive and best method is to use the telnet and ftp utilities built into Netscape Communicator or those within Internet Explorer 4.0. They offer all the options of many third-party application suites and all industry standard features.

Intranet

An intranet, requires integration by using the Web-based services included with Windows NT Server. This includes a highly capable Web server, Internet information server that supports Web, gopher, and anonymous ftp access. However, most corporations use intranets for dispersing information, instead of as an interoperability solution.

Intranets provide far greater flexibility than do groupware solutions (i.e. Lotus Notes). An intranet provides a company with a web-like interface that personnel are familiar with now. An intranet removes a great deal of complexity in learning new software, and allows users to work with a secure solution.

The majority of groupware solutions are expensive and can cost a great deal of time through several version upgrades. An intranet is relatively stable and far less expensive, providing users with the ability to access Web, gopher, and ftp through Windows 2000.

The Windows NT server DNS service can be used to offer name serving to UNIX clients and as a tool designed for UNIX integration. The Windows NT server DNS service provides simple management for both NT and UNIX clients.

Windows NT/UNIX Integration

In order to obtain the highest level of integration between Windows NT and UNIX it is important to have several interoperability requirements that result in:

- ✎ Network File System (NFS) support for real-time, bi-directional file and printer sharing
- ✎ X terminal access from Windows NT systems to UNIX hosts, in order to run native X applications
- ✎ X terminal access from UNIX hosts (or X terminals) to Windows NT, in order to run native Windows applications.
- ✎ Experienced UNIX users migrating to Windows NT systems insisting on a UNIX-like command line environment
- ✎ System administrators demanding tape backup software compatible with UNIX tape formats
- ✎ Software developers requiring a variety of tools to help port programs from UNIX to Windows NT.

NFS Integration

The Network File System (NFS) is the key to contemporary network-based file serving. NFS predates Novell NetWare, Microsoft/3COM LAN Manager, IBM LAN Server, and all other PC-oriented file serving methodologies.

NFS was first created by Sun Microsystems as the file serving component in its Open Network Computing (ONC) architecture. ONC provides several TCP/IP-based networking services, but is best known for its Remote Procedure Call (RPC) and NFS components. The open nature of Sun's ONC architecture permits other UNIX vendors to port ONC components to their own unique environments. NFS early became a de facto standard for file sharing in UNIX networks.

NFS allows a system to access designated directories (including all files and subdirectory entries) on other systems over a TCP/IP network. As with Workgroups (WFW), Windows 95, Windows 98, and Windows NT Workstation, NFS is a peer-oriented solution that permits multiple systems to mount common directories without demanding a dedicated server.

NFS follows a client/server model. Its clients and servers communicate with each other using Sun's RPC architecture over the TCP/IP User Datagram Protocol (UDP) transport. Under this architecture, NFS clients contact a "port mapper" program on the server, and the port mapper translates the RPC service requests into specific TCP/IP sockets serviced by the local NFS server. Under the peer orientation of NFS, a given UNIX system is typically both an NFS client and an NFS server.

To access a directory over the network, the NFS server program must know which directories are available for network access, which client systems can access those directories, and what access rights are associated with various client/directory combinations. This information varies from one UNIX implementation to another. For example, Sun systems use the "share" command to make directories available for network access while most other UNIX implementations usually configure the directory information in a file called *exports*.

An NFS client requests access to a NFS server directory during the boot process or through an interactive "mount" command. The NFS server receives the request though the port mapper program and then compares the requested directory to its list of available directories and authorized client systems. Based on the results of that comparison, the NFS server will either make that directory available to the client or reject the request. Access to specific files and subdirectories in a "mounted" directory is controlled by the access rights assigned to individual users on the client system.

PC Computing

NFS is a UNIX-only offering. Sun Microsystems introduced PCs into NFS with the introduction of PC-NFS. PC-NFS allows PCs to participate in NFS networks as NFS clients. Using PC-NFS, PCs can access UNIX directories as if they were network drives.

Integration of PCs into NFS caused several challenges for developers. For one thing, the PC environment of that time did not support "long" file names; the eight-character file name and three-character extension was the law of the land. Second, PCs did not provide any means of user authentication or access control. Anybody who sat down at a PC keyboard was, in essence, a "superuser" with administrative level rights.

PC-NFS could solve both of these problems. An algorithm was created to translate between UNIX names and legal DOS file names. Thus DOS-based NFS clients could see and access UNIX files with long names, even though the file name might seem more appropriate. This translation occurs on the PC-side of the NFS connection and allows PC-NFS to be compatible with existing NFS server software.

In order to deal with the potential security problem of PC-based users new software was introduced in the NFS server. Sun developed a new server program called the PC-NFS daemon (PCNFSD), which performs two important functions for PC-NFS:

- ✎ **User authentication**—The PC side of PC-NFS includes a logon module that gets invoked before any NFS requests are initiated. The user name and password entered into this module are sent to the PCNFSD program on the NFS server for authentication. A corresponding UNIX user definition must be established on the NFS server, and the access rights for that user will be applied to NFS access through the server.
- ✎ **Print handling**—The PCNFSD program also provides an interface to printers associated with the NFS server. In this scenario, client-side utilities allow the PC user to "mount" printers and direct output to them through local LPT ports. Note that the PCNFSD program delivers the print to the NFS server; PC-NFS does not rely on LPR/LPD services.

TCP/IP's popularity can be seen in the increased use of PC-NFS, making remote file sharing with UNIX systems possible. The number of Web servers operating on UNIX has also increased. NT users often realize they need access to HTML and bit map documents on UNIX Web servers, as well as the ability to modify these. As a result, there has been a trend to provide PC-NFS client software for Windows 2000.

Sun's PC-NFS has been the only significant NFS integration product for the PC market. As the popularity of UNIX increased, however, more and more TCP/IP software vendors introduced NFS products for the PC market. Although these products cannot legally be called PC-NFS, they all support the basic architecture established by Sun's PC-NFS product.

NFS and Windows NT

NFS is important in UNIX networking; the introduction of NFS products to the Windows NT market is significant for several reasons. It allows

Windows NT Workstation and Windows NT Server to be fully integrated into existing UNIX networks. Windows NT users and applications can mount UNIX-based directories and access the information stored in them.

UNIX systems can mount Windows NT directories using standard NFS services and treat those directories just like any other UNIX directory. NFS products for Windows NT are a strategic tool to introducing Windows NT servers into large, or complex multivendor environments. For example, in a mixed PC and UNIX environment, a Windows NT server with NFS services can be placed on the network and provide file, print, and application services for both PC and UNIX systems. PCs can access the Windows NT server using traditional PC LAN services and UNIX systems. PCs can also access the same Windows NT server using NFS. They can even access the same directories.

Added support for NFS is a key element in implementing a successful, fully integrated UNIX-Windows NT environment. The importance of NFS has attracted the attention of a number of software vendors who have developed NFS server and client products for Windows NT. Although there is a great deal of commonality among these third-party products, there are also many differences. These products often differ in how they handle user mapping between UNIX and Windows NT, how they handle file name translation, and how they integrate into the Windows NT environment.

Integrating X Windows

The X Window user interface offers an easy-to-use graphical interface similar to the graphical application interfaces provided by Windows, Windows NT, and Macintosh System 8. The specifications for the X Window System were developed at the Massachusetts Institute of Technology (MIT) under Project Athena. These specifications were subsequently handed over to the non-profit X Consortium (**http://www.x.org**), which now maintains ownership and distribution rights.

The current version of X Window System is commonly referred to as X11. These specifications have undergone a number of revisions; for example, X11R3, X11R5 and X11R6 refer to the third, fifth and sixth revision. X Wsindow System revisions are, for the most part, backward-compatible, although there were a few operational problems with X11R3.

The X11 specifications describe fonts, window controls, and client/server interactions that allow X11 to operate across platforms and UNIX implementations. Despite the flexibility of these specifications, some UNIX vendors have chosen to add proprietary extensions to their X11 implementations.

An important element of X11 is the "window manager," a software module responsible for the appearance and control of individual X window programs in the display area.

More than 24 window managers have been created for X11. Examples include the Universal Window Manager (uwm), the Tab Windows Manager (twm—an earlier version of twm was called Tom's Window Manager), and the Motif Windows Manager (mwm). Most windows mangers are public domain products; however, some UNIX vendors have also developed proprietary windows managers. These include HP's HP VUE, Digital Equipment's DECwindows, and IBM's AIXwindows.

Although an X Window system product can run the full range of "standard" X11 programs, it may be not be able to run mission-critical X programs that depend on proprietary extensions. Consider this a word of caution: pay close attention to any extensions that can make it difficult to achieve true interoperability.

The system displaying the X application is called a "server" and the system where the binary program for the X application resides (and actually runs) is called the "client." Under the X terminology, an X Window terminal is really a server. With this in mind, it might be easier to think of products called "X servers" as X Window terminal emulators.

The X Window server products available for Windows share several operating requirements and features. Most X products run as native Windows NT applications (no underlying services installed). Many of them require an SVGA display subsystem configured for 256 colors (or more). More important these products share the following key capabilities:

✎ They can run X Window programs on the Windows NT desktop. Each X Window program appears in a standard Windows NT window and supports standard Windows NT controls. One way of running X applications under Windows NT is to run each application as a native Windows application

✎ They can run X Window programs within the context of a single Windows NT window. In this configuration, that specific Windows NT window must be accessed in order to access the individual X Window programs running in it

✎ The X applications can also be run in a single terminal window controlled by a remote window manager.

Running X Window programs on the Windows NT desktop is the most natural use of the Windows NT environment. The X Window programs support the same controls as normal Windows programs, and, in more general terms, have the same look and feel as native Windows NT programs. This approach also provides the best performance.

The performance advantage of using the Windows NT desktop for X programs relates to running the X programs under a single Windows NT window. For most X products, there must be a remote window manager (e.g., twm, uwm, mwm, etc.) to manage the X programs that will display in the single window. When a remote window manager is used, every mouse click and control option is being handled remotely. This can be slow. To create an X Window System environment on NT that looks and acts exactly as it does on a UNIX system, this is really your only choice.

Two major areas where X Window software products differ from each other are:

✎ How X Window programs are launched on the remote system
✎ How X Window fonts are handled

Be careful about blind program-launching. Many products do not display error messages generated by the remote system in response to font incompatibilities, command errors, or incorrect parameters. For this reason it may be preferable to use Microsoft's Telnet or rsh facility until command initiation becomes second nature. (An X server product's launch facility does not really have to be used to start X programs).

X Access for Windows Applications

Having the ability to run Windows applications in an X terminal environment provides new power and capabilities to a network. Suddenly, everyone can use the same word processor such as Word for Windows, the same spreadsheet, such as Microsoft Excel, and other common Windows-based applications.

In order to get Word for Windows to run on a X terminal use Citrix's WinFrame technology or rely on technology developed by Prologue Software.

The Citrix architecture offers a thin layer of software placed in a client system (or network computer). This software establishes a link to an NT Server system through a protocol called the Intelligent Console Architecture (ICA) protocol. The purpose of this protocol is to redirect the local screen, keyboard, and mouse actions to the server and post the information received from the server back to the user's system.

ICA offers an effective protocol that can operate over wide as well as local area links. It is similar to the approach used by "remote control" products since both permit doing everything at the user's system that can be done from the server's keyboard, mouse, and monitor.

The most significant difference between Citrix's approach and the approach used by remote control products depends on the server side of the equation. Specifically, Citrix worked with Microsoft to develop a special, multiuser version of NT Server. This special version allows multiple users to access the server system via ICA. Each user can have a separate virtual NT machine. This special version of NT it is marketed only by Citrix and the companies that have relicensed Citrix's technology. Once an ICA client is hooked up to a server, that client can run any program which can be run under Windows NT. This includes 32-bit Windows programs, 16-bit Windows programs, and DOS command-line programs.

Some vendors are trying to access a Citrix WinFrame server directly using X11 by bringing X11 technology to the Citrix environment. The resulting products accommodate either ICA or X clients concurrently. This environment makes it possible to connect to a DOS or Windows application from Windows systems running ICA client software, Windows systems running X terminal emulation software, UNIX workstations supporting X11, Mac systems running ICA or X software, and of course, any networked computer that supports either the ICA or X11 protocol.

These products provide dual X/ICA support and the same core set of features, but differ in available extended options. Some of the products support dynamic NIS integration and UNIX users to be automatically replicated into the Windows NT environment. Others provide only a one-time NIS import facility.

A few of these products support tftp, bootp, and XDM extensions, making it possible to start and manage X terminals from a Windows NT system. Other products require the presence of a UNIX system to load and control the X terminal environment. At present, all of the products in this area are racing to achieve parity with one another, so they are all rapidly becoming more feature-rich. Citrix products include WinFrame and WinFrame Workgroups for up to five users. These application server products permit the effective and efficient enterprise-wide deployment of applications created for Windows operating systems.

With the Prologue architecture, X-enabling software operates as a set of services in a standard Windows NT system. Unlike the Citrix solution, no special version of Windows NT is required. This approach makes it easier to deploy Prologue-based solutions, but it remains to be seen if this architecture can scale as well as the Citrix-based solution, which benefits from highly optimized multi-user services embedded in the Windows NT kernel.

Integration Issues with SAP

When dealing with an SAP implementation, there is now greater understanding of the level of interaction between Windows NT and UNIX. Successful integration of Windows NT into UNIX environments includes NFS, X terminal emulation, and X access to Windows applications. Many third-party options are available in all three areas—as well as other, more specialized aspects of NT/UNIX integration.

The rapid growth of NT/UNIX integration solutions illustrates the increasing interest in moving Windows NT systems into UNIX environments. It also illustrates how fortunate Microsoft is to have such a wide array of third-party companies addressing NT/UNIX integration issues.

Summary

This chapter deals with the ongoing debate over using Windows NT vs. UNIX. In recent years, many organizations have exhibited a mass exodus to the Windows NT platform because of security issues and the fact that Windows NT provides a more user-friendly graphical environment. This chapter deals with the best way of using telnet/ftp utilities, Intranet/internet/extranet integration, and NFS server integration issues.

Integration issues are often prevalent when changing from one operating system to another. However, when changing from one version of a software to another there are an entirely new set of complex issues that must be dealt with.

11-1 How can a high level of integration between Windows NT and UNIX be achieved?

TIP

It is important to know how to evaluate options for integrating UNIX and Windows NT, explore key third-party products which help with the integration, and apply the most straightforward interoperability solutions to common NT configurations. To begin, we will look at the basic UNIX integration services that come with Windows NT.

11-2 Explain what happens when Windows NT is installed. How well do the tools handle UNIX integration issues?

11-3 Can Microsoft's Telnet and FTP access applications share data on UNIX systems?

11-4 What does the standard telnet implementation support?

11-5 Choose a better method of using telnet and ftp utilities. Explain why it is better.

11-6 How can integration be achieved just by having an Intranet?

11-7 Compare and contrast intranets and groupware solutions.

11-8 What does an intranet do for users?

11-9 What does an intranet give users the ability to do?

11-10 How can the Windows NT Server DNS service be used?

11-11 What is the goal of integration between Windows NT and UNIX?

11-12 Explain three integration concerns that may crop up in a typical large organization.

11-13 What are important issues in NFS integration?

BACKGROUND

NFS was originally developed by Sun Microsystems as the file serving component in its Open Network Computing (ONC) architecture. ONC provides a broad range of TCP/IP-based networking services, but is best known for its Remote Procedure Call (RPC) and NFS components. The "open" nature of Sun's ONC architecture allowed other UNIX vendors to port ONC components to their own unique environments. NFS is standard for file sharing in UNIX networks.

11-14 What does NFS allow a system to access?

QUESTIONS

11-15 Explain how NFS clients and servers communicate with one another. What means of communication does NFS use?

11-16 Explain how a "port mapper" program runs on the server.

11-17 Explain the exact method of configuring information for Sun Systems. How does the share command play an important role?

11-18 How does the NFS client request access to an NFS server directory?

11-19 What happens when the NFS server receives a request?

11-20 What happens when the client request is satisfied?

11-21 Illustrate how an NFS client system can initiate the command: mount maven:/users /susers.

11-22 Explain other methods for controlling access to specific files and subdirectories in a "mounted" directory. What controls the directory?

NOTE

There is a high degree of similarity between NFS and the file sharing approach supported by Windows for Workgroups, Windows 95, Windows 98, and Windows NT. This similarity makes it easy for the same client to support both Microsoft and NFS file sharing.

NFS servers assume that the requesting NFS client enforces user authentication and access rights. The NFS server trusts that the client will not allow dangerous users to access important or sensitive files.

BACKGROUND

NFS was always a UNIX-only offering. In the late 1980s Sun Microsystems brought PCs into the NFS fold with the introduction of PC-NFS. PC-NFS was meant to allow PCs to participate in NFS networks as NFS clients. PCs can access UNIX directories using PC-NFS as if they were network drives. This is best illustrated by the fact that the /users directory on NFS server system maven could be mounted on the PC as network drive s:.

11-23 What kind of challenges resulted from the integration of PCs into NFS?

11-24 What changed in PC-NFS to make PC integration more secure?

11-25 Where does filename translation for DOS-based NFS clients take place?

11-26 How was the PC security problem addressed?

11-27 How does user authentication play an important role in security? Explain in detail with respect to PC-NFS.

11-28 What is involved in print handling?

11-29 What makes remote file sharing with UNIX systems possible?

11-30 What is the result of the introduction of NFS products for Windows NT?

11-31 What happens in a mixed PC and UNIX environment?

11-32 What is involved in providing support for NFS?

11-33 Explain how X Windows integration takes place.

11-34 Who developed the specifications for the X Window System?

11-35 What are X11 specifications and what do they describe?

11-36 What is the windows manager?

11-37 What happens when an X Windows system is asked to run proprietary extensions?

TIP

Terminology is often a difficult in the X Window system. The system that is displaying the X application is called a "server" and the system where the binary program for the X application resides and runs is called the "client." Using X terminology, an X Window terminal is really a server. It might easier to think of products called "X servers" as X Window terminal emulators.

11-38 Name a factor common to X Window Server products?

11-39 What two capabilities do X Windows and Windows NT applications share?

11-40 What benefit is there to running X Window programs on the Windows NT desktop?

11-41 Describe in detail the performance advantage gained by using the Windows NT desktop for X programs.

11-42 What happens when a remote windows manager is used?

11-43 What are the two major areas in which X window software products differ from one another?

11-44 What specific questions require careful evaluation when choosing an X server product for font handling?

11-45 What is "blind" program launching?

11-46 What happens when X server software is asked to run in a 16-bit Windows environment?

11-47 What benefits are there to running Windows applications in an X terminal environment?

11-48 How can MS Word run on a X terminal?

11-49 What is the purpose of the ICA protocol?

11-50 Explain where ICA can operate.

11-51 Cite a major difference between the Citrix WinFrame approach and the method employed by remote control products.

11-52 What can the client run when an ICA client is hooked up to the server?

11-53 Explain the server-side hardware requirements necessary to handle multiple users.

11-54 What are the requirements on the client system?

11-55 Is it better directly to access a Citrix WinFrame server using X11?

11-56 In an X Windows environment, what can be connected to a DOS or Windows application?

11-57 What kind of core functionality is offered by dual X/ICA support?

11-58 Explain what extensions these X/ICA products support.

11-59 What do the Citrix products include?

11-60 What is involved in the prologue approach?

11-61 How is the prologue approach different from the Citrix solution?

11-1 It is possible to achieve a high level of integration between Windows NT and UNIX, though few of these integration services come from Microsoft. The majority come from third-party companies with a strong connection to both the UNIX and Windows NT markets. Without these third-party companies, Windows NT and UNIX integration would be virtually impossible.

11-2 After Windows NT is installed, there will be a handful of relatively bland tools for handling UNIX coexistence and interoperability issues. Microsoft provides a TCP/IP stack, but only offers a weak implementation of Telnet and ftp to go with the TCP/IP stack.

11-3 Yes, Microsoft's Telnet and ftp can be used to access applications and share data on UNIX systems, but neither of these tools is as powerful or flexible as any of the commercial versions of Telnet or ftp available from third-party companies.

11-4 Telnet implementation only supports basic VT52 and VT100 emulation and the ftp utility is a command-line, character-mode program.

11-5 The least expensive and best method is to use the telnet and ftp utilities built into Netscape Communicator 4.0 or those within Internet Explorer 4.0. They offer all the options of many third-party application suites and all industry-standard features.

11-6 An intranet can help achieve some level of integration by using the Web-based services included with Windows NT Server. These include a highly capable Web server, Internet Information Server (IIS 4.0), that supports web, gopher, and anonymous ftp access. However, most corporations use intranets primarily for dispersing information, rather than as an interoperability solution.

11-7 Intranets offer greater flexibility than do groupware solutions such as Lotus Notes. An intranet allows a company to have a Web-like interface that personnel already know.

11-8 An intranet removes a great deal of complexity in learning new software, and allows users to work with a secure solution. While many groupware solutions are expensive in both price and time to implement numerous version upgrades, an intranet is relatively stable and far less expensive.

11-9 An intranet gives users the ability to access Web, gopher, and ftp through the Windows NT server simply and efficiently. Complex and expensive software often does not compare to a clearly specified user interface.

11-10 The Windows NT Server DNS service can also be used to provide name serving to UNIX clients. The Windows NT Server DNS service provides the ease of use associated with a Windows NT environment. While

SOLUTIONS

designed primarily for Windows NT clients, it offers simplicity for managing both NT and UNIX clients.

11-11   In most mixed environments, interoperability requirements result in one or all of the following:

1. Network File System (NFS) support for real-time, bi-directional file and printer sharing

2. X terminal access from Windows NT systems to UNIX hosts, in order to run native X applications

3. X terminal access from UNIX hosts (or X terminals) to Windows NT, to run native Windows applications.

11-12   Three integration concerns are:

1. Experienced UNIX users migrating to Windows NT systems may insist on a UNIX-like command-line environment

2. System administrators will demand tape backup software compatible with UNIX tape formats

3. Software developers will require a variety of tools to help them port their programs from UNIX to Windows NT.

11-13   Important issues in NFS integration are X terminal emulation and X access to Windows applications.

11-14   NFS allows a system to access designated directories (including all files and subdirectory entries) on other systems over a TCP/IP network. Analogous to Windows for Workgroups (WFW), Windows 95, Windows 98, and Windows NT Workstation, NFS is a peer-oriented solution that allows multiple systems to mount common directories without demanding a dedicated server (although one can be implemented if desired).

11-15   NFS follows a client/server model. NFS clients and servers communicate with one another using Sun's RPC architecture, which operates over the TCP/IP User Datagram Protocol (UDP) transport.

11-16   NFS clients contact a "port mapper" program on the server, and the port mapper translates the RPC service requests into specific TCP/IP sockets serviced by the local NFS server. Under the peer orientation of NFS, a given UNIX system is typically both an NFS client and an NFS server.

11-17   Sun systems use the share command to make directories available for network access while most other UNIX implementations usually configure the directory information in a file called exports.

11-18   The NFS client requests access to a NFS server directory on the client side during the boot process or through an interactive mount command.

11-19 When the NFS server receives a request through the port mapper program, it compares the requested directory to its list of available directories and authorized client systems. The NFS server will either make that directory available to the client under the control of the associated access rights or reject the request.

11-20 Once the client request is satisfied, the client system can access the NFS directory as though it were a local directory entry.

11-21 An NFS client system named `miller` could initiate the following command: `mount maven:/users /susers`.

    If the NFS server system named `maven` were configured to allow `miller` to mount its `/users` directory, the request would be satisfied. A user working on system `miller` could then change to the `/susers` local directory and attempt to access files and subdirectories stored in the `/users` directory on system `maven`.

11-22 Access to specific files and subdirectories in a "mounted" directory is controlled by the access rights assigned to individual users on the client system. Even though system `miller` can mount the `/users` directory on system `maven`, not all users assigned to `miller` can necessarily access the information in the mounted directory.

11-23 Integration of PCs into NFS presented several challenges for the developers of PC-NFS. The PC environment of that time did not support "long" file names; the eight-character file name and three-character extension was used. PCs did not provide any means of user authentication or access control. Anyone who sat down at a PC keyboard was, in essence, a "superuser" with administrative-level rights.

11-24 PC-NFS developers created an algorithm to translate between UNIX names and legal DOS file names. DOS-based NFS clients can see and access UNIX files with long names, even though the file name may look like `testin~1.tes` instead of `testingfile.test`.

11-25 File name translation for DOS-based NFS clients takes place on the PC side of the NFS connection, which allows PC-NFS to be compatible with existing NFS server software.

11-26 Addressing the potential security problem of PC-based users required the introduction of new software in the NFS server. Sun created a new server program called the PC-NFS daemon (PCNFSD), which performs two important functions for PC-NFS.

11-27 User authentication takes place on the PC side of PC-NFS and includes a logon module that is invoked before any NFS requests are initiated. The

SOLUTIONS

user name and password entered into this module are sent to the PCNFSD program on the NFS server for authentication. A corresponding UNIX user definition must be established on the NFS server, and the access rights for that user will be applied to NFS access through the server.

11-28 In print handling, the PCNFSD program also provides an interface to printers associated with the NFS server. In this situation, client-side utilities allow the PC user to "mount" printers and direct output to them through local LPT ports. The PCNFSD program delivers the print to the NFS server, while PC-NFS does not rely on LPR/LPD services.

11-29 TCP/IP demonstrates the increased use of PC-NFS, enabling file sharing with UNIX systems. The number of Web servers operating on UNIX has also increased. NT users often realize they need access to HTML and bitmap documents on UNIX Web servers, as well as the ability to modify these documents. As a result, there has been a trend to providing PC-NFS client software for Windows 2000.

11-30 Products are fully integrated into existing UNIX networks. Windows NT users and applications can mount UNIX-based directories and access the information stored in them. In the same way, UNIX systems can mount Windows NT directories using standard NFS services and treat those directories just like any other UNIX directory. NFS products for Windows NT are important tools to introduce Windows NT servers into large or complex multi-vendor environments.

11-31 In a mixed PC and UNIX environment, Windows NT server with NFS services can be placed on the network and provide file, print, and application services for both PC and UNIX systems. PCs can access the Windows NT server using traditional PC LAN services such as LAN Manager, Windows for Workgroups, Windows 95, or even Windows NT Workstation. UNIX systems can access the same Windows NT Server using NFS. They can even access the same directories.

11-32 Support for NFS is elemental to implementing a successful, fully integrated UNIX–Windows NT environment. NFS has attracted the attention of a number of software vendors who have developed NFS server and client products for Windows NT. Third-party companies handle user mapping between UNIX and Windows NT, file name translation, and integration into the Windows NT environment.

11-33 The X Window user interface provides a simple and easy graphical interface analogous to the graphical application interfaces provided by Windows, Windows NT, and Macintosh System 8.

SOLUTIONS

11-34 The specifications for the X Window system were developed at the Massachusetts Institute of Technology (MIT) under Project Athena. They were subsequently handed over to the non-profit X Consortium, which now maintains ownership and distribution rights.

11-35 The X11 specifications describe fonts, window controls, and client/server interactions that allow X11 to operate across platforms and UNIX implementations. Some UNIX vendors have chosen to add proprietary extensions to their X11 implementations (just as they do with the UNIX operating system itself). Hewlett-Packard, Digital Equipment Company (DEC), and IBM developed proprietary X tools that use custom fonts. The result is that some X programs are not compatible across platforms.

11-36 X11 also offers the window manager, a software module responsible for the appearance and control of individual X window programs in the display area. There are more than two dozen window managers developed for X11. The more common ones include the Universal Window Manager (uwm), the Tab Windows Manager (twm—an earlier version of twm was called Tom's Window Manager), and the Motif Windows Manager (mwm). Most windows managers are public domain products; however, some UNIX vendors have also developed proprietary windows managers. These include HP's HP VUE, Digital Equipment's DECwindows, and IBM's AIXwindows.

11-37 Although an X Window System product can run the full range of "standard" X11 programs, it may not be able to run mission-critical X programs that depend on proprietary extensions. Remember to look carefully at extensions that can make it difficult to achieve true interoperability. Do not allow hardware-dependent programs to compromise interoperability with any generic equipment. As product vendors change frequently, be sure to have the ability to acquire new extensions for operating environment.

11-38 The X Window server products available for Windows share several common operating requirements and features. The majority of X products function as native Windows NT applications without any underlying services installed. Most of them require an SVGA display subsystem configured for at least 256 colors.

11-39 Both X Windows and Windows NT share many functions and capabilities. They can run X Window programs on the Windows NT desktop. Each X window program appears in a standard Windows NT window and supports standard Windows NT controls. One method of running X applications under Windows NT is to run each application as a native Windows application. X Window programs can run within the context of

SOLUTIONS

a single Windows NT window. However, in this configuration, it is necessary to access a specific Windows NT window in order to access the individual X Window programs running in it. All X applications can also be run in a single terminal window controlled by a remote window manager.

11-40   Running X Window programs on the Windows NT desktop offers the best fit with the Windows NT environment. The X Window programs support the same controls as normal Windows programs do, and have the same look and feel as native Windows NT programs. This approach provides the best performance.

11-41   The performance advantage of using the Windows NT desktop for X programs relates to running the X programs under a single Windows NT window. For most X products, a remote window manager (e.g., twm, uwm, mwm, etc.) must be run to manage the X programs that will display in the single window.

11-42   When a remote window manager is used, every mouse click and control option is being handled remotely. This can be slow. However, if an X Window System environment on NT that looks and acts exactly like it does on a UNIX system is required, this is really the only choice.

11-43   Two major areas where X Window software products differ from one another are: how X Window programs are launched on the remote system and How X Window fonts are handled.

11-44   Font handling encompasses several topics that require careful evaluation before choosing an X server product. These include:

1. Which fonts are included?
2. How are they stored?
3. Are proprietary fonts included?

11-45   Many products do not display any error messages generated by the remote system in response to font incompatibilities, command errors, or incorrect parameters. It is therefore, prudent to use Microsoft's Telnet or rsh facility until realizing command initiation.

11-46   Before trying to run X server software in the 16-bit Windows environment, look hard at X server software running under Windows NT. There is a significant performance difference. The best performance is obtained by running X Windows applications in native windows on the Windows NT desktop. Even though this requires sacrifice of the user-friendly interface of the X11 window manager (i.e., uwn, twm, mwm), the look and feel of native Windows NT windows in return does not sacrifice the user-friendly nature you may enjoy. This approach provides consistency across all applications, regardless of their origin.

11-47 The ability to run Windows applications in an X terminal environment offers new power and capabilities to a network. The result is that everyone uses the same word processor (MS Word), the same spreadsheet (MS Excel), and other common Windows-based applications.

11-48 Two approaches can help achieve the goal of running MS Word on an X terminal. One approach is based on Citrix's WinFrame technology; the other is based on technology developed by Prologue Software. Under the Citrix architecture, a thin layer of software is placed in a client system (or network computer). This software establishes a link to an NT server system using a protocol called the Intelligent Console Architecture (ICA) protocol.

11-49 The purpose of the ICA protocol is to redirect the local screen, keyboard, and mouse actions to the server, and to post the information received from the server back to the user's system.

11-50 ICA is a quick protocol that can operate over wide-area links as well as local-area links. The Citrix WinFrame technology is similar to the approach used by "remote control" products, because both approaches make it possible to do everything at the user's system that can be done from the server's keyboard, mouse, and monitor.

11-51 The most significant difference between Citrix's approach and the approach used by remote-control products lies on the server side of the equation. Citrix worked with Microsoft to create a special, multi-user version of NT server. This special version allows multiple users to access the server system via ICA. Every user can have a separate virtual NT machine. However, this special version of NT Server does not come from Microsoft; it is marketed by Citrix and the companies that have relicensed Citrix's technology.

11-52 Once an ICA client is hooked up to a server, that client can run any program that can be run under Windows NT. This includes 32-bit Windows programs, 16-bit Windows programs, and DOS command-line programs.

11-53 Unfortunately, the server-side hardware requirements to handle multiple users are not insignificant. There must be a server system with a fast CPU (or multiple CPUs), and plenty of memory. The exact requirements depend on the applications, but a good start would be a 400 MHz Pentium processor with 128 MB of memory.

11-54 The requirements on the client system are much less stringent. The ICA client component is a relatively small program and versions of it have been

SOLUTIONS

developed for Windows, Windows 95, Windows 98, Windows NT Workstation, Macintosh, and UNIX environments. Therefore, ICA can be used as a means enable X terminal access to Windows applications. This involves simply running an ICA client program on the X Window terminal.

11-55 Some vendors are trying to bring X11 technology to the Citrix environment. The resulting products make it possible to accommodate either ICA or X clients concurrently.

11-56 You can connect:

- ✎ Windows systems running ICA client software
- ✎ Windows systems running X terminal emulation software
- ✎ UNIX workstations supporting X11
- ✎ Mac systems running ICA or X software
- ✎ Any networked computer that supports either the ICA or X11 protocol.

11-57 The products that offer dual X/ICA support the same core set of functionality, but differ dramatically in available extended options. Some of the products support dynamic NIS integration and allow UNIX users to be automatically replicated into the Windows NT environment. Others provide only a one-time NIS import facility.

11-58 Some of the products supported include tftp, bootp, and XDM extensions. X terminals can be started and managed from a Windows NT system. Other products need the presence of a UNIX system to load and control the X terminal environment.

11-59 Some of the Citrix products include WinFrame and WinFrame Workgroups for up to five users. These application server-products permit the effective and efficient enterprisewide deployment of applications created for Windows operating systems.

11-60 The Prologue approach is an X-only solution with no support for ICA available. Under the Prologue architecture, the X-enabling software runs as a set of services in a standard Windows NT system.

11-61 In contrast to the Citrix solution, no special version of Windows NT is required. This approach makes it easier to deploy Prologue-based solutions, though it remains to be seen if this architecture can scale as well as the Citrix-based solution, which benefits from highly optimized multi-user services embedded in the Windows NT kernel.

SOLUTIONS

SAProcesses in Technology

The open nature of Business Framework satisfies the demands of users who want to keep the interfaces they are already familiar with. A great deal of support must be provided both to experienced R/3 users and those who only occasionally use R/3 to place an order over the Internet.

User Interfaces

SAP concentrates on R/3 development efforts to provide a simple user-friendly interface developed on the most current ergonomic research from an in-house ergonomics laboratory other areas. The graphical user interface is uniform throughout all R/3 applications and opens up the entire system to experienced users.

SAPGUI software supports over 20 languages including the pictographic languages Kanji (Japanese) and Mandarin (Chinese) which, due to their extensive character sets, require two bytes to represent each character in the R/3 system. It is installed on each R/3 front end and handles both this user interface and the communication between the presentation and application servers.

Java is a SAPGUI platform expanding business on the Internet and has established itself as a new, hardware-independent, easy-to-use platform. SAP offers experienced users access to R/3 system functions through the Internet using SAPGUI in Java. The Java-based version of SAPGUI runs on a Web client and provides the same look and feel as the native SAPGUI interface. SAPGUI in Java allows new platforms such as NetPCs or NCs to be used as R/3 clients.

In R/3 4.0, SAPGUI deals with all front-end components such as the reusable program modules or "JavaBeans" that provide the environments for spread-sheet, graphics, and word processing software integrated into SAPGUI. The multimedia R/3 front end is multimedia-based and as easy to use as a Web browser. Various types of information including text, tables, graphics, photographs, and HTML documents can be displayed and edited simultaneously on a single R/3 screen.

Users also have access to a WYSIWYG editor (RTF editor component) to create, edit, and display texts. Components will also be offered for handling tables, HTML documents, graphics, and photos. This technology is implemented using a front-end component framework which supports different components and controls their communication with the R/3 System.

Business Engineer

Business Engineer makes it possible to select only those R/3 components and functions that a company actually needs and uses in productive operation. R/3 offers individualized business application. When a productive R/3 system is customized and installed, Business Engineer helps create the information that describes the specific R/3 implementation.

Session Manager

Session Manager permits access to information that defines the specific R/3 implementation. This represents another step toward a user-specific interface, allowing users to work their way through the R/3 system, and to customize the desktop. It is also possible to navigate through the complete R/3 system from the central Session Manager screen and select a specific view by mouse click.

Session Manager operates on Windows 95 and Windows NT front ends. In R/3 4.0 it can also be used as an Internet session manager via a Web browser. Besides SAPGUI, the R/3 system supports several other user interfaces. Users who rarely work with R/3 or who are accustomed to desktop interfaces like a Windows GUI or a Web browser can benefit from the power of an R/3 system "Inside Out."

Enterprises can take advantage of the potential of the development environments and programming languages underlying other user interfaces as well as associated business applications in combination with the R/3 system "Outside In."

The inside out method allows users to work with a Windows GUI or a Web browser instead of the SAPGUI. Users often deploy these front ends to stay in a familiar environment yet derive full benefit from the R/3 system.

Operation Performance

Daily operation performance offers powerful transaction processing capabilities, and its complicated business application logic is extended from the R/3 system to the workstations of employees who do not normally use R/3.

BAPIs provide assistance, specially designed ABAP applications, so that R/3 can be made available on a controlled business basis. SAP systematically enhances business processes from the R/3 system into the Internet. BAPIs and SAP also provide prefabricated R/3 Internet applications for business-to-business, consumer-to-business or intranet communication.

Employees must contend with everything from business partners to consumers who order products from their home PCs, to employees who implement intranet solutions for communication within the company. These people all use commercial Web browsers to interact with the R/3 system. Internet applications implemented separately in the R/3 system can access core R/3 functions using BAPIs.

SAP Automation provides its own class of dynamic interfaces for application programming. The manual entry of R/3 transactions is automated so that almost any R/3 function can be controlled by an external program from the outside in. In essence, it does not matter whether this is a telephony system, an electronic kiosk, a scanner, a PC program or a new type of self-service application. A customer can query the status of an order over the telephone by keying in the order number. This action triggers the relevant R/3 transaction and the result is output through a speech generator.

SAP Automaton

SAP Automation facilitates the "Outside In" process using SAPGUI communication services to exchange message packets between the application and presentation servers, to pack and unpack data, and to transfer data to the application server or downstream client for further processing. It transfers messages from the program to the application server where processing occurs and interprets data from the application server so it can filter out the data structures required by the program.

With the Outside In process, external applications of all types can utilize R/3 system functions through BAPIs. SAP Automation is an important element in the Business Framework since it offers an additional interface for accessing BAPIs. It also includes the necessary libraries.

SAP has implemented controls that simplify access to BAPI definitions and descriptions in the R/3 system from an external programming environment. These include BAPI controls (ActiveX controls) for Visual Basic that promote direct programming on the control. R/3 system communication is already implemented in the BAPI control.

R/3 can integrate the Internet into business processes with cross-system and enterprise boundaries. In order to satisfy this expansion, the hypertext structure of the World Wide Web has been enhanced by an application structure for business transaction processing. The R/3 system can be accessed directly from the Web without having to store R/3 functions on a Web server.

Internet enterprises offer new ways of redesigning and optimizing business activities with respect to other enterprises (business-to-business), end consumers (consumer-to-business) and among employees (intranet).

The Internet-enabling layer functions as the interface between an HTTP server and the R/3 system when a Web browser or HTTP server is used to access the R/3 system. Each system must map the other's protocols and data formats. An extra R/3 layer enables data exchange between the HTTP server and R/3, specifically the application server where all business transactions are processed.

R/3 uses a series of dynamic programs called Dynpros. Dynpros are composed of a screen and associated process logic. In an Internet-enabling layer Dynpros are compiled into a series of HTML documents which are then transferred through an HTTP server to a Web browser. Whenever data are transferred in the other direction, the field contents of HTML documents are converted into Dynpro data. Changes in core R/3 functions are not required. Enterprises rely on proven performance, stability, and the scope of R/3 business functions in their daily Internet business operations.

Multiple R/3 Internet Application Components (IACs) have been produced with direct input from SAP customers according to the "Inside Out" approach. R/3 Internet components are written in ABAP and represent autonomous entities that run on the application server and add new functions to R/3 core components. Internet and core components can communicate through object-oriented BAPIs.

BAPIs

BAPIs offer an interface technology based on a system of common business semantics. It is independent from the communication and transport foundation technology. The business-oriented character of the BAPIs ensures that R/3 Internet components and R/3 core components can communicate regardless of their release version.

The "Outside-in" approach focuses on responding to the requirements of companies already using the tested R/3 functions and having ABAP as their main development environment.

The openness of Business Framework makes R/3 accessible to other companies as well. When a company has development environments that primarily use Visual Basic, C, C++ or, Java, this often means that there is a strong need for a range of interfaces to deal with legacy systems or database systems and dictionaries not supported by SAP.

BAPI specifications develop the foundation for Business Framework integration that allows for the development of Internet applications using R/3 core components but operating on application servers outside the R/3 system and created in languages including Visual Basic, C, C++, or Java.

These applications function with respect to the "Outside In" approach. This ensures extensive scalability, high-performance transaction processing, and security. Regardless of the option a company chooses to satisfy its business needs, Business Framework BAPIs ensure that specific situations are available for users.

Extended Value Chain

The tasks of the extended value chain are more evenly distributed through business-to-business communication. Business processes are accelerated. Consumer-to-business applications assist global enterprises in opening up new consumer markets and retaining customers. With a simple Web browser, it is possible to access a product catalog at any hour of the day, and place an order right away. Customers can also query the status of an order and determine when delivery is scheduled. Intranet applications enhance the internal flow of information and communications.

Users can deploy an intranet to perform personnel tasks including updating personal data or querying leave or travel expense accounts. This alleviates the strains on the human resources department, allowing a focus on strategic personnel planning. It does not matter which front ends are used to access R/3 functions. Whatever network solutions are implemented within Business Framework, the performance and stability of the R/3 system during productive operation is critical.

ABAP

With ABAP virtual machine (ABAP VM), R/3 can function at a high level of performance. The ABAP VM installed on each application server offers complex mechanisms for optimal results during high-load operation and ensures the scalability needed for growing requirements. The ABAP programs function on the application layer to implement the business logic of R/3 applications. They are executed by the ABAP VM on each application server.

ABAP VM ensures that all R/3 application components can be executed without modification in different system environments. The R/3 runtime environment is implemented ABAP VM. The ABAP VM maintains system independence, high performance, and scalability.

ABAP VM is programmed in ANSI-C and C++, through most R/3 application programs are compiled in 4GL ABAP. Both ABAP programs and Dynpros consist of a screen and the associated process logic. These items are executed by an interpreter. ABAP programs and Dynpros are the two most crucial processes of the ABAP VM and are stored centrally on the database server and dynamically loaded onto the application or presentation server when called by the user.

Business and Database Transactions

There are several major differences between business and database transactions. Some processes executed on the application server at runtime have the sole purpose of overcoming these differences.

Business transactions are functionally related processing units that execute permissible databases changes consistently. They involve debit and credit postings that only make sense together. Most business transactions are more complex and affect a large number of tables in a relational database. These tables must be managed with appropriate locks throughout the entire transaction until completion.

When a production order is created, the system duplicates the bills of material, the price of each material, the routings, the cost of each operation, as well as the material numbers of required materials. It then locks these items as they are processed.

Strict requirements affect all transaction processing in the R/3 system. SAP transactions are implemented as a sequence of logically related, consistent dialog steps. SAP transactions are not always executed within a single work process. Each dialog step in a transaction is processed by one or more work processes. The asynchronous update procedure permits execution of the dialog operations of an SAP transaction and makes the required database updates in different work processes or even on different servers.

The Dispatcher

Each application server incorporates a central dispatcher and several work processes, whose actual number depends on computer performance and the number of processors installed. The dispatcher distributes queued processing requests among the work processes, each of which consists of four main processors:

- ABAP processor
- Dynpro processor
- Database access agent
- Coordinating task handler.

In addition, the dispatcher distributes processing requests to the individual work processes. Special work processes can be installed for dialog processing, updating of change documents, lock management, background processing, and spooling. The dispatcher and work processes map the functions of a TP monitor. An application server has only one dispatcher but several work processes.

Task handlers coordinate activities involved in a work process. If application logic is being processed (i.e. dialogs, updates, and background processing) the task handler activates the Dynpro processor and ABAP processor as required.

Because of the client/server architecture of the R/3 runtime system and use of special work processes controlled by the dispatcher, the R/3 system is optimally equipped for use in multiprocessor environments.

Work Processes

Work processes of an application server can be reserved exclusively for the R/3 Human Resources component, while other application servers are reserved for background processing. There are also work processes meant mostly for spooling.

The message server is crucial within specific scenarios. Each server is installed logically just once in the R/3 system, and its purpose is to assure a consistent view of the different application servers. The message server operates partly as a pure transport mechanism, but also provides internal information on the load distribution across the different application servers. One use of this information is to assure a more uniform distribution of transaction processing among the servers.

Multiprocessor environments.

The *enqueue* work process is associated with the message server that ensures all the necessary locks are set and remain set until transaction processing has been completed, even when complex transactions operate on different application servers. This permits the R/3 system to be scaled with respect to specific enterprise requirements, and allows optimal management of the different application servers and their performance even in complex environments.

Dialog work processes each handle open user sessions one at a time. The two main steps of dialog processing are building the screen (process before output) and checking and processing user entries (process after input).

During these steps, the system receives a Dynpro for processing and the dispatcher places it in a queue. As soon as dialog work processes are available, the first job in the queue is sent for processing. The dialog work process handles exactly one dialog step and creates a response screen that is returned to the session from which the input started. The dialog work process is then free for the next task.

Dialog Programs

R/3 dialog programs for an SAP transaction are composed of several dialog steps and their related screens. The dialog programs create update records for database changes that are processed after the dialog phase has been completed. When the update record has been processed the changes created by the transaction are also made in the database. The update record is composed of data that are changed or updated, with instructions on how this should be carried out and which update routines should be used in making the database changes. To terminate the transaction during the dialog phase or if the transaction fails for other reasons, the update record is not written and the database not updated.

Dialog transactions can perform database changes either directly or indirectly. When dealing with direct changes, the dialog work process renders the update program. Updating must be completed before new entries can be made. This procedure is called synchronous updating.

If the database server processes large volumes of data using the synchronous procedure, this can slow down dialog performance as work processes are blocked while they wait for the database.

Asynchronous updating allows high dialog performance even during times of high system load. The dialog phase of transaction processing is kept separate from the actual update, and database changes are executed by special update work processes. When the application and update are coupled asynchronously, dialog response times are less dependent on communication with the database.

Lock mechanisms in modern relational database systems are not normally sufficient to handle business objects, including customer orders, that affect several relational tables at the database level. SAP offers a supplementary, internal lock management that coordinates simultaneous write access to the same business objects by several applications. This lock management tool is managed by the enqueue work process and is able to handle any number of business objects distributed over several relational tables.

Internal Processes

Internal processes can function properly when lock management assures transactions where dialog steps are processed by different work processes. They keep their locks even when the process changes. This is a critical requirement for implementing the asynchronous update concept. When dialog processing and updating are separated, the update phase of a transaction must be certain that data have not changed since the dialog phase was processed.

Memory Management

A memory manager assures that user contexts such as the data containing the current processing status of a transaction can also be stored in the shared memory or in extended memory. It also makes certain that user contexts can be addressed directly by the work processes.

R/3 memory management performs specific use of the memory capacity of modern computer architectures. User contexts can be addressed directly, whereas transaction processing is accelerated. It is important that shared address space be available, since only a small portion of the user context is recorded in the private address space of a work process. This results in the minimization of the amount of copying required for a context switch. The 64-bit architectures within the extended memory management concept allow optimal use of the new 64-bit architectures in R/3.

Enlarged address space reduces the risk of an address space bottleneck and the consequent loss of performance. It also allows uniform and tolerant customizing of R/3 memory management.

SQL Approach

SAP uses relational database management systems for data storage in the R/3 system. SQL is used as a data definition and manipulation language. The set-based approach of SQL makes it possible for sets of records to be accessed in a single database operation. This significantly reduces the number of network communication operations necessary.

The SQL implementations of various suppliers are different, while the ABAP Development Workbench provides two SQL levels:

✎ **ABAP Open SQL**—The entry level is implemented by ABAP Open SQL. This ABAP language extension ensures that all applications that use only this language to access the database can run on all database systems supported by R/3 without requiring any changes.

✎ **ABAP Native SQL**—ABAP Native SQL allows use of all the functions of a proprietary database system, including all vendor-specific enhancements. In R/3 applications, all locations that need to use Native SQL for performance reasons are encapsulated as database-specific modules. Consequently, only these locations must be taken into account when porting the application to another database system.

Buffers for run-time versions are filled during the dynamic download. Syntax analysis and access optimization take up the biggest share of relational database system resources. In the case of SQL instructions with a small number of hits including reading and customer master record, the preparatory actions may consume more resources than the actual reading of data. Reusability of already-optimized SQL instructions is vital.

Database Suppliers

Various database suppliers provide various means of reusing optimized SQL instructions dealing with their storage in fixed access schedules and dynamic buffering of such instructions.

Database-specific functions are encapsulated in the database interface through a method that does not affect the application programmer. Infrastructure buffers increase performance storage areas. The R/3 system enhances runtime performance through dynamic buffering of the data it requires from an RDBMS. This indicates that all data physically exist only once in the database, and are loaded into the relevant application server buffers when required. These buffers are implemented as storage areas either local to a specific work process or shared by all work processes on an application server.

There will also be high performance through data buffering and portability in different relational database management systems that designate database processing in the R/3 system. This procedure provides the opportunity to load data frequently requested by the applications from the database into the buffers. It significantly reduces the number of physical database access operations and decreases network traffic in distributed solutions. This procedure is advantageous since access to an internal buffer is faster and offers better performance.

Security Standards

Various security mechanisms used to protect the R/3 System include:

- User authentication
- Protection of transmitted data through secure network communications (SNC)
- Secure Store & Forward (SSF), that allows R/3 applications to use functions for protecting data and documents
- The R/3 authorization concept and related access controls
- Authority checks.

R/3 supports security standards and integrates them into internal protection mechanisms based on SNC. The communication between front-end computers and R/3 application servers, and intercommunication between application servers can be protected in this method.

Secure Network Communications (SNC) protects communication that occurs between the front end and application server and application servers through the standard interface, Generic Security Services API (GSS API). These elements are crucial in implementing security mechanisms. The R/3 system can be integrated within any network security product that supports the GSS API.

Integration of R/3 into network security software permits mutual authentication between the user and R/3 System, a single sign-on, and secure data transfer according to state-of-the-art technology.

The R/3 system is integrated into Kerberos, a commonly used standard security product developed by MIT, and SECUDE 5.0, developed by the GMD Research Center for Information Technology.

When these products are used, user authentication and password administration need not be performed in the R/3 system. An enterprise can protect several different applications in its client/server environment by including the R/3 system that has a single security system (single sign-on).

The security software SECUDE supports the use of smart cards, that contain information uniquely identifying the user and offering extra security. The secure formats for R/3 data digital signatures involve Secure Store & Forward (SSF), which makes it possible to protect R/3 data and documents when storing them on data media and transferring them over unprotected communication systems such as the Internet. SSF uses digital signatures and codes.

All data are stored in the same way, regardless of content and the selected transport procedure. Data creation, transmission, and receipt can be carried out at different times. R/3 data and documents are placed in "security wrappers" before being stored on data media or transferred across unprotected communications systems.

Digital signatures ensure that data have not been corrupted, that the sender (signer) can be determined, and that a proof of job request is available. After security checks have been completed, data are placed in a digital envelope and sent to the addressee. This procedure makes certain there are no security gaps along the way or at the final destination.

R/3 data and documents protected using SSF satisfy several basic security requirements including data integrity (protection against corruption), confidentiality of data (protection against unauthorized reading), authentication of the sender (protection against masquerading), and proof of the order request (incontestability of data).

To log on to the R/3 system, enter a user ID and a password. Organizations can define their own impermissible passwords and stipulate at what intervals new passwords must be assigned and after how many unsuccessful logon attempts a session will be terminated. Three incorrect password entries lead to automatic termination of the session. After 12 unsuccessful logon attempts, the user is automatically locked, and an entry is written to the SysLog. Customer default values are set using profile parameters.

R/3 authorization permits designation of general authorizations as well as specific authorizations for individual transactions, fields, and values. User authorizations are managed centrally in user master records. Most authorizations permit the user to handle certain SAP objects, though these authorizations can also relate to specific operations.

R/3 offers a convenient tool for maintaining user authorizations and for setting up authorization profiles. One operation frequently requires several authorizations. To change a material master record, there must be an authorization for the "change" transactions for the material itself, and a general authorization for the company code. The resulting relationships can sometimes become complex. R/3 authorization was created to meet the requirements of these complex relationships. Each authorization object can cover several items needing protection, and is a collection of authorization fields.

To keep maintenance to a minimum, authorizations can be grouped into authorization profiles that can be combined to form composite profiles for specific user groups. The double verification principle can also be implemented.

Authorization profile definitions are based on the company menu. The administrator chooses the specific menu paths and functions for each user group. This selection describes which functions users in a specific group are authorized to perform.

SAProuter

Part of SAP's Online Service System (OSS) for customers is a solution based on the SAProuter product to protect both customers' and SAP's systems against unauthorized access. All communication between the customer and SAP occurs through SAProuters, which should be installed on a firewall for security reasons.

The SAProuter is an OSS component ensuring a high degree of data security. SAProuter is integrated into the SNC concept and permits use of network addresses that have not been officially assigned. Both SAProuters have official IP addresses. Access lists can be used to manage access protection. It is possible to designate specifically who is allowed to access R/3 systems, and to assign passwords. As a result, SAP can only access a customer system with prior consent.

SAProuters are used to protect application servers against unauthorized access from front ends connected over a WAN. Communication occurs between the front end's local SAProuter and the SAProuter in the local network of the application server, which then transfers the messages to the application server, and back.

System Monitoring

Administration of distributed systems must comply with strict system monitoring and control criteria. There are also several additional services required for efficient background processing, spooling, and archiving.

Both system monitoring and control tools facilitate efficient system administration. System administrators can use these tools and benefit from a comprehensive overview of the "system landscape", intervening whenever the situation requires.

The monitor architecture of the Computing Center Management System provides a flexible environment for system monitoring that separates data suppliers from data consumers. The monitor architecture between these two levels assures receipt of system information on various components including the operating system, database, R/3 components, or external components can be combined in a monitor as necessary. In addition, there is user-friendly alert handling within the new monitor architecture so that system administrators to react more quickly to alerts.

System administrators also use the global monitor that has a tree structure to control operation across the R/3 system. In day-to-day operations information and alerts on special areas of the system are available quickly. Sub-trees can be copied from the global monitor, stored, and reused them whenever needed. Different sub-trees can be combined under a virtual node. The system administrator can then analyze and compare the database and CPU utilization in a single monitor.

There are uniform procedures within the monitor architecture which ensure that system monitoring is both flexible and user-friendly. Regardless of how system administrators set up their monitors, the procedure they use is always the same, so that they can quickly know all the different tasks of system monitoring.

The monitor architecture incorporates additional preset monitors for specific typical and routine administration tasks. More efficient system monitoring can be achieved through the handling of alerts. Data suppliers within the monitor architecture send system messages to the attributes of a monitor object including a disk, CPU, and R/3 application components for which these attributes are the literal "leaves" of the system tree. These alerts are executed automatically during monitoring of R/3 components; however in operating and database systems, these data suppliers must be triggered. This ensures that system monitoring is based on consistent messages.

System administrators can establish the threshold values for an alert simply by clicking the relevant node as well as the setup icon to display the screen on which they can make their entries. An alert meant to initiate system administrator intervention is then issued each time the threshold is exceeded in either direction.

Each monitor object has its own alert analysis tools available in the system. They use methods that are most appropriate to the specific problem when presenting information. Clicking on an icon, summons a required tool. This reduces the risk of using different analysis methods for various problems and permits rapid decisions on whether or not a specific alert requires intervention.

The monitor architecture provides benefits in the CCMS that extend beyond the boundaries of a single R/3 system. It is possible to monitor several R/3 systems from the CCMS. Monitors can also be established as APIs permitting the system management tools of external suppliers to be connected. This provides a foundation for system administrators who monitor distributed network solutions within Business Framework.

CCMS

CCMS offers effective control mechanisms for starting and shutting down servers and processors, and for reconfiguring the entire installation. It provides functions that significantly influence the performance and stability of the R/3 system at runtime.

Distributed client/server installations with several processors achieve the best performance when the application load is distributed evenly across the servers, and processing is not limited to just a few servers or processes.

CCMS provides system administrators with three different options for load distribution:

1. **Server assignment**—The CCMS uses "logon load distribution" to assign a user to the application server that currently has the smallest load. CCMS tries to divide its tasks into categories and assign these to specific servers. A new dialog user only has to enter the required R/3 application. One or more servers are assigned in a table to each application area.
2. The **message service** chooses the server with the smallest load from the active servers available.
3. **Modes of operation**—As dialog and background processing cause the load of an R/3 installation to vary throughout the day, it possible to switch to another mode of operation when the situation requires.

CCMS permits definition of different modes of operation to obtain the best possible load distribution. This is best illustrated in the following four conditions:

1. **Online operation**—Most work processes are defined as dialog processes
2. **Night operation**—Most work processes are defined as background processes
3. **Maintenance operation**—Access is restricted to specific users
4. **Open interfaces**—Large R/3 installations with heterogeneous system platforms, multiple network services, and interfaces to external applications may need extra system management services.

CCMS provides several different open interfaces so that SAP can effectively use the system management tools of numerous suppliers. CCMS interfaces can be classified as data collector, service, and management interfaces. Performance-related data are received on the operating and data management systems, and the communications network through data collector interfaces.

CCMS can utilize these interfaces to start and monitor external services that include job scheduling in mainframe environments or the processing of data protection requests by external tools. In the same way, external applications can also send requests to SAP job management for execution.

CCMS can be connected to the system management services of other vendors via open interfaces. This has benefits, especially in large, heterogeneous system environments.

R/3 is integrated into the management services of the Integrated Network and System Management (INSM) platform through appropriate interfaces. INSM is founded on the SNMP and MIB. External systems can interactively query and process management data in the SAP System using a special SNMP MIP. When exceptional situations related to processing in R/3 occur, the SAP system also generates SNMP alarms.

R/3 contains all required interfaces. SAP can certify the use of these interfaces in external applications and use in production systems is logged in the database. Auditing, session management and authorization concepts incorporate security and revision mechanisms in CCMS interfaces. CCMS developments include interfaces as a distributed view of R/3 administration using distributed objects that comply with COM/DCOM and CORBA specifications.

Jobs

Large volumes of data that need to be processed in big enterprises and institutions include planning material requirements and running payroll accounting. R/3 offers complex and flexible service infrastructure for automatic background processing of specific jobs under these circumstances. It provides options such as time-based, calendar-based, and event-based scheduling.

Jobs are defined with a start-time window and with automatic repetition if required. During calendar-based scheduling, a job can be initiated on a specific day of the month (with automatic repetition).

The R/3 factory calendar can be designated for determining whether the day is a workday, and the user can determine how the job should be handled if it is not a workday. Event-based scheduling permits job starts dependent upon predecessor jobs, an operation mode switch, or the triggering of the system or user-programmed event. User-programmed events can be triggered from ABAP programs or from sources external to the R/3 system.

The job/job step concept is critical for R/3 background processing. Each job is composed of one or more job steps processed in sequence. When background processing is scheduled at the same time as several other programs, these programs can be designated as individual steps of the job. All processing steps are logically combined in the job. This offers a better overview of the job and makes it easier to control.

R/3 Spool System

The R/3 spool system is concerned with form and document output. It provides form printing, document printing, and fax services for R/3 users and their applications. Several printers can offer features such as graphics, bar code, and OCR printing, and color printing.

The document output capability in the spool system is platform-independent. The R/3 spool system must be able to produce output for a wide variety of printers. Printing from R/3 is possible even if the formatting options of the operating system platforms differ. Even though it can produce printable output, the R/3 spool system does not directly drive the printers. In the final output stage when data is routed to a printer, R/3 uses the services of the platforms on which it runs.

The R/3 spool system provides many options for communicating with host spool systems. Output data can be transferred to the host system spooler where the R/3 spool server runs. Output can also be transferred across the network to a Microsoft Windows print manager or to a host spooler on a remote system.

The R/3 spool system has the ability to use Windows formatting options. R/3 forms and documents can be output on any device supported by Windows, even if the device is not known to the R/3 system. The R/3 spool system allows integration of selected output management systems (OMS) into large customer systems and existing OMSs. This spool system can transfer jobs to the OMS, obtain status information, and be integrated into the customer's OMS solution for printing using command-line or callback (RFC) interfaces. OMS integration is a form of system management API function that permits R/3 administration functions including spooling to be integrated into existing customer infrastructures.

R/3 Archiving

Archiving is a crucial part of the R/3 system and is based on the Archive Development Kit (ADK), which allows R/3 users to archive application data during online operation. This is made possible by a two-step procedure:

1. Data are retrieved from the database and written to archive files
2. Data are deleted from the database.

This two-step archiving process is advantages because of these primary factors:

1. **Data security**—When data are copied and then deleted, they cannot be lost during the archiving procedure.
2. **Increased capacity utilization**—Keeping the write and delete operations separate and distributing archiving tasks to several parallel jobs assures optimal use of available system resources.

The R/3 archiving solution has the special feature that data can still be accessed by the application after being deleted from the database.

Archive management enables three different types of access depending on the type of application:

1. Read access to a single archive object
2. Evaluation of an archive file for reporting
3. Reloading of archived data.

ADK provides a connection for external archive systems that can be used to integrate optical archiving systems.

R/3 environment availability means that system availability is restored within the shortest possible time following unplanned downtimes, and that planned downtimes are not even noticeable to users. With total availability 365 days a year, SAP offers important services globally around the clock. These include the Hotline, and upon customer request, remote maintenance, and system management with Early Watch. There is also detailed documentation covering all aspects of R/3 system availability; this provides valuable tips on R/3 installation and operation.

Automatic load distribution and the message server's role in logon load distribution make certain that jobs are quickly assigned to one of the other available application servers if the server currently processing the jobs should fail.

Fault Tolerance and Performance

Fault tolerance is based on a dual computer structure with a primary and a standby computer which both have access to shared disks. If the primary computer fails due to a hardware fault, all applications are shifted to the standby computer. The standby computer is given exclusive rights of access to the shared disks. All connections between the primary computer and other computers are reassigned to the standby. If computers are connected by means of TCP/IP, this switchover is effected by transferring the IP address to the standby computer. The entire process is completely automatic and takes only a few minutes. SAP uses functions provided by its hardware partners when implementing the switchover fault-tolerance concept.

Should the faulty computer be a database server, the R/3 DB reconnect procedure used in multi-tier R/3 installations makes certain that the application computers are automatically reconnected to the new database computer.

Performance is improved because R/3 application computers do not need to be shut down and restarted, and because application server buffers retain their contents. Only transactions not yet completed at the time of termination are lost. All manufacturer-specific solutions can be used with the R/3 system. This includes fault-tolerant disk units (mirror disks or RAID systems) and networks, as well as various restore-and-recovery features of database suppliers.

Summary

In this chapter we have learned how an effective user interface can play a critical role in almost any course track. We have seen the importance of SAPGUI zero administration an effective user interface.

12-1 What does the presentation layer of the R/3 system offer?

12-2 Explain exactly what SAPGUI is and provide some background for it.

12-3 What does the SAPGUI software support?

12-4 Where is SAPGUI installed and what does it handle?

12-5 How does Java relate to the SAPGUI platform?

12-6 Where does the Java-based version of SAPGUI run? What does it provide?

12-7 What kinds of new platforms could be expected for SAPGUI in Java?

12-8 What kind of special maintenance is needed for the Java-based SAPGUI?

12-9 What is new with SAPGUI in R/3 Release 4.0?

12-10 What does the multimedia front end provide?

12-11 How are lists produced by the SAP system displayed?

12-12 What will users be able to do in R/3 Release 4.0 in terms of a new GUI?

12-13 How will zero administration of the front end change?

12-14 What is the SUSE and what does it mean to you?

12-15 What does Business Engineer allow you to choose?

12-16 What does R/3 look like from the perspective of the user's enterprise?

12-17 How does Business Engineer promote easier navigation?

12-18 To what does the session manager provide access?

12-19 What does the central session manager screen permit?

12-20 What does the global SAP view present?

12-21 What does the enterprise view show?

12-22 What does the user-specific view illustrate?

12-23 What platforms does Session Manager run on?

12-24 The R/3 system supports several other interfaces; what complementary strategies does this indicate?

12-25 What is involved in the inside-out approach?

12-26 Describe its daily performance operation.

12-27   What benefits can be accrued from BAPIs and specially-designed ABAP applications?

12-28   Explain the R/3 Internet applications components.

12-29   Explain what users can deal with in terms of communication within their company.

12-30   What is the outside-in process?

12-31   How does SAP automation facilitate the outside-in process?

12-32   Describe the SAP automation transfer process.

12-33   How can external applications use R/3 system functions and through what means?

12-34   What critical role does SAP automation play in Business Framework?

12-35   From what specific environment can users access R/3 system functionality?

12-36   Has SAP implemented controls that make it easier to access the BAPI definitions and descriptions from an external programming environment? If so, what are they?

12-37   How does SAP accommodate R/3 expansion into the Internet?

12-38   What does the Internet offer to enterprises with regard to redesigning and optimizing business activities?

12-39   What has SAP done to turn the three-tier R/3 client/server architecture into a multi-tier R/3 network architecture?

12-40   What does R/3 Internet enabling consist of, and what does it usually operate on?

12-41   How does the Internet-enabling layer function?

12-42   What does the additional R/3 layer enable?

12-43   How can the consistency and completeness of business transactions be assured? Define Dynpros.

12-44   What happens when data are transferred in another direction?

12-45   What does the extended R/3 architecture do to enable security?

12-46   What happens when system requirements grow?

12-47   Explain what R/3 IACs are and how they were developed.

12-48   In what language are R/3 IACs written and what do they represent?

12-49 What kind of technology do BAPIs provide?

12-50 Explain outside-in as an alternative approach.

12-51 What does the open nature of Business Framework allow? Explain how BAPI specifications enable the creation of Internet applications.

12-52 How do these applications operate and what approach do they use?

12-53 Explain business processes through the Internet.

12-54 What can vendors use the Web to access?

12-55 What do customer-to-business applications help enterprises to do?

12-56 Describe the benefits a company can receive from Internet applications. Be specific.

12-57 What can employees use an Intranet to perform?

12-58 Why are both the performance and stability of the R/3 system important during productive operation?

12-59 What specific benefit does the ABAP virtual machine offer?

12-60 What do the ABAP programs operating on the application layer implement?

12-61 How is the R/3 runtime environment implemented?

12-62 Explain what ABAP programs and Dynpros consist of. What language are they usually written in?

12-63 Where are ABAP programs and Dynpros stored?

12-64 What does the storage process for ABAP programs and Dynpros mean for both application and user?

12-65 Compare and contrast different transaction concepts.

12-66 Describe business transactions.

12-67 What happens when you create a production order?

TIP

Options such as printing the production order must also be taken into account in production order situations.

QUESTIONS

12-68 What kind of requirements are placed on transaction processing in the R/3 system?

12-69 How are SAP transactions implemented?

12-70 What do a dialog step and input data include?

12-71 What does the system term SAP LUW stand for?

12-72 What is the ACID rule?

12-73 Explain why it may take several work processes to perform SAP transactions.

12-74 What actions does the asynchronous update procedure permit?

12-75 Explain DB LUW.

12-76 When are database updates made?

12-77 What are locking mechanisms?

12-78 What does ABAP VM offer in terms of performance and scalability?

12-79 Explain what the use of different classes of work processes allows the R/3 system to do.

12-80 Can R/3 be used as a standalone installation? Can R/3 operate on a network of several computers?

12-81 How does the operating system see ABAP VM or the R/3 runtime system?

12-82 What does each application server include?

12-83 What does the dispatcher distribute?

12-84 Explain the process of application server processing.

12-85 An application server has how many dispatchers and how many work processes?

12-86 How does SQL affect work processes?

12-87 Where is all other data traffic routed?

12-88 What does a gateway on the application server enable?

12-89 What does a task handler do?

12-90 What does dynamic downloading of software ensure?

12-91 At what times does an ABAP program or Dynpro use the ABAP dictionary?

12-92 How can several application servers meet growing business requirements?

12-93   What do the work processes of an application server do?

12-94   Explain the message server.

12-95   How does the message server function?

12-96   What can the R/3 system do because of its client/server architecture of the runtime system?

12-97   What are enqueue work processes?

12-98   What is elaborate dialog processing?

12-99   What is involved in intelligent updating?

12-100   What happens if the transaction is terminated during the dialog phase?

12-101   What can synchronous update dialog transactions execute?

12-102   Explain how direct changes can be made to a database?

12-103   What happens if the database servers are processing large volumes of data and the synchronous procedure is used?

12-104   What does asynchronous updating enable?

12-105   What happens when the application and update are coupled asynchronously? Explain how to obtain effective lock management.

12-106   How are locks kept when the process changes? What happens when dialog processing and updating are separated?

12-107   What happen to applications programs during the dialog phase?

12-108   What is the significance of recognizing conflicting database operations?

12-109   When a lock is granted, how long is it valid?

12-110   What does the update program automatically do?

12-111   Explain how direct addressing works in R/3 memory management.

12-112   What does a memory manager ensure?

12-113   Are there any circumstances under which user context is required for any steps?

12-114   What does R/3 memory management specifically use?

12-115   What benefit does enlarged address space provide and how does it reduce risk?

12-116   What does SAP use for data storage in RDBMSs?

12-117   What other advantages are derived from RDBMSs?

12-118   What benefit is found in the set-based approach of SQL?

12-119   Explain the portable nature of R/3.

12-120   What do meta-data include?

12-121   What happens in the database access agent?

12-122   Explain how the ABAP development workbench provides two SQL levels.

12-123   Explain the database level and its relationship to the application level.

12-124   Explain how different means of reusing optimized SQL instructions are achieved.

12-125   Explain how database-specific functions are encapsulated?

12-126   What function do infrastructure buffers have?

12-127   Where are infrastructure buffers implemented?

12-128   What characterizes database processing into the buffers?

12-129   Name a benefit of database processing procedures.

12-130   Determine what is specified in the repository.

12-131   What data is especially suitable to be specified in the repository?

12-132   Provide examples of parallel database architectures.

12-133   What was the first parallel database system supported by SAP?

12-134   What can SAP DBA tools be used to administer?

12-135   What database platform does SAP support?

12-136   Describe how data security is implemented in an R/3 operation.

12-137   Name several security mechanisms used to protect the R/3 system.

12-138   Explain the integration of standard security products within R/3.

12-139   What exactly do secure network communications protect?

12-140   What is the internal R/3 SNC interface based on?

12-141   Define the level of integration between R/3 and Kerberos.

12-142   What happens when security products are used?

12-143   What does the security software "SECUDE" support?

12-144   What do secure formats for R/3 data provide? Illustrate in detail with examples.

12-145   What type of independent formats are used to save data, if any?

12-146   At what times are data creation, transmission, and receipt carried out?

12-147   Explain how data and documents are literally "wrapped up" before storing them.

12-148   What exactly does a digital signature ensure?

12-149   What happens after all the checks have been made by the digital signature?

12-150   What is PKCD #7 used for?

12-151   How can both data and documents be protected using SSF?

12-152   Illustrate how authentication takes place.

12-153   Define how password rules can help ensure that an organization remains secure.

12-154   Describe specific user authorizations.

12-155   How are user authorizations managed?

12-156   How does R/3 maintain user authorizations and set up authorization profiles?

12-157   How was the R/3 authorization developed and what requirement does it meet?

12-158   What is the double verification principle?

12-159   Explain how many predefined profiles are within R/3.

12-160   What is the profile generator?

12-161   How can are authorization profiles defined?

12-162   What is involved with the SAProuter and how does it relate to secure SAP/customer communication?

12-163   What kind of component is the SAProuter?

12-164   How does the SAProuter work with network addresses?

12-165   Explain how access lists are used and specify what they manage.

12-166   What controls outgoing connection requests?

12-167   What can a SAProuter protect?

12-168   Explain the administration of distributed systems and what it must comply with.

12-169   Explain the concept of computing center management.

12-170   What is the significance of a flexible system monitoring architecture?

12-171   What does user-friendly alert handling do?

12-172   What can the administrator do with the global monitor?

12-173   Can different sub-trees be combined under a virtual node?

12-174   Explain what a uniform procedure architecture ensures.

12-175   Explain in detail what specific components are included in the monitor architecture.

12-176   What does the tree structure enable?

12-177   Describe how alert handling is an important part of efficient system monitoring.

12-178   What is involved when setting threshold values?

12-179   Explain the significance of alert analysis.

12-180   What benefits result from open system monitoring?

12-181   Describe how CCMS can provide effective control mechanisms.

12-182   What kind of functions does CCMS offer?

12-183   What is load distribution and balancing?

12-184   What three specific options does CCMS offer system administrators?

12-185   What specific modes of operation can be defined in CCMS?

12-186   Does CCMS have different open interfaces? If so, what do they allow?

12-187   How can CCMS interfaces be classified? Name each classification.

12-188   What does the data collector interface do?

12-189   Can CCMS be connected to the system management services of other vendors through open interfaces? If so, what benefits/drawbacks exist?

12-190   Explain how R/3 is integrated in the management services of INSM.

12-191   What happens when exceptional situations related to R/3 processing occur?

12-192 What happens to standard R/3 system-required interfaces in external applications and production systems?

12-193 What do auditing, session management, and authorization concepts incorporate with respect to security?

12-194 What interfaces does CCMS include?

12-195 What is involved with background processing?

12-196 What kind of scheduling options does R/3 offer?

12-197 How are jobs defined?

12-198 What specifications are possible for an R/3 factory calendar?

12-199 What does event-based scheduling allow?

12-200 From where can user-programmed events be triggered?

12-201 Explain the "Job Concept."

12-202 What happens when background processing is scheduled at the same time as several other programs?

12-203 Can different external programs be started from an R/3 background job?

12-204 How can an external program be defined in R/3?

12-205 How can processing runs that require a large amount of system time be divided?

12-206 What does the R/3 spool system provide?

12-207 Specify what document output capability is about.

12-208 What happens in the final output stage?

12-209 What kind of options does the R/3 spool system offer for communicating with the host spool systems?

12-210 What kind of Windows formatting options exist within the R/3 spool system's ability?

12-211 Explain the particulars of the R/3 spool system's integration of selected OMSs?

12-212 What is OMS integration?

12-213 What happens during archiving?

12-214 What do government regulations have to say about archiving data?

12-215   Explain how archiving is based on the ADK.

12-216   What special feature exist within the R/3 archiving solution?

12-217   What three types of access are enabled through archive management? Describe all three type of access in detail.

12-218   What does ADK offer so that external archive systems can integrate optical archiving systems?

12-219   What is the result of hardware and software downtime?

12-220   What is the difference between planned and unplanned downtimes?

12-221   What does "High Availability" in the R/3 environment mean?

12-222   What is round-the-clock availability?

12-223   What are the roles of automatic load distribution and the message server in logon load distribution?

12-224   What do the monitoring functions of the CCMS ensure?

12-225   What happens during unplanned downtime?

12-226   On what is fault tolerance based?

12-227   What happens during database standstill?

12-228   Why is performance be enhanced in R/3?

12-229   What is involved with repository switch technology during planned downtime?

12-1 The presentation layer of the R/3 System provides universal access to users of all types.

12-2 SAP has focused its R/3 development efforts to on producing a user-friendly interface built on the latest ergonomic research completed at the in-house ergonomics laboratory as well as in other areas. The result is the creation of a GUI uniform across all R/3 applications that opens up the entire system functions to experienced users.

12-3 The SAPGUI software supports over 20 languages including the pictographic languages Kanji (Japanese) and Mandarin (Chinese) which, due to their extensive character sets, in the R/3 system require two bytes to represent each character.

12-4 SAPGUI is installed on each R/3 front end and handles both this user interface and the communication between the presentation and application servers.

12-5 Java is a SAPGUI platform that is expanding business on the Internet and has established itself as new, hardware-independent and easy to use. As a result, SAP can offer experienced users access to the range of R/3 system functions through the Internet using SAPGUI in Java.

12-6 The Java-based version of SAPGUI runs on a Web client and provides the same look and feel as the native SAPGUI interface.

12-7 SAPGUI in Java allows new platforms such as NetPCs or NCs to be used as R/3 clients.

12-8 There is no need to perform any special installation, administration, or maintenance work on the client side. When the R/3 system is called over the Internet using the Java-based SAPGUI, the current version of the presentation software is automatically loaded from the Java applet server to the Web client.

12-9 When dealing with R/3 Release 4.0, SAPGUI will also cover all front-end components such as the reusable program modules or JavaBeans that offer the environments for spread-sheets, graphics, and word processing software integrated into SAPGUI.

12-10 The R/3 front-end is multimedia-based and as easy to use as a Web browser. Various types of Information including text, tables, graphics, photographs, and HTML documents can be displayed and edited simultaneously on a single R/3 screen.

12-11 Lists generated by the SAP system are displayed as both tables and graphics in a single screen window.

SOLUTIONS

12-12 In R/3 Release 4.0, users have a WYSIWYG editor (RTF editor component) to create, edit, and display texts. Components are also offered for handling tables, HTML documents, graphics, and photos. This technology is implemented using a front-end component framework which supports different components and controls their communication with the R/3 System.

12-13 Zero administration of the front end is much easier. All front-end components, including ActiveX controls and JavaBeans, are loaded and updated directly from the R/3 system.

12-14 Self-upgrading software environment (SUSE) indicates potential savings, since all front-end components are loaded automatically from the R/3 system to the clients. As a result, end users always have the most up-to-date version of the software without any work on the part of system administrators. This zero administration guarantees a high degree of operating convenience at low cost.

12-15 Business Engineer permits choosing only those R/3 components and functions a company actually needs and uses in productive operation.

12-16 From the user's enterprise perspective, the R/3 system offers individualized business applications.

12-17 When installing and customizing a productive R/3 system, use Business Engineer to create the information that describes the specific R/3 implementation.

12-18 Session Manager provides access to information that describes specific R/3 implementation. This represents another step toward a user-specific interface. It aids in navigation through the R/3 system, and permits customization of the desktop.

12-19 It is possible to navigate through the complete R/3 system from the central Session Manager screen and choose a specific view by mouse click.

12-20 The global SAP view presents the complete system.

12-21 The enterprise view shows the subset of R/3 functions used in an enterprise.

12-22 The user-specific view focuses on the functions set up on the workstation.

12-23 Session Manager runs on Windows 95 and Windows NT front ends. In R/3 Release 4.0 it can also be used as an Internet Session Manager via a Web browser.

12-24 Aside from SAPGUI, the R/3 system supports several other user interfaces in pursuing two complementary strategies:

✎ Users who rarely work with R/3 or who are accustomed to desktop interfaces like a Windows GUI or a Web browser can benefit from the power of the R/3 system (i.e. Inside Out).

✎ Enterprises can benefit from the potential of the development environments and programming languages underlying other user interfaces as well as from associated business applications in combination with the R/3 system (i.e. Outside In).

12-25 The inside-out approach (Figure 12.1) allows users to work with a Windows GUI or a Web browser instead of the SAPGUI. People used to these front-ends can stay in a familiar environment yet derive full benefit from the R/3 system.

FIGURE 12.1
Inside Out Approach

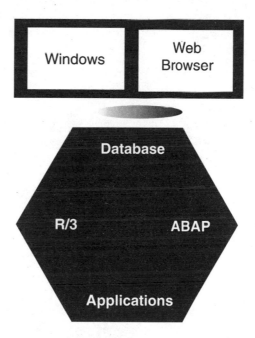

12-26 In Inside Out, performance in daily operation, powerful transaction processing capabilities, and complicated business application logic are all extended from the R/3 system to the workstations of employees who do not normally use R/3.

12-27 With the assistance BAPIs and specially designed ABAP applications, R/3 functions can be made available on a controlled business basis.

12-28 SAP is systematically extending business processes from the R/3 System into the Internet and offers prefabricated R/3 Internet applications for business-to-business, consumer-to-business or intranet communication.

12-29 Users can deal with everything from business partners to consumers who order products from their home PCs, to employees who implement intranet solutions for communication within the company. These people all use commercial Web browsers to interact with the R/3 system. Internet applications, which are implemented as a separate function in the R/3 system, can access core R/3 functions using BAPIs.

12-30 R/3's SAP automation capability offers its own class of dynamic interfaces for application programming. When the manual entry of R/3 transactions is automated, nearly any R/3 function can be controlled by an external program from the outside in (Figure 12.2). It does not matter whether it is a telephony system, an electronic kiosk, a scanner, a PC program, or a new type of self-service application. A customer can query the status of an order over the telephone, by keying in the order number. This action provokes the relevant R/3 transaction and the result is output through a speech generator.

FIGURE 12.2
Outside In Approach

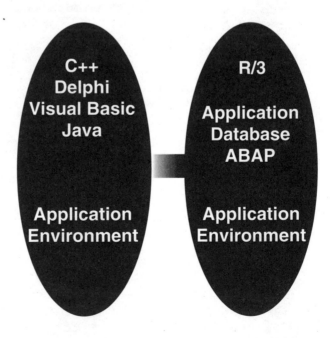

12-31 SAP automation facilitates the Outside-In process (Figure 12.3) using SAPGUI communication services to exchange message packets between the application and presentation servers, to pack and unpack data, and to transfer these data to the application server or downstream client for further processing.

FIGURE 12.3
SAP Automation
Outside In

12-32 SAP automation transfers messages from the program to the application server where processing actually takes place, and also interprets data from the application server in order to filter out the data structures required by the program.

12-33 When dealing with Outside In, external applications of all types can utilize R/3 system functions through BAPIs.

12-34 SAP automation (Figure 12.4) plays a critical role in Business Framework by offering an additional interface for accessing BAPIs. It also includes the necessary libraries.

FIGURE 12.4
SAP Automation

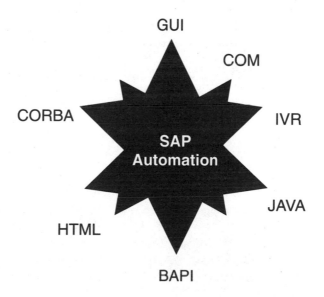

SOLUTIONS

12-35   Users can access all the R/3 functions from standard development environments such as Visual Basic, C, C++ and Java.

12-36   Yes, SAP has already implemented controls which make it easier to access BAPI definitions and descriptions in the R/3 system from an external programming environment. These include BAPI controls (ActiveX controls for Visual Basic that permit direct programming on the control. R/3 system communication is already implemented in the BAPI control.

12-37   R/3 expanded architecture allows the R/3 system to integrate the Internet into business processes with cross-system and enterprise boundaries. In order to accommodate this expansion, the hypertext structure of the Web has been enhanced by an application structure for business transaction processing. The R/3 system functions can be accessed directly from the Web without having to store R/3 functions on a Web server.

12-38   The Internet offers enterprises new ways of redesigning and optimizing their business activities with respect to other enterprises (business-to-business), end consumers (consumer-to-business) and its own employees (intranets).

12-39   In order to gain the greatest advantage technically possible from the business potential of the Internet, SAP has turned the three-tier R/3 client/server architecture into a multi-tier R/3 network architecture by adding a special new layer for Internet business. The primary concept behind this technology is the distinct separation of the presentation, application, database and Internet layers. It offers the perfect foundation for Internet applications.

12-40   The R/3 Internet-enabling layer is an extended HTTP server and usually operates on a separate computer.

12-41   The Internet-enabling layer functions as the interface between an HTTP server and the R/3 system when a Web browser or HTTP server is used to access the R/3 system. Each system has to map the other's protocols and data formats.

12-42   The additional R/3 layer enables data exchange between the HTTP server and R/3, specifically the application server where all business transactions are processed.

12-43   In order to ensure the consistency and completeness of business transactions, R/3 uses a series of dynamic programs called Dynpros. Dynpros consist of screens and associated process logic. In an Internet enabling layer Dynpros are compiled into a series of HTML documents which are then transferred through an HTTP server to a Web browser.

12-44 When data are transferred in the other direction, field contents of HTML documents are converted into Dynpro data. Changes in core R/3 functions are not required. As a result, enterprises can still count on the proven performance, stability, and scope of R/3 business functions in their daily Internet business operations.

12-45 The extended R/3 architecture encompasses security issues that are crucial to doing business over the Internet.

12-46 When system requirements grow, users must only address the one layer that requires upgrading. This is advantageous because of the design principle of distinctive layers. It makes certain that the scalability of the R/3 system is also maintained in Internet-based applications, an important consideration because of the exponentially increasing number of Web users. It is possible to allocate several dedicated application servers to a single HTTP server.

12-47 Several R/3 Internet Application Components (IACs) have already been created with direct input from SAP customers according to the inside-out approach.

12-48 The R/3 Internet components are technically written in ABAP. They represent autonomous entities running on the application server and add new functions to the R/3 core components. Internet and core components can communicate through object-oriented BAPIs.

12-49 BAPIs provide an interface technology based on a system of common business semantics independent of the underlying communication and transport technology. The business-oriented character of the BAPIs makes certain that R/3 Internet components and R/3 core components can communicate regardless of their release version.

12-50 When dealing with the outside-in approach, note that it concentrates on responding to the requirements of companies already using the tested R/3 functions and having ABAP as their main development environment.

12-51 The open nature of Business Framework makes R/3 accessible to other companies as well. These organizations often have development environments that use Visual Basic, C, C++ or, Java. This usually indicates a strong need for a range of interfaces to cater for legacy systems or database systems and dictionaries not supported by SAP. BAPI specifications create the foundation for Business Framework integration to enable the creation of Internet applications that use R/3 core components but operate on application servers outside the R/3 system and have been created in languages including Visual Basic, C, C++, or Java.

SOLUTIONS

12-52 These applications operate according to the outside-in approach, assuring extensive scalability, high-performance transaction processing, and security.

12-53 Whatever option a company chooses to satisfy its business needs, Business Framework BAPIs make certain that specific situations are available for users.

12-54 Vendors can use the Web to access their customers' warehouse systems and manage stocks independently. The tasks of the extended value chain are more evenly distributed through this type of business-to-business communication. Business processes are accelerated.

12-55 Consumer-to-business applications help enterprises worldwide to open up new consumer markets and retain customers. Using a simple Web browser, it is possible to access product catalogs at any hour of the day, and place the order right away. Users can also query the status of their order and determine when delivery is scheduled.

12-56 Intranet applications improve the internal flow of information and communications.

12-57 Employees can use an intranet to perform personnel tasks such as updating their personal data or querying their leave or travel expense accounts. This alleviates the strain on the human resources department of performing routine tasks and allows HR people to focus their efforts on strategic personnel planning.

12-58 Regardless of which front ends are used to access R/3 functionality, the number of users who work in the system, and which network solutions are implemented within Business Framework, the performance and stability of the R/3 system during productive operation is the most important question.

12-59 Using the ABAP virtual machine (ABAP VM), R/3 can operate at it best-possible level of performance. The ABAP VM installed on each application server offer complex mechanisms to provide optimal results during high-load operation and ensure the scalability needed for increasing requirements.

12-60 The ABAP programs that operate on the application layer implement the business logic of R/3 applications. They are executed by the ABAP VM on each application server. The ABAP VM also makes certain that all R/3 application components can be executed without modification, in different system environments.

12-61 The R/3 runtime environment is implemented as an ABAP VM. The ABAP VM maintains system independence, high performance, and scalability.

SOLUTIONS

12-62 ABAP VM is programmed in ANSI-C and C++, though the majority of R/3 application programs are written in 4GL ABAP. Both ABAP programs and Dynpros consist of screens and the associates process logic. These are executed by an interpreter. ABAP programs and Dynpros are the two most crucial processes of the ABAP VM.

12-63 ABAP programs and Dynpros are stored centrally on the database server and are dynamically loaded onto the application or presentation server when called for.

12-64 For the application and user, this procedure assures a high level of consistency in the ABAP programs and Dynpros.

12-65 There is a fundamental difference between a business and a database transaction. The sole purpose of several important processes executed on the application server at runtime is overcoming this difference.

12-66 Business transactions are functionally related processing units that execute permissible database changes consistently. Business transactions include debit and credit postings that only make sense together. The majority of business transactions are usually more complex and affect a large number of tables in a relational database. These tables must be managed with appropriate locks until the entire transaction is completion.

12-67 When a production order is created, the system copies the bills of material, the price of each material, the routings, the cost of each operation, and the numbers of all required materials. It then locks these items while they are being processed.

12-68 Strict requirements are placed on transaction processing in the R/3 system.

12-69 An SAP transaction is implemented as a sequence of logically related, consistent dialog steps.

12-70 A dialog step includes the processing of input data. Input data includes the form itself, sending a data packet, and the resulting response.

12-71 The system term SAP LUW (logical unit of work refers to an entity that makes up all the dialog steps of a transaction including associated database changes and updates.

12-72 By the ACID (atomic, consistent, isolated, durable) rule, LUW is executed either in its entirety or not at all. SAP transactions can be nested using the ABAP statement CALL TRANSACTION. A COMMIT WORK statement normally terminates SAP transactions, and the LUW completes processing by performing an update.

SOLUTIONS

12-73   SAP transactions are not necessarily executed within a single work process. The individual dialog steps of a transaction can be processed by one or more work processes.

12-74   The asynchronous update procedure execution of the dialog operations of an SAP transaction and makes the required database updates in different work processes or even on different servers.

12-75   It is important to be able to distinguish between the atomic processing steps (LUWs) of the SAP system and the database system. There are no cross-process transaction flows in database systems. Each dialog step in an SAP transaction for a database system is a self-contained and complete database transaction (DB LUW).

12-76   Database updates are made during a database transaction.

12-77   The SAP system guarantees the logical coherence of the dialog steps belonging to a single transaction. An application program can issue a lock request so that a user session is given exclusive access to a certain business object for the duration of an SAP LUW (Figure 12.5). It can also undo all database changes made during the course of an SAP LUW from different screens right through successful completion of the SAP LUW.

FIGURE 12.5
Business Object/
Application Link
Enabling

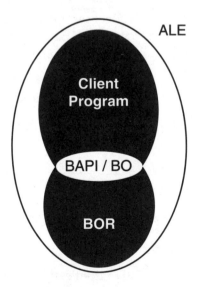

12-78   ABAP VM offers a flexible architecture geared toward performance and scalability. It permits enterprises to acquire excellent performance even during high-load operation.

12-79   Use of different classes of work processes and the same control mechanisms on different application servers and R/3 computers allows the R/3 system to be scaled almost endlessly.

12-80   Yes, R/3 can be used as a standalone installation. R/3 can operate on a network of several computers. This makes even large R/3 systems secure and controllable, even when numerous transactions are being run.

12-81   The operating system sees the ABAP VM or R/3 runtime system as a set of parallel, cooperative processes.

12-82   Each application server includes a central dispatcher and several work processes, whose actual number depends on computer performance and the number of processors installed.

12-83   The dispatcher distributes queued processing requests among the work processes, each of which consists of four main processors:

1.   ABAP processor
2.   Dynpro processor
3.   Database access agent
4.   Coordinating task handler.

12-84   The dispatcher distributes processing requests to the individual work processes. Special work processes can be installed for dialog processing, updating of change documents, lock management, background processing, and spooling. The dispatcher and work processes map the functions of a TP monitor.

FIGURE 12.6
Application Server
Processing

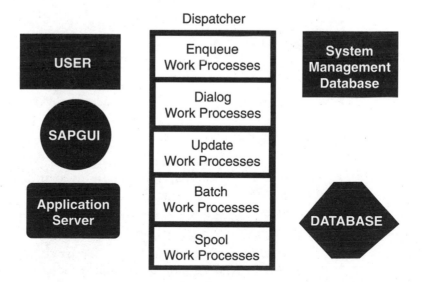

12-85 An application server has only one dispatcher but several work processes.

12-86 Using SQL, work processes can directly access a database in a multi-tier client/server system usually located on a different computer.

12-87 All other data traffic between work processes and the outside world including program-to-program communication or SAPGUI communication is routed via the dispatcher.

12-88 A gateway on the application server enables this data exchange.

12-89 A task handler coordinates the activities involved in a work process. If application logic is being processed (dialogs, updates, and background processing the task handler activates the Dynpro processor and ABAP processor as required.

12-90 Dynamic downloading of software ensures easy maintenance and consistency of ABAP programs and Dynpros (i.e. when dealing with large R/3 environments).

12-91 Every time an ABAP program or Dynpro uses a data structure, it refers to the definition in the central ABAP dictionary. Both ABAP and Dynpro processors use the semantic and technical global view of the R/3 data and functions stored in the ABAP dictionary.

12-92 As corporate business requirements grow, an organization can scale its systems to size by implementing new components as required. Several application servers can operate on one computer or application servers can be distributed among several computers. This allows dedicated tasks to be distributed unambiguously.

12-93 The work processes of an application server can be reserved exclusively for the R/3 human resources component, while another application server is reserved for background processing. Other work processes are meant mostly for spooling.

12-94 The message server plays a crucial role in specific situations. Each is installed just once in the R/3 system, and its purpose is to a consistent view of the different application servers.

12-95 The message server functions partly as a pure transport mechanism but also provides internal information on load distribution across the different application servers. One use of this information is to assure a more uniform distribution of transaction processing among the servers.

12-96 Because of the client/server architecture of the R/3 runtime system and use of special work processes controlled by the dispatcher, the R/3 system is optimally equipped for use in multi-processor environments.

12-97 The enqueue work process connected with the message server makes certain that all the necessary locks are set and remain set until transaction processing has been completed, even when complex transactions operate on different application servers. This permits the R/3 system to be scaled with respect to specific enterprise requirements, and allows optimal management of the different application servers and their performance even in complex environments.

12-98 Dialog work processes each handle open user sessions one at a time. The main steps of dialog processing are: building the screen (process before output) and checking and processing user entries (process after input).

During these steps, the system receives a dynpro for processing and the dispatcher places it in a queue. As soon as a dialog work process is available, the first job in the queue is sent there for processing. The dialog work process handles exactly one dialog step and creates a response screen which is returned to the session from which the input started. The dialog work process is then free for the next task.

12-99 The R/3 dialog programs for an SAP transaction can consist of several dialog steps and their related screens. The dialog programs generate update records for database changes that are then processed after the dialog phase has been completed. Once the update record has been processed (i.e. updating) the changes created by the transaction are also made in the database. The update record contains the data to be changed or updated with instructions on how this should be carried out and which update routines should be used in making the database changes.

12-100 If the transaction is terminated during the dialog phase or fails for other reasons, the update record is not written and the database is not updated.

12-101 Synchronous update dialog transactions can execute database changes either directly or indirectly.

12-102 In direct changes, the dialog work process executes the update program. Updating must be completed before new entries can be made. This procedure is called synchronous updating.

12-103 If the database servers are processing large volumes of data, using the synchronous procedure can slow down dialog performance. As a result, work processes might be blocked while they wait for the database.

12-104 Asynchronous updating enables high dialog performance even during times of high system load. The dialog phase of transaction processing is kept separate from the actual update, and database changes are executed by special update work processes.

SOLUTIONS

12-105   When the application and update are coupled asynchronously, dialog response times are less dependent on communication with the database. The lock mechanisms in modern relational database systems are not usually sufficient to handle business objects, including customer orders, that affect several relational tables at the database level (Figure 12.7). SAP offers a supplementary, internal lock management that coordinates simultaneous write access to the same business objects by several applications. This lock management tool is managed by the enqueue work process and is able to handle any number of business objects distributed over several relational tables.

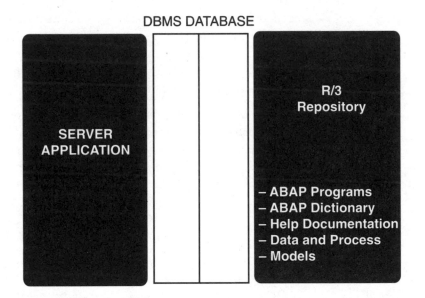

FIGURE 12.7
Database Level

12-106   In order for internal processes to function properly, lock management must assure that transactions where dialog steps are processed by different work processes can be completed. They keep their locks even when the process changes. This is a crucial requirement for implementing the asynchronous update concept. When dialog processing and updating are separated, the update phase of a transaction must be certain that data have not changed since the dialog phase was processed.

12-107   During the dialog phase, application programs request locks for the data objects they want to change.

12-108   Conflicting database operations are recognized so that the application programs can warn the user on time that the requested operation is currently not possible.

12-109   When a lock is granted, it is valid until the entire business transaction has been completed unless explicitly released by the application program.

12-110   The update program automatically deletes all locks in an SAP transaction when the update record created during the dialog phase has been successfully updated.

12-111   This type of highly expandable shared memory contains more than just resources such as ABAP programs, Dynpros, and table contents used by all work processes.

12-112   A memory manager makes certain that user contexts such as the data containing the current processing status of a transaction can also be stored in the shared memory or in extended memory. It also assures that user contexts can be addressed directly by the work processes.

12-113   A special procedure allows the user context required for executing a certain dialog step to be mapped from extended memory to the virtual address space of the relevant work process.

12-114   R/3 memory management (Figure 12.8) makes specific use of the memory capacity of modern computer architectures. User contexts can be addressed directly, while transaction processing is greatly accelerated. As long as sufficient shared address space is available, only a very small portion of the user context is stored in the private address space of a work process. This results in the minimization of the amount of copying required for a context switch. The extended memory management concept allows optimal use of the new 64-bit architectures in R/3.

FIGURE 12.8
Memory Management

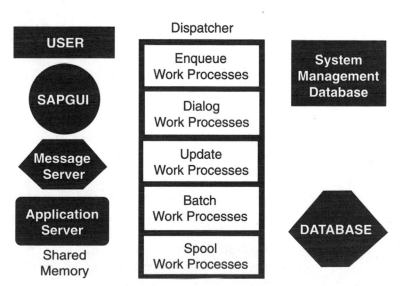

12-115   Enlarged address space reduces the risk of an address space bottleneck and consequent loss of performance. It also allows uniform and tolerant customizing of R/3 memory management.

12-116   SAP uses relational database management systems for data storage in the R/3 system. SQL is used as a data definition and manipulation language.

12-117   Relational database systems offer the advantage of a distributed network solution analogous to that used within Business Framework (Figure 12.9).

FIGURE 12.9
Business Framework

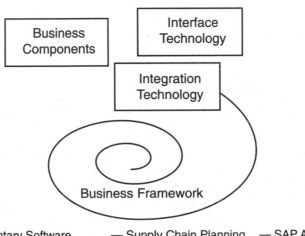

12-118   The set-based approach of SQL makes it possible for sets of records to be accessed in a single database operation. This significantly reduces the number of network communication operations.

12-119   The R/3 system uses these relational database systems to manage more than just operating data. The database documents the entire R/3 system including its meta-data.

12-120   Meta-data include programs, dialogs, and the repository. Regardless of the high degree of standardization of SQL, the R/3 architecture must deal with the different syntax and semantics of the SQL implementations of different vendors.

12-121   In the database access agent (Figure 12.10), one of the four main components of an R/3 work process, differences are isolated in special modules. This maintains the portability of the R/3 system and allows different relational database systems to be supported, provided that their performance satisfies the requirements for the mission-critical OLTP applications of R/3.

FIGURE 12.10
Database
Access Agent

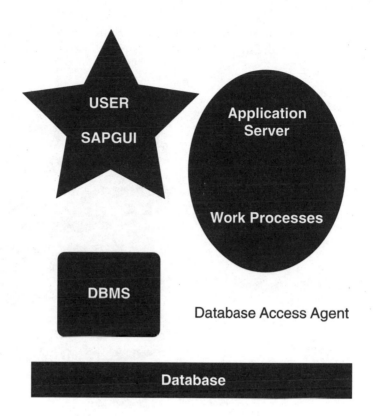

12-122 Since the SQL implementations of different suppliers are different, the ABAP development workbench provides two SQL levels:

  ✎ **ABAP Open SQL**—The entry level is implemented by ABAP Open SQL. This ABAP language extension guarantees that all applications that use only this language to access the database can run on all database systems supported by R/3 without requiring any changes.

  ✎ **ABAP Native SQL**—ABAP Native SQL permits use of all the functions of a proprietary database system, including all vendor-specific enhancements. In R/3 applications, all locations that need to use native SQL for reasons of performance are encapsulated as database-specific modules. Consequently, only these locations must be taken into account when porting the application to another database system.

12-123 Buffers for run-time versions are filled during the dynamic download. Apart from the execution of SQL instructions, syntax analysis and access optimization take up the biggest share of relational database system resources. In the case of SQL instructions with a small number of hits, such as reading a customer master record, the preparatory actions may

SOLUTIONS

consume more resources than the actual reading of data. Reusability of already optimized SQL instructions is elemental.

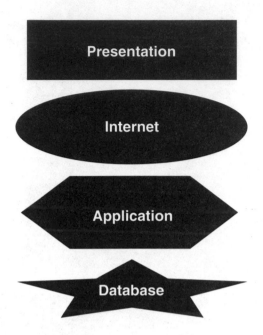

12-124 Different database suppliers offer various means of reusing optimized SQL instructions including storage of optimized SQL instructions in fixed-access schedules and dynamic buffering of such instructions.

12-125 Database-specific functions are encapsulated in the database interface through a method that does not affect the application programmer.

12-126 Infrastructure buffers increase performance storage areas. The R/3 system greatly improves runtime performance through dynamic buffering of the data it requires from an RDBMS. This indicates that all data physically exist only once in the database, and are loaded into the relevant application server buffers when required.

12-127 These buffers are either implemented as storage areas local to a specific work process, or as storage areas shared by all work processes on an application server.

12-128 High performance through data buffering and portability to different relational database management systems characterize database processing in the R/3 system. It is possible to load frequently-requested data from the database into the buffers. This greatly reduces the number of physical database access operations and decreases network traffic in distributed solutions.

12-129 An advantage of the database processing procedure is that access to an internal buffer is fast and offers superb performance.

12-130 Items specified in the repository can include part of a table or the entire table suitable for buffering.

12-131 Data that rarely change, including configuration parameters, ABAP programs, Dynpros, and ABAP dictionary information, is especially suitable. The level at which application data are suitable for this client-caching procedure depends on the application profile.

12-132 The majority of users employ uniprocessor and SMP machines in the R/3 environment. MPP machines and clusters are used in only a few installations.

12-133 The first parallel database system supported by SAP is the Oracle Parallel Server (OPS).

12-134 SAP DBA tools can already be used for OPS administration.

12-135 SAP supports the Informix Online Extended Parallel Server (Online XPS) and IBM's DB2 Parallel Edition. The MPP and cluster systems of parallel CPUs require additional software support. In order to acquire the anticipated performance increase during OLTP operation, the suitability of a customer's transactions for parallel processing must be analyzed—to determine the best method of partitioning the customer data for parallel operation.

12-136 R/3 processes highly sensitive customer and personal data. The topic of data security is crucial in Business Framework as business processes are extended beyond company boundaries.

12-137 Various security mechanisms used to protect the R/3 system include: user authentication and protection of transmitted data through secure network communications (SNC); Secure Store & Forward (SSF) that allows R/3 applications to use functions for protecting data and documents; the R/3 authorization concept, related access controls, and authority checks.

12-138 R/3 supports security standards and integrates them into internal protection mechanisms based on SNC. Both the communication between front-end computers and R/3 application servers, and intercommunication between application servers can be protected.

12-139 Secure Network Communications (SNC) protect communication between the front end and the application server, and between application servers.

SOLUTIONS

The standard interface is Generic Security Services API (GSS API). These elements are crucial in implementing security mechanisms.

12-140   The internal R/3 SNC interface is based on the GSS API. The R/3 system can be integrated into any network security product that supports the GSS API, and has been certified by SAP. Integration of R/3 into network security software allows mutual authentication between the user and R/3 system, a single signon, and secure data transfer according to state-of-the-art technology.

12-141   The R/3 system has so far been integrated into Kerberos, a commonly used standard security product developed by the Massachusetts Institute of Technology (MIT), and SECUDE 5.0, a program developed by the GMD Research Center for Information Technology.

12-142   When these products are used, user authentication and password administration no longer need to be performed in the R/3 system itself. An enterprise can thus protect several different applications in its client/server environment, such as the R/3 system, with a single security system (single signon).

12-143   The security software SECUDE supports the use of smart cards, which contain information that uniquely identifies the user.

12-144   Secure formats for R/3 data digital signatures including Secure Store & Forward (SSF) which permits protection of R/3 data and documents when these are stored on data media and transferred over unprotected communication systems such as the Internet. SSF uses digital signatures and codes.

12-145   All data are stored in the same way, regardless of contents and the selected transport procedure.

12-146   Data creation, transmission, and receipt can be carried out at different times.

12-147   R/3 data and documents are placed in "security wrappers" before being stored on data media or transferred across unprotected communications systems.

12-148   A digital signature assures that data have not been corrupted, that the sender (signer) can be determined, and that proof of job request is available.

12-149   After security checks have been completed, data are placed in a digital envelope and sent to the addressee. This procedure assures that there are no security gaps along the way or at the final destination.

SOLUTIONS

12-150 The international standard format PKCS (Public Key Cryptography Standards) #7 is used for the digital signature and digital envelope.

12-151 Protection of R/3 data and documents using SSF satisfies several basic security requirements including data integrity (protection against corruption); confidentiality of data (protection against unauthorized reading); authentication of the sender (protection against masquerading); and proof of the order request (incontestability of data).

12-152 When logging on to the R/3 system, must enter user ID and a password. Organizations can define their own impermissible passwords and stipulate at what intervals new passwords must be assigned and after how many unsuccessful logon attempts a session will be terminated.

12-153 The R/3 standard is that three incorrect password entries lead to automatic termination of the session. After 12 unsuccessful logon attempts, the user is automatically locked, and an entry is written to the SysLog. Customer-default values are set using profile parameters.

12-154 The R/3 authorization concept makes it possible to designate general authorizations as well as specific authorizations for individual transactions, fields, and values.

12-155 User authorizations are managed centrally in user master records. Most authorizations permit users to handle certain SAP objects, though these authorizations can also relate to specific operations.

12-156 The R/3 system offers a convenient tool for maintaining user authorizations and setting up authorization profiles. One operation frequently requires several authorizations. To change a material master record, there must be an authorization for the "change" transactions for the material itself, and a general authorization for the company code. The resulting relationships can sometimes become extremely complex.

12-157 The R/3 authorization concept was created to meet the requirements of these complex relationships. Each authorization object can cover several items needing protection, and is a collection of authorization fields.

12-158 In order to keep maintenance to a minimum, authorizations can be grouped into authorization profiles that can be combined to form composite profiles for specific user groups. The double verification principle can also be implemented.

12-159 The R/3 system contains a large number of predefined profiles, including those that distinguish among the different tasks of system administration.

SOLUTIONS

12-160 The profile generator simplifies and accelerates the task of setting up the authorization environment for the customer. The administrator only needs to make the customer-specific settings. The profile generator performs all other tasks, such as the selection of the authorization objects. It is integrated in the R/3 system and can be used on all platforms supported by R/3.

12-161 The definition of authorization profiles is based on the company menu. The administrator chooses the specific menu paths and functions for each user group. This selection describes authorized functions for users in a particular group.

12-162 As part of the Online Service System (OSS) for customers, SAP has create a solution based on the SAProuter product to protect both customers' and SAP's systems against unauthorized access. All communication between the customer and SAP runs over SAProuters, which should be installed on a firewall for security reasons.

12-163 The SAProuter is an OSS component which guarantees SAP customers a high degree of data security. The SAProuter will be integrated into the SNC concept.

12-164 The SAProuter permits use of network addresses that have not been officially assigned. Both SAProuters have official IP addresses.

12-165 Access lists are used to manage access protection. Customers can specify who is allowed to access their R/3 systems, and assign passwords. As a result, SAP can only access a customer system with prior consent.

12-166 The customer opens a session and can choose to permit only outgoing connections, blocking any incoming connection requests.

12-167 A SAProuter can be used to protect application servers against unauthorized access from front ends connected over a WAN. In this case, communication occurs between the front end's local SAProuter and the SAProuter in the local network of the application server, which then transfers the messages to the application server, and back.

12-168 The administration of distributed systems must comply with stringent system monitoring and control criteria. Several additional services are also required for efficient background processing, spooling, and archiving.

12-169 The system monitoring and control tools permit efficient system administration. System administrators can use these tools to acquire a comprehensive overview of the "system landscape" and intervene whenever the situation requires.

SOLUTIONS

12-170   The monitor architecture of the computing center management system offers a novel and flexible environment for system monitoring which separates data suppliers from data consumers. The monitor architecture between these two levels ensures that system information on various components, such as operating system, database, R/3 components, or external components, can be combined in a monitor as necessary.

12-171   User-friendly alert handling rounds off this new monitor architecture and allows system administrators to react more quickly to alerts.

12-172   The system administrator can use the global monitor with a tree structure to control operation throughout the R/3 system. In day-to-day operations remember that information and alerts on special areas of the system are available quickly. Sub-trees can be copied from the global monitor, stored, and reused whenever needed.

12-173   It is possible to combine different sub-trees under a virtual node. The system administrator could analyze and compare the database and CPU use in a single monitor.

12-174   Uniform procedures in the monitor architecture ensure that system monitoring is not only flexible but user-friendly. It does not matter how system administrators set up their monitors, the procedure they use is always the same, and therefore permits them to become acquainted quickly with the different tasks of system monitoring.

12-175   The monitor architecture includes additional preset monitors for certain typical and routine administration tasks that facilitate and accelerate its use.

12-176   The tree structure enables convenient setup of individual monitors.

12-177   An important component of efficient system monitoring is handling of alerts. Data suppliers within the monitor architecture send system messages to the attributes of a monitor object such as disk, CPU, and R/3 application components. These attributes are the "leaves" of the system tree. The alerts are performed automatically during monitoring of R/3 components; in operating and database systems, these data suppliers must be triggered. This makes certain that system monitoring is based on consistent messages.

12-178   A system administrator can set the threshold values for an alert just by clicking the relevant node, and then clicking the setup icon to display the screen on which entries can be made. An alert intended to initiate system administrator intervention is then issued each time the threshold is exceeded in either direction.

SOLUTIONS

12-179 Each monitor object has its own alert analysis tools are available in the system; they use methods suited to the specific problem when information is presented. Clicking on an icon calls up the required tool. This eliminates the need for differing analysis methods for differing problems. It is therefore possible to make a quick decision about whether or not a specific alert requires intervention.

12-180 The benefits provided by the monitor architecture of the CCMS extend beyond the boundaries of a single R/3 system. It is technically possible to monitor several R/3 systems from the CCMS. Monitors can also be equipped as APIs, permitting the system management tools of external suppliers to be connected. This provides a foundation for system administrators who monitor distributed network solutions within the business framework.

12-181 CCMS provides effective controls including mechanisms for starting and shutting down servers and processors, and for reconfiguring the entire installation.

12-182 CCMS offers functionality that greatly influences the performance and stability of the R/3 system at runtime.

12-183 Distributed client/server installations with several processors exhibit the best performance if the application load is distributed evenly across the servers and processing is not limited to just a few servers or processes.

12-184 The CCMS offers system administrators three different options for load distribution:

1. **Server assignment**—The CCMS uses "logon load distribution" to assign a user to the application server that currently has the smallest load.

     CCMS tries to divide its tasks into categories and assign these to specific servers. A new dialog user has to enter only the required R/3 application. One or more servers are assigned in a table to each application area.
2. The **message service** chooses the server with the smallest load from the active servers which are available.
3. **Modes of operation**—As dialog and background processing cause the load of an R/3 installation to vary throughout the day, it is possible to switch to another mode of operation when the situation requires.

12-185 In the CCMS, different modes of operation can be defined, and used to achieve an optimal load distribution. This is best illustrated by:

SOLUTIONS

1. **Online operation**—Most work processes are defined as dialog processes
2. **Night operation**—Most work processes are defined as background processes
3. **Maintenance operation**—Access is restricted to specific users
4. **Open interfaces**—Large R/3 installations with heterogeneous system platforms, multiple network services, and interfaces to external applications may need extra system management services.

12-186 The CCMS has different open interfaces that permit SAP is effective use of the system management tools of numerous suppliers.

12-187 CCMS interfaces can be classified as data collector, service, and management interfaces.

12-188 The CCMS receives performance-related data on the operating system, data management system, and the communications network through data collector interfaces. It can use these interfaces to start and monitor external services such as job scheduling in mainframe environments or the processing of data protection requests by external tools. Analogously, external applications can send requests to SAP job management for execution.

12-189 The CCMS can be connected to the system management services of other vendors through open interfaces. This has its benefits, especially in large, heterogeneous system environments.

12-190 R/3 is integrated in the management services of the Integrated Network and System Management (INSM) platform by means of suitable interfaces. INSM is based on the SNMP and MIB. External systems can interactively query and process management data in the SAP System using a special SNMP MIP.

12-191 When exceptional situations related to processing in R/3 occur, the SAP system also generates SNMP alarms.

12-192 The standard R/3 system contains all required interfaces. SAP can certify the use of these interfaces in external applications, and their use in production systems is logged in the database.

12-193 Auditing, session management and authorization concepts incorporate security and revision mechanisms in CCMS interfaces.

12-194 New CCMS developments include interfaces as a distributed view of R/3 administration using distributed objects that comply with COM/DCOM and CORBA specifications.

SOLUTIONS

12-195 Large volumes of data must often be processed in large enterprises and institutions, for planning material requirements or running payroll accounting. In these cases, the R/3 system offers a complex and flexible service infrastructure for automatic background processing of specific jobs.

12-196 The R/3 system offers several scheduling options, such as time-based, calendar-based, and event-based scheduling.

12-197 Jobs can be defined with a start-time window and with automatic repetition if required. In calendar-based scheduling, a job can be started on a specific day of the month (with automatic repetition).

12-198 The R/3 factory calendar can be specified for determining whether the day is a workday; the user can determine how the job should be handled if it is not a workday.

12-199 Event-based scheduling permits job starts dependent upon a predecessor job, an operation mode switch, or the triggering of the system or user-programmed event.

12-200 User-programmed events can be triggered from ABAP programs or from sources external to the R/3 system.

12-201 The job/job step concept is crucial for R/3 background processing. Each job is composed of one or more job steps that are processed in sequence.

12-202 If background processing is scheduled at the same time as several other programs, these programs can be defined as individual steps of the job. All processing steps are logically combined in the job. This provides a better overview of the job and makes it easier to control.

12-203 Yes, different external programs and operating system commands can be started from an R/3 background job.

12-204 An external program is defined in R/3 as an external command with respect to both definition and execution; the latter requires the proper authorizations.

12-205 Processing runs that require a large amount of system time can be divided among several parallel background work processes. These work processes have only a negligible effect on the execution of other background jobs or system processes. It is possible to define which servers may be used for parallel processing.

12-206 The R/3 spool system has to do with form and document output. It provides form printing, document printing, and fax services for R/3 users and their applications. Several printers can be used to offer printing features such as graphics, bar code, and OCR printing, and color printing supported.

12-207 In the document output capability, the spool system is platform-independent. The R/3 spool system must be able to generate output for a wide variety of printers. The document output capability means that printing from R/3 is possible even if the formatting options of the different operating system platforms differ. Even though it can produce printable output, the R/3 spool system does not directly drive the printers.

12-208 In the final output stage, when data are routed to a printer, R/3 uses the services of the platforms on which it runs.

12-209 The R/3 spool system offers various options for communicating with host spool systems. Output data can be transferred to the host system spooler where the R/3 spool server runs. Output can also be transferred across the network to a Microsoft Windows print manager or to a host spooler on a remote system.

12-210 The R/3 spool system has the ability to use Windows formatting options. R/3 forms and documents can be output on any device supported by Windows, even if the device is not known to the R/3 system.

12-211 The R/3 spool system allows integration of selected output management systems (OMS) into large customer systems and existing OMSs. This spool system can transfer jobs to the OMS, obtain status information, and be integrated into the customer's OMS solution for printing using command-line or callback (remote function call) interfaces.

12-212 OMS integration is a form of system management of API functions that permits R/3 administration functions including spooling to be integrated into existing customer infrastructures.

12-213 A significant problem of all production systems is the huge volume of data that accumulates over time and has a negative impact on database performance and administration.

12-214 Even though application data are no longer required for online operation, government laws and company regulations require that this data be kept.

12-215 The archiving which is an integral part of the R/3 system is based on the Archive Development Kit (ADK). The ADK allows R/3 users to archive application data during online operation. This is made possible by a two-step procedure:

1. Data are first retrieved from the database and written to archive files.

SOLUTIONS

2. Data are then deleted from the database.

This two-step archiving process is advantageous because of two primary factors:

1. Data security—When data are copied and the deleted, they cannot be lost during the archiving procedure.

2. Increased capacity usage—Keeping the write and delete operations separate and distributing archiving tasks to several parallel jobs makes certain of optimal use of available system resources.

12-216   The R/3 archiving solution has a special feature in which data can still be accessed by the application even after being deleted from the database.

12-217   Archive management enables three different types of access depending on the type of application:

1. Read access to a single archive object
2. Evaluation of an archive file for reporting
3. Reloading of archived data.

12-218   The ADK provides a connection for external archive systems that can be used to integrate optical archiving systems.

12-219   Hardware and software downtime quickly results in loss of production and service, making it difficult for companies to meet their delivery commitments on time and often resulting in financial losses. The more crucial a system is for company operation, the greater the interdependence between individual system components.

12-220   Planned downtimes occur during hardware and software upgrades or during offline data backup runs. Unplanned downtimes are caused by hardware or software failure.

12-221   "High availability" in the R/3 environment means that system availability is restored within the shortest possible time following unplanned downtimes, and that planned downtimes are not even noticeable to users.

12-222   In order to achieve round-the-clock availability 365 days a year, SAP offers important services globally, 24 hours a day. These include the Hotline, and, upon customer request, remote maintenance; and proactive system management with Early Watch. There is also detailed documentation covering all aspects of R/3 system availability that provides valuable tips on R/3 installation and operation.

12-223   Automatic load distribution and the message server's role in logon load distribution assure quick assignment of jobs to one of the other available application servers if the server currently processing the jobs should fail.

SOLUTIONS

12-224 The monitoring functions of the CCMS also ensure optimal and stable operation of the R/3 system.

12-225 Several hardware suppliers respond to the problem of system downtime caused by computer failure using the switch over fault-tolerance concept. SAP uses the functions offered by its hardware partners.

12-226 Fault tolerance (Figure 12.12) primary and a standby computer which have access to shared disks. If the primary computer fails due to a hardware fault, all applications are shifted to the standby computer. The standby computer is given exclusive rights of access to the shared disks. All connections between the primary computer and other computers are reassigned to the standby. If computers are connected by means of TCP/IP, the switchover is effected by transferring the IP address to the standby computer. The entire process is automatic and takes only a few minutes. SAP uses the functions provided by its hardware partners when implementing the switchover fault-tolerance concept.

FIGURE 12.12
Fault Tolerance

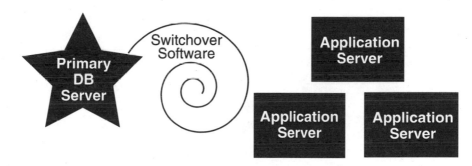

12-227 If the faulty computer is a database server, the R/3 DB reconnect procedure used in multi-tier R/3 installations makes certain that the application computers are automatically reconnected to the new database computer.

12-228 Performance is enhanced because the R/3 application computers do not need to be shut down and restarted, and because application server buffers retain their contents. Only transactions not yet completed at the time of termination are lost. All manufacturer-specific solutions can be used with the R/3 system. This includes fault-tolerant disk units (mirror disks or RAID systems) and networks, as well as various restore and recovery features of database suppliers.

12-229 The R/3 system utilizes the repository switch technology during release upgrades. Depending on the size of the installation, planned production

SOLUTIONS

downtime can be limited to a few hours. Several tasks are performed in parallel with online operation. The R/3 repository is first copied to the background of the productive repository. Customer objects are then copied from the old version to the new database. Only when the production system is switched over to the new repository and customer data are converted to the new release format does the repository have to be shut down. Customer modifications are also adapted during this phase. The R/3 repository switch technology allows quick resumption of production following planned downtime. In order to reduce system downtime as much as possible, SAP recommends using one of two special upgrade strategies.

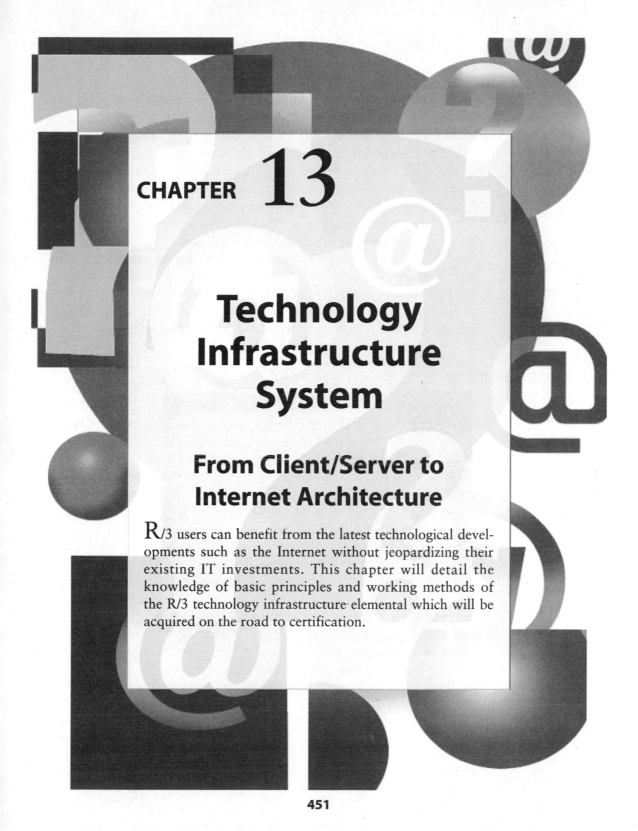

CHAPTER 13

Technology Infrastructure System

From Client/Server to Internet Architecture

R/3 users can benefit from the latest technological developments such as the Internet without jeopardizing their existing IT investments. This chapter will detail the knowledge of basic principles and working methods of the R/3 technology infrastructure elemental which will be acquired on the road to certification.

The bulk of the rapid success achieved by the R/3 system in combination with several business applications functions used in industries worldwide can be attributed to the design of the infrastructure. The open three-tier client/server architecture underlying the R/3 system forms a solid foundation for continuous enhancement of the system.

There are breaks between the presentation, application and database layers. The R/3 system can be distributed flexibly across these three layers with several different client/server scenarios. Cooperative processing can be used in an integrated system together with application components from other vendors.

SAP has grown through the R/3 technology infrastructure into a multi-layer Internet architecture. The addition of object-oriented technology has enhanced development. The Web offers R/3 users especially exciting opportunities. Users are among the first to be able to integrate the power of the Internet into their business processes and do business on the Internet.

Business Workflow

SAP Business Workflow connects information with active control of business processes. It makes employees responsible for specific tasks with access to the right tasks at the right time. One example of a business process which can be controlled using SAP Business Workflow is the complete processing of a customer order from receipt of order through delivery of goods and issuing of an invoice. The specific relationship between the events in the business workflow can be viewed as chronologically specified elements of a business process.

The employee responsible for a specific process in a company can request information about the current status of the corresponding workflow at any time and can also trace the history of the work process.

Business Workflow provides a MAPI-compatible interface for use of MAPI-compatible mail front-ends already installed including: MS Outlook, Lotus CC: Mail or MS Exchange. These can be used for starting workflows both offline and online as well for executing form-based tasks within a business process. Workflow design can be greatly simplified and accelerated by the use of Workflow Wizards integrated into SAP Business Workflow. These Wizards or assistants are the same as those found in many PC applications and lead the designer in a controlled dialog based on carefully prepared questions and decision options to produce an executable workflow definition quickly and safely. It is also possible to start a workflow directly from the Internet or from an intranet. This type of application is illustrated by the use of the Internet for personnel management as a tool for finding candidates for vacant posts.

The basic workflow pattern consists of a preliminary hiring evaluation in the human resources department and immediate rejection or forwarding to the relevant specialist department. This department sends out an invitation to an interview or rejects the candidate (either totally or by referral to a different department). Once the application is submitted, applicants receive a unique identifying code and a password that allows them to check status over the Internet at any time.

SAP Business Workflow couples information with active control of business processes. It offers the employees responsible for specific tasks with access to the right tasks at the right time. A typical example of a business process can be controlled using SAP Business Workflow which is the complete processing of a customer order from receipt of the order through delivery of the goods and issuing of an invoice.

It also offers a MAPI-compatible interface so that you can continue to use MAPI-compatible mail front-ends already installed including: MS Outlook, Lotus CC: Mail or MS Exchange. These can be used for starting workflows offline and online as well for executing form-based tasks within a business process.

Technology Infrastructure

R/3 greatly improves productivity when business applications are implemented. Middleware such as R/3 Technology Infrastructure helps by managing all of the components of a distributed applications system.

R/3 Technology Infrastructure ensures a smooth interoperation of R/3 system applications in combination with graphical user interfaces, database management systems, operating systems, and communications and applications systems from several manufacturers.

The basic structure of the R/3 system is founded on the three-tier model of distributed client/server processing. This model demonstrates the difference between the various processing layers. R/3 Technology Infrastructure distinguishes between the database, application, and presentation layers and clearly identifies the Internet-enabling layer.

R/3 is totally scalable on each of its layers. When more users are added, applications are acquired as the volume of data to be processed increases. New investments required in each of these four layers can be planned, without worry about disruptive side-effects on any of the layers.

The R/3 technology infrastructure guarantees that the complete R/3 system is portable to all hardware, operating systems, and database management systems within the open systems computing concept. The database layer manages an organization's working data, including the master data, transaction data, and the metadata maintained in the repository that describes the database structure.

Applications based on Database Management System (DBMS) compose the second layer. These function with data they acquire from the database layer and write the resulting new data back to this layer. R/3 applications are processed in this layer much as custom-written application enhancements are created using the ABAP Workbench.

The R/3 technology infrastructure provides users with efficient access to the business management functions of the R/3 system while allowing them to choose several different user interfaces.

In SAPGUI, R/3 provides a graphical user interface optimized for business management processes with a design based on the latest ergonomic research. Screen design elements and a work mode familiar from PC applications give new users extra assistance. The goal is for R/3 applications to be quick to learn and simple to use.

Session Manager

The session manager allows users to personalize their desktops and the contents of the desktop menus. It also provides assistance with navigation through R/3 system menus. It offers users three views of the R/3 menu:

1. A comprehensive SAP view comprising all transactions
2. An organization-defined view of only those transactions used within a company
3. A user-defined view. The user-defined menu makes orientation and navigation to transactions easier.

The different menus in the session manager make it simpler to work with R/3. A special session manager window can be customized with frequently used transactions, just by using drag and drop. It provides quick, permanent, and direct access to the selected transactions.

The session manager makes work with R/3 simpler by managing terminal sessions. It can also manage parallel sessions in different R/3 systems as well as different sessions within the same R/3 system. In addition, it provides a permanent overview and direct access to all the activities initiated by using current front-end techniques such as tabs and windows.

SAP R/3 4.0 has organization-defined and user-defined menus that are also available in SAPGUI. A new transaction can be used to access R/3 to choose among menu options and navigate simply and directly to application transactions. SAPGUI also allows frequently-used transactions to be kept in a personal directory.

SAP has integrated new developments in front-end component technology into the latest SAPGUI in Release 4.0. SAP can now integrate both the ActiveX Controls and JavaBeans.

SAPscript is a new PC editor and the R/3 integrated word processing tool. It offers online help based on Explorer and HTML Control and Business Explorer, part of the new Business Information Warehouse. This new technology makes it simpler to integrate R/3 into office products such as Word and Excel. R/3 provides a Java version of the SAPGUI. The three-tier architecture of the R/3 system means that no changes are needed for the system itself. Users can call their normal R/3 transactions directly from the Internet. The Java-based SAPGUI has the same look and feel as the normal SAPGUI. The need for special installation, administration and maintenance work on the client side is completely eliminated.

When R/3 is called from the Internet using a Java SAPGUI, the latest version of the presentation software is automatically loaded onto the Web client. The Java-based SAPGUI also allows new platforms such as Net PCs and NCs to be used as R/3 clients. SAP offers Web users access to the R/3 system business processes through a Web browser. The simple interface of the SAP Internet applications immediately integrates inexperienced Web users into the R/3 business processing flow.

The types of application that can be realized using this Internet connection range from electronic commerce and specialized intranet applications to intercompany business to business applications.

ALE

ALE (Application Link Enabling) technology makes a reality of genuine cooperative processing within a network of loosely coupled applications systems. Ready-made distribution scenarios for ALE have been integrated into the R/3 system. In making the ALE concept an integral element of the R/3 technology infrastructure, SAP has placed a standardized semantic layer for cooperative processing between distributed application systems. The R/3 technology infrastructure extends its functions in a way that might be expected from middleware.

ALE permits loose coupling between different applications and between different R/3 systems. These systems can be configured with respect to a decentralized plan and can be technically independent. They do not all have to use the same software release.

ALE ensures that the business processes in the various installations work in cooperation with each other. It also allows easy integration of applications from other manufacturers (non-SAP systems) and of R/2 systems. Since ALE is based on an exchange of messages controlled by business processes and performed using consistent data, applications are integrated using asynchronous communications mechanisms under time control.

ALE permits business processes from different kinds of systems to be integrated, and synchronizes the business processes of the communicating systems. Whenever ALE exchanges messages containing application data, it uses standardized intermediate documents similar to those used by the R/3 system functions that support the EDI (Electronic Data Interchange) standard.

SAP uses ALE with the R/3 system in several business situations. Should an external system be used for transportation planning, a group of pending shipments can be chosen in the R/3 system and then downloaded through the ALE interface to the planning system.

A system can employ whatever optimization criteria it needs to convert the shipments into actual transport consignments. These consignments are then reported back across the ALE interface to the R/3 system, where they trigger the creation of the shipment documentation.

To deal with shipment handling (i.e. printing the documents and notifying the start of shipping) these functions are performed as part of the usual document processing in the R/3 system. In this situation, it is possible to achieve the fastest implementation of the ALE technology. Attention is concentrated on specific requirements because the preliminary work has already been done, saving time and money. There will be even more integration into the R/3 system, increasing the versatility of ALE as a ready-to-run system.

When working with object technology for the Internet, SAP business objects and the associated BAPIs embody the foundation of SAP's Internet strategy. BAPIs are defined as methods that offer direct communication between applications from different suppliers. SAP business objects have an evolutionary approach to the introduction of object technology into areas such as modeling, workflow design, interface definition, and programming. They make control of the R/3 system more direct and more easily governed by business-related requirements. It makes good business sense to reuse existing application components wherever possible, and to combine them with other components to design new business processes.

SAP Business Objects

A SAP business object is composed of a kernel that possesses the central business management logic and is directly supported by the mature processes, functions and data of the R/3 system. Business objects use the standard functions of object-oriented technology. Each SAP business object is completely documented in the R/3 business object repository and may be accessed there.

BAPIs

BAPIs are crucial to the Internet and the multi-layer R/3 Internet architecture. They are methods of SAP business objects that represent open business management interfaces. Several BAPIs are defined and published, and external companies provide software components that can be used smoothly together with the R/3 system. This is best illustrated by the use of BAPIs to ensure that when two applications systems communicate with each other, the business-related information include: order details, customer number, and part numbers.

Transactions can exchange data with other transactions operating in other companies. BAPIs can be viewed as building on Component Object Model/Distributed Component Object Model (COM/DCOM) to offer interface technology for integrating applications. BAPIs perform as links between the main applications of the R/3 system and the R/3 Internet applications.

In the Business Framework, BAPIs can be used for communication between business components. In combination with the R/3 Internet-enabling layer, they help the three-tier client/server architecture become a multi-layer Internet architecture.

R/3-MIB

The R/3-MIB (Management Information Base) involves interfaces for controlling and monitoring applications and alarm handling. It is important with regards to enterprise mission-critical applications that the least time required for a release upgrade. New technology (i.e. repository switch) and the support provided by comfortable graphical user interfaces and fully automated procedures for importing new releases all help to save large amounts of time and to reduce costs.

Whenever a new release has been imported, the software has to be distributed to the various servers. SAP offers a form of automatic software distribution that allows this version upgrade process to be conducted without interrupting normal operation. Each time a transaction is called, the software on that application server is checked. If the current version of the software is not present, an update is performed automatically. This procedure permits extended periods of unproductive time to be avoided when used commonly during release upgrades. In addition to reducing the planned idle time of systems caused by upgrades and maintenance, SAP creates procedures for reducing the unplanned system idle time resulting from breakdowns.

Availability

SAP ensures that the availability of the R/3 System remains unaffected, even when one of the servers goes down by utilizing the switchover technology of its hardware partners. When the system spots that a server has gone down, it automatically activates a replacement server that takes over the tasks of the lost primary server, without requiring any manual intervention by the system administrator.

Internet Application Components

SAP develops internet application components in R/3 for areas such as consumer-to-business, business-to-business, and intranet solutions. These applications are all decoupled from the R/3 system, but still function on the application server and can access the functions and data of the main applications of the R/3 system via the BAPIs.

It is possible to enforce security for distributed processing, though the primary dealings must be acquiring the highest possible level of security in distributed processing across networks of all kinds.

GSS-API (Generic Security Services API) interfaces are crucial in the implementation of a modern security mechanism for distributed processing. GSS-API has been adopted as part of the R/3 system Secure Network Communications interface (SNC).

R/3 can be integrated with any network security product that itself supports the GSS-API including Kerberos and SecuDE. These systems allow external R/3 users to be authenticated and guarantee that the communications data are secure. In addition, most R/3 users who operate their applications on public networks have installed firewalls.

Internet applications have the SET (Secure Electronic Transactions) standard which SAP integrates into the R/3 System. SET was created by a consortium of technology providers and credit card companies and is based on the Private Communication Technology (PCT) security package from Microsoft and the Secure Socket Layer (SSL) package from

Netscape. These packages handle client authentication, server authentication, confidentiality, connection reliability, and secure payment.

Public networks are commonly used for electronic commerce, and business transactions. Including signing contracts and sending confidential documents must be legally binding. Security requirements for electronic business processes are different from those for online communication between system components. Digital signatures are needed for documents as are encryption mechanisms to prevent unauthorized access to the contents of documents.

SAP has created the technical basis for security to support electronic business processes. This support is provided by Secure Store & Forward (SSF) in R/3 4.0 and allows R/3 data and documents to be encrypted and documents to be signed with digital signatures. R/3 services use external security products that consist of industry-standard processes and formats including X.509, the standard process for asymmetric encryption and PKCS#7, the standard format for signed or encrypted documents.

CCMS

The Computing Center Management System (CCMS) permits continuous monitoring of the R/3 system at database, application-level, operating system, and network. It provides procedures and checklists that help the administrator identify and deal with critical states at an early stage.

CCMS permits fine-tuning of the system using performance monitors (graphical displays that offer the administrator a rapid overview of the whole R/3 system and enable prompt intervention in critical situations. This further contributes to the availability of the system and to the level of user satisfaction.

SAPoffice

SAPoffice, an important component within an organization, is the communication infrastructure for exchange of messages with colleagues and business partners. Most modern communication services include telephone, fax, standard letters, and increasingly, electronic mail. Even now, e-mail largely replaces the current standard means of communication.

In choosing an electronic communication service, look for features including: open nature, integration in existing mail systems, workflow support, ability to send and receive faxes, and integrated inbox. An office communication system should be integrated into the business software used in the company so that it is possible to integrate business processes and business data.

SAPoffice offers an integrated communication service that satisfies all of these requirements. Since the Internet is the most common network for transmitting e-mail, SAPoffice offers the framework for sending and receiving electronic Internet mail. R/3 supports the e-mail standard X.400. SAPoffice can be used as a solid and open basis for global company communication. It also provides an integrated inbox. All messages sent to a user e-mail and faxes and workflow orders are acquired at this point. Users do not need to search manually for their messages in different inboxes or even different systems. The standard point of access to the integrated inbox is the R/3 user interface.

If employees use other mail interfaces, including Microsoft Exchange, these interfaces can also be used to create, send and edit messages administered in SAPoffice because SAP supports the Messaging Application Programming Interface (MAPI) interface. Therefore, employees who do not use any of the R/3 system business functions can have electronic mail.

Backup and Restore

SAP's backup and restore concepts reduce recovery times in the case of hard disk crashes. SAP supports the integration of standard technology for increasing availability at the hardware level, for example redundant hard disk capacity (RAID), redundant networks and uninterruptible power supplies (UPS).

BACKGROUND

Cross-enterprise integration focuses on the flow of business processes is the most effective approach. R/3 addresses this need with SAP Business Workflow that is available within Internet and Intranet solutions.

R/3 acquires flexibility of deployment from its reliable architecture. This means applications can be distributed and there can be an unprecedented degree of integration between SAP and non-SAP components. R/3 forms the foundation of SAP Business Framework architecture: independent business management components, integration technology and open interfaces, which all combine to create a flexible, standards-oriented environment in which the R/3 system and software from external providers can cooperate. Efficient use of R/3 for business management applications that focus on a rapid time to market has a much higher priority than technical problem solving.

Business Framework is composed of both SAP and non-SAP products, forming an integrated and component-based solution. The continued development of R/3 represents an important architectural cornerstone in the pursuit of this integration goal. The highly developed interface based on object-oriented BAPIs is vital. It provides enterprises the chance to devote their complete attention to business goals instead of confronting them with problems that involve feasibility with current IT technology.

Summary

In this chapter we have seen the technology infrastructure moving from client/server into an Internet-based architecture. We looked at the basis of the technology infrastructure course track in order to explain how ALE, SAPoffice, ABAP, and Business Framework are important components in the evolution of a system on the Internet.

In Chapter 14 we move from the evolution of the user interface to the evolution of the client/server infrastructure into the Internet. This growth is representative of the diverse areas of in-depth preparation necessary for passing the certification exam.

13-1   What is middleware?

13-2   Compare middle ware to the R/3 technology infrastructure.

13-3   How does R/3 integrate with the graphical user interface?

13-4   Explain the three-tier model's location in the R/3 system.

13-5   Are the layers of the R/3 system scalable?

13-6   What does the R/3 technology infrastructure guarantee?

13-7   Explain the functionality of the layers within the R/3 system.

13-8   What is SQL used for and what does the acronym stand for?

13-9   What types of databases and applications are supported?

13-10   What does the use of SQL enhancements do with respect to access?

13-11   What do the applications based on DBMS make up?

13-12   Describe the process by which applications are collected from the database then what happens to them?

13-13   Explain the Internet-enabling layer. Above what application layer is it created?

13-14   What is the presentation layer?

13-15   Explain the integration business management functions with different user interfaces. To whom is support offered?

13-16   What does SAPGUI, enable the R/3 system to offer?

13-17   What does the session manager do?

13-18   What do the different menus in the session manager do with regarding working with R/3?

13-19   What does the session manager provide for access in all activities?

13-20   What other alternative user interfaces exist?

13-21   What is the primary means of accessing information for many users?

13-22   What does SAP automation API?

13-23   What helps users to reach interface objective?

13-24   What new items exist in front-end component technology?

13-25   What is SAPscript?

13-26 Is there a Java version of SAPGUI? If so, explain how it functions; if not, explain what versions do exist.

13-27 What happens when the R/3 system is called from the Internet using a Java SAPGUI?

13-28 To what does SAP offer Web-user access?

13-29 What kinds of applications can be realized using an Internet connection?

13-30 What does ALE technology do in a network?

13-31 What does ALE do between different applications?

13-32 Can each of the subsidiaries or divisions of a company work with its own R/3 system?

13-33 What does ALE assure for business processes?

13-34 On what is ALE based?

13-35 How are applications integrated?

13-36 What does ALE do for business processes from different kinds of systems?

13-37 What does ALE do with respect to exchanging messages containing application data?

13-38 With ALE, what does SAP offer its users?

13-39 What is the distribution situation?

13-40 What happens when an external system is used for transportation planning?

13-41 What kinds of optimization criteria are used for a system?

13-42 Where are many of the steps involved in shipment handling performed? What are these steps?

13-43 What do SAP business objects represent?

13-44 What does a SAP business object consist of?

13-45 What kind of functions do business objects use?

13-46 What role do BAPIs play?

13-47 What do BAPIs do in SAP's Internet philosophy?

13-48 How do BAPIs act in the business framework?

13-49 How do BAPIs fit in with Internet applications from SAP?

13-50   How can transaction security be maintained?

13-51   How do you ensure security of distributed processing?

13-52   How does the R/3 technology satisfy the demand for security?

13-53   What is the standard GSS-API?

13-54   Does R/3 offer functions for controlling access to data and functions?

13-55   How does SAP integrate Internet applications, and what does "SET" mean?

13-56   How do the security requirements for electronic business processes different from other security requirements?

13-57   What is a digital signature?

13-58   What has SAP done to create a security foundation to support electronic business processes?

13-59   How do R/3 services use external security products?

13-60   Can secure business transactions be based on the consistent use of standards and extended across R/3 and non-R/3 systems?

13-61   How can continuous system availability be enabled?

13-62   Define CCMS and explain in detail what it does.

13-63   What does SAP offer larger R/3 users who manage their own computing environment with INSM platforms? Explain in detail and define INSM.

13-64   What is the R/3 MIB?

13-65   What happens after a new release is imported?

13-66   What happens each time a transaction is called?

13-67   How does SAP make certain that R/3 system availability remains unaffected?

13-68   What happens when the system realizes that the server has gone down?

13-69   What do SAP's backup and restore concepts reduce?

13-70   What is the focus of cross-enterprise integration?

13-71   What is SAP Business Workflow?

13-72   What kind of relationship exists between events in the business workflow?

13-73 What information can be requested by an employee responsible for a specific company process?

13-74 Define and elaborate on SAP's connection with the WfMC.

13-75 What does the SAP Business Workflow offer?

13-76 How do Workflow Wizards simplify and speed of workflow design?

13-77 What does the basic workflow pattern consist of?

13-78 What is SAPoffice?

13-79 What factors must be considered when choosing an electronic commerce service?

13-80 What does SAPoffice provide?

13-81 What happens if employees use other mail interfaces?

13-82 What is the ABAP workbench?

13-83 What does the ABAP workbench support?

13-84 What do graphical user interfaces and simple working methods do to make tools easy to use? Explain in detail how this relates to the ABAP language.

13-85 Where are development objects stored?

13-86 Who is the primary user of the ABAP dictionary?

13-87 What does the library containing reusable and versatile program modules promote?

13-88 What does the workbench support?

13-89 Describe how applications developed with the ABAP workbench can be ported?

13-90 Explain how R/3 gets its flexibility of deployment.

13-91 Explain the foundation of Business Framework.

13-1   Middleware describes software that enables the smooth mutual functioning of application programs, the operating system, and the communications network.

13-2   R/3 can significantly enhance productivity when business applications are implemented and used. Middleware like the R/3 technology infrastructure achieves this objective by carefully managing the various components of a distributed applications system.

13-3   The R/3 technology infrastructure is created to assure a smooth interoperation of R/3 system applications in combination with graphical user interfaces, database management systems, operating systems, and communications and applications systems from several manufacturers.

13-4   The three-tier model of distributed client/server processing is the cornerstone of the R/3 system. In this model there is a clear distinction among the different processing layers, and the Internet-enabling layer is clearly identified.

13-5   The R/3 system is fully scalable on each of these layers. The number of users grows when new applications are acquired or the volume of data to be processed increases. It is then possible to plan the new investments needed in each of these four layers, without having to worry about disruptive side effects on any of the other layers.

13-6   The R/3 technology infrastructure guarantees that the entire R/3 system is portable to all hardware, operating systems, and database management systems within the open systems computing concept.

13-7   The database layer manages an organization's working data. This includes the master data, transaction data, and also the meta-data maintained in the repository that describes the database structure.

13-8   The standard SQL (Structured Query Language) is used for defining and manipulating all data.

13-9   All relational database management systems (DBMS) that are appropriate for mission-critical applications and have a definite market presence are supported.

13-10   Using proprietary SQL enhancements optimizes access and improves performance without necessitating worry about the technical details.

13-11   The applications based on the DBMS make up the second layer. These applications work with data they collect from the database layer and write the resulting new data back to this layer. The R/3 system applications are processed in this layer, in much the same way as custom-written application enhancements developed using ABAP Workbench.

13-12 Applications can be collected from the database as required, loaded into the application layer, and then run from there.

13-13 Internet technology does not handle business transactions itself, though the Internet-enabling layer has been created above the applications layer. The Internet-enabling layer extends the three-tier R/3 architecture into a multi-layer Internet architecture. R/3 system users can now take advantage of this feature and use the Web as a worldwide transaction web for business applications. The Web can also be integrated with the applications components of other providers.

13-14 The presentation layer is also known as the user interface. It is positioned closest to the user.

13-15 The R/3 technology infrastructure gives users efficient access to the business management functions of the R/3 system while leaving them with their choice of several different user interfaces.

Support is offered both to users for whom the R/3 system is the main IT application and to those who only occasionally use R/3 functions through Web browser or a desktop GUI.

13-16 With SAPGUI (Figure 13.1), the R/3 system offers a graphical user interface optimized for business management processes whose design is based on the latest ergonomic research. Screen design elements and a work mode that are familiar from PC applications give new users extra assistance. The goal is that R/3 applications should be quick to learn and simple to use.

FIGURE 13.1
SAPGUI

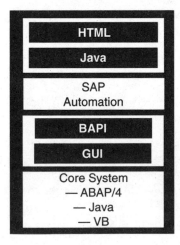

SOLUTIONS

13-17   The session manager allows users to personalize their desktops and the contents of the desktop menus. It also offers assistance in navigating through the R/3 system menus. It offers three views of the R/3 menu:

1. A comprehensive SAP view comprising all transactions
2. An organization-defined view made up of only those transactions used within a company.
3. A user-defined view comprising only those transactions used by individuals. The user-defined menu in particular makes orientation and navigation to transactions easier.

13-18   Just as lists of business items and personal items would be separated for easier location of numbers, different menus in the session manager make it easier to work with R/3. A special session manager window can be customized to contain frequently used transactions simply by using drag and drop. The session manager offers quick, permanent, and direct access to the selected transactions. In addition, it makes work with R/3 easier by managing terminal sessions. It can also manage parallel sessions in different R/3 systems as well as different sessions within the same R/3 system.

13-19   The session manager provides users with a permanent overview of and direct access to all activities initiated, using current front-end techniques such as tabs and windows. In R/3 Release 4.0, organization-defined and user-defined menus are also available in SAPGUI. The new transaction can be used to access R/3: different menu options can be chosen and navigating to required application transactions becomes simple and direct. SAPGUI permits keeping frequently used transactions in a personal directory.

13-20   Besides the R/3 user interface, there are several alternative user interfaces that must be supported. These include kiosk systems, telephone answering systems, and the desktop integration represented by the Microsoft Windows operating system and its associated office products.

13-21   An exponentially growing number of users access information through the Web. These people use browsers from various manufacturers to access information. As a result, an important factor in extending the R/3 System is the ability to open the system to new categories of users by supporting these user interfaces.

13-22   The assistance of the SAP automation API allows users to derive benefit from a variety of user interfaces for developing business processes independent of specific applications.

13-23   It is important to remain current with new technological developments, determining their usefulness, and finding if they are beneficial. It is also important to be able to integrate them quickly into R/3 so that SAP is the front end.

13-24 SAP is using new developments in front-end component technology and has integrated them into the latest SAPGUI in Release 4.0. so that both ActiveX Controls and JavaBeans can be used.

13-25 SAPscript is a new PC editor and the R/3 integrated word processing tool. It offers online help based on Explorer, HTML Control, and Business Explorer, all part of the new Business Information Warehouse. This new technology makes it easier to integrate R/3 into office products such as Word and Excel.

13-26 The R/3 system now offers a Java version of the SAPGUI. The three-tier architecture of the R/3 system means that no changes are required for the system itself. Users can call their normal R/3 transactions directly from the Internet. The Java-based SAPGUI has exactly the same look and feel as the normal SAPGUI. The need for special installation, administration and maintenance work on the client side is completely eliminated.

13-27 When the R/3 system is called from the Internet using a Java SAPGUI, the latest version of the presentation software is automatically loaded onto the Web client. The Java-based SAPGUI also allows new platforms such as Net PCs and NCs to be used as R/3 clients.

13-28 Through the Internet architecture, SAP offers Web users access to the R/3 system business processes through a Web browser. The simple interface of the SAP Internet applications immediately integrates inexperienced Web users into the R/3 business processing flow.

13-29 The types of application that can be realized using this Internet connection range from electronic commerce and specialized intranet applications to intercompany business-to-business applications.

13-30 ALE technology makes a reality of genuine cooperative processing within a network of loosely coupled applications systems. Ready-made distribution scenarios for ALE have been integrated into the R/3 system. In making the ALE concept an integral element of the R/3 technology infrastructure, SAP has effectively placed a standardized semantic layer for cooperative processing between distributed application systems. The R/3 technology infrastructure extends its functions in ways that might be expected middleware.

13-31 ALE allows loose coupling between different applications as well as between different R/3 systems. These systems can be configured with

SOLUTIONS

respect to a decentralized plan and can be technically independent from each other. They do not all have to use the same software release.

13-32 Yes, each of the subsidiaries or divisions of a company can work with its own R/3 system. The implementation and upgrade strategy can be planned separately for each of the subsidiaries.

13-33 ALE ensures that the business processes in the various installations work in cooperation with each other. It also permits easy integration of applications from other manufacturers (non-SAP systems) and of R/2 systems.

13-34 ALE is based on an exchange of messages controlled by business processes and performed using consistent data.

13-35 Applications are integrated using asynchronous communications mechanisms under time control.

13-36 ALE allows business processes from different kinds of systems to be integrated and synchronizes the business processes of the communicating systems.

13-37 When ALE exchanges messages containing application data, it uses standardized intermediate documents similar to those used by the R/3 system functions that support the EDI (Electronic Data Interchange) standard.

13-38 With ALE, SAP offers users more than just technology. The wherewithal to address several business situations in which a company could use ALE with the R/3 system has been designed and supplied with ALE.

13-39 The distribution situation is meant for efficient and optimized transportation planning. In such events, specialized software components have an increasingly important role.

13-40 If an external system is used for transportation planning, a group of pending shipments can be chosen in the R/3 system and then downloaded through the ALE interface to the planning system.

13-41 A system can use whatever optimization criteria are required to convert the shipments into actual transport consignments. These consignments are then reported back across the ALE interface to the R/3 system, where they trigger the creation of the shipment documentation.

13-42 The steps involved in shipment handling including printing the documents and notification of the start of shipping are performed as part of the usual document processing in the R/3 system. This helps achieve the fastest possible implementation of the ALE technology. A company can focus its attention on specific requirements since the preliminary work has been

SOLUTIONS

done, saving the company time and money. Even more integration into the R/3 system will increase the versatility of ALE as a ready-to-run system.

13-43   In the object technology for the Internet, SAP business objects and the associated BAPIs (Figure 13.2) represent the foundation of SAP's Internet strategy. BAPIs are defined as methods providing direct communication between applications from different suppliers. SAP business objects represent an evolutionary approach to the introduction of object technology into areas such as modeling, workflow design, interface definition, and programming. They enable control of the R/3 system to be more directly and more easily governed by business-related requirements. It makes good business sense to reuse existing application components wherever possible, and to combine them with other components to design new business processes.

FIGURE 13.2
Object Oriented BAPIs

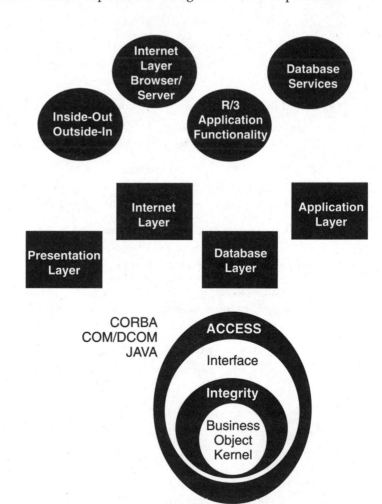

FIGURE 13.3
Business
Object Kernel

13-44 An SAP business object consists of a kernel that contains the central business management logic and is directly supported by the mature processes, functions and data of the R/3 System (Figure 13.3).

13-45 Business objects use the standard functions of object-oriented technology. Each SAP business object is completely documented in the R/3 business object repository and may be accessed there.

13-46 BAPIs play an important role in relation to the Internet and the multi-layer R/3 Internet architecture. BAPIs are methods of SAP business objects and represent open business management interfaces. Several BAPIs are defined and published, and external companies are now offering software components that can be used smoothly with the R/3 system. BAPIs ensure that when two applications systems communicate with each other, the business-related information, such as the order details, customer number or part numbers, the same semantics. In essence, BAPIs assure that the applications systems are communicating correctly. Transactions can even exchange data with other transactions running in other companies. BAPIs can be seen as building on COM/DCOM to offer interface technology for integrating applications.

13-47 In the SAP Internet method, BAPIs act as the links between the main applications of the R/3 system and the R/3 Internet applications.

13-48 In Business Framework BAPIs are used for communications between business components. In combination with the R/3 Internet-enabling layer they charge the three-tier client/server architecture to a multilayer Internet architecture.

13-49 SAP produces Internet application components in R/3 for areas including consumer-to-business, business-to-business, and intranet solutions. These applications are all decoupled from the R/3 system itself, still operate on the application server and can access the functions and data of the main applications of the R/3 system via the BAPIs.

13-50 Transaction security is assured within the R/3 Internet architecture by the R/3 Internet-enabling layer.

13-51 It is possible to ensure security for distributed processing, but the highest possible level of security in distributed processing across networks of all kinds is of critical importance for many businesses.

13-52 R/3's technology satisfies the demand for security by providing a variety of internal and external security mechanisms.

13-53 The standard GSS-API (Generic Security Services API) interface is critical in the implementation of a modern security mechanism for distributed

SOLUTIONS

processing. As a result, the GSS-API has been adopted as part of the R/3 system Secure Network Communications interface (SNC) (Figure 13.4). The R/3 system can be integrated with any network security product that itself supports the GSS-API such as Kerberos and SECUDE (Figure 13.5). These systems allow external R/3 users to be authenticated and guarantee that the communications data are secure. In addition, most R/3 users who operate their applications on public networks have installed firewalls.

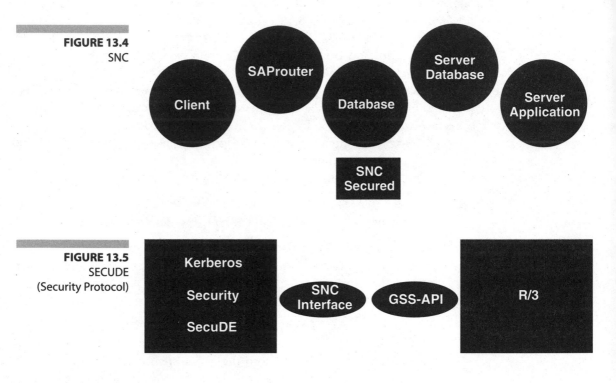

FIGURE 13.4
SNC

FIGURE 13.5
SECUDE
(Security Protocol)

13-54 The R/3 system also offers its own complex ways for controlling access to data and functions in order to prevent unauthorized access.

13-55 Internet applications are the SET (Secure Electronic Transactions) standard by which SAP integrates into the R/3 System. SET was created by a consortium of technology providers and credit card companies and is based on the Private Communication Technology (PCT) security package from Microsoft and the Secure Socket Layer (SSL) package from Netscape. These packages handle client authentication, server authentication, confidentiality, connection reliability, and secure payment. Since public networks are commonly used for electronic commerce, the security measures must be legally binding business transactions as well.

13-56 Security requirements for electronic business processes are different those for online communication between system components.

13-57 Digital signatures are required to sign documents encryption mechanisms prevent unauthorized access to the contents of documents.

13-58 SAP has established the technical basis for security to support electronic business processes. The support offered by Secure Store & Forward (SSF in R/3 Release 4.0 allows R/3 data and documents to be encrypted documents to be signed with digital signatures.

13-59 R/3 services use external security products that consist of industry-standard processes and formats, such as X.509, the standard process for asymmetric encryption and PKCS#7, the standard format for signed or encrypted documents.

13-60 Yes, secure business transactions based on the consistent use of standards can also be extended across R/3 systems and to non-R/3 systems.

13-61 R/3 includes several different services for enabling continuous system availability such as instruments for managing and controlling the ongoing operation of the system, and technology for making certain that stoppages, whether planned or unplanned, are kept as short as possible.

13-62 The Computing Center Management System (CCMS) (Figure 13.6) allows continuous monitoring of the R/3 system at database, application level, operating system, and network. The CCMS offers procedures and checklists to help administrators identify critical states at an early stage and to keep them from worsening. In addition, CCMS allows fine-tuning of the system using performance monitors (graphical displays that offer administrators a rapid overview of the whole R/3 system to facilitate prompt intervention in critical situations). This further contributes to the availability of the system and to the level of user satisfaction.

13-63 SAP has large R/3 users who manage their computing infrastructures with the help of INSM platforms. They can integrate their R/3 systems using the SNMP-MIB (Simple Network Management Protocol–Management Information Base).

13-64 The R/3-MIB involves interfaces for controlling and monitoring applications and alarm handling. It is important for enterprise mission-critical applications that the least time be required for a release upgrade. New technology (i.e. repository switches), the support provided by comfortable graphical user interfaces, and fully automated procedures for importing new releases all help save large amounts of time and reduce costs.

SOLUTIONS

FIGURE 13.6
CCMS

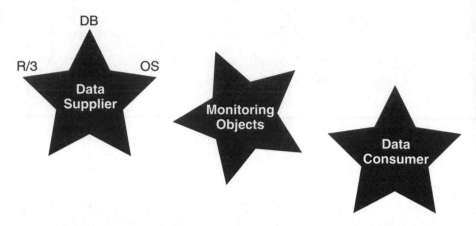

13-65   Once a new release has been imported, the software must be distributed to the various servers. SAP offers a form of automatic software distribution that allows this version upgrade process to be conducted without interrupting normal operations.

13-66   Every time a transaction is called, the software on that application server is checked. If the current version of the software is not present, an update is performed automatically. This procedure permits extended periods of unproductive time to be avoided during release upgrades. In addition, SAP has created procedures for reducing the unplanned system idle time resulting from breakdowns.

13-67   To ensure that the availability of the R/3 system remains unaffected, when one of the servers goes down, SAP uses the switchover technology of its hardware partners.

13-68   When the system spots that a server has gone down, it automatically activates a replacement server that takes over the tasks of the lost primary server, without requiring any manual intervention by the system administrator.

13-69   SAP's backup-and-restore concepts reduce recovery time in the case of hard disk crashes. SAP supports the integration of standard technology for increasing availability at the hardware level, such as redundant hard disk capacity (RAID), redundant networks, and uninterruptible power supplies (UPS).

13-70   In order to benefit from available combinations of business applications and technology, cross-enterprise integration focuses on the flow of business processes. R/3 addresses this with SAP Business Workflow (Figure 13.7), that is available in Internet and intranet solutions.

FIGURE 13.7
Business Workflow

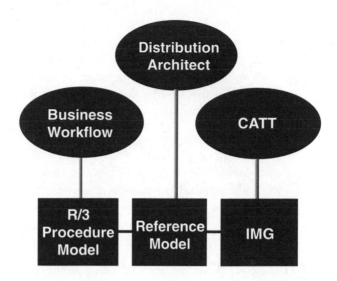

13-71   SAP Business Workflow links information with active control of business processes. It offers the employees responsible for specific tasks access to the right tasks at the right time. A typical example of a business process that can be controlled using SAP Business Workflow is the complete processing of a customer order from receipt of order through delivery of goods and issuing of invoice.

13-72   There is a defined relationship between the events in the business workflow that can be viewed as chronologically specified elements of a business process.

13-73   An employee responsible for a specific process in a company can request information about the current status of the corresponding workflow at any time and can also trace the history of the work process.

13-74   SAP is a founding member of the Workflow Management Coalition (WfMC) and has created the first published workflow standard with an implementation of the Workflow Client application.

13-75   SAP Business Workflow offers a MAPI-compatible interface so that companies can continue to use MAPI-compatible mail front ends already installed including: MS Outlook, Lotus CC: Mail or MS Exchange. These can start workflows both offline and online and execute form-based tasks within a business process.

13-76   Workflow design can be greatly simplified and speeded up by Workflow Wizards integrated into SAP Business Workflow. These Workflow Wizards are assistants analogous to those found in many PC applications.

They lead the designer in a controlled dialog based on carefully prepared questions and decision options and produce an executable workflow definition quickly and safely. In addition, it is also possible to start a workflow directly from the Internet or from an intranet. This kind of application is illustrated by the use of the Internet for personnel management as a tool for finding candidates for vacant posts within a company.

13-77   The basic workflow pattern consists of a preliminary hiring evaluation in the human resources department, immediate rejection or forwarding of the application to the relevant specialist department. This department could issue an invitation to an interview or reject the candidate (either totally or by referral to a different department). Once the application is submitted an applicant receives a unique identifying code and password that permits checking its status over the Internet at any time.

13-78   SAP Office is a crucial component within a company's communication infrastructure. Messages can be exchanged with colleagues and business partners. Today's typical communication services include telephone, fax, standard letters, and, e-mail. If companies that do not use e-mail within the organization can quickly weaken competitiveness.

13-79   When selecting an electronic communication service, look for features including: open nature, integration in existing mail systems, workflow support, ability to send and receive faxes, and integrated inbox. Make certain that the office communication system can be integrated into the business software used within the company so that business processes and data can be integrated.

13-80   SAPoffice provides an integrated communication service that satisfies all of these requirements. The Internet is the most common network for transmitting e-mail. SAPoffice offers the framework for sending and receiving electronic Internet mail. R/3 supports the e-mail standard X.400. Through SAPoffice, R/3 can offer a solid and open basis for global company communication. In addition, SAPoffice provides an integrated in box. All messages sent to user e-mail; faxes and workflow orders are collected at this point. Users do not need to search manually in different in boxes or even different systems for their messages. The standard point of access to the integrated in box is the R/3 user interface.

13-81   If you employees use other mail interfaces, including Microsoft Exchange, these interfaces can also be used to create, send and edit messages administered in SAPoffice. SAP supports the MAPI interface; it is possible to provide e-mail functions to employees who do not use any of the R/3 system business functions.

13-82 Professional client/server applications can be developed with ABAP Workbench, a set of carefully matched professional tools suitable for individualizing R/3 applications and for extending applications. It can be used to develop software independently of SAP standard software.

13-83 ABAP Workbench supports the entire development cycle of organization-wide client/server solutions based on the principles of rapid prototyping.

13-84 Graphical user interfaces and simple working methods with object-oriented navigation make the tools easy to use. The ABAP language is also extended to include object-oriented elements (ABAP objects). These represent a form of component integration using ActiveX and allow additional forms of structuring to be used within the R/3 application components.

13-85 All development objects such as ABAP classes, interfaces, methods, screens, data models, and HTML templates are stored in the R/3 repository (Figure 13.8). This allows fast and easy access to all the objects and provides a clear and intelligible overview of data structures. Development continues on the R/3 repository towards an open repository. This will allow users to store objects they develop themselves in specially assigned name ranges and to integrate them with SAP business objects.

FIGURE 13.8
R/3 Repository

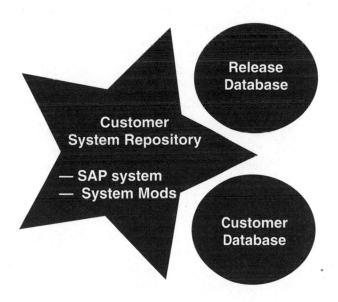

13-86 The ABAP dictionary is the primary information base for developers. This is where all application-specific data is managed and made available in a consistent way to the integrated development tools.

13-87   A library containing reusable and versatile program modules promotes a rational approach to software development within the R/3 system environment and to customers' own developments. Customers' own enhancements and modifications to R/3 applications can be managed individually and compatibility with current releases maintained so that when R/3 is upgraded, enhancements and modifications can easily be transported to the new release.

13-88   The Workbench supports team-oriented development work with a reliable tool for version management. The integrated Workbench Organizer records and documents all the work carried out and makes certain that all changes to programs are coordinated. Web Reporting allows reports and report hierarchies to be displayed as HTML documents in a Web browser. The wide range of features offered by ABAP Workbench offers quality assurance and performance optimization tools. These can evaluate either individual programs or a complete system and then generate detailed statistics of resource consumption and performance.

13-89   Applications developed with ABAP Workbench can easily be ported to a wide range of different platforms, operating systems, databases and graphical user interfaces. R/3 handles the communication with other systems with background; programmers do not need to be involved in the technical details.

13-90   R/3 acquires its flexibility of deployment from the reliable R/3 architecture that allows applications to be distributed and permits an unprecedented degree of integration between SAP and non-SAP components. R/3 forms the foundation of SAP Business Framework.

13-91   The foundations of the business framework architecture are independent business management components, integration technology and open interfaces, which all combine to create a flexible, standards-oriented environment in which the R/3 system and software from external providers can cooperate. Efficient use of R/3 for business management applications that concentrate on a rapid time-to-market has a much higher priority than technical problem solving. Business Framework allows both SAP and non-SAP products to form an integrated and component-based solution. The continued development of R/3 represents an important architectural cornerstone in the pursuit of this goal. The highly developed interface based on object-oriented BAPIs (see Figure 13.9) is extremely important. It gives enterprises the chance to devote their complete attention to business goals rather than being confronted with problems that involve feasibility of current IT technology.

FIGURE 13.9
External
Applications/BAPIs

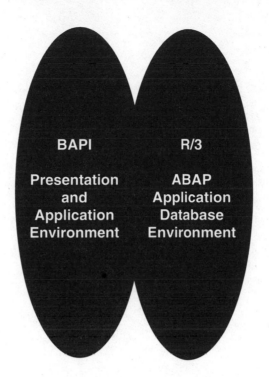

BAPI

R/3

Presentation
and
Application
Environment

ABAP
Application
Database
Environment

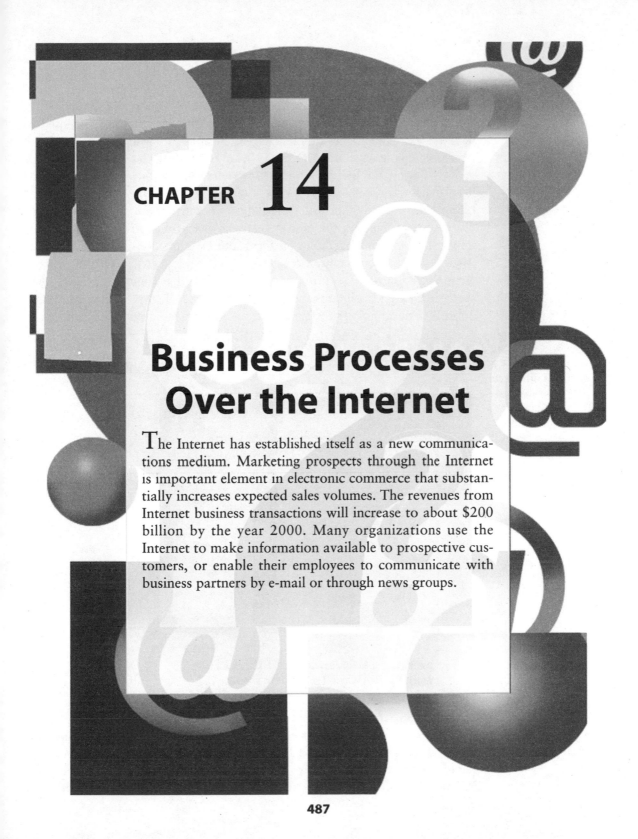

CHAPTER 14

Business Processes Over the Internet

The Internet has established itself as a new communications medium. Marketing prospects through the Internet is important element in electronic commerce that substantially increases expected sales volumes. The revenues from Internet business transactions will increase to about $200 billion by the year 2000. Many organizations use the Internet to make information available to prospective customers, or enable their employees to communicate with business partners by e-mail or through news groups.

Even though the Internet provides cost-effective communications as an instrument for distributing and transmitting data, it is unable to evaluate data received or trigger the performance of certain activities in response to data. The integration of client/server business software supports these processes, bringing innovative momentum to the Internet.

R/3 is optimally prepared for the Internet. SAP offers ready-to-use Internet Application Components for the intranet environment which are important elements for doing business on the Internet. R/3 on the Internet provides several benefits for multilayer network architecture. R/3 Internet applications offer business-to-business and consumer-to-business contacts (Figure 14.1), intranet solutions, BAPI technology, SAP's business object technology, improved security, enhanced R/3 interoperability, expanded ALE scenarios, extended interoperability, accelerated R/3 implementation, business process technology, SAP automation, and a Java-based user interface.

FIGURE 14.1
Internet Commerce
(Business-to-
Business/Consumer-
to-Business)

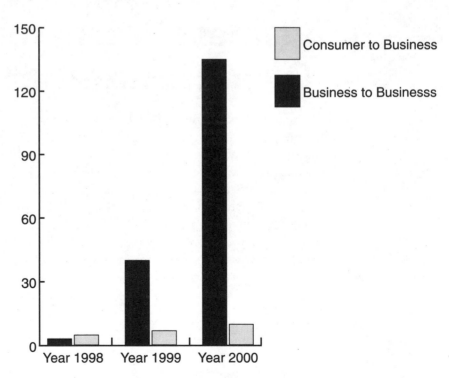

This chapter will discuss factors that will undoubtedly emerge throughout the certification process. The Internet is growing to encompass so many details of the enterprise environment that knowledge of how it relates to R/3 will provide a significant advantage on certification course exams.

Business-to-Business and Consumer-to-Business Applications

Internet-based consumer-to-business applications allow other products and services to be made available to consumers around the world. Information systems are individualized for the needs of these users. Both data entry and administrative tasks can be shifted from the back office to where the data is created.

The business-to-business/consumer-to-business product catalog offers products in situations that include pricing, availability checks, purchase requisitions and order entry. The product catalog offers easy browsing and graphical display. This application is characterized by a well-defined hierarchical structure, an easy-to-use search engine, and the ability to insert pictures and texts.

The application used for retrieving account balances makes it possible to establish a customer information system on the Internet. Customers can have access to such information as current interest rates, account balances, the status of invoices, or consumption. A company benefits from simpler maintenance of master data and better-quality databases, as well as from direct recruiting through the Internet.

In a KANBAN production environment, KANBAN containers are set to EMPTY to trigger replenishment of components for product assembly. The KANBANs and their status can be seen in the KANBAN board.

Business Access

Global Consumer to Business Access For interaction between consumers and companies, customers or prospects use a Web browser to access a vendor's business system to peruse a product catalog, place an order, or find out about a product or service.

You also achieve several benefits from simpler maintenance of master data and better-quality databases. This component is very useful if your company has a large customer base. Using this method, you can be certain that your data is always up to the minute so that you will be able to respond promptly to critical situations.

Service Rates

The rates for different types of services are managed with the aid of an Internal Price List. In order to determine the rate for a given service type, the user can either directly enter it, or use a character string to search through the keys, designations, and descriptions of all service types.

Requirement Requests (MM) In any given enterprise. It is probable that a large number of employees from different departments will constantly be giving notice of their requirements of various items.

Sales Order Creation

The sales order creation component has a typical sales situation, with access to a vendor's home page and the virtual sales office. An electronic catalog on the Web displays products; product descriptions in this online catalog are not restricted to plain text but can be supplemented with photographs, graphics and audio clips or additional information, as needed.

Sales order creation deals with electronic shopping baskets, available-to-promise functions, and customer-specific pricing capabilities. These new business opportunities that allow companies to deal more effectively on the Internet. Organizations that start business processes of this kind on the Internet can deliver more quickly.

The 24-hour order status permits an organization to use the Internet to inform customers of the processing status of sales orders. It is possible to determine if goods have already been shipped. This results in satisfied customers who have ability to inquire about the status of sales orders around the clock.

It is possible to achieve more reliable remote entry of data over the Internet. The Internet application permits entry of the measurement and counter readings through the Internet within the scope of PM.

Application Components

The two application components are:

1. Collective Release of Requisitions
2. Purchase Orders.

This works by greatly simplifying the approval process through a simple easy-to-use browser interface. The system then automatically creates a list of purchase requisition items or purchase orders for processing without requiring the user to know his or her release code.

However, remember that it is necessary is to select an item from a list and release it. Releases that are already effected can also be revoked. This component provides benefits to employees whose daily tasks primarily involve tasks other than the release of purchase requisitions and purchase orders.

Quality Notification

The Internet quality notification component accelerates processing as it reduces the amount of work involved in handling customer complaints. Problems are reported either by inputting a description in textual form, or by choosing from a list of predefined, coded defect types and indicating the object of the complaint, as by specifying the material number.

When a quality notification message is received, the R/3 system (in combination with SAP Business Workflow) starts the proper internal procedures. The processing status of a notification can be queried at any time.

The approval process in R/3 takes the form of a release procedure. Each entity involved in the release procedure uses a release code to grant approval in a release transaction. Executing this action within the R/3 system demands detailed knowledge of the procedure, and cannot be handled without special training. The person giving approval must be able to navigate the R/3 system, know the release code, and be able to work through several screens.

SAPoffice

It is possible to achieve better employee-to-employee communications by using Internet applications as an extension of SAPoffice. This enhances the communication among the employees of large companies by permitting them to access information about one another over the in-house intranet. They can use various search criteria to locate Internet addresses, telephone numbers, fax numbers, room numbers, and photographs of coworkers.

Stored data is constantly updated, so that it is easy to track coworkers who have moved and to send e-mail to workers just by clicking on the appropriate Internet address.

Confirmation Components

Fast confirmation of project status on net projects is not usually confined just to one organization. In many cases, employees or subcontractors must work at customer sites or remote locations.

The project data confirmation component allows authorized users to use an intranet to report on activities executed in a project. They can report the number of hours worked on different days and include a forecast of the amount of work still to be done. This confirmation creates the foundation for evaluating actual schedules and costs in the R/3 project information system.

Workflow Status

Workflow status that pertains to an Internet component permits display of the processing status of workflows. In the release of a purchase requisition through the Internet component, it is possible to view corresponding business processes and determine how far they have progressed, to determine how many worksteps have already been completed, as if a purchase requisition has already been released or a confirmation has already been sent to the requisition's author.

Internet Application Events

The calendar of events intranet application component facilitates a company's events. It makes available a log of events classified according to subject areas for internal and external users through the intranet or Internet.

The events has log information on event dates, content, qualifications obtained, speakers and attendance fees for the events for which places have been reserved.

The booked events intranet application component offers information on education and further training courses and creates a list of training events available through the Internet. In this list the user can obtain information on dates, content, qualifications obtained, trainers and attendance fees for the events booked or reserved.

Internal Activity Allocation

Internal activity allocation is an Internet application component that permits input of services rendered internally, including repairs, Assets produced in-house, tools, and consulting.

This Internet application component permits worldwide data input. Employees can post activity allocations from a remote cost center to a receiver. Receivers can be at other cost centers, orders, or the WSB elements of a project. Internal services can be entered as soon as they are rendered. The cost center for which a service is rendered is charged immediately.

Assets Management Information System

The R/3 Assets Management Information System is directly accessible from the Assets Management component. If you travel to a subsidiary, you could use this component to find out what kind of equipment was available at that location. If your cost center managers do not have direct access to the R/3 System they could use it to create ad-hoc queries about assets in the areas that are needed.

KANBAN

When dealing with an Internet production environment, product suppliers gain access to the customer's KANBAN board. This indicates that they can monitor the KANBANS for which they are responsible. To replenish an empty KANBAN, suppliers produce a shipment in their own system that results in the delivery of the required products. Both organizations take advantage of this visibility that facilitates just-in-time delivery.

There are several benefits of a service improved by accessing R/3 over the Internet. The Internet application "Available to Promise" permits connection to a system, and then input of the material, plant, quantity, and desired delivery date, which results in display of the material provision date and quantity. Each customer can receive information directly without assistance.

Service notification works with fast entry of customer notifications to produce an efficient customer service, very important for both service providers and customers. It is possible to enter Service notifications quickly and simply.

Recruiting

The employment opportunities component supports the recruiting process by offering information to potential applicants through the Internet. Furthermore you gain several benefits of direct Recruiting through the Internet. The Employment Opportunities component supports the recruiting process by offering information to potential applicants through the Internet.

Job Positions

Vacant job positions are structured by showing locations on a map. Just by selecting a geographical region can make all vacancies in that region to be listed. This would permit users to select the job position that interests them most.

The applicant simply inputs the required information for personal details, educational background, qualifications, and previous employers.

Job seekers use the Internet to submit unsolicited applications. Applications arrive for processing in a worker's R/3 inbox folder. When the application arrives, the applicant is assigned a personal number and password. Both the number and password designate the job application, and applicants can use them to check the processing status of their applications at any time. This online method allows companies to obtain the information they need quickly and directly in a form that makes it easy to compare candidates with one another.

Application Status within Human Resources provides you the knowledge of your exact situation at any time. Your personal number and password function together to clearly identify an application.

Internet Business Process Information

R/3 Internet applications can function together effectively to offer a uniform and consistent business environment. The Internet technology of the R/3 system is visible as ALE/WEB brings the benefits of new possibilities for conducting business. There is a great potential for adding value that begins with R/3's Internet applications for developing new market opportunities to allow companies to deal with Internet functionals.

R/3 Internet applications deal with several functions in the areas of accounting, logistics, and human resources management. They enhance the functions of R/3 and can be individualized. Open interfaces are important in an open market. The open infrastructure and architecture necessary to satisfy the requirements for doing business on the Internet are ensured by new, business process-oriented interfaces called BAPIs. BAPIs (Business Application Programming Interfaces) access the logic of the R/3 system, which makes available more than 100 open BAPIs across all application areas of the system. The BAPIs are based on SAP Business Objects, are Microsoft COM/DCOM-compliant and achieve OMG-CORBA compatibility.

The R/3 Internet applications are uncoupled from the R/3 system core. The benefit of this approach is that it allows SAP customers to benefit from new R/3 business processes more quickly. The R/3 Internet architecture provides three tiers to create a multi-layer network architecture that offers the scalability needed to deal with the large and steadily growing number of Internet users.

Business Application Programming Interfaces (BAPIs)

BAPIs facilitate external access to business processes and objects in the R/3 system. They define an open business standard for direct communication between the business applications of different vendors, and this open standard fosters the development of technology partnerships to extend the functions of the R/3 system, including a partnership between SAP and Microsoft. BAPIs are object-oriented interfaces that make it easy to access R/3's business processes.

BAPIs permit more efficient and flexible access to associated business processes independently of the underlying software platforms. They also designate an open business standard for direct communication between the business applications of different vendors. These open interfaces make certain that business objects and data such as an order, a customer number, or a part number are consistently handled in the same way. This allows transactions to be conducted across corporate boundaries.

BAPIs are SAP business-object methods. Because of this, they are implemented in the R/3 business-object repository. They can be called from different platforms. Internet applications use the HTML standard or the Java programming language to access BAPIs. With Microsoft's COM/DCOM foundation, BAPIs can also be used from a program written in Visual Basic or from Excel.

BAPI Functions

BAPIs also enable SAP to take a different approach to the Internet, as the foundation of the R/3 system stays the same. All of these items have increased the BAPIs, while the R/3 Internet applications function outside the R/3 system and need a stable, open interface for accessing the underlying system.

BAPIs allow applications to benefit from the functions and data resources of the R/3 system. SAP is experienced in developing business systems. The company uses its knowledge of business processes to define additional BAPIs.

Support for customer-defined applications increases because of the open standards introduced by BAPIs. R/3 customers can develop their own Internet applications without depending on the R/3 Internet transaction server. BAPIs permit new applications to benefit from the data and functions of the R/3 system. These Internet applications can be implemented with the most convenient programming language ABAP/4, Java, or C++.

BAPIs are also used in SAP Internet applications. A BAPI called `ProductCatalog.GetLayout` designates the structure of the product catalog organized into "shops" and product groups such as software, hardware, and documentation. Should a shopper choose a specific product group, the BAPI `ProductCatalog.GetItems` reads and displays general information on the products it contains. This includes various software products including Excel and Word. The user can then choose specific products to acquire more detailed information. Multimedia information on product catalog entries including sound and graphics is provided by the BAPI `ProductCatalog.GetLayoutDocuments`. Text descriptions of products are gathered by the Internet application using the BAPI `ProductCatalog.GetLayoutDescription`. The consumer can select specific products to buy and place them in a "shopping basket". Orders are placed with the assistance of the BAPI `CustomerOrder.CreateFromData`, the customer is then authenticated by the BAPI `Customer.CheckPassword`.

Business Framework

The business framework integrates different software components such as human resources management system (reporting component) as well as a treasury component. These business components are offered both as products in their own right and as parts of R/3.

The SAP business object's first layer is a kernel with central business logic. The second layer is composed of constraints and business rules responsible for preserving the object's integrity. The third layer is composed of methods, attributes, input event controls, and output events. The outermost layer is the access level (COM/DCOM, COBRA). In addition, SAP business objects implement the standard capabilities of object-oriented technology including encapsulation, polymorphism, and inheritance.

R/3 Repository

The R/3 repository has the documentation on R/3 and detailed descriptions of the R/3 applications. It can export information through an Application Programming Interface (API) to graphics software, modeling tools or BPR tools. The repository is the central warehouse for all R/3 application information on new developments as well as the design and maintenance of applications and components.

Items stored in the repository include process models, function models, data models, SAP business objects, object models, and data. The repository also stores technical information such as data definitions, screens, and program objects used for developing or extending R/3.

The repository API permits other software vendors to access the R/3 repository, retrieve information, and channel it into their own tool or application.

Three-Tier Architecture

The three-tier architecture of the R/3 System allows this system to combine with the uncoupling of business rules from the database. As a result it provides the ideal platform for creating Internet and intranet solutions. The R/3 System's three-tier client/server architecture has grown into a multi-layer network architecture that can run high-data-volume as well as secure and transactional Internet applications.

Business Objects

The Business Object Repository (BOR) is part of the foundation of the R/3 repository. It obtains business data, transactions, and events in R/3 as an integrated set of SAP business objects. SAP business objects offer strong interfaces to a broad range of processes and data accessed through the BOR. SAP business objects are linked to one other to form object models. Remember that a data model defining the internal data structure in the enterprise data model is designated to each business object. Objects are registered by designating object types in the BOR.

During runtime, clients access objects through the BOR that relay requests to objects and report the results to the clients. The source code and location of an object remain unseen by clients. This is important in distributed environments.

The Dynamic Invocation Interface

SAP's BOR has a dynamic invocation interface permitting access to SAP business objects at runtime even if they are not known at compile time. The dynamic invocation interface of the BOR provides late linking to give you increased flexibility to objects because of an object method's parameters, which can be determined at the latest possible moment, even before the method is invoked.

Delegation

The BOR allows for delegation, an important factor if specific types of business objects must be created based on SAP business objects. To achieve this, a subtype of an SAP business object must be developed to receive all the attributes, methods and events from an existing object.

The BOR gives access to SAP business objects for several applications using different interfacing standards such as Microsoft's COM/DCOM and the Object Management Group's (OMG) COBRA. It is also accessible from outside R/3 using RFCs.

Requirement Request

Once an employee has used the application component, a Requirement Request gives notification of that requirement. It is a simple matter to run this component to monitor the status of the request such as ordered or withdrawn from stock.

The Integrated Inbox

An integrated inbox provides you with an easy, global method of maintaining continuous access to messages from workflow, communication, and cooperation services. It is an essential requirement for accelerating business processes. This Internet application allows all employees access their inboxes, outboxes, public folders, and worklists through the Internet/intranet.

SAPGUI and Firewalls

Firewalls monitor external access to your private R/3 data. A firewall is a means of restricting access to your private data through a public network.

SAPGUI has always been secured by firewalls and SAProuter for use in public networks. The main task of SAProuter is to support communications between SAPGUI and R/3 application servers. It is Installed on a firewall and acts as an application-level gateway proxy for the R/3 System. Most of SAP's customers and prospects have installed firewalls because they use a Web server for marketing on the Internet. Resultantly, R/3 only requires reconfiguring an existing firewall.

Security

The Secure Network Communications (SNC) interface permits R/3 to be integrated into company-wide network security products such as Kerberos and SECUDE. This architecture allows the security product to authenticate external R/3 users and to secure the entire communication process between the front end and the application server and between different application servers.

R/3 can be integrated into security products to take advantage of the current and most secure solutions for accessing the system. Because the SNC interface is covered by SAP's certification program, SAP certifies and supporting other network security products.

The security system for the Internet and intranets must deal with both authentication and communication. User authentication is critical to an Internet solution. The user of a system on the Internet must prove identity. When using server authentication, the system must prove it really is the system requested, so that data are not sent to an unauthorized server.

Privacy

Connection privacy is achieved by encrypting transmitted data. Encryption makes certain that no unauthorized lurkers can listen in on messages sent over the Internet. To guarantee message integrity and stop hackers from intercepting messages and modifying them, add additional security information to messages.

Internet Security

Security is crucial for payment transactions on the Internet, because these supply information on the creditworthiness of business partners. Credit card companies are often involved in payment guarantees of goods bought on the Internet. R/3 assigns Web users to R/3 users. SAP Internet Transaction Server (ITS) plays a critical role because the basic user authentication provided by the Web servers can be used to assign Web users or groups of users to specific users in R/3. Public key technology or certificates are also used for this purpose. This offers a means to verify that another party possesses specific attributes to determine whether a particular Web server can communicate with other systems.

Most services provided on the Internet are anonymous. Most people anonymously browse a product catalog before deciding to buy any given product.

R/3 Internet components switch to secure transmission mode before verifying the user account for posting the order into R/3. Secure transmission can be activated by R/3 Internet application components through the "https" URL addressing method.

Firewalls are exceedingly important when monitoring external access to private R/3 data. A firewall is a means of restricting access to private data through a public network. Using a corporate intranet requires at least the same level of security for the enterprise's internal communications as that of Internet communications.

When dealing with intranets, a system recognizes users because they are employees of a company. Whenever they connect to the corporate intranet, the ITS automatically displays a login screen for entry of a user name and password.

Application Link Enabling (ALE) provides the ability to link internal R/3 processes with outside processes, physically to link separate business processes to function as one unit. ALE loosely couples distributed application systems that permit exchange of messages and master data as well as comparison and adjusting of control information. ALE exchanges messages in a time-controlled manner.

Intranet Security

Corporate intranet users have at least the same level of security for their enterprise's internal communications as they enjoy for their Internet communications. Intranets allows for the system to recognize users because they are employees of your company. Whenever they connect to the corporate intranet, the ITS automatically displays a login screen for entry of a user name and a password.

Web Interfaces

The Web Basis improved on the three-tier R/3 architecture for use on the Internet. The Web Basis ties together existing Internet technology with R/3 technology and permits for reliable access to all SAP transactions from the Internet or intranets.

A Web server connects Web clients together with business applications. Web server systems are available from various vendors. They support all major browsers, and can be employed on several different hardware and software platforms.

Internet Notifications

Service notifications are used to request services so that customers can submit service notifications directly through your organization's WWW server.

Customers can use an Internet Browser customer so that they can enter descriptions of problems just by selecting from a list of potential problems or defects. The Web application logs the problem and designates an internal R/3 notification number to it. It interactively documents the problem online using predefined conditions. This makes it easy for the service provider to understand its nature and provide customers with faster, more comprehensive service while simultaneously reducing personnel needed to handle service requests.

Should a requisition item or a purchase order satisfy certain conditions (i.e. when a value is greater than $10,000) then it needs to be approved prior to being processed more during the collective release of requisitions and purchase orders (MM).

Open Application Standards

OAGIS (Open Applications Group Integration Specifications) is the standard for open application integration. The specifications describe data and process sharing and determine how application program methods exchange data with other Open Application Group (OAG)-compliant business applications.

OAGIS satisfies requirements for interoperability at the business process level, and lets users mix and match all OAGIS-compliant solutions to meet their particular requirements. Users who purchase business applications from different vendors, often have a difficult time getting them to work together well. As a result, many people choose to skip the benefits of enterprise application integration. They must also integrate all of their systems to develop a coherent information technology infrastructure to support business. OAG's goal is to define standards to accelerate the connection among software components from different vendors. OAG goes beyond objects and includes business object interoperability among all types of business applications including existing systems.

The Business Object Document (BOD) designates the protocol that different vendors' components used to communicate with one another. The method by which business object documents are distributed across SAP systems is determined by an ALE distribution model. Incoming BOD of the type post to G/L are posted to the general ledger application. Incoming BOD called feedback BODs can be designated to a workflow for further processing.

Open Information Warehouse

The Open Information Warehouse (OIW) incorporates a BAPI that permits consistent access to selected reporting data from FI, HR and logistics. It is possible to determine data available from the R/3 information systems: FIS, HR-IS and LIS are described in the OIW catalog (which also has a BAPI.) This permits an external application to look for data by issuing an appropriate query without knowing any of the R/3 information systems.

Business Engineer

The business engineering workbench provides a fully integrated and comprehensive set of tools for R/3. As customer support for R/3 implementation, the business engineering workbench offers an incremental, integrated procedure concept.

Business Engineer assures integrity and quality within configured business processes throughout the implementation project. It supports analysis and selection of unique business processes, facilitating quick adaptation of the R/3 enterprise structure to specific goals, so that it is possible to choose and model the business areas and processes required. Business Engineer also controls project-related activities including documentation and scheduling. This active guidance for all system configuration procedures guarantees going live quickly with an optimally configured R/3 system.

In the R/3 International Demonstration and Education System (IDES) model enterprise specific options are available in SAP Business Workflow to permit modeling and even automation of processes not included in the R/3 models. Business Engineer automatically transfers all this information to the second phase of the project.

Business Engineer assists in configuring the system. When all the work units have been outlined in the preselection stage, they can be divided into smaller, manageable worksteps. The implementation guide categorizes worksteps as optional, mandatory, or critical activities. This segmentation speeds up the configuration process and assures that all the important steps are taken care of.

Templates

Templates in Business Engineer greatly increase the speed and quality of configuration. Critical activities for R/3 operation including authorization management, setting up the reporting system, creating interfaces, and implementing extensions are concluded during this phase of the project. After the final test Business Engineer proceeds to the next phase to prepare to go live. Structured project management reduces implementation times.

The Procedure Model

Business Engineer offers a procedure model with a complete organizational and administrative structure for implementing R/3, for integrating changes when upgrading to a new release, and for continuous business process reengineering.

The procedure model is an integral component of the R/3 system. It provides several recommendations for installing R/3 and permits calling all the business engineer tools that relate to individual work steps. There is active guidance through the entire process. It is possible to receive online information about the project's status and to look up any project-related information. With a focus on what the system should do, the Business Engineer will manage the project.

The Business Engineer includes a Procedure Model that provides the complete organizational and administrative structure that you need for implementing R/3, for incorporating changes when upgrading to a new release, and for continuous business process reengineering. The Procedure Model is an integral component of the R/3 System.

1. It offers you a variety of recommendations for installing R/3
2. It lets you call all the Business Engineer tools that relate to individual work steps. You are actively guided through the entire process.
3. You can receive online information about the project's status
4. You can look up any project-related information you require.

You can effectively concentrate on what you want the system to do for you, the Business Engineer will manage the project for you.

Profile Generator

The Profile Generator simplifies setting up the authorization environment in the customer system. The administrator needs only to configure the customer-specific settings; the Profile Generator takes care of all the other tasks such as choosing the relevant authorization objects. The Profile Generator is integrated in the R/3 System, and is available on all R/3-supported platforms.

Session Manager

The session manager is part of Business Engineer's team; it gives users a complete overview of their personal work stations. Each workstation is individualized to the user's needs, based on authorizations and profiles created in the system. During this phase, R/3 services such as EarlyWatch, Remote Consulting, or Online Software Service (OSS) can be contacted to arrange for ongoing support.

The Administrator

Profile Generator simplifies the task of setting up the authorization environment in the customer system. The administrator need only configure the customer-specific settings; Profile Generator takes care of all the other tasks such as choosing the relevant authorization objects. Profile Generator is integrated in the R/3 system, and is available on all R/3-supported platforms. In addition, the administrator no longer uses the authorization objects directly to define authorizations for the various user groups. Instead, the authorization profiles are built around the functions to be performed in the R/3 system. Profile Generator chooses the relevant authorization objects and groups them together in a new authorization profile.

SAP Automation

SAP automation is an integration toolkit that offers many components for integrating desktop, server, and Internet applications into the R/3 system. It is composed of C libraries, C++ class libraries and ActiveX components. It enhances R/3's capabilities on the World Wide Web, in telephony, distributed computing, and multimedia kiosks. SAP automation permits integration with the R/3 system at different access levels and using different programming languages.

SAP Automation consists of: RFC Library, RFC Class Library, GUI Library, RFC Component, GUI Component, GUI CodeGen, Transaction Component, BAPI Component, and SAP Assistant.

Stored Data

Due to the fact that stored data is constantly updated, it is easy to track coworkers who have moved. It is also easy to send an e-mail to another worker just by clicking on a person's Internet address.

RFC Library

RFC Library allows users to integrate external applications using existing ABAP RFCs or external RFCs. The library is a good method of accessing the R/3 system. RFC Class Library is built on RFC Library and is designed to facilitate its use. RFC Class Library was created for use by people who do not have low-level knowledge of the RFC API. RFC Class Library can be used with any R/3 system set up to receive remotely-called functions.

RFC Library was created to simplify the programming of external applications that communicate with R/3, RFC Class Library enables users to focus more attention on application logic and less on low-level RFC API details. It also provides a C++ object-oriented framework so that developers can use the benefits within in object-oriented programming.

GUI Library

GUI library permits direct execution of SAPGUI programming. It has a 32-bit dynamic link library for programming the SAPGUI. To create a new interface to an existing application, find out how the application works with the existing interface.

The GUI component is an ActiveX component layered on top of GUI Library. It provides two high-level interfaces: OLE automation interface and terminal interface. The OLE automation interface permits SAP systems to be controlled directly from the OLE automation controller programs including Microsoft Office products, Visual Basic and Hahtsite.

GUI Library API calls have associated calls in the OLE automation interface. The GUI component also provides more thorough error checking and convenient routines to facilitate programming the OLE automation interface within Visual Basic and similar environments. GUI Code-Gen is a code generator for the GUI component and proceeds through an R/3 transaction from a SAPGUI-like screen to generate Visual Basic or HAHTtalk Basic code based on recorded actions. GUI CodeGen eases the construction of alternative GUI interfaces to R/3.

Application Link Enabling

Application Link Enabling (ALE) allows you to link internal R/3 processes with outside processes, thus enabling physically separate business processes to function like one. ALE loosely couples distributed application systems allowing them to exchange messages and master data besides comparing and adjusting control information. ALE exchanges messages in a time-controlled manner.

Synchronous and Asynchronous Communication

Synchronous and asynchronous communications form the basis for demand-driven integration of applications, thereby eliminating the need to link them via a central database such as conventionally structured R/3 Systems.

Java

The Java-based SAPGUI provides manifold benefits to R/3 users, system administrators, and customers. It Java has the same operating environment as the native SAPGUI interface. The SAPGUI in Java benefits from the portability inherent in the Java language. All platforms that include NetPCs and NCs can be used as R/3 clients.

R/3 used over the Internet, automatically downloads Java applets to the client and loads the right version of the Java-based SAPGUI. It is not necessary to install any additional software or perform extra steps to upgrade R/3 on the client. SAPGUI in Java emulates the native SAPGUI and enables R/3 users to access familiar R/3 transactions over the Internet.

Internet Components

Web Reporting

Web Reporting is a WebRFC application that allows Internet users to access information in the R/3 System. This includes the start-up of reports as well as the possibility to call up previously-generated lists which are placed in report trees for reference. In fact, you can also navigate around the report trees by pointing and clicking.

Time Statement Internet Applications

Time statement Internet applications allow employees to query their personal time statements at any time. When working from a company perspective, there is longer necessary to regularly issue time statements in paper form.

RFC Components

RFC components provide access to ABAP RFCs using ActiveX technology. The RFC component is an ActiveX component built on the RFC library and offers an easy access method for ABAP/4 remote functions.

These are used in various development environments including Microsoft Office products, ActiveX Server Page, Visual Basic and Hahtsite.

Transaction Component

The transaction component is an application using the RFC component. It contains details about calling R/3 transactions and remote functions and permits access to R/3 transactions in many development environments and using different programming languages.

BAPI Component

The BAPI component affords high-level access to BAPIs and permits direct access to the SAP BOR and benefit from SAP BAPIs. This component allows rapid implementation of user applications.

Other Helpful Tools

The SAP Assistant serves several purposes. It is a design tool that lets developers create and browse RFCs. It also allows users to browse, execute, and build RFC and transaction objects. SAP Assistant offers efficient runtime access to the R/3 system.

R/3 possesses a three-tier client/server architecture that facilitates Java-enabling without an extensive redesign effort. It is only necessary to insert another layer between the application and presentation levels, and permit Web clients to access the R/3 system. This new Internet layer includes the SAP automation tool to translate the R/3 front-end protocol into a Java-compliant one and the Java server to send Java applets to the Web client. Both components must be installed on a Web server to make them accessible over the Internet.

Summary

In this chapter we learned about Internet business processes in R/3, functions such as ALE, BAPIs, and the details within the KANBAN environment. We discussed the background of the Internet production environment, CORBA, and how to manage encryption.

14-1 How do components running at different locations deal with business processes?

14-2 What do joint customer distribution models ensure?

14-3 What is the function of ALE/WEB?

14-4 What type of benefits are there to ALE/WEB?

14-5 What kinds of functions do R/3's Internet applications offer?

14-6 How do open interfaces and an open infrastructure meet requirements for doing business over the Internet?

14-7 What are BAPIs and how do they relate to the logic of the R/3 system?

14-8 Explain the R/3 system architecture.

14-9 What is the benefit of uncoupling the R/3 Internet applications from the R/3 system?

14-10 What does the Web basis do?

14-11 What does a Web server do?

14-12 Explain consumer-to-business access for interaction between consumers and companies.

14-13 What do Internet-based consumer-to-business applications make possible?

14-14 What does the business-to-business and consumer-to-business product catalog do?

14-15 Name two crucial elements that make the product catalog useful.

14-16 What does customer account information provide?

14-17 What do vendors benefit from?

14-18 Describe employment opportunities. Explain what the employment opportunities components support.

14-19 Explain how vacant positions are structured.

14-20 What can job hunters use the Internet for?

14-21 What does an online approach allow an organization to acquire?

14-22 Describe what is involved with application status.

14-23 What happens in a KANBAN environment?

14-24 What happens in an Internet production environment?

14-25   How is an empty KANBAN supply replenished?

14-26   Who has responsibility for ship-to-line?

14-27   Why do manufacturing processes need an information system?

14-28   How is it possible to cut self-service costs?

14-29   Explain Available-to-Promise with respect to fast ordering over the Internet.

14-30   What are the benefits to ordering over the Internet?

14-31   Describe how service notification works in concert with fast entry of customer notifications.

14-32   What are service notifications used for in the R/3 system?

14-33   What can a customer do through an Internet browser, and what does the Web application do with respect to problems and notifications?

14-34   Explain the sales order creation process.

14-35   What does sales order creation include?

14-36   Define sales order status and explain with specific examples.

14-37   Explain specifically how Web usage is vastly different from either mail or phone inquiries.

14-38   How can reliable remote entry of data over the Internet be created?

14-39   What exactly do counters do?

14-40   Define measurement values.

14-41   Can these measurements be entered through the Internet?

14-42   What are quality certificates?

14-43   What is quality notification?

14-44   What happens upon receipt of a quality notification message?

14-45   What do easy project confirmations on the Internet enable the project manager to do?

14-46   What is involved in the collective release of requisitions and purchase orders?

14-47   What is involved during the approval process?

14-48   What must the person giving approval during the approval process be able to do?

14-49   What two application components simplify the approval process?

14-50   How can employee-to-employee communications be enhanced?

14-51   What makes it easy to track co-workers who have moved?

14-52   What is involved in SAP Web reporting?

14-53   What does R/3 assets management information involve?

14-54   How do time statements play an important role in an intranet solution?

14-55   Describe what is involved in project data confirmation.

14-56   How is it possible to monitor activities and stay informed with respect to project status?

14-57   What does workflow status indicate?

14-58   What is involved in a calendar of events?

14-59   What are booked events?

14-60   Describe internal activity allocation.

14-61   What do internal activities include?

14-62   When can internal services be entered?

14-63   What is involved in an internal price list?

14-64   How can the rates for different types of services be managed?

14-65   Describe the elements in a requirements request status?

14-66   What benefits are derived from an integrated in box?

14-67   Explain the types of access that BAPIs enable.

14-68   What does this open standard promote?

14-69   What kind of interfaces are BAPIs?

14-70   What kind of access do BAPIs allow?

14-71   What standard do BAPIs define?

14-72   What does the BAPI CustomerOrder.CreateFromData do?

14-73   How do BAPIs relate to business object methods?

14-74   BAPIs can be called from different platforms; name some.

14-75   Can the CORBA standard be used?

14-76   What do BAPIs do with respect to the Internet?

14-77   What do BAPIs allow applications to benefit from?

14-78   Define support for customer-defined applications.

14-79   What is different about standalone applications?

14-80   Explain how BAPIs fit within the product catalog.

14-81   What does a BAPI called `ProductCatalog.GetLayout` do?

14-82   What does the BAPI called `ProductCatalog.GetItems` do?

14-83   The available multimedia information on product catalog entries provides what specific BAPI?

14-84   What BAPI is responsible for getting text descriptions of products?

14-85   Explain how the BAPI `CustomerOrder.CreateFromData` relates to the authentication process? Name the BAPI responsible for customer authentication.

14-86   What other elements will BAPIs support? What specific type of communication between business components do they enable?

14-87   How does Business Framework integrate software components? Name some of these components?

14-88   What comprises an SAP business object?

14-89   What do SAP business objects implement?

14-90   What does the business object repository contain?

14-91   Name items stored in the R/3 repository.

14-92   What does the Repository API allow software vendors to access?

14-93   What does the BOR form?

14-94   Explain what types of interfaces SAP Business Objects are. Where can they be accessed?

14-95   Explain where a data model is assigned that describes the internal data structure in the enterprise data model.

14-96   Explain how objects are registered.

14-97   What is the dynamic invocation interface?

14-98   When is delegation required?

14-99 Describe how BOR provides access to a specific item using different interface standards.

14-100 Explain the SNC Interface.

14-101 What happens when R/3 is integrated into security products?

14-102 What specifically must a security system cover for an Internet or intranet?

14-103 Explain user authentication.

14-104 What is involved in server authentication?

14-105 How do can communication privacy be achieved?

14-106 What does encryption ensure?

14-107 How can message integrity be guaranteed?

14-108 How can payment security be achieved?

14-109 What is the main role of the ITS? Define ITS and explain.

14-110 What is public key technology or certificates?

14-111 When do R/3 Internet components switch over to secure transmission mode?

14-112 What do firewalls do?

14-113 What is the main task of the SAProuter?

14-114 How does R/3 verify user accounts?

14-115 What does ALE make possible?

14-116 What forms the basis of demand-driven integration of applications?

14-117 Define OAGIS.

14-118 What do its specifications describe?

14-119 How does OAG define standards to hasten the connection between various software components from different vendors?

14-120 What does BOD define?

14-121 How are BODs distributed across SAP systems?

14-122 What is the SAP OIW?

14-123 What special things does OIW do for Microsoft Excel?

14-124 What benefits can be derived during presentation and further processing of results?

14-125 What does the R/3 analyzer do?

14-126 What can the business engineering workbench do?

14-127 What does the Business Engineer ensure?

14-128 What can be accomplished during the conceptual design phase?

14-129 How does the Business Engineer assist in system configuration?

14-130 What does the Business Engineer's implementation guide categorize?

14-131 What do templates do within the Business Engineer?

14-132 What does structured project management reduce?

14-133 What does the procedure model provide?

14-134 What does the session manager do?

14-135 How are authorization profiles automatically generated in R/3?

14-136 What does the administrator no longer use?

14-137 What is SAP automation?

14-138 What kind of SAP automation is permitted?

14-139 What does SAP automation consist of?

14-140 What does the RFC library allow? How is object-oriented programming used with the RFC class library?

14-141 What does the GUI library allow?

14-142 What is the GUI component?

14-143 What is GUI CodeGen?

14-144 What does the RFC component offer?

14-145 What can the RFC component be used for?

14-146 What does the transaction component do?

14-147 What does the BAPI component allow?

14-148 What does the SAP assistant do?

14-149 What does the Java-based SAPGUI offer?

14-150 What happens when R/3 is started over the Internet?

14-151 Can R/3 be Java-enabled easily?

14-1   Components running at different locations loosely couple together business processes.

14-2   Joint customer distribution models ensure a shared enterprise model with consistent business rules. SAP's R/3 provides Internet applications for large parts of the system's functionality.

14-3   R/3 Internet applications and the R/3 system itself can work together effectively to provide a uniform, consistent business environment. ALE/WEB sets up this integrated business environment for R/3 Internet applications (Figure 14.2).

FIGURE 14.2
Internet-Enabled R/3

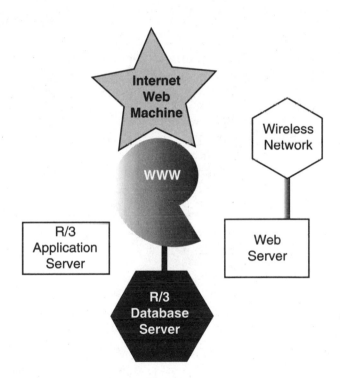

14-4   In the Internet technology of the R/3 System ALE/WEB makes it possible to benefit from new possibilities for conducting business. Its potential for adding and creating value starts with R/3's Internet applications, which create new market opportunities and enable companies to encompass the growing usefulness of the Internet.

14-5   R/3 system's Internet applications cover several functions in the areas of accounting, logistics, and human resources management, expanding the usefulness of R/3 and individualizing it to particular needs.

SOLUTIONS

14-6 Open interfaces are important in an open market. The open infrastructure and architecture necessary to satisfy the requirements for doing business on the Internet are ensured by new, business process-oriented interfaces called BAPIs (Business Application Programming Interfaces).

14-7 BAPIs access the logic of the R/3 system, which makes available more than 100 open BAPIs across all application areas. The BAPIs are based on SAP business objects, are Microsoft COM/DCOM-compliant and are achieving OMG-CORBA compatibility.

14-8 The three-tier architecture of the R/3 system has established itself as the industry's leading technology. The R/3 client only needs a PC as the end-user system. When this is combined with the uncoupling of business rules from the database, it provides the ideal platform for creating Internet and intranet solutions. The R/3 system's three-tier client/server architecture has grown into a multilayer network architecture suitable for running high-data-volume, secure and transactional Internet applications.

14-9 The R/3 Internet applications are uncoupled from the R/3 system core. This approach lets SAP customers benefit from new R/3 business processes more quickly. The R/3 Internet architecture has been extended from three tiers to encompass multiple layers that allow the scalability required to cope with the large and steadily growing number of Internet users.

14-10 The Web basis enhances the three-tier R/3 architecture for use on the Internet. It combines existing Internet technology with R/3 technology and enables reliable access to all SAP transactions from the Internet or intranets.

14-11 A Web server connects Web clients and business applications. Web server systems are available from various vendors and support all major browsers; they have been ported to various hardware and software platforms.

14-12 In worldwide consumer-to-business access for interaction between consumers and companies, customers or prospects use a Web browser to access a vendor's business system to peruse a product catalog, place an order, or find out about a product or service.

14-13 Internet-based consumer-to-business applications make it possible to offer products and services to consumers around the world. Information systems carefully tailored to the needs of these users could vastly increase the potential benefits of business application systems. This can be illustrated by the fact that data entry and administrative tasks can be shifted from the back office to where the data are created.

SOLUTIONS

14-14 The business-to-business/consumer-to-business product catalog presents products in situations that include pricing, availability checks, purchase requisitions and order entry.

14-15 The product catalog offers easy browsing and graphical display. This application is characterized by a well-defined hierarchical structure, an easy-to-use search engine, and the ability to insert pictures and texts.

14-16 The application for retrieving account balances makes it possible to set up a customer information system on the Internet. Customers can have access to information such as current interest rates, account balances, the status of invoices, or (for utilities) gas or electricity consumption.

14-17 Vendors benefit from simpler maintenance of master data and better-quality databases. This component is especially useful if a company has a large customer base. Because data are always current, vendors can respond promptly to critical situations.

14-18 There is the benefit of direct recruiting through the Internet. The employment opportunities component supports the recruiting process by providing information to potential applicants through the Internet.

14-19 Vacant positions are structured by showing locations on a map. Choosing a geographical region causes all vacancies in that region to be listed; allowing users to choose the positions that interest them. The applicant enters the required information on personal details, educational background, qualifications, and previous employers.

14-20 Job hunters use the Internet to submit unsolicited applications. Applications arrive for processing in a worker's R/3 inbox folder. When the application arrives, the applicant is assigned a personal number and password. These two elements of information together designate the job application, and applicants can use them to check the processing status of their applications at any time.

14-21 This online approach allows companies get the information they need quickly and directly in a form that makes it easy to compare candidates.

14-22 Application status within Human Resources gives applicants a definite idea of their situation at all times. The personal number and password together to clearly identify an application.

14-23 In a KANBAN production environment (Figure 14.3), KANBAN containers are set to EMPTY to trigger replenishment of components for product assembly. The KANBANS and their status can be seen in the kanban board.

SOLUTIONS

FIGURE 14.3
KANBAN

Business to Business
– KANBAN
– Quality Certificates

Consumer to Business
– Available to Promise
– Product Catalogs

Intranets
– Requirement Request
– Product Data Confirmation

14-24 In an Internet production environment, product suppliers have access to the customer's KANBAN board. This indicates that they can monitor the KANBANS for which they are responsible.

14-25 In order replenish an empty KANBAN, suppliers create a shipment in their own system that results in the delivery of the required products. Both organizations take advantage of this visibility that facilitates just-in-time delivery.

14-26 The responsibility for ship-to-line is transferred from the manufacturer to the supplier.

14-27 Certain manufacturing processes need an information system for processing commissions, processing contracts, subcontracting, unfinished product inventories, staging materials for in-house and external processing, and processing consignment stocks (such as inventory checks and stock removals).

14-28 SAP customers benefit from improved service by accessing R/3 over the Internet. These benefits are passed on to a company's own customers. Logistical improvements lead to lower costs.

14-29 The Internet application Available-to-Promise makes it possible to connect to a system and then enter the material, plant, quantity and desired delivery date. As a result, the material provision date and quantity are displayed. Additional information on a material itself can be called up.

14-30   The benefits of ordering over the Internet are that each customer can retrieve needed information directly and at any time, without assistance. Fewer telephone calls need to be made. The resulting faster flow of information dynamically speeds up business.

14-31   Service notification works with fast entry of customer notifications to produce an efficient customer service, an important consideration for service providers and customers. Customers to enter service notifications quickly and simply.

14-32   In the R/3 System, service notifications are used to request services. Customers can submit service notifications directly through a company's Web server.

14-33   Using an Internet browser, the customer can enter descriptions of problems by choosing from a list of potential problems or defects. The Web application logs the problem and assigns it an internal R/3 notification number. It interactively documents the problem online using predefined conditions. This makes it easy for the service provider to understand the nature of the problem and to provide customers with faster, more comprehensive service while simultaneously reducing personnel needed to handle service requests.

14-34   The sales order creation component contains typical sales situations in which a consumer navigates to a vendor's home page to access the virtual sales office. An electronic catalog in the Web displays products. The product descriptions in this online catalog are not restricted to plain text but can be supplemented with photographs, graphics and audio clips or additional information, when required.

14-35   Sales order creation includes electronic shopping baskets, Available-to-Promise functions, and customer-specific pricing capabilities. This creates new business opportunities that permit companies to deal more effectively on the Internet. Organizations that start business processes of this kind on the Internet gain a competitive edge by being able to deliver quickly.

14-36   24-Hour order status allows an organization to use the Internet to inform customers of the processing status of sales orders by determining if goods have already been shipped. This results customers satisfied by quick responses and the ability to inquire about the status of sales orders around the clock.

SOLUTIONS

14-37   Unlike mail or phone inquiries, customer requests received over the Web do not produce any additional work for suppliers.

14-38   Reliable remote entry of data is possible over the Internet. The Internet application allows entry of the measurement and counter readings through the Internet within the scope of Plant Maintenance (PM).

14-39   Wear of objects, consumption, or the way in which defined stock is reduced can be monitored by counters linked to technical objects that include functional locations and equipment. Counter readings are periodically taken.

14-40   Measurement values define conditions at a measuring point at a certain time. These include the rotational speed of the rotor of a wind-driven power station, expressed in revolutions per minute.

14-41   Yes, these types of measurements can be entered in the system through the Internet.

14-42   Standard practice in the automotive, chemical and pharmaceutical industries is to certify the quality of products. A quality certificate validates the quality of merchandise by listing the results of quality inspections. An authorized user can create and retrieve quality certificates for products whenever necessary.

14-43   Efficient customer service is important to customers and suppliers. The Internet quality notification component accelerates processing as it reduces the amount of work involved in handling customer complaints. Problems can be reported either by entering a description in text form or by choosing from a list of predefined, coded defect types and indicating the object of the complaint, such as by specifying the material number.

14-44   Upon receipt of a quality notification message, the R/3 system in combination with SAP Business Workflow starts the proper internal procedures. Processing status of a notification can be queried at any time.

14-45   Easy project confirmations in the intranet enable the project manager to work more effectively and quickly identify problems requiring immediate action.

14-46   During the collective release of requisitions and purchase orders (MM), if a requisition item or a purchase order satisfies certain conditions (i.e. when a value is greater than $10,000) it needs to be approved prior to being processed further.

14-47   In R/3, the approval process takes the form of a release procedure. Each individual involved in the release procedure uses a release code to grant

SOLUTIONS

approval in a release transaction. Executing this action within the R/3 system requires detailed knowledge of the procedure and cannot be handled without special training.

14-48   The person giving approval must be able to navigate the R/3 system, know the proper release code, and work through several screens.

14-49   The two application components are: Collective release of requisitions and purchase orders.

They simplify the approval process through an easy-to-use browser interface. The system then automatically creates a list of purchase requisition items or purchase orders for processing without requiring the user to know the release code. The only thing necessary is to choose an item from a list and release it. Releases already effected can also be revoked. This component provides special benefits to employees whose daily work primarily involves tasks other than the release of purchase requisitions and purchase orders.

14-50   There can be better employee-to-employee communications just by using Internet applications that are an extension of SAPoffice. This enhances the communication among the employees of large companies by permitting them to access information about one another over the in-house intranet. They can use various search criteria to locate the intranet addresses, telephone numbers, fax numbers, room numbers, and photographs of coworkers.

14-51   Since stored data are constantly updated, it is easy to track coworkers who have moved. It is also easy to send an e-mail to another worker just by clicking on intranet address.

14-52   SAP Web Reporting is a WebRFC application that allows Internet users to access information in the R/3 system. This includes the start-up of reports as well as the ability to call up previously-generated lists placed in report trees for reference. Navigation around the report trees is by pointing and clicking.

14-53   Multinational companies constantly need basic accounting information about their tangible assets. The R/3 assets management information system is directly accessible from the assets management component. If managers traveling to a subsidiary could use this component to find out what kind of equipment was available at that location. If cost center managers do not have direct access to the R/3 system they could use it to create ad hoc queries about assets in the areas required.

14-54   Time statement Internet applications allow employees to query their personal time schedules at any time. From a company perspective, regular issue of time statements in paper form is no longer necessary.

SOLUTIONS

14-55   Fast confirmation of project status on Internet projects is rarely confined to one organization. In the majority of cases, employees or subcontractors work at customer sites or remote locations.

14-56   The project data confirmation component permits authorized users to use an intranet to report on activities performed in a project. They can report the number of hours worked on different days and include a forecast of the amount of work still to be done. This confirmation provides the basis for evaluating actual schedules and costs in the R/3 project information system.

14-57   Workflow Status in an Internet component that allows display of the processing status of workflows as in the release of a purchase requisition. Through this Internet component, it is possible to view at any time how far the business process has progressed and which work steps have already been completed. A purchase requisition might already have been released or a confirmation might already have been sent to the requisition's author.

14-58   The calendar of events intranet application component makes available a log of events classified according to subject areas for internal and external users through the intranet or Internet. In this log of events, users can acquire information on event dates, content, qualifications obtained, speakers and attendance fees.

14-59   The booked events intranet application component can provide information on education and further training courses. This application makes a list of the training events available through the Internet so that a user can acquire information on dates, content, qualifications obtained, trainers and attendance fees for the events booked or reserved.

14-60   Internal activity allocation is an Internet application component that allows entry of services rendered internally.

14-61   Internal activities could include: repairs, assets produced in-house, tools, and consulting. This Internet application component makes it possible to input data worldwide. Employees can post activity allocations from a remote cost center to a receiver. Receivers can be other cost centers, orders, or the WSB elements of a project.

14-62   Internal services can be entered as soon as they have been rendered. The cost center for which a service is rendered is charged immediately.

14-63   In an internal price list, internal allocation of services; services rendered by a cost center are posted to the receiver.

14-64 The rates for different types of services can be managed with the aid of an internal price list. In order to determine the rate for a given service type, the user can either directly enter it, or use a character string to search through the keys, designations, and descriptions of all service types. In any given enterprise it is probable that a large number of employees from different departments will constantly be giving notice of their requirements for various items.

14-65 Once an employee has used the application component, a requirement request gives notification of that requirement. It is a simple matter to run this component to monitor whether the status of the request is ordered or withdrawn from stock.

14-66 An integrated in box provides an easy, global method of maintaining continuous access to messages from workflow, communication, and cooperation services. It is an essential requirement for accelerating business processes. This Internet application allows all employees access their in boxes, out boxes, public folders, and worklists through the Internet/intranet.

14-67 Business Application Programming Interfaces (BAPIs) enable external access to business processes and objects in the R/3 system. BAPIs define an open business standard for direct communication between the business applications of different vendors.

14-68 This open standard promotes the creation of technology partnerships to extend the usefulness of the R/3 system; there is a partnership between SAP and Microsoft.

14-69 BAPIs are object-oriented interfaces that make it easy to access R/3's business processes. The more than 170 business objects of the R/3 system play a key role by structuring business data and activities.

14-70 BAPIs allow efficient and flexible access to associated business processes independently of the underlying software platforms.

14-71 BAPIs define an open business standard for direct communication between the business applications of different vendors. BAPIs are open interfaces that ensure that business objects and data such as an order, a customer number, or a part number are consistently handled in the same way. This permits transactions to be conducted across corporate boundaries.

14-72 One organization's purchase order can be sent directly to another company's order-entry system and processed there without requiring either predefined EDI transmission routines or manual intervention. This is achieved by a BAPI called CustomerOrder.CreateFromData that uses certain data to produce a sales order object in the R/3 system.

SOLUTIONS

14-73   BAPIs are SAP business object methods and as a result are implemented in the R/3 business object repository.

14-74   BAPIs can be called from different platforms. Internet applications use the HTML standard or the Java programming language to access BAPIs. With Microsoft's COM/DCOM as a foundation, BAPIs can also be used from a program written in Visual Basic or from Excel.

14-75   Yes, the CORBA standard of the object management group will be supported.

14-76   BAPIs enable SAP to take a different approach to the Internet, since the foundation of the R/3 system stays the same. All of these items have been done is to add the BAPIs, while the R/3 Internet applications operate outside the R/3 System and need a stable, open interface for accessing the underlying system.

14-77   The BAPIs let applications quickly benefit from the functions and data resources of the R/3 System. SAP is experienced in developing business systems and uses that knowledge of business processes to define additional BAPIs.

14-78   Support for customer-defined applications is gained through the open standards introduced by BAPIs. R/3 customers can create their own Internet applications without depending on the R/3 internet transaction server. BAPIs allow new applications to benefit from the data and functions of the R/3 system. Another benefit is that these Internet applications can be implemented using the most convenient programming language, such as ABAP/4, Java, or C++.

14-79   Standalone Internet applications have their own mechanisms for assuring the consistency of transactions, data security, and scalability.

14-80   For BAPIs in SAP Internet applications, the product catalog now includes order entry capabilities. When a customer dials into a retailer's system, the Internet application provides information about the product groups available.

14-81   A BAPI called `ProductCatalog.GetLayout` defines the structure of a product catalog organized into "shops" and product groups such as software, hardware, and documentation.

14-82   If the shopper selects a particular product group, a BAPI called `Product-Catalog.GetItems` displays general information on the products it contains, including software products like Excel and Word. The user can then choose to acquire more detailed information on specific products.

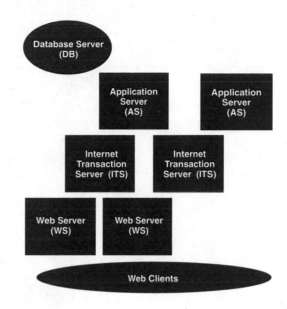

FIGURE 14.4
Internet
Transaction Server

14-83 Multimedia information on product catalog entries including sound and graphics is provided by a BAPI called `ProductCatalog.GetLayout-Documents`.

14-84 Text descriptions of products are gathered by the Internet application using the BAPI `ProductCatalog.GetLayoutDescription`. The consumer can choose specific products to buy and place them in a "shopping basket".

14-85 Before an order is placed with the assistance of a BAPI called `CustomerOrder.CreateFromData`, the customer is authenticated by the BAPI `Customer.CheckPassword`.

14-86 BAPIs will also continue to support the implementation of application software since they enable object-oriented communication between business components within the area of the business framework (Figure 14.5).

14-87 Business framework integrates various software components including the human resources management system reporting component and a treasury Component. These business components are offered both as products in their own right and as parts of R/3.

14-88 SAP Business Object in its first layer is a kernel holding the central business logic. The second layer consists of constraints and business rules responsible for preserving the object's integrity. The third layer contains methods, attributes, input-event controls, and output events. The outermost layer is the access level (COM/DCOM, CORBA).

FIGURE 14.5
Business Framework

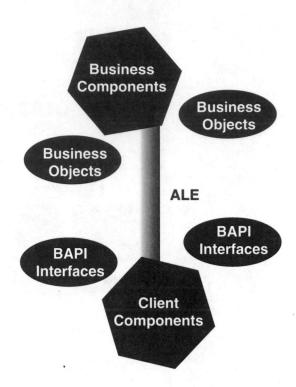

14-89   SAP business objects implement the standard capabilities of object-oriented technology including encapsulation, polymorphism, and inheritance.

14-90   The R/3 repository contains documentation on R/3 and detailed descriptions of R/3 applications. It is able to export information through an Application Programming Interface (API) to graphics software, modeling tools or BPR tools. The repository is the central storehouse for all R/3 application information, including information on new developments as well as on the design and maintenance of applications and components.

14-91   Items stored in the repository include: process models, function models, data models, SAP business objects, object models, and associated data (as well as their connections. The repository also stores technical information such as data definitions, screens, and program objects used for developing or extending R/3.

14-92   The repository API allows other software vendors to access the R/3 Repository, retrieve information, and channel it into their own tools or applications.

14-93   The Business Object Repository (BOR) forms part of the R/3 repository. The BOR draws business data, transactions, and events in R/3 as an integrated set of SAP business objects.

14-94   SAP business objects are powerful interfaces to a broad range of processes and data that can be accessed through the business object repository. SAP business objects are linked to each other to form object models.

14-95   A data model describing the internal data structure in the enterprise data model is assigned to each business object.

14-96   Objects are registered by defining object types in the BOR. At runtime, clients access objects through the business object repository that relays requests to the objects and reports the results to the clients. The source code and location of an object remain hidden from clients. This particularly important in distributed environments.

14-97   The business object repository has a dynamic invocation interface. That makes it possible to access SAP business objects at runtime whose interface was unknown at compile time. The interface allows late linking. This adds flexibility to objects because an object method's parameters can be determined at the latest possible moment. This includes the time just before the method is invoked.

14-98   The business object repository allows for delegation, which is required if SAP customers want to create their own types of business objects based on SAP business objects. In order to accomplish this task, they must first create a subtype of an SAP business object that inherits all the attributes, methods, and events of an existing object. After the new my_order definition is modified, a single instruction is used to tell the runtime component of the BOR to use my_order instead of order.

14-99   The business object repository provides access to SAP business objects for a large number of applications using different interfacing standards including Microsoft's COM/DCOM and OMG COBRA. The BOR is also accessible outside R/3 with Remote Function Calls (RFCs).

14-100   The new Secure Network Communications (SNC) interface allows R/3 to be integrated into company-wide network security products such as Kerberos and SECUDE. It allows the security product to authenticate external R/3 users. In addition, it facilitates securing the entire communication process between the front end and the application server and between different application servers.

14-101   Integrating R/3 into security products makes it possible to take advantage of the current and most secure solutions for accessing the system. Because the SNC interface is covered by SAP's certification program, SAP certifies and supports other network security products.

SOLUTIONS

14-102   A security system for the Internet and intranets will have to cover the various aspects of authentication and communication.

14-103   User authentication is crucial to an Internet solution. A system user on the Internet must prove that identity, an especially important point in banking over the Internet.

14-104   When using server authentication, the system must prove it truly is the system required. This principle is used to prevent data from being sent to an unauthorized server.

14-105   Connection privacy is achieved by encrypting transmitted data.

14-106   Encryption ensures that no unauthorized parties can listen in on messages sent over the Internet.

14-107   In order to guarantee message integrity and prevent hackers from intercepting messages and modifying them, messages must be supplemented by additional security information.

14-108   Security is required for payment transactions on the Internet because these supply information on the creditworthiness of business partners. Credit card companies are often involved here, guaranteeing the payment of goods bought on the Internet.

14-109   R/3 assigns Web users to R/3 Users. The main role is played by the SAP Internet Transaction Server (ITS). The basic user authentication provided by Web servers can be harnessed by assigning Web users or groups of users to specific users in R/3.

14-110   Public key technology or certificates can also be used to verify that another party possesses certain attributes or to check whether a Web server is in fact communicating with a business partner's systems.

14-111   Many services provided on the Internet are anonymous. Prospective customers prefer anonymous browsing in a product catalog before deciding to buy. The corresponding R/3 Internet component switches to secure transmission mode before verifying the user account for posting the order into R/3. Secure transmission can be activated by R/3 Internet application components through the "https" URL addressing method.

14-112   Firewalls monitor external access to private R/3 data. A firewall is a means of restricting access to private data through a public network.

14-113   The SAPGUI has always been secured by firewalls and SAProuter for use in public networks. The main task of SAProuter (Figure 14.6) is to support communications between SAPGUI and R/3 application servers. It is installed on a firewall and acts as an application-level gateway proxy for the R/3 System. Most of SAP's customers and prospects have installed firewalls because they use a Web server for marketing on the Internet. As a result, R/3 only requires reconfiguring an existing firewall.

FIGURE 14.6
SAProuter

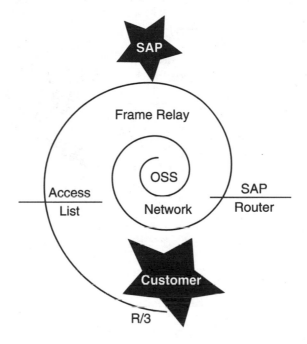

14-114   Users of a corporate intranet have at least the same level of security for their enterprise's internal communications as they enjoy for their Internet communications. In intranets, the system recognizes users because they are employees of a company. Whenever they connect to the corporate intranet, the ITS automatically displays a login screen for entry of a user name and password.

14-115   Application Link Enabling (ALE) permits linking of internal R/3 processes with outside processes, thus enabling physically separate business processes (Figure 14.7) to function as one. ALE loosely couples distributed application systems, allowing them to exchange messages and master data as well as comparing and adjusting control information. ALE exchanges messages in a time-controlled manner.

14-116   Synchronous and asynchronous communications form the basis for demand-driven integration of applications, thereby eliminating for linkage via a central database such as conventionally structured R/3 systems.

SOLUTIONS

FIGURE 14.7
Business Processes

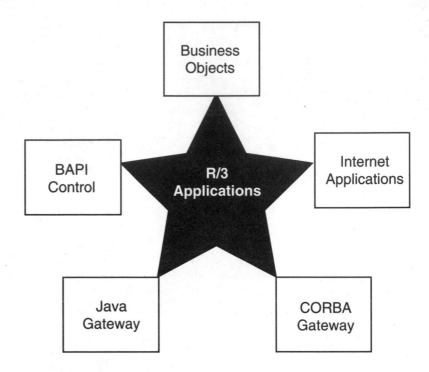

14-117 OAGIS (Open Applications Group Integration Specifications) is the standard for open application integration.

14-118 These specifications describe data and process sharing, and explain how application program methods exchange data with other OAG-compliant business applications. OAGIS satisfies the real need for interoperability at the business process level, lets users mix and match all OAGIS-compliant solutions to meet their particular requirements. When users purchase business applications from different vendors, they often have a difficult time achieving smooth interaction and may skip the benefits of enterprise application integration. They also face the difficult task of integrating all their systems to create a coherent information technology infrastructure to support their business.

14-119 The goal of the OAG is to define standards and hasten the connection among software components from different vendors. The focus of the OAG thus goes beyond objects and includes business object interoperability between all types of business applications, including existing systems.

14-120 The Business Object Document (BOD) defines the protocol that different vendors' components use to communicate with one another.

14-121   The way in which BODs are distributed across SAP systems is defined by an ALE distribution model. Incoming BODs of the type "post to G/L" are posted to the general ledger application. Incoming BODs called "feedback BODs" can be assigned to a workflow for further processing.

14-122   The SAP Open Information Warehouse (OIW) includes a BAPI that allows consistent access to selected reporting data from FI, HR and logistics. Determining which data from the R/3 information systems: (FIS, HR-IS and LIS) are available in the OIWis described in the OIW catalog that also has a BAPI. This allows an external application to search for data by issuing an appropriate query without having to know any of the R/3 information systems.

14-123   For Microsoft Excel, SAP supplies an OIW add-in that permits using simple drag and drop methods to combine OIW queries and insert them into Excel worksheets.

14-124   Presentation and further processing of the results, can benefit from the full functionality of Excel (graphics, pivot tables, automatic recalculation).

14-125   The R/3 analyzer is used to analyze business processes and R/3 customizing.

14-126   The Business Engineering Workbench contains a fully integrated and comprehensive set of tools for R/3. As customer support for R/3 implementation, the Business Engineering Workbench offers an incremental, integrated procedure concept, and is an extensive system configuration kit.

14-127   The Business Engineer ensures the integrity and quality of configured business processes throughout the implementation project. The Business Engineer supports analysis and selection of unique business processes, so that the R/3 enterprise structure can be quickly adapted to your particular goals, choosing and modeling the business areas and processes requires. The Business Engineer also controls project-related activities, such as documentation and scheduling. This active guidance for all system configuration procedures guarantees that going live quickly with an optimally configured R/3 system.

14-128   At the conceptual design phase, a manage knows which system requirements must be met and which interfaces must be set up. A t this stage R/3 users can be involved in the project, working with R/3 prototypes or simulating real-world situations in the R/3 International Demonstration and Education System (IDES) model enterprise. The options available in SAP Business Workflow permit modeling and even automating processes not included in the R/3 models. The Business Engineer automatically transfers all this information to the second phase of the project.

SOLUTIONS

14-129 The Business Engineer assists in configuring the system. Once the work units have been outlined in the preselection stage, they can be subdivided into smaller, manageable work steps.

14-130 The Business Engineer's implementation guide categorizes worksteps as optional, mandatory, or critical activities. This segmentation speeds up the configuration process and ensures that taking care of all the important steps.

14-131 Templates in the Business Engineer also significantly increase the speed and quality of configuration. All the essential activities for subsequent R/3 operation including authorization management, setting up the reporting system, creating interfaces, and implementing extensions are concluded during this phase of the project.

FIGURE 14.8
User Authorization

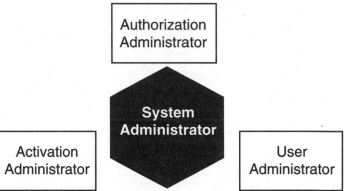

14-132 After the final test the Business Engineer proceeds to the next phase to prepare to go live. Structured project management reduces implementation times.

14-133 The Business Engineer includes a procedure model that provides the complete organizational and administrative structure required for implementing R/3, for incorporating changes when upgrading to a new release, and for continuous business process reengineering. The procedure model is an integral component of the R/3 system.

1. It offers a variety of recommendations for installing R/3
2. It permits calling all the Business Engineer tools that relate to individual work steps and gives active guidance through the entire process.
3. Online information about the project's status is available
4. Any project-related information required can be looked up.

Essentially, the proedure model makes it possible to concentrate on what the system should do; the Business Engineer will manage the project.

14-134 The session manager is one of the Business Engineer's teammates and allows users to have a complete overview of personal workstations. Each workstation is individualized, based on authorizations and profiles generated in the system. During this phase, it is possible to contact R/3 services such as EarlyWatch, Remote Consulting, or Online Software Service (OSS) to arrange for ongoing support.

14-135 The profile generator accelerates the task of setting up the authorization environment in the customer system. The administrator need only configure the customer-specific settings; the profile generator takes care of all the other tasks such as choosing the relevant authorization objects. The profile generator is integrated into the R/3 System and is available on all R/3-supported platforms.

14-136 The administrator no longer uses the authorization objects directly to define authorizations for the various user groups. Instead, the authorization profiles are built around the functions to be performed in the R/3 system. The profile generator chooses the relevant authorization objects and groups them together in a new authorization profile.

14-137 SAP automation is an integration toolkit that provides many components for integrating desktop, server, and Internet applications into the R/3 system. SAP automation consists of C libraries, C++ class libraries and ActiveX components. It extends R/3's capabilities to the Web, telephony, distributed computing, and multimedia kiosks.

14-138 SAP automation permits integration with the R/3 system at different access levels and using different programming languages.

14-139 SAP automation consists of the: RFC library, RFC class library, GUI library, RFC component, GUI component, GUI CodeGen, transaction component, BAPI component, SAP assistant, and the RFC Library (Figure 14.9).

14-140 The RFC library allows users to integrate external applications using existing ABAP RFCs or external RFCs. The library is one of the most efficient ways to access the R/3 system. The RFC class library is built on the RFC library and is designed to facilitate its use. The RFC class library was created to be used by people who do not possess any low-level knowledge of the RFC API and can be used with any R/3 system set up to receive remotely called functions. Created to simplify the programming of external applications that communicate with R/3, the RFC class library enables users to focus more attention on application logic and less on low-level RFC API details. In addition, the RFC class library provides a C++ object-oriented framework so that developers can use the benefits inherent in object-oriented programming.

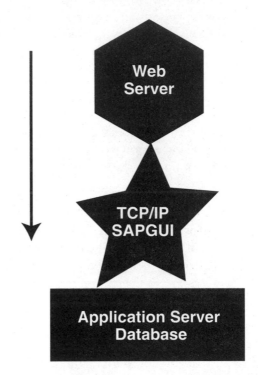

14-141   The GUI library allows direct SAPGUI programming. A 32-bit dynamic link library is available for programming the SAPGUI. To create a new interface to an existing application, find out how the application works with the existing interface.

14-142   The GUI component is an ActiveX component layered on top of the GUI library. It provides two high-level interfaces: OLE automation interface and terminal interface.

The OLE automation interface allows SAP systems to be controlled directly from OLE automation controller programs such as Microsoft Office products, Visual Basic and Hahtsite. All of the GUI library API calls have corresponding calls in the OLE automation Interface. The GUI component also provides more thorough error checking as well as many convenient routines to facilitate programming the OLE automation interface within Visual Basic and similar environments.

14-143 GUI CodeGen is a code generator for the GUI component. It allows users to walk through an R/3 transaction from a SAPGUI-like screen and generate Visual Basic or HAHTtalk Basic code based on recorded actions. GUI CodeGen eases the construction of alternative GUI interfaces to R/3.

14-144 The RFC component offers access to ABAP RFCs using ActiveX technology It is an ActiveX component built on the RFC library and offers an easy access method for ABAP/4 remote functions.

14-145 The RFC component can be used in many development environments, such as many Microsoft Office products, ActiveX Server Page, Visual Basic and Hahtsite.

14-146 The transaction component is actually an application that utilizes the RFC component. It encapsulates details about calling R/3 transactions and remote functions. The transaction component allows access to R/3 transactions in many development environments using different programming languages.

14-147 The BAPI component allows high-level access to BAPIs. Applications can directly access the SAP business objects repository and take full advantage of SAP BAPIs. This component enables rapid implementation of user applications.

14-148 The SAP assistant serves several purposes. It is a design tool that allows developers to create and browse RFCs. It permits browsing, executing, and building of RFC and transaction objects. SAP assistant offers efficient runtime access to the R/3 system.

14-149 The Java-based SAPGUI offers manifold benefits to R/3 users, system administrators, and customers. The SAPGUI in Java has exactly the same look and feel as the native SAPGUI interface. R/3 users will notice no difference between them. The SAPGUI in Java exploits the portability inherent in Java. All platforms that include NetPCs and NCs can be used as R/3 clients.

14-150 Starting R/3 over the Internet automatically downloads Java applets to the client and loads the right version of the Java-based SAPGUI. This requires no installation of any additional software or performance of extra steps to upgrade R/3 on the client. SAPGUI in Java emulates the native SAPGUI and enables R/3 users to access familiar R/3 transactions over the Internet.

14-151 R/3 has a three-tier client/server architecture and can be easily Java-enabled without an extensive redesign effort. It is only necessary to insert another layer between the application and presentation levels, and permit

SOLUTIONS

Web clients to access the R/3 system. This new Internet layer has two main parts:

1. SAP Automation Tool translates the R/3 front-end protocol into a Java-compliant one

2. Java server sends Java applets to the Web client.

Both components must be installed on a Web server to make them accessible over the Internet.

FIGURE 14.10
Java Enabled
Platforms

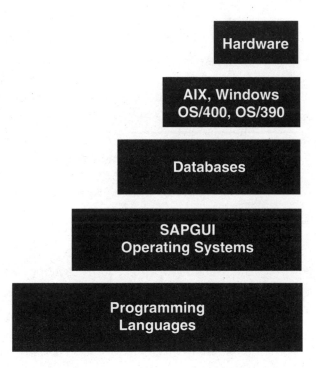

Software Certification and Validation

This chapter will give you a good overview of several very important concepts that will assist you regardless of the certification track you choose to pursue. This chapter will give you the background on several important tools that will advance your pursuits in acquiring your certification from SAP.

In reviewing this chapter you will gain an overview of everything discussed in this book. Achieving your software certification and validation is dependent upon your knowledge of concepts that play a role in all certification courses.

This chapter will delve into concepts including SAPDBA, security, the Executive Information System, solutions that can be used for every industry sector, and business processes that are crucial to your success in real-time project execution.

Personalization Strategy

SAP's personalization strategy is used for applications is to accelerate and simplify the business processes handled with the R/3 System. The transactions of each application are adapted to the business requirements of a company or of different groups of users. Extraneous information and functions in transactions are deactivated, making the processing of business workflows faster and easier. End-users are only offered the transactions that fit their respective work centers, and needless navigation through unnecessary functions in the SAP applications is eliminated. Each end-user has a personal work list of transactions that have been adapted to the business processes.

Both end-users and administrators benefit from the personalization components. Application administrators are provided with tools that adapt their own transactions to their organization's business needs. All of this happens without requiring any modifications.

Standard Transactions

Regular work centers are determined by defining standard or customized transactions to a user group. In this process, appropriate authorization profiles for the members of the work center are defined. It is possible to adapt standard transactions to an organization's business requirements as "transaction variants" are developed. The administrator edits a transaction in a special recording mode, executing the process to be modeled. When each processing step is complete, the administrator can choose to adjust specific parameters. Variants can also be declared valid for the entire company and can act as replacements for the standard transaction. During this event, the user is automatically assigned this variant.

Individual variants are designated for different user groups. In order to facilitate these actions, it is often necessary to separate transactions defined for each variant that are then integrated in the user menu in place of the standard transaction.

During the implementation process, the administrator defines several settings for each individual user. Normally, these settings apply to an entire group of users and more than one work center is described.

To make the user configuration simpler, the administrator defines activity groups that describe the work centers. The activity groups are then assigned to the users and the transactions they perform. The system can automatically create dependent authorization profiles and the appropriate user menu. This profile creation offers a means of identifying the authorization environment.

Authorizations

Authorizations are normally defined through individual authorization objects. Currently, they are defined automatically for the functions that a user group must perform, making authorization designations simpler and more reliable so that only the authorizations that are really required are assigned.

Session Manager

For end-users to use menus more efficiently they must be able to access the graphical user interface called the Session Manager. This interface makes it simpler to operate the applications navigation to the applications is much easier and far more direct.

CCMS

CCMS enables more effective management of an R/3 installation because it works with R/3 front ends through multiple R/3 systems, database systems, and host operating systems, to the network of the R/3 environment.

Integrated CCMS tools offer a simple solution for regular R/3 system operation and management, and help system administrators adapt the system to alter company requirements and analyze and optimize performance.

CCMS is a user-friendly, cost-efficient tool that ensures simple operation of an R/3 installation. It improves customer satisfaction by ensuring high system availability to reduce the total cost of ownership for the R/3 system.

CCMS provides system administrators with a new, object-oriented monitoring environment in R/3 4.0. It allows for management of multiple R/3 installations from a single console. Any software or hardware resources in the R/3 system can be monitored with the addition of "data supplier" programs. Any problems detected are recorded as "service requests;" this provides the operator with a clear overview of the general condition and alert status of every R/3 system.

CCMS offers several job scheduling options that incorporate time-based, calendar-based, and event-driven scheduling. CCMS functions manage print requests that incorporate support for local-language printouts, a failsafe architecture through automatic print rerouting in error cases, load distribution, and an interface for integrating external output management systems (OMS).

Security

Data security and process integrity are important factors in information processing. SAP offers security through precision authorization management, user authentication, the security audit, data transmission through SNC (secure network communications), ITS (Internet Transaction Server), and functions for protecting data and documents (Secure Store & Forward, SSF).

SAPDBA

SAPDBA is SAP's R/3 database administration solution. It provides a special DB monitor that offers:

- Enhanced monitoring architecture
- Monitoring and analysis
- Functions for producing and managing CBO (Cost-Based Optimizer)
- Statistics to provide faster access to business data in the database as well as continuous monitoring of the complete database system based on a new system check function.

R/3 can work with even the largest database systems because of its improved archiving solution. The dataset required for online operations can be small and manageable, while still providing rapid access to the archived data.

CCMS is open and appropriate for integrating external system management tools. It affords the opportunity to integrate current solutions with the new R/3 environment inside a current system management infrastructure.

CCMS has an open nature that keeps implementation and operating costs low, avoids retraining costs, and permits joint management of both legacy systems and R/3. A new version of CCMS has interfaces that are now implemented as BAPIs under the SAP business framework. CCMS interfaces are offered for security, background processing, database back-up and recovery, database management, system monitoring, and output management.

Warehouse Management System

SAP's Warehouse Management (WM) system facilitates the management and monitoring of large warehouses and distribution centers with a high turnover. WM defines the operational structural elements, plans resources and activities, executes goods movements, and supports decision-making through active monitoring. The module supports both planning and operative warehouse staff.

Distribution Resource Planning

The Distribution Resource Planning (DRP) and Deployment components support global inventory planning for production plants and distribution centers. DRP defines the best production plan based on the sales plan, while the deployment component distributes existing warehouse stock to distribution centers for the purpose of offering the maximum service level for distribution to retailers.

Online planning functions allow you to make last-minute changes to the distribution plan caused such as fluctuations in production or forecast errors. Deployment functions enable you to eliminate shortages or surpluses by using algorithms for fair share or push distribution.

Transportation in the Value Chain

Transportation is an important element of the value chain. Transportation costs often account for a sizable amount of the overall costs of logistics. Freight costs are automatically calculated and settled with the service provider. You can store freight rates and agreements in the system and customize calculations for each service provider or type of transportation. Costs can be settled using the credit memo procedure. This makes the freight costs transparent within the overall process.

ALE and PDM

ALE (Application Link Enabling) techniques let you design a distributed, integrated Product Data Management (PDM) scenario. The result of componentization is that product structures can be separately stored. This makes it possible to transfer only released product data, based on its status to the ERP system ALE technology also ensures tight integration between engineering and production systems while synchronizing the data in both systems.

PDM is part of the strategic product architecture of R/3 and thus integral to the Business Framework.

Application Usage

SAP application usage is greatly simplified by personalization. Administrators can quickly and easily adjust the application to the business needs of specific users (or groups). The result is that end-users only navigate in the SAP environment that corresponds to the requirements of their work center.

Company-Specific Menu

A company-specific menu is created automatically during the implementation process. It is based on the selected components. Then, the company menu can be used to form a user-specific menu for each user. This menu is composed only those application components that the end-user needs to execute his or her tasks.

Reporting

Reporting must incorporate information on mission-critical non-monetary factors so that it can reveal changes within an enterprise or in its environment that could impact its operating results. This is the foundation of the balanced scorecard that allows you to monitor the most important factors affecting business success and the key relationships among them and the ways in which they influence financial performance. The result is that the group controlling doesn't focus on capturing and processing financial data, however they do focus on maintaining the reporting system with regard to all critical success factors and on training and advising users.

SAP's Executive Information System

SAP's Executive Information System (EC-EIS) offers more complete control of all mission-critical factors with its user-friendly "inSight" interface for online management reporting. EC-EIS may be combined with a "management cockpit" and can help satisfy requirements of KPI (key performance indicators) reporting or group reporting based on the balanced scorecard concept.

The data structures that pertain to characteristics, key figures, and hierarchies are configured by the user. The system then automatically produces the technical environment such as programs for reporting and data collection. This ensures the best possible level of flexibility together with increased efficiency in configuration and changes. In addition, data collection functions make it easy to extract data from SAP applications, other OLTP systems, and external sources.

Support is offered for multiple-level KPI reporting that deals with everything from the enterprise's operational units to board-level concerns. This support incorporates both a centralized architecture with one EC system for the entire group and a decentralized, distributed architecture with multiple distributed EC systems that are still linked to one another.

EC-EIS functions within Release 4.0 are primarily designed for managing qualitative information. Object-oriented comments can now be stored on transaction data and additional information can be stored with attributes for the characteristics in the EC-EIS database. This information is automatically available in all views and reports. In addition, the EC-EIS module now includes planning functions.

Consolidation (EC-CS) in R/3 4.0 implements a component that can be used at the same time as external and internal consolidation on the basis of flexibly definable consolidation units.

The consolidation monitor offers complex group structures involving a large number of consolidation units. It allows a crucial overview of those consolidation steps already executed or not yet started at different group levels and executes completely automatic consolidation. This is different from other market solutions because this system can be implemented and modified without any programming work.

R/3 can support data transfers from both non-SAP sources and SAP's OLTP applications. The data transfer functions have been much improved. These functions can be integrated with FI, EC-CS, and EC-PCA (Profit Center Accounting). This permits loading of internal accounting data from EC-PCA. These functions also incorporate transaction data and master data and hierarchies into the associated view in EC-CS. In addition, it is possible to load external accounting data from FI. This makes it easy to reconcile external consolidated financial statements with internal statements and greatly simplifies the integration of external and internal accounting systems at the group level.

Profit Center Accounting (EC-PCA) is used to model management-oriented views effectively. It is an accounting system that meets the information needs of the executives responsible for group, profit center, and business unit management without requiring additional entry of transaction data.

Once the EC-PCA master data or profit centers are assigned to objects in Logistics (materials, production orders), and Controlling (cost centers, overhead orders) the system can automatically determine the most appropriate profit center for OLTP transactions and make the appropriate postings to Profit Center Accounting.

Data from EC-PCA can be relayed automatically both to EC-CS for use in internal consolidated financial statements and to EC-EIS for a profit center scorecard. In R/3 4.0, EC-PCA enables the use of transfer prices in profit center controlling.

Valuation

Management does not find the legally oriented valuation method sufficient for representing transfers of goods and services between profit centers. Transfer prices permit control and valuation of exchanges of goods and services between enterprise units in functionally oriented corporate groups.

R/3 3.1 only provided the opportunity to value goods delivered to profit centers at their cost of manufacture. However R/3 4.0 permits valuation based on other approaches, such as managerial valuation bases. These valuation bases can be recorded in EC-PCA in the same manner as prices are recorded in the Sales and Distribution component.

Business Planning (EC-BP) supports the preparation of business plans at a higher level. Its focus is on flexibility in modeling customer-specific operational plans, with respect to how they interact with income statements, balance sheets, and cash-flow plans, and on supporting model-based simulation.

Cockpit

Online Cockpit is an executive information system that facilitates retrieval of more accurate information as well making it possible to communicate better with colleagues.

Management Cockpit supports the implementation of corporate strategies and makes them controllable. Users report that board meetings in the Management Cockpit room become much more productive and take less time. When Management Cockpit is integrated with R/3, the provision of management information can be highly automated. Executives can achieve key performance indicators online at their PCs with EC-EIS and benefit from presentation of the same information in the Cockpit Room during meetings.

Retail Solutions

The retail sector can be described in terms of functions and institutions. Central retail functions incorporate the procurement of merchandise and activities including sorting, merchandising, packing, and selling. Essentially, retailing comprises all the links in the supply chain from the manufacturer to the final consumer.

The retail sector is composed of several different lines of trade: wholesale, direct sales, and mail order. Retail companies split into three core processes: procurement, warehouse operations, and sales. Each core process can be segmented into subprocesses. The subprocesses within procurement can include purchasing, replenishment planning, goods receipt, invoice verification, and accounts payable accounting. The subprocesses within sales are goods issue, marketing, billing, and accounts receivable accounting. The link between procurement and sales is the warehouse.

The main goal of purchasing is to negotiate reasonable prices and price conditions, and conclude contracts. In addition, purchasing has vendor listings that incorporate business with new vendors, and article listings that include new articles in a retail company's assortment.

Sales sets are purchased as single articles and sold to the consumer as a set. Purchased sets are purchased as a set and the articles they contain are sold to the consumer either as a set or individually. As a result, retailers often have to recalculate prices, revaluate inventory, and dedicate more resources to maintaining articles.

Displays are purchased as a pack containing several items. These items are then sold to the consumer individually. Displays are primarily used during sales promotions and are often allocated to stores by the head office, but not purchased by the stores themselves.

Many retailers support empties that are essentially recyclable, returnable packaging on which a deposit is paid, making good organization essential. Managing empties is an often difficult process and can be very expensive; retailers need to plan and organize every detail, setting up special areas for handling empties and returning deposits, providing special storage bins, and transporting the empties back to the vendor.

Computer-aided retailing systems manage datasets in the retail sector, EAN (International Article Number) codes, and bar codes found on almost every piece of merchandise. These items are being used to simplify the handling of articles.

Requirements planning is a core process in the retail cycle that assists retailers in refurnishing their stock as and when required. Requirements planning is based on sales and stock data, and can be carried out both centrally by the head office and by the stores themselves. Purchase orders are sent directly to the vendors.

Requirements planning is crucial to retailers. The frequency with which merchandise needs to be replenished depends on the type of article. Correct planning of the replenishment of stock is a critical success factor for retailers in the apparel industry who often have to purchase their seasonal stock long before it is due to be sold; at the same time they must ensure that their stock will be fashionable when it goes on sale.

It is important for retailers to optimize their system of scheduling purchase orders by determining the most appropriate time to order and to have their merchandise delivered so that it is on the shelves as and when required. Before retail companies accept merchandise from their vendors, they must inspect it as soon as it arrives in their delivery zone. This acceptance of goods represents the first stage of the goods receipt sub-process. The inspection requires that each item be checked on the delivery note to see that the right quantity of goods has been delivered and that the overall quality is acceptable. If the quantity of goods delivered is incorrect, or the quality poor, the delivery, the delivery note, and the purchase order are fixed.

The retailer can either return goods or transport packaging. The quantity of goods actually received defines how much retailers will be invoiced for. The point when data are entered during the delivery note evaluation serves as the foundation for invoice verification. The data are then transferred to the departments responsible for invoice verification and accounts payable accounting.

PM Module

The PM module lets you produce purchase orders for services that are required at periodic intervals. This functionality is used for maintenance plan scheduling, which is consistently linked with the procurement process.

BACKGROUND

R/3 Release 4.0 offers the option of having a service automatically initiated from the sales order and a service assembly order released.

R/3 Management Function

The management function in R/3 Release 4.0 supports flexible planning of sampling procedures, administration of sample master records, and storage of results under sample ID numbers.

Sales Processes

Warehouse logistics deals with the storage and removal of merchandise from stock as well as individual functions within the warehouse that range from mapping and managing the warehouse structure in the retail system, transferring stock, transfer postings, and stocktaking to warehouse control.

The sales process in combination with all its subprocesses concerns all the decisions and negotiations involved in getting goods from the retailer to the consumer. The sales process begins with the goods issue. The retailer needs to supply the goods a store has ordered in the agreed quantity, quality, and time.

Whenever a purchase order is received, "picking" occurs where the required number of goods is removed from storage and prepared for delivery. It is important that all incoming and outgoing goods be recorded to ensure efficient warehouse management. A retail company's warehouses require that the picking data showing what merchandise is to be delivered and to which stores so they can plan delivery routes.

Assortment management is an important element of marketing in a retail company. The assortment is the main control mechanism if the company functions with different types of sales channels and if it has stores that vary in size. Retailers base their choice of assortment on target groups and locations. In addition, they must take into account regional differences in purchasing power and consumer demand.

A retail company faces problems that include planning sales, choosing which items from the assortment to offer in a store or distribution chain, and deciding how many articles to include in a merchandise category. When a retail company has defined the basic structure of its assortment, it must choose whether the central warehouse or the regional warehouses are given responsibility for distributing the articles or if the vendor should deliver the articles directly to the store.

Articles listed differ depending on the retail company and the kind of markets they serve. This is best reflected when a discounter provides customers the same merchandise in all their stores while the assortment of department stores differs from region to region.

Sales prices are determined by sales price calculation, a procedure in which a number of factors are considered: the consumer's price range, the standard market price, the profit margin, and price points.

The effect of special offers on assortments complicates the task of determining prices in the retail sector. Usually, special offers are introduced as part of a sales promotion. In some cases, the price changes affect the sale of other articles in a type of demand effect. The objective is to use this effect to maximize the revenue generated by an assortment.

Sales promotions in the retail sector are an important aspect of marketing. Promotions held at different intervals have the potential to increase a company's public profile as well as increase sales. There is a sizable amount of work necessary to prepare for sales promotions. Retailers must plan the quantity of merchandise to be sold, or negotiate special price conditions with their vendors, or revaluate their current stock.

In the retail sector, subprocesses of sales, goods issue, billing, and accounts receivable accounting all come together at the point of sale (POS). The sales data entered in the various kinds of POS systems can be edited and used as a basis for supporting and, if necessary, adapting purchasing activities and requirements planning. In evaluating point-of-sale data, retailers can gain a detailed insight into sales trends. This information makes it possible to manage purchasing and sales activities for future periods. Its goal is to use POS data to determine what articles are best-sellers and which articles produce the most revenue. Retailers can then get a better idea of which assortments to offer in the future. POS data are used for billing and accounts receivable accounting. The main object of billing is to create the customer's invoice as soon as the merchandise has been delivered or the customer has collected it. Billing is not important to store-based retailing because merchandise is issued at the point of sale. At this point, the sales process has gone full-circle; the retail cycle goes back to the beginning, and the purchasing process starts again.

Most modern retailing systems support the collection of all the data generated during purchasing processes. This provides retailers with all the information they require to make the right decisions on current issues and to work out their future strategies.

Transfer Prices

Transfer prices let you control and valuate exchanges of goods and services between enterprise units in functionally oriented corporate groups. R/3 Release 3.1 only allowed you to valuate goods delivered to profit centers at their cost of manufacture. However R/3 Release 4.0 allows valuation based on other approaches (managerial valuation bases). These valuation bases can be stored in EC-PCA in the same manner as prices in the Sales and Distribution component.

Activity-Based Costing through Enhanced Functionality

Enhanced functions and new components in Controlling includes Activity-Based Costing that offers greater flexibility and enable customers to more efficiently resolve business-related questions.

Public Transportation Module

PT (Public Transportation) is a module for the urban transportation industry that connects to the R/3 system. PT is compiled using the ABAP programming language that is fully integrated in the R/3 system. It allows operators to manage transit card accounts, ticket sales, and criminal offenses such as fines and vandalism.

PT was developed especially for transit providers and provides full sub-ledger functionality. It is integrated with the R/3 FI accounts receivable system. Sales devices are connected to the R/3 system through an open communications interface, PT-COM. PT supports all types of payment cards.

The PT Baseline module has a flexible fare structure management system that can support multiple fare structures at the same time. It also provides multi-currency capability as well as a materials management system tailored specifically to the needs of transportation companies, which can be used to monitor stocks of tickets and merchandise extending to individual salespeople. PT Baseline also offers an interface to R/3's accounts receivable system that includes additional functions for supporting returned unpaid checks and bills as well as an interface to a legal dunning system.

The PT Open Sales module is used for controlling and settling sales of tickets and other articles. PT Open Sales can support several distribution channels including kiosks, ticket vending machines, company and external sales offices. Sales data can be entered manually or fed in from electronic fare payment devices using the PT-COM communications interface. PT Open Sales provides functions for settling commission and managing vouchers; in addition to tickets, the system also supports the sale of merchandise.

The PT Subscriptions function makes it possible to manage transit rider accounts. Besides private passes, the system also supports employer-sponsored transit pass programs (transferable and nontransferable passes) and allows operators to settle student fares with school authorities, taking into account parental contributions where appropriate. The system supports all settlement procedures and payment methods including direct debit, cash payment, and bank transfer. Other services, like accident insurance, can also be sold.

The PT Criminal Offenses module makes it possible to keep track of fines and offenses such as vandalism. Besides the civil law dunning procedure, PT Criminal Offenses also permits pressing charges against repeat offenders automatically identified by the system or prosecution in the event of specific criminal acts. Incidence data and activity reports that are also managed in the system can be entered manually, or data entered into mobile data entry devices by inspectors can be transferred to the system via a standard interface.

The PT-COM sales devices (ticket vending machines, ticket printers, and POS systems are connected to PT through the PT-COM communications interface, created in combination with leading manufacturers of fare payment devices. It permits transit agencies to hook up their devices directly. PT-COM also supports data supply and retrieval (automated operation) for online sales devices. The integrated fault management system enables the current operating status of the devices to be monitored at any time. PT offers a broad span of functionality that can be customized to meet user requirements. All the main import and export interfaces are fully transparent and standardized.

PT's multi-client capability makes it possible to deploy the solution centrally at a computer center for use by several different companies such as multi-provider transportation networks. Because of full integration with R/3 users can leverage the functions of the R/3 system.

Business Transaction Events

SAP's Business Transaction Events are a special type of BAPI. The FI component tailors processes and flows to customer requirements. This special form of BAPI functions together with SAP standard customizing and allow the integration of customer processes without modifications. R/3 algorithms such as the "check for double invoice entry" or "house bank determination" in the payment run can be replaced by the customer's own functions. It is also possible to export credit insurance, credit information, and asset-backed securities. These partner products can easily be linked up along the entire process chain.

SAP's PM module permits production of purchase orders for services that are required at periodic intervals. This functionality is used for maintenance plan scheduling that is consistently linked with the procurement process. The services are provided in combination with products, and R/3 4.0 provides the option of having a service automatically initiated from the sales order and a service assembly order released.

R/3 4.0 management functions support flexible planning of sampling procedures, administration of sample master records, and storage of results under sample ID numbers. Plant maintenance and quality management functions support calibration planning, handling, and testing, as well as decisions on the usage of test and measurement equipment. For continuous flow production and repetitive manufacturing in particular, line design and production scheduling have a definite impact on efficiency. In order to achieve the best possible results, the production sequence is subdivided into processes and a line-loading schedule is created. The line-design function allocates components and production resources to individual line sections and handles the assignment and synchronization of the lines. In continuous flow production, the sequencing function determines the sequence in which orders are handled and also controls line loading.

System Management and Monitoring

SAP's Warehouse Management (WM) system expedites the management and monitoring of large warehouses and distribution centers with a high turnover. WM defines the operational structural elements, plans resources and activities, executes goods movements, and supports decisionmaking through active monitoring. The module supports both planning and operative warehouse staff.

The Distribution Resource Planning (DRP) and deployment components support global inventory planning for production plants and distribution centers. DRP defines the best production plan based on the sales plan, while the deployment component distributes existing warehouse stock to distribution centers for the purpose of offering the maximum service level for distribution to retailers. Deployment functions make it possible to eliminate shortages or surpluses by using algorithms for fair share or push distribution.

Transportation is also an important element of the value chain. Transportation costs often account for a sizable amount of the overall costs of logistics. Freight costs are automatically calculated and settled with the service provider. Freight rates and agreements can be stored in the system and calculations can be customized for each service provider or type of transportation. Costs can be settled using the credit memo procedure. This makes the freight costs transparent within the overall process.

ALE techniques makes it possible to design a distributed, integrated Product Data Management (PDM) scenario. Components allow product structures to be separately stored. This makes it possible to transfer only released product data, based on status to the ERP system. ALE technology assures close coupling between engineering and production systems while synchronizing the data in both systems.

Management and Production

Plant maintenance and quality management functions support calibration planning, handling, and testing, as well as decisions on the usage of test and measurement equipment.

In continuous flow production and repetitive manufacturing in particular, line design and production scheduling have a definite impact on efficiency. In order to achieve the best possible results, the production sequence is subdivided into processes and a line-loading schedule is created. In addition, the sequencing function determines the sequence in which orders are handled and also controls line loading. Exactly when components are supplied and made available depends on the sequence.

NOTE

The line design function allocates components and production resources to individual line sections and handles the assignment and synchronization of the lines.

Payment Cards

Payment cards are replacing cash. R/3 4.0 therefore offers functions for handling transactions involving credit, procurement, and customer cards. The information needed for this is stored in the system. Whenever an order is generated or merchandise is delivered, validity and authorization checks are performed. The data are relayed down the process chain to the billing document and forwarded to financial accounting. SAP R/3 is also equipped to handle card payments in electronic media such as the Internet. This allows for automated entry of orders, product marketing, provision of up-to-date information to customers in the form of electronic catalogues, and electronic payments.

R/3 Release 4.0 offers functions for handling transactions involving credit, procurement, and customer cards. The information required for this is stored in the system. Whenever an order is generated or merchandise is delivered, validity and authorization checks are performed. The data is relayed down the process chain to the billing document and forwarded to financial accounting. SAP R/3 is also equipped for handling card payments in electronic media such as the Internet. This allows for automated entry of orders, product marketing, provision of up-to-date information to customers in the form of electronic catalogues, and electronic payments.

Summary

In this chapter we covered the important theme of software certification and validation. We learned how the CSP program fits into this theme, how testing takes place under very specific circumstances, and how CCMS plays an important role in studies to become certified.

15-1   Explain the SAP Complementary Software Program and how it relates to the SAP Business Framework.

15-2   Describe what special certification and validation programs permit.

15-3   Explain certification interoperability.

15-4   Where is certification available for various software solutions?

15-5   What do SAP's integration and certification centers evaluate?

15-6   Explain the steps involved when third parties apply for certification from SAP.

15-7   Where does testing take place?

15-8   What occurs when a test is successful?

15-9   Does SAP maintain any types of lists? If so, what do they involve and who can look at them?

15-10   What can customers expect when choosing an SAP-certified product?

15-11   What do validated complementary products offer?

15-12   What kind of benefits can a partner expect?

15-13   What are specific software areas covered by certification and validation?

15-14   What has SAP already certified?

15-15   Describe and give an example of partner services.

15-16   Explain which phases of a project are covered under SAP consulting.

15-17   What standard does the quality management process meet?

15-18   What does personalizing applications accomplish?

15-19   How is application usage affected by personalization?

15-20   Describe levels of personalization.

15-21   Explain who benefits from personalization.

15-22   Define a typical work center.

15-23   How can transactions be adapted to individual business requirements?

15-24   What actions do current tools permit?

15-25   What happens if input masks are not needed?

15-26   Can variants be valid for an entire company?

15-27   How are work centers defined?

15-28   Which transactions can a user perform, and which authorizations are associated with these transactions? Which organizational units is a user assigned to?

15-29   How have authorizations changed from the past to the present?

15-30   What is simple navigation?

15-31   When is a company-specific menu created?

15-32   How do end-users use menus efficiently? What user interface must they use?

15-33   What does CCMS offer?

15-34   What do integrated CCMS tools do?

15-35   What does CCMS represent?

15-36   What does CCMS offer administrators?

15-37   What does the alert monitor do?

15-38   How are the monitoring architecture and alert monitor shipped?

15-39   What kind of job scheduling functions does CCMS provide?

15-40   How can long-running jobs be performed?

15-41   What do CCMS functions manage?

15-42   Name two important factors that pertain to information processing.

15-43   Explain SAP's database management solution.

15-44   How does R/3 handle large database systems?

15-45   Explain open system management interfaces.

15-46   What does the open nature help do?

15-47   What does the CCMS interface provide?

KEY CONCEPT

Managing a modern group is difficult. The globalization of companies has ushered in the decentralization of corporate responsibility. The value chains that corporate groups need in order to compete successfully on a global scale have also changed; information needs have increased. This means that management for groups, managerial, and financial accounting departments must meet far more stringent requirements.

15-48 Describe reporting and how it deals with mission-critical factors.

15-49 What is the primary focus of SAP's Executive Information System?

15-50 What requirements can the executive information system meet?

15-51 Who configures the data structures?

15-52 What do the data collection functions do?

15-53 What benefits can be expected from the data collection functions?

15-54 Describe how support is offered for multiple-level KPI reporting.

15-55 What are the new functions in the executive information system designed for?

15-56 What is consolidation?

15-57 What do view capabilities do?

15-58 What does a consolidation monitor do?

15-59 How difficult is it to configure master data, group structures, and consolidation procedures?

15-60 From what sources can a system support data transfers?

15-61 Explain profit center controlling using transfer prices.

15-62 What is EC-PCA?

15-63 What happens when EC-PCA master data are assigned?

15-64 What is the advantage of assigning EC-PCA master data?

15-65 How are profits represented in accounts calculated?

15-66 How can fixed capital be shown?

15-67 How are data relayed from EC-PCA?

15-68 What distinct advantage does EC-PCA gain under R/3 Release 4.0?

15-69 What is it that the valuation method cannot adequately represent?

15-70 What can be controlled and valued by transfer prices?

15-71 What is the purpose of business planning?

15-72 What is the "Online Cockpit?"

15-73 What does the management cockpit support?

15-74 What happens when the management cockpit is integrated with R/3?

KEY CONCEPT

Retailing is concerned with getting the right merchandise at the right time in the right quantity to the right location. There are several functions, processes, and lines of trade involved in this process.

15-75   How can the retail sector be described?

15-76   What do central retail functions include?

15-77   What is the retail sector made of?

15-78   Describe the processes within a retail company.

15-79   What is the most important goal in purchasing?

15-80   What must buyers choose?

15-81   When stores have an extremely large number of items, what crucial factor must the store implement?

15-82   What does a set refer to?

15-83   Between what two sets must retailers make a distinction?

15-84   Explain these two sets in detail?

15-85   What is a display and how is it purchased?

15-86   What is a pre-pack?

15-87   What are empties and how do retailers handle them?

15-88   How are empties managed?

15-89   What do computer-aided retailing systems do?

15-90   What is requirements planning?

15-91   What does requirements planning do for retailers?

15-92   What is replenishment of stock?

15-93   How do retailers optimize their system of scheduling purchases?

15-94   What must retailers do to merchandise before accepting it?

15-95   What retailers do after inspection?

15-96   What does the quality of goods determine?

15-97   How does the warehouse link procurement and sales?

15-98   Explain warehouse logistics.

15-99   What do the sales process and its sub-processes refer to?

15-100 What happens when a purchase order is received?

15-101 What is centralized assortment management?

15-102 What are the main problems a retail company must face?

15-103 What happens when a retail company has created its assortment structure?

15-104 What factors might cause articles to differ?

15-105 What determines sales prices?

15-106 What kind of effect do special offers have on assortments?

15-107 What do sales promotions do in the retail sector?

15-108 Describe the point of sale within the retail sector.

15-109 What results can be expected from the evaluation of point-of-sale data?

15-110 What can POS data be used for?

15-111 What do modern retailing systems support?

15-112 What does the Public Transportation module do?

15-113 For whom was PT created and what type of functions does it offer?

15-114 Where are sales devices connected to the R/3 system?

15-115 What is the PT baseline?

15-116 What do PT open sales do?

15-117 What do PT subscriptions offer?

15-118 What do PT criminal offenses do?

15-119 What does PT-COM do?

15-120 Explain PT's multi-client capabilities.

15-121 Describe in detail what an industry business unit involves.

15-122 What are SAP's business transaction events?

15-123 What is activity-based costing?

BACKGROUND

Companies have a growing need for stronger customer focus and faster purchasing capabilities; it is crucial that they have rapid and flexible access to information about the global availability of materials, resources, and finished products. Large corporations operating globally require more than conventional, transaction-based availability checks. This requirement is met by the Available-to-

Promise (ATP) server that allows companies with high sales and production volumes to perform integrated availability checks in real time throughout the supply chain. Detailed availability checks actively support decisionmaking in connection with sales orders.

It is important to have reliable information about the availability of materials, but businesses also need constantly to reduce internal procurement times. In order for better support, confirmation processes have been significantly automated and accelerated in R/3 Release 4.0, which has ability to support large data volumes and automation of subsequent processing steps. It includes functions such as automatic determination of actual costs, retroactive withdrawal, and confirmation of preceding activities in the processing chain. For confirmation, there are now both time-critical and -uncritical functions; these can be executed as required either online or asynchronously in the background.

There must be optimal assignment of personnel. This function has been supplemented by a time sheet, in which work done can be easily entered in an integrated manner and evaluated.

As with large-scale engineering projects, cash is a key parameter. Release 4.0 supports the overall process of both debit-side and credit-side handling of down payments.

Accurate monitoring of all incoming and outgoing payments, and calculation of interest are possible on a daily basis. Because document management has been integrated into the intranet, any user can easily keep track of all relevant documents.

In order to reduce downtimes, operators of large systems rely heavily on efficient stocking and refurbishing of repairable spares. This is the essential plant maintenance process. With the assistance of refurbishment orders, Release 4.0 supports the entire process of refurbishment culminating in a repairable spare achieving the target state of "refurbished".

15-124 What achievements does the PM module permit?

15-125 What options exist for services provided in combination with products?

15-126 What does the management function in R/3 Release 4.0 support?

15-127 What do plant maintenance and quality management functions support?

15-128 Explain how the production process is subdivided.

15-129 What does the line design function allocate?

15-130 What does the sequencing function determine?

15-131 What does SAP's Warehouse Management system facilitate?

15-1 The SAP Complementary Software Program is a key part of SAP's plans to establish SAP Business Framework as the most open architecture in the software industry. SAP provides the best-quality Business APIs (BAPIs) and supports the specific business processes of customers with a solution consisting of SAP and complementary components. The Complementary Software Program provides resources dedicated to promoting integration projects, providing partner management, technical consulting, validation, and certification of integration.

15-2 SAP has developed special certification and validation programs for third-party complementary products. This gives companies the chance to benefit from short implementation cycles for ready-to-use solutions.

15-3 Certification interoperability indicates the integration of applications and components from different vendors. Interoperability is essential to customers when they select their complementary products. There is no guarantee that this important requirement is met. SAP has introduced a series of measures to validate and certify add-on components that complement and improve the business processes of SAP customers.

15-4 Certification is available for a variety of software solutions integrated with SAP software through BAPIs, IDocs, or lower-level interfaces like RFCs (Figure 15.1).

FIGURE 15.1
RFC

15-5 SAP's Integration and Certification Centers (ICCs) evaluate and test the quality of the complementary software interfaces to SAP components and processes by using integration scenarios so that customers can be sure of getting a technically verified interface that is ready-to-use and release-stable.

SOLUTIONS

15-6   Third parties who apply for certification from SAP receive documentation on the interfaces with which their software integrates. Partners also sign an agreement of cooperation with SAP.

15-7   The testing takes place in one of SAP's ICCs and Certification Centers in California, Germany, or Japan.

15-8   If the test is successful, the partner receives a test report and certificate and is then entitled to use the logo "BAPI-certified" in its marketing materials.

15-9   SAP keeps a list of all certified software that customers, partners, and sales and marketing teams worldwide are free to consult at any time. SAP also maintains lists of complementary solutions.

15-10   When a product is chosen from the list of validated or certified products, reduced implementation times result because this is a ready-to-use solution, costs are reduced with installation of a product with an interface that works with SAP business processes, and there are complementary products that use stable and reliable interfaces to SAP enterprise software.

15-11   Validated complementary products can provide live references to real-world customer situations. An enterprise solution benefits from integrated components, regardless of which vendor sold the software.

15-12   Benefits from the certification and validation processes include fully functional tested and certified interfaces and business and marketing support, and a higher profile through association with SAP.

15-13   Certification and validation of complementary solutions deal with all business processes supported by SAP components.

15-14   SAP has certified ALE converters as well as related data migration tools, archiving and imaging systems, automated test tools, barcode readers, CAD software, credit information tracking, fax and e-mail solutions, development environments, document management systems, EDI subsystems, export invoices, geographical information systems, laboratory information management systems, mobile data recording and radio frequency terminals, sales and use tax systems, point of sale systems, process control systems, shop floor control systems, supervisory control systems (SCADA), supply chain optimization software, system management tools, time and attendance software, warehouse control systems, and weighing devices.

15-15   Complementary software vendors can receive various partner services through the CSP and the associated ICCs. Software vendors who integrate their products with SAP software can make use of technical integration consulting and the education offered by the SAP Partner Academy. Additional services include remote connection to a test system provided by the ICCs and access to a range of test and demo software for partners.

15-16 SAP offers organizational and technical consulting from the planning phase of the project to its execution as well as comprehensive training with 24-hour support.

15-17 The quality management processes implemented in Germany for SAP development and consulting comply with the international standard ISO 9001.

15-18 The goal of the personalization strategy for applications is to accelerate and simplify the business processes handled by the R/3 system. The transactions of each application are adapted to the business requirements of a company or of different groups of users. Extraneous information and functions in transactions are deactivated, making the processing of business workflows faster and easier. End users are offered only the transactions that fit their respective work centers, and needless navigation through unnecessary functions in the SAP applications is eliminated. Each end user has a personal work list of transactions adapted to the business processes.

15-19 SAP applications use is greatly simplified by personalization. Administrators can quickly and easily adjust the application to the business needs of specific users or groups. The result is that end users only navigate in the SAP environment that corresponds to the requirements of their work center.

15-20 Personalization levels include:

- R/3 standard
- R/3 industry solutions
- Corporate-specific
- User Group-specific
- User-centric
- Menus
- Navigation
- Authorizations
- Transactions
- Functions
- Lists.

15-21 Both end users and administrators benefit from personalization components. Application administrators are provided with tools to adapt their own transactions to their organization's business needs. All of this happens without requiring modifications.

SOLUTIONS

15-22   Typical work centers are defined by designating standard transactions or customized transactions to a user group. In this process, appropriate authorization profiles for the members of the work center are designated and an individual user menu for simplified navigation is produced. Effort needed for adjusting the transactions is kept to a minimum.

15-23   In order to adapt the standard transactions to an organization's business requirements, "transaction variants" are created by editing transactions in a special recording mode, executing the process to be modeled. Once each processing step is complete, an administrator can choose to adjust specific parameters.

15-24   The current tools enable fields to be assigned default settings, hidden, or made not-ready for input.

15-25   If entire input masks are not needed, they can be removed. Any number of variants can be created for a standard transaction, as needed for the different business processes.

15-26   A variant can also be declared valid for an entire company. It can act as replacement for the standard transaction. During this event, user automatically assigned this variant. However, individual variants can also be assigned to different user groups. In order to make this happen, transactions must be defined for each variant, then integrated in the user menu in place of the standard transaction.

15-27   Throughout the implementation process, the administrator designates several settings for each individual user.

15-28   Under normal circumstances, these settings apply to an entire group of users that more than one work center is described. In order to make the user configuration simpler, the administrator designates an activity group to describe the work center. The activity group is then assigned to the users and the transactions they perform. The system can automatically create dependent authorization profiles and the appropriate user menu. This profile creation provides a means of identifying the authorization environment.

15-29   In the past, authorizations had to be defined by designating individual authorization objects. Now they are defined automatically for the functions that a user group is to perform. This makes the assignment of authorizations simpler and more reliable, so that only the authorizations really required are assigned.

15-30   An important element of personalization is the simplification of navigation to the individual application functions. The most important aspect of this simplification deals with removing unnecessary functions from the menus and is executed at two levels.

15-31 A company-specific menu is created automatically during the implementation process is based on the selected components. The company menu can then be used to form a user-specific menu for each user. This menu contains only those application components the end user needs to execute tasks.

15-32 In order for end users to use menus efficiently, they must be able to access the graphical user interface called the session manager. This interface makes it much easier to operate the applications. Navigation to the applications is also easier and more direct.

15-33 CCMS offers the complete management of an R/3 installation dealing with R/3 front ends through multiple R/3 systems, database systems, and host operating systems, to the network of the R/3 environment.

15-34 The integrated CCMS tools offer both simplicity and efficiency to regular R/3 System operation and management, as well as helping system administrators to adapt the system to altering company requirements and analyze and optimize performance.

15-35 CCMS is a user-friendly, cost-efficient tool that assures simple operation of an R/3 installation with minimal cost and effort. CCMS enhances customer satisfaction by making certain there is high system availability to reduce the total cost of ownership of the R/3 system (Figure 15.2).

FIGURE 15.2
CCMS/System
Management

15-36 In R/3 Release 4.0, CCMS provides system administrators a new, object-oriented monitoring environment that permits the management of multiple R/3 installations from a single console. Any software or hardware resources within or outside the R/3 system can be monitored with the addition of "data supplier" programs. Problems detected are recorded as "service requests." This gives operators a clear overview of the general condition and alert status of every R/3 system.

15-37   The alert monitor produces analysis tools for processing alerts as well as for offering options for automatic responses to alerts.

15-38   The monitoring architecture and the alert monitor are shipped preconfigured and can be started up immediately without further customization.

15-39   CCMS provides several job scheduling options that include time-based, calendar-based, and event-driven scheduling.

15-40   Long-running jobs can be performed in parallel. R/3 Release 4.0 incorporates improvements and enhancements such as protection against misuse of external commands in background jobs and automatic forwarding of job printouts through e-mail.

15-41   CCMS functions manage print requests that include support for local-language printouts, a failsafe architecture through automatic print rerouting in error cases, load distribution, and an interface for integrating external output management systems (OMS).

15-42   Data security and process integrity are two important factors in information processing. SAP provides security through precision authorization management, user authentication, the security audit, data transmission through SNC, ITS, and functions for protecting data and documents SSF.

15-43   SAPDBA, SAP's R/3 database administration solution, offers a special DB monitor that has hooks for: new monitoring architecture, monitoring and analysis, new functions for generating and managing CBO (Cost-Based Optimizer), statistics to offer faster access to business data in the database, and continuous monitoring of the complete database system based on a new system check function.

15-44   The R/3 system can work even with the largest database systems because of its improved archiving solution. In addition, the data set required for online operations can be kept small and manageable and still provide rapid access to the archived data.

15-45   CCMS is open for integrating external system management tools. It permits integrating of current solutions with the new R/3 environment in an existing system management infrastructure.

15-46   This open nature helps to keep implementation and operating costs low, avoids retraining costs and enables joint management of both legacy systems and R/3. With the new version of CCMS, interfaces are implemented as BAPIs under the SAP business framework.

15-47 CCMS interfaces are provided for security, background processing, database backup and recovery, database management, system monitoring, and output management.

15-48 Reporting must incorporate information on mission-critical non-monetary factors so that it can reveal changes within an enterprise or in its environment that could have an impact on its operating results. This is the foundation of the balanced scorecard that allows monitoring of the most important factors affecting business success, the key relationships among them, and the ways in which they influence financial performance. Group controlling does not focus on capturing and processing financial data but on maintaining the reporting system with regard to all critical success factors and on training and advising users.

15-49 SAP's EC-EIS provides a balanced control of all mission-critical factors with its user-friendly "inSight" interface for online management reporting. EC-EIS may be combined with a "management cockpit."

15-50 EC-EIS is designed to meet the requirements of KPI (key performance indicators reporting or group reporting based on the balanced scorecard concept.

15-51 The data structures involved (characteristics, key figures, hierarchies) are configured by the user, and the system automatically generates the technical environment, including programs for reporting and data collection. This assures the highest level of flexibility, together with efficiency in configuration and changes.

15-52 The data collection functions make it simple to extract data from SAP applications, other OLTP systems, and external sources.

15-53 The user department can create a new application by itself in only a few days, including training users and writing documentation.

15-54 Support provided for multiple-level KPI reporting comes from many locations from the enterprise's operative units to board level. There is a centralized architecture (one EC system for the entire group) as well as a decentralized, distributed architecture (with multiple distributed EC systems still linked to one another).

15-55 The new functions for EC-EIS in Release 4.0 are primarily designed for managing qualitative information. Object-oriented comments can now be stored on transaction data and additional information with attributes for

SOLUTIONS

the characteristics can be stored in the EC-EIS database. This information is automatically available in all views and reports. In addition, the EC-EIS module now also includes planning functions.

15-56 Consolidation (EC-CS) within R/3 4.0 implements a consolidation component that can be used simultaneously with external and internal consolidation on the basis of flexibly definable consolidation units.

15-57 View capabilities have been added to enable storage of parallel consolidation views for external and internal accounting as well as for parallel but different external consolidation views.

15-58 The user-friendly consolidation monitor has a complex group structure involving a large number of consolidation units. It offers an important overview of consolidation steps already executed or not yet started at different group levels and can also carry out fully automatic consolidation. It differs markedly from other market solutions because the system can be implemented and modified without any programming work.

15-59 Master data, group structures, and consolidation procedures are not difficult to configure. Nor is consolidation of investments that can be used to support and automate complex business consolidation steps.

15-60 A system can support data transfers from both non-SAP sources and SAP's OLTP applications. The data transfer functions have been greatly enhanced. They can be integrated with FI and EC-CS and EC-PCA (Profit Center Accounting). This permits loading of internal accounting data from EC-PCA. Transaction data and master data and hierarchies are included in the associated view in EC-CS external accounting data can be loaded from FI. This makes it easy to reconcile external consolidated financial statements with internal statements and greatly simplifies the integration of external and internal accounting systems at the group level.

15-61 There are increasingly complex value chains in corporate groups. Significantly more enterprises are defining local areas of responsibility that include profit centers or (at a higher level of aggregation business units that are managed as independent companies. In addition, they have responsibility for their own operating results without being reflected in the group's legal structure.

15-62 Profit Center Accounting (EC-PCA) can be used to model management-oriented views of this kind effectively. It is an accounting system that satisfies the information requirements of executives responsible for group, profit center, and business unit management without requiring additional entry of transaction data.

15-63 When the EC-PCA master data (or profit centers) are assigned to the objects in Logistics (materials, production orders), and Controlling (cost centers, overhead orders, for example), the system can automatically determine the correct profit center for OLTP transactions and make the appropriate postings to profit center accounting.

15-64 The advantage is that no additional manual postings or account assignments need to be made in daily processing. Values that cannot be directly assigned to a profit center can be collected in a special profit center set up for this purpose and then reallocated to the correct operative profit centers using distribution and assessment functions.

15-65 Profits represented in accounts can be calculated through either period accounting or the cost-of-sales method.

15-66 Fixed capital can also be shown by profit centers if balance sheet items that include fixed assets, receivables and payables, material stocks, and work in process are transferred to profit center accounting. Profits and performance indicators including ROI, working capital, operating cash flow, and economic value added (EVA) can be displayed.

15-67 Data from EC-PCA can be relayed automatically both to EC-CS for use in internal consolidated financial statements and to EC-EIS for a profit center scorecard.

15-68 In R/3 Release 4.0, EC-PCA has the advantage of enabling the use of transfer prices in profit center controlling.

15-69 The legally oriented valuation method is inadequate from a managerial perspective for representing transfers of goods and services between profit centers.

15-70 Transfer prices make it possible to control and value exchanges of goods and services between enterprise units in functionally oriented corporate groups. R/3 Release 3.1 only permitted valuation of goods delivered to profit centers at their cost of manufacture. Release 4.0 allows valuation based on other approaches (managerial valuation bases). These valuation bases can be stored in EC-PCA in the same manner as prices are stored in the sales and distribution component.

15-71 The purpose of Business Planning (EC-BP) is to support the preparation of business plans at a high level of aggregation. The focus is mainly on flexibility in modeling customer-specific operational plans, with respect to how they interact with income statements, balance sheets, and cash-flow plans, and on supporting model-based simulation.

SOLUTIONS

15-72   An "online cockpit" is an online executive information system permits retrieval of more accurate information and facilitates better communication with colleagues.

15-73   The management cockpit supports the implementation of corporate strategies and makes them controllable. Users report that board meetings in the management cockpit room become much more productive and take less time.

15-74   When the management cockpit is integrated with R/3, the provision of management information can be highly automated. Executives can call up key performance indicators online with EC-EIS and benefit from presentation of the same information from the cockpit room during meetings.

15-75   The retail sector can be described in terms of functions and institutions.

15-76   Central retail functions include the procurement of merchandise and activities such as sorting, merchandising, packing, and selling. Retailing consists of all the links in the supply chain from the manufacturer to the final consumer.

15-77   The retail sector consists of several different lines of trade: wholesale, direct sales, and mail order.

15-78   The processes in a retail company are a continuous cycle split into three core processes: procurement, warehouse operations, and sales. Each core process can be divided into subprocesses. The subprocesses within procurement can include purchasing, replenishment planning, goods receipt, invoice verification, and accounts payable accounting. The subprocesses within sales are goods issue, marketing, billing, and accounts receivable accounting. The link between procurement and sales is the warehouse.

15-79   The main goal of purchasing is to negotiate reasonable prices and price conditions, and conclude contracts. In addition, there are vendor listings that involves doing business with new vendors, and article listings that include new articles in a retail company's assortment.

15-80   Buyers must choose how much merchandise to purchase and at what price based on their negotiations with the vendors.

15-81   It is crucial that a retail company have an efficient data management system.

15-82   A set refers to a group of articles with special retail prices.

15-83   Retailers make the distinction between purchased sets and sales sets.

15-84 Sales sets are purchased as single articles and sold to the consumer as a set. Purchased sets are bought as a set and the articles they contain are then sold to the consumer either as a set or individually. Therefore, retailers often have to recalculate prices, revaluate inventory, and dedicate more resources to maintaining articles.

15-85 A display is purchased as a pack containing several items. These items are then sold to the consumer individually. Displays are primarily used during sales promotions. They are usually allocated to stores by the head office, but not purchased by the stores themselves.

15-86 A pre-pack is a prepackaged selection of variations on one item. A good example of a pre-pack is shoes. The retailer purchases them by the pack and each pack contains a dozen different sizes. The pre-pack is only divided up once it has reached the store.

15-87 Many retailers also handle empties, recyclable, returnable packaging on which a deposit is paid; good organization is essential.

15-88 Managing empties is a difficult process and can prove very expensive, so retailers must plan and organize down to the last detail. Special areas for handling empties and returning deposits must be set up, special storage bins provided, and the empties transported back to the vendor.

15-89 Computer aided retailing systems manage data sets in the retail sector, EAN (International Article Number) codes, and bar codes found on almost every piece of merchandise. These items are being used to simplify the handling of articles.

15-90 Requirements planning is a core process in the retail cycle. It helps retailers refurnish their stock as and when required. Requirements planning is based on sales and stock data, and can be carried out centrally, by the head office, and by the stores themselves. Purchase orders are sent directly to vendors.

15-91 Requirements planning is crucial to retailers. The frequency with which merchandise needs to be replenished is dependent on the type of article.

15-92 Planning the replenishment of stock correctly is a critical success factor for retailers in the apparel industry. They often have to purchase their seasonal stock long before it is due to be sold, sometimes up to a year ahead, but at the same time they must ensure that their stock will be fashionable when it goes on sale.

15-93 Retailers must optimize their system of scheduling purchase orders by determining the most suitable time to order and have their merchandise delivered so that it is on the shelves as and when required.

SOLUTIONS

15-94   Before retail companies accept merchandise from their vendors, they must inspect it as soon as it arrives in their delivery zone. This acceptance of goods represents the first stage of the goods-receipt subprocess. Inspection involves checking each item in the delivery note to see that both the right quantity of goods has been delivered and that the overall quality is acceptable. If the quantity of goods delivered is incorrect, or the quality poor, the delivery, the delivery note, and the purchase order are adjusted.

15-95   The retailer can either return goods or transport packaging.

15-96   The quantity of goods actually received determines how much a retailer will be invoiced for. Therefore, when data are entered during the delivery note, evaluation serves as the foundation for invoice verification. The data are then transferred to the departments responsible for invoice verification and accounts payable accounting.

15-97   The warehouse creates the link between the core processes of procurement and sales.

15-98   Warehouse logistics involve storing and removing merchandise from stock as well as individual functions within the warehouse that range from mapping and managing the warehouse structure in the retail system, transferring stock, transfer postings, and stocktaking to warehouse control.

15-99   The sales process and all its subprocesses refer to all the decisions and negotiations involved in getting goods from the retailer to the consumer. The sales process starts with the goods issue. The retailer needs to supply the goods that a store has ordered in the agreed quantity, quality, and time.

15-100   When a purchase order is received, "picking" occurs when the required goods are removed from storage and prepared for delivery. It is important that all incoming and outgoing goods be recorded to ensure efficient warehouse management. A retail company's warehouses need picking data showing what merchandise is to be delivered and to which stores so delivery routes can be planned.

15-101   Assortment management is an important part of marketing in a retail company. A retail company's assortment is its main control mechanism, especially if it functions with different types of sales channels and if it has stores that vary in size. Retailers must base their choice of assortment on target groups and locations. In addition, they must take into account regional differences in purchasing power and consumer demand.

15-102   The main problems a retail company faces include planning sales, choosing which items from their assortment to offer in a store or distribution chain, and deciding how many articles to include in a merchandise category.

15-103 Once a retail company has defined the basic structure of its assortment, it must choose whether the central warehouse or the regional warehouses are given responsibility for distributing the articles or if the vendor should deliver the articles directly to the store.

15-104 Articles that are listed differ depending on the retail company and the kind of markets serve. This is best illustrated when a discounter offers customers the same merchandise in all their stores while the assortment of department stores differs from region to region.

15-105 Sales prices are determined by sales price calculation, a procedure which considers a number of factors. This is best illustrated by the consumer's price range or the standard market price, the profit margin, and price points.

15-106 Special offers have the effect on assortments of complicating the task of determining prices in the retail sector. Usually, special offers are introduced as part of a sales promotion. In some cases, the price changes affect the sale of other articles (a type of knock-on effect). The goal is to use this knock-on effect to maximize the revenue generated by an assortment.

15-107 Sales promotions in the retail sector are an important aspect of marketing. Promotions held at different intervals have the potential to increase a company's public profile as well as increase sales. To prepare for sales promotions, retailers must plan the quantity of merchandise to be sold, negotiate special price conditions with their vendors, or revaluate their current stock.

15-108 In the retail sector, the subprocesses of sales, goods issue, billing, and accounts receivable accounting all come together at the point of sale (POS). The sales data entered in the various kinds of POS systems can be edited and used as a basis for supporting and, if necessary, adapting purchasing activities and requirements planning.

15-109 When point-of-sale data are evaluated, retailers can gain a detailed insight into sales trends. This information helps them manage purchasing and sales activities for future periods. The objective to use POS data to determine which articles are bestsellers and which articles produce the most revenue. Retailers can get then a better idea of which assortments to offer in the future.

15-110 POS data are used for billing and accounts receivable accounting. The main aspect of billing is the customer's invoice created as soon as the merchandise has been delivered or the customer has collected it. Billing is not pertinent to store-based retailing because the merchandise is issued at the point of sale. At this point, the sales process has gone full-circle, the retail cycle goes back to the beginning, and the purchasing process starts again.

SOLUTIONS

15-111   Modern retailing systems support the collection of all data generated during purchasing processes. This provides retailers with the information they require to make the right decisions on current issues and to work out future strategies.

15-112   PT (Public Transportation is a module for the urban transportation industry that links to the R/3 system. PT, is being written using the ABAP programming language and is fully integrated with the R/3 system. It allows operators to manage transit card accounts, ticket sales, and criminal offenses such as fines and vandalism.

15-113   PT was created specifically for transit providers and offers full subledger functions. It is integrated with the R/3 FI accounts receivable system.

15-114   Sales devices are connected to the R/3 system through an open communications interface, PT-COM. PT supports all types of payment cards.

15-115   PT Baseline is a module providing a flexible fare structure management system that can support multiple fare structures at the same time. It also offers multi-currency capability a materials management system, tailored to the needs of transportation companies, which can be used to monitor stocks of tickets and merchandise, as well as individual salespeople. PT Baseline also offers an interface to R/3's accounts receivable system that includes additional functions for supporting returned unpaid checks and bills as well as an interface to a legal dunning system.

15-116   PT Open Sales is a module used for controlling and settling sales of tickets and other articles. PT Open Sales can handle several distribution channels including kiosks, ticket vending machines, and company and external sales offices. Sales data can be entered manually or fed in from electronic fare payment devices using the PT-COM communications interface. PT Open Sales provides functions for settling commissions and managing vouchers, and the system also supports the sale of merchandise.

15-117   The PT subscriptions function permits management of transit rider accounts. Besides private passes, the system also supports employer-sponsored transit pass programs (transferable and nontransferable passes) and allows operators to settle student fares with school authorities, taking into account parental contributions where appropriate. The system supports all settlement procedures and payment methods including direct debit, cash payment, and bank transfer. Other services such as like accident insurance can also be sold.

15-118   The PT criminal offenses module makes it possible to keep track of fines and offenses, such as vandalism. Besides the civil law dunning procedure,

PT Criminal Offenses also offers the ability to press charges against repeat offenders automatically identified by the system or to prosecute in the event of specific criminal acts. Incidence data and activity reports that are also managed in the system can be entered manually, or data entered into mobile data entry devices by inspectors can be transferred to the system via a standard interface.

15-119 PT-COM covers sales devices (ticket vending machines, ticket printers). POS systems are connected to PT through the PT-COM communications interface. The interface was created with the advice of leading manufacturers of fare payment devices. It allows transit agencies to hook up their devices directly with no extra effort. PT-COM also supports data supply and retrieval (automated operation) for online sales devices. The integrated fault management system enables the current operating status of the devices to be monitored at any time. PT offers a broad span of functions that can be customized to meet user requirements. All the main import and export interfaces are fully transparent and standardized.

15-120 PT's multi-client capability allows deployment of a solution centrally at a computer center for use by several different companies, as with multi-provider transportation networks. Full integration with R/3 means that users can leverage the functions of the R/3 System.

15-121 Industry Business Units (IBUs) make certain that the standard product takes exact account of industry-specific requirements and supports the industry infrastructure.

15-122 SAP's Business Transaction Events are a special type of BAPI. In FI they permit the exact tailoring of processes and flows to customer requirements. This special form of BAPI functions together with SAP standard customizing and allows the integration of customer processes without modifications. This means that R/3 algorithms such as the check for double invoice entry or house bank determination in the payment run can be replaced by the customer's own functions. It is also possible to export credit insurance, credit information, and asset-backed securities. These partner products can be easily linked along the entire process chain.

15-123 Enhanced functions and new components in controlling include activity-based costing that offers greater flexibility and enables customers to resolve business-related questions more efficiently.

15-124 The PM module makes it possible to produce purchase orders for services that are required at periodic intervals. This is used for maintenance plan scheduling, which is consistently linked with the procurement process.

SOLUTIONS

15-125   For services provided in combination with products, R/3 Release 4.0 offers the option of having a service automatically initiated from the sales order so that a service assembly order released.

15-126   The management function in R/3 Release 4.0 supports flexible planning of sampling procedures, administration of sample master records, and storage of results under sample ID numbers.

15-127   Plant maintenance and quality management functions support calibration planning, handling, and testing, as well as decisions on the use of test and measurement equipment.

15-128   In continuous flow production and repetitive manufacturing in particular, line design and production scheduling have a definite impact on efficiency. In order to achieve the best possible results, the production sequence is subdivided into processes and a line-loading schedule is created.

15-129   The line design function allocates components and production resources to individual line sections and handles the assignment and synchronization of the lines.

15-130   In continuous flow production, the sequencing function determines the sequence in which orders are handled and also controls line loading. The point when components are supplied and made available depends on the sequence.

15-131   SAP's Warehouse Management (WM) system facilitates the management and monitoring of large warehouses and distribution centers with a high turnover. WM defines the operational structural elements, plans resources and activities, executes goods movements, and supports decision-making through active monitoring. The module supports both planning and warehouse staff.

15-132   Distribution Resource Planning (DRP) and deployment components support global inventory planning for production plants and distribution centers. DRP defines the best production plan based on the sales plan, while the deployment component distributes existing warehouse stock to distribution centers for the purpose of offering the maximum service level for distribution to retailers.

15-133   The online planning function allows last-minute changes to the distribution plan caused by fluctuations in production or forecast errors.

15-134   Deployment functions enable elimination of shortages or surpluses by using algorithms for fair share or push distribution.

15-135 Transportation is an important element of the value chain. Transportation costs often account for a sizable amount of the overall costs of logistics. Freight costs are automatically calculated and settled with the service provider. Freight rates and agreements can be stored in the system and calculations customized for each service provider or type of transportation. Costs can be settled using the credit memo procedure. This makes the freight costs transparent within the overall process.

15-136 ALE techniques permit design of a distributed, integrated Product Data Management (PDM) scenario. The result of creating components is that product structures can be separately stored. This makes it possible to transfer only released product data, based on its status to the ERP system.

15-137 Release changes and upgrades can be performed on operational data without mutual dependencies.

15-138 ALE technology also ensures tight integration between engineering and production systems while synchronizing the data in both systems.

15-139 This PDM scenario is part of the strategic product architecture of R/3 and thus integral to Business Framework.

15-140 Payment cards are increasingly replacing cash; R/3 Release 4.0 offers functions for handling transactions involving credit, procurement, and customer cards. The information required for this is stored in the system. Whenever an order is generated or merchandise is delivered, validity and authorization checks are performed. The data are relayed down the process chain to the billing document and forwarded to financial accounting. SAP R/3 is also equipped for handling card payments in electronic media such as the Internet. This permits automated entry of orders, product marketing, provision of up-to-date information to customers in the form of electronic catalogues, and electronic payments.

SAP Certification

SAP's certification program leads to a higher level of integration between users and complementary software products. This integration plays a crucial role in SAP's strategy to establish R/3 as the most open business framework. In order to support this initiative, SAP has created an open standard, documented interfaces, and BAPIs for the R/3 system and a corresponding certification program.

SAP's Complementary Software Program

Interoperability between and within enterprises provides excellent flexibility and independence for users. Interoperability is designated as interplay between systems and applications of the same or different vendors. This interplay is crucial to SAP's concepts and actions in its complementary software program.

When standards and norms are implemented for interfaces, services, and exchange formats for SAP application systems, it becomes simpler flexibly to custom design how information is managed. In fact, open interfaces assure that communication are maintained between SAP systems and other vendor solutions.

During review of the questions in this chapter, pay special attention to the various facets that make the complementary software program a viable resource for many developers and provide a crucial element to SAP's Business Framework.

Complementary Software Program Information

SAP's Complementary Software Program (CSP) promotes and supports integration of third-party software with the R/3 system through standard interfaces.

CSP is crucial in SAP's strategy to establish R/3 as the most open business framework. SAP and its partners can provide a comprehensive multi-industry business infrastructure to support specific business processes. There is a high level of integration for various complementary software products that increases the scope and the value of R/3 implementation.

CSP offers dedicated resources to identify and recruit complementary software partners, promote integration projects, and offer concentrated partner management and support. Proven, ready-to-use interfaces between the R/3 system and complementary partner products assist in reducing implementation time and costs and safeguarding existing software investments. CSP partners benefit from increasingly efficient partner management, improved information exchange, and efficient coordination of joint business and marketing activities.

CSP Program and Third-Party Software Vendors

The Complementary Software Program supports independent third party software vendors with products that are interfaced with the R/3 System through one of SAP's standard certifiable interfaces or BAPIs (Business Application Programming Interfaces). It may also be interfaced with a standard partner interface that uses one of several SAP-endorsed interoperability methods.

However, SAP does not endorse companies or their products. The Complementary Software Program ensures the interfaces through business and technical evaluation of the partner's interfaces.

When you work with R/3 Compatible Component Partners, the Complementary Software Program ensures that partners and their integration scenarios are judged by SAP from both a business and technical point of view. R/3 Compatible Component Partners must also be able to provide customer reference sites which are productively using the integration method. A formal technical interface test is not executed. When dealing with Independent Software Vendors, these have neither a formal agreement with SAP nor do they provide an SAP-recognized interface.

Complementary Software Program

SAP developed the complementary software program to provide dedicated support for partners in business, sales, and marketing activities. The CSP team provides support to Certification Partners in various areas, including SAP's internal partner database.

Certification Partners are maintained in SAP's complementary software web pages where SAP has information on companies, contact parties, interface and partners products.

Partners who successfully complete the formal interface certification process receive SAP's Certified Partner Logo. This is globally accepted and made available for marketing purposes such as brochures and advertisements. Partners must restrict the logo's use to brochures and public relations activities specifically dealing with the certified interface. The logo cannot be used in headers of letters or for products not involved in the certification evaluation.

Certification partners can participate in customer events including regional SAPPHIRE events or local sales events like industry-specific or application-specific information days. SAP allows several Certification Partners who have especially interesting products and comprehensive service offerings to demonstrate their products at the SAP Partner Academy or at sales workshops.

SAP provides a number of certifiable interfaces to integrate to the following third party software products, including:

- ALE Converters (XA-ALE)
- Bar code readers (MM-MOB, PP-PDC)
- Computer-aided design software, electronic catalogs (PP-CAD)
- Database backup tools for Oracle databases (BC-BRI)
- Document management systems (PP-DMS, SAP ArchiveLink)
- EDI subsystems (XA-EDI)
- Export invoices (SD-EXP)
- Fax and e-mail software (SAPconnect)
- Financials/accounts receivable interface (FI-AR)
- Generic Security Service (XA-GSS)
- Geographical information systems (PP-GIS)
- Hand-held devices
- Radio-frequency input devices (MM-MOB)
- Imaging, optical archives (SAP ArchiveLink)
- Laboratory information management systems
- Quality inspection systems (QM-IDI)
- Production optimization schedulers (PP-POI)
- Mobile data recording (MM-MOB)
- Modeling software
- Data modeling software (Repository API)
- Point-of-sales system (XA-POS)
- Process control systems
- Shop floor control systems (PI-PCS)
- Product data management software (PP-EC)
- Production order systems (PP-PDC, channel 2)
- Sales and use tax systems (XA-TAX)
- Sales force automation systems (SD-SFA)
- System management systems (XA-SMS)
- Time and attendance systems (PP-PDC), channel, distribution and transportation planning systems (SD-TPS)
- Treasury management online data feed (TR-TM)
- Warehouse control systems (WM-LSR)
- Weighing instruments (MM-MOB).

Software vendors are not restricted to creating interfaces in those areas where SAP has available certifiable interfaces. SAP promotes R/3 is open nature and support through a variety of integration scenarios. SAP also offers interoperability techniques including Object Linking and Embedding (OLE), Remote Function Call (RFC), Intermediate Documents (IDocs), SAP Automation (via SAP-GUI interface), and BAPIs, to support integration with the R/3 system.

Product Releases

SAP certification is only valid for certain software versions. Certification confirms that the integration between a certain release of the complementary product and the R/3 System has been correctly tested and functions correctly. The certification is valid for the tested release combination of the respective products.

Certified release combination is printed on the certificate to make certain that customers receive precise information about tested interfaces.

Future partner product releases or changes to SAP's certified interfaces and BAPIs require recertification. Normally, recertification involves minimal effort and cost and makes certain to maintain the long-term quality and compatibility of the interfaces. Recertification services are offered at half the standard flat-rate certification fee.

SAP first requires further information about a company and product. Software vendors can then contact the alliance management team in their local SAP subsidiary to acquire the Partner Profile Form. This form can be sent directly to the regional Complementary Software Program team for further processing.

When the form is received, the organization and product are automatically included in SAP's Complementary Software Partner Database, then used by SAP's global sales, consulting and marketing organizations. This information forms the foundation for assisting the CSP team; the certification program is the best partnership opportunity to satisfy an organization's needs when certification interfaces or BAPIs are appropriate. SAP can forward to the vendor the relevant certification agreement and the certification interface or BAPI documentation.

When the software vendor has signed the agreement, an appointment is made with the regional ICC for the consultancy days included as part of the certification agreement. Technical consulting services are offered to help answer any open questions concerning the interface/BAPI or certification test, and effectively accelerate the certification process. When the vendor has completed the development of the interface, actual certification can take place at one of the regional ICCs. There is a technical evaluation as part of the SAP AG predefined test program. When this test is successfully completed, the vendor is awarded a certificate and a copy of the certification logo for marketing purposes.

The certification procedure tests the quality of the partner's interface to the R/3 system, but not the partner's product itself. The partner is responsible for the quality of the software.

The length of time involved in the certification process depends on the scope of the interface, the software partner's resources and the time schedule for interface development.

Certification Course Information

SAP's certification program permits third-party vendors to have their interface certified by SAP. Certification indicates that SAP's regional Integration and Certification Centers (ICCs) have formally evaluated and tested the quality of a software vendor's interface and data exchange with the R/3 system. The ICCs evaluate only the connection between the complementary product's interface and SAP's interface.

Ready-to-Use Interfaces

Ready-to-use interfaces allow customers to purchase third-party software knowing that the certified interface to SAP software has been tested and proven. It is possible to gain a quality interface that permits plug-and-play implementation.

There are significant advantages to ready-to-use, standard interfaces, including avoiding individual customer projects or lengthy development time and implementation costs. SAP's certifiable interfaces and BAPIs are standards and open for use by all third-party vendors to facilitate usage by partners.

R/3 release-stable interfaces and BAPIs reduce costly updates. Stress is placed on avoiding interface changes with new R/3 releases. When interface enhancements are required, they are completely documented and the changes are communicated to partners with certified interfaces. The certification program confirms SAP's dedication and permits third-party vendors to update their certified interfaces to be compatible with new releases. As a result, customer investments in existing software and interfaces are protected.

Interfaces certified by SAP are completely documented and delivered with all standard R/3 installations. The SAP certification program is a quality guarantee and customers specifically request SAP certification or refer to our certified software partner list prior to selecting a software vendor.

Interface Changes

Try to avoid interface changes with new R/3 releases. Should interface enhancements become necessary, they must be completely documented and partners would gain early notification of the pertinent changes.

Alliance Management

The CSP is part of SAP's Alliance Management Program. Alliance Management supports SAP partners by dealing with hardware, technology, and consulting partners for R/3 solution providers and complementary software partners.

CSP offers dedicated teams of experienced managers who concentrate on the specific needs of the complementary software partners. Regional CSP teams work in America, Europe, Asia and Japan and are supported by the general Alliance Managers or by dedicated CSP Managers in local SAP subsidiaries. Regional CSP managers concentrate on specific focus industries and interface situations.

These CSP teams work with customers and analysts as well as internal SAP departments that involve SAP's Product Management, Industry Centers of Expertise (ICOE's), consulting and marketing, integration of industry-specific concepts; application-specific and customer-specific needs are also woven into the program.

CSP partners are independent third-party software vendors with products that are interfaced with the R/3 system. They meet criteria that pertain to partners who need to provide a software product that improves R/3's core business processes, and adds value to the R/3 solution. The software product must be owned and sold by the software vendor, whereas software product partners interoperate with the R/3 system via a standard interface that uses SAP-supported enabling technologies or BAPIs.

Products may also have a standard partner interface that employs one of several SAP-endorsed interoperability methods. In addition, component partners provide standard, proven interfaces. Certification partners produce interfaces that have been formally tested as part of SAP's certification program. Development partners work in combination with SAP development to offer joint software solutions or interfaces.

Alliance Partners

Third party software vendors can contact the alliance management team in your local SAP subsidiary to acquire the Partner Profile Form.

Partner Logos are a primary element of our packages and are available to CSP members to be used in all joint marketing and sales activities. They give your software product a unique image, giving you that all-important head start in the marketplace. The Internet has become an important tool for any convincing marketing strategy. SAP gives you the option of presenting your products on your own web page on SAP's popular Internet site. They give you an Internet page where you can list product information and important contact addresses for prospects. In addition, you can add your company logo to the page to make it even more unique. Should you wish present your software and its integration with the R/3 System in more detail, they will also create a link to your own product page or home page. Every CSP partner gets an individual web page.

NOTE

International Demonstration and Education System (IDES) is a complete pre-installed R/3 System that includes data for core business processes. The IDES System was created for testing, demonstration, and training purposes. It can be enhanced by partner-specific demonstration examples. IDES can be ordered by partners at no cost once they have acquired an R/3 Test and Demo License, or have become an R/3 customer.

PartnerNet Packages

Providing information electronically or on paper is a crucial element of CSP PartnerNet packages. They offer you technical reports, presentations, and the SAP Annual Report. You also gain a free subscription to SAP Company's magazine. As a user of CSP PartnerNet packages, you also get access to SAPNet, SAP's multimedia information system.

In order to satisfy user needs, SAP integrates desktop software into several R/3 applications. Desktop integration allows end users to execute their tasks in an integrated, consistent environment.

Costs and Courses

Certification costs depend on the size and scope of the interface being certified. The functions, scope and customer base of the complementary product are not important. The size of the company applying for certification has no influence on certification costs. The certification fee is usually between $10,000 and $20,000.

Certification courses deal with the formal technical evaluation of the partners' interfaces as well as technical consulting with respect to the relevant interface or BAPIs, interoperability techniques, remote access to an R/3 system, receipt of the certification partner logo for marketing purposes, and inclusion in both SAP's Partner Database and complementary software web pages.

Individual solutions created at a customer site can be certified but only if the developed interface that integrates with the R/3 system is in an area in which SAP already offers a corresponding certification interface or BAPI.

Object Technology

Object technology is an important part of the R/3 system when dealing with integration between R/3 applications, external systems, and desktop applications. Business data and functions are encapsulated in objects, whereas ALE messages can also be sent through an EDI subsystem to EDI-capable application. Objects can be defined based on object types and managed in the business object repository. When dealing with the enterprise data model, business objects are derived by assigning data models. Each data model defines the internal structure of a business object. Business objects, technical objects like texts, and graphics can be stored in the business object repository.

SAP's object model is geared to the COM and CORBA standards (OMG). An RFC dynamic invocation interface permits access to attributes and methods of the objects types defined in the business object repository. An OLE Automation server based on this RFC interface permits PC applications to use business objects much as other desktop objects do. The objects have a standard interface to SAP business workflow. R/3 will make it possible to connect external systems using standard object interfaces like OLE Automation or CORBA to establish links.

Open Application Group

The Open Applications Group (OAG) was founded by major software vendors with the goal of speedily defining a standard interface for linking different applications within and outside of enterprises. The specifications emerging from this group call for communication based on Business Object Documents will allow applications from different vendors to speak with one another.

NOTE

SAP supports many corporate routines with assistance from appropriate business objects and business function libraries.

SAP Automation

SAP Automation concentrates on offering tools and utilities to enable external programs to read and write to visible fields in the SAPGUI. Partners can use communication standards like SQL or ODBC to access the tables of relational database systems used by SAP.

When work with desktop integration is concerned, both SAP users and vendors benefit from R/3 function modules, calling them from the outside to link PC applications such as office programs and the R/3 system. They can also be called in the opposite direction from R/3 to the PC software. Remote Function Calls (RFCs) or Object Linking and Embedding (OLE) must be used.

Application Link Enabling

ALE permits loosely coupled distributed applications and integrated business processes across multiple systems. It will be easy to integrate special-purpose subsystems, as for CAD or plant-data capture. Desktop programs can be linked, in the same way as word processors or spreadsheets, to R/3 applications. In addition, workflow techniques and electronic mail effectively support automation and control of cross-system work routines.

SAP provides its ALE technology for distributed application systems. ALE makes possible secure communication for business data transmitted between technically independent systems. In a coordinated architecture, ALE provides distribution models and technologies for application linking as well as tools for the design and operation of distributed applications. Frequently requested distribution situations are configured as distribution models in R/3, providing a proven business foundation for customized solutions.

ALE supports business processes for the distribution of accounting and logistics, sales/invoicing and shipping, local and central profitability analyses, as well as central and local sales and operation planning (SOP). It combines autonomous distributed application systems through a configurable distribution model, ensuring exchange of business information messages, updates of master data, and the coordination of control information.

ALE technology is founded on a business-event-controlled, time-driven exchange of business information messages. Synchronous and asynchronous communication mechanisms (RFCs) provide need-driven integration of applications. It is no longer necessary to connect through a central database.

The ALE architecture is composed of application, communication services, and distribution services. This layer supports the system or release-based conversion of message contents, where R/2 and external applications can also be integrated.

External Interfaces

External interfaces let you link in supplemental solutions of other vendors. These interfaces are commonly referred to as Business APIs. SAP will make certain that they provide stability and support for them. The methods on which the individual interfaces are based encompass OLE Automation and Remote Function Call (RFC), Electronic Data Interchange (EDI), and Intermediate Documents (IDocs). You will see a large amount of interplay for business applications as well as their supplementary components. SAP practices quality control by executing a certification program for the application specific interfaces.

Standards and Open Interfaces

SAP employs standards and open interfaces. The most important one involves Object Linking and Embedding (OLE) which is an industry standard incorporated into R/3 system. You will also find Remote Function Call (RFC) as well as SAP's open programming interface.

NOTE

The SAP Intelligent Terminal will allow easy linking of supplemental software to SAP business processes via the SAP-GUI.

Integrating with Microsoft Excel

You may wish to integrate Microsoft Excel into the XXL List Viewer for more flexible reporting. You can use MS Excel for costing, project planning, and consolidation. Microsoft Work is available in the Human Resources module as well as for users of the ABAP/4 Development Workbench to compose online documentation. In addition, mobile users can benefit from Microsoft Access to enter travel expenses. SAP-EIS integrates both Word and Excel. There are still other desktop programs such as applicant administration and calendar management that is integrated by R/3.

Summary

In this chapter we have examined SAP's Complementary Software Program. We have seen how CSP plays an important role in SAP's business framework and the benefits obtained by complementary software partners. Certification, marketing, and PartnerNet packages benefits and how a software company can be part of CSP were discussed.

Chapter 17 looks at the differences between R/3 Release 4.0 and R/3 Release 3.x and illustrates the improvements present in the new version of R/3.

16-1   What does the certification program support?

16-2   What is the benefit of maintaining a level of certification?

16-3   Explain the significance of achieving SAP certification.

16-4   What does the SAP certification program allow third-party vendors to do?

16-5   What does certification mean, and what are ICCs?

16-6   What does certification guarantee?

16-7   Describe some benefits of obtaining certification.

16-8   What are ready-to-use interfaces?

16-9   Explain how it is possible to benefit from reduced implementation time and costs.

16-10   Explain the process of achieving multi-vendor integration.

16-11   What are "stable interfaces?"

16-12   What are safeguard investments?

16-13   Explain how certification partners can benefit from certification.

16-14   Explain the level of integration with SAP standard interfaces.

16-15   What is a renowned program and SAP-acknowledged interface?

16-16   Explain SAP's philosophy of dedicated business, marketing and sales support and what this means to the certification process.

16-17   Describe SAP's connection with release-stable interfaces.

16-18   Describe in detail how access is granted to an R/3 system for partners.

16-19   Describe SAP's sales and marketing support for certification partners.

16-20   How do vendors benefit as SAP certified software partners?

16-21   Describe the inclusion of partner and product profiles in SAP's Web pages.

16-22   What is a dedicated certification partner logo and what is involved achieving it?

16-23   Specify where the partner logo has restricted use.

16-24   Explain how certification partners have the opportunity of participating at customer events.

16-25   What is the procedure for dealing with product demonstration for SAP sales and consulting organizations?

16-26   What are PartnerNet packages?

16-27   Does SAP sells its partners' certified interfaces? If so, tell why, if not, specify why not.

16-28   How does SAP support and promote its certification partners?

16-29   What kinds of information are provided to customers?

16-30   Who performs the coordination of partner software sales and software delivery?

16-31   Describe which interfaces SAP certifies.

16-32   Are there other interface opportunities besides certification interfaces?

16-33   Who does SAP automation focus on?

16-34   Explain the concept of desktop integration.

KEY CONCEPT

The complementary software program offers a specific type of partnership for specific support for "R/3-Compatible component partners." These partners offer a software product that integrates with the R/3 system via a standard interface through SAP-endorsed interoperability technology. The complementary software program does not certify these interfaces, but does evaluate partners and their integration scenarios from both business and technical perspectives.

16-35   What must R/3-compatible component partners provide?

16-36   Explain whether certification is only valid for specific software versions.

16-37   Where is the certification release combination printed?

KEY CONCEPT

SAP is dedicated to making certain to provide upward-compatibility of its interfaces. Emphasis is placed on avoiding changes to certification interfaces and BAPIs with new R/3 releases. As a result, certification is valid for subsequent R/3 releases, as long as change has taken place to SAP's interface or the partner software.

16-38   Do new partner product releases or changes to SAP's certified interfaces require recertification?

16-39   With reference to the certification process, explain how an organization should proceed if it wishes to participate in SAP's certification program.

16-40   What happens when the software vendor has signed the appropriate certification agreement?

16-41   What types of services are offered to answer questions?

16-42   What step must the interface go through?

16-43   Who specifically certifies the partner's product, and/or about the partner's interface?

16-44   Who is responsible for the quality of the software?

16-45   How much time is required for the certification procedure?

16-46   When do software vendors receive the appropriate interface documentation?

16-47   When can technical consulting days be reserved?

16-48   How much notice do the ICCs request for an appointment for the certification evaluation?

16-49   How much does certification cost and what factors change the costs involved?

16-50   What do the courses generally offer?

16-51   Can an individual solution developed at a customer's site can be certified.

16-52   Is certification a possibility for a customer-individual interface for R/3?

16-53   What exactly is the SAP Complementary Software Program (CSP)?

16-54   How does the CSP play a critical role in an open business framework?

16-55   How well are CS products integrated?

16-56   What kind of resources does the CSP provide?

16-57   How do Complementary Software Partners benefit?

16-58   Explain the organization of the CSP and how it relates to SAP's Alliance Management Program?

16-59   What level of management experience can be expected for the CSP?

16-60   Explain team collaboration in the CSP.

16-61   Explain exactly who is a complementary software partner.

16-62   Explain specifically the types of complementary software partners supported by the program.

16-63   Explain if SAP and the CSP support software companies and their products.

16-64   Explain how certification plays an important role achieving the best software solution.

16-65 How does the CSP deal with R/3-compatible component partners?

16-66 Explain the type of support that the CSP provides its partners.

16-67 Who needs to apply for an ABAP/4 Development Workbench license?

16-68 What does the certification package offer?

16-69 What do marketing packages provide?

16-70 Describe the methods for gaining access to the R/3 system.

16-71 Who is responsible for installing the software and customizing a system?

16-72 What is IDES?

16-73 What factors determine the best access method?

16-74 How can a software company apply be included in the CSP?

16-75 What can third-party software vendors do if they would like to join SAP's CSP?

16-76 Explain SAP's CSP PartnerNet packages.

16-77 How important are partner logos to the PartnerNet packages?

16-78 Describe the information and training for CSP partners.

16-79 What does SAPNet offer?

16-80 Define EDI standards.

16-81 What options does ALE permit?

16-82 Describe how ALE can benefit loose coupling of distributed applications.

16-83 What common event happens during both the setup and operational phases of distributed application systems?

16-84 Explain what benefits synchronous and asynchronous communication methods offer.

16-85 Explain what the ALE architecture makes up.

16-86 Explain how integrating desktop applications can improve the working environment with R/3.

16-87 Define situations that illustrate desktop integration.

16-88 How do standards and open interfaces come into play?

16-89 What is a desktop development kit?

16-90   What is SAP's Intelligent Terminal?

16-91   Explain open applications integration.

16-92   What are Business APIs?

16-93   What do external interfaces do?

16-94   Explain the significance of business objects.

16-95   How are objects defined?

16-1 The certification program supports complementary software partners who need to integrate their products with the R/3 system and have their interface formally certified by SAP. It promotes close integration of a wide range of partner software products to increase the scope and the value of R/3 implementation.

16-2 It is possible effectively to reduce implementation time and costs and safeguard existing implementations.

16-3 Since customers need a higher level of integration between distributed systems and different software vendor products through a standard interface, knowledge can play a critical role in making an SAP implementation proceed as smoothly as possible. Organizations usually deal with individual integration solutions that can be very time-consuming to develop and implement and very costly to maintain. This situation made SAP create a certification program for its business interfaces and BAPIs.

16-4 The certification program allows third-party vendors to have their interfaces certified by SAP.

16-5 Certification means that SAP's regional Integration and Certification Centers (ICCs) have formally evaluated and tested the quality of a software vendor's interface and the data exchange with the R/3 system. The ICCs only evaluate the connection between the complementary product's interface and SAP's interface. SAP does not assess the function or quality of the third-party application itself.

16-6 Certification is a guarantee of obtaining a technically verified link to the R/3 system. It promises a stable and ready-to-use interface between the partner product and the R/3 System.

16-7 The certification program offers several benefits, including a list of certified interfaces; customers can access the most recent list of SAP certified interfaces, certified partners, and product information on SAP's complementary software Web pages.

16-8 Ready-to-use interfaces can be purchased by customers for third-party software, with the knowledge that the certified interface to SAP software has been tested and proven by one of SAP's ICCs. A ready-to-use certified interface is a quality interface that permits plug-and-play implementation.

16-9 Ready-to-use, standard interfaces. are beneficial because users avoid having to construct individual customer projects or face lengthy development time and implementation costs.

SOLUTIONS

16-10   SAP's certifiable interfaces and BAPIs standards are open for use by all third-party vendors to facilitate widespread use by partners.

16-11   R/3 release-stable interfaces and BAPIs reduce costly updates. Emphasis is placed on avoiding interface changes with new R/3 releases. When interface enhancements are necessary, they are completely documented and the changes are communicated to partners with certified interfaces.

16-12   Safeguard investments are those in complementary products guaranteed to interface reliably with SAP software. The certification program affirms SAP's dedication and allows third-party vendors to update their certified interfaces so they are compatible with new releases. That way, customer investments in existing software and the interface itself are both safeguarded.

16-13   Certification partners can benefit from a wide range of technical advantages and marketing support when their interface is certified by SAP.

16-14   SAP's certifiable interfaces are standard interfaces; completely documented and delivered with all standard R/3 installations.

16-15   The SAP certification program is well established in the market and recognized as a quality guarantee by its customers. As a result, customers often specifically request SAP certification or refer to the certified software partner list before choosing a software vendor.

16-16   Certification partners can benefit from the support offered by the complementary software program. The program was created to offer dedicated resources for more efficient partner management, improved information exchange, and efficient coordination of joint business and marketing activities.

16-17   An emphasis is placed on avoiding interface changes with new R/3 releases. Should interface enhancements be necessary, they are completely documented and partners gain early notification of the pertinent changes.

16-18   Partners who have signed the certification contract may apply for remote access to an R/3 system to support development and testing of their interface. Partners can also obtain an R/3 installation for a reduced fee or IDES for demonstration purposes.

16-19   SAP has created the complementary software program (Figure 16.1) to offer dedicated support to partners in business, sales, and marketing activities. The CSP team provides support to certification partners in areas including SAP's internal partner database.

FIGURE 16.1
CSP

Certification/Validation
Process

Software Vendor
Contacts

Complementary
Software
Partner

CSP Membership

Software Vendor Information

16-20 As SAP-certified software partners, vendors benefit from having an SAP-acknowledged interface. They are automatically included in SAP's partner database, which is used by SAP worldwide sales, marketing, and consulting organizations.

16-21 Certification partners are maintained in SAP's complementary software Web pages where SAP has information about companies, contact people, interfaces and partners' products.

16-22 Partners who have successfully completed the formal interface certification process receive SAP's certified partner logo. This logo is recognized worldwide and is made available to certified partners for marketing purposes such as brochures, advertisements.

16-23 Partners must restrict the logo's use to brochures and public relations activities specifically dealing with certified interfaces. The logo cannot be used in headers on letters or for products not involved in the certification evaluation. Places for logo use include: public relations support for press

SO\LUTIONS

releases or product articles, and participation at SAP customer events and in trade fairs.

16-24 Certification partners have the opportunity to participate in customer events including regional SAPPHIRE events or local sales events like industry-specific or application-specific information days.

16-25 SAP permits a few certification partners with especially interesting products and comprehensive service offerings to demonstrate their products at the SAP partner academy or at sales workshops.

16-26 PartnerNet packages exist in the complementary software folder.

16-27 SAP does not currently sell the partners' certified interfaces. SAP has strategic partnerships with a restricted number of development partners who give SAP the right to sell their products.

16-28 SAP supports and promotes certification partners on a neutral basis.

16-29 Customers are provided with partner information that includes sales contacts and product profiles of all available certification partners for interfaces or BAPIs.

16-30 The coordination of partner software sales and software delivery is performed by the partner, independently from SAP.

16-31 SAP offers several certifiable interfaces to integrate to the following third-party software products. The specific interfaces involve ALE converters (XA-ALE), Bar code readers (MM-MOB, PP-PDC), computer-aided design software, electronic catalogs (PP-CAD), database backup tools for Oracle databases (BC-BRI), document management systems (PP-DMS, SAP ArchiveLink), EDI subsystems (XA-EDI), export invoices (SD-EXP), fax and e-mail software (SAPconnect), a financials/accounts receivable interface (FI-AR), generic security service (XA-GSS), geographical information systems (PP-GIS), hand-held devices, radio-frequency input devices (MM-MOB), imaging, optical archives (SAP ArchiveLink), laboratory information management systems, quality inspection systems (QM-IDI), production optimization schedulers (PP-POI), mobile data recording (MM-MOB), modeling software, data modeling (Repository API), point-of-sales (XA-POS), process control systems, shop floor control systems (PI-PCS), product data management software (PP-EC), production orders (PP-PDC, channel 2), sales and use tax (XA-TAX), sales force automation (SD-SFA), system management systems (XA-SMS), time and attendance systems (PP-PDC), channel, distribution and transportation planning systems (SD-TPS), treasury management online data feed (TR-TM), warehouse control systems (WM-LSR), and weighing instruments (MM-MOB).

FIGURE 16.2
Automation

16-32 SAP provides several interface opportunities. Software vendors are not restricted to creating interfaces in those areas where SAP has available certifiable interfaces. SAP promotes R/3 open nature and support through a variety of integration scenarios. SAP provides several interoperability techniques including Object Linking and Embedding (OLE), Remote Function Call (RFC), Intermediate Documents (IDocs), SAP Automation (via the SAPGUI interface), and BAPIs, to support integration with the R/3 system.

16-33 SAP automation focuses on providers of tools and utilities and enables external programs to read and write to visible fields in the SAPGUI. Partners can use communication standards like SQL or ODBC to access the tables of relational database systems used by SAP.

16-34 When dealing with desktop integration, both SAP users and vendors benefit from R/3 function modules calling them from the outside to link PC applications such as office programs and the R/3 system. They can also be called in the opposite direction from R/3 to the PC software. This is done with RFCs or OLE.

16-35 R/3 compatible component partners must be in a position to provide customer reference sites which are productively using the integration scenario.

16-36 Certification is only valid for certain software versions. Certification confirms that the integration between a certain release of the complementary product and the R/3 system has been successfully tested and functions correctly. The certification is valid for the tested release combination of the respective products.

16-37 The certified release combination is printed on the certificate to make certain that customers receive precise information about tested interfaces.

16-38 Yes, new partner product releases or changes to SAP's certified interfaces and BAPIs require recertification. Usually, recertification involves minimal effort and cost. It assures the long-term quality and compatibility of the interfaces. Recertification services are offered at 50 percent of the standard flat-rate certification fee.

16-39 The organization must first provide SAP with further information about the company and its product. Software vendors can then contact the alliance management team in their local SAP subsidiary to acquire the partner profile form. SAP's partner profile form can also be sent directly to the regional complementary software program team for further processing. When the form is received, the company and product will be automatically included in SAP's complementary software partner database. The information is then used by SAP's global sales, consulting and marketing organizations. It forms the foundation for assisting the CSP team in understanding that the certification program is the best partnership opportunity to meet an organization's needs and which certification interfaces or BAPIs are appropriate. SAP can then forward to the vendor the relevant certification agreement and the certification interface or BAPI documentation.

16-40 A software vendor who signed the agreement can make an appointment with the regional ICC for the consultancy days included as part of the certification agreement.

16-41 Technical consulting services are offered to help answer any open questions concerning the interface/BAPI or certification test, and effectively accelerate the certification process. When the vendor has completed the development of the interface, actual certification can take place at one of the regional ICCs.

16-42 The interface undergoes a technical evaluation as part of an SAP AG predefined test program. When this test is successfully completed, the vendor is awarded a certificate and a copy of the certification logo for marketing purposes.

16-43 The certification procedure tests the quality of the partner's interface to the R/3 system, but not the partner's product itself. Users of a certified interface know they are receiving a tested and proven interface between the partner product and the R/3 system to allow plug-and-play integration.

SOLUTIONS

16-44 The partner is responsible for the quality of the software.

16-45 The length of time involved in the certification process depends on the scope of the interface in question. The most important aspect involves the software partners' resources and the time schedule for interface development.

16-46 Software vendors receive the appropriate interface documentation directly after having sent the CSP team a completed partner profile form.

16-47 Technical consulting days can be reserved as soon as SAP has received a signed certification agreement from the vendor.

16-48 The ICCs request two weeks' notice for an appointment for the certification evaluation.

16-49 Certification costs depend on the size and scope of the interface being certified. The function, scope and customer base of the complementary product are not important. As a result, the size of the company applying for certification has no influence on certification costs. The certification fee is usually between $10,000 and $20,000.

16-50 Certification courses cover the formal technical evaluation of the partner's interface as well as technical consulting with respect to the relevant interface or BAPIs, and interoperability techniques, remote access to an R/3 system, receipt of a certification partner logo for marketing purposes, and inclusion in both SAP's partner database and complementary software Web pages.

16-51 Yes, an individual solution developed at a customer site can be certified, but only if the developed interface that integrates with the R/3 system is in an area in which SAP already offers a corresponding certification interface or BAPI.

16-52 No, certification is not possible for a customer-individual interface to the R/3.

16-53 SAP's Complementary Software Program (CSP) has as (Figure 16.3) a goal the promotion and support of seamless integration of third-party software with the R/3 system through standard interfaces.

16-54 The CSP plays a critical role in SAP's strategy for establishing R/3 as the most open Business Framework in the software industry. Both SAP and its partners can offer a complete, multi-industry business infrastructure to support the specific business processes.

16-55 There is a very high level of integration for a wide variety of complementary software products that increases the scope and the value of an R/3 implementation.

SOLUTIONS

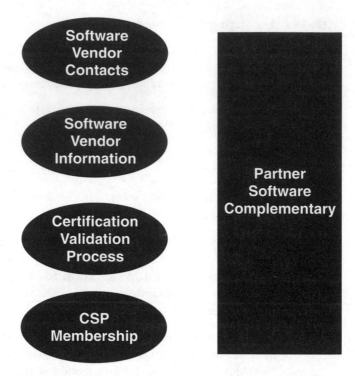

FIGURE 16.3
CSP Overview

16-56   The CSP provides dedicated resources to identify and recruit complementary software partners, promote integration projects, and offer concentrated partner management and support. Benefits are accrued from several proven, ready-to-use interfaces between the R/3 system (Figure 16.4) and complementary partner products. This assists in reducing implementation time and costs, and safeguarding existing software investments.

16-57   Complementary software partners benefit from increasingly efficient partner management, improved information exchange, and efficient coordination of joint business and marketing activities.

16-58   The CSP is part of SAP's Alliance Management Program. Alliance management supports SAP partners, dealing with everything, including hardware, technology, and consulting partners for R/3 solution providers and complementary software partners.

16-59   The CSP has dedicated teams of experienced managers to focus on the specific needs of the complementary software partners. Regional CSP teams have been initiated in the Americas, Europe, Asia and Japan and are supported by the general alliance managers or by dedicated CSP managers in local SAP subsidiaries. Regional CSP managers focus on specific focus industries and interface scenarios.

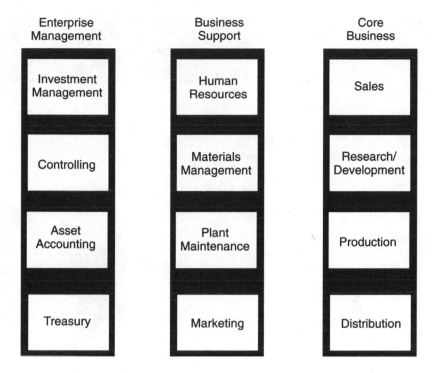

FIGURE 16.4
R/3 System

16-60 The CSP teams work closely with customers, analysts, and internal SAP departments including SAP's Product Management, Industry Centers of Expertise (ICOE's), consulting and marketing, and integration of industry-specific concepts. Application-specific and customer-specific needs are also woven into the program.

16-61 Complementary Software Partners are independent third-party software vendors with products that are interfaced with the R/3 system. They satisfy criteria relating to partners who must offer a software product that improves R/3's core business processes and adds value to the R/3 solution. The software product must be owned and sold by the software vendor, while software product partners interoperate with the R/3 system through a standard interface that uses one of the wide variety of SAP-supported enabling technologies or BAPIs.

16-62 The CSP supports independent third-party software vendors with products that are interfaced with the R/3 system through one of SAP's standard certifiable interfaces or BAPIs It may have a standard partner interface (Figure 16.5) that uses one of several SAP-endorsed interoperability methods.

SOLUTIONS

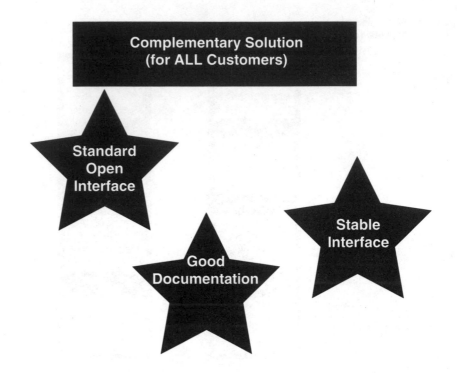

FIGURE 16.5
Standard Solutions

16-63 SAP does not endorse companies or their products. The CSP ensures the interfaces through business and technical evaluation of the partners' interfaces.

16-64 Component partners must offer standard, proven interfaces. Certification partners provide interfaces that have been formally tested as part of SAP's certification program. Development partners work in close collaboration with SAP development to offer joint software solutions or interfaces.

16-65 When dealing with R/3-Compatible Component Partners, the CSP makes certain that partners and their integration scenarios are judged by SAP from both business and technical points of view. R/3-Compatible Component Partners must also be able to provide customer reference sites which are productively using the integration method. A formal technical interface test is not executed. Independent software vendors have no formal agreement with SAP nor do they provide an SAP-recognized interface.

16-66 Several PartnerNet packages are offered to support our partners with development, certification, and marketing of their interfaces. Technical consulting services and access to an R/3 system can be provided to support the development and testing phases of partner interfaces.

FIGURE 16.6
Certification

16-67 Partners who want to develop interfaces or R/3 enhancements in ABAP/4 need to apply for an ABAP/4 Development Workbench license. A development package is planned to provide BAPI documentation, development tips, and early notification on BAPI updates.

16-68 The certification package offers concentrated support for partners who wish to connect with one of SAP's certification interfaces or BAPIs and have data exchange formally certified by SAP. Partners gain a certification contract and interface documentation, avail themselves of technical consulting and can have their interface certified. Partners whose interfaces have successfully passed the certification procedure can use the certification partner logo.

16-69 Marketing packages provide complementary software partners with concentrated sales and marketing support in areas dealing with partner management, provision of partner logo/stamps, and partner training as well as joint marketing activities including public relations, participation in SAP events, or partner entry in SAP's partner database and complementary software Web pages.

16-70 SAP provides the access to R/3 software through remote access (Figure 16.7) through a SAPGUI Kit. The SAPGUI kit is a CD-ROM that con-

SOLUTIONS

tains the necessary SAP gateway, the RFC libraries, and other software to permit a login to a remote R/3 system for test purposes. There is also gain access through the R/3 test and demo license. This license allows complementary software partners to install an R/3 system at their own local sites for a limited fee.

FIGURE 16.7
Remote Access

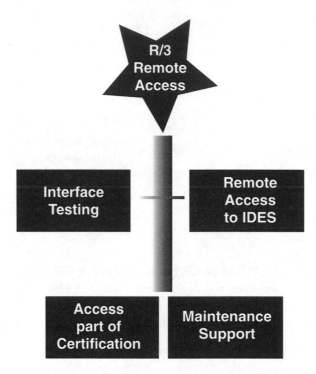

16-71 The partner is responsible for installing the software and customizing the system. The R/3 test and demo license permits demos of the integration of the partner's product with R/3, testing of the interfaces, and training of the partner's employees.

16-72 International Demonstration and Education System (IDES) is a complete preinstalled R/3 system that includes data for core business processes. The IDES system was created for testing, demonstration, and training purposes and can be enhanced by partner-specific demonstration examples. IDES can be ordered by partners at no cost once they have acquired an R/3 test and demo license, or have become an R/3 customer.

16-73 SAP determines which access method is best by considering the type of partnership involved, i.e. development partner, certification partner, R/3 compatible component partner, or ISV. Other factors that help determine the access method include the partner's knowledge of the R/3 system, participation in SAP training classes and available partner resources for an R/3 system installation.

16-74 A software company must first provide SAP with further information about the company, the product, and the type of integration scenario desired. This information gives the CSP team better understanding of which program best meets specific corporate needs.

16-75 Third-party software vendors can contact the alliance management team in the local SAP subsidiary to acquire the partner profile form.

16-76 SAP's CSP PartnerNet packages help increase the profile of the software solution in the industry while solidifying a partnership with SAP. CSP PartnerNet packages are a comprehensive collection of communication tools. Our proven partner management strategy will correctly position a company and products in the R/3 market. PartnerNet packages combine marketing and business-oriented services tailored to meet the specific needs of complementary software partners and help them gain the maximum possible benefit from their cooperation with SAP. CSP PartnerNet packages offer high quality, and concentrated support for marketing and business activities.

16-77 Partner logos are a primary element of our packages and are available to CSP members to be used in all joint marketing and sales activities. They give the software product a unique image, that all-important head start in the marketplace. The Internet has become an important tool for any convincing marketing strategy. SAP provides the option of presenting products on a personalized Web page on SAP's popular Internet site. The company's Internet page can list product information and important contact addresses for prospects. The company logo can be added to the page to make it unique. If a company wishes to present its software and integration with the R/3 system in more detail, SAP will also create a link to the company's product page or home page. Every CSP partner gets an individual Web page.

16-78 The ability to provide information electronically or on paper is a crucial element of CSP PartnerNet packages, which offer you technical reports, presentations, and the SAP Annual Report, as well as a free subscription to SAP Info (the SAP company magazine). A user of CSP PartnerNet packages, has access to SAPNet, SAP's multimedia information system.

16-79 In SAPNet, software partners gain access to documents and information not available on SAP's public Web site. The program attempts to provide

CSP partners with continuous training opportunities. Employees can attend special SAP Partner Academy training courses to enhance their knowledge of integration techniques. SAP also offers CSP PartnerNet package owners a discount for these courses.

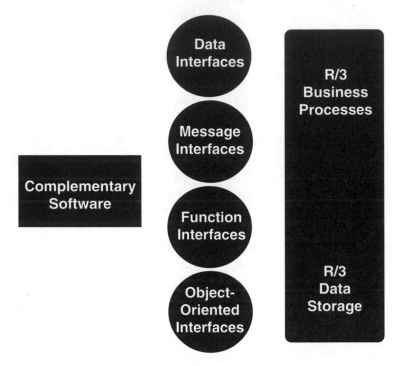

FIGURE 16.8
Integration
Techniques

16-80   The standards for Electronic Data Interchange (EDI) automate exchange of data between SAP and third-party application systems.

16-81   ALE permits loose coupling of distributed applications and integration of business processes across multiple systems. It is easy to integrate special-purpose subsystems as for CAD or plant data capture. Desktop programs can be linked as necessary much as word processors or spreadsheets are, to R/3 applications. In addition, workflow techniques and e-mail effectively support automation and control of cross-system work routines.

16-82   SAP offers its ALE technology for distributed application systems. ALE clears the way for efficient, secure communication of business information between technically independent systems. When dealing with a coordinated architecture, ALE offers distribution models and technologies for application linking as well as tools for the design and operation of distributed applications. Frequently requested distribution scenarios are configured as distribution models in R/3, thereby providing a proven business foundation for customized solutions. ALE also supports business processes for the distribution of accounting and logistics, sales/invoicing and shipping, local and central profitability analyses, as well as central and local sales and operation planning (SOP). ALE couples autonomous distributed application systems through a configurable distribution model, making certain that exchange of business information messages, updates of master data, and the coordination of control information takes place.

16-84   During both the setup and operational phases of distributed application systems, transparency and ease of handling are preserved no matter how detailed the methods. Distributable process units such as inventory management guarantee data uniformity throughout distribution.

16-85   ALE technology is based on a business event-controlled, time-driven exchange of business information messages. Synchronous and asynchronous communication mechanisms (RFCs) offer need-driven integration of applications, through connecting through a central database is no longer required.

16-86   The ALE architecture develops application and communication as well as distribution services. This layer handles the system-or release-based conversion of message contents, where R/2 and external applications can also be integrated.

16-87   In order to protect their computing investments, many modern companies need an open software landscape. Users also want their companies' business software to embrace personal productivity tools such as word processors, spreadsheets, and PC databases. It is important to satisfy user needs, SAP integrates desktop software into several R/3 applications. Desktop integration allows end-users to execute their tasks in an integrated, consistent environment.

16-88   Microsoft Excel can be integrated into the XXL List Viewer for more flexible reporting. MS Excel can be used for costing, project planning, and consolidation. Microsoft Work is available in the human resources module as well as for users of the ABAP/4 Development Workbench to compose online documentation. In addition, mobile users can benefit from Microsoft Access to enter travel expenses. SAP-EIS integrates both Word and Excel. There are still other desktop programs, such as applicant administration and calendar management, that are integrated by R/3.

16-89   SAP makes sure to use standards and open interfaces. The most important of these involves Object Linking and Embedding (OLE) an industry stan-

SOLUTIONS

dard incorporated into the R/3 system. Remote Function Call (RFC) and SAP's open programming interface are also available.

16-90   Desktop development kits support software developers in these areas.

16-91   The SAP Intelligent Terminal will allow easy linking of supplemental software to SAP business processes via the SAPGUI.

16-92   The Open Applications Group (OAG) was founded by major software vendors with the goal of speedily defining a standard interface for linking different applications within and outside of enterprises. The specifications emerging from this group call for communication based on business-object documents that will allow applications from different vendors to speak with one another.

16-93   SAP supports many corporate routines with assistance from appropriate business objects and business function libraries.

16-94   External interfaces make it possible to link in supplemental solutions of other vendors. These interfaces are commonly referred to as Business APIs. SAP will make certain they provide stability and support for BAAs. The methods on which the individual interfaces are based encompass OLE RFC, EDI, and Intermediate Documents (IDocs). There is also a great deal of interplay for business applications and their supplementary components. SAP practices quality control by executing a certification program for the application-specific interfaces.

16-95   Object technology is coming to the forefront of the R/3 system for integration of R/3 applications, external systems, and desktop applications. Business data and functions are encapsulated in objects, while ALE messages can also be sent through an EDI subsystem to EDI-capable applications.

16-96   Objects can be defined based on object types and managed in the business object repository. When dealing with the enterprise data model, business objects are derived by assigning data models. Each data model defines the internal structure of a business object. Business objects, technical objects such as texts, and graphics can be stored in the business object repository. SAP's object model is geared to the COM and CORBA standards (OMG). An RFC dynamic invocation interface allows access to attributes and methods of the object types defined in the business object repository. An OLE automation server based on this RFC interface allows PC applications to use business objects much as they use as other desktop objects. The objects possess a standard interface to SAP Business Workflow. R/3 makes it possible to connect external systems using standard object interfaces like OLE Automation or CORBA to establish links.

SOLUTIONS

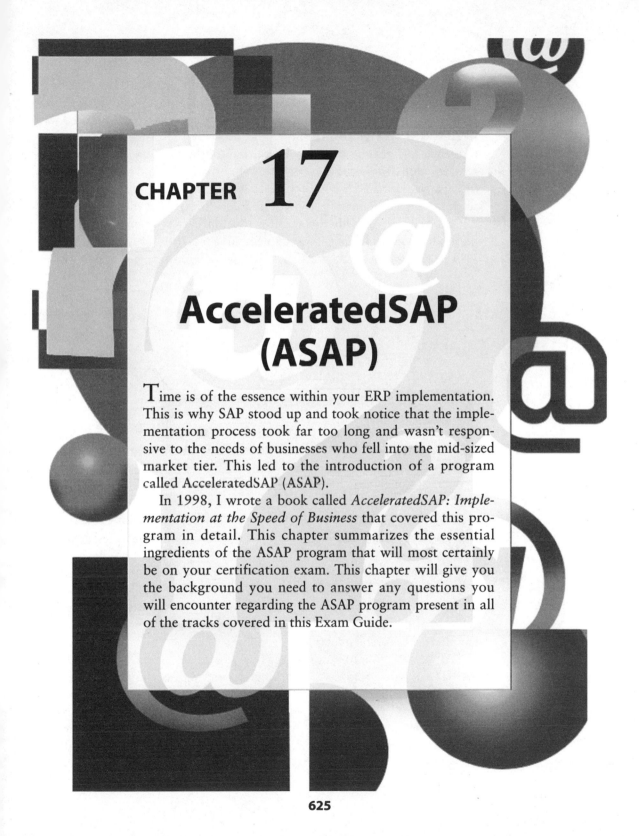

CHAPTER 17

AcceleratedSAP
(ASAP)

Time is of the essence within your ERP implementation. This is why SAP stood up and took notice that the implementation process took far too long and wasn't responsive to the needs of businesses who fell into the mid-sized market tier. This led to the introduction of a program called AcceleratedSAP (ASAP).

In 1998, I wrote a book called *AcceleratedSAP: Implementation at the Speed of Business* that covered this program in detail. This chapter summarizes the essential ingredients of the ASAP program that will most certainly be on your certification exam. This chapter will give you the background you need to answer any questions you will encounter regarding the ASAP program present in all of the tracks covered in this Exam Guide.

Pay special attention to how you can go live with AcceleratedSAP program in months instead of years. Make mental notes on how the implementation of R/3 rests on important concepts such as pre-configured templates, the ASAP Roadmap, and how you can further reduce implementation time through several key outlined methods in this chapter. Remember how these concepts apply directly to mid-sized companies, but watch how ASAP has become so popular as a significant time-saver during your implementation process. In addition, you will note that during your career you will also see how most larger companies are using this methodology for departmental implementations too. You will see how the ASAP program ties into every facet of SAP R/3 implementations now and in the future.

ASAP: The Beginnings

In order to achieve a successful SAP R/3 implementation, you need to develop a program that can deploy a solution in months instead of years. Industries have hungered for a solution, and SAP realized this need through the development of its program called AcceleratedSAP or ASAP.

Your business is determined to stay ahead of its competition and ahead of the market. Information is the driving force behind your business, and that data is the catalyst in your business operations for current and future endeavors. The way in which you use that information, as well as how you make it work for you, determines your status in the marketplace. That status will ultimately determine your customer base and your future projects.

You need to make your business ready for a better return on information and a better return on investment (ROI). SAP R/3 allows you to start enhancing your efficiency using a method that is compatible to the way in which your business uses information. ASAP makes that process faster, simpler, and more productive.

SAP permits you to attain faster business results with R/3. AcceleratedSAP allows you to have R/3 working in less time so you can be ready for new business decisions come the year 2000. ASAP allows you to utilize best business practices based on several years of implementation experience. AcceleratedSAP results in a rapid implementation solution created for your enterprise to achieve a quick and observable return on your R/3 investment.

Assistance

A great deal of resources exists to help you within every level of AcceleratedSAP. In addition, ASAP allows you to specifically designate how R/3 fits into your specific business objectives to accurately determine the price and scheduling of your R/3 implementation. AcceleratedSAP gives you the essential ingredients for success. The elements for a successful implementation involve the process, tools, training, and services. SAP's goal is to place the cornerstone within your business processes to form a solid foundation for future R/3 upgrades. The integration between SAP R/3 and an effective business model is illustrated in Figure 17.1. AcceleratedSAP is the bridge that will take you from where you are today to a higher level of integrated business processes tomorrow. ASAP links together everything you need to successfully implement R/3 quickly, effectively, and accurately.

FIGURE 17.1
Integration of
Business
Model and R/3

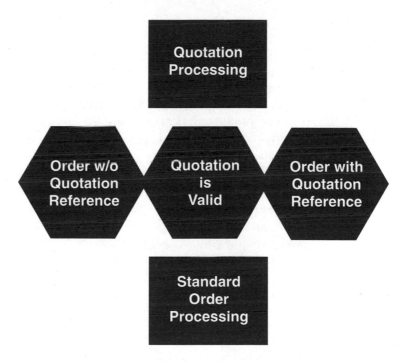

The ASAP Expressway

AcceleratedSAP produces a process-oriented, direct project plan to specifically yield direction throughout your R/3 implementation.

The expressway to implementation is paved with several SAP tools that make an important difference. Your primary task is to communicate with the Implementation Assistant for answers and gain a direction to move you through your implementation program. The following steps provide you with a simple and easy reservoir of information on some very key issues:

1. What needs to be done?
2. Who will achieve it?
3. How long does it take?

ASAP uses the detailed configuration capabilities of R/3's Business Engineer. Within this toolbox are tools that are used for modeling, implementation, continuous improvement, as well as documentation. There are also established models and industry templates that will directly act as catalysts to speed your implementation time and provide you with an accurate solution now.

Team Training

SAP offers a pyramid approach that integrates the training process and allows you to create an effective, total training program for faster, superior retained learning throughout your organization.

The fundamental objective is to integrate SAP's support and services network in an effort to provide answers to questions that may occur during your implementation. However, in any implementation, it is not just your installation effort, but also the knowledge that you can get answers after you've gone "live" that really counts. The goal is to provide you with assistance in every phase of your project. Nobody purchases a car without buying a "roadside assistance" plan from the automobile club. Why should your investment have anything less?

TeamSAP

TeamSAP is a major component of your implementation effort. It represents a coordinated network of products, processes, and people who are key to making certain that you acquire a successful SAP solution. TeamSAP enhances AcceleratedSAP and Business Framework programs with the goal of adding critical components, solutions expertise, assuring project coordination, leadership, and cross-customer knowledge sharing.

We will first examine the Business Framework that is SAP's strategic product architecture that permits complementary software partners to constantly convey new solutions into your R/3 implementation.

Then you can add solutions expertise, which is the culmination of the specialized expertise, experience, and training that exists for every Team-SAP member who contributed to the success of your project. TeamSAP makes certain that you have SAP-certified partner resources organized and in a logical, integrated, and comprehensive presentation that supports the knowledge base and experiences with SAP's most effective implementations. You have the resources to utilize both the power and information of TeamSAP to enhance your R/3 implementation time, and reduce costs throughout your effort to allow you to go live and beyond.

ASAP Consultant Specifics

SAP Consultants include SAP's Application Consultants, Remote Consultants, and Technical Consultants. They add a great deal of functionality and technical expertise to your efforts, especially if your business is multinational, because Global Support Managers are available to assist you throughout the specific items that occur within multiphased implementations.

AcceleratedSAP offers certified partners Powered by AcceleratedSAP, which permits the use of certain sections of ASAP techniques together with their own implementation practices. Customers who are part of a program with a Powered by AcceleratedSAP partner have a greater chance of speeding up their enterprisewide efforts in addition to complementing continuous efforts when a rapid implementation is required.

AcceleratedSAP Partners involve organizations that are certified as ASAP partners who have nearly three-quarters of their consultants achieve training in AcceleratedSAP and who have totally adopted the ASAP style to their duties. When you select to use an AcceleratedSAP Partner, it is a comfort to know that your partner will utilize the techniques in AcceleratedSAP and link both consistency and speed to your R/3 implementation. Speed, performance, and knowledge are all exemplified within the SAP consultant team. Having a good implementation is only part of the puzzle; the remainder involves acquiring an accurate solution in as little time as possible.

ASAP: Defined

ASAP is SAP's extensive, reproducible implementation solution meant to refine R/3 projects. ASAP acts as an efficiency expert with respect to time, quality, and productive use of resources in implementations.

ASAP possesses components that make your implementation successful. These components include:

1. **SAP Roadmap**—This is a gradual project structure designed to create refined implementations that incorporate designations regarding the specifics for each activity on the Roadmap. You can see the various steps involved in this Roadmap in Figure 17.2.

2. **SAP toolkit**—The ASAP Implementation Assistant is the navigation tool for the SAP Roadmap that includes all of the specific examples, templates, forms, and checklists. The implementation tools within the R/3 Business Engineer (BE) compose the cornerstone of Accelerated-SAP and expedite configuration of R/3 in the most efficient and productive pathway.

3. **SAP consultant training**—SAP offers much more than simple consulting and training. Their service and support products include Early-Watch, OSS, concept review, and Going Live check. Each of these tools is used as a quality assurance and quality check. In addition, they also provide active tuning of the R/3 system.

FIGURE 17.2
AcceleratedSAP
Roadmap (Six Steps)

| Project Preparation | Business Blueprint | Simulation | Validation | Final Preparation | Go Live and Support |

Accelerators

One of the most important mechanisms of the AcceleratedSAP program is the addition of components called accelerators. Each of these accelerators is used for all types of implementations. They can either be used together or independently, depending upon your specific needs. In terms of partners, the Roadmap can be substituted by their own techniques, however, they still use the accelerators in order to achieve an effective implementation goal for your organization.

These implementation goals can best be defined specifically to provide you with:

- Much quicker implementation
- Speedier delivery of business results
- Certified quality
- Specific knowledge acquisition during implementation

✎ Most efficient use of resources
✎ Communion and utility of results for future implementation phases
✎ Shortened implementation cost
✎ Speedier return on investment

Approaching ERP in a New Direction

AcceleratedSAP is wisdom born from time-proven practices and standards that employ the best implementation and business practices from SAP customers. ASAP allows partner consultants to have a uniform approach that allows rapid implementation. The implementation tools of the R/3 Business Engineer are the cornerstones of the configuration support present in SAP's R/3.

The new direction SAP America is taking with ASAP started in the United States. However, the project team, called Fox, has offered AcceleratedSAP on a global solution scale. This project had already begun to blossom in the latter portion of 1997, and promises a great deal of potential in the future. At the present time, several countries have begun using the current version of AcceleratedSAP, as well as several of its components. There are numerous AcceleratedSAP projects in Europe, and a European ASAP customers went live in 1997.

Now that we have discussed the past and present directions of ASAP, the future holds even greater potential with more and more businesses coming online with significantly greater implementation times. SAP is dedicating a great deal of resources designed to continually strengthen and broaden AcceleratedSAP. These decisions are the result of both the United States and Germany working together in combination with the Business Engineering Center in SAP development.

In terms of SAP's R/3 release 4.0, SAP is adapting AcceleratedSAP to assimilate new R/3 functionality. This begs the question of how SAP methodology is altered with respect to its consulting partners. The answer lies in the fact that SAP and its partner consultants are trying to achieve a common goal to provide an accurate R/3 solution that is both quick and inexpensive. The most recent release of SAP R/3 is release 4.0, illustrated in Figure 17.3. SAP works together with its consulting partners as a whole-team unit to ensure the success of your implementation efforts. This methodology lends itself to the creation of TeamSAP, and illustrates how teamwork can accomplish realistic achievements in a reasonable time frame.

FIGURE 17.3
SAP R/3 Release 4.0

Business Functions

Several SAP partners have begun ASAP training in the United States, while some current AcceleratedSAP implementations are supported by SAP in combination with its consulting partners.

Functionality

AcceleratedSAP is a comprehensive program that has a great deal of functionality that supports both tools and templates. ASAP is effectively implemented in several customer R/3 implementations on both a domestic and global scale.

Compare and Contrast ASAP

It is important to point out how ASAP compares to the R/3 Business Engineer and R/3 Procedure Model. AcceleratedSAP employs the R/3 Business Engineer tools at all pertinent steps throughout the implementation process. ASAP's Roadmap is closely related to the R/3 Procedure

Model. Each effectively handles various concepts of an implementation. The R/3 Procedure Model shows a far less specific view at a higher level.

AcceleratedSAP is a complete implementation solution with tools for R/3 service and support provisions that ensure time savings and quality with respect to your implementation.

Essentially, every customer can use AcceleratedSAP because its components are used as accelerators in any kind of implementation. The correct approach will be constructed from the Roadmap as part of project planning.

Since the majority of AcceleratedSAP tools and templates can be used in most implementations, ASAP can even be used if you are working on a project that involves different techniques. It is important to note that questionnaires, how-to guides, and standard forms can all be used separately and in combination with the ASAP Roadmap.

Most customers try to disassociate AcceleratedSAP with business process reengineering (BPR). However, the fact is that ASAP does not support techniques that involve how to reengineer your business or how to support a given level of change with your company. If a great deal of BPR is needed, you should partner with a consulting company who specializes in your area. In addition, all projects can profit from AcceleratedSAP, including questionnaires, forms, and how-to guides.

Since there is only one version of the AcceleratedSAP Roadmap tools and templates, there is less chance of confusion from different implementation efforts. One of the most beneficial features is ICOEs (industry centers of expertise) which handle the development of industry-specific ASAP tools and templates that enhance the overall service.

AcceleratedSAP can also be used in future phases of your implementation project. You will need to watch the next phases of your implementation effort because ASAP results can be used several times to enhance and improve the acceleration since they represent a company-specific starting point for all project methods.

Cost

No extra expense is incurred in using AcceleratedSAP because all of the contents of ASAP are part of the services offered by SAP and ASAP partners. Essentially, all tools, templates, and completed deliverables go to customers through their implementors. There are, however, optional services, such as EarlyWatch, that are priced separately from ASAP, as shown in Figure 17.4.

FIGURE 17.4
Showing How an SAP
EarlyWatch Works

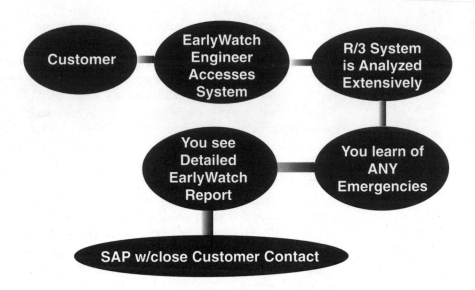

Training

SAP America and SAP in Europe offer three AcceleratedSAP-related training courses, and this is how customers are trained on AcceleratedSAP.

At this point in the implementation, the SAP implementor designates the specific training for their AcceleratedSAP customers and trains the appropriate staff. ASAP is SAP's total implementation solution to refine R/3 projects. AcceleratedSAP optimizes time, quality, and effective resources in implementations. This complete solution is composed of elements that ensure its success:

1. Roadmap
2. Toolkit
3. Service and support
4. Training

The Roadmap comprises five elements:

1. Project preparation
2. Business blueprint
3. Realization
4. Final preparation
5. Go live and support

The Roadmap also incorporates descriptions in the form of overview information as well as how-to's or best practices.

The toolkit designates all the tools employed in ASAP such as the R/3 Business Engineer and several other software products including Microsoft Project. AcceleratedSAP's Best Estimator tool allows you to correctly determine the needed resources, costs, and time frame for the implementation. The AcceleratedSAP Implementation Assistant is effectively a how-to guide that assists you through the unique phases of implementation such as the checklists and project plans.

Service and support is an area that needs to be fostered from the first planning stages through completion of implementation and beyond. Services incorporate consulting and training. ASAP also uses the service and support provision for services relating to the SAP environment. Early-Watch, concept reviews, and GoingLive checks are all components of the service palette that ensures total quality and allows you to actively refine your R/3 system.

Training strategies for the project team training, in addition to end-user training, are integrated into the plan. Usually, the project team is trained in a combination with standard level 1–3 training classes, as well as onsite training. With respect to end users, the main strategy is a train-the-trainer technique for effective knowledge transfer from the project team.

Rapid Deployment

AcceleratedSAP is becoming a global industry standard for rapid deployment of SAP's R/3. ASAP allows organizations to benefit from reliable implementation best practices founded on the experience of SAP customers. ASAP gives companies around the world one technique for implementing R/3 across global operations. AcceleratedSAP gives customers a much quicker return on investment, as well as significant cost savings that allows you to realize greater operational efficiency now. ASAP is focused on your goals, it supports backward scheduling from your go-live time frame, and makes certain that all functions add value and help you reach your objective.

Teamwork

Teamwork is an essential ingredient in helping to meet your goal. SAP consultants and implementation partners experienced in AcceleratedSAP objectives are dedicated to your success. SAP professionals work as a tightly knit team with your organization from the initiation of your project through your ultimate go-live date.

Teamwork occurs through automated means such as ASAP's Implementation Assistant. This product includes templates, forms, questionnaires, and checklists that provide you with several implementation tools with which to start your project. All of these tools help to organize your systems by evaluating the configuration of core business processes that deal with cycles throughout your departments. This makes certain that you achieve a cross-functional, integrated implementation. Once that implementation is complete, your team tests your system for quality assurance. The ASAP Roadmap in Chap. 2 demonstrates the totality and coherence of your project. It designates exactly what must be accomplished throughout each phase.

When your implementation is completed, you can reuse these very same standard procedures to deploy R/3 more widely within your organization. You can accomplish your task by defining and coordinating project team roles for aspects including application design, technical installation, and project management throughout all phases of your implementation. This allows you to make certain that all activities function as one cohesive entity.

AcceleratedSAP Ingredients

The ASAP Roadmap gives you a detailed plan for all of your implementation activities that offers you a greater level of detail. The R/3 Implementation Assistant is composed of tools that allow you to invent implementation pathways once one already exists that is right for you, resulting in significant time savings. The R/3 Business Engineer is a tool that creates a foundation for your system configuration. It has an automated configuration functionality that supports the continuous improvement of your business processes. Service and support are essential ingredients for any consultant working with your implementation partners. This effort allows you to work with customers as one team during your implementation. You can achieve an even greater level of support with EarlyWatch, GoingLive checks, and Online Service and Support programs to help you on your implementation journey.

The ASAP Roadmap Legend

The Roadmap takes you from the initial stages of your project to completion. This very specific layout helps you achieve several important goals in order to complete implementation as fast as possible. The first step is project preparation during which you work toward achieving executive commitment. Then, you can form a project team that has the ability to make critical decisions and develop a definitive project plan.

The next step is to bring your plan to fruition through the phase called Business Blueprint. Your project team combined with ASAP consultants establish a detailed blueprint of your business on R/3 and provide a copy to your company executives to be approved. At this point you are ready for your simulation. Both your consultants and the project team configure and install four-fifths of your standard R/3 systems just by using the Business Blueprint to simulate business transactions with real master data. This procedure refines and confirms the blueprint. That refinement is then validated. Your project team works with SAP consultants to allow the system to grow into a completely integrated solution. Then, the final preparation involves completion of systems testing, training of end users, and coordination of your "go-live" strategy. The point at which you go live and provide support is achieved once you have a productive R/3 environment. This is accomplished by both consultants and project team members who make certain your business environment is completely supported by validating the accuracy of transactions and meeting end users' needs.

Business Engineer

One of the aspects this book deals with is SAP's R/3 Business Engineer (BE), a very important configuration tool that allows much quicker and more efficient R/3 implementation of enterprise business solutions. It also allows greater improvement of business processes. R/3 Business Engineer 4.0 allows you to configure R/3 simply and easily and provides support for your entire R/3 environment. In addition, R/3 Business Engineer permits you to implement changes quickly—at any time and at any place—within your existing enterprise system.

R/3 Business Engineer Benefits

Version 4.0 contains a very detailed level of configuration for R/3 that permits simple, rapid implementation support for ongoing business growth. It also results in a higher return on investment for R/3 Flexible in an open configuration environment.

R/3 Business Engineer's knowledge-based configuration makes implementation simpler through an interactive interface that offers a question-and-answer type configuration process. Its purpose is to provide structure through your R/3 configuration and determine if any problems exist. In addition, it excites the R/3 process chains to determine how configuration decisions influence business processes across the integrated system. It also emulates a live R/3 solution that will operate traditional enterprise modeling with the live R/3 system. It then connects business models and deploys them to make certain that process design integrity and decisions are executed during system configuration. The last step is to ensure there is both consistent and supported R/3 features that have a standard interface which makes R/3 Business Engineer accessible to partners, consultants, and customers. It allows you to enhance industry solutions and create corporate rollout templates.

Easy Configuration

The R/3 Business Engineer greatly simplifies configuration. For example, it contains 100 distinct business scenarios that aggregate R/3's 1000 business processes into controllable views of the best business practices. Industry templates yield an efficient industry-centered R/3 solution. These solutions are useful for consumer-packaged goods and chemical and steel industries. SAP provides these templates for all of its vertically focussed industries.

Business Engineer is improving constantly. It allows customers to support change and regularly execute system improvements by handling nine-tenths of daily business changes, such as adding or subtracting items from within your corporate structure. These tasks involve business units, production plants, and warehouses. Other tasks include the addition of new staff, promotions, reallocation of work duties, and maintaining authorization profiles for both new and concurrent currencies. These functions may play a critical role with global business clients who have modified legal requirements, including new tax rates or revised employment legislation. In short, you have access to new business process optimization support for current or future implementations of R/3.

Versatility

R/3 Business Engineer permits customers to configure several versions of R/3, which allows them to utilize new releases and add new projects into the operating system such as standard APIs and support for major interfaces like COM/DCOM and ActiveX. The goal is to facilitate integration with third-party software, tools, and techniques. There is also a web-browser front-end and HTML-based documentation so that R/3 Business

Engineer is not platform specific. In addition, it provides simpler and easier access.

SAP's Business Framework is maintained by the R/3 Business Engineer, which handles component-centered implementation that is updated with the delivery of R/3 components.

Reengineering Questions

Although SAP is increasing its profits from one of its popular enterprise software platforms, users believe that implementing SAP software is a prelude to organizational reengineering. Company marketing allows users to make certain that these practices are indicative of a powerful change in management. The corporate business structure that is in place is the cornerstone for current and future planning that guides the organization through the support services migration. In the event that companies are not prepared for such an extensive transition, they will have to pay for very costly SAP consultants and technical support.

The time frame for a very fast SAP implementation is about 2 years, however, it is important to inform your financial officers about the corporate migration costs. SAP realizes the importance that its customers place on technical support. Therefore, they are creating software modules that are simple to install and inexpensive to enhance your organization's ability to handle specific support problems.

SAP is growing rapidly in terms of number of users. When you buy an SAP system, the importance lies in the product you own, indicating that your company realizes the need for extensive, continuous SAP support and consulting.

Consultant Focus

Independent consultants can be very costly, especially when you consider that many of the sessions don't deal directly with technology but on the method of system adoption. For example, how to manage a 24-month migration (a time frame that is more than exemplary for a large corporate implementation) to a completely new computing system that often uses a totally different method for your business, thus requiring that your business be reengineered.

After several sessions, many organizations realize that managing a total system change is even more important than the SAP applications. The most important guideline is the importance of keeping track of your return on investment and business case problems. It is important to note that you may require a special group whose purpose is just to manage change. If you find yourself in a cost overrun, you may wish to discuss your options with your financial officer so you can continue your implementation efforts and put them back on track.

Some large companies warrant special attention from SAP, such as an onsite SAP engineer who can support issues as they come up. In addition, an SAP engineer can act as a liaison between your company and SAP. However, only billion-dollar companies warrant SAP's sending out a highly trained account manager.

SAP is working diligently to take advantage of the support situation by producing an accelerated solution with several preconfigured or easily customized modules. They are creating more vertical business applications, such as bank modules, that are configured to order as opposed to being built to order. This is an effective time-saver that accelerates the R/3 implementation process.

Making a Plan

The first step is project preparation. Your preparation will involve all of your decision makers. Everyone must be in agreement on the various steps in your R/3 implementation project. At this point, you will be able to form your internal and external implementation team. These primary tasks will allow you to start your implementation effort with greater speed and efficiency.

Several layers of preparation must be adhered to when approaching your ASAP solution. Once you have completed all of the preliminary preparation steps described here, you will then be able to go on to your final preparation. At this point, you will need to examine your overall game plan to determine what type of testing and adjustments will be needed in order for you to ensure a successful implementation. This stage is your chance to test all interfaces, train all end users, and migrate your business data to your new R/3 system.

After preparation is complete, then you can design your business blueprint. At this stage, you realize that your company is prepared to embark on an AcceleratedSAP solution. Now, you will need to record your organization's business requirements. The Business Blueprint gives you a visual model of your company's future environment once the R/3 installation is complete. This blueprint can help you in your planning process, as illustrated in Figure 17.5. In addition, it will permit your project team to specifically designate your objectives. These objectives can further be strengthened by the fact that your resources are concentrated on the R/3 processes required to operate your business.

FIGURE 17.5
Process Planning

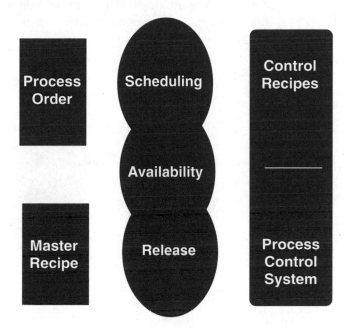

Once your final preparation is done, you have reached the level to go live and support. This is the final step to your implementation effort that will allow you to reach your destination and go live. Knowing your time frame will allow you to set your implementation efforts into motion so you can achieve your ASAP goal in a timely manner. Implementation is tempered by the fact that you may run into problems along the way. However, the road you take will be eased through SAP's support and services program.

Once your preparation is complete, it is time for realization of all of your hard work. Now you must configure your R/3 system to meet all of your individual business needs. Your Business Blueprint can be used by your team to both configure and fine-tune the specific elements of your implementation. In this plan, you can accurately control all aspects involving your AcceleratedSAP implementation of R/3.

Finally, it is reasonable to conclude that no implementation of R/3 operation is static. You must be prepared to deal with continuous change within your environment. Your support is not over once your operations are functional because you must have the power to get answers to your problems once you have gone live. At any given time, SAP has a large network of professionals to provide global access to R/3 expertise, product support, and maintenance services throughout the entire year, without exception.

Since this is an accelerated solution, you need to have the resources available to meet your changing needs. SAP is constantly creating new services to satisfy your changing needs, answer your questions, and support your implementation. Maintenance service needs are shown in Figure 17.6.

FIGURE 17.6
Maintenance Service

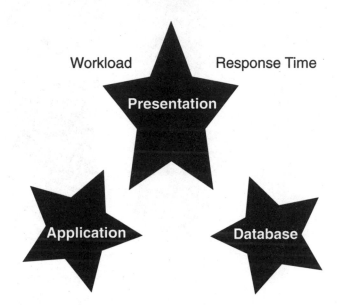

Implementation Assistant

ASAP's Implementation Assistant provides several solutions for any component that may be problematic during your implementation effort. The Implementation Assistant is simply a storehouse of information that designates what needs to be done, who should do it, and the length of time it should take to complete. It can be consulted at any time to make certain that your project is a success. You will learn how to do specific tasks, complete checklists, review examples, consult questionnaires, and check with technical guidelines.

The Implementation Assistant provides details on specific tasks such as designating who should be on a specific project team and determining the project team's duties. It helps you develop the necessary details and guides you through every task in the AcceleratedSAP Roadmap.

Following the Roadmap

As you progress with your implementation, you need to consider several key factors that will ultimately make you successful. You need to determine the following factors:

1. Cost
2. Time
3. Length of implementation
4. R/3 implementation tools
5. Required resources

Review of these factors is essential to determine how you can best proceed with the planned ASAP steps outlined in the previous section. Specifically, a detailed list of the steps required to guide you through your implementation effort will assist you in achieving your ultimate goal of running R/3 live in your organization.

Phase 1: Project Preparation

You must first collect your resources so you can adequately deal with your entire implementation effort. You can achieve a timely and efficient implementation by planning ahead to make sure your organization is ready for this upgrade. The planning stage can be somewhat simplified through the AcceleratedSAP program.

Full agreement of all of your corporate decision makers who are responsible for this project is needed before you can proceed any further. Once you have total agreement that R/3 will support the majority of your business needs, you will be in a position to make decisions more quickly and efficiently. Garnering acceptance is a key component to accelerating your implementation. The next component is developing a very clear project goal. Your decision-making process will be much more efficient once you determine your primary goals and objectives. Your company can more easily accept change and work together as an effective implementation team composed of people from all areas of your business. At this point you can begin the first phase of your project effort with the confidence that your primary barriers have be removed.

When you effectively eliminate problems at the beginning of your effort, change will occur much more quickly. Your TeamSAP consultants will work together with your organization to effectively determine your needs and requirements.

The ASAP Project Estimator is a tool that leads your team through several predefined questions. It facilitates interviews with your organization's senior executives, as well as key operating managers, in terms of their respective objectives. Since these objectives are tempered by the actual speed of your deployment, they become the objectives of your AcceleratedSAP solution.

TeamSAP consultants will assess each of these responses and determine the overall project scope and resources needed. These needs include three basic elements:

1. Time
2. Cost
3. Personnel

This is the jumping-off point that allows you to prepare your internal team members through introductory training to create R/3 awareness. You will find that product awareness allows you to tailor your expectations to meet product development. Level 1 training allows you to analyze SAP's architecture for service and support, the cornerstone of your implementation, and SAP terminology. The R/3 program is organized around essential business processes that cross application modules as well as emulate your organization's business processes.

The team you assemble can utilize realistic business process flows, scenarios, and models to permit both quick and cost-effective execution of business tasks. Standard service inspections will allow you to keep business processes flowing smoothly as you move down the ASAP roadmap that leads to your ultimate implementation. This journey is fortified by the quality of your business processes. That quality is further realized through use of an SAP quality assurance professional who performs inspections on a regular basis.

This very detailed quality assurance check and independent audit ensures that your implementation efforts have been worthwhile and are proceeding according to schedule. You have the confidence that your implementation is supported by your top-level executives, therefore, you can be certain you are ready for your team to develop the details of the project plan, as well as all of the key benefits that will assist both top-level management and all personnel.

At this point, you can enumerate all of the issues relevant to goals, budgets, and timing. Subsequently, you can acquire the required level of approval for your R/3 implementation plan from the decision makers within your organization. You can then instruct your team to complete all of its preparation duties and then proceed with the next phase of your implementation effort.

Phase 2: The Business Blueprint

The Business Blueprint allows you to record and designate your R/3 implementation. At this point, you will need to answer several questionnaires within such events as executive sessions, group discussions, and individual interviews. The answers you provide will assist TeamSAP consultants in determining your core business strategy. This information permits them to specify your future business processes and requirements.

AcceleratedSAP balances the power of the Business Engineer. The Business Engineer (BE) provides a total toolkit of specific business processes to accelerate your activities. This acceleration not only works in the present but also in the future to keep R/3 operating as the cornerstone of change as your business needs grow. A blueprint created for the methodology you use now can meet your growing needs, and is designed to keep track of your needs as your market changes.

Throughout the Business Blueprint phase, TeamSAP professionals refine R/3 to meet your industry-specific business processes. As you use both the questionnaires and the models from the Business Engineer, your project team will determine your business processes to depict the future of your business. Industry templates also work as an accelerator to facilitate your implementation process by designating industry best practices for your business. The end result of this effort is a total blueprint of your business. Your business plan will form the foundation for your ultimately successful R/3 implementation.

ASAP can be an integral part of any project regardless of its scale. It does not concentrate on projects that need to be reengineered or require operational enhancements. However, TeamSAP professionals will assist you in developing new approaches for your business processes. They will help you to create a basis by which you can achieve continuous improvement for your R/3 implementation. These phases essentially define the blueprint for the remainder of your implementation in addition to that of future upgrades.

In order to concentrate on the blueprint that is being created for your specific industry focus, your project team members will initiate Level 2 training on R/3 integrated business systems. Furthermore, an invaluable element of basic training exists across application modules, in addition to that of learning key success factors necessary in implementing total business solutions. Level 2 training will walk you through a detailed education level of R/3 business process skills. Your project team will be able to construct and maintain R/3 to meet your individual business processes.

ASAP Business Process Inquiries often helps to determine your focus areas. You may find it useful to determine how your customers are linked with your sales cycle, pricing, and discounts. In fact, you can tailor your individual setup to detect the most commonly used techniques to determine cost factors by product, customer type, and geographical location. Then you can set factors that detail sales processing within your organization, as well as the level of centralization involved in determining individual aspects associated with it. Finally, you may wish to look at the methods your company uses for reporting sales figures with respect to specific customers, regions, and districts.

Essentially, this example helps you to determine how to best use your Business Blueprint to specifically configure all of the details of your own R/3 system. You can use this information to create an environment that answers your growing organizational needs—both as an organization today and in the future.

You can use your established Business Blueprint to initiate a two-level process to configuring your R/3 system. The first level involves your TeamSAP professional who will efficiently configure your standard system. The next level is where your project team refines the system to satisfy all of your business and process requirements.

In terms of the previous sales example, imagine that most of the orders for your business are through the Internet. Your TeamSAP professional will configure your standard system. This is the basis of most of your transactions. Your standard system will be made up of four-fifths of your daily business transactions. Due to the fact that your original configuration is rooted in the blueprint that your team has created, your standard system will provide you with a realistic view of how your business transactions will operate in R/3. It is possible for you to continue to gain speed as the AcceleratedSAP process constructs every element of your implementation for the most efficiency in terms of resource utilization.

Parallel activities will be completed together and initiated earlier in the process, effectively reducing your time constraints significantly. Next, you need to focus on the full configuration that incorporates the remaining one-fifth of your business transactions. Your project team will now be able to configure the exception transactions, such as sales orders, that come in via fax or telephone. Your TeamSAP professional will segment your business processes into cycles of associated business areas. The cycles act as project landmarks and permit you to test distinct sections of the business process. The end result is an instantaneous report providing specific feedback. It is at this point that detailed learning by example enables you to comprehend the specifics about your R/3 system.

While you configure your system's exceptions, it is important to check your Implementation Assistant for specific tips and examples. Your organization will profit from the extensive consultant experience within each industry that has made R/3 live on a global scale. The Implementation Assistant has an extensive testing guide within it to assist your group and configure associated business processes. These time-savers offer increased configuration efficiency, as well as the most direct path. An automatic travel log will designate your pathway to implementation.

Phase 3: Simulation

At the simulation phase, you can proceed with balancing your Business Engineer functionality with its Implementation Guide (IMG). You can then utilize your blueprint and objectives and link them to the IMG. The result is a clearly laid out guide that explains what must be configured for each process. At this point, you can utilize the guidelines, steps, and configuration data for every element of R/3 functionality. In addition, IMG permits you to record your implementation pathway to R/3. It also allows you to establish a detailed implementation log that records each step along your roadmap or pathway. It designates each and every change or addition you make to your R/3 system. Your IMG travel log accesses the most current configuration status at any time frame in your pathway. This action will greatly simplify reporting to top-level management and keep communication and support at a highly accelerated level.

Phase 4: Validation

The next step is to enhance your skills to Level 3 training. At Level 3, the training gets even more fast-paced because you are closing in on your validation. By utilizing advanced training, your project team can gain the expertise they need to manage your R/3 system. This detailed training incorporates advanced topic workshops to create expertise specific to your organization's individual requirements. Furthermore, your project team will have access to industry workshops, as well as self-directed reference and training for continuing education.

The purpose is to capture the future and incorporate all associated enhancements that will be incorporated into your overall R/3 implementation plan. The system your team creates during the realization phase acts as the platform for continuing business modifications. These processes and tools are used constantly to refine business changes, expansions, and system improvements during and after your implementation.

It is important to create corporate guidelines for a simple deployment for all associate areas within your organization when changes, upgrades, and improvements are required. Knowledge transfer allows you to control your project and make certain that its team is in control of the implementation of R/3 now and its operation in the future. You will become very self-sufficient when your TeamSAP professionals transfer R/3 system knowledge to your project team. Then your R/3 standard system can become fully configured and move on to the next phase.

Phase 5: Final Preparation

The final preparation phase takes your system through a very detailed level of testing. At the same time, it takes your end users through a very detailed level of training. It is at this stage that you can refine your R/3 system prior to your "Go Live" stage. You have the power to execute any needed modifications in order to prepare both your system and your business for production initialization. As you prepare to Go Live, it is important to execute final system tests, as well as end-user training. Figure 17.7 illustrates the pathway to performance management, as well as guiding you through your strategy implementation. The next stage is to migrate business data to your new system. Then you must test and tune your system for optimum performance.

FIGURE 17.7
Pathway to Performance Management and Implementing a Strategy

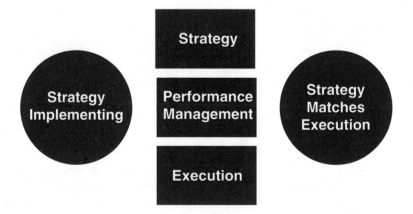

Your testing time is minimized due to the fact that you have been testing your system throughout your implementation process. At the final preparation, you will need to execute volume and stress tests. Each of these tests is essential for optimizing performance of your system. Integration tests are also important so that you can emulate live conditions. These conditions will test your conversion and interface applications for both accuracy and usability. In addition, you will test your system to be certain that your end users will accept their new system for a seamless transition to Go Live.

Preventative maintenance is an excellent check that allows you to make certain you achieve optimal performance of your R/3 system. The R/3 GoingLive Check permits SAP professionals to log on to your R/3 system via a remote connection that allows them to analyze the configuration of each of your individual systems, resulting in important recommendations that allow you to optimize your system. Education is a key component to the success of your R/3 implementation as it allows your end users to become more familiar with the system. Your goal is to promote a level of familiarity with your new R/3 system.

One method that is used to gain acceptance is called the train the trainer method since users will be trained by experienced coworkers within your organization. Your end users will then be prepared to utilize the skills they learned to operate and optimize R/3 for their daily business tasks. Training specific to each person's job is important so that each end user will know exactly how to use the R/3 system for his or her daily tasks. Then, you must be prepared to Go Live as your project team prepares a production initialization method. Your straightforward data conversion plan will ensure that all of the data from your old systems is transferred correctly into your R/3 integrated information system.

Your preparation to Go Live is analogous to preparing for your end users' questions as they begin to use their new R/3 system. The point at which you Go Live is an important transition that must foster the general feeling that every user and manager is going to be supported. Each worker will need to know whom to call for any questions or reports about system performance.

The Help Desk is key to protecting your internal system and providing end users with the answers they need to successfully perform their daily tasks. Ultimately, your project team will create the first audit procedures, as well as a project team support structure as part of the final stage of preparation. Once that final preparation is completed, you must proceed with the fifth phase of your project which involves your system actually going live with support.

Phase 6: Go Live and Support

The actual point at which your organization is Going Live is more than simply flipping a switch, as you have seen in all of the preparatory steps detailed in this chapter. Since you have carefully detailed all of your objectives, you have been able to create a rapid form of implementing R/3 that allows your company to realize significant business benefits that have taken place as soon as possible.

During this final phase of your project, it is important to create procedures and measurements to provide details on all of the benefits of your R/3 investment at regular intervals. As your business travels take you further along the ASAP Roadmap, you will begin to feel comfortable with the convenience of key elements including:

1. R/3 expertise
2. Product support
3. Preventative maintenance

Support and services allow you to keep R/3 working perfectly along with SAP support and services that help you make certain that your system will continue to run efficiently and effectively. Since your business is always working on new areas and projects, it is important to note that support does not conclude once you have gone live. SAP assists you during each and every phase of your R/3 project. An expansive network of consultants is available whenever you need them. They effectively yield global access to R/3 support and maintenance services all the time. These support services can provide assistance via a remote connection or through your local SAP office.

The Online Service System (OSS) is a centralized communications network that exists between you, your SAP partners, and SAP itself. OSS enables you to electronically transmit your problems or questions to SAP via a remote connection. In addition, you can automatically monitor their progress toward an ultimate solution. The OSS (shown in Figure 17.9) permits you to access a library of notes detailing specific event solutions that have been achieved by other SAP customers. Remote Consulting Services allows SAP professionals to log onto your R/3 system through a direct remote connection (e.g., video conferencing). Then you have the ability to transmit your Remote Consultant requests and questions from technical assistance to process- or application-specific support.

Once you do Go Live, EarlyWatch gives you a proactive system diagnosis. SAP can diagnose possible problems and resolve them at an early stage so you can be certain you achieve optimal system availability and performance. SAP's support and services are created to help your organization, realizing that every company is an individual. Furthermore, as your requirements grow, SAP helps you continue with your roadmap to gain an even more successful solution. Utilizing both speed and skill allows you to gain a competitive edge when your R/3 system is live. Knowing that ASAP helps you implement a working solution quickly and efficiently, permits you to use your business resources more effectively at a greater profit. When you have your R/3 system working at its full potential, your company can realize a far greater return on its information investment.

FIGURE 17.8
Online Service System

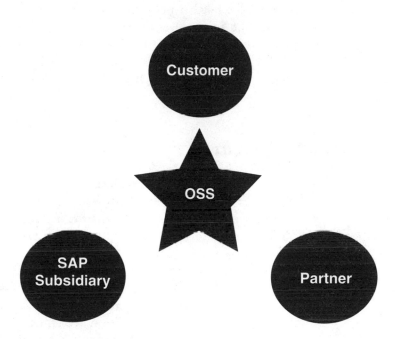

SAP Modules Ease Implementation

SAP produces both modules and versions for its ERP solutions to cater to their client/server software. SAP has created sales and implementation tools to make R/3 suite-applicable to midsized companies. SAP has two new tools to help midsized companies with its CBS (Certified Business Solutions) program that involves more front-end planning for R/3 implementations.

SAP salespeople who function under AcceleratedSAP come to new accounts at midsized companies and make projections with SAP's Estimator tool. This tool allows SAP to evaluate both your business and equipment needs. The objective is to provide a practical idea of your project's cost in terms of both time and money.

SAP's Implementation Assistant desktop application acts as a guide to take you through the six-step process above. It permits you to have a closely configured system with the Business Engineer configuration tool.

In addition, SAP offers a new development environment that permits your organization to integrate third-party components into the pre-cast R/3 enterprise system much simpler. ABAP Objects is a component of SAP's CIM software Business Framework method. IT builds on the backbone of SAP's ABAP programming language and object programming technology. Furthermore, this development environment allows both individual and team development tools as well as a virtual machine to produce cross-platform application portability. Its functionality also includes both publish & subscribe and event-trigger mechanisms to support business application needs. ABAP Objects is part of R/3 4.0, due in the second quarter of 1999.

AcceleratedSAP Benefits

There are several benefits from using the AcceleratedSAP program. ASAP improves time, quality, and efficient resources utilization throughout your implementations. Its primary benefits include quicker R/3 implementation and improved business results. It offers a standard approach to R/3 implementation for your partners and consultants, so that you are confident in the quality and guaranteed implementation knowledge. It results in more effective use of available resources, and these results can be used in future implementation stages to decrease your overall implementation costs for a better return on your information investment.

Accelerated R/3

The largest drawback to R/3 has been that it takes far too long to implement. The AcceleratedSAP program was designed specifically to refine and produce a standard implementation approach to cut the implementation time to less than 2 years and reduce costs, making it an acceptable solution for smaller businesses.

The ASAP program implementation of R/3 has six stages beginning with collecting and assessing your resources and ending with the final Go Live and support stage. This program reduces the time it takes to learn the system, and places you in a distinct advantage in terms of time, so that everyone within your organization is working together as a cohesive unit.

When dealing with CBS, the process is further shortened. The CBS version ties together some stages to offer an even shorter, less-labor-intensive start-up process for organizations that must work within daily work hours. The CBS implementation program is founded on the premise that its customers are too busy for a full system analysis.

The CBS program offers a complete process and ASAP speeds implementation. This system includes a questionnaire as part of the planning process, but the most disturbing fact is that many people simply don't define their project requirements before starting. This is an important step that ensures your success.

The best program benefit is that it defines a course of action prior to implementation, however, you don't receive any documentation as to how your system works after you Go Live with the product. SAP's average time to implement is approximately 6 months, a time frame that can vary either way, depending on the size and complexity of your organization. It is important for your project team to have an understanding of how a business works. Implementations are managed successfully when a company knows and can communicate its business needs.

This program neither resolves all implementation issues nor deals with reengineering issues. Therefore, if your company has just migrated from legacy systems, you need to deal with issues that this plan doesn't support.

It is important to make your R/3 business investment viable to accumulate a high return on your investment in the shortest time possible. One of the methods to assure you receive the best possible ROI is to investigate the integrated service solution shown in Figure 17.9.

AcceleratedSAP was created originally for North American customers whose annual revenues were between $200 million and $2.5 billion. However, the ASAP program is not utilized domestically or globally by multibillion dollar customers who need to gain more rapid returns on an SAP investment. SAP and several of their implementation partners use this program. It is an option for enterprises that need to complete their tasks, migrate from legacy applications, and at the same time meet year 2000 compliancy.

AcceleratedSAP is not effective for all R/3 implementations. Enterprises that require a great deal of operational improvement via large-scale reengineering can benefit from a more standardized R/3 implementation effort that stresses process improvement over rapid deployment. However, the factors of accelerated implementation are what AcceleratedSAP is about as it applies to almost everyone across many different R/3 implementations.

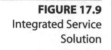

FIGURE 17.9
Integrated Service
Solution

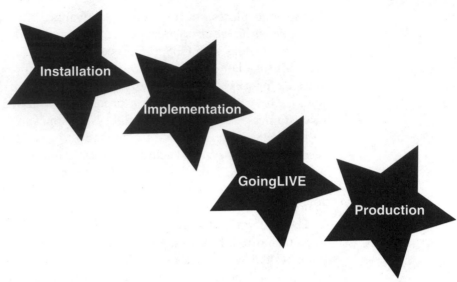

ASAP Differentiators

ASAP is the first implementation solution created and supported directly by SAP. It provides you with a straightforward SAP-derived preliminary estimate of resource requirements. It ties together elements that lead to success. It reduces time, cost, and people to form a solution that relies heavily on your needs. ASAP can be used by any of SAP's implementation partners that wish to offer this accelerated methodology. AcceleratedSAP is used as the foundation for R/3 customers around the world, as they can utilize a standard method for their R/3 implementations throughout any department, region, or country. The best goal is that it provides an excellent foundation for future R/3 upgrades, due to the fact that the ASAP program has only small software modifications. In that way, you are in a superior position to utilize the benefits from SAP's research and development from current and future releases.

Business Engineer Benefits

Significant improvements have been made in SAP's R/3 Business Engineer (BE) (see Figure 17.10). BE is a configuration, modeling, implementation, and ongoing improvement tool that provides distinct advantages in speed for any organization that wishes to compare specific business requirements to R/3's capabilities. The Business Engineer is the foundation tool for AcceleratedSAP, as it permits rapid implementation and ongoing process improvement.

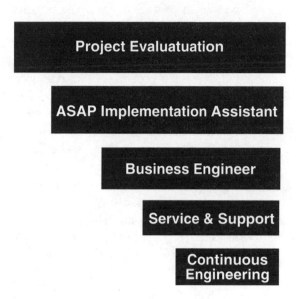

AcceleratedSAP is different from any other traditional software implementation efforts due to the fact that executives need to be ready for rapid software deployment, which is of significance to any enterprise resource planning (ERP) package implementation that includes R/3. This preparedness requires that you are highly motivated to make effective decisions about business processes, execute definable business objectives, and agree to carry the project to completion in the most timely manner possible.

Upper management needs to be ready to estimate the level to which their business can utilize R/3's best practice processes as opposed to the possible modifications needed for their own operational needs. For executives who are confident that their enterprises do not need a great deal of change management, reengineering, or R/3 modification requirements, AcceleratedSAP provides a great deal of time and resource savings as it forms the foundation for ongoing operational improvements.

AcceleratedSAP: Six Phases

Before your business selects AcceleratedSAP as an implementation program, SAP consultants help determine the suitability of this program for your particular location. Consultants utilize the SAP Project Estimator kit that incorporates predefined questionnaires to interview upper management and operating managers regarding their expected results and objectives from using R/3 for their business, and the level of speed they need for their deployment. Their responses are compared with a database of past implementation information, and the responses should be similar to those in the database. After the analysis of the responses, the consultant will develop a potential plan, resource utilization chart, and cost estimates for your entire implementation process.

The result is several initial estimates that are very important due to the fact that the amounts often form the foundation for discussion, opposition, and enhancements at the beginning of your R/3 implementation. Often, the R/3 implementation starts with implicit and incompatible expectations by both the customer and independent professional services consultants. This 2-day process adjusts expectations and permits SAP consultants to suggest the best AcceleratedSAP approach, so that you will be prepared to implement R/3 quickly with the fewest system changes. This action assists SAP consultants by recommending the level and type of R/3 consulting support the customer requires.

Phase 1: Project Preparation

This step determines how ready your organization is to proceed with its implementation effort. When your organization selects AcceleratedSAP as its implementation path, it is ready to learn about business solutions within R/3. This first stage allows your organization's management to come to an agreement as to which R/3 best practice processes work to support the majority of your business requirements. In addition, the major modifications to R/3 are reduced, which leads to a much smoother implementation. This acceptance of R/3 integrated processes will allow you to save a great deal of implementation time.

Upper management can feel more confident in the fact that a thorough decision-making process is being used to confirm your project's objective with the least amount of change and a written agreement to refine the scope of your project. When your project guidelines are developed, an implementation team of managers throughout your organization come together to complete the preparation phases and begin your implementation effort. The project start involves executive overview training about the product as well as the process for the implementation team members.

Phase 2: Business Blueprint

In order for you to define your business needs, the next phase of your ASAP implementation is perhaps the most difficult. SAP consultants utilize several very detailed questionnaires collected from individual interviews, group discussions, and executive sessions to determine your core business and to list the specific processes that your company uses. Throughout a typical 6-month implementation, this phase will take 3 to 4 weeks of very focused work. The result will be a detailed blueprint of your business needs. At the same time, your implementation team members attend a week of training to distinguish between different types of business systems.

This process defines your business requirements and provides you with several benefits, including a clearly defined project scope for your implementation team. You also have the opportunity to acquire R/3 solutions and benefits without knowing R/3 tables. Implementing R/3 will provide you with enhanced efficiency. Figure 17.11 shows the change before and after implementing R/3. Finally, as an R/3 customer, you will see what your business will look like after your accelerated R/3 implementation.

The Business Blueprint phase doesn't require you to make a major reengineering effort. AcceleratedSAP concentrates on meeting business requirements so that superior advancements to processes can be determined by SAP consultants and highlighted for you to use. AcceleratedSAP doesn't offer a great deal of reengineering capabilities, however, it provides the cornerstone for ongoing business process improvement.

FIGURE 17.11
Before and After
Implementing R/3
Improved Efficiency
Copyright by SAP AG

Before R/3	After R/3
• Very limited shop floor control capabilities	• Fully automated, integrated shop floor control
• Only one bill of material per item, company-wide	• Bills of material maintained by plant
• No facility for tracking raw material substitutions	• Full-cycle tracking of substitutions
• Trouble reports prepared manually and faxed to buyers	• Schedulers and buyers have online access to shortages and scheduled receipts

Phase 3: Simulation

When you have agreed on a Business Blueprint, the members of the AcceleratedSAP team start to focus their training on your R/3 system to transfer knowledge directly to your project team. At the same time, AcceleratedSAP consultants begin to configure your R/3 system, based on your Business Blueprint. As an AcceleratedSAP customer, you realize that your implementation project should use as many of R/3's integrated processes as practical so that your system can be configured when your project team members complete their training.

The benefits from the simulation phase include continued knowledge transfer of the software and technology to the customer, as well as an initial R/3 system configuration that must resemble your enterprise's business processes. The simulation phase permits your AcceleratedSAP team of internal managers and consultants to demonstrate the proposed system for your entire user community. Then you can start the critical communication and buy-in regarding the reason why these changes will improve each worker's individual work environment.

Phase 4: Validation

In an attempt to finalize your configuration, knowledge is continually transferred to your project team. The Business Blueprint permits the configuration of most of your R/3 system. In addition, there will always be distinct business scenarios that must be handled. This is the critical, detailed work where the AcceleratedSAP team must make certain that your final R/3 configuration best supports your organization's business processes. Your employee team members are sent for additional technical or module training on an as-needed basis while all these events are taking place.

Throughout the validation phase, your implementation team concentrates on the time and available resources for any business exceptions that were not configured in the simulation phase. It is at this point that the AcceleratedSAP technique permits your project team to focus on and customize areas where your organizational business processes are unique. During this process, your team members learn the R/3 system that your business is deploying.

Phase 5: Final Preparation

Once you have completed testing and have trained your end users, it is time to see how AcceleratedSAP is designed to test your system throughout the implementation. The results from this phase concentrate on testing interfaces and get end-user approval. Complimenting end-user approval is end-user training. The final preparation phase offers the skills that your users need to best operate and utilize R/3 for their jobs. ASAP concentrates on speed, but that focus does not negate the need for training end users in order to make R/3 successful. As an AcceleratedSAP customer, you need to work with your SAP consultants to make certain that training is done in a complete and timely manner so that you achieve your goals. However, while that process is often complex to coordinate, it offers you a chance to satisfy your enterprise resource planning requirements in an effective manner, without wasting time.

Phase 6: Go Live and Support

In order to quantify your ERP investment, you need to determine if the employees within your organization are self-sufficient enough to operate their own R/3 system. SAP consultants must be available for specific additional work, including the financial close at the end of each year. The AcceleratedSAP program offers your business the system, tools, and skills to operate and quantify the benefits of your R/3 investment. This leads to a productive system with a team that is trained for future AcceleratedSAP module implementations run by trained personnel.

TeamSAP and ASAP

TeamSAP defines SAP and its large, global structure of customers, partners, and suppliers that SAP has put together through its years of operation. Linking together a team of the best in many industries offers you complete SAP solutions. As an R/3 customer, you trust SAP staff for direct support and advice regarding specific implementation needs. The creation of AcceleratedSAP is part of an ongoing effort to make certain that you have both the partner resources and SAP support necessary to achieve your business objectives. TeamSAP, in relation to AcceleratedSAP, specifies SAP's partners, as well as Global Logo Partners, National Logo Partners, National Implementation Partners, and customer representatives that all have an important sense of urgency and direction on your R/3 implementation team.

Global Logo Partners

SAP's Global Logo Partners are made up of the largest of consulting firms who provide business and technology functionality that deals with reengineering assistance, change management, and education in cross-platform expertise. These firms provide the best implementation options for bigger R/3 customers who are proceeding with core business changes. Current Global Logo partners offer comprehensive implementation services to help you achieve your accelerated business objectives successfully.

Global Logo Partners find that AcceleratedSAP provides them a chance to supplement continuous enterprisewide efforts where there is a need for a rapid roll-out in a particular region, business unit, or pilot project. This program can provide time-sensitive services that are required for you to achieve a successful conversion effort in the year 2000.

The designation "AcceleratedSAP Inside" is provided by the Global Logo Partners to identify the use of this SAP-sponsored implementation program. SAP's Global Logo partners offer their own programs to meet customer demands for quicker returns on their R/3 investments. These partners hasten R/3 deployments by using preconfigured industry templates, tools, and techniques that complement the modeling functionality of the Business Engineer. They also expand their knowledge of Intranets to quickly share best-practice information on a global basis. In addition, implementation decisions must offer you a set price and time and risk-sharing options. You also gain the benefit from SAP consultant teams in SAP Solution Centers. AcceleratedSAP offers extra options so that Global Logo partners can satisfy your implementation requirements.

Implementation Partners

SAP's National Implementation Partner Program participants first see advantages from utilizing the AcceleratedSAP program with its customers. Consulting firms often function as the primary R/3 implementor for businesses with revenues below $1 billion. AcceleratedSAP was designed to deal with the requirements of small enterprises. In contrast to its bigger industry competitors, smaller businesses examining R/3 have less resources to deploy, however, they need to rapidly create an information infrastructure to support development. Therefore, midsized organizations were the initial target for utilizing AcceleratedSAP. Currently, SAP's National Logo and National Implementation Partners include:

- Affiliated Computer Services
- Holland Technology Group
- Applied Integration Services
- Intelligroup
- ARIS Corporation
- Honeywell
- Arthur Andersen
- IDS Prof. Scheer, Inc.
- Bureau van Dijk
- IMI Systems
- Card America, Inc.
- Kurt Salmon Associates
- CCAI
- MultiVision Consulting
- Chaptec Group
- Osprey Systems, Inc.
- CISCorp
- Plaut
- Clarkston Potomac Group
- RCG Information Technology
- Computer Aid
- RSA
- Comsys Information Technical
- SAIC Services
- D.A. Consulting
- Seltmann, Cobb & Bryant
- DDS
- Softline, Inc.
- Decision Consultants, Inc.
- Software Consulting Partners
- Deno Morris Group, Inc.
- Software Consulting Services
- EMAX Solutions Partners
- Spearhead Systems Consultants
- Global Core Strategies
- SPO America, Inc.
- Grom Associates
- Technology Solutions Company
- Hewlett-Packard
- Waypointe Information Technologies
- HJM Consulting, Inc.

✎   Whittman-HartMost

National Implementation Partners has been successful with Accelerated-SAP and plan to integrate its service offerings. It is important to choose the right TeamSAP partner for your AcceleratedSAP implementation. You may wish to examine your AcceleratedSAP program in order to locate consultants working for SAP, however, you may find that SAP does not have sufficient consultants to directly support all its customers. Further-more, SAP will not integrate this service because there are several partners that have over 25,000 SAP consultants globally for each IT industry.

SAP focuses on its own consultants' efforts to support the Accelerat-edSAP program with respect to assisting customers with the size and scope of their project before and during the preparation phase. They also make certain that there is always an SAP manager available for cus-tomers and consultants during all six phases. They offer specialized SAP product knowledge and quality assurance for continuous implementa-tions. The result is that the majority of AcceleratedSAP customers are in a position where they can evaluate potential professional service providers to enhance their internal capabilities and the support that SAP consultants offer.

The majority of R/3 implementation customers choose their R/3 imple-mentor on the basis of how much confidence they have in that person. This confidence is based on a past relationship or on the confidence of strong colleague references. When an organization is not familiar with the market or is looking for additional information about implementation partner options, SAP can recommend certain consultants that satisfy unique implementation requirements for your organization.

AcceleratedSAP and TeamSAP Support

AcceleratedSAP is fostered by centralized SAP support for training, soft-ware, and SAP consulting support. SAP offers several programs that sup-port both the AcceleratedSAP and TeamSAP program.

SAP has a professional services organization. When AcceleratedSAP was initiated in 1996, it paralleled the development of a new professional services organization at SAP America. There are more than 1200 consul-tants within SAP's professional services organization. This number will continue to grow to make certain there is extensive coverage and contin-ued contact with customers and partners implementing R/3 rapidly.

There is dedicated SAP field support for you. SAP makes certain there is continuous customer support via a field services organization. In larger organizations, there is a senior SAP manager who acts as a full-time liaison on your project. In smaller organizations, there is a similar senior SAP manager who supports several customers, resulting in direct, continuous customer communication of both SAP experts and resources.

SAP also provides technology and applications consulting that involves technology planning, knowledge transfer, execution, and quality assurance meant to assist your implementation of R/3 as quickly as possible. It also makes sure that you are self-sufficient during your productive operations. This group also works hand in hand with SAP development groups to transfer knowledge on changing customer requirements.

AcceleratedSAP Training

In order to support the initiation of AcceleratedSAP, SAP offered what is called "spring training" classes for implementation partners as an overview of the people, tools, and processes that make up this program. Although spring training is no longer offered, SAP still offers partners classes in the AcceleratedSAP techniques.

These classes lead to partner certification. SAP is on track to certify implementation partners to effectively utilize AcceleratedSAP. Certification will indicate that specific training and SAP experience conditions have been satisfied before certification is granted.

Business Engineer configuration functionality is further increased by R/3 version 4.0. This enhanced functionality continues to improve the ability of AcceleratedSAP to quickly configure, deploy, and constantly modify R/3. As the foundation tool for AcceleratedSAP, Business Engineer's improvements will continue to enhance the AcceleratedSAP program.

Customer benefits from AcceleratedSAP are increasing exponentially. While AcceleratedSAP was designed for companies with revenues between $200 million and $2.5 billion, it was believed that these organizations would have the greatest need for a rapid implementation option that didn't require as many resources. However, the result was that customers from all sized companies and locations discovered advantages in using the AcceleratedSAP techniques. The reasons for the broad acceptance of ASAP was seen in benefits that allow customers to achieve significant goals in a shortened period of time.

ASAP produced much quicker returns on their R/3 investment. It acquired rapid returns for each R/3 investment and was the motivating factor for the creation of AcceleratedSAP in the first place. Many customers found that they benefited from this program with a quick return on their investments. This often meant restricting an implementation to three or four modules in order to make certain that rapid deployment could be met, while the remainder could be deployed in either the second or third AcceleratedSAP phase. The results indicate realizable returns in a shortened time frame.

ASAP for Accelerated Year 2000 Transitions

The year 2000 problem is growing in complexity, and the time for dealing with it continues to diminish significantly each day. One way to counter this problem is to transition your computer systems from legacy applications. Once you accomplish this goal, you can replace many noncompliant, older systems with new systems that offer enhanced functionality. The largest factor against deploying R/3 involved satisfying your year 2000 functionality which, under a normal implementation time frame, would sacrifice too much time to accomplish your compliance goals. The utilization of AcceleratedSAP permits any size organization to rapidly replicate existing functionality.

Standard Global Production

There are several large businesses that have deployed R/3 globally only to find that each R/3 implementation was managed by a leading consulting firm that varied from site to site. In this sense, you would not acquire sufficient benefits from reusing or learning from one implementation site to another. However, this standardization permits a much simpler enterprisewide production of R/3 functionality. AcceleratedSAP provides a common technique that can be used by various consulting firms throughout various geographic or business boundaries in simultaneous implementations.

Reusable Technique for R/3 Deployment

When you reuse techniques, as either a pilot or a first-phase R/3 production, the knowledge of AcceleratedSAP and R/3 exists within the client organization. Customers who initiate a second phase through an AcceleratedSAP implementation require less external resources for their next implementation phase.

One of the benefits is that it offers an optimal basis for R/3 upgrade. One of the most important lessons acquired from different organizations who have implemented R/3 is that the more modifications executed on the R/3 system, the more challenging it is to benefit from its advanced functionality in R/3 upgrades. This is due to the fact that SAP spends several hundred million dollars in research and development every year to enhance its R/3 solution. At that point, customers often believe that they have modified R/3, but instead become upset because they lack the ability to easily migrate from one version to another. The functionality of AcceleratedSAP rests in the fact that it can help you find solutions within R/3. It can successfully result in an optimal foundation that allows you to upgrade from one R/3 version to the next.

Deploying R/3 Effectively

Regardless of whether AcceleratedSAP is chosen, the process that enterprise management uses to make this determination offers a great deal of information on the R/3 implementation path that is selected. AcceleratedSAP does not optimize all R/3 implementations, however, making that decision makes executives deal with compromises between a rapid R/3 deployment and the efforts necessary for fundamental business changes while deploying R/3.

R/3 System Release 4.0

This chapter focues on enchancements to the R/3 system for Release 4. These enhanceents fall into main areas:

- General enhancements to the R/3 system from 3.1
- Specific enhancements to the HR module
- Specific enhancements to the FI module
- Industry solutions.

SAP pioneered three-tier client/server architecture with the initial release of R/3. In its following releases, SAP continuously enhanced R/3's business processes and functions. The introduction of R/3 Release 3.1 allowed SAP to take R/3 business processes to the Web by adding Internet application components.

SAP has now produced R/3 Release 4.0 which can support the entire value chain from point of sale to point of production. It offers enhanced key logistics, human resources, and financial functions that extend the enterprise, providing better methods to discuss with business partners. R/3 Release 4.0 contains a variety of new functions that enhance value-chain management and time-to-market.

R/3 can assist users in matching the need for speed within the supply chain against the need to control costs and manage risk. It can also help organizations meet the upcoming challenge of switching to the Euro—the new European currency—and prepare businesses for the coming millenium.

General Enhancements

R/3 4.0 Information

Value chain innovation is a method of constantly improving a business. It offers a means to produce flexible business processes that can respond to changing market conditions. It enhances the enterprise and helps identify and create new business processes now.

R/3 offers advanced production planning and manufacturing processes that maximize time-to-market efficiencies in manufacturing environments. Its components use Advanced Application Link Enabling (ALE) to permit execution of distributed planning and manufacturing processes.

R/3 Release 4.0's enhanced engineer-to-order capabilities makes it possible to streamline the supply chain and discover new features to assist in setting priorities and optimizing the shipping of goods to customers.

R/3 4.0 provides a comprehensive distribution resource planning component for the creation of sales channels. Business application programming interfaces (BAPIs) refine communication with transportation partners.

SAP offers a BAPI-based solution for managing the environmental and regulatory requirements associated with processing hazardous goods.

SAP provides a global enterprise management consolidation component to give corporate controllers critical, business information with new management consolidation and transfer pricing tools useful in managing decentralized business units. It also provide target costing and activity-based cost management capabilities for optimizing internal processes.

R/3 4.0 offers corporate finance solutions that provide treasurers with the tools for enterprise-wide investment and risk management. These tools include functions such as joint venture accounting and group investment controlling.

Business Framework

SAP's Business Framework features several SAP and non-SAP products that create a component-based, integrated solution. A company can deploy new R/3 functionality incrementally to curtail disruptions in the organization. Business Framework allows a company to meet changing business conditions quickly by deploying new processes, usually by adding or changing business components.

Protecting Sensitive Documents

Applications can use Secure Store and Forward (SSF) mechanisms to protect sensitive data and documents. This is especially important if data is stored on external data media or transferred across insecure networks. R/3 Release 4.0 uses digital signatures and encryption to make certain of the integrity of the data, authenticity of the sender, non-repudiation, and confidentiality.

Business Engineer

R/3 Business Engineer has been improved to configure R/3 faster and easier. It supports phased implementations and changes to existing configurations without disrupting continuous business activities. The R/3 Business Engineer allows you to define organizational structures and the business processes needed using familiar language while walking you through an implementation step by step.

Templates

Industry-specific templates reduce the number of functions displayed speeding up implementation even more. Existing configurations can be easily changed when the support of new business goals or shifting market demands is needed.

Electronic Batch Record

The electronic batch record is enhanced by inspection results through data collected in post-process controls after production. You can allocate the batches of the manufactured product to the record. An approval procedure for master recipes exists using the change requests of engineering change management. You can use change requests to represent a procedure in which changes to be made in a master recipe must first be requested, and then be checked and approved by different persons before the change can actually be carried out in the master recipe. The approval procedure is implemented in the inspection plan. The new active ingredients processing functionality is used to manage materials that contain one or more concentrates or active ingredients. This functional solution supports complete integration of product data management, engineering change management, and the financial aspects of cash flow and cost control. It is imperative that you have the ability to track changes in the product structure. SAP can effectively handle serial numbers as well as other parameters.

Resource Planning

Workforce planning tools are highly important to the success of research and development departments or the design phase of a product.

Resource and workforce planning function together as a specific function specially developed for the engineering SAP Aerospace & Defense R/3 Release 4.0. This release further extends the solution for designers, manufacturers, or maintainers of high value capital equipment. All primary and auxiliary business processes deal with business acquisition through product design and manufacturing to delivery and subsequent maintenance, are effectively supported.

Transfer Pricing

Transfer Pricing handles the valuation of material stocks and goods movements from the group as well as from divisions, organizational units, or profit centers.

Managing the Approval Process

Appropriation requests help organizations manage the corporate approval process from idea through implementation. Users rate requests by their viability and priority in order to create an investment wish list. The projects are produced directly from there. Users can then create global reports in Investment Management and they import data from any source including the local R/3 systems, R/2 applications, or non-SAP systems into a central R/3 system.

Investment Management summarizes the data. Users can analyze the data using a variety of reports. A link from the investment program to plant maintenance orders opens a global window on capital investment.

Plant maintenance orders are used to manage repairs or new assets under construction and link them to corporate budgets. Flow Manufacturing provides effective manufacturing capabilities as well as improved information flow for demand-driven manufacturing.

Work Cycles

Work cycles are calculated to control material flow and to calculate the time the material is retained on the line. Manufacturers must also allocate products to lines and operations, and components, production resources, and tools to parts of the line. This is where you will designate feeder lines to main lines to make certain that the two are synchronized.

Customizing Functionality

Companies can use customizing functions to modify the transfer of data from one system to another. Special Business Application Programming Interfaces (BAPIs) (that exchange data between systems) support specific information and comparison functions.

Virtual Value Chains

You can create virtual value chains just by placing your product catalogs on the Internet. Many vendors provide industry-specific catalogs containing products and services offered by a number of different vendors. In R/3 Release 4.0, external catalogs can communicate with R/3. This allows organizations to become fully integrated and motivated by SAP the maintenance of the virtual marketplace. You can search for materials in a catalog on the Internet and assign the vendor as the supply source in the purchase requisition. You can use information from the requisition such as the description, quantity, delivery date, or a maximum price to search through an external catalog. You can adopt various data from that search for items that include material description, vendor number, confirmed quantity, or price in the purchase requisition.

The specific information passed to R/3 depends on the external catalog. When dealing with the procurement of external services, you can
treat standard service catalogs like external catalogs. These features are
critical to extending business access traditional boundaries and generate
competitive advantage in virtual value chains.

The Procurement Process

Establishing consignment stores frees capital. SAP has extended the
process of handling vendor consignment stocks in R/3 Release 4.0. A
warehouse can contain stocks owned by different consignment vendors.
Settlement is based on the material withdrawn from the consignment
stock. The result is that Inventory Management and Invoice Verification
must satisfy special requirements.

You can support the procurement process for consignment material,
you can define conditions for consignment processing that are valid for
specific periods. It is possible for you to input specific conditions in foreign currencies and include alternative units of mea-sure. When you deal
with inventory postings made for deliveries, good issues, confirmations
for run schedule headers, and in the relevant preparatory phases you will
note that the system can suggest the stocks from which to withdraw
material.

Warehouse Structure

Complex warehouse structures Strategies for stock placement and stock
removal Optimization of space usage The R/3 Warehouse Management
System supports both load distribution and operative activities in the
warehouse regardless of whether you manage inventory by storage bin.

The warehouse complex is extended to include gates, material staging
areas, and picking areas General planning and detailed planning of the
workload in the warehouse from beginning to end for incoming and outgoing deliveries based on the number of packing units, the number of
items, or weight.

The Warehouse Management System supports the processes in the
warehouse or distribution center with respect to: the definition of the
operative structure elements: support during planning of resources and
activities, processing of goods receipts, goods issues, and stock transfers,
and methods for decision making and monitoring.

Goods and Distribution

Goods issues and distribution functions are fully integrated in the system, and the flow of goods is supported throughout the entire process. Distribution of work into waves for picking purposes, packing, loading, and goods issue. These activities can be triggered by transports or route schedules. DRP calculates the net requirements of the distribution centers and offers a distribution plan to guarantee the pertinent stock levels in the distribution centers. This plan considers lead times and is represented by stock transfer requisitions. Requirements can be satisfied by more than one supply center. Deployment is short term unlike DRP. Your deployment objectives help you cope with deviations from the DRP run. Deviations can occur in the production process or they can occur because of imprecise sales forecasts. Deployment uses algorithms for fair-share and push distribution to help you take appropriate action when shortfall or surplus situations happens.

All of the activities for incoming and outgoing goods in the warehouse are supported by the system. The system is then fully integrated in the goods receipt and goods distribution processes.

Event Handling

Users can handle multi-session events or conventions where several sessions of a main event are held in parallel. They can also perform all processing functions such as resource reservation for the individual sessions of a convention. R/3 Release 4.0 includes several enhancements and extensions that improve usability, flexibility, and performance. The Human Resources ad-hoc query is a simple and powerful tool for choosing and processing personnel information that is based on information types within Personnel Administration that can be composed for particular areas using ABAP Query. Companies can also use selection criteria to make the query in the most efficient manner possible.

Interfaces

Publish-and-subscribe interfaces allow users to determine specific events that have occurred in the application to make data available. These events trigger other processes illustrated by a master record created because documents can be entered, parked, changed or reverse. This allows clearing to be executed or canceled a workflow to be started.

Process interfaces control business processes similar to payments but differ from the standard system. With the new process interfaces, an organization can choose payment methods or other features with respect to defined selection criteria.

ATP Server

Available-To-Promise (ATP) server provides real-time integrated availability-to-promise checks for high-volume, high-order line-item environments across the complete logistics supply chain. Organizational entities are complex and often availability checks do not occur within a conventional, transaction-based system.

An ATP server permits methods that include rules-based or optimized availability checks. It can set delivery expectations when demand occurs and perform against those expectations with the objective of providing ATP information throughout the company.

An ATP server allows you to perform availability checks and performance improvements in production planning and high volume capability.

Backflushing

Fast response times are critical when creating confirmations for production orders or run schedule headers. Extra processing steps must be automatically triggered when confirmation occurs. These steps involve functions that result directly from the confirmation of the operation, including the determination of current costs or backflushing and confirmation of previous operations in the processing chain.

To execute detailed process chains, a company must distinguish between functions where time is critical and where it isn't. It must then transfer processing steps to the background, aggregate them, and place them in parallel.

Individual confirmation functions are encapsulated and can be executed online as a confirmation in an asynchronous background task, or as a periodic background job. These functions include:

- Updating actual data
- Capacity adjustment
- Automatic goods receipt
- Backflushing of material components.

External Processing

External processing is significant for distributing work in virtual value chains. R/3 4.0 supports these processes by integrating production and purchasing. External processing also includes creation of a subcontract, and purchase requisition at order creation, allocation of components, copy of the parts to be provided from the order to the purchase order, processing of a subcontract purchase requisition, update of material costs, workflows, scheduling an external operation, and integration of quality assurance during goods receipt for the purchase order.

Line Design

Designing production lines and planning the production process are two of the most important tasks for flow and repetitive manufacturers. Within these types of environments, production is segmented into distinct processes and the sequence of these processes is used as a basis for developing the plan for loading a line. This is the reason that line is subdivided into line segments and work cycles.

Line design functions have been enhanced to meet the special requirements of flow and repetitive manufacturers. R/3 4.0 incorporates the following functions:

- Line designing and line processing using a graphical interface
- Calculation of key figures for optimizing lines
- Product-to-line allocation
- Allocation of processes to line segments
- Allocation of operations, components, operating facilities, and documents to line segments
- Definition of work cycle areas in a line
- Calculation of workcycle times Synchronization of main and feeder lines
- Creating and printing
- Operational method sheets (instruction sheets for line work centers)
- Sequencing
- Flow shop and variant manufacturing with a high volume of orders
- Sequencing functions to plan order quantities, finding the sequence for flow-shop manufacturing.

In this process, the system loads the workstations of a line and takes sequencing restrictions into account. When dealing with customer-oriented assembly processing in the automobile and computer industries sequence planning is a significant part of production planning.

KANBAN

KANBAN is a procedure for controlling production and material flow. Material is not restocked or produced until a certain production level is reached. Significant parameters for production control with KANBAN incorporate several KANBANs that circulate in a control cycle. These parameters can be used to define material circulation and material stock. Optimizing these parameters, helps minimize inventory levels.

The goal is to guarantee material replenishment with the lowest possible inventory. Since inventory needs fluctuate greatly, it is important to adjust these parameters periodically. R/3 4.0 automatically calculates the number of KANBANs and the quantity per KANBAN.

A system proposes a number of KANBANs and quantity per KANBAN using a report based on either the results of material requirements planning or long-term planning. It is possible to designate which valuation period the system uses to make the calculation.

PDM & ERP Systems

Product Data Management has several functions. The PDM components of R/3 4.0 extend the supply chain from component manufacturers through suppliers to customers for total product life-cycle management. They can now be used in an individual R/3 system.

Tight coupling between the integrated, distributed PDM system, and the Enterprise Resource Planning (ERP) system makes certain the necessary data are exchanged. Distributing data between systems allows companies to store design data separately from production data. Releases and maintenance levels in the PDM and ERP systems can be upgraded at different times. An integrated, distributed PDM solution in R/3 is part of the R/3 Business Framework strategy.

Data are exchanged between the PDM system and the ERP system using ALE. In R/3 4.0, ALE interfaces have been extended for material master records bills of material, document management, engineering change management classes, characteristics, and object dependencies.

ABAP VM

ABAP has grown into an object-oriented programming language. ABAP Objects have evolved into the new generation of the ABAP virtual machine that support the new interfacing technologies and enhances the interoperability with external object architectures. The ABAP VM also ensures that all R/3 application components can be executed without modification in different system environments.

ALE and BAPI

ALE supports BAPIs that have Application Link Enabling (ALE) because companies can utilize a technology that integrates components into network solutions independent of their release version. They integrate business processes between different R/3 Systems or business components. ALE controls the exchange of business messages between these components and makes certain of their semantic synchronization. BAPIs (methods of SAP Business Objects) can now also be invoked asynchronously by ALE.

Management

Sample Management permits flexible planning of the actual samples to be drawn and the assignment of inspection results to a sample record. The new enhancement satisfies the requirements of Good Manufacturing Practice (GMP) for the documentation and verification of samples used in inspection processing.

Sample management is integrated with the existing quality management functions and includes inspection planning, inspection lot processing, and results recording.

It is important to determine methods for saving on transportation and logistic costs while quickly shipping goods to satisfy customers. Transportation functions offer an interface to transportation planning and optimizing. R/3 4.0 integrated functions for freight charge processing, include defining freight rates and agreements using the SAP condition technique. SAP pricing can be used to compute transportation costs for each phase of a shipment.

The R/3 time sheet component standardizes cross-application time recording. Time Sheet rolls the time recording functions of several applications into a single transaction. With time sheet an organization can supply information on work times to applications including:

- Attendance in Human Resources (HR)
- Internal activity allocation in Controlling (CO)
- Confirmations in Plant Maintenance (PM)
- Project System (PS)
- Service Management (SM)
- Entry of services performed in External Services Management (MM-SRV).

After components SAP were created in R/3 4.0, Human Resources (HR) and Travel Management were split off from R/3 as separate components with a dedicated database and an independent release cycle. The HR and Travel Management incorporate several workflow, Internet, and intranet enhancements.

ESS

In R/3 4.0, SAP Human Resources incorporates Employee Self-Service (ESS) solutions allow employees to view and maintain data in R/3 easily through a Webbrowser. The whole enterprise community can connect with R/3 and maintain own human resource data through the Internet or corporate intranet.

ESS benefits include 24-hour, 365-days-a-year access, low-cost business transactions, access to the most up-to-date information, and direct data entry in order to accelerate business processes and cut costs.

Web-enabled SAP Business Workflow

SAP has enhanced Web-enabled SAP business workflow to make it even simpler for users to access and execute business workflow 24 hours a day from corporate intranets or the Internet. Users can trigger workflow through the Web using HTML forms. This enhances operations by adding an important option to the existing possibilities of triggering workflow through BAPIs or Internet application components.

Users can access their integrated inboxes via the Web to execute transactions, create attachments, or forward items to co-workers. SAP offers Workflow Wizards to make it easier and faster to implement workflow. A company can add workflow to a customer-developed transaction and an R/2 transaction using a Workflow Wizard that automatically generates a workflow task.

Form-Based Business Workflow

Form-Based SAP Business Workflow in HR Many administrative processes in Human Resources simply consist of an employee processing business transactions, like pay increases, applications for leave, and personnel requirements. In R/3 Release 4.0, you can create simple forms using tools like VisualBasic or JetForms and integrate them with SAP Business Workflow to create self-service Human Resources applications.

SAP has extended the Web-enabled SAP Business Workflow to make it even simpler for users to access and execute business workflow 24 hours a day from corporate intranets or the Internet. New in R/3 Release 4.0, SAP Business Workflow allows users to trigger workflow through the Web using HTML forms. This adds an important option to the existing possibilities of triggering workflow through BAPIs or Internet Application Components. Users can access their integrated inboxes through the Web to execute transactions, create attachments, or forward items to co-workers. SAP provides more Workflow Wizards to make it easier and faster to implement workflow. Organizations can add workflow to a customer-developed transaction and an R/2 transactions using a Workflow Wizard that automatically generates a workflow task.

Specific Enhancements to HR

HR Country-Specific Versions

The HR country versions are extensions of the general, international functionality with respect to personnel administration and payroll. They offer additional functions that specifically meet a country's legal requirements and specific business procedures.

SAP produces new country versions for the Personnel Administration component for Mexico and the Personnel Administration and Payroll components for Indonesia, Malaysia, New Zealand, and Taiwan. SAP has 30 different country versions of R/3. Travel Management has been adapted for Germany, Austria, Switzerland, the U.S., and Japan. In R/3 Release 4.0, country versions are also available for Great Britain, the Netherlands, Belgium, France, and Denmark. R/3 Release 4.0 supports the statutory and the enterprise-specific provisions for trip cost accounting in country versions that allows enterprises to reengineer business processes in travel management to account for statutory regulations and company policy. Multinational companies will profit from the parallel operation of several country versions when setting up international Human Resources Service Centers.

SAP/ADP USA Payroll Interface

The SAP/ADP USA payroll interface outsources gross payroll data to an ADP DOS system product for net payroll processing. R/3 Release 4.0. It adds an interface to ADP PC/Payroll for Windows through a master data extract so you do not need to configure payroll schemas and rules. In R/3

Release 4.0, external recruitment systems and R/3 can exchange data using an independent interface.

Before any employee can participating in insurance plans, they must provide evidence of insurability (EOI). This includes a medical affidavit for proof of good health. R/3 Release 4.0 can store employees' elections before EOI is provided by creating active plans, pending plans, or no plans at all. Companies can then enroll employees when an EOI is received or enroll them in an interim plan. They can also define and monitor grace periods and then delete pending plans whose grace period has expired.

Time Sheet Component

The time Sheet component is where actual work is recorded across applications. Simulation or "what if" analysis is needed at the start of a project or product life cycle when many factors are unknown. Even when the product is almost ready for shipment customer changes may require a simulation to determine the consequences in terms of costs and schedules. A flexible and comprehensive simulation tool places the information needed for efficient decision making is at the ready.

Earned value analysis, profit analysis forecast, and various project reports illustrate many of the features supporting both engineering and construction requirements.

HR Reporting Tools

You can use the standard HR reporting tools to perform simple evaluations for selected payroll results. Payroll results can be retrieved by employee using configurable info-types. Eligibility rules govern which employees can participate in the plan. Enterprises can set up the salary structure based on salary groups or grades and their associated salary ranges. Companies can also designate salary grades at the position or job level and by employee. In addition, salary planning allows you to create salary budgets from bottom to top with a roll-up over the organizational structure. The time intervals in R/3 Release 4.0 are more specific so companies can define requirements and find match-ups. You can also designates qualifications as part of the requirements definition.

HR-Career/Succession Planning

In Career Planning, personnel departments can create potential career paths within your company. This type of planning assists you in motivating ambitious, qualified employees by showing the options available to them. Succession Planning provides information about employees who currently fulfill the requirements of a particular position now or in the future. This makes it easier to fill vacant positions from within your company. In both Career Planning and Succession Planning, the system compiles a hit-list of people, sorted in order of their suitability. Matching personnel profiles and position profiles shows in detail how to further train employees to broaden their skills to meet future requirements.

COBRA

SAP has enhanced R/3's COBRA functions to integrate COBRA processing for health plans and spending accounts. R/3 4.0 processes completed COBRA election forms and updates and tracks the status of beneficiaries. An organization can notify COBRA-qualified beneficiaries when election periods have expired, can track payments, send out late payment notices, confirm COBRA election changes, and cancel COBRA participation.

Compensation Management

Compensation Management controls and administers an organization's remuneration policies. The compensation plan definition can be used to create multiple compensation plans and assign them, using the organizational structure. The compensation plans have flexible eligibility and individual processing rules.

Eligibility rules define which employees can participate in the plan. Enterprises can set up a salary structure based on salary groups or grades and their associated salary ranges. Companies can also designate salary grades at the position or job level and by employee. In addition, salary planning helps in creating salary budgets from bottom to top with a roll-up over the organizational structure.

Personnel departments can create potential career paths within a company. This type of planning assists in motivating ambitious, qualified employees by showing the options available to them. Succession planning provides information about employees who fulfill the requirements of a specific position now or in the future. This makes it easier to fill vacant positions from within a company.

In addition, matching personnel profiles and position profiles shows in detail how further to train employees to broaden their skills to meet future requirements.

Specific Enhancements to FI

Treasury Management

Treasury Management has applications for money market, foreign exchange, derivatives, securities, loans, and market risk management. Treasury Management offers functions for input and managing of transactions, developing and analyzing portfolios, position management, transition to financial accounting, flexible reporting and data-feed interfaces.

The market risk management component supports interest and currency exposure analysis. It also emulates collections of real and fictitious financial transactions and offers market-to-market valuation.

Measurements and Indicators

Traditional capacity measurements of machine time and product throughput volume are now improved to integrate Activity Based Costing to help manage overhead cost by identifying idle capacities of overhead resources.

Consolidation

Consolidation Enterprise Controlling's Consolidation application component aggregates data from all parts of the R/3 system. Data collection occurs at the company, business, or profit-center level, offering valuation and elimination methods that permit consolidation to be the foundation for optimizing group reporting within an organization. Consolidation links to the centralized Executive Information System. Its main functions involve multiple dimensions to simultaneously represent different areas of consolidation in group reporting, consolidation units in hierarchies by time periods and versions, multiple charts of accounts collection of company, business area, and profit-center data from R/3 systems.

The consolidation component was developed for corporate groups that must use various sets of tools to create internal and statutory group reports to standardize on a single tool. The component helps organizations reconcile internal and external data using uniform functions and a common user interface.

Self-Audit

Self-Audit enhances audit quality and makes the auditing process smoother and more straightforward. The audit report tree provides various auditing functions and default configurations, including auditing procedures and documentation, auditing evaluations, and downloading audit data. The self-audit component supports continuous controlling and intcrim audits as well as year-end closing statements and year-end audits.

Joint-Venture Accounting

Joint Venture Accounting allows an organization to combine monetary and personal resources for projects with high-risk, large-capital investment, and extended payback periods. Joint Venture Accounting allocates periodic expenses to venture partners based on their contribution and working interests.

This component:

- Distributes revenues and expenses among partners with regard to individual working interests
- Transfers material and assets between ventures
- Allows change management and suspense by groups of equity holders
- Permits expense and revenue netting by equity partner.

Joint venture accounting:

- Processes partner-carried interest
- Inputs venture transactions in more than one currency in parallel
- Bills partners and receives payment.
- Processes venture partner cutbacks as well as cutbacks to other divisions of the corporation
- Offers a variety of tools.

Activity-Based Costing

Activity Based Costing makes it possible to define cross-functional processes as well their cost drivers. Process, activity, and quantities are determined automatically from operational cost driver data in the integrated R/3 system environment.

Process costs can be traced to products by multiplying the consumed process quantities with the process price. They can be allocated directly to profitability segments. Activity-based costing handles the strategic decision making process by concentrating on the right products for the right customers in the right markets.

Payment Cards

Payment cards are replacing cash. Because payment cards have gained in popularity, card technology has greatly advanced. SAP has a flexible payment card solution for entry-level and sophisticated systems accepting all sorts of payment cards while conducting business with several partners.

Payment card functions support sales processes for credit cards used for purchasing goods and services with regular billing with or without extended credit, procurement cards that are issued on behalf of companies to employees for purchasing small-ticket items, cards used by customers to buy goods and services from a merchant or group of merchants, and payment card processing. These items support card data in the sales order.

Information necessary for payment card processing is stored at various levels in the sales order. The header contains payer information (items contain pricing information), schedule lines contain delivery dates and quantities, and a payment card plan attached to the order contains the card number, card type, and authorization information.

An organization can store all relevant data in a payment card master record and control whether the authorization check is performed at order entry or later. The system can be set up to determine card numbers. It then checks to make certain that the authorization is still valid for delivery creation and goods issues. Should the authorization no longer be valid, the system instructs the user to reinitiate an authorization check in the sales order.

The system then copies payment card information from the sales order to the billing document or uploads it directly into the billing document from the point of sale. Whenever a billing document is released to financial accounting, the system copies the payment card information, billing amount, and authorization information from the payment card plan into the accounting document. Financial accounting determines the card category used in payment, then starts the appropriate settlement process.

SAP payment card software is compatible with electronic marketplaces, allowing fully automatic order entry, product marketing on a national, and international scale, up-to-date customer information in electronic catalogs and product brochures, and electronic payment.

In working with point of sale, authorization are executed from an external system. Relevant data is imported into the R/3 system where a billing document is created. The authorization process starts when a customer uses a payment card and the card number is recorded in the sales order. The card number together with the payer, address, and sales order amount are forwarded to the clearing house for authorization to make certain that payment is received. Until authorization has been granted for the transaction, the sales order is blocked for delivery.

An SAP payment card solution involves authorization functions so that authorization checks occur in the background to reduce the costs of transferring data, authorization checks in real-time, and manual entry of authorization information in sales orders. Documentary credits reduce the risks of foreign trade transactions. Documentary support of payments provides the buyer with power of disposal over the goods because the documents are given only on or after payment. The documents offer the vendor confirmation that the quantity, quality, and that the nature of the goods delivered are the same as determined in the contract.

Payment types include payment against documentary collection, documents against payment, documents against acceptance, and payment using letter of credit. SAP supports documentary business processing through the development of documentary letters of credit without reference to orders or deliveries, assigning documentary letters of credit to one or more orders, checking the validity of a letter of credit for one or more orders, updating the value of goods delivered against the letter of credit, blocking an order or delivery if credit rules are not satisfied, and monitoring.

These functions have been integrated into the credit management section of the sales and distribution component so letters of credit are guaranteed to be coordinated with other forms of payment security.

Industry Solutions

Utilities

SAP Automotive and the automotive industry require dynamic, global, and customer-focused business processes. These support shorter product cycles, reaction to cost pressures, and the call of product variety for new manufacturing methods.

SAP Utilities

SAP Utilities for R/3 4.0 provides a crucial industry solution and I's supplemented with the industry component IS-U/CCS (Industry Specific Utilities/Customer Care and Service), the first client/server customer care and information system that is completely integrated with standard enterprise business application software.

IS-U/CCS provides many functions of standalone, "specialized" customer care and customer information systems. It offers the benefits of tight integration of essential business systems and processes that utility companies need in order to remain competitive.

IS-U/CCS offers a comprehensive customer information and billing system for customer services, marketing, and sales support, consolidated billing, mass billing, and metering. The Internet and intranet abilities allow utilities to offer real-time information for employees, suppliers, partners, and customers. With IS-U/CCS it is easy to customize the needs of the individual utilities company, which benefits from SAP's Business Engineer and ASAP.

R/3 4.0 satisfies requirements by offering support for flow manufacturing. This incorporates automated KANBAN calculation, line design to illustrate the line structure, and sequencing as a tool for graphical demonstration of line covering. ATP servers make it possible to perform availability checks and achieve improvements in production planning and high volume capability.

SAP Retail

SAP Retail integrates business practices into enterprise-wide software with both functionals and flexibility. It allows retailers to respond to changes in customers' buying behavior, and helps them gain control over the whole supply chain, from point of sale to point of production. SAP Retail completely integrates and supports store systems and EPOS (Electronic Point of Sale) including credit card payment, down payments, layaways, and billing transactions. SAP Retail also includes a predefined set of information structures that offer lean information.

Category Manager Workbench is a specialized process-oriented environment that focuses on the activities involved in grouping merchandise. It combines the distributed activities of planning and controlling categories of merchandise, costs, and profitability.

SAP Retail has the ability to support electronic commerce on the World Wide Web. It provides the ability to link to third-party systems including Microsoft's Commerce Server or IBM's Netcommerce and offers an SAP Internet component called the "Product Catalog with Sales Order Entry".

SAP Chemicals

SAP Chemicals results from the enhancement of the existing R/3 system to satisfy the requirements of the process industry. Hazardous Goods

Management functions to enhance current application components of R/3 to support hazardous goods processing. SAP's Environment, Health and Safety component for hazardous goods management for R/3 4.0 works with hazardous goods master data. Prior to shipping, products must be classified with respect to legislation. This classification must work with the hazard potential of the product as well as with the traffic carrier. The data are stored in the traffic carrier-specific material master and are necessary for both hazardous goods checks and the development of hazardous goods documents.

Product safety enhancements with respect to SAP's EH&S component an incorporate the substance information system so that companies can create complex drill-down reports on substance properties. Queries and results can be recorded and displayed in customer-specific layouts. Report management functions support various work processes including material safety data sheets (MSDS) and labels. Enhanced functions allow for the designation of status registration and the import/export substance, phrase, and source data.

The preconfigured industry system represents the R/3 business processes needed by the chemical industry. This live R/3 system comprises the industry model, systems settings, and master data specific to the industry and additional documentation to supplement the standard SAP documentation.

SAP Pharmaceuticals

SAP Pharmaceuticals R/3 4.0 supports FDA requirements, including the use of smartcard readers for electronic signature, a forgery-proof method of identifying people executing transactions in the R/3 system. An organization can activate the electronic signature feature to complete the processing of a phase in the PI-Sheet, release the electronic batch record and inspection results record, finalize inspection lots, release master recipe/inspection plan changes, and release documents.

To complement the existing PP-PI (Production Planning for Process Industries) module, the new component Process Flow Scheduler (PFS) provides a finite-capacity scheduling system that is part of supply chain planning. Supply chain planning was created to assist manufacturing plant planners in process industries. There are extra process control system integration models that permit linking to an external PI-Sheet.

SAP Consumer Products in R/3 4.0 offers features to improve the promotion planning process, permitting flexible promotional budgeting as well as the ability to track real-time billing activity to gauge a promotion's effectiveness. The free goods function offers a flexible method of defining buy-one-get-one-free promotions.

R/3 gives planners the extra capability of tracking promotional commitments to provide marketing a clear idea of the objective market's intent before starting the actual program. In addition, SAP's payment card functions handle the processing of all types of payment cards while conducting business with several partners.

Distribution resource planning is used for planning of complex distribution networks. It offers production planning with accurate requirement plans to optimize the distribution of available stock levels in the distribution network.

The consumer products process modeling is based on R/3 Business Engineer and is a knowledge-based configuration that guides customers quickly through initial implementation and uses the same intuitive, and question/answer procedure to support ongoing changes and adaptations in business processes.

SAP Engineering and Construction

SAP Engineering and Construction supports the entire product life-cycle from design through planning and manufacturing to final assembly at the customer site. It also deals with the post-sales and service phases, and permits companies to concentrate on business and be more responsive to changes in product structures, whether in the design phase or later in production. R/3 organizations can acquire control over the entire life-cycle and the supply chain from suppliers and subcontractors to customers with Release 4.0.

SAP supports complete integration of product data management, engineering change management, and the financial aspects of cash flow and cost control. It is important to have the ability to track changes in the product structure.

Accurate workforce planning tools are crucial to the success of research and development departments or the design phase of a product. Plan key resources with workforce planning through a function specially developed for the engineering SAP Aerospace & Defense R/3 4.0. Release 4.0 enhances the solution for designers, manufacturers, and maintainers of high-value capital equipment. All primary and auxiliary business processes work with business acquisition, through product design and manufacturing to delivery, as well as subsequent maintenance.

SAP Aerospace & Defense

SAP Aerospace & Defense provides a variety of industry-specific features that allow users to adhere to commercial and governmental contracts. Cross-contract planning functions support inventory and production flexibility while tracking the ownership and cost of individual contracts. SAP Aerospace & Defense represents an integrated and comprehensive solution that satisfies the needs of the industry.

The integrated character of SAP Aerospace & Defense permits a detailed overview and online retrieval and analysis functionality for critical information required for program management success.

In combination with already existing functionality such as earned value management, time recording, and billing, SAP Aerospace & Defense represents an integrated and comprehensive solution that satisfies the needs of the industry.

Summary

In this chapter we have covered specific details of the new R/3 4.0. This is a significant upgrade from Release 3.x because its material will be present in several of SAP's course tracks. We discussed the new features of this release, how enhanced BAPIs play a critical role, and how each industry benefits from the new functions.

18-1   Explain the concept of value chain Innovation?

18-2   How does R/3 Release 4.0 respond to market conditions?

18-3   What does R/3 provide in order to increase time-to-market efficiency?

18-4   What do R/3 components use to running distributed planning and manufacturing processes?

18-5   What do manufacturers benefit from?

18-6   What new features does R/3 Release 4.0 offer?

18-7   What new BAPIs are present in the new release of R/3?

18-8   What does SAP's global enterprise management consolidation component offer?

18-9   Describe the level of customer service features in R/3.

18-10   What does R/3's corporate finance solution offer in release 4.0?

18-11   What are the features of the business framework?

18-12   Describe SAP automotive and the industry with which it works.

18-13   Describe the SAP utilities-based industry.

18-14   What does IS-U/CCS offer?

18-15   R/3 Release 4.0 meets what type of requirements by providing support for what?

18-16   What does an ATP server allow?

18-17   How does R/3 Release 4.0 help manage product-related information?

18-18   How does SAP Retail function in R/3 Release 4.0?

18-19   What is the category manager workbench?

18-20   SAP Retail is able to support what on the Web? Name the two solutions it offers retailers.

18-21   Explain SAP Chemicals.

18-22   What does good hazard management do?

18-23   What must happen before products are shipped?

18-24   What do the product safety enhancements of SAP's environment, health, and safety component include?

18-25   What do report management functions support?

18-26   What does the active ingredients processing function include?

18-27   How can an existing PP-PI module be supplemented?

18-28   What do additional process control integration modules provide?

18-29   Which industry requires a preconfigured industry system?

18-30   Describe the SAP pharmaceuticals industry.

18-31   What is an electronic signature?

18-32   How is the electronic batch record enhanced?

18-33   Describe how the approval procedure is implemented.

18-34   How effective is the active ingredient from batch to batch?

18-35   How does the process flow scheduler fit in?

18-36   What is supply chain planning designed to do?

18-37   What are process control systems based on and what do they do with R/3 component communication?

18-38   What do SAP consumer products provide?

18-39   What does free goods functionality provide users?

18-40   What do SAP's payment card functions handle?

18-41   What is distribution resource planning designed for?

18-42   Explain the consumer products process modeling.

18-43   What is SAP engineering and construction?

18-44   Describe the integration of functionality within R/3 Release 4.0.

18-45   Describe precise workforce planning tools.

18-46   Describe what is involved with the planning of a key resource in workforce planning.

18-47   Describe the industry-specific features offered by SAP aerospace and defense.

18-48   What does cross-contract planning functionality support?

18-49   Describe and name a means of effectivity handling support.

18-50   Name three elements of functionality that, when coupled together, represent the integration of SAP aerospace and defense.

18-51   What is the time sheet component?

18-52   Explain enhanced cast and cost control management functionality.

18-53   Name features that support engineering and construction requirements.

18-54   Explain SAP's intranet strategy with R/3.

18-55   Explain SAP's treasury management functionality.

18-56   What does the market risk management component handle?

18-57   Explain the consolidation application component and discuss who makes it.

18-58   What are the consolidations application component's main functions?

18-59   Describe the self-audit component in R/3 Release 4.0.

18-60   What are the self-audit component functions?

18-61   What does joint venture accounting allow companies to do?

KEY CONCEPT

Many large organizations organize themselves by groups composed of legal entities. These legal entities make analyzing the whole group much more difficult. Besides monitoring the individual legal entities, companies usually require a management-oriented structure like business areas, divisions, or profit centers. In the past, this was oriented toward the legal entities.

18-62   Explain what transfer pricing supports.

18-63   What is activity-based costing?

18-64   Where can process cost be allocated to?

18-65   Are there any changes to the traditional capacity measurements of machine time and product throughput volume?

18-66   What are appropriation requests and how do they help organizations?

18-67   What does investment management do?

18-68   What are plant maintenance orders used for?

18-69   What are publish and subscribe interfaces?

18-70   What do process interfaces control?

18-71   What is the ATP server? State what it provides.

18-72   Explain where availability checks occur and why.

18-73   What does the ATP server allow?

18-74   How is highly automated confirmation achieved?

18-75   What does customizing allow?

18-76   What are individual confirmation functions?

18-77   How does R/3 support external processing?

18-78   What functions are included in external processing?

18-79   What does flow manufacturing provide?

18-80   Name two of the most important tasks for flow and repetitive manufacturers.

18-81   How are work cycles calculated in R/3 Release 4.0?

18-82   How have line design functions been enhanced?

18-83   How does the system use the information from sequencing?

18-84   What does sequencing determine in flow shop manufacturing?

18-85   How exactly is the line load displayed?

18-86   What can be determined using colors?

18-87   How are external optimization or model-mix procedures linked?

18-88   Define KANBAN in detail.

18-89   Describe the relationship between the demand and supply source and explain where this relationship is defined.

18-90   What are the most significant parameters for production control with KANBAN?

18-91   How does the system calculate the number and quantity of KANBANs?

18-92   What factor helps display detailed information for the control cycle?

18-93   What are PDM functions?

18-94   How can it be assured that the necessary data are exchanged?

18-95   What does distributing data between systems allow organizations to do?

18-96   How are data exchanged between the PDM system and the ERP system?

18-97   How can companies use customizing functions?

18-98   How do you enable companies to put their catalogs on the Internet?

18-99   What is the limiting factor that dictates what specific information is passed onto R/3?

18-100 Explain the process of vendor consignment.

18-101 What can a warehouse contain?

18-102 What is settlement based on?

18-103 How is the procurement process supported?

18-104 Does R/3 provide enhanced functionality to allow settlement of consignment liabilities?

18-105 Define a complex warehouse structure strategy.

18-106 Explain the level of integration present for both the goods issues and distribution functions.

18-107 Explain the process for the distribution of work in waves; why is this done?

18-108 What does DRP (Distributed Resource Planning) calculate?

18-109 How can requirements be satisfied?

18-110 How can deviations occur in the production process?

18-111 What does deployment use when a shortfall or surplus happens?

18-112 Describe the warehouse management system and what it supports.

18-113 Are all activities for incoming and outgoing goods in the warehouse supported by the system?

18-114 Explain the process of payment card processing.

18-115 Explain what the new payment card functionality supports.

18-116 Where is the information stored for payment card processing?

18-117 Where can companies store data and what can they control?

18-118 What does the system need to check to be valid?

18-119 How are card data dealt with in billing documents?

18-120 How and for what purpose are card data used in financial accounting?

18-121 How are accounts for payment card transactions dealt with?

18-122 Explain the concept of bill-back processing.

18-123 Define the standard payment card interface.

18-124   What is the SAP payment card software compatible with?

18-125   What are point-of-sale functions?

18-126   Describe the authorization process.

18-127   Describe the authorization functions of the SAP payment card solution.

18-128   What does documentary handling of payments provide?

18-129   There are two payment types; describe them fully.

18-130   How does SAP support documentary business processing?

18-131   What is the sample management component and what does it make possible?

18-132   How is the administration of sample data in a sample record handled?

18-133   What is sample management integrated with?

18-134   What is plant maintenance equipment used for?

18-135   What do calibration inspections monitor?

18-136   What is a value contract?

18-137   Is it possible to define restrictions on the customer or the material that is to be defined?

18-138   Against what does the system check the released materials?

18-139   Can a value contract be billed directly or per call-off?

18-140   Explain free goods functionality.

18-141   Explain the concept of freight charge processing?

18-142   What is cross-application time recording?

18-143   Describe the ease of use involved in the time recording interface.

18-144   Explain the components in the business framework architecture.

18-145   What can customers do to deploy HR functionality?

18-146   Explain HR globalization.

18-147   How does R/3 Release 4.0 deal with country versions?

18-148   How can HR be used as a self-service and outsourcing system? Start by defining what ESS is and how it relates directly to SAP human resources.

18-149   How are ESS components implemented?

18-150 Describe the benefits administration for CORBA enrollment.

18-151 Describe claim processing.

18-152 Name some benefits that ESS provides.

18-153 What are the two main functions of outsourcing?

18-154 What is the interface toolbox?

18-155 Explain the SAP/ADP USA payroll interface.

18-156 Describe the elements of an external recruitment system.

18-157 Explain EOI.

18-158 Describe the particulars of human resource training and event management.

KEY CONCEPT

R/3 Release 4.0 includes functions for booking and canceling attendance at training, event management, employee participation information, enrollment in benefits, and the use of form-based workflow in SAP business workflow.

18-159 How is human resource reporting handled in R/3 Release 4.0?

18-160 What can the standard HR reporting tools be used to perform?

18-161 What does the compensation management component do?

18-162 What do eligibility rules govern?

18-163 Explain the time intervals in R/3 Release 4.0 and how they are more specific for a company requirements.

18-164 Explain career and succession planning.

18-165 What do matching personnel profiles and position profiles show?

18-166 What does form-based SAP business workflow consist of?

18-167 How are forms created in SAP Release 4.0?

18-168 What does SAP deliver front-end components for?

18-169 How are ABAP objects different in R/3 Release 4.0, and what is ABAP VM?

18-170 What does ABAP VM ensure?

18-171 How does ALE support BAPIs?

18-172 How has R/3 Release 4.0 embraced secure internet applications?

18-174 How has R/3 Business Engineer changed with R/3 Release 4.0?

18-175 Through what does knowledge-based configuration guide users?

18-176 What do industry-specific templates reduce?

18-177 How has SAP extended its Web-enabled business workflow?

18-177 What benefits can users experience by accessing their integrated in boxes through the Web to execute transactions?

18-178 Does SAP Business Workflow extend support for electronic forms in R/3 Release 4.0? If so, how?

18-1 Value chain innovation is a means of constantly enhancing a business and producing flexible business processes that can respond to changing market forces. Value chain innovation extends the enterprise and assists in identifying and creating new business processes now. It can dramatically affect constant change management.

18-2 SAP makes it easier to respond to changing market conditions because the tight integration of the R/3 System permits coordination of all aspects of a business.

18-3 R/3 provides advanced production planning and manufacturing processes that maximize time-to-market efficiencies in manufacturing environments.

18-4 R/3 components use advanced Application Link Enabling (ALE) for execution of distributed planning and manufacturing processes.

18-5 Manufacturers benefit from R/3 Release 4.0's enhanced engineer-to-order capabilities, which streamline the supply chain. There are also new features that assist in prioritizing shipping goods to customers.

18-6 R/3 Release 4.0 offers a detailed distribution resource planning component for deploying new sales channels, new processes for managing payment-card operations, and enhanced warehouse and transportation-management features for better control and tracking of transportation costs.

18-7 New BAPIs refine communication with transportation partners. SAP has produced a BAPI-based solution for managing the environmental and regulatory requirements connected with processing hazardous goods.

18-8 SAP's global enterprise management consolidation component offers corporate controllers critical, timely business information with new management consolidation and transfer pricing tools for managing decentralized business units. It also offers target costing and activity-based cost management capabilities for optimizing internal processes.

18-9 SAP has improved the customer service features of R/3's service management software so that a service department can track configuration information about shipped products more simply, manage product and component life-cycle information, and better service installed products.

18-10 R/3 Release 4.0's corporate finance solution gives treasurers detailed tools for enterprise-wide investment and risk management and includes such capabilities as joint venture accounting and group investment controlling.

18-11 The business framework (Figure 18.1) features SAP and non-SAP products that form a component-based, integrated solution. An organization can

SOLUTIONS

deploy new R/3 functionality incrementally, which minimizes disruption of the organization. The business framework allows a company to adapt quickly to changing business conditions by deploying new processes. This change can be as simple as adding or changing business components.

FIGURE 18.1
Business Framework
(Automation)

Business Information Warehouse

Sales Force Automation

R/3
Application
Link Enabling

Electronic Commerce

Advanced Planner and Optimizer

18-12 The automotive industry needs dynamic, global, and customer-focused business processes. SAP automotive supports shorter product cycles, relieves cost pressures, and assists with product variety calling for new philosophies and methodologies in manufacturing.

18-13 SAP utilities for R/3 Release 4.0, the industry solution, is supplemented by the industry component IS-U/CCS (Industry Specific Utilities/Customer Care and Service), the first client/server customer care and information system completely integrated with standard enterprise business application software. It provides the full functionality of standalone, "specialized" customer care and customer information systems and the benefit of close coupling of essential business systems and processes that utility companies need to manage in order to remain competitive.

18-14 IS-U/CCS offers a detailed customer information and billing system and customer services, marketing, and sales support, consolidated billing, mass billing, and metering. The Internet and intranet abilities help utilities provide real-time information for employees, suppliers, partners, and customers. IS-U/CCS is easy to customize to the specific needs of a utilities company and benefits from SAP's Business Engineer and ASAP.

18-15 R/3 Release 4.0 meets those requirements by providing the support for flow manufacturing. This includes automated KANBAN calculation, line design to illustrate the line structure, and sequencing of tools for graphic demonstration of line covering.

18-16 An ATP server makes it possible to execute availability checks and performance improvements in production planning and high-volume capability.

18-17 Both the MAIS pickup sheet and evaluated receipt settlement produce PDM functionality, the better to manage product-related information during the entire product life cycle.

18-18 SAP retail integrates proven business practices into enterprise-wide software with both usefulness and flexibility. It permits retailers to respond to changes in their customers' buying behavior, and helps them gain control over the whole supply chain, by dealing with everything from point of sales to point of production. SAP retail completely integrates and supports store systems and EPOS such as credit card payment, down payments, layaways, and billing transactions. SAP retail also includes a predefined set of information structures that offer lean information.

18-19 The category manager workbench is a specialized process-oriented environment that concentrates on the activities involved in grouping merchandise. It ties together distributed activities of planning and controlling categories of merchandise, their costs, and their profitability. A central tool such as this is the prerequisite for cross-company projects such as efficient consumer response.

18-20 SAP retail is able to support electronic commerce on the Web, offering retailers two solutions:

1. A link to third-party systems such as Microsoft's Commerce Server or IBM's Netcommerce
2. An SAP Internet component called the "Product Catalog with Sales Order Entry".

18-21 SAP chemicals is the result of enhancing the existing R/3 system to satisfy the requirements of the process industry.

18-22 Hazardous goods management works to improve existing application components of R/3 to support hazardous goods processing. SAP's Environment, Health and Safety (EH&S) component for hazardous goods management for R/3 Release 4.0 deals with hazardous goods master data.

18-23 Before shipping, products must be classified with respect to legislation. This classification must deal with the hazard potential of the product as well as the traffic carrier. Data are stored in the traffic carrier-specific material master and are required for both hazardous goods checks and the creation of hazardous goods documents.

18-24 The product safety enhancements of SAP's EH&S component include a substance information system where companies can generate complex drill-down reports on substance properties. Queries and results can be stored and displayed in customer-specific layouts.

18-25 Report management functions support the various work processes involved in the management of reports such as material safety data sheets (MSDS) and labels. Enhanced functions permits the designation of status registration and the import/export substance, phrase, and source data.

18-26 The active ingredients processing function is used to manage materials that contain one or more concentrates or active ingredients. The strength of the active ingredient varies from batch to batch and is applied throughout the supply chain.

18-27 The existing PP-PI module can be supplemented, through SAP's process flow scheduler. This finite capacity scheduling system is part of the supply chain planning designed to assist planners at the manufacturing plant in process industries.

18-28 Additional process control integration modules permit linking to an external PIsheet using the latest information presentation technology for plant-floor user interaction.

18-29 A preconfigured industry system represents the R/3 business processes required by the chemical industry. This live R/3 system consists of the industry model, systems settings, and master data that are specific to the industry, as well as additional documentation to supplement the standard SAP documentation.

18-30 SAP Pharmaceuticals R/3 Release 4.0 supports FDA requirements, including the use of smartcard readers for electronic signatures.

18-31 An electronic signature is a forgery-proof method of identifying people executing transactions in the R/3 system. An organization can activate the electronic signature feature to complete the processing of a phase in the PIsheet, release the electronic batch record or inspection results record, finalize inspection lots, release master recipe/inspection plan changes, and release documents.

18-32 The electronic batch record is enhanced by inspection results through data collected in post-process controls after production. Batches of the manufactured product can be allocated to the record. An approval procedure for master recipes exists and uses the change requests of engineering change management. Change requests can be used to represent a procedure in which changes to be made in a master recipe must first be requested, and then be checked and approved by different people before the change can actually be carried out in the master recipe.

18-33 The approval procedure is implemented in the inspection plan. The new active ingredients processing function is used to manage materials that contain one or more concentrates or active ingredients.

18-34 The effectiveness of the active ingredient varies from batch to batch and is applied throughout the supply chain.

18-35 In order to complement the existing PP-PI module, the new component Process Flow Scheduler (PFS) offers a finite capacity scheduling system as part of supply-chain planning.

18-36 Supply-chain planning is designed to assist planners in the manufacturing plant in process industries. Extra process control system integration models that offer the possibility of linkage to an external PIsheet.

18-37 Process control systems are based on easily set up program-to-program communication with R/3 components.

18-38 SAP consumer products (in R/3 Release 4.0) offers powerful new features that improve the promotion planning process permitting flexible promotional budgeting as well as providing ability to track real-time billing activity to gauge a promotion's effectiveness.

18-39 The free-goods function provides users with a flexible method of defining buy-one-get-one-free promotions. Release 4.0 of R/3 offers planners the extra capability of tracking promotional commitments to provide a clear idea of the objective market's intent before starting the actual program.

18-40 SAP's payment card functions handle the processing of all types of payment cards while conducting business with numerous partners.

18-41 Distribution resource planning was designed for planning of complex distribution networks. It offers production planning with accurate requirement plans to optimize the distribution of available stock levels in the distribution network.

SOLUTIONS

18-42   Consumer products process modeling, based on the R/3 Business Engineer, is knowledge-based configuration that guides customers quickly through initial implementation and uses the same intuitive, question-and-answer procedure to support ongoing changes and adaptations in business processes.

18-43   SAP engineering and construction supports the entire product life cycle from design through planning and manufacturing to final assembly at the customer site. In addition, it covers the post-sales and service phases. It allows companies to concentrate on business and be more responsive to changes in product structures, whether in the design phase or later on in production. With Release 4.0, R/3 organizations can gain control over the entire life-cycle and the supply chain from suppliers and subcontractors to customers.

18-44   The usefulness in SAP's solution supports complete integration of product data management, engineering change management, and the financial aspects of cash flow and cost control. It is imperative that there be the ability to track changes in product structure. SAP can effectively handle serial numbers as well as other parameters.

18-45   Precise workforce planning tools are highly important to the success of research and development departments or the design phase of a product.

18-46   Planning of key resources with workforce planning is a specific function specially developed for the engineering SAP aerospace and Defense R/3 Release 4.0. This release further extends the solution for designers, manufacturers, or maintainers of high-value capital equipment. All primary and auxiliary business processes dealing with business acquisition, through product design and manufacturing to delivery and subsequent maintenance, are effectively supported. The integrated character of SAP aerospace and defense permits a detailed overview and online retrieval and analysis functions for critical information required for program management success.

18-47   SAP aerospace and defense offers a vast array of industry-specific features that allow users to adhere to commercial and governmental contracts.

18-48   Cross-contract planning functions support inventory and production flexibility while tracking the ownership and cost of individual contracts.

18-49   Model-unit effectiveness and other flexible means of handling offer support for industry-specific manufacturing processes and serial number traceability, and build capabilities that allow conformance to the strictest requirements of regulating authorities.

SOLUTIONS

18-50 Coupled with already existing functions of earned value management, time recording, and billing, SAP aerospace and defense represents an integrated and comprehensive solution that satisfies the needs of the industry.

18-51 It is in the time sheet component where actual work is recorded across applications. Simulation or "what if" analysis is needed at the start of a project or product life-cycle when many factors are unknown. Even when the product is almost ready for shipment, customer changes may require a simulation to determine the consequences in terms of costs and schedules. A flexible and comprehensive simulation tool readies the information needed for efficient decision making.

18-52 Enhanced cash and cost control management functions are designed to assist the controller's daily work.

18-53 Earned value analysis, profit analysis forecast, and various project reports illustrate many of the features supporting both engineering and construction requirements.

18-54 SAP's intranet communication permits companies to have an overview of all documents assigned to a specific product structure as well as to concentrate quickly on a single drawing.

18-55 The treasury management function includes applications for money market, foreign exchange, derivatives, securities, loans, and market risk management. Treasury management includes functions for input and managing transactions, developing and analyzing portfolios, position management, transition to financial accounting, flexible reporting and data-feed interfaces.

18-56 The market risk management component handles interest and currency exposure analysis. It also emulates portfolios composed of real and fictitious financial transactions and provides mark-to-market valuation.

18-57 Consolidation Enterprise Controlling's Consolidation application component aggregates data from all parts of the R/3 system. Data collection takes place at either the company, business, or profit-center level. The component has valuation and elimination methods that allow consolidation to be the foundation for optimizing group reporting within an organization. Consolidation links to the centralized executive information system.

18-58 Consolidation's main functions include: multiple dimensions for simultaneously representing different areas of consolidation in group reporting, consolidation units in hierarchies by time periods and versions, multiple charts of accounts, and collection of company, business area, and profit center data from R/3 systems. The consolidation component was created

SOLUTIONS

for corporate groups that must use different sets of tools to generate internal and statutory group reports and want to standardize with a single tool. The component helps organizations reconcile internal and external data using uniform functions and a common user interface.

18-59   The self-audit component enhances audit quality and makes the auditing process smoother and more straightforward.

18-60   It contains the audit report tree that offers various auditing functions and default configurations, including auditing procedures and documentation, auditing evaluations, and downloading audit data. The self-audit component supports continuous controlling and interim audits as well as year-end closing statements and year-end audits.

18-61   The joint venture accounting component lets companies combine monetary and personal resources for projects with high risk, large capital investment, and extended payback periods. Joint venture accounting allocates periodic expenses to venture partners based on their contribution and working interests. This component distributes revenues and expenses among partners with respect to their working interests, transfers material and assets between ventures, allows changes of management and suspense by groups of equity holders, and permits expense and revenue netting by equity partners. Joint venture accounting processes partner-carried interest, inputs venture transactions in more than one currency in parallel, bills partners and receives payment using EDI, and processes venture partner cutbacks as well as cutbacks to other divisions of a corporation.

18-62   Transfer pricing supports the valuation of material stocks and goods movements from the group as well as from divisions, organizational units, or profit centers.

18-63   Besides performing traditional cost accounting, activity-based costing makes it possible to define cross-functional processes as well as their cost drivers. Process, activity, and quantities are determined automatically from operational cost-driver data in the integrated R/3 system environment. Process costs can be traced to products by multiplying the consumed process quantities by the process price.

18-64   Process cost can also be allocated directly to profitability segments. Activity-based costing supports the strategic decision making process by concentrating on the right products for the right customers in the right markets.

18-65   Traditional capacity measurements of machine time and product throughput volume are now improved to integrate activity-based costing to help manage overhead cost by identifying idle capacities of overhead resources.

18-66 Appropriation requests help organizations manage the corporate approval process from idea through implementation. Users rate requests by their viability and priority in order to create an investment wish list. The projects are produced directly from this list. Users can then create global reports in investment management and import data from any source including the local R/3 systems, R/2 applications, or non-SAP systems into a central R/3 system.

18-67 Investment management summarizes the data. Users can analyze this data with a variety of reports. A link from the investment program to plant maintenance orders opens a global window on capital investment.

18-68 Plant maintenance orders are used to manage repairs or new assets under construction and link them to corporate budgets.

18-69 Publish-and-subscribe interfaces let users know that certain events have occurred in the application and make data available. These events trigger other processes. This is best illustrated by a master record created because documents can be entered, parked, changed or reversed, effectively allowing clearing to be executed or canceled or having a workflow started.

18-70 Process interfaces control business processes as payments that are different from the standard system. In using the new process interfaces, an organization can individually choose payment methods or other features with reference to defined selection criteria. In addition, the note to payee entries in a payment can be industry-specific.

18-71 The Available-To-Promise (ATP) server offers real-time integrated availability-to-promise checks for high-volume, high-order line-item environments across the complete logistics supply chain.

18-72 Organizational entities have become sophisticated, and availability checks cannot occur within a conventional, transaction-based system.

18-73 The ATP server allows methods including rules-based or optimized availability checks. It can set delivery expectations when demand occurs and perform against those expectations with the objective of providing ATP information throughout the entire company.

18-74 Quick response times are essential in creating confirmations for production orders or run-schedule headers. Extra processing steps that should be automatically triggered when confirmation occurs include functions that result directly from the confirmation of the operation: the determination of current costs or backflushing and confirmation of previous operations in the processing chain. In order to execute these detailed process chains, there must be a distinction between functions where time is critical and where it is not. Then processing steps must be transferred to the background, aggregated, and placed in parallel.

18-75   Customizing makes it possible to specify which functions can be executed when an operation is used and also when it is executed.

18-76   Individual confirmation functions are encapsulated and can be run online as a confirmation as an asynchronous background task, or as a periodic background job. This applies to functions that includes: updating actual data, capacity adjustment, automatic goods receipt, backflushing of material components, determination of expected receipt surplus/deficit, updating HR incentive wage data, actual cost determination, integration of subcontractors, and external operations, all important parts of production.

18-77   External processing is significant for distributing work in virtual value chains. R/3 Release 4.0 supports these processes by integrating production and purchasing.

18-78   External processing includes the functions for:

- The creation of a subcontract
- Purchase requisition at order creation
- Allocation of components (in the externally processed operation as parts to be provided for the purchase requisition)
- Copies of the parts to be provided from the order to the purchase order
- Processing of a subcontract purchase requisition (with materials management functions)
- Update of material costs (for the parts to be provided in the production order at goods receipt for the purchase order)
- Purchasing objects including purchase requisitions, purchase orders, and purchase order histories in the Order Information System
- Workflows (when orders are modified and existing purchase orders are affected)
- Scheduling an external operation (by either planned delivery time or a standard time).
- Integration of quality assurance during goods receipt for the purchase order.

18-79   Flow manufacturing provides effective manufacturing capabilities as well as improved information flow for demand-driven manufacturing.

18-80   Line design of production lines and planning the production process are two of the most important tasks for flow and repetitive manufacturers.

Within these types of environments, production is segmented into distinct processes and the sequence of these processes is used as a basis for developing the plan for loading a line. This is why the line is subdivided into line segments and work cycles.

18-81 Work cycles are calculated to control material flow and to the time the material is retained on the line. Manufacturers must also allocate products to lines and operations, and components, production resources, and tools to parts of the line. This is where to designate feeder lines to main lines to assure the two are synchronized.

18-82 Line design functions have been enhanced to meet the special requirements of flow and repetitive manufacture. R/3 Release 4.0 incorporates the following functions for line design:

1. Line designing and line processing using a graphical interface
2. Calculation of key figures for optimizing lines
3. Product-to-line allocation
4. Allocation of processes to line segments
5. Allocation of operations, components, operating facilities, and documents to line segments
6. Definition of work cycle areas in a line
7. Calculation of work cycle times
8. Synchronization of main and feeder lines
9. Creating and printing
10. Operational method sheets (instruction sheets for line work centers)
11. Sequencing
12. Flow shop and variant manufacturing of a high volume of orders
13. Sequencing functions to help you plan order quantities and finding the sequence for flow-shop manufacturing.

In this process, the system loads the workstations of a line and takes sequencing restrictions into account. In customer-oriented assembly processing in the automobile and computer industries sequence planning is a significant part of production planning.

18-83 The system uses the information from sequencing to compute the exact delivery times for staging components.

18-84 In flow-shop manufacturing, sequencing determines the order in which products are processed on a production line.

18-85 The line load is displayed graphically on a time axis folded so as to display as many orders as possible at once.

18-86   Use of colors can help show the status of orders or assembly areas where the orders are located. Sequence plans can be manually maintained.

18-87   External optimization or model-mix procedures are linked through a Production Optimization Interface (POI).

18-88   KANBAN is a procedure for controlling production and material flow. Material is not restocked or produced until a certain production level is reached.

18-89   The relationship between the demand source and the supply source is defined in a control cycle.

18-90   Significant parameters for production control with KANBAN include the number of KANBANs that circulate in a control cycle. These parameters can be used to define material circulation and material stock. Optimizing these parameters minimizes inventory levels. The objective is to guarantee material replenishment with the lowest possible inventory. Since inventory needs fluctuate greatly, it is important to adjust these parameters periodically.

18-91   R/3 Release 4.0 automatically calculates the number of KANBANs and the quantity per KANBAN. The system proposes a number of KANBANs and a quantity per KANBAN using a report based on the results of material requirements planning or of long-term planning. It is possible to designate which valuation period the system must use to make the calculation.

18-92   An aid in displaying detailed information for the control cycle is an online transaction to check and possibly change or accept the system's proposals. This transaction can be used as a basis for displaying detailed information for the control cycle to help check the proposals.

18-93   Product Data Management (PDM contain a variety of PDM functions. The PDM components of R/3 Release 4.0 extend the supply chain from component manufacturers through suppliers to customers for total product life-cycle management. They can now be used in an individual R/3 System.

18-94   Close coupling between the integrated, distributed PDM system, and the Enterprise Resource Planning (ERP) system make certain the necessary data are exchanged.

18-95   Distributing data between systems allows companies to store design data separately from production data. Releases and maintenance levels in the PDM and ERP systems can be upgraded at different times. An integrated, distributed PDM solution in R/3 is part of the R/3 business framework strategy.

18-96 Data are exchanged between the PDM system and the ERP system using ALE. In R/3 Release 4.0, ALE interfaces have been extended with respect to: material master records, bills of material, document management, engineering change management, classes, characteristics, and object dependencies.

18-97 Companies can use customizing functions to modify the transfer of data from one system to another. Special BAPIs that exchange data between systems support specific information and comparison functions.

18-98 In order to enable virtual value chains, an increasing number of vendors place their product catalogs on the Internet. Many vendors provide industry-specific catalogs containing products and services offered by a number of different vendors. In R/3 Release 4.0, external catalogs can communicate with R/3. This allows organizations to become fully integrated. SAP helps maintain the virtual marketplace. A search for materials in a catalog can be done on the Internet and the vendor assigned as the supply source in the purchase requisition. Information from the requisition such as description, quantity, delivery date, or a maximum price, can be used to search through an external catalog. Data from that search can be adopted for items in the purchase requisition that include material description, vendor number, confirmed quantity, or price.

18-99 The specific information passed to R/3 depends on the external catalog. In dealing with procurement of external services, treat standard service catalogs like external catalogs. These features are elemental to extend business access across traditional boundaries and generate competitive advantage in virtual-value chains.

18-100 Establishing consignment stores frees capital. SAP has extended the process of handling vendor consignment stocks in R/3 Release 4.0.

18-101 A warehouse can contain stocks owned by different consignment vendors.

18-102 Settlement is based on the material withdrawn from the consignment stock. The result is that inventory management and invoice verification must satisfy special requirements.

18-103 To support the procurement process for consignment material, it is possible to define conditions for consignment processing that are valid for specific periods. Specific conditions can be input in foreign currencies and include alternative units of measure. In dealing with inventory postings made for deliveries, good issues, and confirmations for run schedule headers, and in the relevant preparatory phases note that the system can suggest the stocks from which to withdraw material.

18-104   Yes, the R/3 system provides enhanced functions for settling consignment liabilities. To make the process more transparent to the vendor, create consignment settlement documents and send them to the vendor.

18-105   Complex warehouse structures includes strategies for stock placement and stock removal and optimization of space usage. The R/3 warehouse management system supports both load distribution and operational activities in the warehouse regardless of whether or not inventory is managed by storage bin. The warehouse complex is extended to include gates, material staging areas, and picking areas, as well as general planning and detailed planning of the workload in the warehouse from beginning to end for incoming and outgoing deliveries, based on the number of packing units, the number of items, or weight.

18-106   The goods issue and distribution functions are fully integrated in the system, and the flow of goods is supported throughout the entire process.

18-107   Distribution of work into waves for picking purposes, packing, loading, and goods issue can be triggered by transports or route schedules.

18-108   DRP calculates the net requirements of the distribution centers and offers a distribution plan to guarantee the pertinent stock levels in the distribution centers. This plan considers lead times and is represented by stock transfer requisitions.

18-109   Requirements can be satisfied by more than one supply center. Deployment is short-term unlike with DRP. The deployment objective is to facilitate reaction to deviations from the DRP run.

18-110   Deviations can occur in the production process or because of imprecise sales forecasts.

18-111   Deployment uses algorithms for fair-share and push distribution to suggest appropriate action when shortfall or surplus situations happen.

18-112   The warehouse management system supports processes in the warehouse or distribution center with respect to definition of the operative structure elements: support during planning of resources and activities, processing of goods receipts, goods issues, and stock transfers, and methods for decision making and monitoring.

18-113   Yes, all activities for incoming and outgoing goods in the warehouse are supported by the system. The system is then fully integrated in the goods receipt and goods distribution processes.

18-114 Payment cards are replacing cash. Since payment cards have gained in popularity, card technology has advanced greatly. SAP is producing a flexible payment card solution for entry-level and sophisticated systems accepting all sorts of payment cards while conducting business with several partners.

18-115 The new payment card function supports sales processes for card types including: credit cards used for purchasing goods and services with regular billing, with or without extended credit; procurement cards issued on behalf of companies to employees for purchasing small-ticket items; customer cards used by customers to buy goods and services from a merchant or group of merchants; and payment-card processing. These items support card data in the sales order.

18-116 The information required for payment-card processing is stored at various levels in the sales order. The header contains payer information, items contain pricing information, schedule lines contain delivery dates and quantities, and a payment card plan attached to the order contains the card number, card type, and authorization information.

18-117 Companies can store all relevant data in a payment card master record and control whether the authorization check is performed at order entry or later. The system can be set up to determine card numbers.

18-118 The system checks to make certain that the authorization is still valid for delivery creation and goods issues. Should the authorization no longer be valid, the system requires reinitiation of an authorization check in the sales order.

18-119 The system copies payment card information from the sales order to the billing document or uploads it directly into the billing document from the point of sale.

18-120 When a billing document is released to financial accounting, the system copies the payment card information, billing amount, and authorization information from the payment card plan into the accounting document. Financial accounting determines the card category used in payment, then starts the appropriate settlement process.

18-121 An open item-managed, general ledger account is established for each clearinghouse.

18-122 In bill-back processing, R/3 supports the reverse billing process when disputes occur between the customer and merchant.

18-123 SAP has defined a standard payment-card interface to use to create protocols for clearinghouses. It is compatible with the Internet.

SOLUTIONS

18-124   SAP payment-card software is compatible with electronic marketplaces permitting fully automatic order entry, product marketing on a national and international scale, up-to-date customer information in electronic catalogs and product brochures, and electronic payment.

18-125   At the point of sale, authorizations are executed from an external system. Relevant data are imported into the R/3 system where a billing document is created.

18-126   The authorization process occurs when a customer uses a payment card and the card number is recorded in the sales order. The card number together with the payer, address, and sales order amount are forwarded to the clearinghouse for authorization, to make certain that payment is received. Until authorization has been granted for the transaction, delivery of the sales order is blocked.

18-127   The SAP payment card solution includes authorization functions such as: authorization checks (occur in the background to reduce the costs of transferring data), authorization checks in real-time, and manual entry of authorization information in sales orders.

18-128   Documentary credits help reduce the risks of foreign trade transactions. Documentary handling of payments gives the buyer power of disposal over the goods because the documents are given only on or after payment. The documents offer the vendor confirmation that the quantity, quality, and nature of the goods delivered are the same as determined in the contract.

18-129   The payment types include payment against documentary collection, documents against payment, documents against acceptance, and payment using letter of credit.

18-130   SAP supports documentary business processing through:

- Creation of documentary letters of credit without reference to orders or deliveries
- Assigning documentary letters of credit to one or more orders
- Checking the validity of a letter of credit for one or more orders
- Updating the value of goods delivered against the letter of credit
- Blocking an order or delivery if credit rules are not satisfied monitoring.

These functions have been integrated into the credit management section of the sales and distribution component so letters of credit are guaranteed to be coordinated with other forms of payment security.

18-131   The sample management component makes possible flexible planning of the actual samples to be drawn.

18-132 Administration of sample data in a sample record is handled by the assignment of inspection results to a sample record. The new enhancement satisfies the requirements of Good Manufacturing Practice (GMP) that regulate the documentation and verification of samples used in inspection processing.

18-133 Sample management is integrated with the existing quality management functions that include inspection planning, inspection lot processing, and results recording.

18-134 Plant maintenance equipment is used to manage individual test and measurement equipment. R/3 Release 4.0 supports calibration inspections for these individual items of equipment.

18-135 The calibration inspections monitor calibration deadlines and define and record calibration characteristics (also known as inspection characteristics).

18-136 A value contract is an agreement with a customer to release materials up to a certain value during a certain time. The value contract defines the outline agreement. It has a validity period and an agreed total value, and contains rules that determine which types of releases are allowed.

18-137 Yes, restrictions on the customer or the material can be defined. Special pricing agreements contain discounts that can be stored at any level in the value contract. The value contract can contain prices for individual materials or discounts for each released material. Releases from the value contract can be executed by sales orders.

18-138 The system checks the released materials against the rules of the value contract and the validity period, while the value is checked against the remaining open value. A company can easily determine whether or not the total value of the contract can be exceeded.

18-139 The value contract can be billed directly or per call-off. If the value contract is billed directly, a billing plan can be stored to invoicing of the value contract at several deadlines and for proportional values.

18-140 The free goods function is new in R/3 Release 4.0. It offers users a flexible way to define buy-one-get-one-free promotions aimed at a specific key account or an entire sales region. Free goods agreements are then automatically applied to relevant sales orders.

18-141 It is crucial to find ways to save on transportation and logistics costs while quickly shipping goods to satisfy customers. Transportation functions offer an interface to transportation planning and optimizing. R/3 Release 4.0 incorporates functions for freight charge processing that includes defining freight rates and agreements using the SAP condition technique. SAP pricing can be used to compute transportation costs for each phase of a shipment.

18-142   The R/3 time sheet component standardizes cross-application time recording. The time sheet rolls the time recording function of several applications into a single transaction. The time sheet can be used to supply information on work times for applications including:

- Attendance in human resources (HR)
- Internal activity allocation in controlling (CO)
- Confirmations in plant maintenance (PM)
- Project System (PS)
- Service Management (SM)
- Entry of services performed in External Services Management (MM-SRV).

18-143   The time recording interface is so easy to use that even those with little R/3 experience can work with the time sheet.

18-144   After numerous components were created by SAP in R/3 Release 4.0, HR and travel management were split off from R/3 as separate components with a dedicated database and an independent release cycle. The human resource and travel management components incorporate several workflow, Internet, and intranet enhancements.

18-145   Customers are able quickly and easily to deploy new HR functionality, gain additional business flexibility, and reduce the time needed to complete business processes.

18-146   The HR country versions are extensions of the general, international functionality with respect to personnel administration and payroll. They offer additional functions that specifically meet a country's legal requirements and business procedures.

18-147   SAP has produced new country versions for the personnel administration component for Mexico and the personnel administration and payroll components for Indonesia, Malaysia, New Zealand, and Taiwan. SAP offers 30 distinct country versions of R/3. Travel management has been adapted for Germany, Austria, Switzerland, the U.S., and Japan. In R/3 Release 4.0, country versions are also available for Great Britain, the Netherlands, Belgium, France, and Denmark. R/3 Release 4.0 supports statutory and enterprise-specific provisions for trip cost accounting in country versions that allow enterprises to reengineer business processes in travel management to account for statutory regulations and company policy. Multinational companies will profit from the parallel operation of several country versions when setting up international human resources service centers.

18-148   In R/3 Release 4.0, SAP HR incorporates new Employee Self-Service (ESS, Figure 18.2) solutions that permit employees to view and maintain data in R/3 through a Web-browser. This allows the whole enterprise community to connect with R/3 and maintain individual human resource data through the Internet or corporate intranet.

FIGURE 18.2
ESS

18-149   The ESS components are implemented using BAPIs.

18-150   SAP has enhanced R/3's COBRA functions to incorporate COBRA processing for health plans and spending accounts. R/3 Release 4.0 processes has completed COBRA election forms and updates and tracks the status of beneficiaries. Companies can notify COBRA-qualified beneficiaries when election periods have expired, and can track payment, and send out late-payment notices. They can also confirm COBRA election changes and cancel COBRA participation.

18-151   The money an employee saves in a Flexible Spending Account (FSA must be available during the course of the year. In R/3 Release 4.0 it is possible

SOLUTIONS

to process claims made against an employee's FSA and monitor the balance for a single employee or for a group of employees. Companies can also specify a grace period during which employees can submit claims for expenses incurred in a previous year.

18-152 ESS provides numerous benefits including 24-hour, 365-days-a-year access, low-cost business transactions, access to the most up-to-date information, and direct data entry, which speeds up business processes and cuts costs.

18-153 Outsourcing's two main functions provide interfaces to enable third-party processing of SAP data and to use R/3 to process data provided by third-party services.

18-154 Outsourcing is executed in the interface toolbox, which will be used to create the interfaces required for outsourcing.

18-155 The SAP/ADP USA payroll interface outsources gross payroll data to an ADP DOS system product for net payroll processing. R/3 Release 4.0 adds an interface to ADP PC/Payroll for Windows through a master data extract payroll schemes and rules.

18-156 In R/3 Release 4.0, external recruitment systems and R/3 can exchange data using an independent interface.

18-157 Any employee who wants to participate in insurance plans, must provide evidence of insurability (EOI). This includes a medical affidavit as proof of good health. R/3 Release 4.0 can store employees' elections before EOI is provided by creating active plans, pending plans, or no plans at all. Companies can then enroll employees when an EOI is received or enroll them in an interim plan. They can also define and monitor grace periods and then delete pending plans whose grace period has expired.

18-158 Users can handle multi-session events or conventions where several sessions of a main event are held in parallel. They can also perform all processing functions such as resource reservation for individual sessions of a convention.

18-159 R/3 Release 4.0 includes several enhancements and extensions that improve usability, flexibility, and performance. The human resources ad hoc query is a simple and powerful tool for choosing and processing personnel information; it is based on information types within personnel administration that can be composed for particular areas using ABAP Query. Companies can also use selection criteria to make the query in the most efficient manner possible.

18-160 The standard HR reporting tools can be used to perform simple evaluations for selected payroll results. Payroll results can be retrieved by employees using configurable information-types.

18-161 The compensation management component controls and administers an organization's remuneration policies. Using the compensation plan definition, companies can create multiple compensation plans and assign them using the organizational structure. Compensation plans have flexible eligibility and individual processing rules.

18-162 Eligibility rules govern which employees can participate in a plan. Enterprises can set up the salary structure based on salary groups or grades and their associated salary ranges. Companies can also designate salary grades at the position or job level and by employee. In addition, salary planning permits creation of salary budgets from bottom to top with a roll-up over the organizational structure.

18-163 The time intervals in R/3 Release 4.0 are more specific so companies can define requirements and find matchups. It is also possible to designate qualifications as part of the requirements definition.

18-164 In career planning, personnel departments can create potential career paths within a company. This type of planning assists in motivating ambitious, qualified employees by showing the options available to them. Succession planning provides information about employees who fulfill the requirements of a particular position now or will do so in the future. It becomes easier to fill vacant positions from within the company. In both career planning and succession planning, the system compiles a list of people, sorted in order of suitability.

18-165 Matching personnel profiles and position profiles shows in detail how further to train employees to broaden their skills to meet future requirements.

18-166 Form-based SAP business workflow is used in HR. Many administrative processes in Human Resources simply consist of an employee's processing business transactions, like pay increases, applications for leave, and personnel requirements.

18-167 In R/3 Release 4.0, simple forms can be created using tools like VisualBasic or JetForms and integrated with SAP business workflow to create self-service human resources applications.

18-168 SAP delivers the front end for the next generation of client/server software. It enhances the ease-of-use and simplifies the administration of R/3.

SOLUTIONS

Based on the integration of front-end components, the R/3 Release 4.0 GUI can display different kinds of information at the same time, much as a Web browser does. Although processing of the business logic remains on the application server, the new front-end component framework supports desktop performance with local processing of user interaction and presentation logic. The front-end components are automatically downloaded from the R/3 system to the client on demand, simplifying and reducing the costs of administration. SAP has implemented these enhancements to the SAPGUI architecture using ActiveX technology from Microsoft and JavaBeans from Sun Microsystems.

18-169 ABAP has grown into an object-oriented programming language. ABAP objects have evolved into the new generation of the ABAP virtual machine that supports the new interfacing technologies and enhances interoperability with external object architectures.

18-170 The ABAP VM (Figure 18.3) also ensures that all R/3 application components can be executed without modification in different system environments.

FIGURE 18.3
ABAP VM

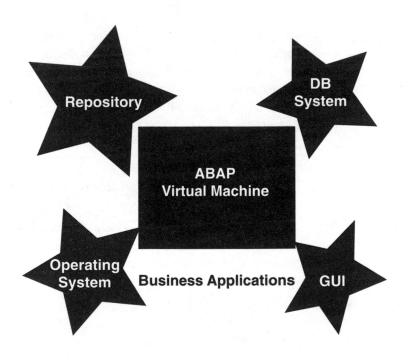

18-171 ALE supports BAPIs with application link enabling because companies can utilize a technology that integrates components into network solutions independent of their release version. ALE integrates business processes between different R/3 systems or business components (Figure 18.4). It controls the exchange of business messages between these components and makes certain of their semantic synchronization. BAPIs (methods of SAP Business Objects can now also be invoked asynchronously by ALE.

FIGURE 18.4
Business Components

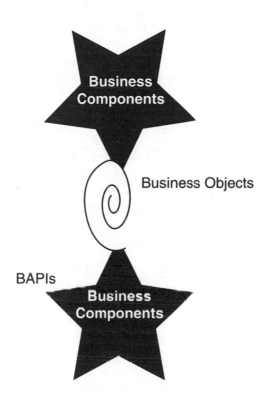

18-172 Applications can use Secure Store and Forward (SSF) mechanisms to protect sensitive data and documents. This is especially important if data are stored on external data media or transferred across insecure networks. R/3 Release 4.0 uses digital signatures and encryption to assure the integrity of the data, authenticity of the sender, non-repudiation, and confidentiality.

18-173 SAP has significantly improved R/3 Business Engineer to configure R/3 faster and more easily. It supports phased implementations and changes to existing configurations without disrupting continuous business activities. R/3 Business Engineer allows definition of organizational structures and the business processes needed using familiar language as it walks users through implementation step by step.

SOLUTIONS

18-174 Knowledge-based configuration guides users through the implementation automatically.

18-175 Industry-specific templates reduce the number of functions displayed, speeding up implementation even more. Existing configurations can easily be changed when the support of new business goals or shifting market demands is needed.

18-176 SAP has extended the Web-enabled SAP business workflow to make it even simpler for users to access and execute business workflow 24 hours a day from corporate intranets or the Internet. New in R/3 Release 4.0, SAP Business Workflow allows users to trigger workflow through the Web using HTML forms. This adds an important option to the existing possibilities of triggering workflow through BAPIs or Internet application components.

18-177 Users can access their integrated in boxes through the Web to execute transactions, create attachments, or forward items to coworkers. SAP provides more Workflow Wizards to make it easier and faster to implement workflow. Organizations can add workflow to a customer-developed transaction and R/2 transactions using a Workflow Wizard that automatically generates a workflow task.

18-178 Yes, SAP Business Workflow extends support for electronic forms. Occasional or mobile users are better incorporated into the information and decision-making processes of the company. Active support for evaluating workflow-related process information is further extended and can be provided through the business information warehouse.

Gold Level
SAP Contacts

Want to know more about each industry sector at SAP? Finding contacts is often difficult or next to impossible when trying to find information through the Web or brochures.

The following contacts will give you a key to contacting individuals at SAP to help you gain as much information as possible about the specific industry sector you need for training, information, or practical purposes. The information is organized with respect to each industry sector at SAP.

SAP Aerospace and Defense

Americas
Robert Johnson
SBU Director
SAP AG, Walldorf
robert.johnson@sap-ag.de

Frank Colantuono
Regional Industry Group
SAP AG, Walldorf
frank.colantuono@sap-ag.de

North East Asia
Larry Hoshi
Regional Industry Group
larry.hoshi@sap-ag.de

South Asia Pacific
Mark Jarvis
Regional Industry Group
mark.jarvis@sap-ag.de

Europe, Africa
Hanne Schultz Andersen
Regional Industry Group
hanne.schultz.andersen@sap-ag.de

Emmanuelle Morice
Product Management
emmanuelle.morice@sap-ag.de

Marketing related issues:
Christian Knab
Global Industry Marketing
christian.knab@sap-ag.de

SAP Automotive

Industry Marketing/Corporate
Kerstin Fabarius
Corporate Industry Marketing
SAP Automotive
SAP AG, Walldorf, Germany

k.fabarius@sap-ag.de

North America
Michael Morris
Business Development Consultant
SAP America, Detroit
michael.morris@sap-ag.de

Japan
Shigeo Hara
Automotive Group, Japan
SAP Japan
shigeo.hara@sap-ag.de

SAP Banking

Bernd Dexheimer
Global Industry Business Director—
Banking, SAP AG, Walldorf
+49 6227 747097
bernd.dexheimer@sap-ag.de

Hubert Spaeth
Product Manager—SAP Banking/SEM
SAP AG, Walldorf
+49 6227 745194
hubert.spaeth@sap-ag.de

John Macdonald
Industry Marketing Manager—Financial
Services
SAP UK, London
+44 181 818 1775
john.macdonald@sap-ag.de

SAP Chemical

Global Industry Marketing
Ian Kimbell
Corporate Marketing Manager
Chemical / Pharmaceutical Industry
ian.kimbell@sap-ag.de

Regional Support Group

Americas
Stephen Gaines
Regional Support Group
Chemical / Pharmaceutical Industry
SAP America, Lester, PA
stephen.gaines@sap-ag.de

Europe
Volker Anders
Regional Support Group
Chemical / Pharmaceutical Industry
SAP AG, Walldorf, Germany
volker.anders@sap-ag.de

Dr. Thomas Reiss
Regional Support Group
Chemical / Pharmaceutical Industry
SAP AG, Walldorf, Germany
t.reiss@sap-ag.de

SAP Consumer Products

Global Industry Marketing
Stefanie Glenk
Corporate Vertical Marketing
Consumer Products Industry
SAP AG, Walldorf, Germany
stefanie.glenk@sap-ag.de

North America
Mark Smith
Americas Industry Center Director
SAP America, Philadelphia, PA, USA
mark.smith@sap-ag.de

Europe
Christian Koch
ICOE Consumer Products, Europe
SAP AG, Walldorf, Germany
christian.koch@sap-ag.de

SAP Engineering and Construction

Global Industry Marketing
Gino Kremmler
SAP AG, Walldorf
gino.kremmler@sap-ag.de

Europe
Regional Industry Group
Oliver Sachse
SAP AG, Walldorf
oliver.sachse@sap-ag.de

Product Management
Emanuelle Morice
SAP AG, Walldorf
emanuelle.morice@sap-ag.de

Americas
Regional Industry Service Group
Gerhard Meinecke
SAP Labs, Palo Alto, California, USA
gerhard.meinicke@sap-ag.de

SBU Director
Vince Beacom
vince.beacom@sap-ag.de

South Asia Pacific
SBU-Manufacturing
Nandkishore Man Kalambi
nandkishore.man.kalambi@sap-ag.de

North East Asia
SBU-Manufacturing
Haruyuki Uchijama
haruyuki.uchijama.@sap-ag.de

SAP Healthcare

Corporate Industry Marketing
Ingo Glaser
Corporate Marketing—Healthcare
SAP AG, Walldorf
ingo.glaser@sap-ag.de

Industry Business Unit Public Sector
Dietmar Pfaehler
Director Industry Business Unit Public Sector
SAP AG, Walldorf
dietmar.pfaehler@sap-ag.de

Leo Schneider
Product Manager–Healthcare
SAP AG, Walldorf
leo.schneider@sap-ag.de

Americas
Lawrence Sinkuler
ICOE Manager—Healthcare
SAP America, Lester
lawrence.sinkuler@sap-ag.de

Asia
Poh Hiang Tan
ICOE Manager—Healthcare
SAP Asia, Singapore
poh.hiang.tan@sap-ag.de

SAP High Tech

Europe
Stefanie Gruen
Corporate Industry Marketing
SAP AG, Walldorf, Germany
stefanie.gruen@sap-ag.de

Americas
Christine Clevenger
Regional Industry Support Group Manager
SAP Labs, Inc., Palo Alto, USA
chistine.clevenger@sap-ag.de

Asia
Chee Tong Leow
Regional Industry Support Group Manager

SAP Taiwan
chee.tong.leow@sap-ag.de

SAP Insurance

Ingo Huber
Product Manager
SAP Insurance
Walldorf, Germany
Phone: +49 6257 95 2620
ingo.huber@sap-ag.de

Richard Page
Industry Marketing
SAP Insurance
SAP UK, London
Phone: +44 181 917 6267
richard.page@sap-ag.de

Manfred Stephan
Sales Manager
SAP Insurance
Walldorf Germany
Phone: +49 6227 7 1291
manfred.stephan@sap-ag.de

Robert Koffler
National Sales Manager
Financial Services SBU
SAP America, USA
Phone: +001 212 349 5331
robert.koffler@sap-ag.de

Timothy Singer
Senior Marketing Specialist
Financial Services SBU
SAP America, USA
Phone: +001 610 595 5566
timothy.singer@sap-ag.de

SAP Insurance—Sales Contacts

Australia
John Pitcher
+61 2 99354 907

Austria
Christian Arbeiter
+43 1 28822 296

Belgium
Patrick van Lishout
+32 2 7780 511

Canada [East]
Daniel Lefebvre
+1 514 350 7300

Canada [West]
Shawna Kovacs
+1 403 269 5222

Canada [Central]
Randy Wheeler
+1 416 229 0574

Czech Republic
Petr Pihera
+420 2 651 9701

Denmark
Henrik Sanden
+45 4326 3900

Germany
Manfred Stephan
+49 6227 741356

Japan
Yasuo Kainosho
+81 3 5531 3333

Takeshi Tanaka
+81 78 362 7880

Netherlands
Peter Lanting
+31 73 6 45 7562

Portugal
Joao Matos
+351 1 3030300

Singapore/SE Asia
Ed Musiak
+65 249 1327

Slovak Republic
Peter Manda
+421-7 834 663

Spain
Gabriel Lapuerta
+34 1 456 7200

Sweden
Charlotte Darth
+46 8 80 96 80

Switzerland
Christian Arbeiter
+411 8711 506

Peter Mock
+41 1 8711 515

United Kingdom
Henry Blythe
+44 181 917 6056

U.K. [North East]
Paul Grillo
+1 610 595 4900

U.K. [Mid West]
Bill Macdonald
+1 708 947 3400

U.K. [South East]
Michael Murphy
+1 770 730 4110

SAP Insurance Marketing Contacts

Richard Page
+44 181 917 6267

United States
Rich Blumberg
+1 610 595 5503

Tim Singer
+1 610 595 4900

Australia
Robert Fowler
+61 2 99354 4965

Germany
Martino Milcovic
+49 6227 344241

United Kingdom
Anne-Marie Lavelle
+44 181 917 6211

France
Alain Bohan
+33 1 55 30 20 12

SAP Media

Global Industry Marketing
Nadia Durante
Corporate Marketing Manager—SAP Media
SAP AG, Walldorf
nadia.durante@sap-ag.de

Global Product Management
Manfred Gärtner
Corporate Product Manager—SAP Media
SAP AG, Walldorf
manfred.gaertner@sap-ag.de

SAP Metal, Paper and Wood

Reinhild Gefrerer
Director MPW IBU
SAP AG Walldorf
reinhild.gefrerer@sap-ag.de

Prashanth Narasimha
Corporate Industry Marketing
SAP AG Walldorf
prashanth.narasimha@sap-ag.de

North America
Chip Reichhard
Process Industry Business Unit Director
leonard.reichhard@sap-ag.de

Sonny Hathaway
bueford.hathaway@sap-ag.de

Gregory Peay
gregory.peay@sap-ag.de

Europe
Niels Molzen
ESBU Sponsor
MD Nordic
niels.molzen@sap-ag.de

Esa Parjanen
esa.parjanen@sap-ag.de

South Asia Pacific
Nandkishore Manhar Kalambinand
kishore.man.kalambi@sap-ag.de

North East Asia
Masaki Sawabe
masaki.sawabe@sap-ag.de

SAP Oil and Gas

Corporate Industry Marketing
Prashanth Narasimha
Manager
SAP AG Walldorf
prashanth.narasimha@sap-ag.de

Regional Industry Support Group
Europe/Middle East/Africa
Peter Maier
Senior Manager

SAP AG, Walldorf
peter.maier@sap-ag.de

Regional Industry Support Group
North East Asia
Gerold Kaske
Manager
SAP AG, Tokyo
Gerold.Kaske@sap-ag.de

Sales Business
Americas
Lester Amidei
Director
SAP America, Houston
lester.amidei@sap-ag.de

Sales Business Unit
South Asia Pacific
R. Kashiviswanath
SAP South Asia Pasific, Singapore
kashiviswanath.r@sap-ag.de

SAP Pharmaceutical

Global Industry Marketing
Ian Kimbell
Corporate
Marketing Manager
Chemical / Pharmaceutical Industry
ian.kimbell@sap-ag.de

Regional Support Group
Americas
Stephen Gaines
Regional Support Group
Chemical / Pharmaceutical
Industry SAP America, Lester, PA
stephen.gaines@sap-ag.de

Europe
Volker Anders
Regional Support Group

Chemical / Pharmaceutical
Industry SAP AG, Walldorf, Germany
volker.anders@sap-ag.de

Dr. Thomas Reiss
Regional Support Group
Chemical / Pharmaceutical Industry
SAP AG, Walldorf, Germany
t.reiss@sap-ag.de

SAP Public Sector

Dietmar Pfähler
Director Industry Business Unit Public Sector
SAP AG, Walldorf
dietmar.pfaehler@sap-ag.de

Norbert Vilvorder
Products Management Public Sector
SAP AG, Walldorf
norbert.vilvorder@sap-ag.de

Ingo Glaser
Corporate Industry Marketing Manager Public Sector
SAP AG, Walldorf
ingo.glaser@sap-ag.de

Frank Schabel
Corporate Industry Marketing Manager Public Sector
SAP AG, Walldorf
frank.schabel@sap-ag.de

North America
John Greaney
Public Sector Center of Expertise
SAP America Public Sector, Washington
john.greaney@sap-ag.de

Lori Goss
Director Marketing Public Sector America
Public Sector SAP America
lori.goss@sap-ag.de

SAP Retail

Global Business Development
Dr. Ferri Abolhassan
Business Development Manager Retail and Consumer Products
SAP AG, Walldorf
ferri.abolhassan@sap-ag.de

Global Industry Marketing
Dagmar Fischer-Neeb
Director Industry Marketing
SAP AG, Walldorf
dagmar.fischer-neeb@sap-ag.de

Christian Koch
Industry Marketing Manager Retail
SAP AG, Walldorf
christian.koch@sap-ag.de

Regional Industry Support Groups

Europe/Mideast/Africa
Guido Anterist
RISG Manager Europe/Mideast/AfricaSAP AG, Walldorf
guido.anterist@sap-ag.de

Americas
David Lubert
RISG Manager Americas
david.lubert@sap-ag.de

Northeast Asia and Greater China
Jochen Bethke
RISG Manager Northeast Asia and Greater China
jochen.bethke@sap-ag.de

Christa Koppe
Industry Marketing Manager, Service Provider
SAP AG, Walldorf
ch.koppe@sap-ag.de

Dr. Martin Przewloka
Professional Services, IBU
SAP AG, Walldorf

martin.przewloka@sap-ag.de

Hanna Gradzka
Railway, Technical Services, IBU
SAP AG, Walldorf
hanna.gradzka@sap-ag.de

Josep Cortadellas Huguet
Tourism, IBU
SAP AG, Walldorf
josep.cortadellas.huguet@sap-ag.de

Dr Paul Centen
Real Estate Management, IBU
SAP AG, Walldorf
paul.centen@sap-ag.de

Dr Werner Sommer
IBU Director
SAP AG, Walldorf
werner.sommer@sap-ag.de

Barbara Wanner
Assistant, IBU
SAP AG, Walldorf
barbara.wanner@sap-ag.de

SAP Telecomunications

Global Industry Marketing
Holger Rupp
Industry Marketing Manager—SAP Telecommunications
SAP AG, Walldorf
holger.rupp@sap-ag.de

North America
William Rogers
SAP Telecommunications SBU Director
SAP America
william.rogers@sap-ag.de

Lori Zelko
Industry Marketing
SAP America
lori.zelko@sap-ag.de

Europe
Christoph Wobbe
RIS Director
SAP AG, Walldorf
christoph.wobbe@sap-ag.de

Asia
Kwai Seng Lee
Industry Marketing Utilities and Telecom
SAP Asia, Singapore
kwai.seng.lee@sap-ag.de

SAP Transportation

Christa Koppe
Industry Marketing Manager, Service and Transportation
SAP AG, Walldorf
ch.koppe@sap-ag.de

Hanna Gradzka
Railway, Technical Services, IBU
SAP AG, Walldorf
hanna.gradzka@sap-ag.de

Dr Werner Sommer
IBU Director
SAP AG, Walldorf
werner.sommer@sap-ag.de

Barbara Wanner
Assistant, IBU
SAP AG, Walldorf
barbara.wanner@sap-ag.de

Marie-Laurence Poujois
Storage, Shipping and Distribution, IBU
SAP AG, Walldorf
marie-laurence.poujois@sap-ag.de

SAP Utilities

Global Industry Marketing
Christopher Knoerr

Corporate Industry Marketing – Utilities
SAP AG, Walldorf
christopher.knoerr@sap-ag.de

North America
Andrew Zetlan
SAP Utilities, SBU Director
SAP America, Lester
andrew.zetlan@sap-ag.de

Lori Zelko
Industry Marketing Utilities
SAP America
lori.zelko@sap-ag.de

Europe
Christoph Wobbe
RIS Director, Europe
SAP AG, Walldorf
christoph.wobbe@sap-ag.de

Asia
Kwai Seng Lee
Industry Marketing Utilities and Telecom
SAP Asia, Singapore
kwai.seng.lee@sap-ag.de

Australia
James McClelland
Utilities Director
SAP Australia, Sydney
james.mcclelland@sap-ag.de

Contacts

CBT Systems [Corporate Headquarters]
1005 Hamilton Court
Menlo Park, CA. 94025
Telephone# (415) 614-5900
Fax# (415) 614-5901
Sales# (800) 387-0932
Toll-Free Tech Support: (800) 938-3247
Web Site: http://www.cbtsys.com/

SAP America, Inc.

Strategic Planning and Support Office
100 Stevens Drive
Philadelphia, PA 19113
(610) 595-4900

SAP America District Offices

Atlanta
6 Concourse Parkway
Ste. 1200
Atlanta, GA 30328
(770) 353-2900

Austin
Austin Center
Ste. 800
701 Brazos
Austin, TX 78701
(512) 425-2300

Boston
Bay Colony Corporate Ctr.
950 Winter Street
Waltham, MA 02154
(781) 672-6500

Chicago
Five Westbrook Corp. Ctr.
Ste. 1000
Westchester, IL 60154
(708) 947-3400

Cincinnati
312 Walnut Street
Ste. 2470
Cincinnati, OH 45202
(513) 977-5400

Cleveland
127 Public Square
Ste. 5000

Cleveland, OH 44114
(216) 615-3000

Dallas
600 E. Las Colinas Blvd.
Ste. 2000
Irving, TX 75039
(972) 868-2000

Denver
4600 South Ulster Street
Ste. 700
Denver, CO 80237
(303) 740-6696

Detroit
One Town Square
Ste. 1550
Southfield, MI 48076
(248) 304-1000

Houston
2500 City West Blvd.
Ste. 1600
Houston, TX 77042
(713) 917-5200

Irvine
18101 Von Karman Ave
Ste. 900
Irvine, CA 92612
(714) 622-2200

Minneapolis
3530 Dain Bosworth Plaza
60 S. 6th Street
Minneapolis, MN 55402
(612) 359-5000

New York
One Liberty Plaza
165 Broadway, 51st Floor
New York, NY 10006
(212) 346-5300

Pittsburgh
301 Grant Street
One Oxford Center
Ste. 1500
Pittsburgh, PA 15219
(412) 255-3795

Philadelphia
100 Stevens Drive
Philadelphia, PA 19113
(610) 595-4900

Pittsburgh
301 Grant Street
One Oxford Center
Ste. 1500
Pittsburgh, PA 15219
(412) 255-3795

Parsippany
Morris Corporate Ctr.
300 Interpace Parkway, Bldg. A, 4th Floor
Parsippany, NJ 07054
(973) 331-6000

San Francisco
950 Tower Lane
12th Floor
Foster City, CA 94404
(650) 637-1655

Seattle
800 Bellevue Way N.E.
4th Floor
Bellevue, WA 98004
(206) 462-6395

St. Louis
City Place One
Ste. 430
1 City Place
St. Louis, MO 63141
(314) 213-7500

INDEX

C